Lecture Notes in Computer Science 3273

Thomas Baar   Alfred Strohmeier
Ana Moreira   Stephen J. Mellor (Eds.)

«UML» 2004 – The Unified Modeling Language

Modeling Languages and Applications

7th International Conference
Lisbon, Portugal, October 11-15, 2004
Proceedings

Volume Editors

Thomas Baar
Alfred Strohmeier
Swiss Federal Institute of Technology Lausanne (EPFL)
Software Engineering Laboratory
1015 Lausanne, Switzerland
E-mail: {thomas.baar,alfred.strohmeier}@epfl.ch

Ana Moreira
Universidade Nova de Lisboa, Faculdade de Ciências e Tecnologia
Departamento de Informática
Quinta da Torre, 2829-516 Caparica, Portugal
E-mail: amm@di.fct.unl.pt

Stephen J. Mellor
Mentor Graphics, Corp., Accelerated Technology
Suite 365, 7400 N. Oracle Road, Tucson, AZ 85704, USA
E-mail: Stephen_Mellor@Mentor.com

Library of Congress Control Number: 2004112978

CR Subject Classification (1998): D.2, D.3, K.6, I.6

ISSN 0302-9743
ISBN 3-540-23307-5 Springer Berlin Heidelberg New York

Springer is a part of Springer Science+Business Media

springeronline.com

Printed in Germany

Typesetting: Camera-ready by author, data conversion by Boller Mediendesign
Printed on acid-free paper SPIN: 11329060 06/3142 5 4 3 2 1 0

Preface

This volume comprises the final versions of the technical papers presented at the ≪UML≫ 2004 conference held in Lisbon (Portugal), October 11–15, 2004.

≪UML≫ 2004 was the seventh conference in a series of annual ≪UML≫ conferences. The series started in 1998 and was located at Mulhouse (France); the following years saw the conference move to Fort Collins (USA) in 1999, York (UK) in 2000, Toronto (Canada) in 2001, Dresden (Germany) in 2002, San Francisco (USA) in 2003, and now Lisbon (Portugal) in 2004. During this time, the ≪UML≫ conference became one of the leading conferences in the area of object-oriented modeling. While in the first years the focus of the conference was on the scientific investigation of the Unified Modeling Language (UML), which had just been adopted by the Object Management Group (OMG) at the time, the focus has changed in recent years to innovations in techniques such as metamodeling, model transformations, model validation and verification, aspect orientation, and beyond. Many recent research activities have been especially stimulated by the Model Driven Architecture (MDA) initiative, started in 2000 by the OMG. The goal of MDA is the definition of a framework to enable the development of software purely based on models. In order to reflect the changes of recent years, the conference series ≪UML≫ will be continued, from 2005 onwards, under the name MODELS (MOdel Driven Engineering, Languages and Systems).

The call for papers for ≪UML≫ 2004 encouraged authors around the world to submit 157 abstracts and 135 technical papers. Each submission was reviewed by at least three referees, in most cases by four. Based on the reviews, the whole program committee discussed in four rounds the submissions' quality, leading to the selection of 30 submissions (26 research papers, 4 experience reports) for publication. In addition, the program committee selected one paper for the *Best Paper Award ≪UML≫ 2004*. After a detailed discussion of selected candidates the committee came to the conclusion that the paper by Alexandre Correa, Cláudia Werner (Brazil), "Applying Refactoring Techniques to UML/OCL Models", deserved the award. Congratulations to the authors!

For managing the review process, the free version of Cyberchair (`http://www.cyberchair.org`) was used. We are grateful to its author Richard van de Stadt who also helped with advice. We also want to take the opportunity to express our greatest gratitude to Arnaud di Clemente whose work on the technical side was invaluable for managing the review process and preparing the conference proceedings.

Besides the presentation of technical papers in 10 sessions, the scientific program of ≪UML≫ 2004 included 3 keynote talks, "Generative Software Development", given by Krzysztof Czarnecki (University of Waterloo), "Goals, Viewpoints, and Components — an MDA Perspective", given by Desmond D'Souza (Kinetium), and "Putting Change at the Center of the Software Process", given by Oscar Nierstrasz (University of Bern), 12 workshops, including a doctoral symposium, 6 tutorials, and a special track with industry papers. In addition to this proceedings, a postconference book entitled *≪UML≫ 2004 Satellite Activities* was published by Springer as LNCS volume 3297. This book includes the papers of the industry track, summaries of the workshops, tool papers and poster papers.

We are glad to express our gratitude to all persons and organizations who were involved in the organization of the conference: to the sponsors and supporters for the financial, organizational, and moral aid, to the reviewers for their dedication in writing reports and contributing to the discussion, and to the members of the local organization committee for their incredible work in coordinating all activities and making the local arrangements.

July 2004

Thomas Baar
Alfred Strohmeier
Ana Moreira
Stephen J. Mellor

Organization

Executive Committee

General Chair	Stephen J. Mellor (Mentor Graphics, USA)
Conference Chair	Ana Moreira (New University of Lisbon, Portugal)
Program Co-chairs	Thomas Baar (EPFL, Switzerland) Alfred Strohmeier (EPFL, Switzerland)
Industry Track Chair	Bran Selic (IBM Rational Software, Canada)
Tutorial Chair	Ezra K. Mugisa (University of the West Indies at Mona, Jamaica)
Workshop Chair	Ambrosio Toval (University of Murcia, Spain)
Panel Chair	Jon Whittle (NASA Ames Research Center, USA)
Poster Chair	Nuno Jardim Nunes (University of Madeira, Portugal)

Organizing Team

Publicity Chairs	João Araújo (New University of Lisbon, Portugal) Geri Georg (Colorado State University, USA)
Local Arrangements Chair	Isabel Sofia Brito (Politécnico de Beja, Portugal)
Tools Exhibition Chair	Alberto Silva (Technical University of Lisbon, Portugal)
Local Sponsors Chair	Fernando Brito e Abreu (New University of Lisbon, Portugal)
Web Chair	Miguel Goulão (New University of Lisbon, Portugal)

Program Committee

Mehmet Aksit (The Netherlands)
Omar Aldawud (USA)
Colin Atkinson (Germany)
Doo-Hwan Bae (Korea)
Jean Bézivin (France)
Marko Boger (Germany)
Ruth Breu (Austria)
Jean-Michel Bruel (France)
David Bustard (UK)
Alessandra Cavarra (UK)
Betty Cheng (USA)
Siobhán Clarke (Ireland)
John Daniels (UK)
Stéphane Ducasse (Switzerland)
Gregor Engels (Germany)
Andy Evans (UK)
Robert France (USA)
Sébastien Gérard (France)
Martin Gogolla (Germany)
Jeff Gray (USA)
Constance Heitmeyer (USA)
Brian Henderson-Sellers (Australia)
Heinrich Hussmann (Germany)
Pankaj Jalote (India)

Stuart Kent (UK)
Jörg Kienzle (Canada)
Haim Kilov (USA)
Philippe Kruchten (Canada)
Tim Lethbridge (Canada)
Richard Mitchell (USA)
Hiroshi Miyazaki (Japan)
Pierre-Alain Muller (France)
Ileana Ober (France)
Gunnar Overgaard (Sweden)
Ernesto Pimentel Sanchez (Spain)
Gianna Reggio (Italy)
Laurent Rioux (France)
Bernhard Rumpe (Germany)
Peter H. Schmitt (Germany)
Andy Schürr (Germany)
Bran Selic (Canada)
R.K. Shyamasundar (India)
Keng Siau (USA)
Jos Warmer (The Netherlands)
Alain Wegmann (Switzerland)
Jon Whittle (USA)

Additional Reviewers

Aditya Agrawal
Muhammad Alam
Carsten Amelunxen
Gabriela Arévalo
Egidio Astesiano
Richard Atterer
Pavel Balabko
Elisa Baniassad
Alexandre Bergel
Lodewijk Bergmans
Egon Börger
Marius Bozga
Richard Bubel
Fabian Büttner
Robert D. Busser
Maura Cerioli
Alexey Cherchago
Joanna Chimiak-Opoka
Olivier Constant
Steve Cook
James Davis
Gregory Defombelle
Birgit Demuth
Min Deng
Ludovic Depitre
Manuel Díaz
Cormac Driver
Hubert Dubois
Francisco J. Durán
Cristian Ene
Brit Engel
Alexander Förster
Per Fragemann
Markus Gälli
Geri Georg
Cesar Gonzalez-Perez
Orla Greevy
Jiang Guo
Michael Hafner
Nabil Hameurlain
Michel Hassenforder
Jan Hendrik Hausmann
Reiko Heckel
Karsten Hölscher
Hardi Hungar
Andrew Jackson
Bernhard Josko
Frédéric Jouault
Andreas Kanzlers
Stephen Kelvin
Dae-Kyoo Kim
Alexander Knapp
Alexander Königs
Matthias Köster
Sascha Konrad
Holger Krahn
Jochen Küster
Juliana Küster-Filipe
Ivan Kurtev
Pierre Laforcade
Benoit Langlois
Lam-Son Lê
Alexander Lechner
Yuehua Lin
Arne Lindow
Chang Liu
Sten Loecher
Marc Lohmann
Shiu Lun Tsang
Viviana Mascardi
Girish Maskeri
Dan Matheson
Wei Monin
Stefan Müller
Andronikos Nedos
Thierry Nodenot
Joost Noppen
Iulian Ober
Jean-Marc Perronne
Andreas Pleuss
Erik Poll
Tadinada V. Prabhakar
Birgit Prammer
Raghu Reddy
Gil Regev
Wolfgang Reisig
Arend Rensink
Robert Rist
Tobias Rötschke
Andreas Roth

Suman Roychoudhury
Enrico Rukzio
Irina Rychkova
Goiuria Sagardui
Paul Sammut
Tim Schattkowsky
Steffen Schlager
Jean-Marc Seigneur
Magdy Serour
Vibhu Sharma
Andrew Simpson
Randy Smith
Jonathan Sprinkle
Thomas Sproesser
Dominik Stein
Ryan Stephenson
Philippe Studer
Thorsten Sturm
Bedir Tekinerdoğan
Bernard Thirion
Stavros Tripakis
Dinh-Trong Trung
Ambrosio Toval
Antonio Vallecillo
Klaas van den Berg
Pim van den Broek
Jesco von Voss
Barbara Weber
Reinhard Wilhelm
James Willans
Alan Cameron Wills
Mariemma I. Yagüe
Zhenxiao Yang
Jing Zhang
Paul Ziemann
Steffen Zschaler

Sponsors

SINFIC
http://www.sinfic.pt

Springer
http://www.springeronline.com

Mentor Graphics
http://www.mentor.com

IBM France
http://www.ibm.com/fr

Supporters

ACM Special Interest Group on Software Engineering
http://www.acm.org

IEEE Computer Society
http://www.ieee.com

New University of Lisbon
http://di.fct.unl.pt

Turismo de Lisboa
http://www.tourismlisbon.com

Object Management Group,
http://www.omg.org

Table of Contents

Metamodeling

Aspects

Profiles and Extensions

OCL

Model Transformation

Verification and Model Consistency

Security

Methodology

Workshops and Tutorials

Empirically Driven Use Case Metamodel Evolution*

Amador Durán[1], Beatriz Bernárdez[1], Marcela Genero[2], and Mario Piattini[2]

[1] University of Seville
{amador,beat}@lsi.us.es
[2] University of Castilla–La Mancha
{marcela.genero,mario.piattini}@uclm.es

Abstract. Metamodel evolution is rarely driven by empirical evidences of metamodel drawbacks. In this paper, the evolution of the use case metamodel used by the publicly available requirements management tool REM is presented. This evolution has been driven by the analysis of empirical data obtained during the assessment of several metrics–based verification heuristics for use cases developed by some of the authors and previously presented in other international fora. The empirical analysis has made evident that some common defects found in use cases developed by software engineering students were caused not only by their lack of experience but also by the expressive limitations imposed by the underlying use case metamodel used in REM. Once these limitations were clearly identified, a number of evolutionary changes were proposed to the REM use case metamodel in order to increase use case quality, i.e. to avoid those situations in which the metamodel were the cause of defects in use case specifications.

Keywords: metamodel evolution, use cases, empirical software engineering

1 Introduction

Metamodel evolution is usually based on a previous theoretical analysis. The usual *evolution vectors* are elimination of internal contradictions, simplification of unnecessary complexities, or enhancement of expressiveness in order to model unforeseen or new concepts [1, 2]. In this paper, the evolution of the use case metamodel implemented in the REM requirements management tool [3] is described. This evolution has been driven not by a theoretical analysis but by the analysis of empirical data obtained during the assessment of several metrics–based verification heuristics for use cases developed by some of the authors (for a description of the verification heuristics and their implementation in REM using XSLT, see [4]; for their empirical assessment and review, see [5]). This empirical analysis has revealed that some common defects in use cases developed by software engineering students had their roots in the underlying REM metamodel, therefore making its evolution necessary in order to increase requirements quality.

The rest of the paper is organized as follows. In the next section, the initial REM use case metamodel is described. The metrics–based verification heuristics that originated the metamodel evolution are briefly described in section 3. In section 4, the results of the

* This work is partially funded by the following projects: AgilWeb (TIC 2003–02737), Tamansi (PCB–02–001) and MESSENGER (PCC–03–003–1).

T. Baar et al. (Eds.): UML 2004, LNCS 3273, pp. 1–11, 2004.

empirical analysis in which the problems in the metamodel were detected are presented. The proposed changes to the metamodel and their analysis are described in section 5. In section 6, some related work is commented and, finally, some conclusions and future work are presented in section 7.

2 Initial Use Case Metamodel

The initial use case metamodel, i.e. the REM metamodel [4], is shown in Fig. 1. This metamodel was designed after a thorough analysis of several proposals for natural language use case templates like [6, 7, 8, 9]. One of the goals in mind when this initial metamodel was developed was to keep use case structure as simple as possible, but including most usual elements proposed by other authors like conditional steps or exceptions.

Apart from inherited requirements attributes, a use case in REM is basically composed of a *triggering event*, a *precondition*, a *postcondition*, and a *ordinary sequence* of steps describing interactions leading to a successful end. Steps are composed of one *action* and may have a condition (see Fig. 1). Three classes of actions are considered: *system actions* performed by the system, *actor actions* performed by one actor, and *use case actions* in which another use case is performed, i.e. UML *inclusions* or *extensions*, depending on whether the step is conditional or not [10]. Steps may also have attached *exceptions*, which are composed of an exception condition (modeled by the *description* attribute), an action (of the same class than step actions) describing the exception treatment, and a *termination* attribute indicating whether the use case is resumed or canceled after the performance of the indicated action.

Another metamodel goal was to make XML encoding simple so the application of XSLT stylesheets were as efficient as possible. In REM, XML data corresponding to requirements is transformed into HTML by applying a configurable XSLT stylesheet, thus providing a WYSIWYG environment for requirements management (see Fig. 2).

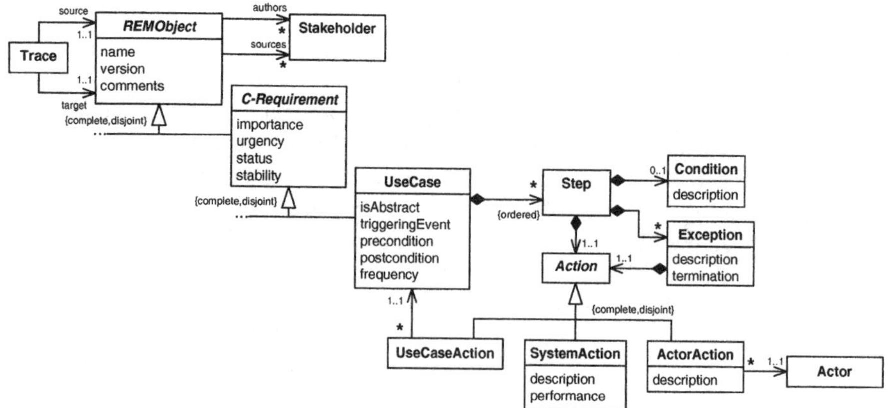

Fig. 1. Initial REM use case metamodel

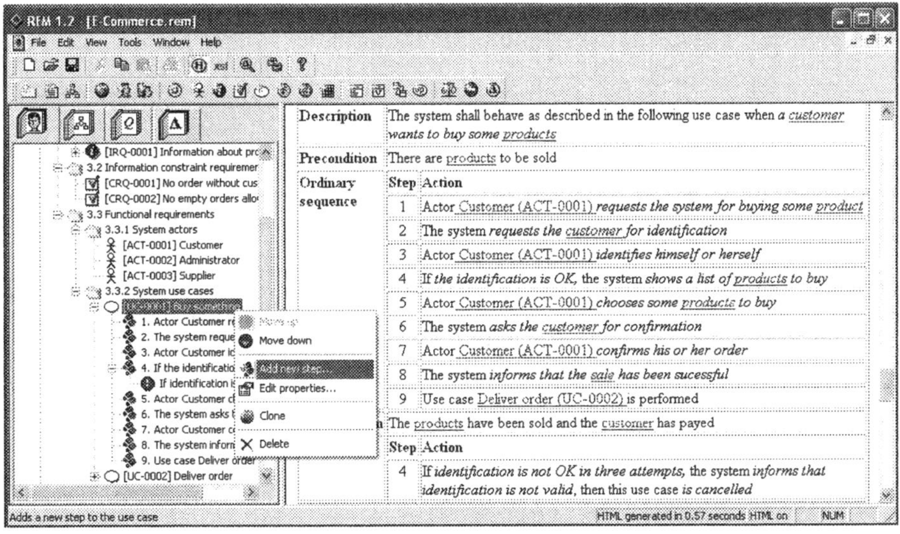

Fig. 2. REM user interface for use cases

In this way, all composition relationships (*black diamonds*) in Fig. 1 are easily mapped into XML hierarchies.

3 Verification Heuristics

As described in [4], the experience of some of the authors in the verification of use cases developed by students using REM led to the definition of several metrics–based, defect

```
context UseCase def:
  -- helper definition
  let NOS_TYPE( t:OclType ) : Sequence( Action ) =
        step->select( action.oclIsTypeOf( t ) )

  -- metrics definition
  let NOS   = step->size()                        -- number of steps
  let NOAS  = NOS_TYPE( ActorAction   )->size()  -- number of actor steps
  let NOSS  = NOS_TYPE( SystemAction  )->size()  -- number of system steps
  let NOUS  = NOS_TYPE( UseCaseAction )->size()  -- number of use case steps
  let NOCS  = (step.condition)->size()            -- number of conditional steps
  let NOE   = (step.exception)->size()            -- number of exceptions
  let NOAS_RATE = NOAS / NOS                      -- actor steps rate
  let NOSS_RATE = NOSS / NOS                      -- system steps rate
  let NOUS_RATE = NOUS / NOS                      -- use case steps rate
  let NOCS_RATE = NOCS / NOS                      -- conditional steps rate
  let NOE_RATE  = NOE  / NOS                      -- exceptions rate
  let CC        = NOCS + NOE + 1                  -- cyclomatic complexity

  -- some metrics relationships
  inv: NOAS + NOSS + NOUS = NOS
  inv: NOAS_RATE + NOSS_RATE + NOUS_RATE = 1
```

Fig. 3. Use case metrics definition in OCL

detection heuristics. These heuristics are based on a simple idea: there are some use case metrics for which a range of *usual* values can be defined; if for a given use case, its metric value is out of its corresponding usual range, then the use case is considered as potentially defective and it should therefore be checked.

In Fig. 3, the OCL definition of the metrics used in the verification heuristics, based on the metamodel in Fig. 1, is shown. As described in [4], these metrics can be easily computed in XSLT and the heuristics can be applied automatically in REM using the XML representation of use cases.

The metrics–based heuristics that led to metamodel evolution and their rationales are briefly described below. The usual ranges were chosen after a statistical analysis of 414 use cases developed by students using REM. For a comprehensive discussion and other metrics–based verification heuristics see [4].

Heuristic (A): NOS should be in $[3, 9]$.
Rationale: A use case with just a few steps is likely to be incomplete. Too many steps usually indicate too low level of detail and make the use case too complex to be understood and defect–prone.

Heuristic (B): NOAS_RATE should be in $[30\%, 70\%]$.
Heuristic (C): NOSS_RATE should be in $[40\%, 80\%]$.
Rationale: A use case describes system–actor interactions, so the rate of actor and system steps should be around 50%.

Heuristic (D): NOUS_RATE should be in $[0\%, 25\%]$.
Rationale: An abusive use of use case relationships makes use cases difficult to understand — customers and users are not familiar with procedure call semantics. Use them to avoid repetition of common steps only.

Heuristic (E): CC should be in $[1, 4]$.
Rationale: A high value of the cyclomatic complexity implies many conditional steps and exceptions, probably making the use case too complex to be understood and defect–prone.

4 Empirical Analysis

The empirical assessment and analysis of the verification heuristics introduced in previous section was carried out by manually verifying 127 use cases in 8 requirements documents developed by students of Software Engineering at the University of Seville. The whole process and detailed results are described in [5]. In this section, only most relevant results are presented, especially those related to the REM use case metamodel evolution.

4.1 Analysis of Heuristic A

This heuristic was widely validated by empirical data: 85% of the use cases out of the usual range of the NOS metric were identified as defective. A subsequent analysis of the detected defects revealed that whereas those use cases with too low NOS were usually either incomplete or trivial or described no interaction at all, use cases with too high NOS were usually at a too low level of detail. On the other hand, for the most part of the 15% of the use cases that were wrongly identified as potentially defective, NOS was high because of the *writing style* or because of the presence of *actor–to–actor* interactions.

Writing Style The writing style has been identified as a very important factor for the accuracy of heuristic A. Whereas some students used only one step for specifying a sequence of consecutive actions carried out either by the system or by a given actor, others used one step for each action, thus increasing NOS (see [7] for a comparison of both styles). This heuristic was designed with the former writing style in mind, but as commented in [5], a further analysis for identifying another usual range for the latter writing style is currently being carried out.

Actor–to–Actor Interactions The inclusion of actor–to–actor interactions cannot be in anyway considered as a defect in use cases, but it dramatically affects the accuracy of heuristic A by increasing NOS without making use cases defective (heuristics B and C are also affected, see below). This is one of the metamodel evolution factors that will be taken into consideration in section 5.

4.2 Analysis of Heuristics B and C

Heuristics B and C were also confirmed by empirical data with 80% and 70% respectively of defective use cases out of usual ranges. Both heuristics are tightly coupled because a high value of one of them implies a low value of the other. Use cases with high NOAS_RATE (and therefore low NOSS_RATE) are usually use cases in which system behavior has been omitted or in which a lot of actor–to–actor interactions have been considered (usually *business use cases*), as commented above. On the other hand, use cases with high NOSS_RATE (and therefore low NOAS_RATE) are usually defective use cases describing *batch* processes or internal system actions only.

4.3 Analysis of Heuristic D

Heuristic D, confirmed with 75% of use cases out of usual range being defective, usually detects use cases with a high number of extensions due to a *menu–like* structure, i.e. use cases without a clear goal in which, depending on an actor choice, a number of different use cases are performed. Nevertheless, most of the 25% of use cases out of usual range but presenting no defects were use cases in which the impossibility of the metamodel of representing *conditional blocks* of steps, i.e. a group of steps with the same condition, forced students to create extending use cases in order to avoid the repetition of the same condition along several consecutive steps. The same happened when the treatment of an exceptional situation required more than one single action to be performed (the metamodel in Fig. 1 only allows one action to be associated to an exception). In this case, students were also forced to create an extending use case that was performed when the exception occurred. An example of this situation using a different use case metamodel (Leite's metamodel for scenarios [11]) can be also seen in [12].

4.4 Analysis of Heuristic E

This heuristic was confirmed by empirical data with 87% of use cases out of usual range being defective. The usual cause of defect was the abusive use of conditional steps of the form "*if ¡condition¿, the system goes to step X*", making use cases almost impossible to understand. As commented above for heuristic D, the lack of conditional blocks was the usual case for abnormally high values of CC in non–defective use cases when students decided not to create an extending use case but repeating the same condition along several steps, thus artificially increasing CC value.

5 Metamodel Evolution

Taking into consideration the analysis of empirical data presented in previous section, three main evolution vectors were identified: one for evolving the metamodel in order to be able to represent conditional branches, another for allowing complex treatments of exceptions, and another for introducing new specializations of actions.

5.1 Conditional Branches

The analysis of empirical data has made evident the inadequacy of use case metamodels in which alternative branches consisting of more than one step can be represented only by means of extension relationships or by repeating the same condition along several steps. The analysis has detected that students have overcame this problem either creating an excessive number of *abstract use cases* [13] which extend one use case only (i. e. *singleton abstract use cases*), or repeating the same condition along several consecutive steps. Both situations are clearly undesirable and must therefore be avoided by enhancing the underlying use case metamodel.

In order to allow conditional branches of more than one step, two tentative evolved metamodels were initially proposed (see Fig. 4). The main difference between them is that whereas the former allows the nesting of conditional branches, the latter does not. Keeping the initial goal of having a simple use case structure, and taking into consideration that non–software professionals find nested conditional structures difficult to understand, we decided to allow only one level of conditional branches in the ordinary sequence (a second level is introduced by exceptions, see section 5.2).

A question raised during the discussion of the metamodel evolution was whether conditional branches should have an *else* branch or not. Once again, the goal of keeping use case structure simple made us discard the *if–then–else* structure, which is not often familiar for customers and users. If an *else* branch is necessary, another conditional branch with the explicit negation of the *if* condition can be added to the ordinary sequence of the use case.

Another issue considered during metamodel evolution was the termination of conditional branches. Considering the excellent study of alternatives in use cases presented in [2], we found necessary to specify if a conditional branch: *(a)* resumes the ordinary sequence after performing its last step; *(b)* leads to a goal success termination of the use case; or *(c)* leads to a goal failure termination. This information is modeled as the enumerated attribute termination in class ConditionalBranch. See Fig. 5 for the explicit visual representation adopted for the three different situations in REM.

Thus, the second metamodel in Fig. 4 was finally adopted for the next version of REM. Notice that in both models composition associations can be easily mapped into XML hierarchies, thus keeping the original goal of having a direct mapping into XML.

5.2 Exception Treatment

The analysis of heuristic D pinpointed the need of allowing exceptions to have more than one associated action so *singleton abstract use cases* could be avoided. In order to do so, the composition relationship between exceptions and actions has increased its maximum cardinality from 1 to many in the evolved metamodel (see Fig. 4).

Although conditional branches and exceptions have a lot in common in the evolved metamodel, we decided to keep them as different classes because no empirical evidence pinpointed this as a problem. Notice that keeping exceptions as part of steps, instead of considering as conditional branches, introduces a second nesting level, i.e. a step in a conditional branch can have an attached exception. This situation, which was already present in previous metamodel, presented no empirical evidence of being a source of problems, so we considered there was no need for any change.

See Fig. 6 for the new visual representation of exceptions, in which actions are represented by the same icon than steps for the sake of usability, and exception termination (*resuming* or *canceling* the use case) has been made visually explicit coherently with visual representation of conditional branches shown in Fig. 5.

5.3 Specializations of Actions

The metamodel evolution for the inclusion of new specializations of actions (see Fig. 7) might seem not as obviously necessary as the changes described in previous sec-

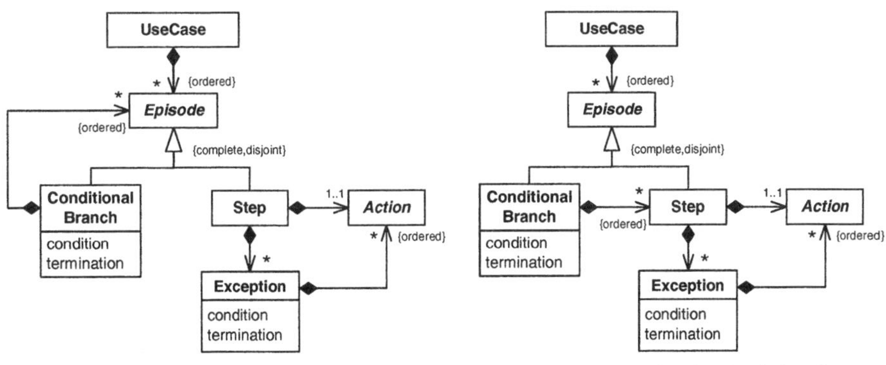

Fig. 4. Tentative evolved metamodels for conditional branches

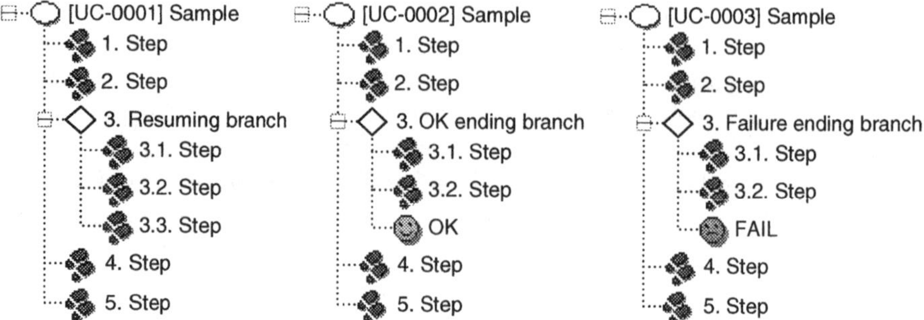

Fig. 5. Visual representation of conditional branches (evolved metamodel)

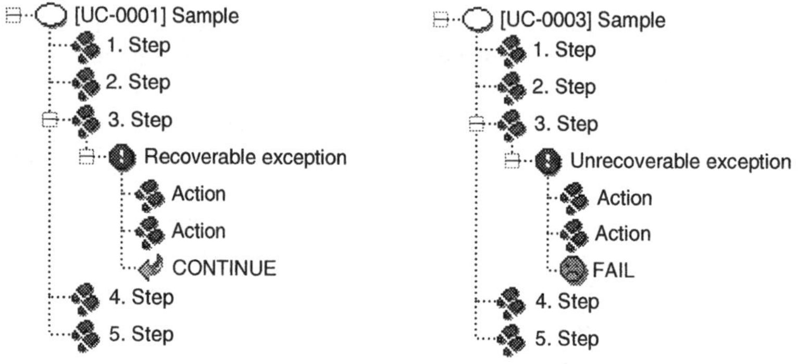

Fig. 6. Visual representation of exceptions (evolved metamodel)

tions. Nevertheless, this evolutive change makes possible the definition of new use case metrics (see Fig. 8) that allow the redefinition of the verification heuristic B in order to increase its accuracy. These new metrics also make possible the definition of new heuristics for defect detection considering different types of actor actions (see section

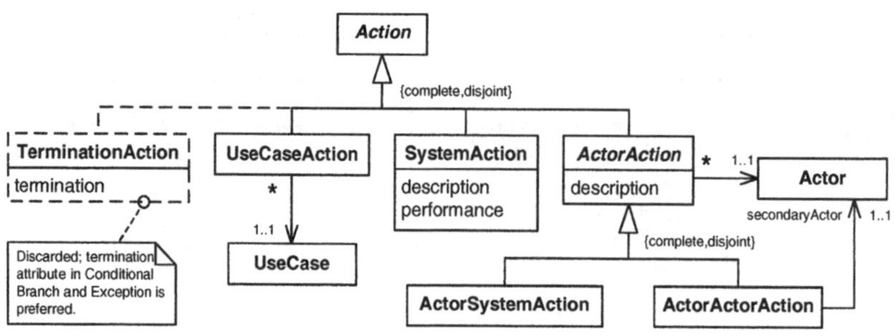

Fig. 7. Evolved metamodel for new specializations of actions

```
context UseCase def:
  -- helper definitions
  let allSteps : Sequence( Step ) =
    episode->iterate( e : Episode; acc : Sequence( Step ) = Sequence{} |
      if   e.oclIsTypeOf( Step ) then acc->including( e.oclAsType( Step ) )
      else acc->union( e.oclAsType( ConditionalBranch ).step )
      endif
    )

  let allBranches : Sequence( ConditionalBranch ) =
    episode->select( e | e.oclIsTypeOf( ConditionalBranch ) )

  let NOS_TYPE( t:OclType ) : Sequence( Action ) =
    allSteps->select( action.oclIsKindOf( t ) )

  -- metrics definition
  let NOS   = allSteps->size()                     -- no. of steps
  let NOAAS = NOS_TYPE( ActorActorAction )->size()  -- no. of actor-actor steps
  let NOASS = NOS_TYPE( ActorSystemAction )->size() -- no. of actor-system steps
  let NOAS  = NOS_TYPE( ActorAction )->size()       -- no. of actor steps
  let NOSS  = NOS_TYPE( SystemAction  )->size()     -- no. of system steps
  let NOUS  = NOS_TYPE( UseCaseAction )->size()     -- no. of use case steps
  let NOCB  = allBranches->size()                   -- no. of cond. branches
  let NOE   = (allStep.exception)->size()           -- no. of exceptions
  let NOAS_RATE  = NOAS / NOS                       -- actor steps rate
  let NOAAS_RATE = NOAAS / NOS                      -- actor-actor steps rate
  let NOASS_RATE = NOASS / NOS                      -- actor-system steps rate
  let NOSS_RATE  = NOSS / NOS                       -- system steps rate
  let NOUS_RATE  = NOUS / NOS                       -- use case steps rate
  let NOCS_RATE  = NOCS / NOS                       -- conditional steps rate
  let NOE_RATE   = NOE  / NOS                       -- exceptions rate
  let CC         = NOCB + NOE + 1                   -- cyclomatic complexity

  -- some metrics relationships
  inv: NOAS = NOAAS + NOASS
  inv: NOAS + NOSS + NOUS = NOS
  inv: NOAS_RATE = NOAAS_RATE + NOASS_RATE
  inv: NOAS_RATE + NOSS_RATE + NOUS_RATE = 1
```

Fig. 8. New use case metrics definition in OCL

7). Moreover, the explicit identification of the secondary actor in actor–to–actor actions adds important information for use cases; in the previous metamodel, the secondary actor in an actor–to–actor actions was *hidden* in the text of the action description.

As shown in Fig. 7 in dashed line, a new kind of action, namely TerminationAction, was temporarily considered for expressing the termination of conditional branches and exceptions. This change was eventually discarded in favour of the termination attribute because this new kind of action made possible the termination of the use case at any point, something that would require adding complex constraints to the metamodel in order to be avoided.

5.4 Evolutive Changes Summary

The evolutive changes in the finally adopted use case metamodel are the following:

1. A new abstract class, Episode, has been introduced for representing both steps and conditional branches in the ordinary sequence of use cases.

2. A new class, ConditionalBranch, has been introduced for representing conditional branches inside ordinary sequence of use cases. Conditional branches are composed of a sequence of steps. Notice that this is a non–recursive composition, i.e. conditional branches cannot contain other conditional branches. Conditional branches also have an enumerated attribute, termination, that can take one of the following values: *resumes, OK_ending, failure_ending.*
3. The cardinality of the composition between Exception and Action classes has changed from 1–to–1 to 1–to–many in order to allow the specification of more than one Action as the exception treatment, thus avoiding the need of creating singleton abstract use cases for such situations.
4. The attribute description of class Exception has been renamed as condition in order to make its semantics more evident.
5. The ActorAction class has been specialized into two new subclasses, ActorSystemAction and ActorActorAction. The latter has an association with the Actor class representing the secondary actor.

6 Related Work

As far as we know, this is the only work on empirically driven metamodel evolution, i.e. metamodel evolution motivated after the analysis of empirical data about the quality of the models that are *instances of* the metamodel. Other works on metamodel evolution and use case metamodels are commented below.

Henderson–Seller's works [1, 14] are an excellent example of a proposal for metamodel evolution driven by a thorough theoretically analysis, although not directly related to use cases. He focuses on metamodel deficiencies in the UML.

In [2], several changes to the UML 1.3 use case metamodel are proposed in order to support several types of alternative courses, namely *alternative stories*, *use case exceptions*, and *alternative parts*. This work has had a strong influence on the evolution of the REM use case metamodel, especially on the evolution of conditional branches, as commented in section 5.1.

In [15], an evolution of the UML 1.3 use case metamodel is proposed in order to support a viewpoint–oriented approach to requirements engineering. In [16], a refactoring–oriented use case metamodel is described, including a rich set of use case relationships.

7 Conclusions and Future Work

In this paper, we have presented an evolution of the REM use case metamodel. Unlike other metamodel evolutions which are driven by theoretical analysis, the evolution presented in this paper has been driven by the analysis of empirical data. We consider that, specially in an informal realm like use cases, empirical evidence should be the main metamodel evolution force, even above theoretical analysis. In our case, the REM use case metamodel has experienced a significant evolution that would have not probably taken place without an empirical approach.

Following our empirical philosophy, the immediate future work is to validate the metamodel evolution, i.e. to check if the evolved metamodel increases the quality of use cases. By the time the next version of the REM tool will be available, we will be able to drive the corresponding empirical studies with our students.

We are also investigating new defect detection heuristics, but for the moment, the lack of use cases developed using the new metamodel allows only speculative approaches.

References

[1] Henderson-Sellers, B.: Some problems with the UML V1.3 metamodel. In: Proc. of 34th Annual Hawaii International Conference on System Sciences (HICSS), IEEE CS Press (2001)

[2] Metz, P., O'Brien, J., Weber, W.: Specifying Use Case Interaction: Types of Alternative Courses. Journal of Object Technology **2** (2003) 111–131

[3] Durán, A.: REM web site. http://rem.lsi.us.es/REM (2004)

[4] Durán, A., Ruiz-Cortés, A., Corchuelo, R., Toro, M.: Supporting Requirements Verification using XSLT. In: Proceedings of the IEEE Joint International Requirements Engineering Conference (RE), Essen, Germany, IEEE CS Press (2002) 141–152

[5] Bernárdez, B., Durán, A., Genero, M.: An Empirical Evaluation and Review of a Metrics–Based Approach for Use Case Verification. Journal of Research and Practice in Information Technology (2004) To be published in a special collection on Requirements Engineering.

[6] Coleman, D.: A Use Case Template: Draft for Discussion. Fusion Newsletter (1998)

[7] Cockburn, A.: Writing Effective Use Cases. Addison–Wesley (2001)

[8] Schneider, G., Winters, J.P.: Applying Use Cases: a Practical Guide. Addison–Wesley (1998)

[9] Durán, A., Bernárdez, B., Ruiz, A., Toro, M.: A Requirements Elicitation Approach Based in Templates and Patterns. In: WER'99 Proceedings, Buenos Aires (1999)

[10] OMG: Unified Modeling Language Specification, v1.5. The Object Management Group, Inc. (2003)

[11] Leite, J.C.S.P., Hadad, H., Doorn, J., Kaplan, G.: A Scenario Construction Process. Requirements Engineering Journal **5** (2000)

[12] Ridao, M., Doorn, J.: Anomaly Modeling with Scenarios (in Spanish). In: Proceedings of the Workshop on Requirements Engineering (WER), Valencia, Spain (2002)

[13] Jacobson, I., Griss, M., Jonsson, P.: Software Reuse: Architecture, Process and Organization for Business Success. Addison–Wesley (1997)

[14] Barbier, F., Henderson-Sellers, B., Le Parc–Lacayrelle, A., Bruel, J.M.: Formalization of the Whole–Part Relationship in the Unified Modeling Language. IEEE Transactions on Software Engineering **29** (2003)

[15] Nakatani, T., Urai, T., Ohmura, S., Tamai, T.: A Requirements Description Metamodel for Use Cases. In: Proc. of 8th Asia–Pacific Software Engineering Conference (APSEC), IEEE CS Press (2003)

[16] Rui, K., Butler, G.: Refactoring Use Case Models: The Metamodel. In: Proc. of 25th Computer Science Conference (ACSC). (2003)

Applying OO Metrics to Assess UML Meta-models

Haohai Ma[1, 2], Weizhong Shao[1], Lu Zhang[1], Zhiyi Ma[1] and Yanbing Jiang[1]

[1] Software Institute, School of Electronics Engineering and Computer Science, Peking University, Beijing 100871, P.R. China
{mahh, wzshao, zhanglu, mzy, jyb}@sei.pku.edu.cn
[2] Department of Computer Science, Inner Mongolia University, Hohhot 010021, P.R. China

Abstract. UML has been coming of age through more than seven years development, in which there are not only minor revision like from UML 1.1 to UML 1.2, but also significant improvement like final adoption of UML 2.0 submissions. However there is so far lack of an objective assessment to UML meta-models, which can be used to control and predict the evolution of the UML. In this paper we regard UML meta-models as the equivalent of Object-Oriented (OO) design models. Therefore, we can adapt OO design metrics and criteria as a method to assess UML meta-models. Our method conducts the assessment of stability and design quality to UML meta-models in versions of 1.1, 1.3, 1.4 (with Action Semantics), 1.5, and 2.0. Based on the results we analyze the evolution of the UML versions and provide the applicability suggestions to the method.

1. Introduction

The Unified Modeling Language (UML) was first standardized in 1997 as the end of the methods wars, and it quickly grew to become a de facto modeling language [10]. As with all software, the UML evolves through a number of iterations during seven years down the road. Each iteration leads to a newly designed or reinforced UML meta-model, in which meta-classes are instantiated as modeling constructs. The evolution of the UML results from incorporating new technologies, refining semantics and notations, as well as catering to better usage requirements and rectifying faults. As the UML meta-model evolves, the abstract syntax of the meta-model changes due to the modification of meta-classes and relationships between them, the addition of new meta-classes, and the removal of obsolete meta-classes. Each step of the evolution of the UML meta-model has done significant reworks to meet the changes or augments of responsibilities and requirements as a modeling language.

Once a new UML version is released, it may be costly and time-consuming for testing the compatibility and upgrading modeling tools and models that built with the previous versions. This fact together with the high costs of developing and revising the UML specifications indicates the importance of understanding and characterizing the evolution of UML meta-models.

A number of papers, especially those presented by the UML revisers, such as [4], [10], [11], [17], have made surveys to delivered UML versions and expectations to

T. Baar et al. (Eds.): UML 2004, LNCS 3273, pp. 12-26, 2004.

the latest one, UML 2.0. However, there is so far lack of objective assessment of UML evolution. The assessment can not only qualitatively make sure that UML will stay up to date with the latest developments in the software industry [25], but also quantitatively evaluate the complexity of released UML versions so as to control and predict its future evolution. This requires that there must be a method assisting the assessment of UML meta-models as each version is released. Particularly, a maneuverable assessment method for identifying structural flaws or quality descending in an UML meta-model will provide more reliable suggestions for effectively improving the design of the meta-model.

Inspired by metrics research for measuring systems developed with the object-oriented (OO) paradigm [6] [12] [15], we propose a method for assessing UML meta-models, which can identify and characterize stability and design quality of the meta-models. In our empirical studies, the method is applied to five meta-models in UML specifications, including versions of 1.1, 1.3, 1.4 (with Action Semantics), 1.5, and 2.0. Our assessment of UML 2.0 only focuses on its Superstructure part [26] since it is actually on behalf of UML 2.0 meta-model. We omit UML 1.2 since it does not include any significant technical improvements to the language [10].

The remaining of this paper is organized as follows. Section 2 overviews the assessment method and reasons its feasibility. Section 3 and section 4 present experiments for applying the method to assess UML meta-models. Section 5 analyzes the results of the assessment to characterize the UML evolution. A discussion of our method's applicability is presented in section 6. Finally the conclusion of the paper and further works are provided in section 7.

2. UML Meta-models Assessment Using OO Metrics

2.1 Approach Overview

Over the last decade, object-orientation has become the overwhelming paradigm of choices for developing software. A key research area in this field is to leverage a suite of metrics for measuring systems developed with OO paradigm [6] [12] [15]. Research in proposing, applying, validating, and extending metrics for object-oriented systems has been popular. The literatures of [8], [15] summarize OO metrics into two perspectives: One is the internal perspective, i.e. metrics are collected and computed from attributes of entities in the system using clearly defined rules. The other one, the external perspective, allows the use of the metrics in response to prediction or assessment needs of quality characteristics of system development.

According to the two perspectives, we adapt two practical and straightforward methods from OO metrics researches as our groundwork.

The foundation of our method for assessing the stability of UML meta-models roots in the methods of Bansiya [2] and Mattsson [14]. The former carries out the stability assessment from the level of the architecture, the latter conduct the same assessment from the level of individual class. Accordingly, our method for the assessment is studied from the corresponding levels. For each level of the stability assessment, firstly, we select some suitable OO metrics in the literatures and adapt them for the assessment of UML meta-model characteristics. Additionally, we define some more metrics especially for assessing UML meta-models. Secondly, we apply these metrics to the five versions of UML meta-models and collect a suite of metrics values. Finally, based on the collected metrics values, we compute respectively: 1) the *normalized extent-of-change* which reflects the architectural stability of the meta-models; and 2) the *relative extent-of-change* which evaluates the changeability between successive UML meta-models at the level of individual meta-classes. Both *extent-of-changes* can be used as the complement and consistent verification to each other.

The base of our assessment of design quality of UML meta-models comes from Bansiya's hierarchical model for OO design quality assessment [3]. Although there is no universally agreed definition of software quality, many methods for quality assessment are based on the assumption that evaluating a product's internal characteristics some reasonable conclusions can be drawn about the product's external quality attributes [9]. In this paper, we adapt such a method (i.e. [3]) for assessing UML meta-models. On the basis of a set of computation formulas adopted from [3], our method can evaluate six quality attributes such as functionality, effectiveness, understandability, extendibility, reusability, and flexibility from eleven design properties including design size, hierarchies, abstraction, encapsulation, coupling, cohesion, composition, inheritance, polymorphism, messaging, and complexity. Then the design properties can be mapped into one or more metrics that have been used in the stability assessment. Since the values of these metrics for UML meta-models are all set, we can easily draw conclusions of the quality assessment of UML meta-models.

2.2 Feasibility

The UML meta-model is defined as the layer of M_2 in a four-layer meta-modeling architecture (M_3-M_0). The syntactical view of the UML meta-model is the abstract syntax, which is composed of instances of limited meta-meta-classes of the M_3 layer, such as meta-class, meta-attribute and meta-association. We take the abstract syntax as our main aim to assess through leveraging OO metrics because we believe that the abstract syntax is homogenous with the class diagram of general OO design. The reasons lie in the following facts. 1) The abstract syntax is provided as a model described in a subset of UML, consisting of a UML class diagram [20] [21] [22] [23]. 2) The four-layer architecture can be applied recursively many times so that what is a meta-model in one case can be a model in another case [24]. 3) The "meta" notion is not a property of a model, but of the role a model plays in relation to another model: a meta-model relates to a model in the same way that a model relates to an instance model [1]. Thus it is reasonable that we regard UML meta-models as a kind of OO design model for measurement.

In such a case, we can map the components of the abstract syntax in the UML meta-model into that of the class diagram in OO design, simply as:

$$\begin{aligned} &meta\text{-}class \rightarrow class \\ &meta\text{-}attribute \rightarrow attribute \\ &meta\text{-}association \rightarrow association \end{aligned}$$

Usually, the design of classes is consistently declared to be central to the OO paradigm [6] [27]. The metrics outlined in research specifically focus on measuring class diagrams of the system. This makes it possible that implementation details of the system may not be needed when carrying out a measurement to OO systems, thus the measurement may be used in the early phase of Software Development Life Cycle (SDLC), such as analysis-time or design-time [3] [16]. Although there is no implementation for meta-classes in the UML meta-model, many OO metrics can be adapted for meta-model assessment because they are independent of implementation. Therefore, we can find enough metrics for our assessment. Particularly, we adapt some implementation independent metrics in [2], [14], and [3], which are only based on the class declarations in OO frameworks without any additional source code information required.

Of course, we have to admit that class diagrams that define the abstract syntax of UML meta-models are completely static since these diagrams only represent UML modeling constructs and their relationships, i.e. a kind of information model, but are short of operational methods which represent collaborations amongst instances in OO programs. However, meta-classes in UML meta-models have well-formed rules and additional operations for depicting semantic constraints in the meta-model. In a sense, they are similar to operational methods of the classes in OO programs. Thus we view well-formed rules and additional operations as the methods in the meta-classes.

3. Experiment 1: Assessing Stability of UML Meta-models

3.1 Architectural Level Assessment

The outcome of the assessment in this sub-section is the *normalized extent-of-change* metric which indicate the stability of UML meta-models at the architectural level. The assessment process consists of the following steps.

Step 1: Selecting metrics for assessment

Several literatures have proposed and studied metrics for OO programming [6] [8], and some for OO frameworks in particular [2] [14]. We firstly select suitable metrics from them. These metrics are related to the relationships amongst meta-classes and the structuring of meta-classes in inheritance hierarchies. Taking UML meta-model specialties into account, it leads to the definition of six new metrics, ANS, AWF, AAP, NAC, NCC, and NEK. The architectural meta-model metrics are listed in Table 1. The metrics especially for UML meta-models are in bold fonts.

Step 2: Data Collection

The metrics data was collected from [20], [21], [22], [23], and [26] by four M.S. students who are familiar with UML specifications because they take part in designing and implementing our UML modeling tool, JBOO (Jade Bird Object-Oriented tools) [13]. JBOO is upgrading to version 4.0 based on UML 2.0, pervious versions of JBOO are designed to follow UML 1.3 and 1.4 in turn. The data collected for each version of UML meta-models have been verified consistency with corresponding versions of UML Meta-Model code packages in JBOO, thereby reducing the possibility of human errors. Table 2 shows the data collected for the architectural metrics described in Tables 1 from five versions of UML meta-models.

Table 1. Architectural metrics descriptions

Metric	Description
DSC	Design size in meta-classes.
NOH	Number of hierarchies. It is a count of the number of non-inherited classes that have children in a meta-model.
MNL	Maximum number of the level of inheritance.
NSI	Number of single inheritance meta-classes.
NMI	Number of multiple inheritance meta-classes.
ADI	Average depth of the meta-class inheritance structure.
AWI	Average width of the meta-class inheritance structure.
ANA	Average number of ancestors.
ANDC	Average number of distinct meta-classes that a meta-class associates with.
ANAT	Average number of meta-attributes.
ANAG	Average number of meta-aggregations.
ANS	**Average number of stereotypes.**
AWF	**Average number of well-formed rules.**
AAP	**Average number of additional operations.**
NAC	**Number of abstract meta-classes.**
NCC	**Number of concrete meta-classes.**
NEK	**Number of meta-classes who have no parent and no child in meta-model. Most of them stand for enumeration kinds.**

Table 2. Actual architecture assessment metric values of UML meta-models

Metric	UML1.1	UML1.3	UML1.4	UML1.5	UML2.0
DSC	120	133	192	194	260
NOH	2	2	3	3	1
MNL	6	6	7	7	9
NSI	83	94	157	159	209
NMI	5	7	7	7	18
ADI	2.46	2.45	2.92	2.93	3.87
AWI	0.77	0.81	0.89	0.89	0.95
ANA	2.50	2.68	2.95	2.97	4.26
ANDC	0.86	0.90	1.40	1.65	1.03
ANAT	0.64	0.62	0.55	0.66	0.39
ANAG	0.32	0.29	0.51	0.70	0.65
ANS	0.38	0.35	0.32	0.29	0.22
AWF	1.2	1.29	1.49	1.49	1.37
AAP	0.28	0.33	0.44	0.43	0.31
NAC	10	13	25	26	46
NCC	110	120	167	168	214
NEK	30	30	25	25	32

We see that UML meta-models have had an increase of the number of meta-classes (DSC) more than double times, from 120 meta-classes in version 1.1 to 260 meta-classes in version 2.0. The values of MNL, NSI, ADI, AWI, ANA, ANS, NAC, and NCC agree with the increasing value of the number of meta-classes (DSC). The number of hierarchical tree (NOH) coexisting in a meta-model decreases from the maximum of 3 in version 1.4 and 1.5 down to 1 in version 2.0. Adversely, the number of multiple inheritance meta-classes (NMI) has a dramatically increase from 5 in UML 1.1 to 18 in UML 2.0. There are a minor change of the values of ANDC, ANAT, ANAG, AWF, and AAP except for a few peaking values appearing in UML 1.4 or 1.5. Another decrease number appears on ANS, it implies that the number of stereotypes (=ANS*DSC) of UML meta-models is nearly the same. UML 1.1, 1.3 and 2.0 hold more enumeration kinds than UML 1.4 and 1.5 according to the value of NEK.

Step 3: Computing Normalized Extent-of-Change

In order to calculate values of different ranges together, the architectural metrics values are normalized in Table 3 with respect to the metric's values in the version pervious to the current one (the first version are assigned with 1 as a base). For example, the normalized DSC of UML 1.4 is $DSC_{1.4}$(=192) / $DSC_{1.3}$ (=133) = 1.44. The normalized metric values of versions are summed to compute *aggregate-changes*. The *normalized extent-of-change* value for versions is computed by taking the difference of the *aggregate-change* of a version (V_i, with i > 0) with the *aggregate change* value of the first version (V_1). For example, the *aggregate-change* of UML 1.4 is V_3 (=21.92) – V_1 (=17) = 4.92

Table 3. Normalized architecture assessment metric values and extent-of-change

Metric	UML1.1	UML1.3	UML1.4	UML1.5	UML2.0
DSC	1	1.11	1.44	1.01	1.34
NOH	1	1.	1.5	1.	0.33
MNL	1	1.	1.17	1.	1.29
NSI	1	1.13	1.67	1.01	1.31
NMI	1	1.4	1.	1.	2.57
ADI	1	1.	1.19	1.	1.32
AWI	1	1.05	1.1	1.	1.07
ANA	1	1.07	1.1	1.01	1.43
ANDC	1	1.05	1.56	1.18	0.62
ANAT	1	0.97	0.89	1.2	0.59
ANAG	1	0.91	1.76	1.37	0.93
ANS	1	0.92	0.91	0.91	0.76
AWF	1	1.08	1.16	1.	0.92
AAP	1	1.18	1.33	0.98	0.72
NAC	1	1.3	1.92	1.04	1.77
NCC	1	1.09	1.39	1.01	1.27
NEK	1	1.	0.83	1.	1.28
Aggregate change	17	18.25	21.92	17.71	19.53
Normalized Extent-of-change	0.00	1.25	4.92	0.71	2.53

According to [2], the *normalized extent-of-change* metric is an effective indicator for assessment of stability of meta-models from an architectural perspective. Fig. 1 shows the *normalized extent-of-change* values of UML meta-models. Higher values of the indicator are the reflective of higher instability of the architecture, values closer to zero indicate greater stability.

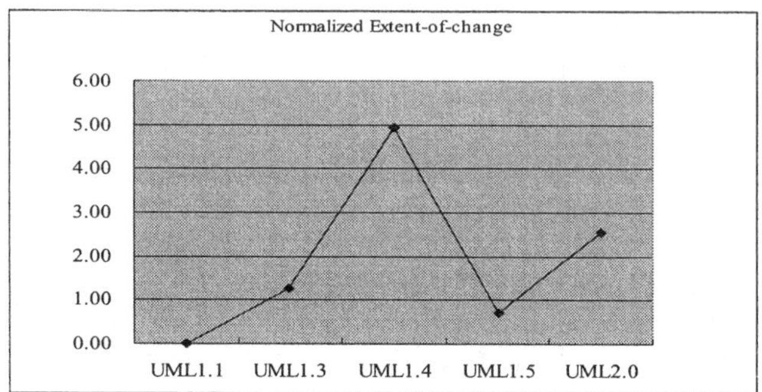

Fig. 1. Normalized extent-of-change metric values for UML meta-models

3.2 Meta-class Level Assessment

The outcome of the assessment in this sub-section is the *relative extent-of-change* metric [14], which is somewhat similar to the *normalized extent-of-change* metric. The *relative extent-of-change* metric, however, focuses on individual meta-class level. The calculation of the measurement is based on successive UML meta-model versions. For example, UML1.1/UML1.3 means it is measured between UML 1.1 and UML 1.3. The used ten meta-class metrics are listed in Table 4, in which the bold NOS, NWF, and NOP are also special for UML meta-models.

Table 4. Meta-class metrics descriptions

Metric	Description
VPC	Parent meta-classes
NAT	Number of meta-attributes
DOI	Depth of the meta-class inheritance
NOC	Number of directed children
NOA	Number of ancestors
NDC	Number of distinct meta-classes that a meta-class associates with
NAG	Number of the meta-aggregations
NOS	**Number of Stereotypes**
NWF	**Number of well-formed rules**
NOP	**Number of additional operations**

Each metric in Table 4 depicts a meta-class characteristic and its value can be changed between successive UML versions. If the value of a particular metric of a meta-class changes from one version to the next, this is defined as one *unit-of-change*. In Table 5, the values of ten meta-class metrics obtained from UML versions are presented. Taking VPC as an example, there are totally 17 *unit-of-changes* happened between UML1.1 and UML 1.3, which means that the parents of 17 meta-classes in UML 1.1 have changed when UML evolves to version 1.3.

In order to calculate the *total unit-of-changes*, firstly, we have to know the *growth units* between successive meta-models, since a number of meta-classes are removed from the predecessor version or added to the successor version (see Table 6). The value of the *growth units* is a product of *growth number of meta-classes* between successive versions in Table 6 and 10 (number of metrics that can change for a meta-class). Then, the *total unit-of-changes* is the sum of *unit-of-changes* in all metrics and *growth units* between successive versions.

Table 5. Meta-class assessment metric values and relative extent-of-change

Metric	UML1.1/ UML1.3	UML1.3/ UML1.4	UML1.4/ UML1.5	UML1.5/ UML2.0
VPC	17	6	0	57
NAT	52	11	10	27
DOI	36	2	0	68
NOC	15	8	2	24
NOA	25	20	0	74
NDC	66	29	41	55
NAG	42	9	17	33
NOS	14	7	1	11
NWF	73	75	51	69
NOP	20	32	16	21
Growth units	130	590	20	660
Total unit-of-changes	490	789	158	1099
Maximum unit-of-changes	1200	1330	1920	1940
Relative extent-of-change	40.8%	59.3%	8.2%	56.6%

Table 6. Change and growth numbers of successive UML versions

Metric	UML1.1/ UML1.3	UML1.3/ UML1.4	UML1.4/ UML1.5	UML1.5/ UML2.0
Removed meta-classes	18	20	0	101
Added meta-classes	31	79	2	167
Growth number of meta-classes	13	59	2	66

To understand what the *total unit-of-changes* in Table 5 really means, we compare it with the *maximum unit-of-changes*. The *maximum unit-of-changes* represents the case where all the metrics would have changed values for all meta-classes in a version. We define the *relative extent-of-change* metric as the *total unit-of-changes* relative to the *maximum unit-of-changes*. For example, version 1.1 of UML has 120 meta-classes which give a theoretical maximum of 120 * 10 = 1200 *unit-of-changes*. The *total unit-of-changes* between version 1.1 and 1.3 is 490. Thus the *relative extent-of-change* between version 1.1 and 1.3 is (490 / 1200) * 100 = 40.8%. Fig.2 illustrates the *relative extent-of-change* metric values fluctuating with UML evolution. Higher values of the metric reflect more changes happened between successive UML meta-models, values closer to zero indicate higher similarity between two versions. Except for UML1.4 evolving to UML 1.5, we can see that almost half of meta-classes changed during UML's version upgrading.

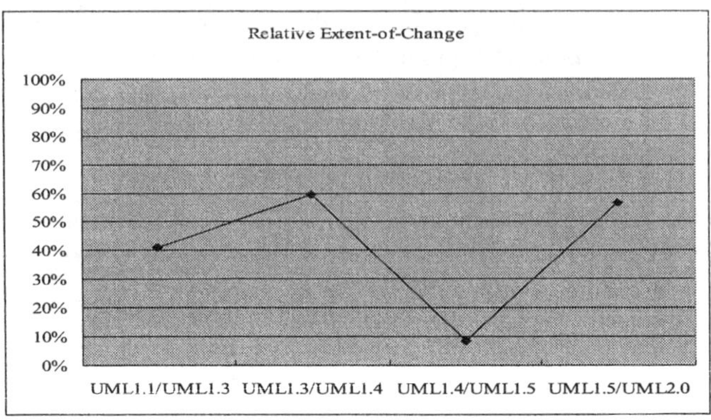

Fig. 2. Relative extent-of-change metric values for successive UML meta-models

4. Experiment 2: Assessing Design Quality of UML Meta-models

First of all, we define six quality attributes of UML meta-model with reference to [3]. Table 7 summarizes the definitions of the attributes.

Table 7. Quality attribute definitions

Quality Attributes	Definition
Reusability	A lower coupled and higher cohesive meta-model design is provided that is reused by different domains.
Flexibility	Characteristics that allow the incorporation of changes in a meta-model design.
Understandability	The properties of the meta-model design that enable it to be easily learned and comprehended.
Functionality	The responsibilities assigned to the meta-classes of a meta-model design.
Extendibility	The meta-model design allows for the incorporation of new requirements.
Effectiveness	This refers to a design's ability to achieve the desired functionality.

Secondly, the quality attributes could be calculated by eleven design properties (see Table 9). The relative significance of individual design properties that influence a quality attribute is weighted proportionally. A schema for weighting the influences is presented in Table 8, adopted from [3].

Table 8. Computation formulas for quality attributes from design properties

Quality Attributes	Definition
Reusability	-0.25*Coupling+0.25*Cohesion+0.5*Messaging+0.5*Design Size
Flexibility	0.25*Encapsulation-0.25*Coupling+0.5*Composition+0.5*Polymorphism
Understandability	-0.33*Abstraction+0.33*Encapsulation-0.33*Coupling+0.33*Cohesion-0.33*Polymorphism-0.33*Complexity-0.33*Design Size
Functionality	0.12*Cohesion+0.22*Polymorphism+0.22*Messaging+0.22*Design Size+0.22*Hierarchies
Extendibility	0.5*Abstraction-0.5*Coupling+0.5*Inheritance+0.5*Polymorphism
Effectiveness	0.2*Abstraction+0.2*Encapsulation+0.2*Composition+0.2*Inheritance+0.2*Polymorphism

Thirdly, each of these design properties can be directly mapped into one or more metrics which assess stability of UML meta-models in Table 1. Table 9 summarizes the mapping and the values of those metrics that are excerpted from Table 2. The mapping rules of design properties and the metrics are deduced according to the principles in [3]. However, there are no direct mappings from the metrics to the design properties of *encapsulation* and *cohesion* since both of them are derived from relative complete OO class declarations that possess private attributes and method parameters. We simply assign 1 to both of them due to the fact that the meta-class represents a single, well-encapsulated, and semantically meaningful concept in UML meta-model, which is viewed as the most desirable cohesion in [7].

Table 9. Mapping design metrics to design properties and actual property values for UML meta-models

Design Property	Design Metric	UML 1.1	UML 1.3	UML 1.4	UML 1.5	UML 2.0
Design Size	DSC	120	133	192	194	260
Hierarchies	NOH	2	2	3	3	1
Abstraction	ANA	2.50	2.68	2.95	2.97	4.26
Encapsulation	—	1	1	1	1	1
Coupling	ANDC	0.86	0.90	1.40	1.65	1.03
Cohesion	—	1	1	1	1	1
Composition	ANAG	0.32	0.29	0.51	0.70	0.65
Inheritance	ADI	2.46	2.45	2.92	2.93	3.87
Polymorphism	NAC	10	13	25	26	46
Messaging	ANAT	0.64	0.62	0.55	0.66	0.39
Complexity	ANS+AWF+AAP	1.86	1.97	2.25	2.21	1.90

Because actual design property values of different ranges are combined in the computation of the quality attributes, the property values have to be normalized with respect to the properties' values in the first version of UML meta-models. The actual property measures in Table 9 are replaced by their normalized values in Table 10.

Table 10. Normalized properties values for UML versions

Design Property	UML1.1	UML1.3	UML1.4	UML1.5	UML2.0
Design Size	1.00	1.11	1.60	1.62	2.17
Hierarchies	1.00	1.00	1.50	1.50	0.50
Abstraction	1.00	1.07	1.18	1.19	1.70
Encapsulation	1.00	1.00	1.00	1.00	1.00
Coupling	1.00	1.05	1.63	1.92	1.20
Cohesion	1.00	1.00	1.00	1.00	1.00
Composition	1.00	0.91	1.59	2.19	2.03
Inheritance	1.00	1.00	1.19	1.19	1.57
Polymorphism	1.00	1.30	2.50	2.60	4.60
Messaging	1.00	0.97	0.86	1.03	0.61
Complexity	1.00	1.06	1.21	1.19	1.02

Table 11 shows the computed values of the six quality attributes for UML meta-models based on the normalized values in Table 10 and formulas in Table 8.

Table 11. Computed quality attributes for UML meta-models

Quality Attribute	UML1.1	UML1.3	UML1.4	UML1.5	UML2.0
Reusability	1.00	1.03	1.07	1.09	1.34
Flexibility	1.00	1.09	1.89	2.16	3.27
Understandability	-0.99	-1.18	-2.02	-2.15	-2.87
Functionality	1.00	1.08	1.54	1.60	1.85
Extendibility	1.00	1.16	1.62	1.53	3.34
Effectiveness	1.00	1.05	1.49	1.63	2.18

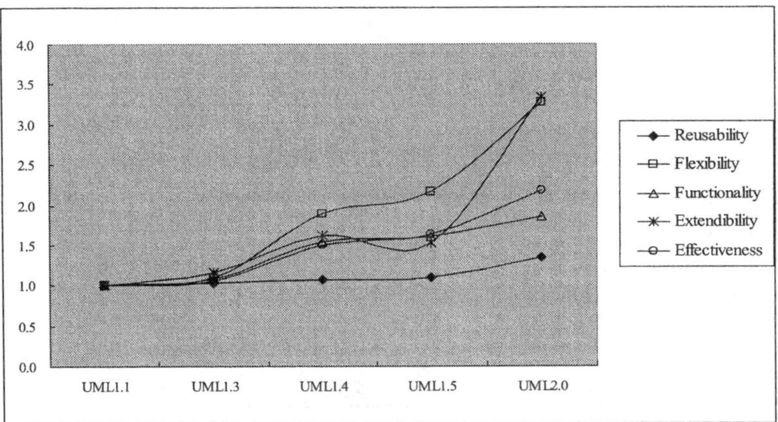

Fig. 3. Plot of computed quality attribute values for UML meta-models

Fig 3 is a plot of quality attribute values, which are basically increasing with the evolution of UML meta-models (except for understandability which is decreasing). The tendency appearing in Fig. 3 agrees with the common belief of people that the "overall quality" of the software (UML) should increase from one release to the next [3].

5. Results Analysis

From quantitative stability and design quality perspectives, not much has changed between UML 1.1 and UML 1.3. This assessment result is identical with the opinion of [10].

We can see there is an actual similarity between Fig.1 and Fig.2. Both plots tell us that UML 1.4 is the most unstable meta-model due to the fact that UML underwent a radical modification from UML 1.3 to UML 1.4 (most of time the case is disguised). This is in opposition to most people who considered the stability shake-up should belong to UML 2.0. The amplitude of modifications between remaining successive meta-models observed from Fig.2 is decreasing from UML1.3/UML1.4 to UML1.5/UML2.0, then to UML1.1/UML1.3 and the minimum is UML1.4/UML1.5. Thus the evolution from UML 1.4 to 1.5 is so far a minimal revision to the UML meta-model. A little inconsistence between Fig.1 and Fig.2 lies in the values of two kinds of *extent-of-change* regarding UML 2.0. In Fig. 1 the stability of UML 2.0 is two times as higher as that of UML 1.4, but the *relative extent-of-change*s of UML1.5/UML2.0 and UML1.3/UML1.4 in Fig.2 are nearly the same. A possible explanation is the assessment in Fig.2 focuses on meta-classes level and UML 2.0 has much more removed and added meta-classes than other versions (see Table 6), but the assessment in Fig.1 does not take the matter into account.

Accordingly, we think that UML 1.4 is not a very successful release of UML because architectural constraints were relaxed or ignored by revisers so that there is a meta-model structural surge compared to UML 1.3. This may result from introducing *Action semantics* and being failure in maintaining the integrity of the meta-model architecture. For instance, an unintelligible hierarchical tree is constructed from the root of *LinkEndData* meta-class in UML 1.4 so that its number of hierarchical trees (NOH) reaches up to 3 (see Table 2). In addition to that, nearly two times as more as couplings and aggregations are used in the meta-model. Unfortunately, UML 1.5 is worse since it neither addresses the problems inherited from UML 1.4 nor tries to use less coupling relationships, which incur that the extendibility of the meta-model is lower than that of UML 1.4 (see Fig. 3). However, we have to admit that the improvements of the design quality of UML 1.4 are much greater than that of UML 1.3, which may owe to the fact that many augments has been done by the revisers to finalize UML 1.4 [11] [17].

UML 2.0 possesses a cleaner and more complex meta-model. Since UML 2.0 intends to fit a number of different stakeholders, which leads to be a fairly large language [4]. For example, the number of meta-classes (DSC) has reached double times and the understandability decreased three times respectively than both metrics of the original UML version. In spite of more meta-classes being contained, the UML 2.0 meta-model adjusts its meta-class hierarchies so that hierarchical trees coexisting in a meta-model (NOH) is only 1. Thus all meta-classes in UML 2.0 are inherited from the root meta-class of *Element,* rather than of *Element* and *Expression* in UML 1.1

and 1.3, as well as of *Element*, *Expression* and *LinkEndData* in UML 1.4 and 1.5. The meta-model of UML 2.0 has a deeper and wider inheritance structure according to the increasing value of the metrics of ADI, ANA, and AWI. UML 2.0 even has triple inheritance for the first time, such meta-classes as *Classifier*, *StructuralFeature*, and *StructuredActivityNode*.

In Fig.3, UML 2.0 makes dramatic enhancements to the design quality of its meta-model compared with previous versions. The extendibility and the flexibility of the meta-model are increased more than three times; the functionality and the effectiveness are increased nearly two times. In spite of there being a little increase in the reusability of UML 2.0 meta-model, the reusability of all meta-models keeps relatively constant. This may imply that the UML does not intend to cover a wide range of application domains (the works should be left for various Profiles).

Based on the observations of the assessment results, we deduce that UML 2.0 satisfies the expectations in [11] and [17], which are in hopes of achieving an architectural moderation (see Fig. 1, 2) and consolidating existing features (e.g. seamlessly integrating *Actions* into the overall architecture of the UML 2.0 mate-model). This results in a more agile and more extensible UML (see the quality attributes of the extendibility and the flexibility in Fig. 3), which is crucial to avoid the infamous "language bloat syndrome" [17] [18] or "second-system syndrome" [5] [10] [11] [19].

6. Discussion

The method for assessing UML meta-models makes it possible to evaluate UML versions with respect to the stability and design quality. It contributes to the issues pertaining to the controllable and predictable evolution of UML.

Firstly, empirical information collected from the assessment of UML meta-models can be valuable in guiding the development and evolution of new versions of UML and can be used to further develop heuristics for estimation activities. So far little information of how effectively and efficiently the development of UML meta-model exists. Empirical information about the stability and design quality of meta-models will help in the process of allocating specialists and resources to the UML developments as well as effort estimations.

Secondly, the UML meta-model assessment can be used to select tenets for deciding when to incorporate a new requirement or not during UML evolving to the next version. It supports decisions on the incorporation of new features in the UML, since the impact is made explicit. For example, a primary strategy for the revision of UML is to rule out those augments which are stretching the limits on the stability or quality of the UML meta-model. In addition, UML revisers can decide when the next UML version can be released based on the assessment, avoiding the shipping of the UML version that does not fulfill stability or quality requirements.

Thirdly, the UML meta-model assessment can be used by modeling tool vendors or users who model systems with UML. They evaluate the impact of changes for adopting a newer UML version. On the basis of the assessment results, tool vendors and users can predict required effort for tools upgrade and consistence testing of the system models.

Finally, UML 2.0 infrastructure supports two extensibility mechanisms, by which users can not only define new dialects of UML by using Profiles, but also define new members of the UML family of languages [24]. This indispensable leads to the situation of the family of meta-models. The method for assessing meta-models, therefore, will become a strong tool which can be extended for assessing the family of meta-models.

7. Conclusion

This paper introduces a quantitative method to assess stability and design quality of UML meta-models. The method carries out objective assessments to UML meta-models using adapted object-oriented metrics. All metrics take meta-classes in UML meta-models as the basis, which results from the fact that most of object-oriented measurement technologies take the class as central measuring target. Metric values are used to compute two kinds of extent-of-changes between versions. The extent-of-change is regarded as an indicator of stability in UML evolution. In addition, these metric values can be utilized to assess quality attributes of UML meta-models, such as functionality, effectiveness, understandability, extendibility, reusability, and flexibility. On the observations of the results of the empirical assessments, our method can draw consistent conclusions about the UML evolution with other literatures. Furthermore, the method for assessing UML meta-models can be used to control and predict the UML evolution.

The future work is to reinforce our metrics to measure well-formed rules and additional operations in meta-classes, since in this paper we only count the number of metrics per meta-class without conducting a more deliberate semantics analysis of them.

Acknowledgements The work is funded by the National High-Tech Research and Development Plan of China (No. 2001AA113070) and the National Grand Fundamental Research 973 Program of China (No. 2002CB31200003), administered by the China National Software Engineering Research Institute. We thank Zhe Ji, Guodong Yang, and Le Zhang for their great patient and excellent job in analyzing meta-models data for supporting this effort.

References

[1] Alhir, S. S.: Extending the Unified Modeling Language. At home.earthlink.net/ salhir (1999).

[2] Bansiya, J.: Evaluating framework architecture structural stability. ACM Computing Surveys (CSUR), Vol. 32, Issue 1es, No. 18 (2000)

[3] Bansiya, J. and Davis, C.G.: A hierarchical model for object-oriented design quality assessment. IEEE Transactions on Software Engineering, Vol. 28, Issue 1 (2002) 4-17

[4] Björkander, M.: Model-Driven Development and UML 2.0. The End of Programming as We Know It?. UPGRADE, European Journal for the Informatics Professional, Vol. IV, No. 4 (2003) 10-14
[5] Brooks, F.: *The Mythical Man-Month*, Anniversary Edition. Addison-Wesley, Reading, PA (1995)
[6] Chidamber, S. R. and Kemerer, C. F.: A Metrics Suite for Object Oriented Design. IEEE Transactions on Software Engineering, Vol. 20, Issue 6 (1994) 476 - 493
[7] Eder, J., Kappel, G. and Schrefl, M.: Coupling and Cohesion in Object-Oriented Systems. Technical Report, University of Klagenfurt, (1994)
[8] Fenton, N. and Pfleeger, S. L.: *Software Metrics, A Rigorous and Practical Approach*, 2nd ed. International Thomson Computer Press (1997).
[9] Kitchenham, B. and Pfleeger, S. L.: Software Quality: The Elusive Target. IEEE Software, Vol. 13, No.1 (1996)12-21
[10] Kobryn, C.: UML 2001: A Standardization Odyssey. Communications of the ACM, Vol. 42, No. 10 (1999)
[11] Kobryn, C.: Will UML 2.0 Be Agile or Awkward? Communications of the ACM, Vol. 45, No. 1 (2002) 107-110
[12] Lorenz, M. and Kidd, J.: *Object-Oriented Software Metrics*, Prentice Hall, Englewood Cliffs, NJ (1994).
[13] Ma, Z., Jang, Y., Li, J. and Dai, Y.: Research and Implementation of JBOO Based on UML. ACTA ELECTRONICA SINCA, Vol.12A (2002). (in Chinese)
[14] Mattsson, M. and Bosch, J.: Characterizing Stability in Evolving Frameworks. In Proceedings of the 29th International Conference on Technology of Object-Oriented Languages and Systems (TOOLS EUROPE '99), Nancy, France (1999) 118-130
[15] Purao, S. and Vaishnavi, V.: Product metrics for object-oriented systems. ACM Computing Surveys (CSUR), Vol. 35, Issue 2 (2003) 191-221
[16] Reißing, R.: Towards a Model for Object-Oriented Design Measurement. Fifth International ECOOP Workshop on Quantitative Applications in OOSE (QAOOSE) (2001)
[17] Selic, B., Ramackers, G. and Kobryn, C.: Evolution, Not revolution. Communications of the ACM, Vol. 45, No. 11 (2002) 70-72
[18] Selic, B.: An overview of UML 2.0. Proceedings of the 25th International Conference of Software Engineering (ICSE'03) (2003)
[19] Thomas, D.: UML - Unified or Universal Modeling Language? UML2, OCL, MOF, EDOC - The Emperor Has Too Many Clothes. Journal of Object Technology, Vol. 2, No. 1 (2003)
[20] Unified Modeling Language Semantics, Version 1.1, OMG Document: ad/97-08-04
[21] Unified Modeling Language Specification, Version1.3, OMG Document: formal/00-03-01
[22] Unified Modeling Language Specification, Version 1.4 with Action Semantics, OMG Document: formal/01-09-67
[23] Unified Modeling Language Specification, Version 1.5, OMG Document: formal/03-03-01
[24] UML 2.0 Infrastructure Specification, OMG Document: ptc/03-09-15
[25] UML 2.0 Superstructure RFP, OMG Document: ad/00-09-02
[26] UML 2.0 Superstructure Specification, OMG Document: ptc/03-08-02
[27] Xenos, M., Stavrinoudis, D., Zikouli K. and Christodoulakis, D.: Object-Oriented Metrics - A Survey. Proceedings of the FESMA 2000, Federation of European Software Measurement Associations, Madrid, Spain (2000)

An OCL Formulation of UML2 Template Binding

Olivier Caron, Bernard Carré, Alexis Muller, and Gilles Vanwormhoudt

Laboratoire d'Informatique Fondamentale de Lille
UMR CNRS 8022
Université des Sciences et Technologies de Lille
F-59655 Villeneuve d'Ascq cedex, France

Abstract. After being considered only as documentation for a long time, models are gaining more and more importance in the software development lifecycle, as full software artefacts. The UML standard contributes a lot to this mutation, with the identification and the structuration of models space dimensions and constructs. Models can nowadays be explicitly manipulated through metamodeling techniques, dedicated tools or processes such as model transformation chains. This is "Model Driven Engineering". Once it is clear that models are full software ingredients, we are faced with new problems (needs!) such as the possibility of their reusability and composability. As a consequence, specific constructs are introduced in order to facilitate this, such as the template notion initiated by UML1.3. Applications of this notion are growing more and more so that it was deeply revisited and strengthened in UML2. Though, its specification still lacks precision, particularly concerning the "binding" mechanism that allows to obtain models from templates. We propose a set of OCL constraints which strengthens the definition and helps in verifying the correctness of resulting models. These constraints apply to the UML2 metamodel and were implemented in an OCL verifier that we integrated in the Eclipse environment.

1 Introduction

After being considered only as documentation elements for a long time, models are gaining more and more importance in the software development lifecycle, as full software artefacts. The UML [2] standard contributes a lot to this mutation, with the identification and the structuration of models space dimensions and constructs. Models can nowadays be explicitly manipulated through metamodeling techniques, dedicated tools or processes such as the MDA [1] transformation chains. This is "Model Driven Engineering" [9]. The main motivation is the reduction of delays and costs by the capitalization of design efforts (models) at each stage, and the automation, as far as possible, of transitions between these stages. So it would be possible to separate high level business oriented models from low level architectural and technological ones, but also to reuse these models from one application to another.

T. Baar et al. (Eds.): UML 2004, LNCS 3273, pp. 27–40, 2004.

Indeed, once it is clear that models are full software ingredients, we are faced with new problems (needs!) such as the possibility of their reusability and composability. As a consequence, models stand more and more as good candidates for the "design for reuse" quest and specific constructs are introduced to make them generic. It is the case of the UML template notion which helps in specifying parameterized models. Applications are patterns formulation [3] [4], modelization of reusable subjects in [5] or frameworks in Catalysis [6]. We also use templates to specify modeling components which capture reusable functional aspects [10].

UML templates applications are numerous and various, with the result that its initial introduction in UML1.3 was deeply revisited and strengthened in the UML2 standard. Though its specification remains much more structural and verbal in [3]. Particularly, constraints lack for the precise definition of the related "binding" relation which allows to obtain models from templates. These constraints are needed to verify the correctness of the resulting models. That is why we propose here a set of OCL constraints [11] which could strengthen the notion of model templates and facilitate the above verification. These constraints apply to the UML2 metamodel.

In the following section, we show the notion of templates through examples of parameterized model elements. Then (section 3), we present the UML metamodels of templates and the template binding as they are specified in [3] and explain them with the help of the preceding examples. We so (section 4) propose a set of OCL constraints which could complete this specification and help in verifying the correctness of resulting models. These constraints were checked in an OCL verifier that we integrate in the Eclipse environment (section 5).

2 The UML 2 Template Notion

In UML standard, a template is a model element which is parameterized by other model elements. Such parameterizable elements can be classes or packages, so called respectively *class templates* or *package templates.* To specify its parameterization, a template element owns a signature. A template signature corresponds to a list of formal parameters where each parameter designates an element that is part of the template. Template elements have also a specific notation which consists in superimposing a small dashed rectangle containing the signature on the right-hand corner of the standard symbol.

A template can be used to generate other model elements using template binding relationship. A bind relationship links a "bound" element to the signature of a target template and specifies a set of template parameter substitutions that associate actual elements to formal parameters. The binding of a bound element implies that its contents are based upon the contents of the target template with any element exposed as formal parameter substituted by the actual element specified in the binding.

Figure 1 shows a class template on the left. This class, *Stack*, is graphically represented as a standard UML class with a dashed rectangle containing its sig-

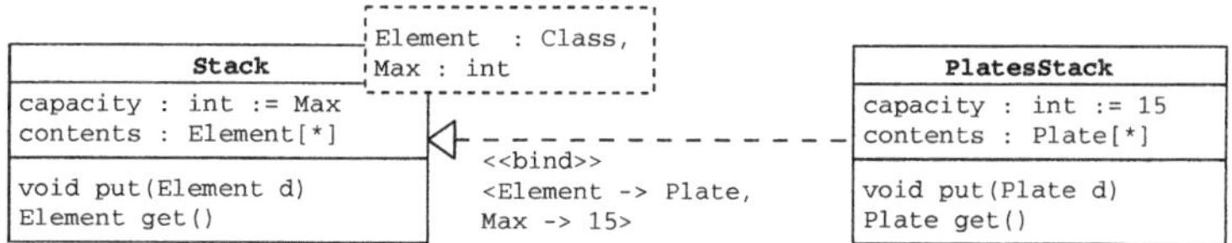

Fig. 1. Class Template

nature. Here, the signature states two elements as formal parameters: *Element* of type class and *Max* of type int. The right side of this figure shows the class *PlatesStack* which is bound to the *Stack* template through a "bind" relationship. This class is the result of the substitution in the template of its formal parameters, *Element* and *Max* by the actual values *Plate* and *15* respectively. This substitution is stated by the bind relationship.

Figure 2 is another example of a template which shows that they can also apply to packages. Here, the notion of template is used to model the well-known observer pattern. The content of this template reflects the structure of this pattern and includes the classical *Subject* and *Observer* classes. As indicated by the signature attached to the template, these classes and their respective *value* and *value_view* attributes are identified as formal parameters.

Figure 2 illustrates the use of the previous template for specifying a *HeatFlowRegulation* package that models a part of a home heating system. This package has its own content which is composed of *RoomSensor*, *HeatFlowRegulator* and *Furnace* classes. In this example, the bind relationship is used to render the collaboration between *RoomSensor* and *HeatFlowRegulator*. This is specified by associating *RoomSensor* to *Subject*, *HeatFlowRegulator* to *Observer* and their respective *value* and *value_view* attributes to *currentTemperature* and *measuredTemperature*. As a result of this binding, *RoomSensor* and *HeatFlowRegulator* have respectively the same elements (operations and association) than *Subject* and *Observer*. Note that actual classes may have contents in addition to those specified for the formal parameters.

3 The UML 2 Template Metamodel

The templates package in the UML 2 metamodel [3] introduces four classes : *TemplateSignature*, *TemplateableElement*, *TemplateParameter* and *ParameterableElement* (see Figure 3). *TemplateBinding* and *TemplateParameterSubstitution* metaclasses are both used to bind templates (see Figure 4).

UML 2 elements that are sub-classes of the abstract class *TemplateableElement* can be parameterized. *Classifier*, in particular classes and associations, *Package* and *Operation* are templateable elements.

The set of template parameters (*TemplateParameter*) of a template (*TemplateableElement*) are included in a signature *TemplateSignature*. A *TemplateSignature* correspond to a small dashed rectangle superimposed on the symbol for

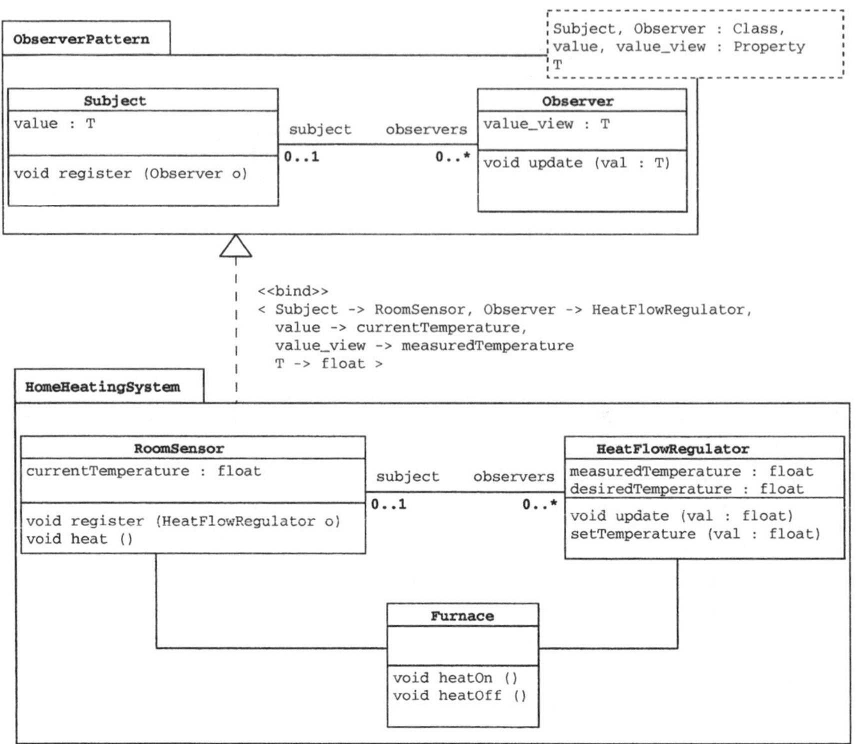

Fig. 2. Package Template

the templateable element. A *TemplateParameter* corresponds to a formal template parameter and exposes an element owned by the template thanks to the *parameteredElement* role.

Only parameterable elements (*ParameterableElement*) can be exposed as formal template parameter for a template or specified as actual parameters in a template binding. Such UML 2 elements are : *Classifier*, *PackageableElement*, *Operation* or *Property*[1].

The notion of template binding (*TemplateBinding*) describes the use of a template for a given system (cf. Figure 4). A template binding is a directed relationship labeled by the << *bind* >> stereotype from the bound element to the template (*boundElement*). The template binding owns a set of template parameter substitutions (*TemplateParameterSubstitution*). A parameter substitution associates an actual parameter of the bound element to a formal template parameter of the template signature.

[1] The *Property* class that is introduced in UML 2 mainly substitutes the UML 1.4 *Attribute* class.

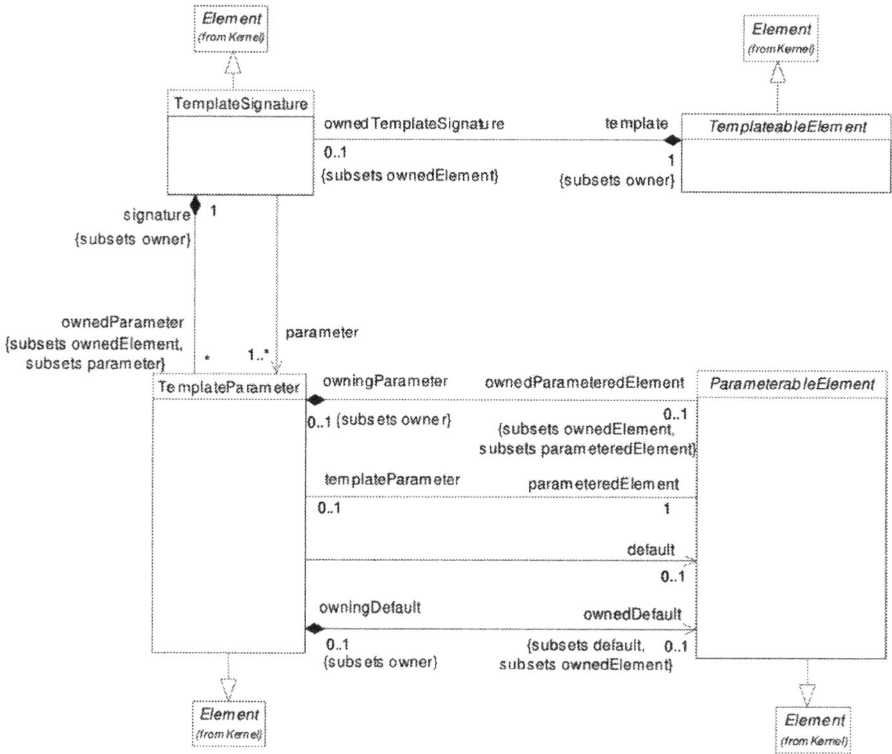

Fig. 3. Template Metamodel

Figure 5 shows an extract of the instantiation of this metamodel for the example described in Figure 2. It depicts the substitution between the *Subject* formal template parameter and the actual *RoomSensor* parameter of the bound *HomeHeatingSystem*.

UML 2 introduces the notion of partial binding when not all formal template parameters are bound. In that case, the unbound formal template parameters are formal template parameters of the bound element.

In case of multiple bindings, each binding is evaluated to produce intermediate results which are then merged to produce the final result.

4 Constraints

The UML 2 specification defines the *binding* relation as a copy of all template elements into the *boundElement* modulo parameters substitution. *"The presence of a TemplateBinding relationship implies the same semantics as if the contents of the template owning the target template signature were copied into the bound*

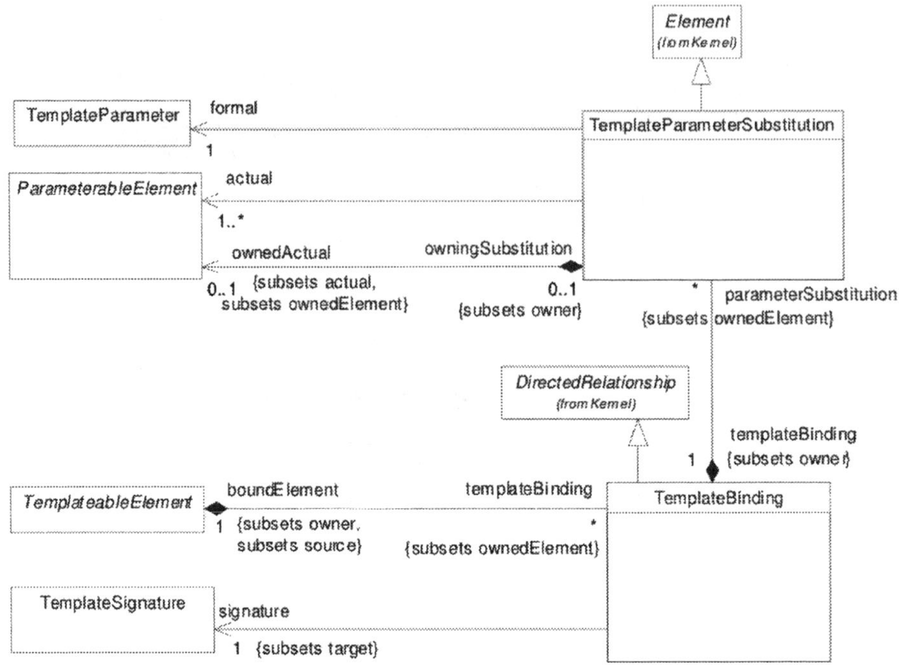

Fig. 4. Template Binding Metamodel

element, substituting any elements exposed as formal template parameters by the corresponding elements specified as actual parameters in this binding." [3].

We propose here to formalize this definition with a set of constraints expressed in the OCL language. Note that the standard constraints only check that the type of each actual parameter is compatible with the type of the related formal template parameter.

4.1 Overall Structure of the Binding

The above definition requires that the structure formed by the template elements is well preserved in the *boundElement*. To verify this property we define one constraint and two operations. These operations allow to check the matching of complex elements thanks to a recursive and polymorphic call. Indeed they must be enriched to check specific properties to operations and associations. It will be done in the next subsection.

Before checking if the bound element is well formed according to a particular binding, it is necessary to check that elements used as parameters are also elements of the bound element. This is done by the first constraint. The standard *allOwnedElement* query gives both direct and indirect owned elements.

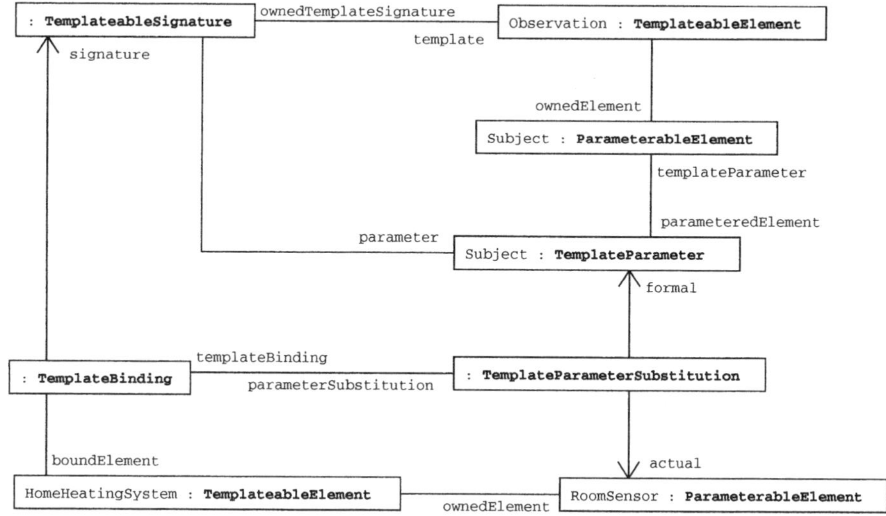

Fig. 5. Extract of the Object Diagram for the *HomeHeatingSystem* Package

```
[1] The elements used as current parameters of a substitution must belong
    to boundElement.
```

```
context TemplateBinding inv :
     self.parameterSubstitution.actual->forAll (p |
          self.boundElement.allOwnedElement()->includes (p))
```

The following constraint checks that each element of the template, parameter or not, has a matching element in the *boundElement*. This matching uses an *isBound* metaoperation defined on the *Element* metaclass (see constraint 4).

In case of multiple substitutions, it is necessary to check that each actual parameter match the formal parameter (see constraint 3).

```
[2] For any element of the template, a matching element in the
    boundElement must exist.
```

```
context TemplateBinding inv :
  self.signature.template.ownedElement->forAll (template_element |
          self.boundElement.ownedElement->exists
                  (b | b.isBound (template_element, self)))
```

```
[3] Each actual parameter of a TemplateParameterSubstitution must match
    the formal parameter.
```

```
context TemplateParameterSubstitution inv :
self.actual->forAll (a | a.isBound (self.formal, self.templateBinding)
```

The following *isBound* metaoperation checks if an element of the *boundElement* matches a template element *te* according to a given binding.

For the matching, we must handle two cases : whether the element is the result of a substitution of the binding (lines 4-5) or a simple copy (lines 6-9). In case of a partial binding,

the constraint 2 verifies for free that copies of unsubstituted parameters exist into the bound element.

In order to treat complex elements (classes, packages...), this checking is done recursively on their content. It is the role of the *bindOwnedElement* metaoperation (line 10)[2].

```
[4] An element is related to another element by a binding relationship if
    they have the same name and the same type or if there is a
    substitution between these two elements in the binding relationship,
    and if it checks the bindOwnedElement operation.
```

```
1 context Element
  def : isBound (te : Element,
3                binding : TemplateBinding) : Boolean =
    binding.parameterSubstitution
5     ->exists (p | p.formal = te and p.actual->includes (self)) or
    (self.oclIsKindOf (NamedElement) implies
7       self.oclAsType (NamedElement).name =
                 te.oclAsType (NamedElement).name
9       and self.oclIsTypeOf  (te.oclType))
    and self.bindOwnedElement (te, binding)
```

```
[5] An element e binds an element te if there exists, for each element
    te_owned contained in te, an element contained in e which matches
    te_owned.
```

```
context Element
def : bindOwnedElement (te : Element,
                        binding : TemplateBinding) : Boolean =
  te.ownedElement->forAll (te_owned |
    self.ownedElement->exists (self_owned |
      self_owned.isBound (te_owned, binding)))
```

In Figure 6, *att1* is an attribute of *ClassA* in the template and there is no attribute matching in the *X* class of the *boundElement.* This kind of error is checked by the previous constraints.

4.2 Specialized Constraints

In order to deal with specificities of *Operation*, *Property* and *Association* the *isBound* operation is specialized[3].

---

[2] The used recursion is analogous to the *allOwnedElements* operation specified on UML 2.0.

[3] Each specialization always starts with a call to the basic checking (expressed by *self.oclAsType (Element).isBound (te, binding))* and then adds specific complements

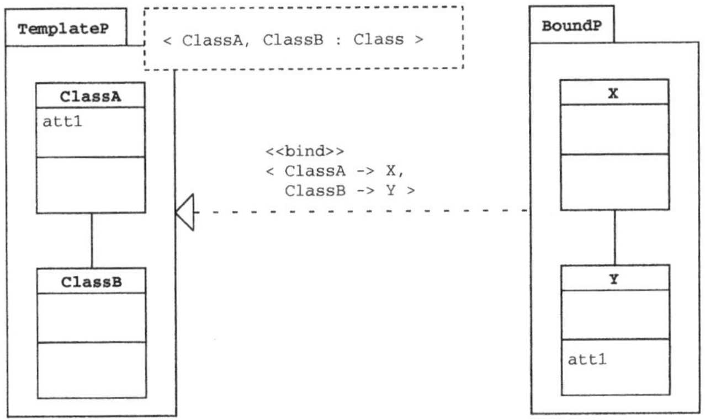

Fig. 6. Containment Error

Concerning operations, it is necessary to check, for each operation of the *boundElement* related to an operation of the template, if their signatures are compatible : types of the operations arguments must be identical or the result of a binding substitution.

The constraint 6 checks this property and prohibits errors like the ones illustrated Figure 7, where the parameter t of the *foo* operation of *ClassA* in the *boundElement* is typed Z instead of Y. Indeed, the type of t in the template (X) is substituted by Y in the *boundElement*.

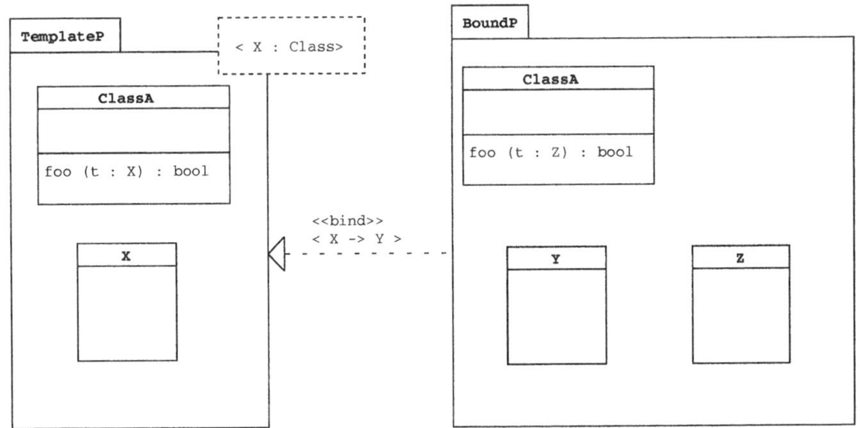

Fig. 7. Operation Signature Error

[6] An operation of the bound element match an operation of the template if their signatures match according to the isBound operation.

```
1 context Operation::isBound (te : Element,
                               binding : TemplateBinding) : Boolean
3 body :
    self.oclAsType (Element).isBound (te, binding) and
5     self.formalParameter->size() =
        te.oclAsType (Operation).formalParameter->size () and
7     Sequence {1..self.formalParameter->size ()}->forAll (i : Integer |
       self.formalParameter->at (i).type.isBound
9        (te.oclAsType (Operation).formalParameter->at (i).type,
          binding) and
11     self.returnResult->size() =
        te.oclAsType (Operation).returnResult->size ()
13  and Sequence {1..self.returnResult->size ()}->forAll (i : Integer |
      self.returnResult->at (i).type.isBound
15       (te.oclAsType (Operation).returnResult->at (i), binding))
```

Lines 5 to 10 check for compatibility of arguments. Lines 11 to 15 do the same for results types.

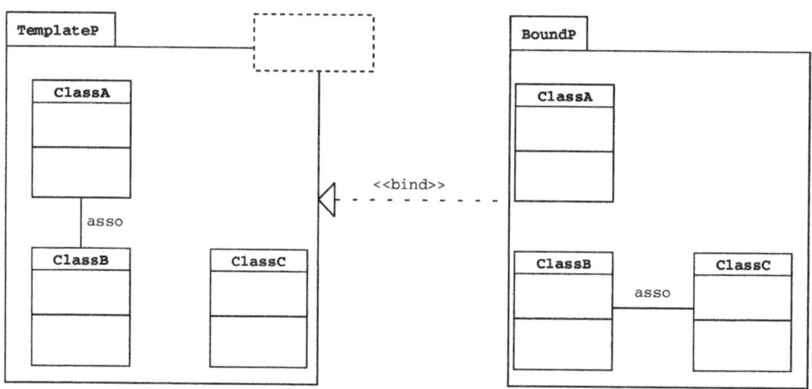

Fig. 8. Association Error

The following stands for property specificities. First of all it is necessary to check if a *Property* of *boundElement* and his matching *Property* in the template are compatible (line 5). Secondly a property may play a role in an association modeling (figure 9). Indeed in UML2, unlike UML 1.X, there is no more *AssociationEnd* metaclass. The latter is replaced by a *Property* playing the role of *ownedAttribute* for a class and is connected to an association. This is why this constraint is defined on the *Property* metaclass to check the respect of connections between classes and associations.

If a *Property* is related to an association in the template (line 6), it checks that the connected *Property* in the *boundElement* is related to the matching association (lines 7-8).

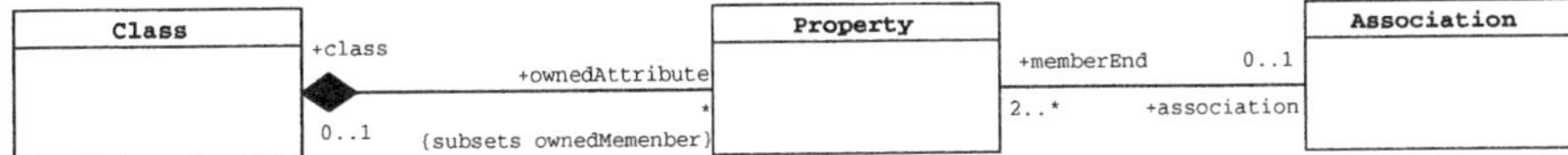

Fig. 9. Class-Property-Association Metamodel

```
[7] If a property of the template is end of an association A then the
    dependent property must be end of association related to A.

1 context Property::isBound (te : Element,
                             binding : TemplateBinding) : Boolean
3 body :
    self.oclAsType (Element).isBound (te, binding) and
5     self.type.isBound (te.oclAsType (Property).type, binding) and
        te.oclAsType (Property).association->notEmpty () implies
7         self.association.isBound (te.oclAsType (Property).association,
                                    binding)
```

This constraint prevents the kind of errors presented Figure 8, where *asso* "is moved" from an association between *ClassA* and *ClassB* to an association between *ClassB* and *ClassC*. This constraint also works for associations identified as template parameters thanks to the *isBound* call (line 7). The error illustrated Figure 10 is thus also detected.

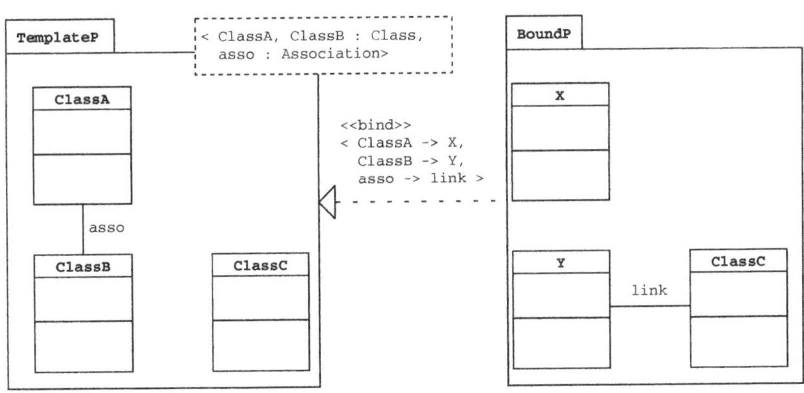

Fig. 10. Parameterized Association Error

Lastly, in order for an association of the *boundElement* to match an association of the template, it must have the same arity, which prohibits for example constructions like that of the Figure 11. This property is checked using the constraint 8.

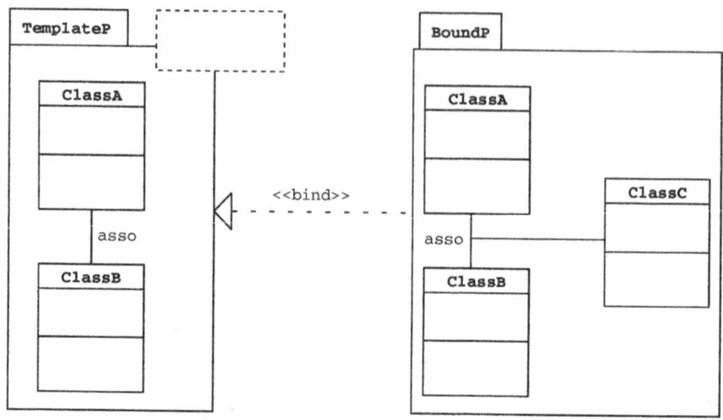

Fig. 11. Association Arity Error

```
[8] The arity of an association must be the same as that of the
    matching association of the template.

context Association::isBound (te : Element,
                              binding : TemplateBinding) : Boolean
body :
    self.oclAsType (Element).isBound (te, binding) and
      self.memberEnd->size () =
          te.oclAsType (Association).memberEnd->size ()
```

5 Integration to Case Tools

To validate our set of constraints, we have extended the Eclipse modeling Framework plug-in of the Eclipse environment and coupled this framework with the Dresden OCL Toolkit [8]. EMF [7] (based on Essential MOF) is a Java modeling framework that includes a metamodel for describing models and provides tools and runtime support to produce a set of Java classes for these models and a basic editor. For instance, EMF facilities have been used by its designers to represent the UML2 metamodel and generate an UML2 plug-in [4] that supports representation and editing of UML2 models.

Our integration of EMF and OCL Toolkit gives the ability to annotate any EMF models with OCL constraints and verify the expression of these constraints.

Figure 12 shows the annotation of the UML2 metamodel described as an EMF model. By selecting an element, the user can easily associate OCL constraints. Here, the selected element is the TemplateBinding class. As it is expanded, we can see that this element owns two of the OCL constraints defined in the previous section. The attachment of constraints to model elements was

[4] see UML2 project at http://www.eclipse.org

made possible by extending the EMF metamodel with the introduction of a EConstraint metaclass (similarly to the MOF metamodel).

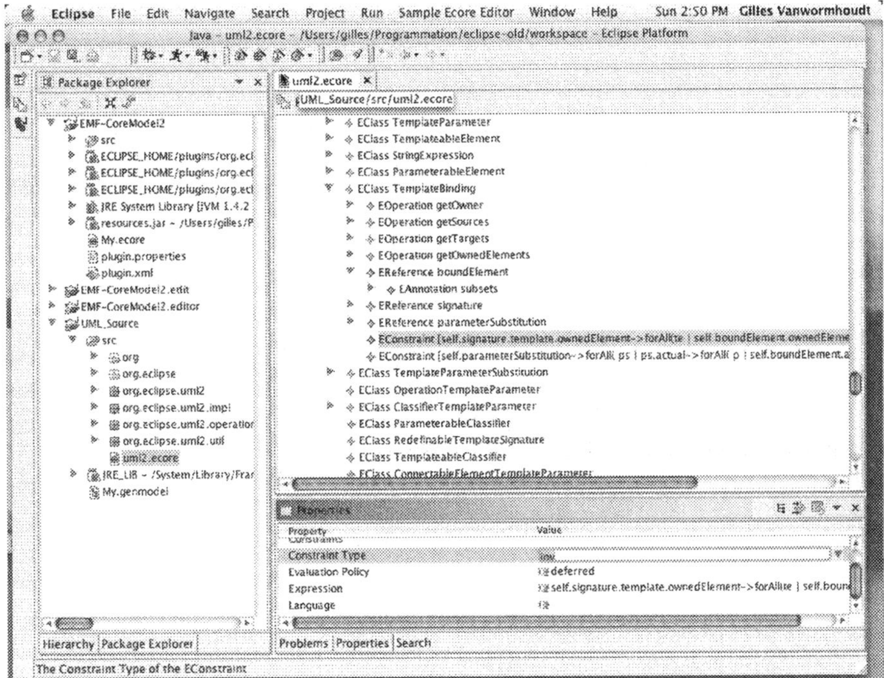

Fig. 12. Annotation of the UML2 metamodel with OCL constraints

Constraints attached to elements of EMF models are checked for syntactical and semantic correctness (i.e type checking and consistency rule). This checking is done by the verifier module of the OCL Toolkit. To implement the checking, we have developed a bridge that provides linkage between OCL expressions and the EMF model over which the expression should be evaluated. All types defined in the EMF model are legal types in an OCL expression belonging to the model. This bridge provides type information from the EMF model to the OCL verifier and ensures the proper handling of navigation and operation call in OCL expression. Each time the verifier needs to check an expression, it can acquire the necessary information from the model by interacting with the bridge. In our current implementation, we extend some implementation classes of the EMF metamodel (Package, Class, Operation, ...) so that they fulfill the bridge functionality.

By using this checking facility, we are able to test and validate the expression of our constraints. We do so by annotating the UML2 metamodel that serves to generate the UML2 plug-in.

6 Conclusion

In this paper, we have studied the notion of model template and the associated binding mechanism. We pointed out that the current specification of this notion remains much more structural and verbal [3]. The set of constraints presented in this paper gives a more precise formulation of template binding and clarify its semantics. Another interest of these constraints is that the correctness of models using templates can be checked. Moreover, template checking can be integrated into modeling case tools. By integrating an OCL verifier into the Eclipse environment, we can now specify any (meta)model with OCL constraints. This functionality was used to verify the correctness of our constraints in relation to the UML 2 metamodel described with this plug-in.

In the context of this work, we formulate OCL constraints for the current core of the template specification. These constraints could be completed to treat other parts of the specification such as template inheritance or diagrams other than structural ones.

References

[1] OMG Model-Driven Architecture Home Page, http://www.omg.org/mda.
[2] U.M.L. Home Page, http://www.omg.org/technology/uml, 2001.
[3] Auxiliary Constructs Templates, http://www.omg.org/docs/ptc/03-08-02.pdf, pages 541-568. UML 2.0 Superstructure Specification, 2003.
[4] Biju K. Appukuttan, Tony Clark, Andy Evans, Girish Maskeri, Paul Sammut, Laurence Tratt, and James S. Willans. A pattern based approach to defining the dynamic infrastructure of UML 2.0. Technical report, March 2002.
[5] S. Clarke. Extending standard uml with model composition semantics. In *Science of Computer Programming, Elsevier Science*, volume 44, 2002.
[6] Desmond D'Souza and Alan Wills. *Objects, Components and Frameworks With UML: The Catalysis Approach.* Addison-Wesley, 1999.
[7] F. Budinsky, D. Steinberg, E. Merks, R. Ellersick, and T. Grose. *Eclipse Modeling Framework.* Addison Wesley, 2004.
[8] Heinrich Hussmann, Birgit Demuth, and Frank Finger. Modular architecture for a toolset supporting ocl. In *Proceedings of UML.* Elsevier North-Holland, Inc., June 2002.
[9] S. Kent. Model Driven Engineering. In *Proceedings of IFM 2002*, http://www.cs.kent.ac.uk/pubs/2002/1594, pages 286–298. Springer-Verlag, May 2002.
[10] A. Muller, O. Caron, B. Carré, and G. Vanwormhoudt. Réutilisation d'aspects fonctionnels : des vues aux composants. In *Langages et Modèles à Objets (lmo'03)*, pages 241–255, Vannes, France, January 2003. Hermès Sciences.
[11] Jos Warmer and Anneke Kleppe. *The Object Constraint Language – Second Edition, Getting Your Models Ready for MDA.* Addison-Wesley, 2003.

A Metamodel for Generating Performance Models from UML Designs

Dorin B. Petriu, Murray Woodside

Dept. of Systems and Computer Engineering
Carleton University, Ottawa K1S 5B6, Canada
{dorin,cmw}@sce.carleton.ca

Abstract. Several different kinds of performance models can be generated from sets of scenarios that describe typical responses of a system, and their use of resources. The Core Scenario Model described here integrates the scenario and resource elements defined in a UML model with performance annotations, preparatory to generating performance models. It is based on, and aligned with the UML Profile for Schedulability, Performance and Time, and supports the generation of predictive performance models using queueing networks, layered queueing, or timed Petri nets. It is proposed to develop it as an intermediate language for all performance formalisms.

1. Performance Analysis of Software Specifications

Preliminary performance analysis can be effective in avoiding performance disasters in software projects [11]. However, it takes time and effort to derive the necessary performance models. The UML Profile for Schedulability, Performance and Time (SPT) [6] was developed to assist the capture of performance data, and automation of the model-building step. This should make the analysis more accessible to developers who are concerned about performance issues in their designs. Figure 1 illustrates the type of processing that is envisaged by the Profile.

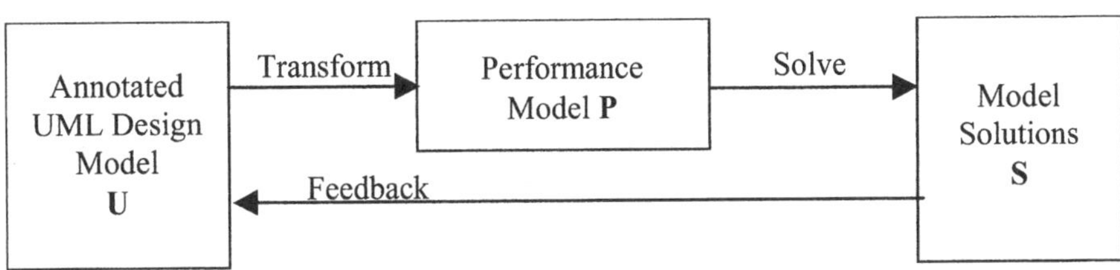

Fig. 1. Transformations and performance model solutions as envisaged in the UML SPT Profile

The range of applications covered by the SPT Profile is broad, ranging from embedded systems with schedulability concerns, to business systems. The present paper is directed to applications with probabilistic behaviour and statistical performance

T. Baar et al. (Eds.): UML 2004, LNCS 3273, pp. 41-53, 2004.

requirements, which are common in distributed information processing such as telecom, business systems and web services.

The relevant information in the UML design U is scattered in behaviour and deployment submodels, and possibly in other submodels. Some of it is expressed in the stereotypes and tag values of the SPT Profile, and some (e.g. the sequence of actions) is implicit in the UML. The Core Scenario Model (CSM) collects and organizes all this into a form that is convenient for generating P, and allows us to check for consistency and completeness of this information from the viewpoint of P. We thus propose a two-step processing sequence as shown in Fig. 2, with two transformations: U2C extracts the scenario model and C2P to derives a performance model, Different C2P transformations may support different performance formalisms for P.

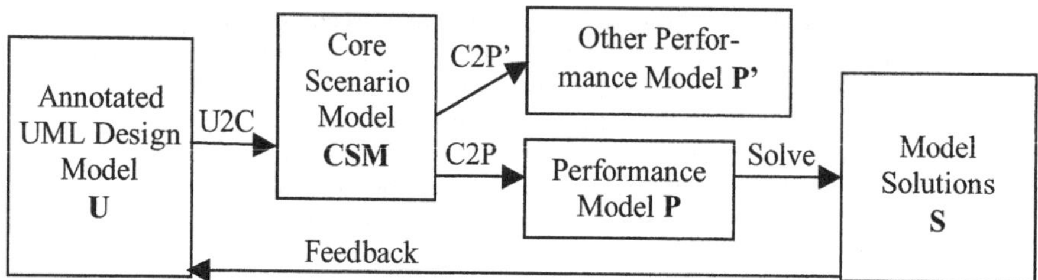

Fig. 2. Two-step transformation supporting consistency-checking and a variety of performance formalisms

The purpose of this work is to describe the CSM, demonstrate that it captures all the information defined by annotations in the profile, and discuss its feasibility for deriving performance models.

2. UML Profile for Schedulability, Performance, and Time (SPT)

The SPT Profile [6] extends the UML standard by defining stereotypes and tags which can be applied to object instances, and to instances of action executions in behaviour specifications. The UML specification together with the stereotypes determines structural properties of a performance model, and the tags provide parameter values. The profile is based on domain sub-models for resources and for performance, which are the basis of the CSM metamodel described below.

The SPT domain model for performance is summarized in Fig. 3. It is centered on a Scenario class, representing behaviour for one kind of system response. A scenario is an ordered sequence of steps, each of which can be a sub-scenario. The ordering supports forks, joins and loops in the flow. Stereotypes and tagged value names are prefixed by P or PA for “performance” or “performance analysis”.

Each scenario has a “workload” which describes the intensity of its execution. It may be an open workload, with arrivals from the environment (described by their rate), or a closed workload in which a fixed number of potential arrivals are either in the system, or are waiting to arrive again.

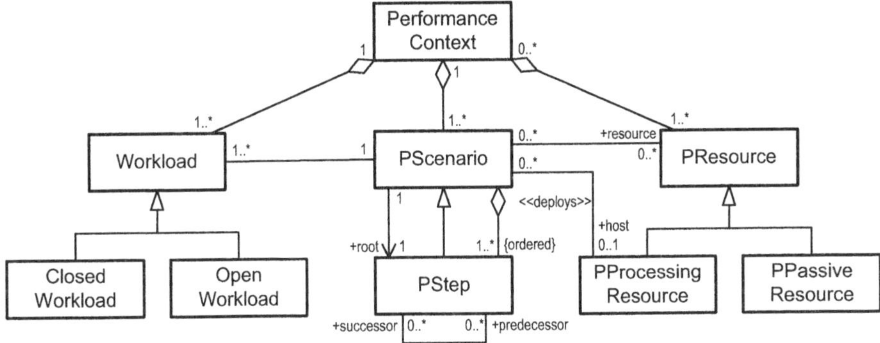

Fig. 3. The Performance domain model of the UML SPT Profile (from Fig. 8-1 of [6])

Resources may be attached to a scenario. The domain submodel for resources (in Chapter 4 of [6]) distinguishes between active resources (such as a user) which spontaneously generate events, and passive resources that respond to requests. Both types of resource may be protected, (in which case a client gets exclusive use of one or more units of the resource), or unprotected, in which case they can be shared without control. Chapter 8 distinguishes between processing resources (devices) and logical resources (created by the software, such as buffers, tasks, or semaphores). Every primitive Step has a host processing resource or CPU, which executes the step.

3. The Core Scenario Model (CSM) Metamodel

The CSM metamodel captures the essential entities in the domain model which are required for building performance models, and it makes explicit some facts which have to be inferred from the UML and the SPT Profile data. The class structure of CSM, consistent with the Meta-Object Facility (MOF, [7]) is shown in Fig. 4.

The CSM provides explicit representation of the scenario flow in a Path Connection type. The Profile depends on a simple successor association between Steps. Here, there is a PathConnection object between each pair of Steps, with subtypes which correspond to the sequential relationship types common in path models for real-time software: Sequence for simple sequence, one step after another; Branch for an OR-fork with Merge for an OR-join, to describe alternative paths, and Fork and Join for AND-fork and AND-join respectively (to describe parallel paths). Probabilities for a Branch are attributes of the target Steps. Explicit Path Connections (instead of just successor associations) simplify the later generation of a performance model, when the UML context is stripped away.

Each PathConnection subtype takes a different number `m` of source steps, and `n` of successor steps, and these are labeled with the subtypes in the diagram. For example, a Sequence has exactly one source and one target Step, while a Fork or Branch has one source Step and multiple target Steps.

Explicit subtypes of Step, for Resource Acquire and Release, and for Start and End of a Scenario, also support checking of the model, and performance model generation.

A Message class, which may be associated to any path connection, has been added for future use (it is not supported in [6]), to describe the size of network messages sent between system nodes.

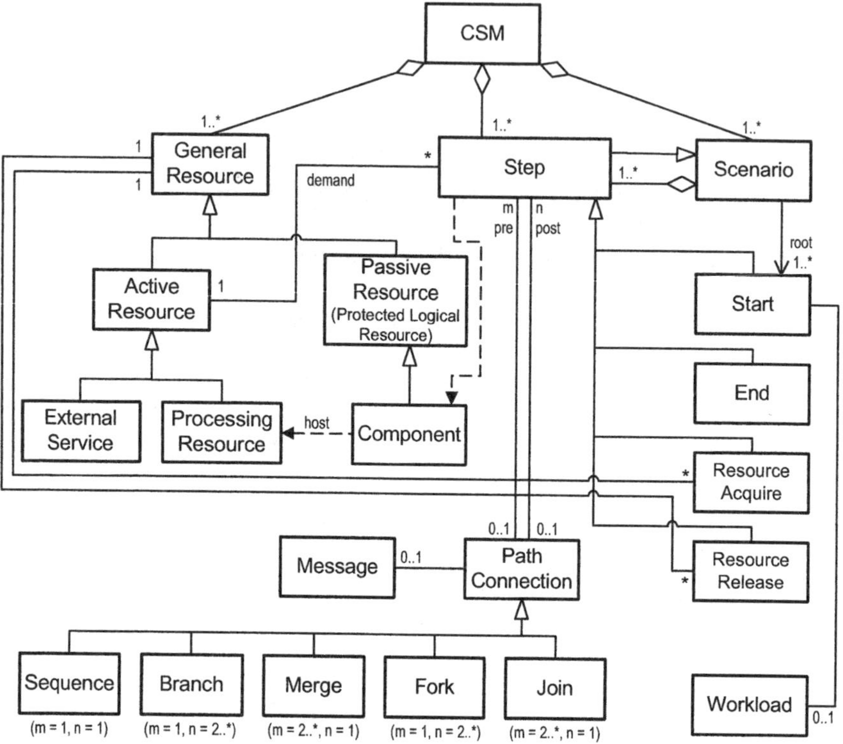

Fig. 4. Classes in the Core Scenario Model meta-model. Attributes are described in Table 1

Active and passive resources represent the resources defined in the Profile. Active resources include devices (Processing Resources) and subsystems (captured by a placeholder called External Service). The latter are service operations executed by some resource outside the design document. Passive resources include operating system processes (or threads) identified as Components, and hosted by Processing Resources. In this way a primitive Step (but not an abstract Step) has a host resource through its Component. Unprotected resources have been combined with protected resources, based on a multiplicity parameter which defines the number of units of the resource, such as a number of buffers, or of threads. An exclusively-held resource has multiplicity one, while an unprotected resource is indicated by an infinite multiplicity. This avoids the need for separate classes and is consistent with resource notation in queueing models. The attributes of the CSM correspond to tagged values in the Profile and are described in Table 1. These include ID-ref attributes representing meta-associations which are not shown in Fig. 4 to avoid cluttering the diagram.

4. A Building Security System (BSS) Example

An example which has been used in previous work to describe the use of the SPT Profile [9][13], will be used here to describe the use of CSM. It is a Building Security System (BSS), which controls access and monitors activity in an institutional building. The BSS is deployed on a main processing node, a database node, and a set of other resources all communicating over a LAN, as shown in Fig 5.

Table 1. Attributes of the CSM Metaclasses (ID is a unique identifier generated automatically, opt stands for optional, and ref stands for an object reference)

CSM Class	Attributes
Component	ID; name; host ProcessingResource ID ref; 'is active' flag; description (opt); multiplicity (opt); containing component ID (opt)
ActiveResource	ID; name; time per operation; scheduling policy; description (opt)
Scenario	ID; name, collection of Steps
Step	ID; name; Component ref, host ProcessingResource demand, optional collection of pairs of ExternalService ID refs and demands; probability (opt); repetition count (opt); subscenario ref to nested Scenario (opt); description (opt); selection policy (opt)
Start	*Step attributes* + Workload ID ref
End	*Step attributes*
ResourceAcquire	*Step attributes* + Resource ID ref; resource units (opt); priority (opt)
ResourceRelease	*Step attributes* + Resource ID ref; resource units (opt)
Workload	ID; arrival stream type (open or closed); arrival process; distribution type; closed system population size (opt); mean inter-arrival delay (opt); lower bound on the inter-arrival delay (opt); upper bound on the inter-arrival delay (opt); inter-arrival process description (opt)
PathConnection	ID; Message ID ref (opt); condition (opt); label (opt)
Sequence	*Path Connection attributes* + source Step ref; target Step ref
Branch	*Path Connection attributes* + source Step ref; target Step refs
Merge	*Path Connection attributes* + source Step refs; target Step ref
Fork	*Path Connection attributes* + source Step ref; target Step refs
Join	*Path Connection attributes* + source Step refs (2 or more); target Step ref
Message	type (none, asynchronous, synchronous, reply); size; multiplicity (opt)

In Fig. 5, the nodes are either host ProcessingResources (`<<PAhost>>`) which execute the steps of the various components, or other physical ProcessingResources stereotyped as `<<PAresource>>`. The software components are concurrent processes (the stereotype `<<PAresource>>` has not been shown, but is shown in Fig. 6) and a buffer pool called Buffer (also `<<PAresource>>`), associated with the Buffer Manager. The size of the buffer pool is given by the tag PAcapacity, which takes the default value of 1 for the other resources.

A performance-sensitive scenario for video surveillance is presented as a UML Sequence Diagram in Fig. 6. Video frames are captured periodically from a number of web cameras located around the building, and stored in the database as needed. The example is explored in greater detail, including Activity Diagrams and an additional scenario for managing building access, in [13].

In Fig. 6 (and also Fig. 5) the annotations use the stereotypes and tagged values defined in the SPT Profile. A *performance context* (labeled <<`PAcontext`>>) defines the overall scenario made up of *steps* (<<`PAstep`>>). The first step is driven by a *workload* (<<`PAclosedLoad`>>). The step use resources, with a host resource (<<`PAhost`>>) for its processor. Each step is a focus of control for some concurrent component (<<`PAresource`>> in Fig 6). The stereotype can be applied to the focus of control or to the message that initiates it, and can be defined directly or in a note.

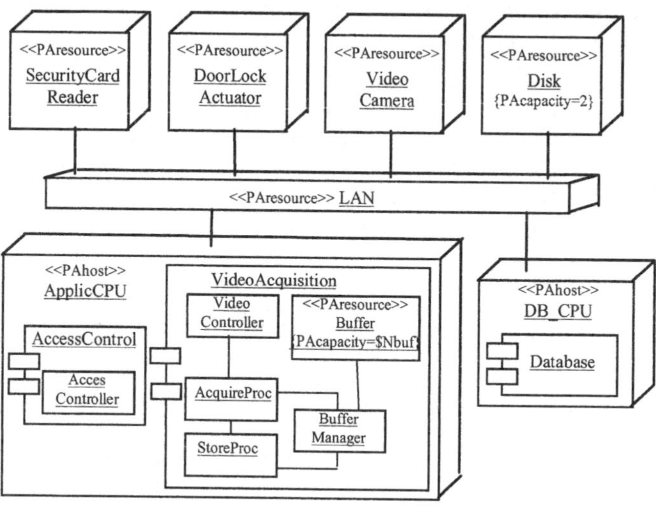

Fig. 5. Deployment and software components in the Building Security System (BSS)

The steps are tagged with a CPU demand value for processing time (tag `PAdemand`). The PAworkload stereotype is also tagged with a response time requirement, indicated by the tag PAInterval with parameter 'req', that the interval between successive frames be less than 1 second 95% of the time, and a placeholder with name $Cycle is defined for the model prediction for the 95th percentile.

The getImage step requires a network operation which is not included in the Sequence Diagram. It is described as a demand for an ExternalService (tagged as <<PAextOp>> on the getImage step), shown by the tag PAextOp = (Network, $P), indicating a number of network operations (and latencies) defined by the variable $P. The time for a network latency is not defined in the UML specification or the Profile, and is meant to be supplied by the modeler. If it is supplied during the U2C transformation, it can be included as an attribute of the corresponding ExternalService ActiveResource object.

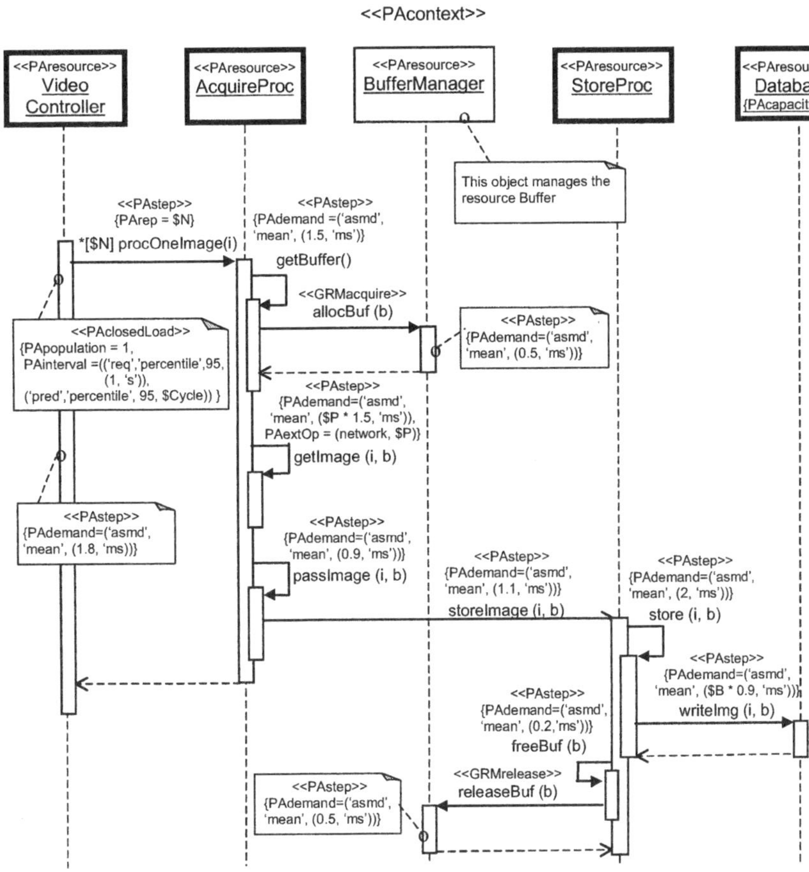

Fig. 6. The Acquire/Store Video scenario for the Building Security System

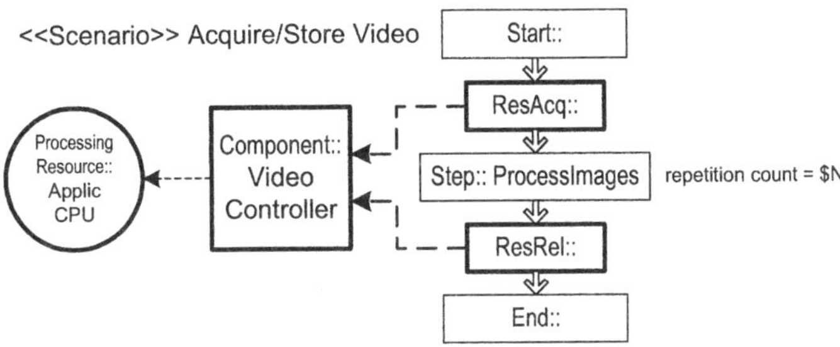

Fig. 7. The CSM representation of the information in Figures 5 and 6: the high-level loop

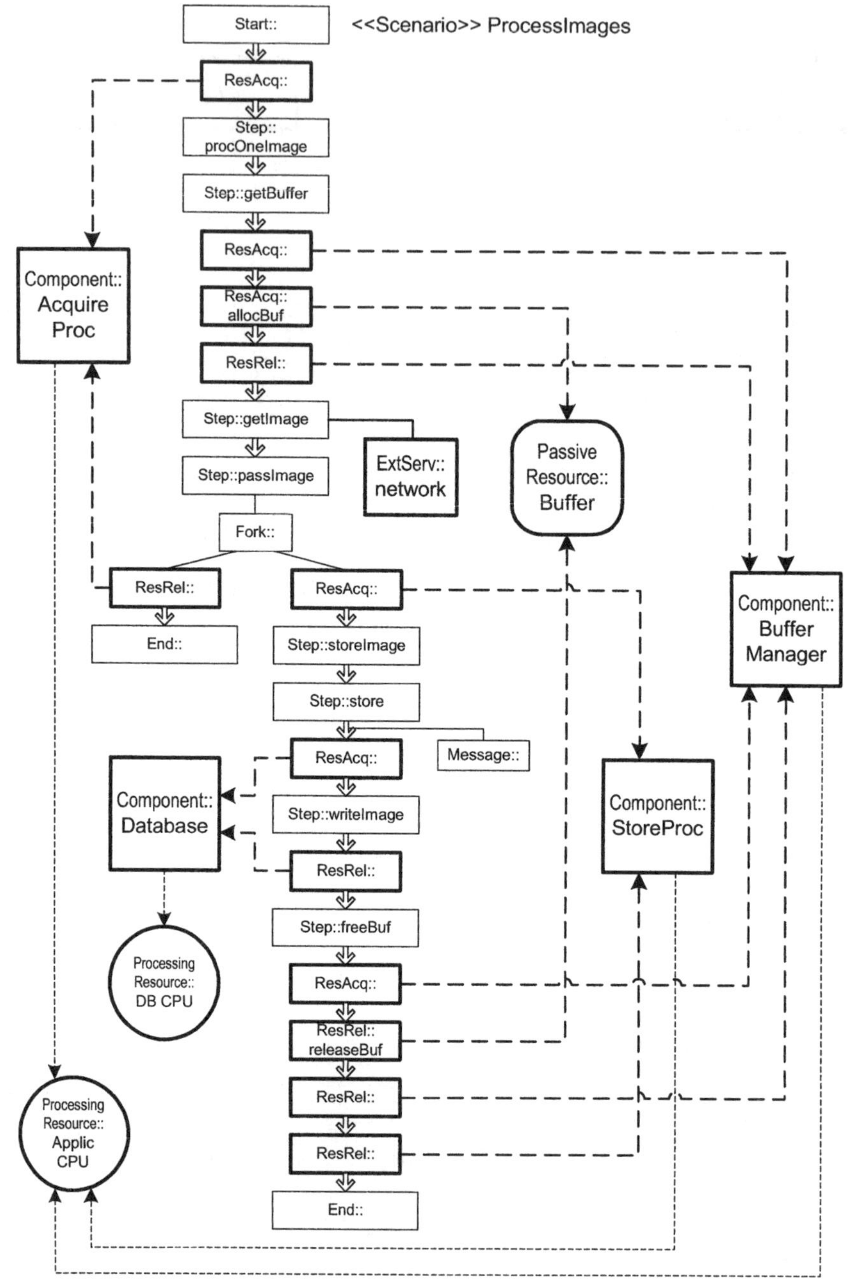

Fig. 8. The CSM representation of Figures 5 and 6: refinement of the loop step

Figs. 7 and 8 show the corresponding CSM model, using some abbreviations for CSM types (such as ResAcq for ResourceAcquire) which should be clear. The loop which is indicated by the parameter *$N on the procOneImage message in Fig. 6, has been realized as a CSM Step processImages with a repetition parameter $N in Fig. 7. It is refined by a subscenario also named processImages, in Fig. 8. Figs. 7 and 8 use some special graphical notation. They use bold outlines for Resources and for ResourceAcquire and ResourceRelease Steps, and bold arrows for dependencies between them. There is also a special hollow arrow representing a Sequence path connection and its associations with its predecessor and successor Steps.

It can be confirmed that Figs. 7 and 8 capture the sequential scenario information from the Sequence Diagram, and the resource relationships from it and the Deployment Diagram, without loss of information.

A place has also been provided in the CSM representation for a description of the Message sent to the database to log the video frame. The UML specification does not provide message parameters, but a modeler could provide them for the CSM.

The power of the CSM representation can be observed in its clear representation of the Buffer buffer pool resource, which is important in this system. In the UML specification its existence is defined in Fig. 5, and its use is indicated by the GRMAcquire and GRMrelease stereotypes on the messages to the Buffer Manager in Fig 6, and the note that associates the Buffer Manager with the Buffer resource. The U2C transformation assembles the information and connects the acquisition and release points to the resource. If the UML models failed to define the buffer pool resource, or to associate it correctly with the messages to allocate and deallocate buffers, the missing information could be discovered during the U2C transformation and supplied through queries to the modeler.

5. The Transformations to Generate a Performance Model

The implementation of the two transformation steps in Fig. 2 (U2C and C2P) can exploit a variety of established techniques.

U2C is a model transformation as envisaged in the proposals for Queries, Views and Transformations (QVT) at the OMG, such as [1]. As performance is platform-dependent, other QVT transformations to incorporate platform-specific elements may also be a part of U2C, or a preliminary to it. Work with QVT is for the future. At the time of writing we are creating a direct ad hoc transformation from an XMI representation of the UML design, to an XML representation of the CSM, following the CSM metamodel.

5.1. Transformation U2C, from UML to a Core Scenario Model

The transformation that is currently being developed reads XMI files representing the UML design model, builds a data structure to represent the UML objects, and uses it to create a DOM (Domain Object Model) tree for the CSM, which can be output in XML. The formal definition of this U2C transformation, based on the UML metamodel, will be described in a planned report on the transformation. Here, the status of the transformation and its general approach will be described. At present, only Deployment Diagrams and Activity Diagrams are included; Sequence Diagrams will be approached later. The Activity Diagram for the example (corresponding to Figure 6) is given in [9].

The first step is to create resource and component objects for the resources and components in the UML description, using the stereotypes (possibly provided by notes) in the UML, and the one-to-one correspondences shown in Table 2. Attributes are obtained from tagged values. Then each Activity Diagram (AD) in the UML is examined. A CSM Scenario is established, and the AD Partitions (swimlanes) are identified with Components in CSM, constructed from the Deployment information. If this is not straightforward through component names, the user is asked about creating Component objects for them. From the Initial PseudoState, a Start Step is created. If a State following this has a <<PAworkload>> stereotype, the workload parameters become attributes of the Start Step. The rest of the AD is used to create a set of Steps and Connectors from the correspondences in the second part of Table 2. If an activity is of type CompositeState, with another diagram to refine it, the Step in CSM has a reference to a nested Scenario created for the second diagram.

Table 2. Objects in CSM, created in direct correspondence to objects in a UML Deployment or Activity Diagram

Type of Object in UML	**Stereotype in STP Profile**	**Type of Object in CSM**
Deployment Diagram		
Node	PAresource	Passive Resource
Node	PAhost	Processing Resource
Component	PAresource	Passive Resource
Component	none	Component
Activity Diagram		
SimpleState	PAstep	Step
CompositeState	PAstep	Step with nested Scenario
PseudoState: Initial	none	Start Step
PseudoState: Fork	none	Fork PathConnector
PseudoState: Join	none	Join PathConnector
PseudoState: Branch	none	Branch PathConnector
PseudoState: Merge	none	Merge PathConnector
FinalState	none	End Step

The sequential relationships in the Scenario are constructed by linking the Steps through IDrefs to PathConnectors, as described by the attributes shown in Table 1. They are based on the Transitions in the Activity Diagram, and their source and target States. If both are States (SimpleState or CompositeState) the Transition provides a Sequence PathConnector linked to the corresponding Steps. If one is a Fork, Join, Branch or Merge PseudoState, the Transition provides only a pair of links (in both directions) between the corresponding PathConnector and the Step for the other. If both are PseudoStates then a dummy Step is introduced between the PathConnectors in the CSM.

A loop can be described in the Activity Diagram by a CompositeState activity (referencing another diagram for a subscenario), stereotyped as <<PAstep>> with a repetition count tagged value. This can be translated directly to the CSM representation as a high-level Step with a nested Scenario and a repetition count attribute. However another possible representation of a loop in an AD is a sequence of activities delimited by a Merge at the loop head (where the repetition begins) and a Branch at the loop end (with a Transition back to the Merge for the next repetition); we can call this an "informal loop". Informal loops must be detected and then transformed to the subscenario structure just described, but this has not yet been addressed.

In a diagram with swimlanes representing different Components, a Transition from one swimlane to another implies releasing one Component Resource and acquiring the other. A Resource Release Step, Sequential PathConnector and Resource Acquire Step are introduced into the sequence for that Transition, possibly with Sequential PathConnectors at the beginning and end, depending on the source and target.

External Operations (with operation counts) are created in CSM for every ExternalService in the Activity Diagram, named in a tagged value attached to a <<PAStep>> stereotype. They are placeholders for calls to services defined outside the design, and are intended to be described by submodels introduced at the CSM level or at the performance model level (as in [12] for instance).

Since most of the CSM metamodel corresponds one-to-one to elements in the domain model underlying the SPT Profile, most of the U2C transformation is straightforward. Most of the transformations described above have been implemented and tested at this point; some details are incomplete.

Clearly some parameters or resource specifications may be missing, and the process of CSM extraction will include reports to the user, and provision of default values. Some translations have not yet been addressed, including informal loops (mentioned above) and the "Message" objects in CSM (which are not derived from the current Profile). Our current approach to any gap or ambiguity is to ask the tool user to resolve it.

Traceability from objects in the UML design to objects in the CSM (and on into the performance model) is presently provided only by the use of names, such as the names of Resources, Components, and Steps. Some UML tools provide a unique object identifier which could be carried into the CSM along with the name, to provide a stronger traceability.

5.2. Transformation to a Performance Model

There is not space here to describe the possible C2P transformations in any detail, but typical performance models use Queuing Networks, Layered Queues, or timed Petri nets. For systems with only processing devices and no nested resources Smith has shown how to create a Queueing Network model from a similar scenario model which she calls an Execution Graph [11] (she also deals with nested resources on an ad hoc basis). For nested resources, a systematic algorithm which traverses a scenario model almost identical to CSM, and generates a layered queueing (LQN) performance model [3] was described in [10]. The LQN that emerges for the BSS example in this paper was described in [13], with an analysis that illustrates the use of the model to study bottlenecks and scalability.

Other authors have created performance models using different intermediate models. Shen and Petriu extracted a graph model of the scenario from UML activity diagrams and used graph transformations to create an LQN [8]. Kahkipuro [4] defined his own intermediate model expressing the UML information he needed to create a model similar to a LQN. Cortelessa et al define a kind of Execution Graph to extract the scenario [2], and derived queueing models. Lopez-Grao et al [5] derive a timed Petri net in an interesting way. They create subnets for the individual Steps with labels that allowed them to compose the fragments of scenarios, bottom-up, to arrive at a model for the entire behaviour. However, their approach is suitable only for the particular style of Petri nets they use, and at this point their model does not address processor contention.

6. Conclusions

The Core Scenario Model defined here has the capability to open up the use of predictive models for performance of software designs, by providing a core of information needed in building performance models of different kinds. It provides a kind of "Unified Performance Model", at one remove from the actual modeling formalisms.

This paper described the model and showed, using an example, how it captures the required information. CSM provides a bridge between UML and the SPT Profile, and existing techniques to generate performance models which are based on the queueing and layered queueing formalisms. While it is not demonstrated here, it seems clear that Petri net models may be obtained with equal ease, and that new features introduced in UML 2 are easily accommodated.

Acknowledgments
This research was supported by the Natural Sciences and Engineering Research Council of Canada, through its program of Strategic Grants. The U2C transformations outlined here are the work of Kathleen Shen and will be described in detail elsewhere.

References

[1] DSTC et al, *MOF Query/Views/Transformations: Second Revised Submission*, OMG document ad/04-01-06, Jan. 2004.

[2] V. Cortellesa, "Deriving a Queueing Network Based Performance Model from UML Diagrams," *in Proc. Second Int. Workshop on Software and Performance (WOSP2000)*, Ottawa, Canada, 2000, pp. 58-70

[3] G. Franks, S. Majumdar, J. Neilson, D. Petriu, J. Rolia, and M. Woodside, "Performance Analysis of Distributed Server Systems," *Proc. 6th Int. Conf. on Software Quality (6ICSQ)*, Ottawa, Ontario, 1996, pp. 15-26.

[4] P. Kahkipuro, "UML-Based Performance Modeling Framework for Component-Based Systems," in *Performance Engineering*, R. Dumke, C. Rautenstrauch, A. Schmietendorf, and A. Scholz, Eds. Berlin: Springer, 2001.
[5] J. P. Lo'pez-Grao, J. Merseguer, and J. Campos, "From UML Activity Diagrams To Stochastic Petri Nets: Application To Software Performance Engineering," in *Fourth Int. Workshop on Software and Performance (WOSP 2004)*, Redwood City, CA, Jan. 2004, pp. 25-36.
[6] Object Management Group, "UML Profile for Schedulability, Performance, and Time Specification," OMG Adopted Specification ptc/02-03-02, July 1, 2002
[7] Object Management Group, *Meta Object Facility (MOF) 2.0 Core Specification*, OMG Adopted Specification ptc/03-10-04, Oct. 2003.
[8] D. C. Petriu and H. Shen, "Applying the UML Performance Profile: Graph Grammar-based derivation of LQN models from UML specifications," in *Proc. 12th Int. Conf. on Modeling Tools and Techniques for Computer and Communication System Performance Evaluation,* London, England, 2002.
[9] D. C. Petriu and C. M. Woodside, "Performance Analysis with UML," in *"UML for Real"*, ed. B. Selic, L. Lavagno, and G. Martin, Kluwer, 2003, pp. 221-240.
[10] Dorin Petriu, Murray Woodside, "Software Performance Models from System Scenarios in Use Case Maps", *Proc. 12 Int. Conf. on Modeling Tools and Techniques for Computer and Communication System Performance Evaluation (Performance TOOLS 2002*), London, April 2002.
[11] C. U. Smith and L. G. Williams, *Performance Solutions.* Addison-Wesley, 2002.
[12] Xiuping Wu and Murray Woodside, "Performance Modeling from Software Components," *in Proc. 4th Int. Workshop on Software and Performance (WOSP 2004)*, Redwood Shores, Calif., Jan 2004, pp. 290-301
[13] Jing Xu, Murray Woodside, Dorina Petriu "Performance Analysis of a Software Design using the UML Profile for Schedulability, Performance and Time", *Proc. 13th Int. Conf. on Computer Performance Evaluation, Modeling Techniques and Tools (TOOLS 2003*), Urbana, Illinois, USA, Sept 2003, pp 291 – 310.

On the Classification of UML's Meta Model Extension Mechanism

Yanbing Jiang[1], Weizhong Shao[1], Lu Zhang[1], Zhiyi Ma[1], Xiangwen Meng[1], and Haohai Ma[1,2]

[1]Software Institute, School of Electronics Engineering and Computer Science, Peking University, Beijing 100871, P.R. China
{jyb, wzshao, zhanglu, mzy, Mengxiangwen, mhh}@sei.pku.edu.cn
[2]Department of Computer Science, Inner Mongolia University , Hohhot 010021, P.R. China

Abstract. Although the UML meta model extension mechanism has been used in many modeling fields in which extension of UML is needed, UML specification has little necessary classification and application guidance on the meta model extension mechanism. This paper defines four levels of UML's meta model extension mechanism, and discusses the readability, expression capability, use scope and tool support on the basis of precise definitions of each level. The work on the paper reinforces the maneuverability of the UML meta model extension mechanism, and provides a reliable theoretical base for the development of modeling tools that support meta model extension.

1. Introduction

To suit for different modeling requirements in different domains, UML1.X defines several extension mechanisms, such as tag definition, constraints and stereotype[1]. UML2.0 puts forwards a powerful extension mechanism, the meta model extension mechanism[2]. The introduction of these extension mechanisms makes UML no longer a close system. According to their actual model requirements, modelers can select a relevant extension mechanism to extend UML in order to precisely describe special modeling domains.

The meta model extension mechanism directly extend UML's meta model, which means new meta model constructs can be directly added to the original meta model and original meta model constructs can be directly modified. Although UML1.X does not formally introduce this kind of extension mechanism, many researchers and modelers have used meta model extension mechanism in practice [1]. However, the meta model extension mechanism is so powerful that the expression capability of it may be vary from very limited to very large scope and users can use it to extend UML's syntax and semantics at large. Because of the lack of necessary classification and application guidance, many modelers often misuse meta model extension mechanism. As Cris Kobryn once pointed out [3], "many modelers are anxious to apply this new solution sledgehammer to problems where a claw hammer or a tack hammer would suffice."

T. Baar et al. (Eds.): UML 2004, LNCS 3273, pp. 54-68, 2004.

In [4], Ansgar Schleicher and his fellows put forwards a method of classifying meta model extension. They divide the meta model extension into two kinds: the controlled and none-controlled. In the none-controlled meta model extension, new meta model constructs can be added to original meta model arbitrarily, and associations can be defined between any two meta model constructs. In the controlled meta model extension, any new meta model construct must have parents in the original meta model, and only when a new association is a specialization of an existing association in the original meta model, could it be added to meta model. However, the classification is not enough meticulous and exact.

In UML2.0, the meta model extension is formally introduced as a kind of extension mechanism, which makes UML's extension capability enhanced largely. However, there is lack of a precise classification and essential application guidance of meta model extension mechanism in UML2.0. Furthermore, although UML2.0 indicates that the meta model and stereotype extension mechanism have some overlap in the aspects of extension capability, it dose not explain in which circumstances the two extension mechanism are equivalent.

In summary, although the UML meta model extension mechanism has been used in many modeling fields in which extension of UML is needed, UML specification has little necessary classification and application guidance on the meta model extension mechanism. The paper defines four levels of UML's meta model extension mechanism, and discusses the readability, expression capability, use scope and tool supporting on the basis of precise definition of each level. The work in this paper reinforces the maneuverability of the UML meta model extension mechanism, makes modelers select a relevant level to extend UML's meta model according to actual modeling requirements and provides a reliable theoretical base for the development of modeling tools that support the meta model extension mechanism.

2. The Definition of UML's Meta Model Extension Classification

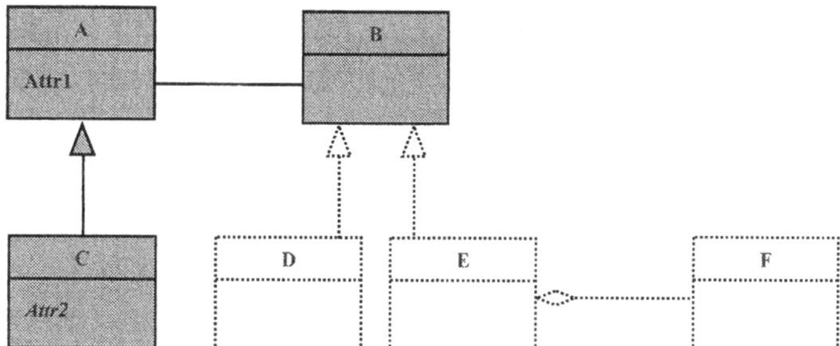

Fig 1. A brief illustration of UML's meta model extension mechanism

The abstract syntax and semantics of model elements in UML are described in the meta model level (M_2). The abstract syntax is described by UML's class diagram. If it is necessary to extend the abstract syntax of UML's meta model, relevant segments of the class diagram which describe UML's abstract syntax should be modified or extended. For example, new classes, associations and generalizations may be added to the original meta model to implement an extension.

The expression of meta model extension is showed in Fig1, in which grayed meta model constructs represent the original constructs in the meta model, white ones with dashed lines represent extended meta model constructs; italic attributes represent extended attributes, otherwise is original ones; grayed generalizations represent original relations, white ones with dashed lines represent extended relations and so on.

When modelers extend the abstract syntax of UML's meta model, they can follow different levels of constraint rules. According to the different constraint degree expressed by the meta model extension, this paper divides the meta model extension into four levels. Different levels mean different expression capability and application boundaries. When modelers extend UML's meta model according to their real modeling requirements, they can select a appropriate extension level to make the extension more reasonable and operable and avoid the extension blindness caused by insufficiency of expression capability or absence of constraints. To describe the classification of UML's meta model extension precisely, a formal definition of UML's meta model is given in definition 1.

Definition 1 (meta model.) The meta model can be defined as a tuple: $M<C, A_S, A_G, G>$, where C stands for the set of meta model constructs, which is defined in definition 2; A stands for the set of association relations and $A_S \subseteq C \times C$; A_G stands for the set of aggregation and $A_G \subseteq C \times C$; and G stands for the set of generalization and $G \subseteq C \times C$.

Definition 2 (meta model construct.) The meta model construct can be defined as a tuple: $M_C<M_N, F, A_T, C_O, N, S>$, where

M_N is the name of the meta model construct;

F is the sets of fathers of the meta model construct, which are still meta model constructs;

A_T is the set of attributes: A_T={<*attributename*, *attributetype*>}, where *attributename* is the name of attribute of the meta model construct, and *attributetype* is its type;

C_O is the set of constraints of the meta model, which is also called the static semantics set;

N is the notation description of the meta model constructs; and

S is the semantics description of the meta model constructs.

On the base of the two definitions, the following section precisely defines the four levels of meta model extension according to the different constraints imposed on it. Fig 2 illustrates the four levels of meta model extension. The grayed meta model constructs stand for the original ones, and the white meta model constructs stand for extended ones. The italic attributes stands for the extended attribute.

2.1 The First Level of Meta Model Extension

In this level of meta model extension, modelers can extend the original meta model at their will. For example, attributes, operations and relationships can be directly added to the original meta model without any constraints, such as shown in Fig 2(a). Definition 3 shows the precise definition of this level.

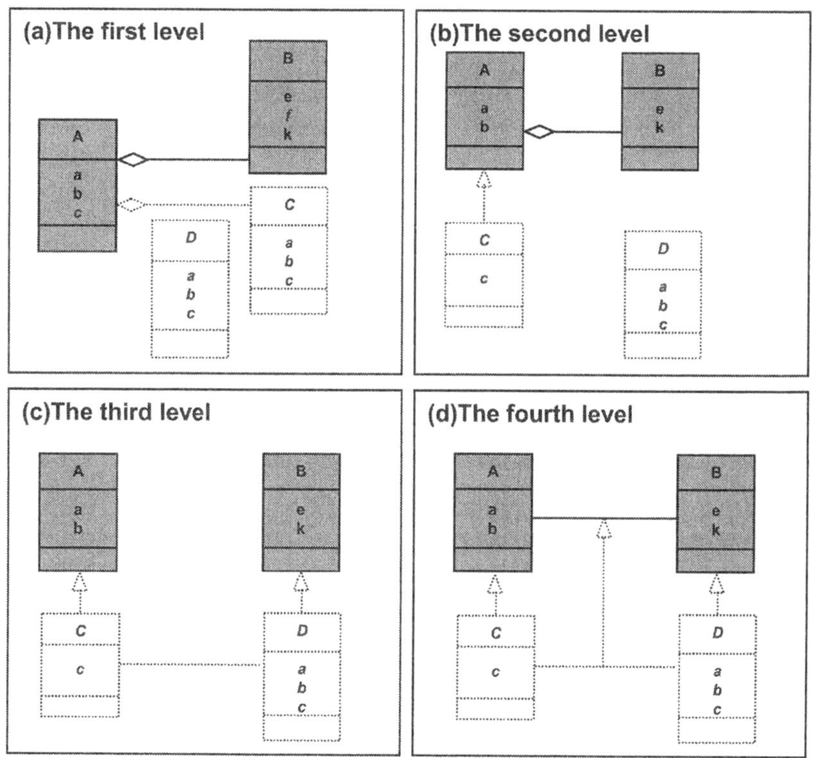

Fig 2. The four levels of meta model extension

Definition 3 (The first level of meta model extension.) Original meta model is $M<C, A_S, A_G, G>$. If there is another meta model $M_e<C_e, A_{Se}, A_{Ge}, G_e>$, and $C_e \geq C$, $A_{Se} \supseteq A_S$, $A_{Ge} \supseteq A_G$, $G_e \supseteq G$, then M_e extends M with the first level of meta model extension, which can be formally described as $M \xrightarrow{1} M_e$.

The operator $\geq$ is defines as follows. There are two sets of meta model constructs, C_1 and C_2. For any meta model construct $Mc<M_N, F, A_T, C_O, N, S>$ in C_2, if there is a meta model construct $Mc'<M_N', F', A_T', C_O', N', S'>$ in C_1, and $Mc \, \Delta \, Mc'$, which means Mc′is a generalization of Mc, or $(M_N'=M_N) \wedge (A_T' \supseteq A_T)$, then we call $C_1 \geq C_2$.

2.2 The Second Level of Meta Model Extension

In this level of meta model extension, modelers cannot modify constructs in the original meta model, but can add new constructs without any constraints, such as Fig 2(b) shows. Definition 4 shows the precise definition of this level.

Definition 4 (The second level of meta model extension.) The original meta model is M<C, A_S, A_G, G>, and there is another meta model M_e<C_e, A_{Se}, A_{Ge}, G_e>, where we have $C_e \supseteq C$, $A_{Se} \supseteq A_S$, $A_{Ge} \supseteq A_G$, $G_e \supseteq G$. Besides, if meta model constructs Mc_1 and Mc_2 are in C, and <Mc_1, Mc_2> $\notin A \cup A_S$, then we have <Mc_1, Mc_2> $\notin A_e \cup A_{Se}$; if either Mc_1 or Mc_2 is in C, then we also have <Mc_1, Mc_2> $\notin A_e \cup A_{Se}$. If meta model M_e satisfies the above conditions, then M_e extends M with the second level of meta model extension, which can be formally described as $M \xrightarrow{2} M_e$.

2.3 The Third Level of Meta Model Extension

In this level of meta model extension, the extended meta model satisfied constraints of the second level of meta model extension, and all new constructs must have a parent constructs in original meta model, such as Fig 2(c) shows. Definition 5 shows the precise definition of this level.

Definition 5 (The third level of meta model extension.) Original meta model is M<C, A_S, A_G, G>, and there is another meta model M_e<C_e, A_{Se}, A_{Ge}, G_e>, which satisfies $M \xrightarrow{2} M_e$. Besides, for any construct Mc in C_e but not in C, if there is a construct Mc′in C and ralation <Mc′, Mc> in G_e, then M_e extends M with the third level of meta model extension, which can be formally described as $M \xrightarrow{3} M_e$.

2.4 The Fourth Level of Meta Model Extension

In this level of meta model extension, the extended meta model satisfied constraints of the third level of meta model extension, and all new constructs must not have new relations between each other, except the one which is a specialization of an existed relation between original constructs, such as Fig 2(c) shows. Definition 6 shows the precise definition of this level.

Definition 6 (The fourth level of meta model extension.) Original meta model is M<C, A_S, A_G, G>, and there is another meta model M_e<C_e, A_{Se}, A_{Ge}, G_e>, which satisfies $M \xrightarrow{3} M_e$. Besides, if relation <a, b> is in A_{Se} but not in A_S, then there is a relation <a′, b′> in A_S, which satisfies a′ Δ a, b′ Δ b, and <a′, b′> Δ <a, b>. and if relation <a, b> is in A_{Ge} but not in A_G, then there is a relation <a′, b′> in A_G, which satisfies a′ Δ a, b′ Δ b, and <a′,b′> Δ <a,b>. The operate Δ here means generalization relation between father and child. If meta model M_e satisfies the above conditions, then M_e extend M with fourth level of meta model extension, which can be formally described as $M \xrightarrow{4} M_e$.

According to the definition of four levels of meta model extension, it can be conclude that the higher level of meta model extension modelers adopt, the more constraints are added in the abstract syntax extension of meta model extension. The inclusion relationship can be illustrated in Fig 3. In the following part of this paper, we have a detailed analysis of the four levels of meta model extension from different points of view, such as readability, expression capability, application scope, equivalence and tools support.

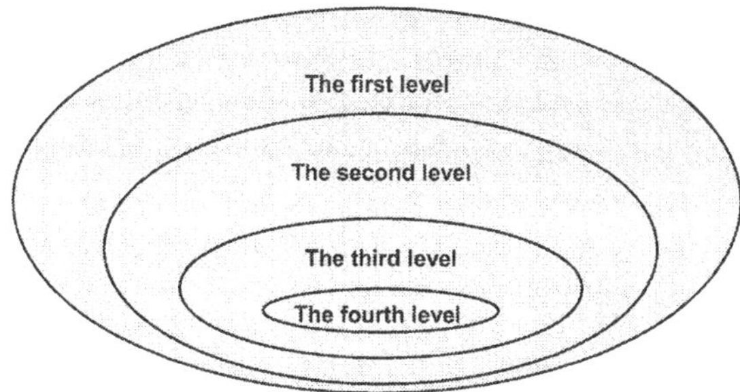

Fig 3. The inclusion relationship of the four levels of meta model extension

3. Different Aspects of the Four-Leveled Meta Model Extension

According to the definitions of the four levels of meta model extension mechanism, different levels have different constraints. Therefore, these four levels of meta model extension have different features in aspects such as readability, expression capability, use scope and tool supporting. In this section, these aspects are discussed in detail to help the modelers select right meta model extension level in expressing the necessary extension to UML.

3.1 Readability

When modelers use the first level of meta model extension, they do not have any constraints, and can make their extension directly on original meta model. Therefore, the extended language elements and the original language elements might exist in a same meta model construct. Because of this kind of phenomena, there is a close coupling between the original meta model and the extension. That is to say, after extension, some original meta model constructs no longer exist as a complete construct, but a part of the extended constructs. In summary, from the aspect of readability, this level of meta model extension cannot clearly distinguish extended meta model constructs from the original ones.

Because direct modification of the constructs in original meta model is not allowed in the second level, extended and original syntax elements are not in the same meta model construct. It is easy to distinguish the extended part form the original part of the meta model.

The third level of meta model extension does not allow adding new meta constructs without foundation. That is to say, new meta model constructs must has at least a generalization. Because all the new meta model constructs in the third level are built on the original meta model constructs, the modelers would not be puzzled by a new constructs without any foundation, when they read the extended meta model. Further more, the modelers can easily comprehend the extended meta model, which is founded on the original meta model. In summary, the third level of meta model extension has a better readability than the second level of meta model extension.

The fourth level does not allow defining new structure of extended meta model construct. In other words, an extended meta model construct must have the same structure as its parent. Hence, modelers can deduce the structure of extended meta models according to the original ones. The readability of the fourth level is the strongest among the four levels.

3.2 Expression Capability

The first level of meta model extension can be used to construct any new syntax structure. However, this level allows directly modifying original meta model constructs, which makes a directly modified meta model construct no longer independently existing, but evolving into a new meta model construct. Therefore, the directly modified original meta model construct cannot be instantiated as a dependent meta model construct.

The expression capability of the second level is the same as that of the first level. The second level can also express all syntax structure expressed by the first level. What is different is that the second level completely preserves all original meta model constructs. In the second level, when it is necessary to extend original meta model constructs, modelers need to create a new meta model construct, let it be a specialization of an original meta model construct, and add expansion information to the new meta model construct. The benefit of this level is that the original meta model construct can still be instantiated as a separated meta model construct.

Because the third level meta model extension dose not allow the appearance of meta model constructs which have no parents, the expression capability of this level is limited. The third level only allows extending the meta model constructs on the basis of original ones, so the new meta model constructs which have completely different features with original constructs cannot be expressed with this level.

The expression capability of the third level meta model extension is determined by the abstraction degree of the top meta model constructs. If the top meta model constructs in original meta model are quiet particular, the newly added meta model constructs must specialize these meta model constructs, so the expression capability of extended meta model is quite limited. On the contrary, if the top meta model constructs in original meta model are quiet abstract, then the expression capability of extended meta model is quite strong.

The fourth level does not change the structure of original meta model, so the only thing the modelers can modify is to add new feature to an original meta model. This level is so restrict that it cannot express new meta model constructs that have different structure with original ones, but just add new features to them.

3.3 Application Scope

The first level of meta model can be used to describe any new modeling structure. However, because this level cannot guarantee that instances of the original meta model constructs and extended ones coexist in a same model system, it does not suit for the circumstances where both original meta model constructs and extended ones are needed. That is to say, this level suits for the circumstances where original meta model constructs are no longer needed after being extended.

The second level can completely be used to express any newly added modeling structure. Moreover, this level can guarantee that the original and extended constructs coexist in a modeling system. Therefore, this level suit for circumstances in which both the original meta model constructs and extended ones are needed for modeling.

The third level of meta model extension can be used to express new meta model constructs which have common features, structure and relations as original meta model constructs. The new meta model constructs are the specialization of original ones. Therefore, this level cannot suit for the extension requirements which need a suite of brand-new meta model constructs, but suit for the extension requirements which just extend the original meta model constructs to describe a certain special domain more precisely.

The fourth level can be used to express the new meta model constructs with the same structure as original ones. On the premise of keeping the structure of its parent, new feature can be added. Therefore, this level does not suit for circumstances where new structure must be imported, but for circumstances where new features can be imported.

3.4 Tools Support

According to the degree of supporting the expansibility, modeling tools can be divided into two types, the un-extensible modeling tools and extensible modeling ones. The un-extensible modeling tools have fixed meta models, which cannot be modified by users. If we wanted an un-extensible modeling tool to support an extended meta model, then there is nothing to do but ask the provider of this tool to modify the source code. On the contrary, extensible modeling tools permit users to extend their meta models. To achieve this goal, extensible modeling tools must have a kind of instantiation mechanism that helps users to transform meta models into models. Just because the first level cannot clearly distinguish extended meta models from original meta models, the original instantiation process cannot be reused in the instantiation process of the extended meta models.

When the meta model of a modeling tool is extended with the second level, the extended modeling tool supports the instantiation of original meta model constructs. Moreover, because the second level clearly distinguishes the extended meta model constructs from the original ones, it is easy to reuse the original instantiation process in the instantiation process of new-added meta model construct which specializes an original meta model construct.

The third level enhances the reuse degree of the original meta model, and every newly added meta model construct reuses some original meta model construct more or less. Therefore, it is convenient for reusing the meta model in modeling tools to use this level of meta model extension.

The fourth level more enhances the reuse degree to the original meta model. The meta model extended with this level not only reuses the features of original ones, but also the structure. Therefore, the modeling tool extended with this level can reuse the architecture of the meta model used by the original modeling tools. The only thing left to do is to add some new features to the original meta model constructs.

3.5 Summary

A brief summary on the four aspects of different levels of meta model extension is given in Table 1. In Table 1, the number of the symbol * means the degree of some aspect of a certain level of meta model extension.

Table 1. A summary on the four aspects of different levels of meta model extension

	Readability	Expression capability	Application scope	Tool supporting
The first level	*	***	***	*
The second level	**	***	***	**
The third level	***	**	**	***
The fourth level	****	*	*	****

According to Table 1, we can see that with the growth of the level the extended meta model belongs to, the readability increases, the expression and application scope decrease, and modeling tool support is easier. Considering the real modeling requirements, modelers can select the right level to extend the meta model on the guidance of the framework of four-leveled meta model extension.

4. Transformation

To help the modelers optimize the extended meta model and set up a bridge between meta model and stereotype extension, we give the transformations from the first level to the second level and from the third level to stereotype in this section.

4.1 Transformation from the First Level to the Second Level

Because the first level and the second level have same expression capability, it is possible to transform the first level to the second level in order to reduce the coupling and enhance the capability of tool support. Transformation 1 formally describes the transformation from the first level to the second level.

Transformation 1: There are meta models $M<C, A_S, A_G, G>$ and $M_{e1}<C_{e1}, A_{Se1}, A_{Ge1}, G_{e1}>$. If $M \xrightarrow{1} M_{e1}$, then there is meta model $M_{e2}<C_{e2}, A_{Se2}, A_{Ge2}, G_{e2}>$ which makes $M \xrightarrow{2} M_{e2}$ and M_{e2} has the same expression capability of M_{e1}. The prerequisites of the transformation are:

i) For meta model construct $Mc<M_N, F, A_T, C_O, N, S>$ in C, if there is a construct $Mc'<M_N', F', A_T', C_O', N', S'>$ in C_{e1}, and $(M_N'=M_N) \wedge (A_T' \supseteq A_T)$, then there are constructs $Mc<M_N, F, A_T, C_O, N, S>$ and $Mc''<M_N'', F'', A_T, C_O, N, S>$ $c''<MN'', F'', A'', C'', N'', M''>$, and relation $<c, c''>$ is in G'_{e2}, which is the transitive closure set of C_{e2}.

ii) If constructs c_1 and c_2 are in C, and relation $<c_1, c_2>$ is in $A_{e1} \cup A'_{e1}$ but not in $A \cup A'$, then $<c_1, c_2>$ is not in $A_{e2} \cup A'_{e2}$, and there are constructs c'_1 and c'_2 in C_{e2}, which makes the relation $<c'_1, c'_2>$ exist in $A_{e2} \cup A'_{e2}$, and relation $<c_1, c'_1>$ and $<c_2, c'_2>$ in G'_{e2}, which is the transitive closure set of G_{e2}.

iii) If construct c_1 is in C, c_2 is not in C but in C_{e1}, and relation $<c_1, c_2>$ is in $A_{e1} \cup A'_{e1}$, then relation $<c_1, c_2>$ is not in $A_{e1} \cup A'_{e1}$, and there is construct c'_1 in C_{e2}, which makes the relation $<c'_1, c_2>$ exist in $A_{e2} \cup A'_{e2}$, and relation $<c_1, c'_1>$ in G'_{e2}, which is the transitive closure set of G_{e2}.

Transformation 1 can be explained in plain English as follows:

i) If a new feature is directly added to the meta model construct in the first level, then in the transformation to the equal second level, we add a new meta model construct which specializes the original construct, and add new feature to the new construct.

ii) If a new relation is directly linked between two original meta model constructs, then in the transformation to the equal second level, we add two new meta model constructs which specializes the original constructs respectively, and add a new relation between them.

iii) If a new relation is directly linked between an original and a new meta model constructs, then in the transformation to the equal second level, we add a new meta model construct which specializes the original construct, and add a new relation between the two new constructs.

The Fig 4 illustrates Transformation 1. In the first extension level, a new attribute *Attri1* is added to the meta model construct A, and a new association relation is added between meta model constructs A and B. The expression capability of A, which conforms to the first level of extension, is equal to the expression capability of A′, which conforms to the second level of extension. In the first extension level, because the construct A is a generalization of construct C, the addition of a new attribute to A makes C have the same attribute. Similarly, the addition of a new association to A also makes C have the same association. So the expression capability of C is equal to C′. In the same way, the expression capability of D is equal to D′. Thus the meta model extended by the second extension level preserves original meta model constructs, and has the same expression capability as the first level.

4.2 Transformation from the Third Level to the Stereotype

Stereotype is an important extension mechanism in UML. In UML, a stereotype is a model element that defines additional values (based on tag definitions), additional constraints, and optionally a new graphical representation [1]. Stereotype can only add some attributes and constraints to the existing meta model constructs, but cannot reduce some attributes and constraints or create new meta model constructs from beginning. From this point, we can conclude that the expression capability of stereotype is equal to the third level of meta model extension, and a equal

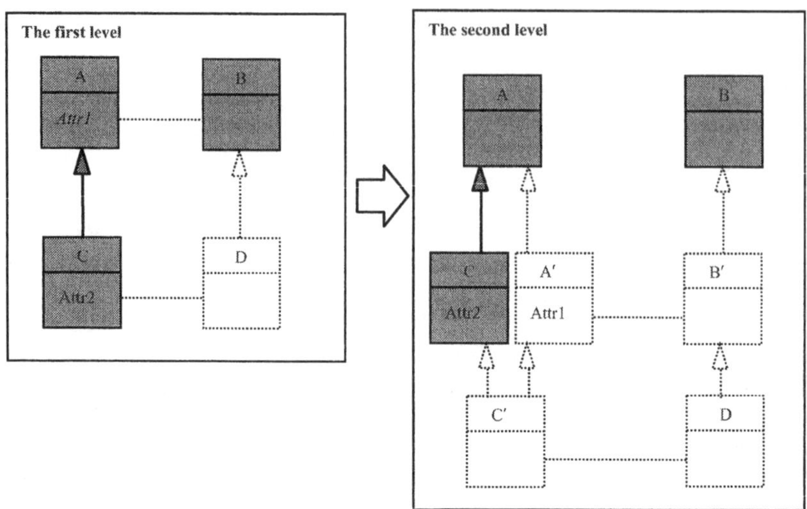

Fig 4. Transformation from the first level to the second level

transformation can be made between stereotype and the third level of meta model extension.

To describe the transformation precisely, we need first formally define the stereotype and the stereotype extension mechanism.

Definition6 (stereotype): Stereotype can be defined as a tuple: Stereotype<S, B, P, T, C, N, M>, where

S is the stereotype name;

B is the base class name, which is the name of meta model construct extended by stereotype;

P is the set of father stereotypes of S;

T is the set of tag definition, and T={<*tagname*, *tagvaluetype*>}, where *tagname* is the name of tag definition, *tagvaluetype* is the type of the tag definition;

C is the constraint set of S;

N is notation of S; and

M is the semantics of S.

Definition7 (stereotype extension mechanism): Let original meta model be M<C, A, A′, G>. There is a stereotype set Y. For any stereotype y<S, B, P, T, C, N, M> in Y, if B is in the set of M.C, which means the meta model constructs in M; and for any t in T, if its *tagvaluetype* is in C ,Y or the other stereotype set of M, then we call that Y extends M by the stereotype type, which can be formally noted as $M \xrightarrow{S} Y$.

On the basis of these definitions, Transformation 2 formally describes the transformation between stereotype and the third level of meta model extension.

Transformation 2: If meta model M<C, A, A′,G> and M_e<C_e, A_e, A'_e, G_e> satisfy $M \xrightarrow{3} M_e$, then we have a profile Y, which satisfies $M \xrightarrow{S} Y$, and Y and M_e have the same extension capability. The detailed transformation is listed as follows:

i) If meta model construct c_1<MN_1, F_1, A_1, C_1, N_1, M_1> is in C of M, and meta model construct c_2<MN_2, F_2, A_2, C_2, N_2, M_2> is not in C of M, but in C_e of M_e, then there is a stereotype y<S, B, P, T, C, N, M> in Y, where

$S=MN_2$;

$B= c_2$;

A_2 is transformed to T, concretely, every attributes in A_2 is transformed to tag definitions in T;

C_2 is transformed to C, concretely, every piece of constraints in C_2 is transformed to constraints in C;

N_2 is transformed to N, concretely, every piece of notations in N_2 is transformed to notations in N;

M_2 is transformed to M, concretely, every piece of semantics in N_2 is transformed to semantics in M.

ii) If meta model constructs c_2 and c_3 are in C_e, but not in C, and relation $<c_2,c_3>$ is in $A_e \cup A'_e$, then for the stereotype y<S, B, P, T, C, N, M> which is transformed from c_2, there is tag definition t in T, the tag name of t is the name of association $<c_2, c_3>$, and the tag type is the type of c_3 or its reference.

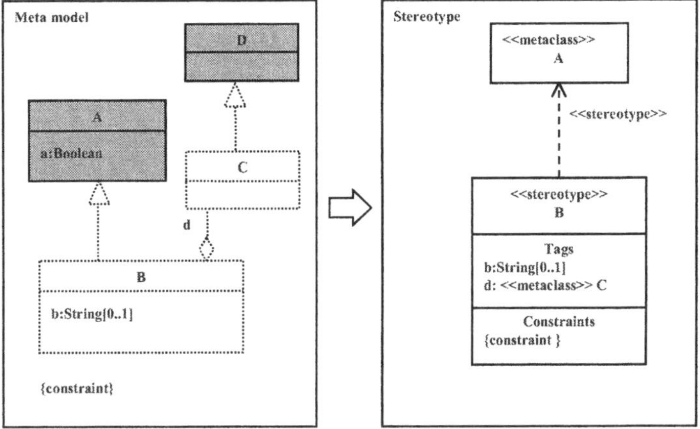

Fig 5. Transformation from the third level to stereotype

In Transformation 2, the extended meta model construct is transformed to a stereotype; the parent of the meta model construct is transformed to the base class of the stereotype; the newly added attributes or associations of the extended meta model construct are transformed to tag definition of the stereotype; constraints of the extended meta model construct are transformed to constraints of stereotype and so on, just as Fig.5 illustrates.

Thus it can be seen that only extended meta model that satisfies the third level of meta model extension can be transformed to stereotype extension. Therefore, the expression capability of meta model extension is much stronger than stereotype. Stereotype just equals to a kind of restrict meta model extension.

5. Case Study

To validate that the classification of meta model extension is helpful in practice of meta model extension, we study a case of meta model extension according to the framework of meta model classification which we put forward in this paper, and use the process of transformation between different levels of meta model extension to optimize the practical meta model extension solution.

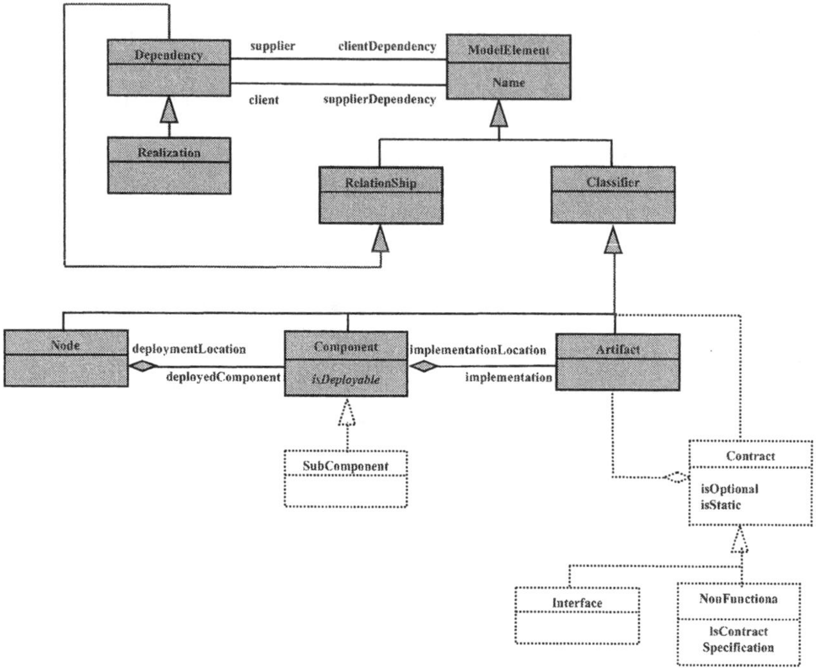

Fig 6. The extended meta model to support modeling to contract aware component (T. Weis)

In order to solve the problem how to trust a component in a mission-critical system, references [5] and [6] put forward the concept of contract aware components. T. Weis puts up the extended UML meta model to support modeling contract aware components in [7].

As illustrated in Fig 6, the extended meta model imports new meta model constructs (for example, *subcomponent* and *contract*), and directly adds new attributes to original meta model constructs (for example, *component*). Under the framework of classification of meta model extension that we put forward in this paper, we can conclude that extended meta model belongs to the first level. The first level has some shortcomings such as weak readability and difficulty of tool support. As to the case, for example, the original meta model construct *Component* is directly added an attribute *isDeployable*, which makes the original and newly-added attributes coexist in a same meta model construct, and as a result, modeler cannot distinguish them easily.

In this case, because no brand-new meta model is imported, the extension of the meta model can be expressed with the third level. According to the transformation 1 in the section 4, we transform the extended meta model that T. Weis had put forward to the second level. This meta model in the second level accidentally satisfies the third level. As illustrated in Fig 7, the original and extended meta model constructs are clearly distinguished. The transformation enhances the readability of the extended meta model, and makes modeling tools support this extension much easier.

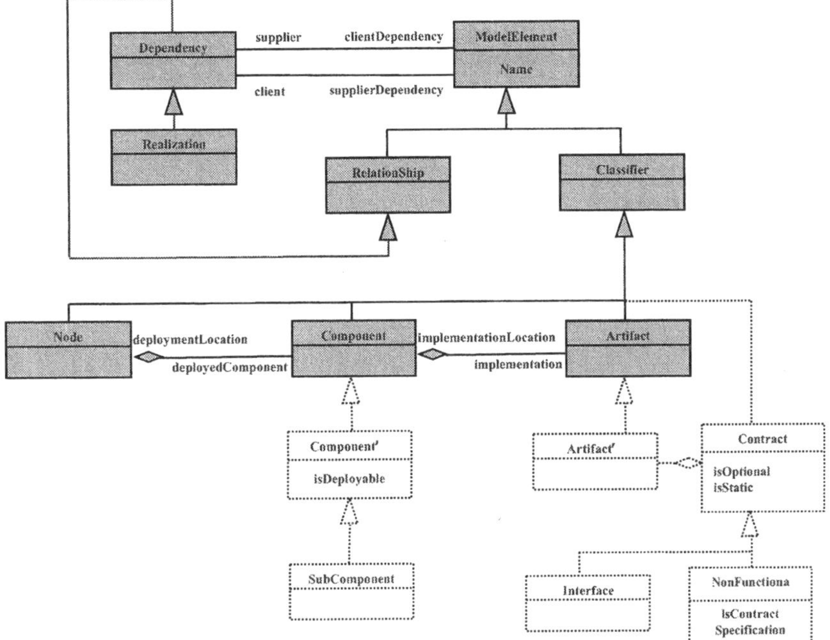

Fig 7. Transformed meta model that satisfies the third level

6. Conclusion

As to the problem that UML has little necessary classification and application guidance on the meta model extension mechanism, we put forward a classification definition to UML's meta model extension. On the basis of precise definitions of each level of meta model extension, the readability, expression capability, application scope, and tool support are discussed detailedly. Some conclusions can be drawn as following:

1. Along with the increase of the level of meta model extension, more and more constraints are imposed on the extended meta model, more and more original meta model elements can be reused by the extended meta model, the readability increases, the expression and application scope decrease, and tool support becomes easier.

2. In the aspect of expression capability, the first and the second levels are equivalent. The first level can be transformed to the second level to reduce coupling and enhance reusability.

3. The third level has same expression capability as stereotype extension. The third level can be transformed to stereotype.

4. When modelers use the meta model extension mechanism, they should first consider the higher level of meta model extension. Only when the high level cannot express the extension requirements, can they resort to a lower level of meta model extension.

In summary, the work of this paper enhances the maneuverability of UML's meta model extension mechanism, provides an instructive method and strategy for modelers to select appropriate meta model extension.

Acknowledgements The work is funded by the National High-Tech Research and Development Plan of China (No. 2001AA113070) and the National Grand Fundamental Research 973 Program of China (No. 2002CB31200003), administered by the China National Software Engineering Research Institute. We thank Mr. Zhidao Zhu and Mr. Nengbin Zhang for their help.

References

1. OMG Unifed Modeling Language Specification 1.3 ,1.4
2. UML 2.0 Infrastructure, 3rd Revision, OMG document ad/03-03-01. Object Management Group, 2003
3. C. Kobryn,UML2001:A STANDARDIZATION ODYSSEY Communication Of The ACM October 1999/Vol.42 No.10
4. A. Schleicher,B. Westfechtel, Beyond Stereotyping:Meta model ing Approaches for the UML, 34th Annual Hawaii International Conference on System Sciences (HICSS-34)
5. J.-M. Jézéquel and B. Meyer, Design by Contract: The Lessons of Ariane, *Computer*, Jan. 1997, pp. 129-130
6. E.J. Weyuker, Testing Component-Based Software: A Cautionary Tale, *IEEE Software*, Sept. 1998, pp. 54-59
7. T. Weis, C. Becher, K. Geihs,N. Plouzeau, A UML Meta-model for Contract Aware Components, UML'2001-Modeling Language,Concepts, and Tools,Springer October 2001

Modeling Business Processes in Web Applications with ArgoUWE*

Alexander Knapp[1], Nora Koch[1,2], Gefei Zhang[1], and Hanns-Martin Hassler[1]

[1] Ludwig-Maximilians-Universität München, Germany
{knapp@pst,kochn@pst,zhangg@pst,hassler@cip}.ifi.lmu.de
[2] F.A.S.T. GmbH, Germany
koch@fast.de

Abstract. The CASE tool ArgoUWE supports the systematic design of Web applications using the UML-based Web Engineering (UWE) approach. The design methodology of UWE is based on a metamodel which is defined as a lightweight extension of the UML metamodel in the form of a profile and comprises the separate modeling of the different aspects of a Web application: content, structure, layout, and business logic. ArgoUWE is implemented as a plugin into the open-source tool ArgoUML. In this paper, we focus on the latest improvements of the ArgoUWE tool: On the one hand, ArgoUWE supports the design of workflow-driven Web applications where business logic can be captured by process structure and process flow models. On the other hand, ArgoUML's design critic mechanism has been extended to indicate deficiencies and inconsistencies in UWE models based on the UWE metamodel and its OCL well-formedness rules.

1 Introduction

Most of the existing approaches supporting the development process of Web applications were born with the aim to develop Web Information Systems (WIS) [3, 6, 9, 14], whose main focus is to retrieve, adapt and present information to the users. However, Web applications are evolving to software systems supporting complex business processes in the same way as non-Web software does. To address the complexity of these business processes software development methods usually include the definition of an explicit business process view. In contrast, such business processes have been only tangentially tackled in most existing Web Application development approaches. This work centers its attention on such a business process view in the design of Web applications.

Web engineering always implies the employment of systematic, disciplined and quantifiable methods and tools in the construction of the applications. UWE and ArgoUWE are such a method and such a tool, respectively. UWE is the acronym for "UML-based Web Engineering" [9]. The model elements of UWE are defined in a UML profile—a conservative extension of the UML [13]—and the iterative and incremental development process is based on the Unified Software Development Process [7]. The extension comprises appropriate elements to permit separate modeling of

* This work has been partially supported by the EU project AGILE (IST-2001-32747), the DFG project InOpSys (WI 841/6-1), and the BMBF project MMISS (08NM070D).

T. Baar et al. (Eds.): UML 2004, LNCS 3273, pp. 69–83, 2004.

the conceptual, navigational, business logic and presentational aspects of Web applications, guaranteeing the consistency between these models.

We have extended the CASE tool ArgoUML into a tool for UWE-based Web application development, called ArgoUWE[3] [8]. The distinguishing features of ArgoUWE are support of visual modeling, UML conformance and open source characteristics. This tool provides on the one hand tailored editors for the UML-based notation used for the conceptual, navigation, presentation and business process modeling of Web applications. On the other hand, it offers several semi-automatic model transformations that are defined in the UWE development process [9]. As these model transformations are based on the UWE-metamodel, both consistency between the different models and integrity of the overall Web application model with respect to UWE's OCL constraints are ensured by the tool. In particular, in a conceptual model classes can be marked for navigation and navigation classes can be derived from annotated conceptual classes. Furthermore, in the navigational model ArgoUWE can add automatically access primitives such as queries and menus. ArgoUWE is implemented as a plugin module of the open-source ArgoUML [16] modeling tool. It fully integrates the UWE metamodel [10] and provides an XMI extension. The construction process of Web applications is supported by incorporating the semi-automatic UWE development steps as well as the OCL well-formedness rules of the UWE metamodel which can be checked upon request.

We present in this work a new version of ArgoUWE, which includes new modeling facilities to support the design of process-driven Web applications. A business process model and new stereotyped classes are included as well as a set of additional constraints that are used for consistency checks and semi-automatic generation of process models. In contrast to the old version, consistency of models is now checked in the background during modeling. This way the developer is supported but not constrained in his modeling activities with suggestions for corrections and improvements.

In contrast to the Web application development tool VisualWADE, which is based on the Web engineering method OO-H [6], UWE and ArgoUWE use the UML throughout the complete development process. Furthermore, ArgoUWE does not rely on proprietary standards, like the Web modeling language WebML [1] that is used in the WebRatio tool. ArgoUWE can be viewed as complementary to work focusing on the technological aspects of Web applications, such as [2, 12].

This paper is organized as follows: Section 2 provides an overview of the UWE approach. Section 3 describes how ArgoUWE supports the systematic design of Web applications focusing on the modeling of the business logic. Section 4 presents those special features of ArgoUWE implemented to guarantee model consistency. Section 5 presents the novel implementation aspects of business logic and the so-called design critics in the current version of ArgoUWE. Section 6 gives an overview of related work. Finally, in the last section some concluding remarks and future work are outlined.

2 UML-based Web Engineering

UML-based Web Engineering (UWE) has been continuously extended since 1999; for a summary see [10]. UWE supports Web application development with special focus on

[3] http://www.pst.ifi.lmu.de/projekte/argouwe

systematization. Being a software engineering approach it is based on the three pillars: process, notation and tool support. The focus of this article is the tool support and we will only give a brief overview of the UWE approach and the underpinning UWE metamodel here. Section 3 gives some details about the UWE process and the notation used when showing how the ArgoUWE tool supports the design of Web applications.

The UWE process is object-oriented, iterative and incremental. It is based on the Unified Process [7] and covers the whole life cycle of Web applications focusing on design and automatic generation [10]. The UWE notation used for the analysis and design of Web applications is a lightweight UML profile [13] published in several previous articles. It is a UML extension based on the extension mechanisms defined by the UML itself, i.e., the extension is performed by the definition of stereotypes, tagged values and OCL constraints. These modeling elements are used in the visual representation of the requirements and in the design of the conceptual model, the navigation structure, the business logic and the presentation aspects of Web applications (see Sect. 3).

We defined the UWE metamodel as a conservative extension of the UML 1.5 metamodel. Conservative means that the model elements of the UML metamodel are not modified. Instead, all new model elements of the UWE metamodel are related by inheritance to at least one model element of the UML metamodel. We define additional features and relationships for the new elements. Analogous to the well-formedness rules in the UML specification, we use OCL constraints to specify the additional static semantics of these new elements. The resulting UWE metamodel is profileable, which means that it is possible to map the metamodel to a UML profile. In particular, UWE stays compatible with the MOF interchange metamodel and therefore with tools that are based on the corresponding XML interchange format XMI. The advantage is that all standard UML CASE tools which support UML profiles or UML extension mechanisms can be used to create UWE models of Web applications. If technically possible, these CASE tools can further be extended to support the UWE method. ArgoUWE presents an instance of such CASE tool support for UWE based on the UWE metamodel.

We only briefly review the UWE metamodel here; for further details see [10]. The extension of the UML metamodel consists of adding one top-level package UWE to the three UML top-level packages. This UWE package contains all UWE model elements, which are distributed in sub-packages (see Fig. 1(a)). The structure of the packages inside the UWE package is analogous to the UML top-level package structure (shown in grey). The package Foundation contains all basic static model elements, the package BehavioralElements depends on it and contains all elements for behavioral modeling and finally the package ModelManagement, which also depends on the Foundation package, contains all elements to describe the models themselves specific to UWE. These UWE packages depend on the corresponding UML top-level packages. Figure 1(b) shows part of the UWE metamodel classes in UWE::Foundation::Core::Process. Note that the separation of concerns of Web applications is reflected by the package structure of the package UWE::Foundation of the UWE metamodel in Fig. 1(a).

The UWE methodology provides guidelines for the systematic and stepwise construction of models for Web applications. The precision can be augmented by the definition of constraints in the OCL.

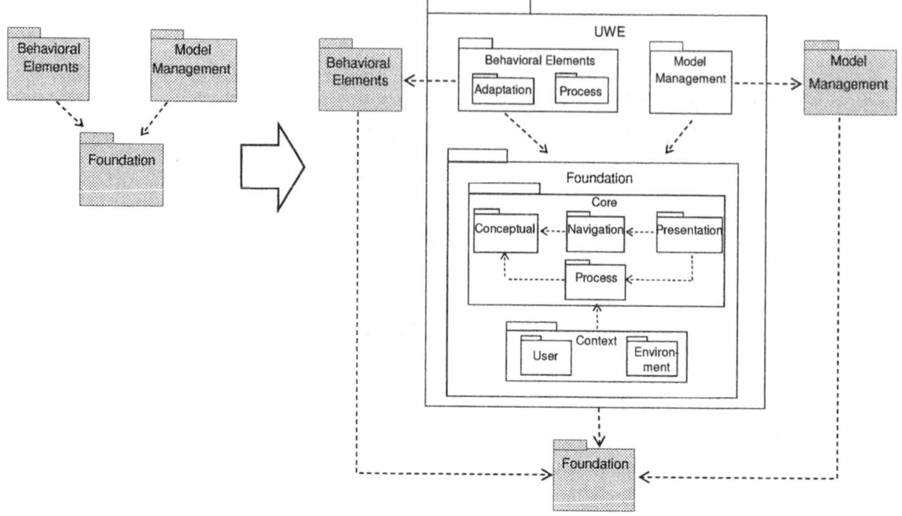

(a) UWE metamodel embedded into the UML metamodel

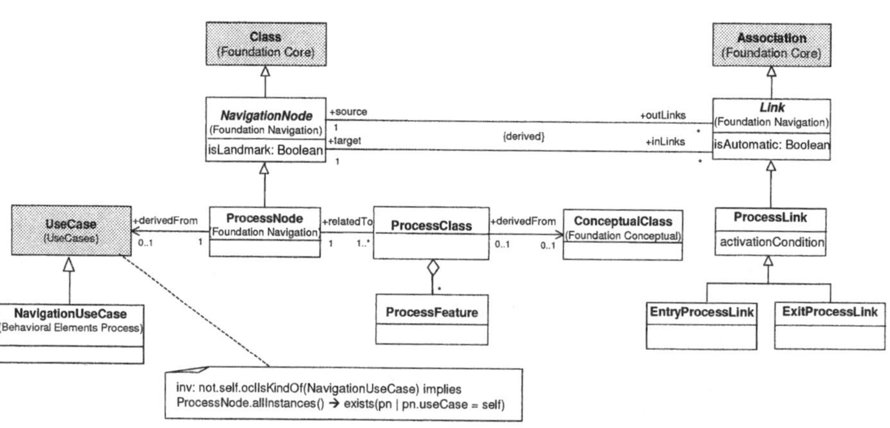

(b) Part of UWE metamodel classes in UWE::Foundation::Core::Process

Fig. 1. UWE metamodel

3 Modeling with ArgoUWE

We present the main steps of modeling Web applications using the CASE tool ArgoUWE by means of a simplified example of an e-shop. The user of this e-shop can search for and select products, add them to his shopping cart, and view the content of the shopping cart. If he has signed in as a customer, he can also order the items stored in his shopping cart following a checkout process.

Working with ArgoUWE is intuitive to ArgoUML users. In particular, ArgoUWE makes use of ArgoUML's general graphical user interface. The *project browser* is divided into several panes, see Fig. 4. The *navigation pane* (1) lists all diagrams and model elements of the current project in a tree view. A single UWE diagram is edited in the *multi-editor pane* (2). In the *critique pane* (3) a list of design critics issues is shown. The *detail pane* (4) serves several different purposes: besides a to do list, details of the currently selected model element are shown and edited here: meta attributes, stereotypes, tagged values, and OCL constraints. Even code skeletons can be generated for a selected model element and shown in the detail pane.

3.1 Starting with the Use Case Model

The first step towards modeling a Web application using UWE is the elicitation of requirements which is laid down in a use case model, see Fig. 2.

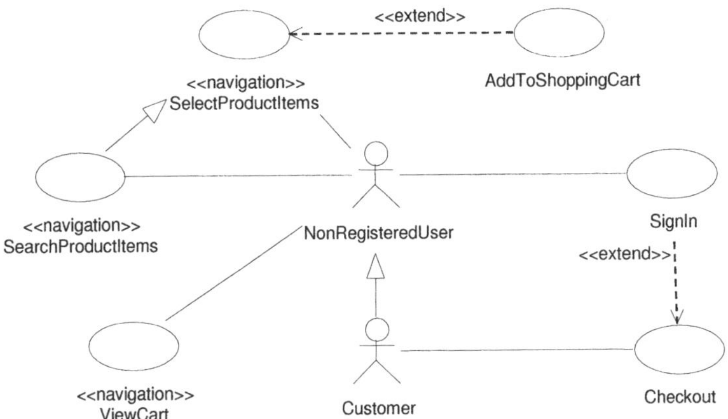

Fig. 2. Use case model of the e-shop example

UWE distinguishes between two kinds of use cases: ≪navigation≫ use cases represent navigational activities of the user, like the selection of product items and viewing the shopping cart. On the other hand, standard UML use cases capture the business logic of the Web application. These use cases will be refined later in the step of process modeling. Both types of use cases can be integrated in the same use case model.

For implementation reasons of ArgoUWE as a plugin module a new type of diagram UWE use case diagram is defined, which only differs from the UML use case diagram in that it allows for ≪navigation≫ use cases.

3.2 Building the Conceptual Model

Based on the requirements analysis, the content of a Web application in UWE is modeled in a conceptual model, represented by a UML class diagram. The main model

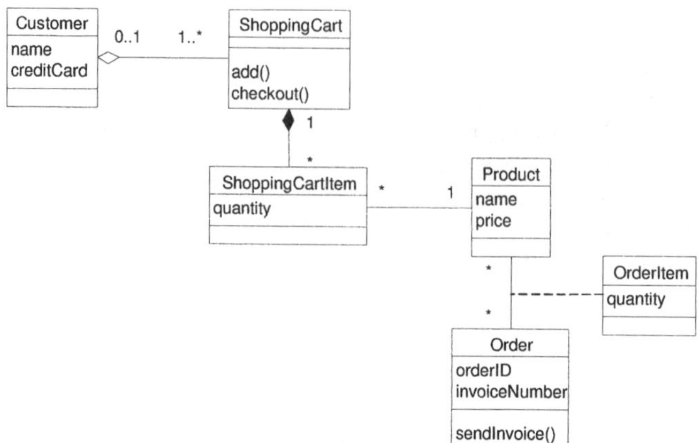

Fig. 3. Conceptual model of the e-shop example

elements are conceptual classes, associations, and packages. Figure 3 shows the conceptual model of the e-shop example, where a Customer has one or more ShoppingCarts which contain a set of ShoppingItems that can be ordered by the customer.

The conceptual model does not contain any information pertaining to the navigational aspects of the Web application, but it forms the basis for constructing the navigation model. In fact, by marking conceptual classes as relevant to navigation the designer indicates that the instances of these classes contain information that will be shown to the user. In the e-shop example, all conceptual classes are marked as navigation relevant; ArgoUWE supports the selection via a pop-up menu.

3.3 Generating and Enriching the Navigation Model

Based on the requirement analysis and the content modeling, the navigation structure of a Web application is modeled. Navigation classes are navigable nodes of the hypertext structure, navigation links represent direct links between navigation classes. Alternative navigation paths are handled by menus. Access primitives are used to reach multiple instances of a navigation class (≪index≫ or ≪guided tour≫), or a selection of items (≪query≫).

ArgoUWE supports the Web application designer in generating a navigation model from the conceptual model. When the designer selects Navigation Diagram from the menu Create Diagram, ArgoUWE generates navigation classes and associations for all "navigation relevant" conceptual classes and all associations between them into a new navigation model. The modeler can add some links after automatic creation of the navigation diagram. ArgoUWE automatically generates indexes and menus when one of the encircled buttons in Fig. 4 is selected: An index is added between two navigation classes related by an association whenever the multiplicity on the target end is greater than one. Menus are added to every class that has more than a single outgoing association (for a more detailed account see [8]). For instance, CustomerOrders and MainMenu will be automatically included in the e-shop example (see Fig. 4).

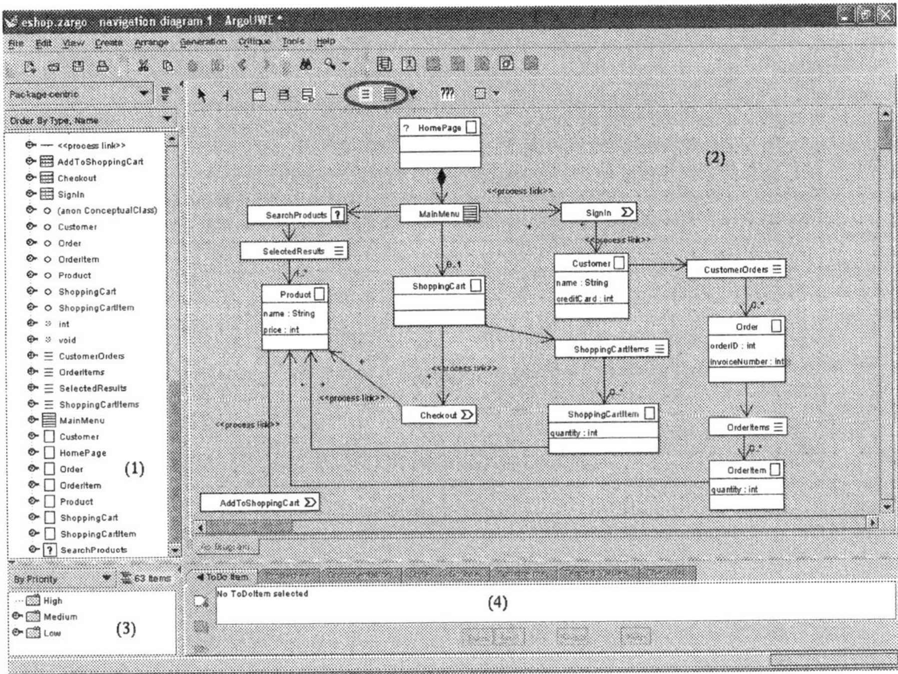

Fig. 4. Navigation model of the e-shop example after integration of business processes

In Web applications which are business logic intensive the business processes have to be integrated into the navigation structure indicating entry and exit points to the process nodes, see Fig. 1(b). In UWE, each business process that is modeled by a use case can be added to the navigation model as a corresponding ≪process node≫. A link connecting such a process node to a navigation node is called a ≪process link≫. Figure 4 shows the enriched navigation model of the e-shop example where SignIn, AddToShoppingCart, and Checkout have been integrated.

3.4 Constructing the Process Model

In this step of the UWE design process each process node is refined in a process model, consisting of a process structure model and a process flow model. A process structure model is represented by a UML class diagram and describes the relationship of a ≪process node≫ and other ≪process class≫es whose instances are used to support this business process. The logic of the business process is described by a process flow model visualized as a UML activity diagram.

ArgoUWE generates a process node in the navigation model for each (non-navigational) use case that is manually selected by the modeler. Thereby, a process class is generated for the process node of the selected use case and automatically included in the process structure model. Auxiliary process classes can be added manually. Figure 5(a) shows that the process node Checkout is supported by the process classes Customer, ShoppingCart, Order, and PaymentOption.

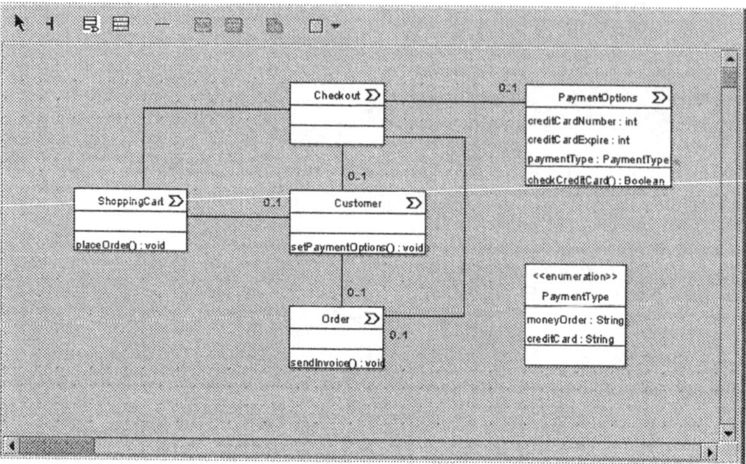

(a) Process structure model

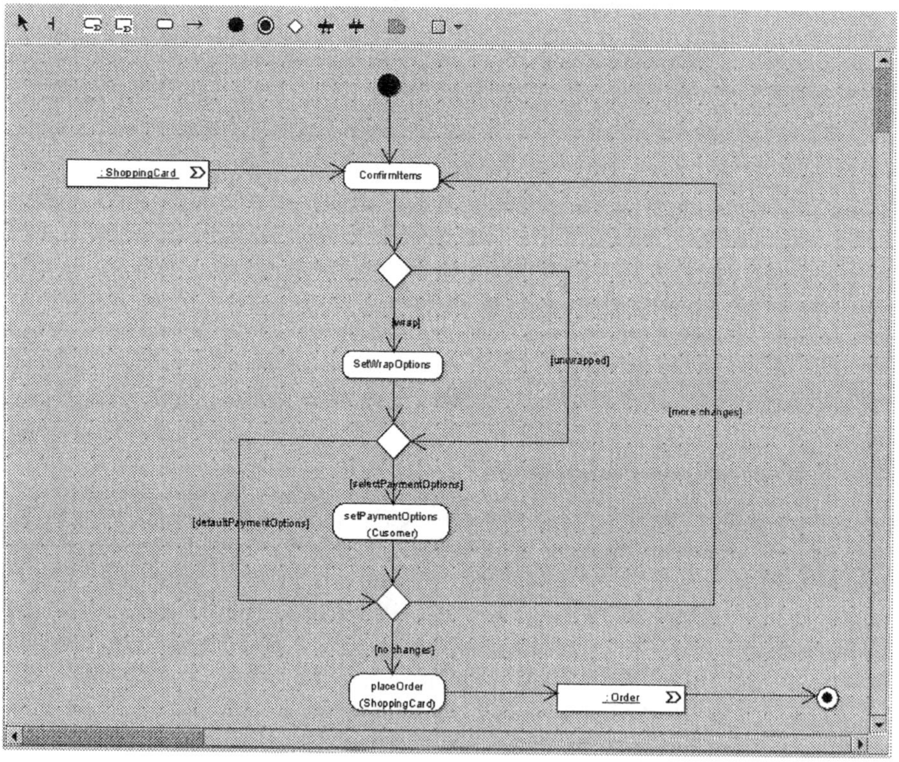

(b) Process flow model

Fig. 5. Process model of checkout of the e-shop example

Figure 5(b) shows a part of the process flow model of the check out process in the e-shop example. In the business process Checkout a user can confirm the product items he gathered in his shopping cart. Additionally, he can set wrapping and payment options. The activity setPaymentOptions has been included in the process flow model by selecting the corresponding operation of class Customer from the process structure model. Similarly, the objects ShoppingCart and Order are instances of classes in the process structure model.

3.5 Sketching the Presentation Model

Based on the navigation model, a presentation model is created in the UWE design process to model the abstract layout of the Web pages. In ArgoUWE, a logical presentation model can be inferred from the navigation model by choosing the menu item Presentation Diagram from the menu Create Diagram. For each navigation node, each access primitive, and each process node a corresponding presentation element is created and added to the presentation model (for a more detailed account see [8]). Such a presentation model only sketches the Web pages. Layout details like relative position, colors and size of layout elements cannot be represented in presentation diagrams.

4 ArgoUWE Design Critics

One of the distinguishing features of ArgoUML compared to other modeling tools is the support of cognitive design critics offered to the designer. During run time, a thread running in the background keeps checking if the model built by the user shows deficiencies. For each deficiency found a design critique item will be created and added to the design critique pane. Design critics not only warn the user that his design is still not perfect but can also, by means of a wizard, help the user improve the design. The design critics range from incompleteness, such as lacking names of model elements, to inconsistency, such as name collisions of different attributes or operations in a class. Furthermore, design critics also suggest the use of certain design patterns such as the singleton pattern [5]. Design critics are not preemptive and never interrupt the designer. Instead, they simply give warnings and post items to the designer's "to do" list shown in the detail pane.

ArgoUWE inherits the design critics feature from ArgoUML. In fact, all well-formedness constraints of UWE have been fully integrated and are continuously checked by ArgoUWE in the background at runtime. In Fig. 6 the highlighted design critique item in the design critique pane indicates that a process use case does not show a corresponding process node yet; this critique corresponds to the following UWE metamodel constraints:

```
context ProcessNode
inv: not self.useCase.oclIsKindOf(NavigationUseCase)

context UseCase
inv: (not self.oclIsKindOf(NavigationUseCase)) implies
     ProcessNode.allInstances()->exists(pn | pn.useCase = self)
```

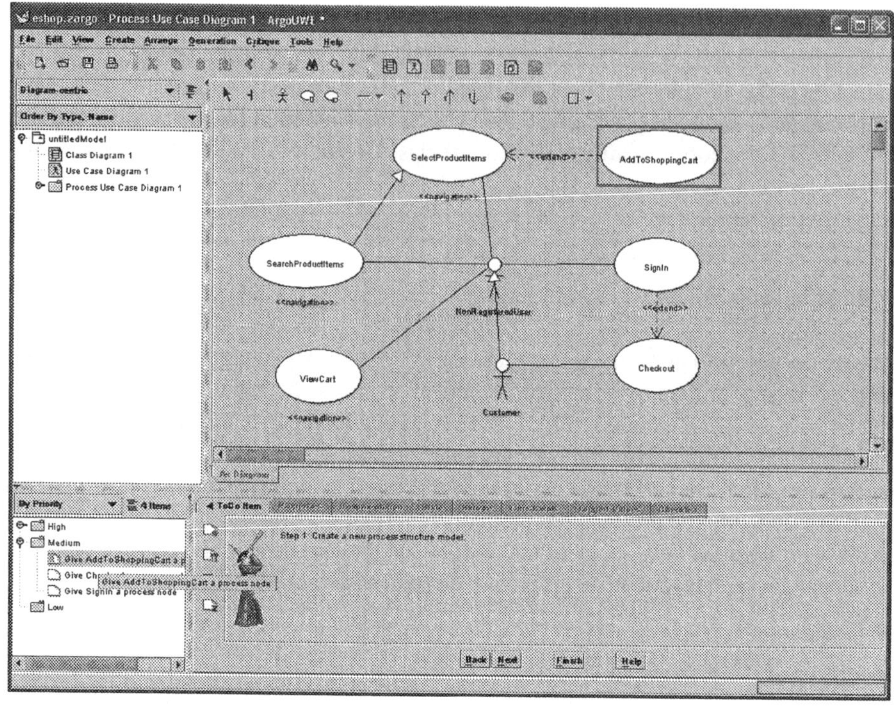

Fig. 6. Design critique concerning the checkout use case

In the detail pane, a two-step wizard designed for this critic is leading the user to correct this defect by creating a process model. In the first step, a new process structure model has to be created and in the second step, a new process flow model.

5 Architecture of ArgoUWE

The ArgoUWE tool is implemented as a plugin into the open-source UML modeling tool ArgoUML (version 0.15.7), both written in Java. ArgoUML provides a suitable basis for an extension with UWE tool support by being based on a flexible UML metamodel library (NSUML [18], version 1.3/0.4.20) and a general graph editing framework (GEF [17], version 0.10.2), as well as featuring an extendable module architecture. These feature characteristics and also the fact that ArgoUML is an open-source tool with an active developer community lead us to favoring ArgoUML as development basis over other commercial tools—although the open source code of ArgoUML has sometimes to offset its rather poor documentation. However, tools like Rational Rose™ or Gentleware's Poseidon™ would also afford the necessary extension prerequisites, perhaps with the exception of metamodel extensions.

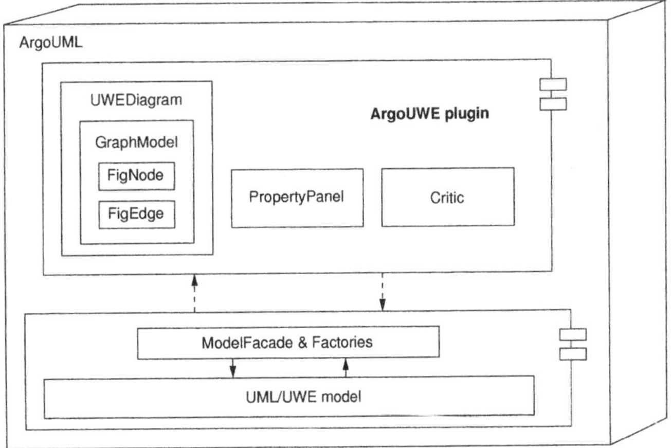

Fig. 7. Overview of the ArgoUWE plugin architecture

5.1 ArgoUWE Metamodel

The "Novosoft UML library" (NSUML), on which ArgoUML is based, not only provides a library for working with UML 1.3 models in terms of Java objects, but also contains an XML/XMI-based generator for arbitrarily changed and extended (UML) metamodels. As UWE uses additional modeling concepts targeted onto Web applications, ArgoUWE uses NSUML to generate an extended UML/UWE metamodel that again allows the programmer to handle UWE entities in a seamless manner. In particular, we chose a "heavyweight extension" for the physical metamodel that is generated by NSUML. Alternatively, we could employ the UWE lightweight UML profile directly. However, stereotyping and tagging is not compatible with the concept of overloading in object-oriented programming. For the current ArgoUML version, the adaptations of the UML metamodel merely consist of extending the NSUML generator resource files by the UWE metaclasses ConceptualClass, NavigationNode, ProcessNode, etc.

5.2 Plugin Architecture

In ArgoUML, the model is encapsulated in an instance of the (extended) NSUML library class ru.novosoft.uml.model_management.MModel and accessed through the facade org.argouml.model.ModelFacade. Thus, manipulations of the model have a single access point, all effects of model manipulations are disseminated to other components by a general observer mechanism following the Model-View-Controller paradigm. Figure 7 summarizes the general structure of the ArgoUML model, view, and control devices as used in ArgoUWE. The UWE diagram kinds: conceptual diagram, navigation diagram, process structure diagram, process flow diagram, and presentation diagram are straightforwardly supported by introducing new subclasses of org.argouml.uml.diagram.ui.UMLDiagram, more specifically the common superclass org.argouml.uml.diagram.ui.UWEDiagram.

A UMLDiagram captures the graphical presentation and manipulation of model elements. It is based on a bridge, the graph model, between the model realized by NSUML library classes and the graphical presentation using the "Graph Editing Framework" (GEF) library classes. The bridges for the structural UWE diagrams are all derived from the class org.argouml.uml.diagram.static_structure.ClassDiagramGraphModel whereas the bridge for the process flow diagram inherits from the class org.argouml.uml.diagram.state.StateDiagramGraphModel.

Each UWE model element is linked to a figure node (org.tigris.gef.presentation.FigNode) or a figure edge (org.tigris.gef.presentation.FigEdge) of the GEF library. In addition to manipulating the model elements graphically, they can also be changed and edited by using property panels that are implemented as subclasses of org.argouml.uml.ui.PropPanel. ArgoUWE adds property panels for conceptual classes, navigation classes, etc., which are installed on the ArgoUML platform automatically with the diagram counterparts by reflection. Finally, the ArgoUWE semi-automatic editing functionalities induced by the UWE method (see Sect. 3) are triggered in a UWEDiagram.

The ArgoUWE consistency checking mechanisms are packaged into ArgoUML design critics: Each well-formedness rule of a UWE model is implemented as a class inheriting from CrUWE, i.e., the abstract UWE model critic that extends org.argouml.cognitive.critics.Critic. By registering a critic with org.argouml.cognitive.critics.Agency a so-called designer thread of class org.argouml.cognitive.Designer will continuously check whether the critic applies to the current model; the critic will then post a critique in form of a org.argouml.cognitive.ToDoItem to the designer thread.

The UWE extensions are packaged in a plugin module. The original ArgoUML user interface is extended by a class implementing the extension point class org.argouml.application.api.PluggableMenu, registering the new diagram types and their support. This extension, when put into the extension directory (./ext) of ArgoUML, is loaded automatically on ArgoUML start-up. However, it must be noted that the UWE extension of ArgoUML is not completely orthogonal to ArgoUML as the underlying metamodel has been changed. Nevertheless, packaging the UWE extensions as a plugin module insulates these extensions from the continuous changes to ArgoUML.

6 Related Work

Many methods for the development of Web applications have been proposed since the middle of the nineties. An excellent overview is presented by Schwabe [15] where the most relevant methods, such as OOHDM [14], OO-H [6], WSDM [3], and UWE [9] are described on the basis of a same case study. But only some of these methods support the systematic development with a CASE tool. The most advanced tool support is offered for both, the method OO-H and the modeling language WebML.

VisualWADE is the tool, which provides an operational environment supporting the OO-H method. In contrast to our ArgoUWE, it uses the UML only in the first phase of the development process. A default presentation is obtained from the navigation model similarly as in ArgoUWE. VisualWADE includes authoring tool features that allow the designers to render the final look and feel of the application. VisualWADE provides model compilers for PHP/mySQL, PHP/Oracle and PHP/SQL server technologies.

In WebRatio, Web applications are specified using an entity-relationship (ER) model for data requirements, and the proprietary Web Modelling Language (WebML [1]) for the functional requirements. This approach differs from UWE as it does not perform a clear separation of the navigation and presentation aspects. The WebRatio development architecture includes a graphic interface for editing ER and WebML schemas, and customizable code generators for transforming ER specifications into relational table definitions for any JDBC or ODBC compliant data source, and WebML specifications into page templates for the J2EE and .NET architectures. WebRatio internally uses XML and XSL as the formats for encoding both the specifications and the code generators: XML is used for describing data and hypertext schemas, whereas XSL is used for generating the graphic properties and layout of the page templates, for validity checking, and for automatic project documentation.

A more architecture-oriented approach is proposed by Conallen [2]. It extends the UML to support the design of Web applications focusing on current technological aspects of the implementation and is based on the generic RUP [11] development process. The notation is supported by the Rational Rose™ tool, but in contrast to ArgoUWE it neither supports a systematic development process nor guides the developer through the Web-specific process.

Another metamodel for modeling Web-based user interfaces and an associated notation is proposed by Muller et al. [12]. The modeling elements of this approach are defined as specializations of the very general UML ModelElement. A kind of graph is used to represent the interface behavior and a class diagram is used to represent business classes. The action language Xion that augments OCL with Java-like structures is used to describe the behavior of the methods. The main disadvantage of such an approach is that it requires the implementation of its own editor and development environment.

Our approach focuses on the structures and the workflows of business processes in Web applications. Furthermore, ArgoUWE supports the integration of business processes into the navigation structure. In contrast, languages like ebXML [4] concentrate on the inter-process aspects—the collaborations and the choreography between business processes—rather than the intra-process aspects of business processes.

7 Conclusions and Future Work

We have presented the CASE tool ArgoUWE [8] that we have developed for the computer aided design of Web applications using the UWE methodology. The focus of this paper is to show how ArgoUWE was enhanced to support the development of more complex Web applications which include business processes like those that are frequently used in e-commerce systems.

ArgoUWE is built as a flexible extension of ArgoUML due to the plugin architecture facilities provided by the ArgoUML tool. We claim that the core of the CASE tool is the underlying UWE metamodel [10] defined as a conservative extension of the UML metamodel. ArgoUWE provides platform-independent models (PIMs) that will be used in the OpenUWE tool suite environment, which is currently under development, to achieve a model-driven generation of Web applications.

We outlined in this work the basic ideas behind the UWE methodology [9] and presented a running example to show how the tool supports the design of the main UWE models: use case model, conceptual, navigation, process and presentation models in a semi-automatic development process where user and tool-activities are interleaved. The support of the designer activities is also improved by the UWE well-formedness rules included in the design critics mechanism assisting the modeler in finding design errors or enhancing the models while designing with better modeling constructs. This consistency checking mechanism allows the continuous verification of the rules in contrast to the former checking process that had to be explicitly triggered by the modeler.

We are currently working on minor improvements of the usability of ArgoUWE and to include better support for iterative and incremental modeling. Further, we will improve ArgoUWE to provide new UWE modeling elements as well as additional well-formedness rules needed in the design of personalized Web applications. Finally, we will enhance ArgoUWE to build platform-specific models (PSMs) for frequently used frameworks like Zope or Struts and architectures such as J2EE and .NET.

References

[1] S. Ceri, P. Fraternali, A. Bongio, M. Brambilla, S. Comai, and M. Matera. *Designing Data-Intensive Web Applications*. Morgan-Kaufmann, San Francisco, 2002.

[2] J. Conallen. *Building Web Applications with UML*. Addison-Wesley, Reading, Mass., &c., 2nd edition, 2003.

[3] O. de Troyer and C. J. Leune. WSDM: A User Centered Design Method for Web Sites. *Computer Networks and ISDN Systems*, 30(1–7):85–94, 1998.

[4] ebXML. Business Process Specification Schema, Version 1.01. Specification, ebXML, 2001. http://www.ebxml.org/specs/ebBPSS.pdf.

[5] E. Gamma, R. Helm, R. Johnson, and J. Vlissides. *Design Patterns*. Addison-Wesley, Boston, &c., 1995.

[6] J. Gómez, C. Cachero, and O. Pastor. On Conceptual Modeling of Device-Independent Web Applications: Towards a Web-Engineering Approach. *IEEE Multimedia*, 8(2):26–39, 2001.

[7] I. Jacobson, G. Booch, and J. Rumbaugh. *The Unified Software Development Process*. Addison-Wesley, Reading, Mass., &c., 1999.

[8] A. Knapp, N. Koch, F. Moser, and G. Zhang. ArgoUWE: A CASE Tool for Web Applications. In *Proc. 1st Int. Wsh. Engineering Methods to Support Information Systems Evolution (EMSISE'03)*, Genève, 2003. 14 pages.

[9] N. Koch and A. Kraus. The Expressive Power of UML-based Web Engineering. In D. Schwabe, O. Pastor, G. Rossi, and L. Olsina, editors, *Proc. 2nd Int. Wsh. Web-Oriented Software Technology (IWWOST'02)*, pages 105–119. CYTED, 2002.

[10] N. Koch and A. Kraus. Towards a Common Metamodel for the Development of Web Applications. In J. M. C. Lovelle, B. M. G. Rodríguez, L. J. Aguilar, J. E. L. Gayo, and M. del Puerto Paule Ruiz, editors, *Proc. Int. Conf. Web Engineering (ICWE'03)*, volume 2722 of *Lect. Notes Comp. Sci.*, pages 495–506. Springer, Berlin, 2003.

[11] P. Kruchten. *The Rational Unified Process — An Introduction*. Addison-Wesley, Reading, Mass., &c., 2nd edition, 2000.

[12] P.-A. Muller, P. Studer, and J. Bézivin. Platform Independent Web Application Modeling. In P. Stevens, J. Whittle, and G. Booch, editors, *Proc. 6th Int. Conf. Unified Modeling Language (UML'03)*, volume 2863 of *Lect. Notes Comp. Sci.*, pages 220–233. Springer, Berlin, 2003.

[13] Object Management Group. Unified Modeling Language Specification, Version 1.5. Specification, OMG, 2003. http://www.omg.org/cgi-bin/doc?formal/03-03-01.

[14] G. Rossi and D. Schwabe. Object-Oriented Web Applications Modeling. In M. Rossi and K. Siau, editors, *Information Modeling in the New Millennium*, pages 463–484. IDEA Group, 2001.

[15] D. Schwabe, editor. *Proc. 1st Int. Wsh. Web-Oriented Software Technology (IWWOST'01)*, 2001. http://www.dsic.upv.es/ west2001/iwwost01/.

[16] http://www.argouml.org.

[17] http://gef.tigris.org.

[18] http://nsuml.sourceforge.net.

Model Composition Directives

Greg Straw, Geri Georg, Eunjee Song, Sudipto Ghosh, Robert France, and James M. Bieman

Department of Computer Science
Colorado State University, Fort Collins, CO, 80523
{straw, georg, song, ghosh, france, bieman}@cs.colostate.edu

Abstract. An aspect-oriented design model consists of a set of aspect models and a primary model. Each of these models consists of a number of different kinds of UML diagrams. The models must be composed to identify conflicts and analyze the system as a whole. We have developed a systematic approach for composing class diagrams in which a default composition procedure based on name matching can be customized by user-defined composition directives. This paper describes a set of composition directives that constrain how class diagrams are composed.

1 Introduction

Solutions to design concerns (e.g., security and fault tolerance concerns) may cross-cut many modules of a design model. The cross-cutting nature of these solutions can make understanding, analyzing and changing the solutions difficult. This complexity can be addressed through the use of aspect-oriented modeling (AOM) techniques, where the design of a cross-cutting solution is undertaken in an independent fashion, and the resulting *aspect* models are composed with *primary* models of core functionality to create a complete system design. Composition is necessary to identify conflicts across aspect and primary models, and to identify undesirable emergent properties in composed models.

We have developed an AOM technique in which aspect and primary models are expressed using the UML [12]. Each model consists of a variety of UML diagrams. Composition of aspect and primary models involves composing diagrams of the same types. For example, the class diagram in an aspect model is composed with the class diagram in a primary model. The AOM technique uses a default, name-based composition procedure in which model elements with the same syntactic type and name are merged to form a single element in the composed model. The default procedure assumes that elements of the same syntactic type with the same name represent different and consistent views of the same concept. This may not be the case if the aspect and primary models are developed independently. Often, a more sophisticated form of composition is needed to produce composed models with desired features. Composition directives can be used to modify the default composition procedure [6]. In this paper we rigorously define and significantly extend a set of composition directives informally described in our previous work [6], and show how the composition direc-

T. Baar et al. (Eds.): UML 2004, LNCS 3273, pp. 84-97, 2004.

tives can be used to alter the basic default composition procedure. We also give examples of how composition directives can be used to resolve conflicts in composed models produced by the default composition procedure.

2 Composition in AOM

An aspect-oriented design model consists of a primary model and aspect models [6]. A primary model consists of one or more UML diagrams that each describes a view of the core functionality. The core functionality determines the primary structure of a design. In our AOM approach an aspect model describes a family of solutions for a design concern that each cross-cuts the primary model. Aspect models consist of parameterized UML artifacts that describe generic solutions to design concerns [7,11]. An aspect model cannot be directly composed with a primary model. A *context-specific aspect model* must first be created by binding the aspect model's template parameters to application-specific values. The context-specific aspect can then be composed with the primary model.

Conflicts across aspect and primary model views and undesirable emergent properties can be identified during composition or during analysis of the composed model. Composition directives can be used to resolve conflicts or remove undesirable emergent properties during composition. For example, a composition directive can (1) indicate that properties in aspect models override conflicting properties in primary models (or vice versa), (2) specify that particular primary model elements must be removed or added during composition, and (3) determine the order in which two or more aspects are composed with a primary model.

Figure 1 illustrates a simple composition example. Figure 1(a) shows an aspect model consisting of a single class diagram template. The aspect model describes a family of solutions (from a structural perspective) in which entities that produce outputs (buffer writers) are decoupled from output devices through the use of buffers. Template parameters are preceded by the symbol "|". Figure 1(b) shows a context specific aspect model created from the aspect model in Figure 1(a). The context specific aspect model is obtained using the following name bindings:

```
(|Buffer<-Buffer), (|Output<-FileStream),
  (|BufferWriter<-Writer), (|write()<-writeLine())
```

The result of composing the context-specific aspect class diagram shown in Figure 1(b) with the primary model class diagram shown in Figure 1(c) is shown in Figure 1(d). In the primary model the output producer sends outputs directly to the output device. In the composed model a buffer is introduced between the output producer and the output device. Composition of the context-specific aspect model and the primary model is carried out using a default name-based composition procedure. The procedure merges model elements that have the same name and syntactic type to produce a single model element in the composed model. If the matching model elements are associated with invariants (e.g., expressed in the OCL) the invariant associated with the merged element in the composed model is formed by taking the logical 'AND' of the invariants. Operation specifications, expressed as OCL pre and post-conditions, can also be merged for matching operations. The precondition of the merged operation in the composed model is formed by taking the logical "OR" of the preconditions associated with the matching operations, and the postcondition is formed by taking the logical "AND" of their postconditions. Composition using the simple default procedure can produce undesirable results. In Figure 1(d) an association between *Writer* and *FileStream* exists in the composed model, but the intent is that the writer be completely decoupled from the output device, and thus the association should be removed. A composition directive can be used to alter the composition so that it includes removal of this association.

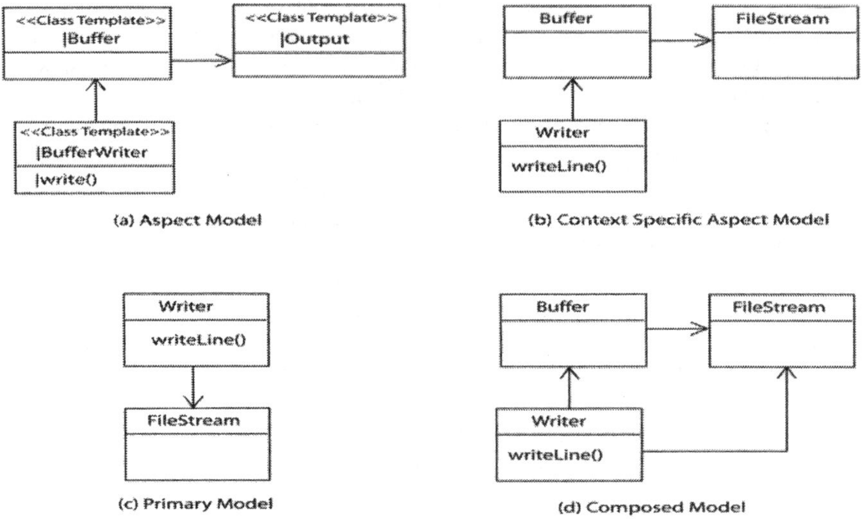

Fig. 1. Default Composition Example

3 Requirements for Composition Directives

In this section we motivate the need for composition directives and identify some of the directives that can be used to resolve conflicts. We restrict our attention to models that consist only of class diagrams.

Consider operations *addUser(u: User, mId: MgrID)*, *doAddUser(u: User)* in a class *Repository* that is part of a context specific aspect model, and an operation *addUser(u: User)* defined in a primary model class named *Repository*. The *addUser* operation in the primary model adds a user (instance of *User*) to a collection of users (instance of a class *Users*). The *addUser* operation in the context specific aspect model calls the *doAddUser* operation if and only if the client calling the operation is authorized to add a user. The *doAddUser* operation adds a user to the collection. Composition of the two matching *addUser* operations produces a conflict because the two operations have different specifications. This is an example of a *property conflict* – a property conflict occurs when two matching elements (elements with the same name and syntactic type) are associated with conflicting properties (in this case pre and postconditions). In this example, the intention is to merge the *doAddUser(u:*

User) operation in the context specific aspect model with the *addUser(u: User)* operation in the primary model. To resolve this conflict, composition directives should rename the *addUser* operation in the (context specific) aspect model to *checkAndAddUser*, and rename the *doAddUser* operation in the aspect model to *addUser*.

In some cases, renaming elements may not be the appropriate way to resolve a property conflict. Consider a context specific aspect model that includes a class *FileStream* with an attribute *maxWriters: int* that is associated with the constraint {*maxWriters = 1*}. Now consider a primary model with a class named *FileStream* that contains an attribute *maxWriters: int*, with the constraint {*maxWriters = 2*}. If the matching attributes are merged, a property conflict will arise because the merged constraint ({*maxWriters = 1 and maxWriters = 2*}) is inconsistent. This conflict can be resolved by specifying, through a composition directive, that one operation overrides the other, such that properties from the overriding element take precedence over those in the element being overridden. However, override relations can produce a *cyclic-override* conflict when a cycle exists between two elements such that there are override relations specifying both as dominant elements.

In some cases, elements may need to be added or deleted during composition in order to produce a composed model that has desired properties. For example, associations may be added to provide correct access to other elements, or may be removed if they pose a security risk. Composition directives can be used to add or delete model elements during composition.

With the ability of renaming, adding, and removing elements comes the risk of yet another type of conflict: the *nonexistent-reference conflict.* A nonexistent-reference conflict arises when a reference in one of the models refers to an element that no longer exists, or exists under a different name. To resolve this conflict, the reference elements in a model must be updated.

In a system with multiple aspects, the order in which aspect models are composed with a primary model may be important in the cases where different orderings produce different composed models [6]. Composition directives can be used to specify the order in which multiple aspects are composed with a primary model.

With the addition of ordering relationships, an additional type of conflict becomes possible. A *cyclic-ordering conflict* occurs when there is a cycle among ordering relationships defined over multiple aspects. These conflicts can be resolved by analyzing the aspects to correct the order relationships.

The above examples give rise to the following set of actions that can be specified by composition directives:

- Creating new elements.
- Adding elements to a Namespace.
- Deleting elements from a Namespace.
- Renaming elements.
- Changing references to an element.
- Specifying override relationships between matching elements.
- Specifying ordering relationships among multiple aspects.

4 Composition Directives

In this section, short descriptions of the composition directives are followed by illustrated examples. For more detailed specifications of the directives, refer to our technical report [13]. Many of these descriptions refer to *ModelElements*, *Names*, and *Namespaces* from the UML meta-model [12]. References to *Aspect* in these descriptions refer to a context specific aspect model. Two types of composition directives are used in our AOM approach: Low-level composition directives are used to customize the composition of a single context specific aspect model and a primary model, and high-level composition directives are applied to two or more aspect models and are used primarily to specify the order in which aspect models are composed with a primary model. The set of composition directives defined in this paper is not intended to be a complete set, but serves as a starting point for the eventual definition of a complete set of composition directives.

4.1 Low-Level Composition Directives

Creating New ModelElements. The directives for creating new ModelElements are collectively referred to as *constructors*. Each constructor will have a different set of operands, but each will consist of the necessary properties to define each (see Example 2 in section 4.2). The use of a constructor results in the creation of a reference to a new ModelElement. The constructors are used as follows:

```
newHandle = create<ModelElement.name> { parameters …}
```

Adding ModelElements to a Namespace. Once a new ModelElement is created, it is not yet a member of a Namespace. The directive for adding ModelElements to a Namespace is `add`. The add directive has two operands: (1) The ModelElement to be added, and (2) the Namespace the ModelElement is being added to. The `add` directive is used as follows:

```
add addition :ModelElement to owner :Namespace
```

Removing ModelElements. The directive for removing ModelElements from a Namespace is `remove`. It has two operands: (1) The ModelElement to be removed, and (2) the Namespace to remove the ModelElement from. The `remove` directive is used as follows:

```
remove member :ModelElement from owner :Namespace
```

Renaming ModelElements. The directive for renaming ModelElements is `rename`. The rename directive has two operands: (1) The ModelElement to rename, and (2) the new Name. The `rename` directive is used as follows:

```
rename target :ModelElement to newName :Name
```

Replacing References to a ModelElement. Removing a ModelElement may lead to invalid references that refer to a non-existent ModelElement. The `replaceReferences` directive can change these references to a different ModelElement. This directive has three operands: (1) The original Name of the ModelElement the references refer to, (2) the replacement Name for the references, and (3) the Namespace containing the references. The third operand defines a scope for the replacement of references. The `replaceReferences` directive is used as follows:

```
replaceReferences originalName :Name
 with replacementName :Name in owner :Namespace
```

Overriding ModelElements. An override relationship specifies that one ModelElement's properties take precedence over properties of another ModelElement. The `overrides` directive has two operands: (1) The ModelElement that will take precedence, and (2) the ModelElement that will be overridden. When an override relation is defined for two ModelElements, the relationship is honored for all contained ModelElements. This directive is used as follows:

```
superior :ModelElement overrides inferior :ModelElement
```

4.2 Composition Examples

Illustrated examples show the use of the composition directives for composing a single primary and context specific aspect. Each aspect model may be woven into multiple areas of a primary model. For simplicity, these examples only show only one portion of the primary model, which represents one portion of the design for which the aspect is to be woven.

Example 1. Consider the example in Figure 2. In the context specific aspect model, the *UserMgmt* class contains a operation called *getRepositorySize()* that retrieves the size of *SystemMgmtAuthRepository*. Note that this operation has been created from the aspect model with a name that will cause a property conflict. The conflict is with the operation of the same name in *UserMgmt* in the primary model. The operation *primary::UserMgmt::getRepositorySize()* returns the size of *UserRepository*, which is a different operation. To resolve this conflict, the `rename` directive can rename one or both operations, and the `replaceReferences` directive can update any references to the old Name. The following composition directives are applied:

```
(1) rename aspect::UserMgmt::getRepositorySize()
      to aspect::UserMgmt::getAuthRepositorySize()

(2) replaceReferences
      aspect::UserMgmt::getRepositorySize()
      with aspect::UserMgmt::getAuthRepositorySize()
      in aspect
```

```
(3) rename primary::UserMgmt::getRepositorySize()
     to primary::UserMgmt::getUserRepositorySize()

(4) replaceReferences
     primary::UserMgmt::getRepositorySize()
     with primary::UserMgmt::getUserRepositorySize()
     in primary
```

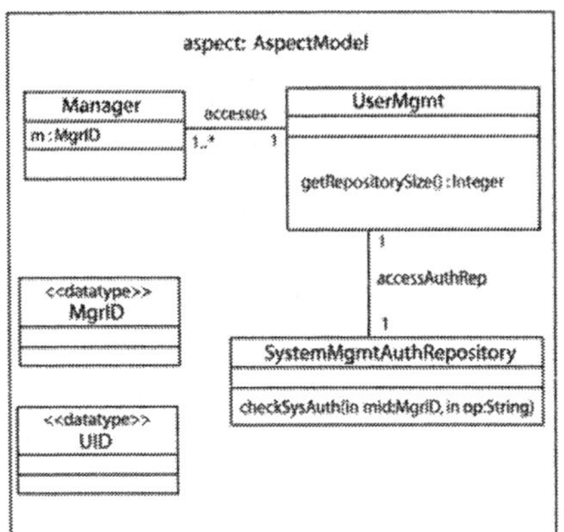

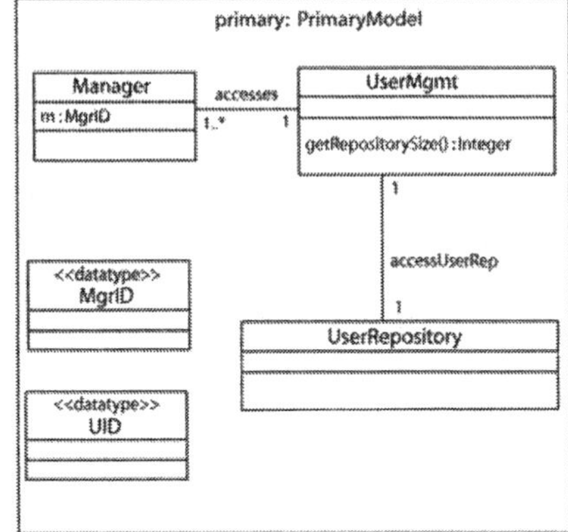

Fig. 2. Example 1: Before Application

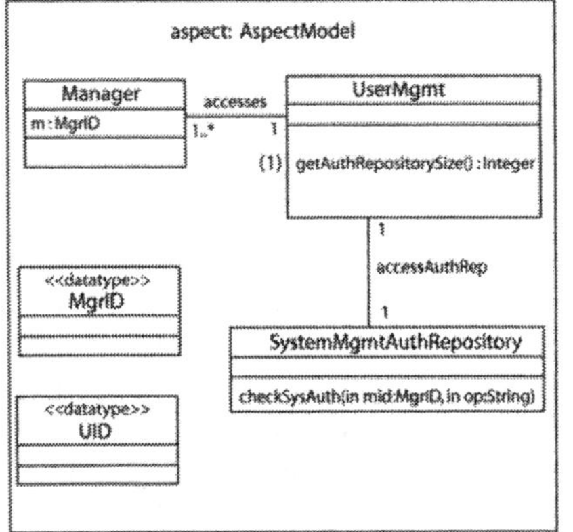

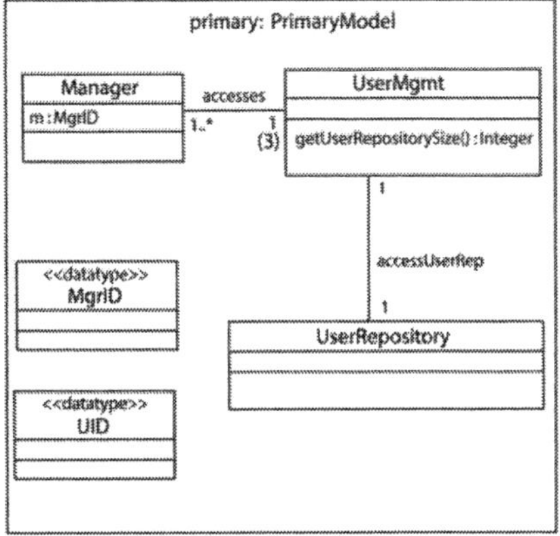

Fig. 3. Example 1: After Application. (1) and (3) note the name changes

The result of applying the directives is shown in Figure 3. Where applicable, the effects of the composition directives are denoted in the composed model using the corresponding numbers. The names of *getRepositorySize()* in `aspect` and `primary` are changed to *getAuthRepositorySize()* and *getUserRepositorySize()*, respectively. The references to the operation names are changed throughout each model to reflect the name change, and to avoid reference conflicts.

Example 2. The following example, from France *et al.*[6], illustrates the use of the `create`, `add`, `remove` and `replaceReferences` directives. In Figure 4, the *UserAuth* class performs authorization checks for *Managers* requesting the addition or deletion of users from the system. In the primary model, *Manager* has a direct association with *UserMgmt*, which provides the *addUser* and *deleteUser* services. In the composed model, *Manager* needs to make these requests to *UserAuth* and should have no direct access to the *UserMgmt* class. The first step to specifying this composition is to recognize the *accesses* association as a prohibited element to be removed:

```
(1) remove primary::Manager::accesses
     from primary::Manager
```

This does not result in a well-formed primary model however, since there may be references to the *accesses* association in *Manager*. References to *accesses* in the primary model must be changed to *uaccesses* in the context specific aspect model, since it is the association intended for making the *addUser* and *deleteUser* requests, and replaces *accesses*:

```
(2) replaceReferences primary::Manager::accesses
     with aspect::Manager::uaccesses
     in primary::Manager
```

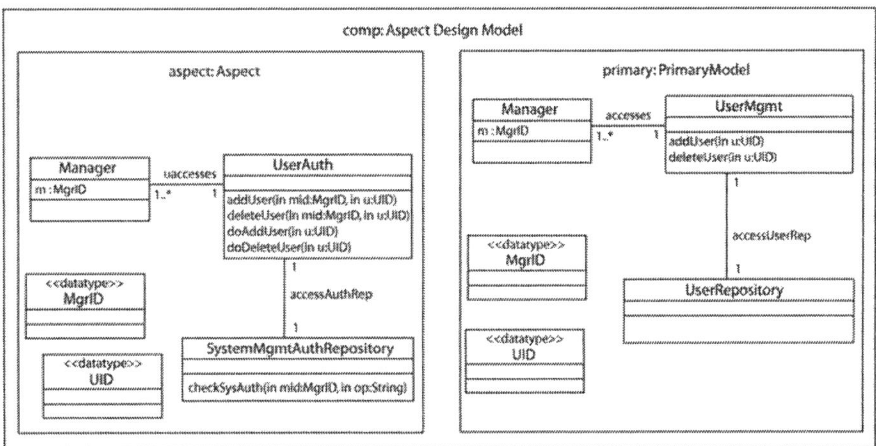

Fig. 4. Example 2: Before Application

The definitions of the *addUser* and *deleteUser* operations in *UserAuth* include an authorization check for a given *MgrID*, and if the *Manager* is authorized its request, a call is made to the appropriate operation *doAddUser* or *doDeleteUser*. The *doAddUser* and *doDeleteUser* operations are intended to request the add and delete services, however there is no connection to the *UserMgmt* class that provides these services. The first step to solving this problem is to create an association between *UserAuth* and *UserMgmt*:

```
(3) userAuthEnd = createAssociationEnd {
                      isNavigable = true,
                      aggregation = aggregate,
```

```
                          participant = aspect::UserAuth,
                          multiplicity = 1  },
userMgmtEnd = createAssociationEnd  {
                          isNavigable = true,
                          aggregation = none,
                          participant = primary::UserMgmt,
                          multiplicity = 1  },
userAuth-userMgmt = createAssociation {
                          name = "UserAuth-UserMgmt",
                          connection = [userAuthEnd,
                          userMgmtEnd]  }
```

Once the new Association is created, we need to add it to the appropriate Namespace, which in this case is the composable aspect design model (i.e., a single primary model and a context specific aspect) since the association spans both the primary and context specific aspect models. The new AssociationEnds must be added to their respective participants as well:

```
(4) add userAuth-userMgmt to comp,
    add userAuthEnd to aspect::UserAuth,
    add userMgmtEnd to primary::UserMgmt
```

There are two options for specifying the correct operation calls: The first option is to define *doAddUser* and *doDeleteUser* to delegate to *UserMgmt* via the new association. The second option is more concise, and simply replaces the call of *doAddUser* and *doDeleteUser* to the appropriate operations in *UserMgmt*, and deletes *doAddUser* and *doDeleteUser*. This is the option we will use, and results in the following composition directive:

```
(5) replaceReferences aspect::UserAuth::doAddUser
      with primary::UserMgmt::addUser()
      in aspect,

    remove aspect::UserAuth::doAddUser
      from aspect::UserAuth,

    replaceReferences aspect::UserAuth::doDeleteUser
      with primary::UserMgmt::deleteUser()
       in aspect,

    remove aspect::UserAuth::doDeleteUser
      from aspect::UserAuth
```

The result of the composition is shown in Figure 5. The **X**'s mark the ModelElements removed by the composition directives. The dependencies from the *addUser* and *deleteUser* operations in *UserAuth* illustrate the calls to the respective operations in *UserMgmt*.

Example 3. Figure 6 illustrates the need for defining an override relationship. The primary model shows a simple system for writing to a *FileStream*. This system only supports one *Writer*, as there is no concurrency control.

The following invariants are defined for *maxWriters* in the context specific aspect model and primary models:

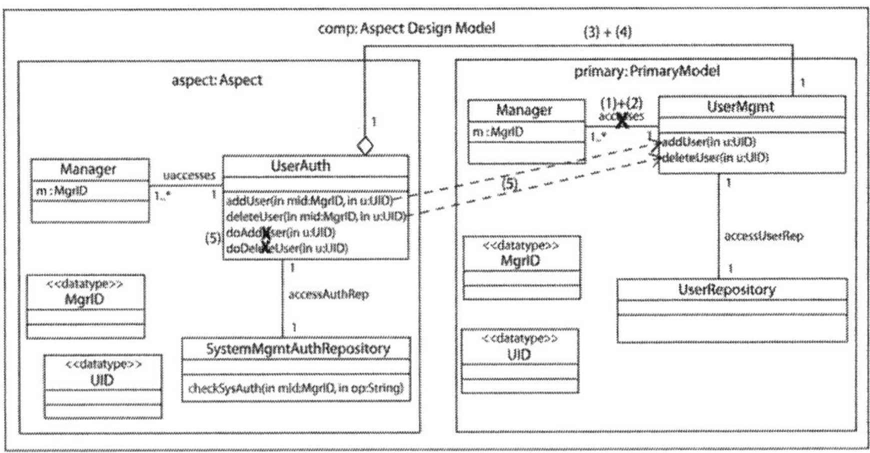

Fig. 5. Example 2: After Application

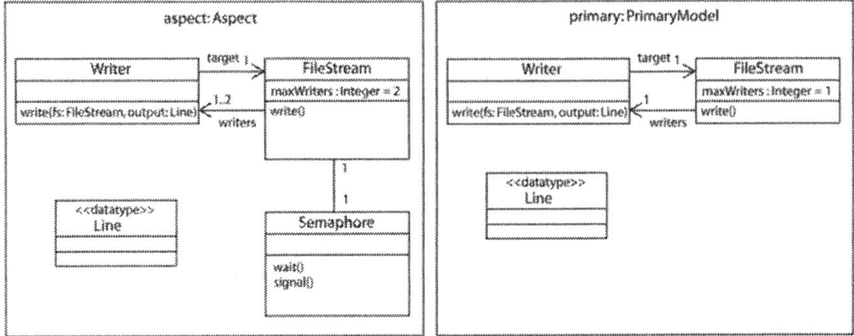

Fig. 6. Example 3: Before Application

```
context primary::FileStream::maxWriters
  inv: maxWriters = 1

context aspect::FileStream::maxWriters
  inv:  maxWriters  = 2
```

The *FileStream* in the context specific aspect model supports up to two *Writer*s, while in the primary model, it only supports one. The default composition behavior is to take the logical 'AND' of constraints over matching properties, but in this case that behavior would not be appropriate. In the composed model, the intended result is the support of up to two *Writers*, so the following override relationship is defined:

```
(1) aspect::FileStream::maxWriters
     overrides primary::FileStream::maxWriters
```

Another override relationship is needed. The definition of *write()* in *primary::FileStream* simply writes the *Line* to the *FileStream* without any checks. The definition for *write()* in *aspect::FileStream* supports multiple *Writer*s, and thus obtains the semaphore through calls *wait()* and *signal()* in the *Semaphore* class. This is the desired behavior in the composed model, so the following override relationship is defined:

```
(2) aspect::FileStream::write()
      overrides primary::FileStream::write()
```

All properties of *primary::FileStream* are overridden by their respective properties in *aspect::FileStream*. This same behavior can be achieved using the following composition directive, since any declared override relationship is honored for contained, matching ModelElements:

```
(3) aspect::FileStream overrides primary::FileStream
```

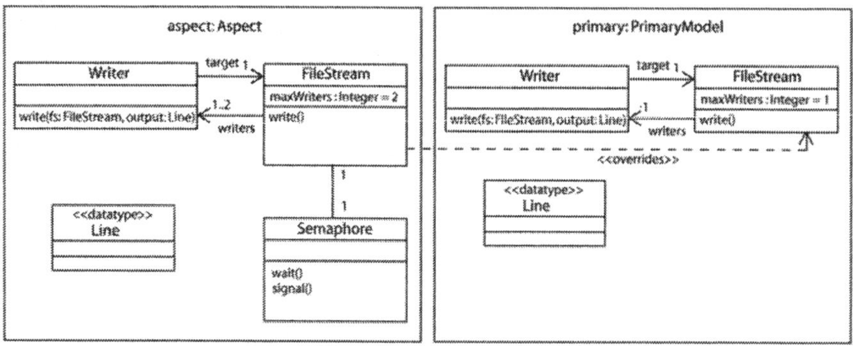

Fig. 7. Example 3: After Application

Figure 7 shows the result of applying the composition directive (3). The dependency from *aspect::FileStream* to *primary::FileStream* illustrates the created override relationship between the two classes. When composition is performed, the definitions and constraints for *write()* and *maxWriters* in the context specific aspect model are used rather than those for the respective properties in the primary model.

4.3 High-Level Composition Directives

In a system with multiple aspects, the order in which aspect models are composed with a primary model is important: Different ordering can result in different composed models [6]. The weave order for an aspect design model containing multiple aspects can be defined using weave-order relationships that specify that one aspect is to be woven before another. Any ordering of multiple aspects can be achieved using binary relations [13], which allows a developer to specify the important relationships in the weave order. A weave ordering relationship can be created using either the `follows` directive or the `precedes` directive. The `precedes` directive has two operands: (1) the aspect to be woven first, and (2) the aspect to be woven second.

```
former :Aspect  precedes latter :Aspect
```

Conversely, the same relationship can be created using the `follows` directive, both directives are only provided for convenience.

```
later :Aspect follows earlier :Aspect
```

4.4 Weave-Ordering Example

Example 4. Consider the following aspect design model in Figure 8(a). There are three different aspects and the primary model. Without any direction, the aspects will be woven in an arbitrary order. In this example, the aspect *authentication* needs to be woven before the aspect *authorization*, since authorization without authentication is meaningless. Therefore, we declare the following composition directive to make the order explicit.

```
(1) authentication precedes authorization
```

We could have also defined a composition directive using the `follows` directive with the operands reversed to achieve the same result. Suppose we also wish to weave the *errorChecking* aspect last. The following composition directives achieve this:

```
(2) errorChecking follows authorization
(3) errorChecking follows authentication
```

The result is shown in Figure 8(b). The dependency from *authentication* to *authorization* illustrates the weave-order relationship that specifies that *authentication* must be woven before *authorization*, and the dependencies from *errorChecking* to

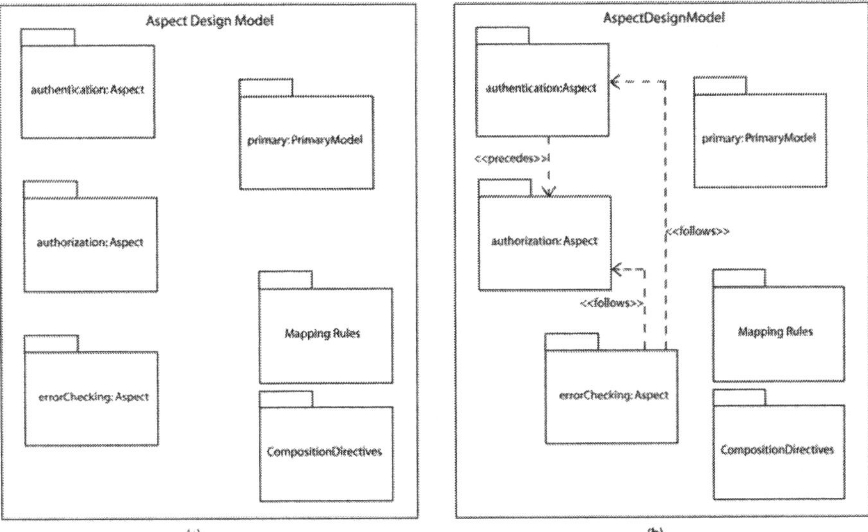

Fig. 8. Example 4: Specifying Weave Order

each of the other aspects illustrates the two binary weave-order relationships that specify *errorChecking* as the last aspect to be woven.

5 Related Work

Clarke *et al.* describe an approach similar to AOM which is based on *subjects* [3,4,5], where a subject is a particular view of the comprehensive system. There is no primary design; instead everything is a subject and the overall system design is obtained through the composition of all subjects. The compositions of subjects include the addition or overriding of named elements in a model. One limitation of this approach is that there is no support for the merging of constraints associated with a model. There is also no support for the deletion of elements, except when an element is implicitly deleted as a result of being overridden. The operation supports conflict reconciliation through precedence and override relationships between conflicting elements, but nothing further. We describe directives that support the composition of constraints, and the deletion of model elements.

Brito and Moreira describe an aspect composition process that identifies match points in a design element and defines composition rules [2]. Rules use identified match points, a binary contribution value (either positive or negative) that quantifies the affects on other aspects, and a priority for a given aspect. In the context of AOP [10], Kienzle *et al.* describe composition rules based on dependencies between aspects [9]. Both papers [2,9] focus primarily on relationships that can exist between aspects. We describe the possible relationships between aspects as weave-order relationships and override relationships instead of priority and dependency as done by Brito and Moreira. This paper expands further on composition directives that are meant for varying the default composition behavior.

6 Conclusions and Future Work

This paper defines a set of composition directives that facilitate the customization of model composition. These directives can form the basis for the development of tools to support the AOM approach described in France *et al.* [6]. The directives also provide a common vocabulary for describing composition actions. Illustrated examples demonstrate the use of each directive.

The defined directives are *expressive* [1] in the sense that they possess the following two properties. First, the directives can specify common composition actions such as renaming and replacing classes and operations. Second, the directives can be used to specify creation and removal of model elements, making it possible to significantly alter how models are composed.

Empirical evaluation is needed to validate the AOM approach in real world design settings. Specifically (1) the amount of effort required to specify the kinds of compositions that are required in real world designs needs to be empirically evaluated; (2) the development of a tractable method of identifying conflicts in a composed model needs to be investigated; and (3) the currently defined composition directives need to be tried in a real design setting, and evaluated for their ability to support the kinds of composition actions that actually occur. This evaluation could result in the specification of some common composition strategies [8] to manage the complexity of specifying compositions and is an area of future work.

We are also exploring how to express the applicability and consequences of using composition directives in terms of pre and postconditions for directives. We plan to investigate the use of the Object Constraint Language [12] for this purpose.

Acknowledgements

This material is based in part on work supported by the U.S. National Science Foundation under grants CCR-0098202 and CCR-0203285, and by the AFOSR under grant FA9550-04-1-0102. Any opinions, findings and conclusions or recommendations expressed in this material are those of the authors and do not necessarily reflect the views of the National Science Foundation or the AFOSR.

References

1. R. Allen, and D. Garlan. 1997. A Formal Basis for Architectural Connection. *ACM Trans on Software Engineering and Methodology*. vol 6, no 3, pp.213-249, July 1997
2. I. Brito, and A. Moreira, Towards a Composition Process for Aspect-Oriented Requirements. In *Proceedings of the Workshop on Early Aspects: Aspect-Oriented Requirements Engineering and Architecture Design*. Boston, MA, March 2003.
3. S. Clarke and J. Murphy. Developing a tool to support the application of aspect-oriented programming principles to the design phase. In *Proceedings of the International Conference on Software Engineering (ICSE '98)*, Kyoto, Japan, April 1998.
4. S. Clarke, W. Harrison, H. Ossher, and P. Tarr. Separating concerns throughout the development lifecycle. In *Proceedings of the 3rd ECOOP Aspect-Oriented Programming Workshop*, Lisbon, Portugal, June 1999.
5. S. Clarke. Extending standard UML with model composition semantics. Science of Computer Programming, Volume 44, Issue 1, pp. 71-100. Elsevier Science, July 2002.
6. R. B. France, I. Ray, G. Georg, and S. Ghosh. An Aspect-Oriented Approach to Design Modeling. IEE Proceedings - Software, Special Issue on Early Aspects: Aspect Oriented Requirements Engineering and Architecture Design. (To Appear)
7. R. B. France, D. K. Kim, S. Ghosh, and E. Song. A UML-Based Pattern Specification Technique. IEEE Transactions on Software Engineering, Volume 30, No 3, March, 2004.
8. G. Georg, R. B. France and I. Ray, Composing Aspect Models. In *Proceedings of the Workshop on Aspect Oriented Modeling with UML*, San Francisco, CA, October 2003.
9. J. Kienzle, Y. Yu, and J Xiong. On Composition and Reuse of Aspects. In *Proceedings of the Foundations of Aspect-Oriented Languages Workshop* , Boston, MA, March 2003.
10. G. Kiczales, J. Lamping, A. Mendhekar, C. Maeda, C. V. Lopes, J-M. Loingteir and J. Irwin. Aspect-oriented programming. In *Proceedings of the European Conference on Object-Oriented Programming (ECOOP '97),* volume 1241 of *Lecture Notes in Computer Science*, pages 220-242, Jyvaskyla, Finland, June 1997.
11. D. K. Kim, R. France, S. Ghosh. A UML-Based Language for Specifying Domain-Specific Patterns. *Special Issue on Domain Modeling with Visual Languages, Journal of Visual Languages and Computing*, 2004. (To Appear).
12. The Object Management Group (OMG). Unified Modeling Language. OMG, http://www.omg.org/docs/formal/03-03-01.pdf. Version 1.5, March 2003.
13. G. Straw, G. Georg, E. Song, S. Ghosh, R. France, J. M. Bieman. Primitives of Composition Directives. *Technical Report CS 04-103, Computer Science Department, Colorado State University, 2004.*

Query Models

Dominik Stein, Stefan Hanenberg, and Rainer Unland

University of Duisburg-Essen
Essen, Germany
{dstein, shanenbe, unlandR}@cs.uni-essen.de

Abstract. The need for querying software artifacts is a new emerging design issue in modern software development. Novel techniques such as Model-Driven Architecture or Aspect-Oriented Software Development heavily depend on powerful designation means to allocate elements in software artifacts, which are then either modified by transformation or enhanced by weaving processes. In this paper we present a new modeling notation for representing queries using the UML. We introduce special symbols for common selection purposes and specify their OCL selection semantics, which may be executed on existing UML models in order to allocate all selected model elements therein. By doing so, we aim to give forth the advantages of modeling to query design: Our query models facilitate the specification of queries independent from particular programming languages, ease their comprehension, and support their validation in a modeling context.

1 Introduction

Querying software artifacts is a new emerging design issue in modern software development. Novel software development techniques, such as Model-Driven Architecture (MDA) [9] and Aspect-Oriented Software Development (AOSD) [6], focus on the allocation of elements, which are then either modified by transformation (in MDA) or enhanced by weaving processes (in AOSD). The primary goal of these approaches is to apply common refinements to multiple points in target artifacts. At the same time, refinements are kept separate from the points being affected in order to allow reuse of refinements in different application domains.

Prerequisite to querying software artifacts is the existence of accurate query specification means since only accurate specification of the selection criteria on target elements may lead to desired results and avoid unpredicted effects. Accordingly, the need for query specification means in MDA is manifested in the "MOF 2.0 Query / Views / Transformation (QVT)" Request For Proposal (RFP) [10]. The RFP calls for suggestions for a standard model transformation language. One part of the RFP demands appropriate designation means to allocate model elements in existing models that will serve as sources to transformations. Most submissions to the RFP (e.g., [4], [12], [1]) propose a textual language – in particular, the Object Constraint Language (OCL) [17] – in order to query existing user models. However, using a textual language (like OCL) quickly leads to very complex expressions even when defining a relatively small number of selection criteria. Hence, as query comprehension is difficult, accurate query specification is not easy and error-prone. We feel that a

T. Baar et al. (Eds.): UML 2004, LNCS 3273, pp. 98-112, 2004.

graphical notation could help. However, no graphical notation is currently around that assists the specification of selection queries in a more feasible manner.

In AOSD, the need of query specification means emerges from the need to specify sets of points in the target program (so-called "join points" [6]) at which aspect-oriented refinement shall take place. In order to designate such sets of join points, aspect-oriented programming languages provide special constructs, called "crosscuts" [3] (examples are "pointcuts" in AspectJ [7] and "traversal strategies" in Adaptive Programming [8]). Crosscuts are usually expressed using textual means. As with any textual pattern description, crosscuts as well tend to be difficult to comprehend as soon as they become more complex. Again we think that a graphical notation could help in understanding and specifying crosscuts. However, although there are various modeling approaches around to model aspect-oriented software (e.g., [2], [14], [5]), they all lack a suitable notation to represent selections of join points graphically.

In conclusion, we think that there is a need for a general graphical representation to express selection queries on software artifacts for the various domains. Indeed, we believe that such a suitable modeling notation is indispensable for technologies like MDA and AOSD to become popular software developing techniques. Such a graphical visualization would facilitate the comprehension of selection queries, as well as the estimation of where refinements actually take place. It would assist the software developer to communicate his/her ideas to colleagues or to document design decisions for maintainers and administrators. At last, provided with precise selection semantic, the modeling notation would permit reasoning on design decisions and validation of final results.

In this paper, we present a novel modeling notation for specifying selection queries: "Join Point Designation Diagrams" ("JPDD"). JPDDs are special kinds of diagrams that are used to visualize the selection criteria that elements must satisfy in order to be selected by the query. The notation is based on the modeling means provided by the Unified Modeling Language (UML) [11], making its comprehension easy and intuitive to a broad range of developers. The modeling notation is accompanied by a set of OCL operations that outline the allocation of elements in existing models according to the specifications made in a JPDD. These OCL operations allow for the validation of selection queries in a modeling context.

The remainder of this paper is structured as follows: At first, we emphasize the urgency of having a common graphical notation to represent queries giving real-life examples from the MDA and AOSD domains. After that, we introduce the selection means that we have defined and specify their selection semantics with the help of OCL expressions. We further describe the general syntax of JPDDs in order to elucidate the ways that our selection means may be combined. Finally, we demonstrate the applicability of our diagrams by applying them to the examples given in the problem statement. We conclude the paper with a short summary.

2 Problem Statement

In order to motivate the need to visualize query specifications, we present three daily-life sample implementations of queries as we can find them in MDA and AOSD.

2.1 Query Specification in OCL

The first example shows an (excerpt from an) OCL query statement as it may be used in MDA transformations. The statement selects all classes which are named "cn" and that either have an attribute named "an" or – in case not – have an association to some other class named "cn1" which in turn has an attribute named "an". The example is adopted from [12]. There it is used within a transformation that translates classes into tables. Fig. 1 shows a possible application area for such a transformation: Imagine we want to store all instances of "Person" in a database table together with the "Street" the person lives on. In some cases (A), the developers may have decided to implement "Street" as a direct attribute of "Person". In other cases (B), they may have chosen to associate class "Person" with another class "Address" which in turn includes the attribute "Street". The query we specify here covers both solutions.

```
->select(c: Class |
     (c.name='cn' and
      c.allAttributes->exists(att | att.name='an') )
or   (c.name='cn' and not
      c.allAttributes->exists(att | att.name='an') and
      c.oppositeAssociationEnds->exists(ae |
          let c1 : Class = ae.participant in
          c1.name='cn1' and
          c1.allAttributes->exists(att | att.name='an') ) ) )
```

The example demonstrates the complexity that the textual notation of OCL imposes on the developer when specifying or comprehending a selection query: He/she needs to be have a profound knowledge on what properties (e.g., `name` or `participant`) of what elements (e.g., classes and associations) may be constrained, and how. Further, the precise way to refer to the element's relationships to other model elements must be well understood (e.g., by using the collection operation `->exists` on properties like `allAttributes` or `oppositeAssociationEnds`). The assignment of variables (e.g., `c1`) using the `let` expression and the scoping of variable names by means of brackets is another source of significant complexity. Last but not least, the placement of Boolean operators is crucial to the selection result, and therefore must be carefully investigated.

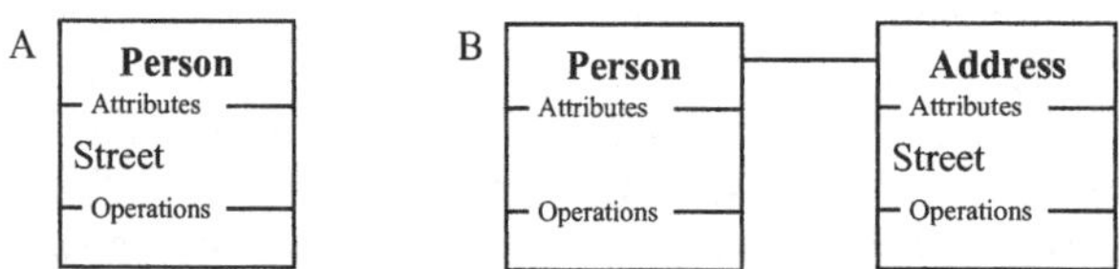

Fig. 1. Application areas for the OCL query

2.2 Query Specification in AspectJ

The next example shows a "pointcut" as we can find it in AspectJ [7]. AspectJ is a very popular general-purpose aspect-oriented programming language based on Java. Its "pointcut" construct is used to designate a selection of join points. A specialty of AspectJ is to allow aspect-oriented refinements (i.e., crosscutting) based on the runtime context of join points.

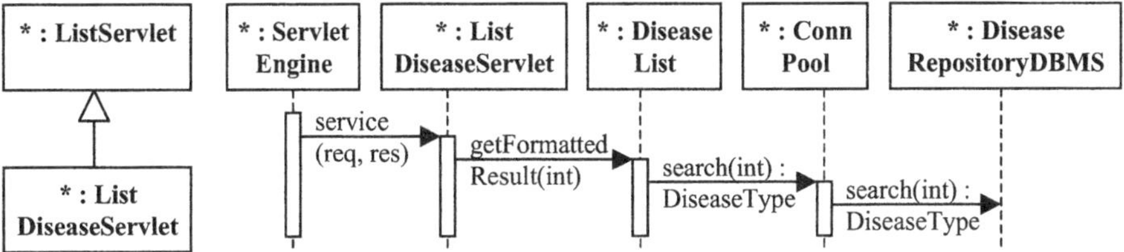

Fig. 2. Application area for the AspectJ pointcut

The sample pointcut shown here selects all those messages as join point that invoke (`call`) method "search" on class[1] "DiseaseRepositoryDBMS" (taking an integer value as parameter and returning an instance of class "DiseaseType") that come to pass within the control flow (`cflow`) of any (`*`) method called from (`this`) class[1] "ServletEngine" on class[1] "ListServlet" (or any of its subclasses[1] (`+`)), taking any number (`..`) of parameters and returning any or none (`*`) return value. The pointcut is adopted from an example in [13] and its main purpose is to reduce loading time of complex data objects ("DiseaseType") when only partial information is needed. Fig. 2 shows a possible scenario for our sample pointcut. In this scenario, class[1] "ServletEngine" invokes method "service" on class[1] "ListDiseaseServlet", which is a subclass of class[1] "ListServlet". After two hops via "DiseaseList" and "ConnPool", the message sequence ends invoking method "search" on class[1] "DiseaseRepositoryDBMS". At this point the selection criteria specified in the pointcut are satisfied and message "search" is added to the list of selected join points.

```
pointcut aspectj_pc():
    call(DiseaseType DiseaseRepositoryDBMS.search(int)) &&
    cflow(call(* ListServlet+.*(..)) && this(ServletEngine))
```

This example points out the absolute need of being familiar with keywords (such as `call` and `cflow`) and operators (like `+`, `*`, and `..`) for the comprehension of selection queries. In response to this indispensable prerequisite, we carefully related our explanations in the previous paragraph to the terms and characters used in the pointcut. However, in order to compose a new query, knowing the meaning of keywords and operators is not enough. Developers must be aware of what arguments may be specified within a particular statement (such as `call` and `cflow`), and what consequences these have. They need to know, for example, that the selection of `calls` can be further refined to operations having a particular signature pattern, or being invoked by certain instances (using the `this` construct). In the end, it requires high analytical skills in order to combine these statements (by means of Boolean operators) in such a way that only those join points are selected that we actually want to crosscut.

2.3 Query Specification in Demeter/C++

Our last example is from the domain of Adaptive Programming [8]. The goal of Adaptive Programming is to implement behavior in a "structure-shy" way. That means that methods should presume as little as possible about the (class) structure

[1] i.e., an instance of that class/those classes

they are executed in. For that purpose, Adaptive Programming makes use of special kinds of crosscuts, so-called "traversal strategies".

The following traversal strategy is taken from [8]. It selects a path from class "Conglomerate" to class "Salary" that passes class "Officer", however, that does not include an association (end) of name "subsidiaries". The strategy is part of a method that sums up the salaries of "Officers" in the "Conglomerate". Fig. 3 shows a possible class hierarchy that the method can cope with. The actual summation is accomplished by visitor methods that are appended to the individual classes on the strategy path. Note that according to the traversal strategy, calculation does not consider officers employed by the company's subsidiaries.

```
*from* Conglomerate
     *bypassing* -> *,subsidiaries,*
     *via* Officer
*to* Salary
```

Looking at this example, we are once again faced with new keywords and new operators whose meaning and consequences must be well understood by the developer. A major part of complexity arises from the various kinds of relationships – denoted as construction, alternation, inheritance, and repetition edges – that can be specified in traversal strategies: Developers need to be aware of the distinctive meaning of each of those edge types, and they must remember their precise notation (`->`, `=>`, `:>`, and `~>`, respectively) in order not to designate the wrong relationship. At last, they have to keep in mind what specific information they may provide with each relationship. For example, restrictions to the relationship labels may only be specified for construction edges.

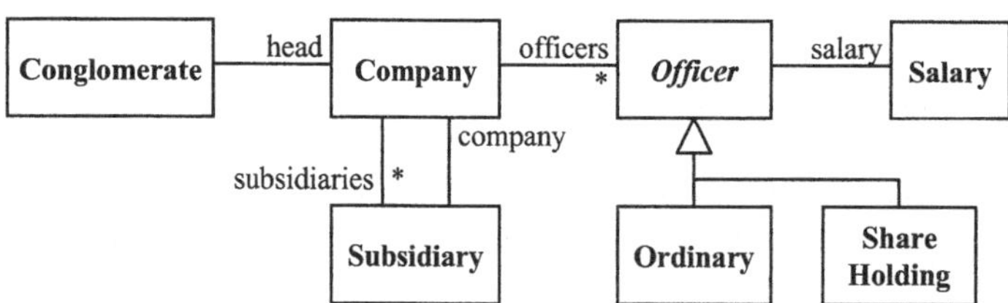

Fig. 3. Application area for the Demeter/C++ traversal strategy

2.4 Preliminary Conclusion

As a conclusion from the previous investigations, we attest textual notations to leave developers stranded with a heavy load of complexity: Developers are required to have a profound understanding about the usage of keywords and operators in order to specify queries properly. They must know what properties of what elements they may refer to, and how. Finally, they must have high analytical capabilities in order to assess the grouping of selection criteria as well as their semantic interdependencies, so that they can estimate what elements will be actually retrieved.

Opposed to so much complexity, developers urgently call for a graphical notation that help them with the composition and comprehension of selection queries. That notation should give them a visual conception of the selection semantics they are currently specifying using textual keywords. It should facilitate the specification of selection criteria on elements and their properties. Furthermore, it should depict the grouping of such selection criteria and visualize their interdependencies.

In order to come up with more concrete characteristics that our graphical notation must possess, we revisit the examples of the previous sections and investigate what different kinds of selections we have used: First of all, we may observe that – even though each notation comes with its own, most individual syntax, keywords, and operators – they are all concerned with the selection of (more or less) the same program elements, namely classes and objects, as well as the relationships between them (i.e., association relationships, generalization relationships, and call dependencies). Further, we recognize that selection is almost always based on the element names (only sometimes the elements name does not matter). Apart from that, selection may be based on the element's structural composition; for example, based on the (non-)existence of features in classes or of parameters in a parameter list. The last observation we make is that selection of elements is often based on the general context they reside in; meaning that query specifications abstract from (a set of) direct relationships between elements and merely call for the existence of paths.

Having identified these core objectives of a graphical query language, we now explain how we deal with these issues in our query models.

3 Modeling Selection Criteria

In this section we present the core modeling means we developed for the specification of selection criteria in selection queries. We explain their graphical notation, describe their objectives, and define their selection semantics using OCL meta-operations. Due to space limitations, only important meta-operations are shown.

Before discussing the modeling means in detail, we like to emphasize some general facts: Each model element is selected based on the values of their meta-attributes. In doing so, we extrapolate our observation that selections may be based on the value of the element's meta-attribute "name", and allow selections based on the values of the other meta-attributes, as well. Further, selection may be based on the model element's meta-relationships to other elements. That way we cope with the occasions when elements need to be selected based on their structural composition. Evaluation of meta-attributes and meta-relationships is accomplished by special OCL meta-operations, which we append to various meta-classes in the UML meta-model (see Table 1 for an example). These OCL meta-operations take a selection criterion from a JPDD as argument and compare it with an actual model element in a user model.

Within the meta-operations, name matching is generally accomplished using name patterns. Name patterns may contain wildcards, such as "*" and "?", in order to allow the selection of groups of elements (of the same type) following similar naming conventions. Within a JPDD, each model element's name is considered to be a name pattern by default. A name pattern may be given an identifier in order to reference the name pattern's occurrences at another place within the JPDD. Graphically, such identifiers are prepended by a question mark and are enclosed by angle brackets. They are placed in front of the name pattern whose occurrences they reference (see "<?C>Con*" in Fig. 4 for an example). Technically, name patterns which are given an identifier are stored in a special tagged value, named "namePattern". Is such a tagged value present, the OCL meta-operation evaluates the tagged value for name matching rather than the model element's proper name (see Table 1, block I, for details).

A JPDD must always show all characteristics that are considered relevant for selection. If any meta-attribute is not explicitly set to a value, or if any meta-relationship is not explicitly defined to be present, they are regarded irrelevant for selection (like the publicity specification in Fig. 4, for example). In doing so, we allow selections based only on partial information. Special treatment is necessary whenever selection criteria are defined on values of meta-attributes that are mapped to standard representations in diagrams. For example, every class in a UML class diagram is non-abstract by default – unless explicitly stated otherwise. Without additional means, it would not be possible to select classifiers regardless of the value of those meta-properties. To overcome this dilemma, the values of meta-attributes may always be explicitly defined using standard constraint notation (see Fig. 4 for an example).

3.1 Classifier Selection

To demonstrate the general facts mentioned above, let us have a look at the way that classifier selections may be specified. Fig. 4 depicts the graphical means that we provide for defining selection criteria on classifiers. Table 1 details how such means are evaluated on existing UML models using OCL expressions. As you can see, the OCL meta-operation first evaluates the model element's name (or the tagged value "namePattern", if present). Then, it compares the element's meta-attributes. And finally, it considers the element's meta-relationships to other model elements.

When specifying selection criteria on classifiers, special regards must be given to the features they must or must not possess. As illustrated in Fig. 4 (see attribute "att1"), we can use the Boolean operator "{not}" in order to require the non-existence of a particular element for selection. Technically, the matching result is inverted by the OCL meta-operation in that case (see [16] for further details).

Further, you can choose the multiplicity of attributes to indicate exact upper and/or lower limits or to designate upper and/or lower bounds which the multiplicity of an attribute must not exceed or underrun (respectively). The lower multiplicity limit of "att2" in Fig. 4, for example, is an exact lower limit (indicated by "!"). Attributes are only selected, if their lower limit equates "2". The upper multiplicity limit of "att2" in

Table 1. OCL meta-operation for matching classifiers

```
context Classifier::
matchesClassifier(C : Classifier) : Boolean
post: result =                                          -- block I. evaluate name pattern
if C.taggedValue->exists(tv | tv.type.name = 'namePattern') then
  self.matchesNamePattern(C.taggedValue->select(tv |
      tv.type.name = 'namePattern').dataValue->asSequence()->at(1))
else
  self.matchesNamePattern(C.name)
endif                                                   -- block II. evaluate meta-attributes
and (self.isRoot = C.isRoot or C.isRoot = '')
and (self.isLeaf = C.isLeaf or C.isLeaf = '')
and (self.isAbstract = C.isAbstract or C.isAbstract = '')
                                                        -- block III. evaluate meta-relationships
and (C.allAttributes->forAll(ATT | self.possessesMatchingAttribute(ATT))
  or C.allAttributes->size() = 0)
and (C.allOperations->forAll(OP | self.possessesMatchingOperation(OP))
  or C.allOperations->size() = 0)
```

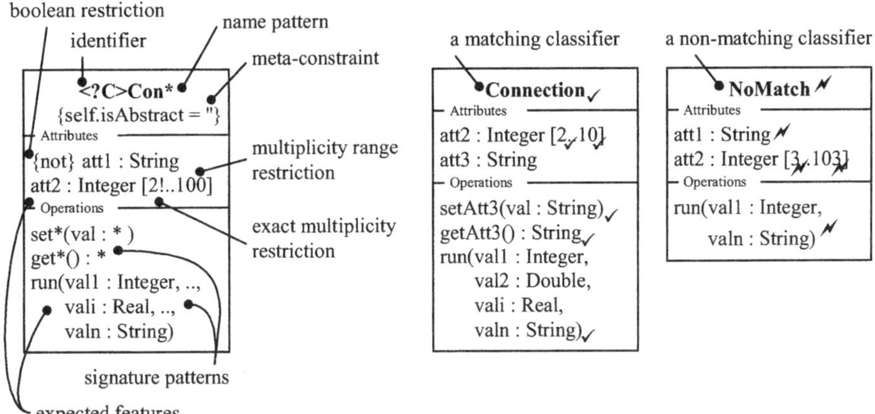

Fig. 4. Classifier selection

Fig. 4 denotes an upper bound. Attributes are selected if their upper multiplicity limit does not exceed "100" (see Fig. 4, right part, for examples). Technically, fix upper and lower limits are indicated by special stereotypes: Attributes of stereotype "fixed-LowerLimit" determine a fixed lower limit. Attributes of stereotype "fixedUpper-Limit" determine a fixed upper limit (see [16] for further details). Graphically, attributes of both stereotypes are indicated by appending an "!" to the respective multiplicity limit (see Fig. 4 for example).

Finally, operations are specified using signature patterns, which may contain wildcard ".." in order to abstract from an arbitrary number of parameters in the operation's parameter list (see Fig. 4 for an example). Matching is accomplished by comparing the overall order of the parameters in the operation's parameter list, as well as their particular order at the beginning and the end of the parameter list (see [16] for further details on the OCL matching expressions).

3.2 Relationship Selection

As pointed out in section 2, the presence of relationships and in particular the existence of paths between elements plays an important role in selection queries. In the following we present the graphical means we provide to deal with both association, generalization, and specialization relationships and paths, respectively.

Association Selection. Fig. 5 depicts the graphical means we provide for specifying selections based on association relationships. Table 2 details how such means may be evaluated on existing UML models using OCL expressions. Note that, similar to features, we may restrict the multiplicity of association ends and/or require an association (end) *not* to be present (see Fig. 5, center part, for an example). Special regards must be given to "indirect" associations, or association paths. Graphically, indirect associations are depicted as double-crossed lines. Fig. 5, left part, for example, signifies that there must be an association path from class "C" to class "AC". Technically, indirect associations are indicated using a special stereotype "indirect" (see Table 2 for details).

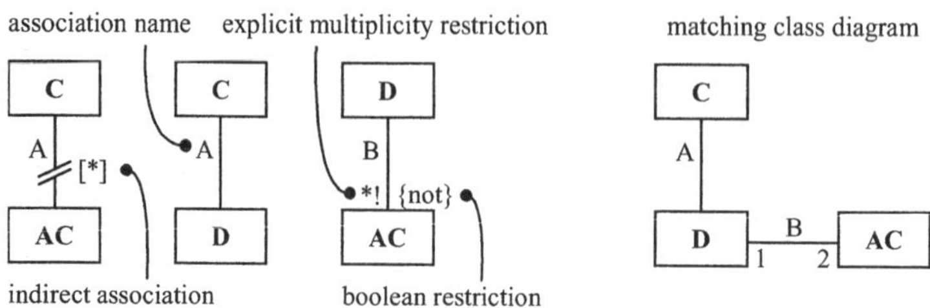

Fig. 5. Association selection

Matching of paths essentially means comparing the ends of the path in a UML model with the ends of the indirect association in the JPDD. Table 2 details how this is accomplished using OCL expressions: Operation "indirectNeighbors" returns all navigable association ends of a given association. Operation "allIndirectNeighbors" returns all navigable association ends that are reachable via a given association. Operation "possessesMatchingAssociation" then makes use of this operation to evaluate whether one of such association ends matches the opposite association end of the indirect association (see block I).

Generalization and Specialization Selection. Fig. 6 depicts the graphical means we provide for defining selection criteria on generalization and specialization relationships. Table 3 details how such means may be evaluated on existing UML models using OCL expressions. Note that, as with association relationships, we may

Table 2. OCL meta-operation for matching association relationships

```
context Classifier::
possessesMatchingAssociation(a : Association, c : Classifier) : Boolean
post: result =                                  -- block I. evaluate indirect neighbors
if a.stereotype->exists(st | st.name='indirect') then
  self.associations->exists(A | A.matchesAssociation(a) and
  a.allConnections->select(ae | ae.participant = c)->forAll(ae |
    A.allConnections->select(AE | AE.participant = self)
      ->exists(AE | AE.matchesAssociationEnd(ae) and
       a.allConnections->select(ae | ae.participant <> c)
      ->forAll(ae2 | self.allIndirectNeighbors(A)
      ->exists(AE2 | AE2.matchesAssociationEnd(ae2))))))
else                                            -- block II. evaluate direct neighbors
  self.associations->exists(A | A.matchesAssociation(a) and
  a.allConnections->forAll(ae | A.allConnections
      ->exists(AE | AE.matchesAssociationEnd(ae))))
endif
```

```
context Classifier::
allIndirectNeighbors(a : Association): Set(AssociationEnd)
post: result = self.indirectNeighbors(a)->union(
  self.indirectNeighbors(a)
  ->collect(AE | AE.participant.allAssociations->reject(A | A = a)
  ->collect(A | AE.participant.allIndirectNeighbors(A))))->asSet()
```

```
context Classifier::
indirectNeighbors(a : Association): Set(AssociationEnd)
post: result = self.allOppositeAssociationEnds
  ->select(AE | AE.association = a and AE.isNavigable)
```

specify a generalization/specialization relationships *not* to be present (see Fig. 6, center part, for an example).

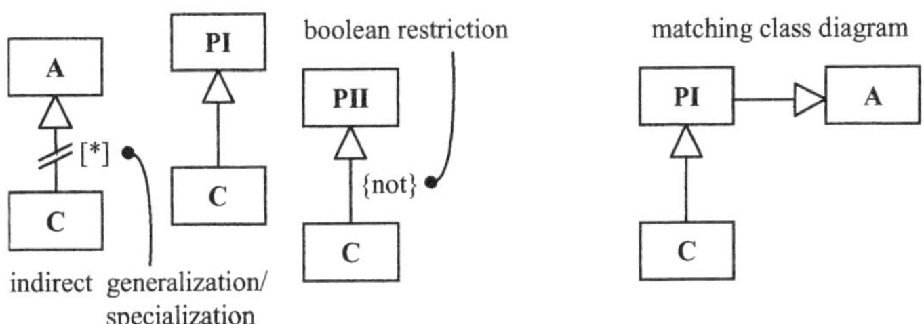

Fig. 6. Generalization selection

Special regards must be given to "indirect" generalization and specialization relationships, or inheritance paths (see Fig. 6). Graphically, indirect generalizations and specializations are depicted as double-crossed lines. According to the specification made in Fig. 6, left part, for example, class "C" must have class "A" among its ancestors in order to be selected, and class "A" must have class "C" among its descendants. Technically, inheritance paths are represented as special stereotype "indirect" of the generalization relationship. Table 3 exemplifies how inheritance path matching is accomplished in UML models in case of an generalization relationship (see block I).

Table 3. OCL meta-operation for matching generalization relationships

```
context Classifier::
possessesMatchingParent(g : Generalization) : Boolean
post: result =                                   -- block I. evaluate indirect parents
if g.stereotype->exists(st | st.name='indirect') then
   self.generalization->exists(G | G.matchesGeneralization(g) and
   G.parent->union(G.parent.allParents)->exists(C |
       C.matchesClassifier(g.parent) and
       C.matchesRelationships(g.parent)))
else                                             -- block II. evaluate direct parents
   self.generalization->exists(G | G.matchesGeneralization(g) and
       G.parent.matchesClassifier(g.parent) and
       G.parent.matchesRelationships(g.parent))
endif
```

3.3 Message Selection

As demonstrated in section 2, selections are not confined to the structural properties of software artifacts, but may be based on their behavior, as well. In the following, we describe the graphical means we provide to specify such selections. In doing so, we concentrate on the symbols used in UML sequence diagrams (i.e., messages).

Messages are selected based on the actions they are associated with. Signature patterns may be used to restrict such actions (see Fig. 7, left part, for example). Besides that, messages may be selected based on the control flow they occur in or which they invoke. Such control flow is sketched using predecessor and successor messages, respectively: All messages complying to message "?msg1" in Fig. 7, center

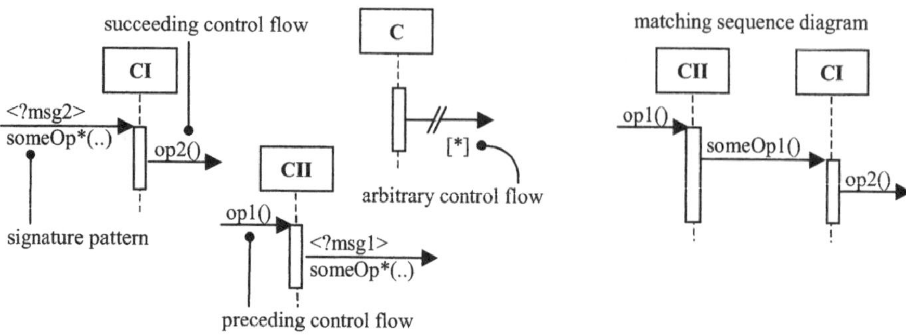

Fig. 7. Message selection

part, for example, must occur in the control flow of message "op1". All messages selected by message "?msg2" in Fig. 7, left part, must invoke some message "op2". Special regards must be given to "indirect" messages, which may be used to indicate an arbitrary control flow. Graphically, indirect messages are depicted as double-crossed arrows (see Fig. 7, center part, for example). Technically, they are represented as messages of the special stereotype "indirect". Last but not least, it is important to note that messages are selected based on the base classifiers of their sender and receiver roles (rather than on the roles themselves). This is accomplished deeming that selections should execute on the full specification of classifiers rather than on restricted projections. The same is valid for the associations used for transmitting the messages. See [16] for the precise OCL code used for message matching.

4 A Technical Perspective

Having specified the graphical notation and their semantics in the previous section, we now want to describe briefly how those means are integrated into the UML. Fig. 8 depicts the general syntax of a JPDD: It consists of at least one selection criterion, some of which delineate selection parameters. A JPDD represents a selection criterion itself, and thus may be contained in another JPDD (e.g., for reuse of criteria specifications). Fig. 8 illustrates how we can map the syntax of JPDDs to the general syntax of UML namespace templates: In terms of the UML meta-model, a JPDD represents a (special stereotype of a) namespace which may contain several model elements, each representing a selection criterion. The namespace is provided with a set of template parameters that indicates the model elements to be returned by the query. We do not further restrict the particular kind of namespace that a JPDD may reify since different application domains may have different demands. Therefore, JPDDs may be specified as classifier templates, collaboration templates, or package templates, etc. – whatever suits the needs of the particular query specification best.

It is important to note that JPDDs do not quite comply with the semantic of conventional UML templates. In fact, the meaning of JPDDs is rather "inverse" to that of conventional UML templates: While conventional UML templates are generally used to instantiate multiple model elements from one common mould (or a "generation pattern"), JPDDs are used to identify all model elements that share one common shape (a "selection pattern"). Correspondingly, template parameters of

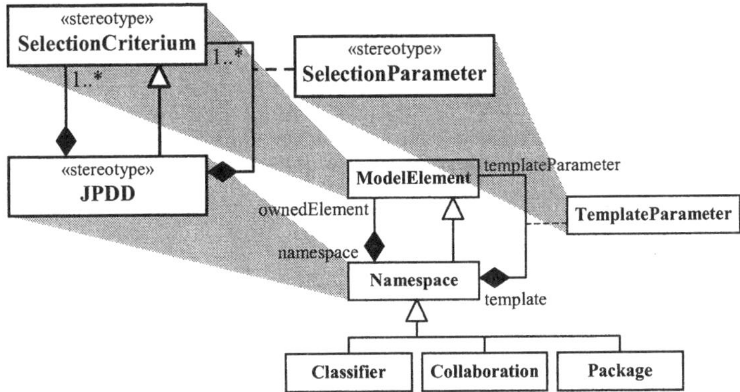

Fig. 8. Abstract syntax of JPDDs, and its mapping to UML's meta-classes

JPDDs are meant to return actual arguments rather than being bound to actual arguments. To indicate this important difference in meaning visually, we place template parameter boxes to the bottom right corner of JPDDs (rather than to their conventional position at the top right corner of the template). In the following section we give examples of what a fully specified JPDD looks like.

5 Application to Software Development Techniques

In this section we demonstrate how our notation may be put to use in actual software development techniques, namely in MDA and AOSD. To do so, we revisit the examples given in section 2 and show how these sample query specifications can be represented using JPDDs. We demonstrate the benefits that our modeling notation yields to the comprehension of query specifications and compare it to other possible approaches to visualize selection queries.

5.1 Model-Driven Architecture

It has been already mentioned that the need to specify model queries in the field of MDA is manifested in OMG's "MOF 2.0 QVT" RFP. While most submissions to the RFP are content with proposing textual notations (in particular OCL) to specify model queries, only one [12] comes up with a graphical representation. In the following we compare that graphical notation with the one presented here. To do so, we make use of the OCL selection statement described in section 2.1.

Let us first have a look at the JPDD (see Fig. 9, left part). The JPDD depicts three classes (together with their features) and one relationship. The elements are grouped into two alternative selection patterns, which are interconnected by a Boolean "{or}". Attribute "?att" in the upper class of the right selection pattern is annotated with a Boolean "{not}", stating that no matching attribute must be present in the respective classifier for the selection to succeed. Class names and attributes names are specified using name patterns ("cn", "cn1", and "an"), which are given identifiers ("?c", "?c1", and "?att"). Two of those identifiers ("?c" and "?att") reappear in the template parameter box of the query, meaning that the selection is supposed to return all class/attribute-pairs that satisfy the specified selection criteria in the JPDD.

Fig. 9, right part, shows a graphical representation of the same query using the notation presented in [12]. The approach aims to define general meta-model mappings in MDA. Therefore, queries are defined in terms of meta-model entities and meta-model properties rather than in terms of user model entities and user model properties (as in our approach). In consequence, the approach can be considered to be in parts more general than ours: Its notation allows the specification of model queries for any (MOF) meta-model and is not confined to the UML meta-model. However, we think that the gain of higher generality is at cost of lower feasibility and readability: Users have to learn and understand the meta-models they are (unawarely) working with before they can write their model queries. Further, the need to express selection criteria in terms of meta-model entities may often lead to unnecessary and distracting noise in selection diagrams. For example, in order to define a simple association between two classes, we need to draw three meta-model entities (see Fig. 9, right part). Apart from such pragmatic problems, the approach does not provide for the selection based on indirect relationships and/or name/signature patterns.

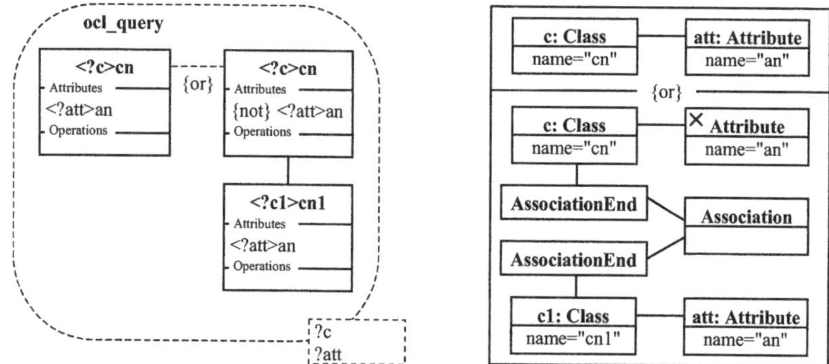

Fig. 9. Representation of the OCL query (from section 2.1). *Left part*: Using a JPDD. *Right part*: Using the notation presented in [12]

5.2 Aspect-Oriented Software Development

In AOSD, a major design issue is where and when to apply crosscutting enhancements implemented by aspects. Aspect-oriented programming techniques provide various textual means to define the conditions under which crosscutting has to take place. Even though various aspect-oriented modeling approaches are around [2] [14] [5], none of them presents a solution to represent such conditions graphically. By means of JPDDs, we now have a graphical notation at hand to visualize the criteria under which a join point is to be enhanced by an aspect. To demonstrate this, we exemplify in the following how JPDDs may be used to represent pointcuts in AspectJ. We are using the example given in section 2.2[2]:

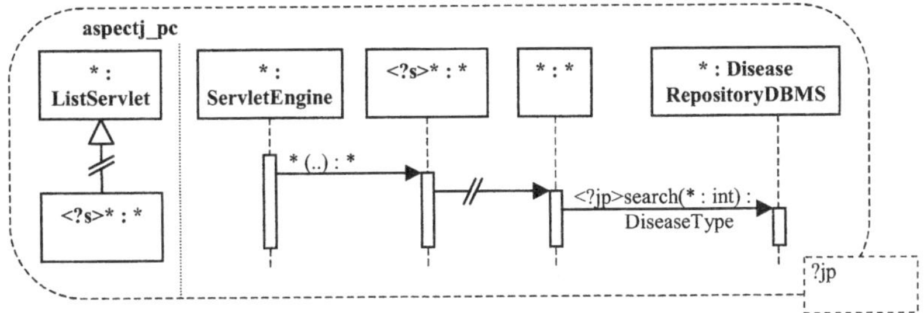

Fig. 10. Representation of the AspectJ query (from section 2.2) using a JPDD

To visualize the pointcut, we draw a JPDD consisting of two parts (see Fig. 10), one specifying the behavioral selection criteria (right part) and one specifying the structural constraints (left part). The parts are linked to each other via identifier "?s". According to the structural constraints, "?s" refers to all children of "ListServlet". In the behavioral part, "?s" is then used to portray a control flow from a "ServletEngine" to one of its children. That control flow must go on, passing any arbitrary number of messages, until an invocation of operation "search" on a "DiseaseRepositoryDBMS" (taking any integer value as parameter and returning a "DiseaseType") is reached. This is the point that the AspectJ pointcut is supposed to retrieve. Therefore, it is given an identifier "?jp", and is placed in the JPDD's template parameter box.

6 Summary and Future Work

In this paper, we presented a graphical notation to define query models. The specification of queries is a new emerging design issue. Queries lie at the heart of novel techniques such as MDA or AOSD. Despite that fact, though, no suitable graphical notation is around to our knowledge that supports the definition of selection queries. An appropriate query modeling language is considered indispensable, though, for techniques like MDA and AOSD to allow them to become widespread. Software developers demand programming language-independent modeling facilities that ease their comprehension on where (MDA- and AO-) refinements actually take place.

In this paper, we have identified frequent selection criteria in query specifications on software artifacts. We presented a comprehensive set of easy to use, yet powerful modeling means to specify such selection criteria in selection queries. We supplemented them with precise OCL semantics that can be executed on existing UML models in order to allocate model elements meeting such criteria. At last, we proved the applicability of our notations with different programming languages using daily-life examples as we can find them in MDA and AOSD.

To the best of our knowledge, our modeling notation is the first approach that provides an essential set of modeling means for the explicit design of queries based

[2] A visualization of the Demeter/C++ traversal strategy presented in section 2.3 is omitted here due to space limitations. Please refer to [15] for a graphical representation.

on the UML. The major advantage of adopting UML's existing modeling means is that query models are easy to write and easy to understand by a broad community of software developers. They do not need to learn a new modeling language, nor do they need to deal with the meta-model (as in other approaches) in order to define query models.

In order to advance the support for software developers in designing queries to a further extent, the following issues are focus of future work: The capabilities allowing the composition of new selection queries from existing ones – like, for example, query aggregations or query specializations – must be improved. Further, suitable abstraction means must be found that enable software developers to reason on selection queries (and their relationships to each other) without bothering about the exact details.

References

[1] Alcatel, Softeam, Thales, TNI-Valiosys, Codagen Technologies Corp, *Revised Submission for MOF 2.0 Query / Views / Transformations RFP*, 18. August 2003

[2] Clarke, S., Walker, R.J. *Composition Patterns: An Approach to Designing Reusable Aspects.* in Proc. of ICSE '01 (Toronto, Canada, May 2001), ACM, pp. 5-14

[3] Gybels, K., Brichau, J., *Arranging language features for more robust pattern-based crosscuts*, in: Proc. of AOSD'03 (Boston, MA, March 2003), ACM, pp. 60-69

[4] Interactive Objects Software, Project Technology, *Revised Submission for MOF 2.0 Query / Views / Transformations RFP*, 18. August 2003

[5] Kandé, M.M., PhD Thesis, EPFL, Lausanne, Swiss, 2003

[6] Kiczales, G., Lamping, J., Mendhekar, A., Maeda, Chr., Lopes, C.V., Loingtier, J-M., Irwin, J.: *Aspect-Oriented Programming*, in: Proc. of ECOOP '97 (Jyväskylä, Finland, June 1997), Springer, pp. 220-242

[7] Laddad, R., *Aspectj in Action: Practical Aspect-Oriented Programming*, Manning Publications, Greenwich, 2003

[8] Lieberherr, K., *Adaptive Object-Oriented Software: The Demeter Method with Propagation Patterns*, PWS Publishing Company, Boston, 1996

[9] OMG, *MDA Guide Version 1.0*, 2003 (OMG Document omg/2003-05-01)

[10] OMG, *Request for Proposal: MOF 2.0 Query / Views / Transformations RFP*, 2002 (OMG Document ad/2002-04-10)

[11] OMG, *Unified Modeling Language Specification*, Version 1.5, 2003 (OMG Document formal/03-03-01)

[12] QVT-Partners, *Revised Submission for MOF 2.0 Query / Views / Transformations RFP*, 18. August 2003 (http://qvtp.org/downloads/1.1/qvtpartners1.1.pdf)

[13] Soares, S., Laureano, E., Borba, P., *Implementing Distribution and Persistence Aspects with AspectJ*, in: Proc. of OOPSLA '02 (Seattle, WA, November 2002), ACM, pp. 174-190

[14] Stein, D., Hanenberg, St., Unland, R., *A UML-based Aspect-Oriented Design Notation For AspectJ*, in: Proc. of AOSD '02 (Enschede, The Netherlands, April 2002), ACM, pp. 106-112

[15] Stein, D., Hanenberg, St., Unland, R., *Modeling Pointcuts*, Early Aspect Workshop, AOSD '04 (Lancaster, UK, March 2004)

[16] Stein, D., Hanenberg, S., Unland, R., *A Graphical Notation to Specify Model Queries for MDA Transformations on UML Models*, Workshop on MDAFA 2004 (Linkoeping, Sweden, June 2004)

[17] Warmer, J., Kleppe, A., *The Object Constraint Language: Precise Modelling with UML*, Addison-Wesley, 1998

Specifying Cross-Cutting Requirement Concerns

Geri Georg, Raghu Reddy, Robert France

Colorado State University
[georg, raghu, france]@cs.colostate.edu

Abstract. Addressing non-orthogonal software concerns that arise from requirements can significantly contribute to the complexity of developing large systems. Difficulties arise from the need to: locate related requirements, reason about the software concerns they represent, and analyze the impact of changing requirements. We address these issues through the use of requirements aspects. We present a method to identify requirements aspects from viewpoints, to associate requirements aspects with generic design solutions based on domain experience, and to specify the generic solutions using the UML. We demonstrate these techniques using a smart home controller application.

Keywords: cross-cutting concerns, requirements aspects, specification, UML

1 Introduction

Complexity in large systems development can begin as requirements are gathered, analyzed, and synthesized to become the driving forces of system design objectives. During requirements analysis, software concerns are identified. Jackson [14] defines a software concern as anything of interest to a stakeholder. Software concerns may relate to specific system functionality or to other issues. Developers group requirements they perceive as being related to each other into more generalized software concerns such as usability or security. Software concerns may also impose additional requirements on the system. Requirements complexity during the analysis process is driven by the number of: 1) requirements sources (e.g. users, developers, hardware/firmware components, physical environments, etc.), 2) requirements, and 3) interacting software concerns represented in the requirements. The related requirements that make up a software concern often come from different requirements sources, so it can be difficult to locate all the requirements related to a particular concern.

Determining the impact of requirements changes on software concerns can also be a complex task, since the requirements related to a particular concern are spread across multiple requirements sources. However, analysis is necessary since requirements changes may cause software concerns to become important in different requirements sources, cause new concerns emerge, or cause new relationships between concerns. The issues of locating related requirements, being able to reason about the software concerns they represent, and being able to analyze the impact of changing them

T. Baar et al. (Eds.): UML 2004, LNCS 3273, pp. 113-127, 2004.

contribute significantly to the complexity faced by the developers of large software systems.

We address these issues through the use of requirements aspects. Requirements aspects are aspects identified during requirements gathering and analysis, and they help structure requirements and related software concerns, in particular concerns that cross-cut the requirements specification. Requirements aspects can be used to structure functional software concerns or non-functional software concerns such as security and maintainability. Requirements aspects can provide a link between requirements and design by providing experienced-based design solutions. Analysis of these potential solutions identifies conflicts between cross-cutting system objectives that are not orthogonal.

In this paper we present an approach to 1) identify requirements aspects from multiple requirements sources, 2) associate requirements aspects with generic experienced-based solutions that address the concern, and 3) specify generic solutions using the UML [23-25]. We also briefly discuss how generic solutions can be analyzed and outline how these solutions can be used in later stages of the development process.

The rest of this paper is organized as follows. Section 2 contains a background discussion of requirements and requirements aspects. Section 3 presents a method to identify and use requirements aspects. Section 4 applies this method to a case study under development at Colorado State University. Section 5 presents related work, and in Section 6 we discuss conclusions and future work.

2 Background

Software requirements are derived from many sources. Among these are users of the system, both within the organization building the system, and outside organizations that must interact with it. Other requirements sources include system developers and maintainers, firmware or hardware portions of the system that place constraints on the system software, and the business context and physical environment in which the system is used. We term each of these different sources a viewpoint. This notion of a viewpoint generalizes the definition of viewpoints given in Kotonya and Sommerville's Viewpoint-Oriented Requirements Definition (VORD) technique. VORD defines a viewpoint as a requirements source external to the system that either receives services or provides data or control to services (see [19]).

Requirements that are related to each other can be grouped into software concerns that may be related to the system's required functionality or to other desired system qualities such as availability or security. Software concerns that cross-cut multiple viewpoints are called requirements aspects. We limit the focus of this paper to software concerns related to non-functional system behavior, although the approach presented can also be used for other software concerns that cross-cut multiple viewpoints.

Figure 1 shows the concepts used in the aspect-oriented requirements modeling approach described in this paper. Requirements may be described using different forms. Examples are static structure diagrams (including OCL constraints), text, scenario sequence diagrams, use case diagrams, and state machine diagrams. A *requirements document* therefore may consist of several different types of information, both textual and graphical. A single requirement may be associated with any number of viewpoints. Viewpoints can be hierarchical.

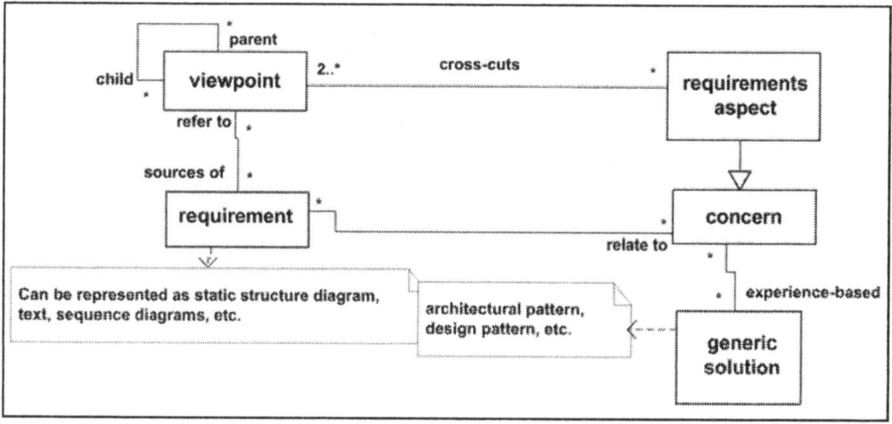

Fig. 1 The structure and relation of system requirements and requirements aspects

Requirements aspects are logical groupings of requirements that relate to a software concern, with the added constraint that the requirements must cross-cut two or more viewpoints. Requirements aspects may give rise to additional requirements that are not present in any other viewpoints. There may be a hierarchical decomposition of requirements aspects. Rashid, et al. [26] present a similar structure of viewpoint requirements and requirements aspects.

Requirements aspects related to many non-functional behaviors can be addressed with a set of standard solutions, developed through research and experience, that have been shown to effectively address the software concerns. For example, encryption is a generalized solution to the concern of data privacy when data is traveling over an un-trusted communication medium. Figure 1 shows that standard, or generic, solutions consist of different elements. Common examples are architectural patterns of system structure such as three-tier or blackboard, design patterns, and invariants.

The specification of a generic solution consists of a set of packages, where each package is a collection of elements. The types of element are: 1) a collection of functional design patterns specified as static diagrams and/or behavioral diagrams, 2) architectural patterns, and 3) system constraints. Each collection is specified as a set of templates. Constraints are thus written in terms of the template elements. When the solution is actually applied, it must be instantiated in the context of the software system. Details of this process are beyond the scope of this paper; see [10] for details on instantiation and composition of aspect models.

3 Requirements Aspect-Oriented Modeling (RAM) Method

Cross-cutting concerns are often identified directly from textual requirements. It is also necessary to understand the system use-scenarios to determine where and how these concerns affect system behavior. We therefore create static and dynamic diagrams of a requirement model. The static portion of this model consists of a description of the problem concepts and the relations between them represented using UML static diagrams. The behavior diagrams describe the behavior of key concepts identified in the static diagram. We use sequence diagrams to specify these scenarios although activity or state diagrams can also be used. Once we have constructed static and dynamic diagrams we can analyze system requirements and identify cross-cutting, non-functional, concerns.

We group similar requirements into software concerns, and identify requirement aspects as those concerns with requirements that cross-cut multiple viewpoints. Requirements are originally presented at different levels of abstraction. Developers must work to evolve or decompose very abstract requirements into more detailed requirements that contain statements of acceptance criteria. A requirement that is very abstract (e.g. "*the smart home system must be user-friendly*") must be decomposed into a set of more detailed requirements that contain measurable acceptance criteria (e.g. "*a user must be able to program the heating system in the smart home in one minute*"). The original and the detailed requirement both deal with the same non-functional concern, usability. Usability can be addressed by best practices developed through experience.

Requirements aspects are analyzed and addressed according to current best engineering practices. Best practices for many concerns have been identified through both research and practical use. They have been used in differing circumstances as patterns for solutions, and through time have been adjusted to meet changing conditions. We take advantage of the expertise already developed in these areas, and utilize their standard solutions.

It must be noted that just because a requirements aspect cross-cuts multiple viewpoints and can be addressed by a generic solution design pattern, that pattern may not become a design aspect. This is because a design aspect cross-cuts the primary modularization of system design, and a generic solution pattern may not. However, if a generic solution pattern cross-cuts sequence diagrams that deal with different areas of the system's primary functionality, the pattern may cross-cut multiple modules of the design and be a design aspect. Requirements aspects that are best addressed through system structure will not be realized as design aspects. Requirements aspects that are addressed by constraints will remain constraints through the design phase. Examples of each of these generic solution cases are given in the case study described in Section 4.

The overall Requirements Aspect-oriented Modeling (RAM) method is outlined below. Input to the method is a set of viewpoints and their associated requirements.

(1) Group requirements with similar features/properties. The result is a set of software concerns. System designers rely on their expertise and experience to relate requirements to each other and more generalized software concerns.

(2) Identify concerns that cross-cut viewpoints. These are requirements aspects. Identify additional requirements based solely on the requirements aspects.

(3) Associate requirements aspects with generic solutions based on experience in the domain. Generic solutions include architectural patterns, functional patterns, and system constraints.

(4) Add detail to generic solutions as applicable. This can include detailing patterns or making constraints more specific.

Steps 5 and 6 are analysis steps:

(5) If applicable, compose generic solution pattern models with design models to identify interactions and potential conflicts.

(6) Use analysis information from step 5 during initial system structuring. If patterns cross-cut the system modularization, they become design aspects. Constraints identified in step 3 help direct software design, and may be used to ensure that the related software concern is adequately represented in the design.

We demonstrate steps 1-4 of the RAM method in the next section. Steps 5 and 6 use aspect-oriented modeling (AOM) composition and analysis techniques we developed for aspect-oriented design and are not discussed further in this paper. Please see our previous work for a discussion of model composition and conflict analysis [10-12].

4 Case Study – A Smart Home System

The smart home control system is being used as a research vehicle at Colorado State University and is the basis of a set of design problems used in senior-level classes in the Computer Science Department. The smart home consists of several devices that can be controlled through software, and the system software is responsible for both acquiring data from these devices and controlling them. Devices capable of being part of the system include heating and air conditioning subsystems, a sprinkler subsystem, an alarm system, water heaters, etc.

There are several stakeholder viewpoints represented in the initial system requirements. These include:

- a consumer who configures the smart home system and gets it running
- a consumer who analyzes reports generated by the smart home controller, generally for the purposes of conserving resources
- repair personnel called in to fix particular device failures
- devices that are part of the smart home system
- installation personnel who add new devices to a home

Requirements that result as interaction with ancillary organization include those from:

- emergency response personnel
- electric, water, and gas companies who own the meters associated with a home

Sample requirements from two of these stakeholders are given below. The example stakeholders are the consumer who configures the smart home system and the consumer who analyzes reports. Requirements are identified with the stakeholder code and a number. These requirements were chosen from a much larger set of requirements for the purposes of illustration. In some cases the same requirement is present in multiple viewpoints, as demonstrated by requirements CSA-2 and CA-2.

Consumer System Administrator (configures overall system – code is CSA):
- system must be easily used by someone not familiar with computers (CSA-1)
- multiple user interfaces are needed to accommodate user preferences (CSA-2)
- it must be easy to check device configurations (CSA-3)
- a configuration has to be coherent (e.g., no air conditioning in the winter) (CSA-4)
- configurations and other information presented to the user must reflect the actual state of the devices controlled by the system (CSA-5)

Consumer Analyzer (analyzes reports to conserve resources – code is CA):
- system must be easily used by someone not familiar with computers (CA-1)
- multiple user interfaces are needed to accommodate user preferences (CA-2)
- reports need to suggest ways to save money on electricity, gas, and water (CA-3)
- reports must be accurate (CA-4)
- reports must be available on demand or automatically (CA-5)

System designers group the requirements given above into generalized software concerns, based on experience. For example, requirements CSA-1, 2, 3 and CA-1, 2, 5 all relate to the software concern of usability. Requirements CSA-4, 5 and CA-4 relate to correctness, and requirements CSA-2 and CA-2, 5 relate to availability. In all three cases the concerns cross-cut multiple viewpoints, so each is a requirements aspect. We will address the usability requirements aspect in detail in the following discussion.

We analyze a requirements model in order to understand how the usability requirements aspect will affect system behavior. A portion of the static diagram for this model is shown in Figure 2, and a use-scenario in Figure 3. We use an interaction diagram to show the use-scenario rather than a use-case diagram in order to show more detail about the interactions. The extra detail allows us to identify locations where a requirements aspect generic solution needs to be applied.

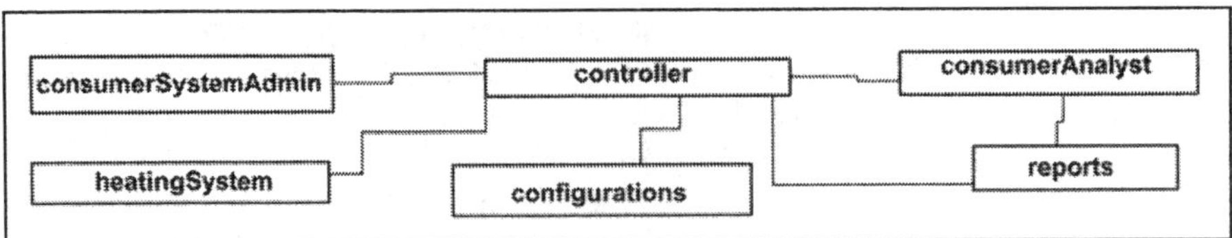

Fig. 2 Portion of the requirements model static diagram for the smart home system

The major classes shown in Figure 2 are two consumer users, the system administrator and an analyst, a controller, a heating sub-system, reports to be analyzed, and storage for device configurations. We define a configuration for the heating sub-system to consist of a target temperature for the home, and a state, either *on* or *off*. The current house temperature is also part of this sub-system. The static structure shown in Figure 2 does not include specific device components of the heating sub-system, although these devices (a heater and a fan) are shown in Figure 3.

Figure 3 shows the use-scenario for changing the configuration of the heating system. This scenario is shown as a sequence diagram.

This sequence is initiated when the consumer system administrator chooses the heating system. The system controller gets the configuration of the heating system and the current house temperature. The consumer system administrator requests the controller to show this configuration so it is presented to the user. The user must decide whether or not to change the configuration. If there are no changes to be made, the sequence is complete.
If there are changes to be made, the user may request to view settings used at some other time using *getSpecificConfig*. In this case the controller must access the configuration storage to obtain the configuration of interest. The user can decide what changes to make to the configuration and request that the controller make them. The controller needs to perform consistency and correctness checks on the proposed configuration, and if it is acceptable, request the heating system to change. If the configuration is in error, then the controller must present an error to the user via *showConfigError*. Once the heating system has made changes the new configuration can be saved to storage.

Once a requirements aspect has been identified, it may impose additional requirements on the system. For example, in the area of usability, various researchers have described usability as dealing not only with the user interface, but also with a system's structure and underlying concepts [1, 3, 8, 17]. This description leads to the addition of usability requirements that address concepts such as the user's ability to learn how to use the system, efficiency at completing tasks, knowledge retention over time, error rate, and overall satisfaction with the system [8]. Different researchers identify slightly different requirements for usability; an alternative definition of usability is the user's perception of the system's simplicity, understandability, and ease-of-use [3]. These additional requirements are related to the usability requirements aspect, but not to any other viewpoint in the system. Rashid, et al. [26] also identify requirements that are part of a requirements aspect, and not a stakeholder viewpoint.

The change configuration sequence diagram has three areas where interaction with the user can be designed to address usability requirements: getting input from the user, presenting information to the user, and the mental model used to provide consistency in these actions. In particular the mental model can directly influence usability requirements. For example, when a user's mental model is compatible with the underlying metaphor of the software, learning, efficiency, retention, and error rate are all positively affected. Satisfaction can be positively affected by compatible metaphors. A consumer metaphor may differ from the metaphor used for other users, such as a heating system installer.

We next identify best practices that address input, output, and metaphor usability requirements. For example, the user input experience can be improved by generic solutions such as remembering previous input choices, making suggestions for input, and performing error checking on the fly. Providing different kinds of input technologies such as graphical, audio, keyboard, and remote capabilities also can improve usability. Output functionality that uses consistent concepts and allows different presentation mediums is also part of a generic solution to usability. Finally, the use of a consistent metaphor that is a simple model employing familiar terminology, and that is consistent across the system is another generic solution [1, 3, 4, 8, 17, 21].

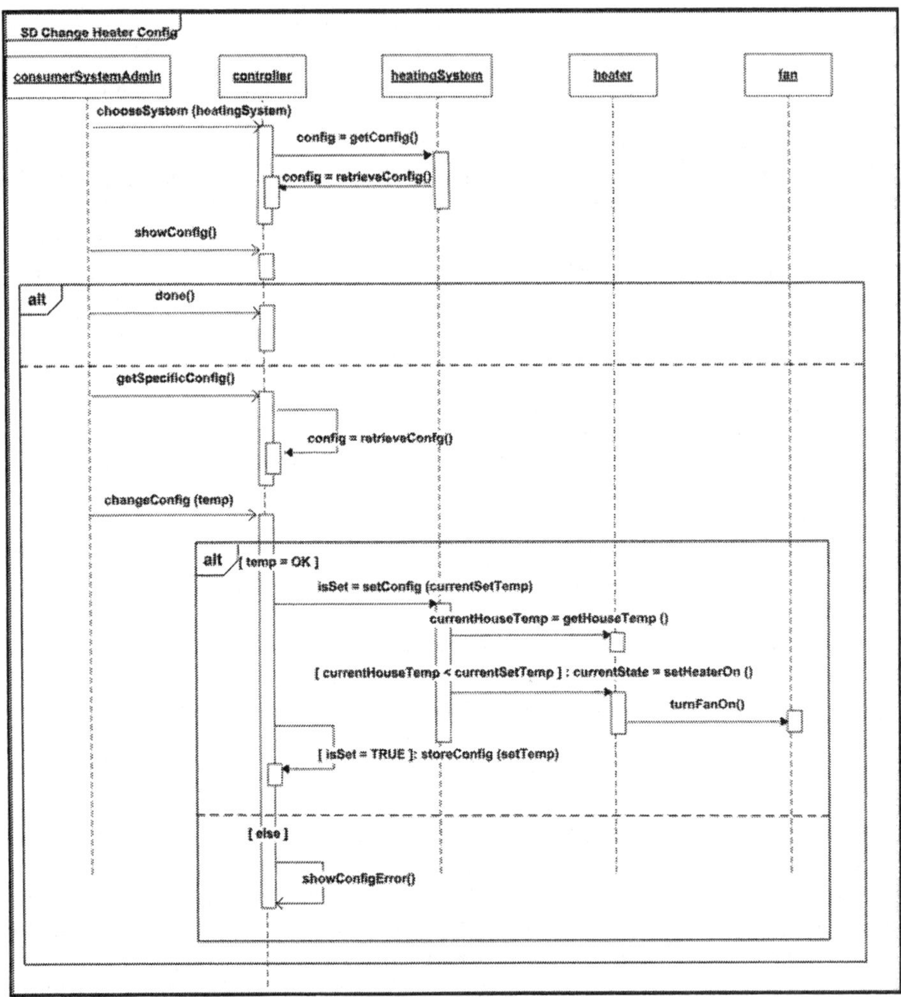

Fig. 3 Sequence diagram to change heating system configuration

Some of these generic solutions can be treated as constraints on the design, for example the consistent use of a metaphor. Sometimes generic solutions are architectural patterns, for example a 2- or 3-tier architecture. The metaphor model is a design pattern.

Not all usability generic solutions are needed for every user interaction; they do not all pertain to every use-scenario. We therefore need to be able to specify generic solutions, and also to note where specific solutions will be applied in the system. We achieve this by specifying the generic solutions as UML packages, and annotating the requirements model diagrams with references to them.

We specify generic solutions after providing more detail to them. We demonstrate this detailing using the metaphor solution. A metaphor is the mental model a user uses to interact with a system.

We also define the dynamic behavior of the metaphor as translating information that needs to be presented to the user into the terminology and preferred representation for that user, and performing the inverse of this translation for information the user is putting into the system. Constraints associated with the metaphor include the constraint that all user input and output must go through the metaphor, with appropriate translation for different users. This is the informal specification of the metaphor generic solution.

We next discuss this generic solution specification according to the notation presented in Section 2. The definition of the metaphor solution can be specified in static diagrams. Since the definition is generic, we use the template notation developed for generic aspects in our AOM research. Dynamic behavior diagrams that specify metaphor operation are specified as template sequence diagrams. Metaphor constraints are specified using natural text. These three items comprise the metaphor generic solution. If architectural structure patterns were also a part of this generic solution they would be specified using the UML architectural notation. Due to space constraints we do not show the complete package notation described in Section 2, but examples of static and behavioral diagrams are presented in Figures 4 and 5.

Figure 4 shows the major structural roles and relationships between them that are needed to add the generic metaphor solution to an application. The only addition to this static diagram over the metaphor definition discussed above is that of a *target* which is the ultimate source or sink of the information provided to or from the user.

In the smart home system, two different user types might be a consumer and the installer of a heating subsystem. The items that are to be represented during user interactions would be the controller and the elements of the heating subsystem, a thermostat (with its own controller), a heater, and a fan. The terminology would include terms for all of these items in the case of an installer, but perhaps only terms for the smart home controller, heating subsystem, and fan for a consumer. Part of the metaphor terminology mapping would include the fact that the installer concepts of heater and thermostat with its own controller are not part of the consumer concept of a heating subsystem.

Each element name in Figure 4 that is preceded by the | symbol may be mapped to a model element in the requirements model when the generic solution is applied to an application. For example, the model element |*userType* in the metaphor diagram corresponds to both the *consumerSystemAdmin* and the *consumerAnalyst* classes in the smart home requirements model shown in Figure 2. Similarly, the generic solution element |*itemsToRepresent* corresponds to the *heatingSystem* class. Finally, the |*target* generic solution element corresponds to the *controller* class. A direct communication between a user and the target is prohibited once the metaphor solution has been applied to an application. This is shown using the *<<prohibited>>* stereotype. OCL statements in Figure 4 constrain relationship multiplicities.

When a generic solution is applied to an application it must be instantiated from the template and then composed with the requirements model of the application. Composition follows the same approach as that outlined in our other aspect-oriented modeling work. See [9, 11] for details on AOM composition.

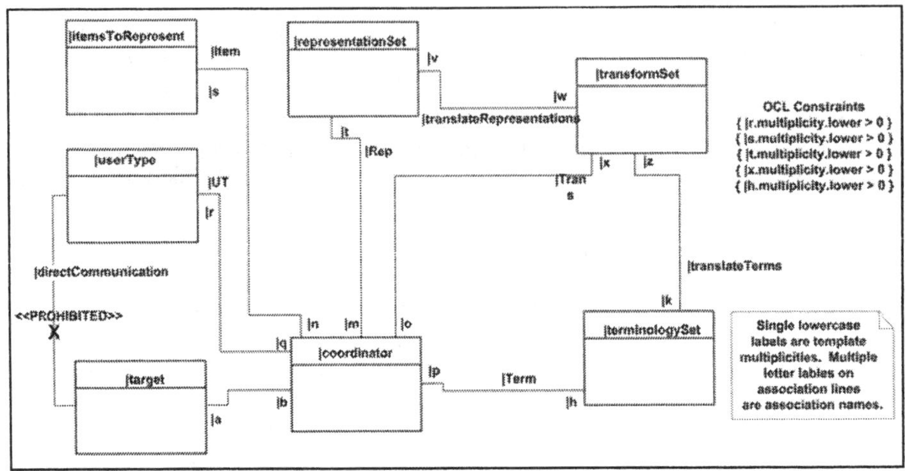

Fig. 4 Static diagram of metaphor pattern

Figure 5 shows the dynamic behavior for user input and output using the generic metaphor solution.

The sequence diagrams shown in Figure 5 also use the aspect notation developed in our previous AOM research. Model elements whose names are preceded by the | symbol may be mapped to model elements in the target application requirements sequence diagrams. The first metaphor sequence shows that input from the user is translated by the metaphor and passed onto the target. The output sequence is the inverse of this behavior. For simplicity, we have not detailed the sequence used by the metaphor in the actual translation, which includes the *|itemsToRepresent*, *|representationSet*, *|terminologySet*, and *|transformSet* elements from the structural diagram shown in Figure 4.

The constraints for the metaphor aspect are:

- all input and output between *|target* and *|userType* must pass through the metaphor
- the correct terminology must always be used for each user type
- the preferred representation set must always be used for each user type

The metaphor generic solution consists of the static and behavioral diagrams shown in Figures 4 and 5, and the constraints noted above. These constraints are specified informally using template elements and constitute the constraint package of the metaphor generic solution. This generic solution is associated with the usability requirements aspect. Other generic solutions can be similarly specified and associated with the usability requirements aspect. Since different generic solutions can be applied to different user interactions, annotations referencing these solutions can be applied to the interactions, and further aid requirements traceability.

We annotate requirements model diagrams with requirements aspect information as follows. An *A* icon is appended with the defined abbreviation of the requirements aspect. If there is a generic solution that can be applied, an abbreviation of the generic solution is added. This annotation is placed on the requirements model where it is affected by the requirements aspect. For example, we define a usability requirements aspect for the smart home system and give it the abbreviation *U*. We assign an abbreviation *m* to the metaphor generic solution. Thus, the annotation for the metaphor solution of the usability requirements aspect is *A-U-m*. Similarly, *A-U-ui*, *A-U-i*, and *A-U-o* are the annotations for the user interface, input, and output generic solutions.

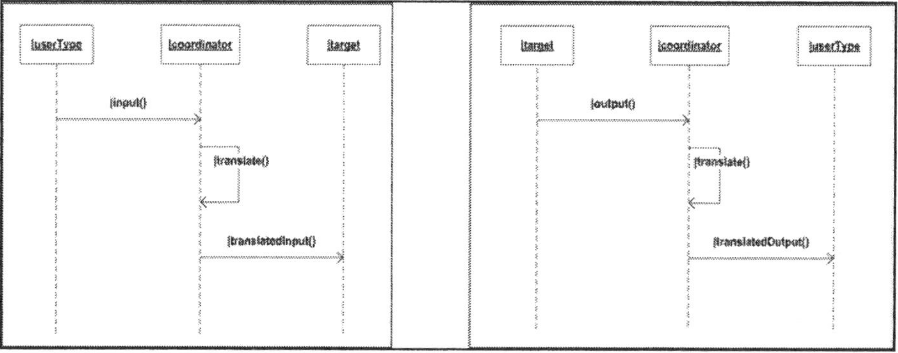

Fig. 5 Dynamic behavior of the metaphor (a) input behavior and (b) output behavior. The metaphor is a translator between user input and some portion of the target system

All user interactions between *consumerSystemAdmin* and *controller* in Fig 3 can be annotated to indicate that the metaphor pattern solution to the usability requirements aspect affects the sequence at these points. In addition, the Fig 3 sequence in *controller* that presents an error to the user (*showConfigError*) is also a point where this pattern needs to be applied. Generic solution information can also be added to the diagram as general constraints. Example constraints for the metaphor pattern are: 1) all input and output between any target and user must go through the metaphor, 2) the correct terminology must always be used for each user type, and 3) the preferred representation set must always be used for each user type.

In cases where a requirements aspect or sub-aspect can be addressed with a design pattern, such as in the case of the metaphor generic solution, this pattern can be composed with the existing requirements model in a similar fashion to that described in our work on design aspect model composition [10-12]. Aspect model composition and subsequent analysis are useful to system architects as part of the process of identifying and mitigating conflicting software concerns at the requirements level.

5 Related Work

Researchers have presented different approaches for identifying/modeling aspects at higher levels of abstraction. Several methods have been proposed for separating concerns at the design level, but very few at the requirements level. Rashid et al. [26, 27] propose an approach for modularizing cross cutting concerns. The approach involves identifying requirements using stakeholders' viewpoints, use cases/scenarios, goals or problem frames. The aim is to establish an approach that can help in conflict resolution and critical trade-offs between concerns before the architecture is derived. The approach basically uses a set of matrices consisting of the viewpoints and concerns represented in XML. The approach is supported by the Aspectual Requirements Composition and Decision support tool (ARCaDe). This is very similar to initial steps in our technique, but it does not include the generic solutions that can help in determining how to address the requirements aspect. AOM complements this work by supporting requirements aspect identification, identifying generic solutions to address requirements aspects, composition of generic solutions with requirements models to identify potential conflicts, and traceability between requirements, requirements aspects, and generic solutions.

Araujo and Coutinho [2] provide a viewpoint-oriented requirements method for managing crosscutting requirements. This is similar to the approach presented in this paper except that they consider the system as a black-box. The approach described by Araujo and Coutinho only represents use cases, whereas other types of requirements representation may be necessary. Ebert's work [7] gives a set of guidelines for specifying, measuring and tracing quality attributes namely performance, usability, reliability, and maintainability. The work is not rigorous and only shows a set of guidelines. This method does not address the problem of software concern identification.

Jacobson [15, 16] describes the development of design aspects based on use-cases, which are then composed to create different views of the system. This work maps directly to program level aspects, using the composition techniques originally developed for AspectJ [18]. Our approach is more general since we deal with software concerns from viewpoints other than end users, we address requirements that cannot easily be represented as use-cases (e.g. requirements resulting from a business context). Our composition techniques do not impose the assumptions of the AspectJ model and therefore can be used to perform a wider range of compositions (see [10] for details). We also use analysis to identify conflicts between interacting concerns, and to provide guidance in the resolution of these conflicts. This topic is not addressed in Jacobson's use-case driven aspect work.

Gray et al. [13] use aspects in domain-specific models that target embedded systems specifically. Requirements, architecture and the environment of a system are captured in the form of formal high-level models that allow representation of concerns. The work in this research can complement theirs by providing UML based approach for representing aspects, and making trade-offs. Zarate and Botella [28] use UML to represent non-functional requirements. They use stereotypes, class compartments and stereotyped dependencies to represent the non-functionality aspect and OCL to represent the constraints. The approach shows the representation of different non-functional requirements on a simple set of functionality, but it does not show a way to handle non-functional requirements that crosscut functionalities.

The subject-oriented design approach presented by Clarke et al. [5, 6] is a UML based approach similar to the AOM approach used in this research. In the subject-oriented approach every requirement is treated as a subject and a comprehensive design is obtained by composing the views provided by these subjects. Their work is more at the design level and complements our design-level AOM approach. Suzuki and Yamamoto [29] propose an extension to UML to support aspects. They describe aspects as a classifier in the meta-model. Their approach is restricted to design aspects that can be represented as aspects in an aspect-oriented program.

Mylopoulos et al. [20, 21] describe a technique called *soft-goals* that can be used to decompose requirements. Soft-goals are especially useful for refining the affects of non-functional behavior. Direct validation can be provided to show that behaviors represented by soft-goals are present in a specification. Soft-goals are useful in making trade-off decisions during design. Our method does not make trade-off decisions during requirements analysis. Instead we present best practices, and the potential interactions between them, to system architects for their consideration when creating the system architecture.

Nuseibeh [22] defines ViewPoints™ as cross-cutting, partial knowledge of the system and its environments from the perspective of different stakeholders. Nuseibeh notes challenges in composing ViewPoints™ and analyzing interactions across them. Our work is complimentary in that we use requirements aspects to locate potential interactions between requirements viewpoints and we have developed composition and analysis techniques to address these interactions.

6 Conclusions and Future Work

The issues of locating related requirements that are spread across the system, determining the software concerns they represent, specifying these concerns in an understandable way, tracing the concerns through design, and analyzing conflicts between non-orthogonal concerns need to be addressed at early stages of software development. We address these issues through the use of requirements aspects. We define requirements aspects as software concerns whose related requirements cross-cut two or more viewpoints. We presented a method called Requirements Aspect-oriented Modeling (RAM) to identify requirements aspects from viewpoint-based requirements, and to identify best practice design solutions based on domain experience. We specified generic solutions using the UML.

A simplified smart home case study that contains cross-cutting concerns was presented. Usability, availability and correctness requirements aspects were identified using the RAM method. We expanded on the usability requirements aspect using the generic solutions based on domain experience. The RAM method allows architects to identify software concerns and their generic solutions at the requirements level, which gives them a better idea about the possible design alternatives. The use of architectural patterns and constraints can result in resolution of conflicts. Although the paper has not shown the traceability to design and composition of usability aspect with the smart home system (which is possible as shown in our earlier design level AOM work), it does provide us with an approach to handle these problems.

We plan to further expand the smart home example to identify more requirements aspects and establish a concrete traceability mechanism with our design aspect-oriented modeling. We also intend to identify some architectural patterns and other generic solutions to compose with the sequence diagrams for identification and resolution of conflict resolutions.

The work presented in this paper shows that it is possible to identify aspects from requirements, and to track the relation between original requirements and their associated aspects. We are currently working to make the approach more methodical, including the issue of grouping requirements and identifying software concerns from these groupings.

References

1. J. Anderson, F. Fleek, K. Garrity, and F. Drake, "Integrating Usability Techniques Into Software Development," *IEEE Software*, vol. 18, no. 1, pp. 46-53, 2001.
2. J. Araujo and P. Coutinho, "Identifying Aspectual Use Cases Using a Viewpoint-Oriented Requirements Method," in *Early Aspects 2003: Aspect-Oriented Requirements Engineering and Architecture Design Workshop.* 2nd International Conference on Aspect-Oriented Software Development. Boston, MA, 2003.
3. S. Becker and F. Mottay, "A Global Perspective on Web Site Usability," *IEEE Software*, vol. 18, no. 1, pp. 54-61, 2001.
4. L. Chung, B. A. Nixon, E. Yu, and J. Mylopoulos, *Non-Functional Requirements in Software Engineering.* Boston, Dordrecht, London: Kluwer Academic Publishers, 2000.
5. S. Clarke, "Extending Standard UML with Model Composition Semantics," *Science of Computer Programming*, vol. 44, no. 1, July, pp. 71-100, 2002.
6. S. Clarke, W. Harrison, H. Ossher, and P. Tarr, "Separating Concerns Throughout the Development Lifecycle," in *Proceedings 3rd ECOOP Aspect-Oriented Programming Workshop*. ECOOP. Lisbon, Portugal, 1999.
7. C. Ebert, "Dealing with Nonfunctional Requirements in Large Software Systems," *Annals of Software Engineering*, vol. 3, September, pp. 367-395, 1997.
8. X. Ferre, N. Juristo, H. Windl, and L. Constantine, "Usability Basics for Software Developers," *IEEE Software*, vol. 18, no. 1, pp. 22-30, 2001.
9. R. France, I. Ray, G. Georg, and S. Ghosh, "An Aspect-Oriented Approach to Design Modeling," *IEE Software*, to be published.
10. G. Georg, R. France, and I. Ray, "Designing High Integrity Systems Using Apsects," in *Proceedings of the 5th IFIP TC-11 WG.* 11.5 Working Conference on Integrity and Internal Control in Information Systems (IICIS 2002), 2002.
11. G. Georg, R. France, and I. Ray, "Composing Aspect Models," in *4th AOSD Modeling with UML Workshop*. UML 2003. San Francisco, CA, October, 2003.
12. G. Georg, I. Ray, and R. France, "Using Aspects to Design a Secure System." Proceedings of the 8th IEEE International Conference on Engineering of Complex Computer Systems (ICECCS 2002). Greenbelt, MD, 2002.

13. J. Gray, T. Bapty, S. Neema, and J. Tuck, "Handling Cross-Cutting Constraints in Domain-Specific Modelling," *Communications of the ACM*, vol. 44, no. 10, October, pp. 87-93, 2001.
14. M. Jackson, *Problem Frames*. Addison-Wesley, 2001.
15. I. Jacobson, "Case for Aspects – Part I", *Software Development Magazine*, October, pp 32-37, 2003.
16. I. Jacobson, "Case for Aspects – Part II", *Software Development Magazine*, November, pp 42-48, 2003.
17. N. Juristo, H. Windl, and L. Constantine, "Introducing Usability," *IEEE Software*, vol. 18, no. 1, pp. 20-21, 2001.
18. G. Kiczales, E. Hilsdale, J. Hugunin, M. Kersten, J. Palm, W. Griswold, "Getting Started with AspectJ", *Communications of the ACM*, vol. 44, no. 10, October, pp 59-65, 2001.
19. G. Kotonya and I. Sommerville, "Requirements Engineering with Viewpoints," *IEE Software Engineering Journal*, vol. 11, no. 1, pp. 5-18, 1998.
20. J. Mylopoulos, L. Chung, and B. Nixon, "Representing and Using Nonfunctional Requirements: A Process-Oriented Approach," *IEEE Transactions on Software Engineering*, vol. 18, no. 6, June, pp. 483-497, 1992.
21. J. Mylopoulos, L. Chung, and E. Yu, "From Object-Oriented to Goal-Oriented Requirements Analysis," *Communications of the ACM*, vol. 42, no. 1, January, pp. 31-37, 1999.
22. B. Nuseibeh, "Crosscutting Requirements", in *Proceedings of the 3rd International Conference on Aspect-Oriented Software Development (AOSD 2004)*, Lancaster, UK, 2004.
23. OMG, "Response to the UML 2.0 OCL RfP," 1/7/2003, 2003.
24. OMG, "UML 2.0 Infrastructure Specification," Http://www.omg.org/docs/ptc/03-09-15.pdf, 9/15/2003, 2003.
25. OMG, "UML 2.0 Superstructure Specification," Http://www.omg.org/docs/ptc/03-08-02.pdf, 8/2/2003, 2003.
26. A. Rashid, A. Moreira, and J. Araujo, "Modularization and Composition of Aspectual Requirements." 2nd International Conference on Aspect-Oriented Software Development. Boston, MA: ACM, 2003, pp. 11-20.
27. A. Rashid, P. Sawyer, A. Moreira, and J. Araujo, "Early Aspects: A Model for Aspect-Oriented Requirements Engineering." IEEE Joint International Conference on Requirements Engineering. Essen, Germany, 2002, pp. 199-202.
28. G. Salazar-Zarate and P. Botella, "Use of UML for Non-Functional Aspects." 13th International Conference Software and Systems Engineering and Their Applications (ICSSEA 2000). Paris, France, 2000.
29. J. Suzuki and Y. Yamamoto, "Extending UML with Aspects: Aspect Support in the Design Phase," in *Proceedings 3rd ECOOP Aspect-Oriented Programming Workshop.* ECOOP. Lisbon, Portugal, 1999.

A UML Profile to Model Mobile Systems

Vincenzo Grassi, Raffaela Mirandola, and Antonino Sabetta

Università di Roma "Tor Vergata", Italy

Abstract. The introduction of adaptation features in the design of applications that operate in a mobile computing environment has been suggested as a viable solution to cope with the high heterogeneity and variability of this environment. Mobile code paradigms can be used to this purpose, since they allow to dynamically modify the load of the hosting nodes and the internode traffic, to adapt to the resources available in the nodes and to the condition of the (often wireless) network link. In this paper we propose a UML profile to deal with all the relevant issues of a mobile system, concerning the mobility of both physical (e.g. computing nodes) and logical (e.g. software components) entities. The profile is defined as a lightweight customization of the UML 2.0 metamodel, so remaining fully compliant with it. In the definition of this profile, the underlying idea has been to model mobility (in both physical and logical sense) as a feature that can be "plugged" into a pre-existing architecture, to ease the modelling of both different physical mobility scenarios, and of different adaptation strategies based on code mobility. Besides defining the profile, we give some examples of use of its features.

Keywords: mobile computing, code mobility, UML profile.

1 Introduction

Mobile computing applications have generally to cope with a highly heterogeneous environment, characterized by a large variance in both the computing capacity of the hosting nodes (that span portable devices and powerful fixed hosts) and in the available communication bandwidth, that can range from tens of Kbps to tens of Mbps, depending on the type of wireless or wired network [12]. Moreover, these environment conditions can also rapidly change because of the physical mobility, that can cause a mobile node to connect to different nodes, or to enter zones covered by different wireless networks, or not covered at all.

As a consequence, mobile computing applications should be designed so that they are able to adapt to their execution environment, to successfully cope with the problems caused by its high heterogeneity and variability. In this respect, mobile code paradigms and technologies can be exploited to devise possible adaptation strategies [7], for instance by dynamically modifying the current deployment of the application components, to better exploit the new communication and computing features that have become available.

T. Baar et al. (Eds.): UML 2004, LNCS 3273, pp. 128–142, 2004.

The main goal of this paper is to provide a modeling framework for mobile computing applications, where both the *physical* mobility of the computing nodes and the *logical* mobility of software elements are taken into account, since both kinds of mobility deserve consideration, for the reasons explained above. However we would like to remark that, even though our focus is on mobile computing where both physical and logical mobility are present, logical mobility is a valuable design paradigm also in other fields (e.g. wide area distributed applications [7]). To enhance the usability of our framework, we have defined it as a UML 2.0 lightweight extension, exploiting the Profile mechanisms, so remaining fully compliant with the UML 2.0 metamodel [3].

For what concerns the modeling of the physical and logical mobility, we would like to point out that they play different roles from the viewpoint of a mobile computing application designer. Indeed, physical mobility is an environment feature that is generally out of the control of the designer; in other words, it is a sort of constraint he has to deal with, to meet the application requirements. On the other hand, logical mobility is really a tool in his hands, that he can exploit to better adapt the application to the environment where it will be deployed. Despite this basic difference, we have adopted a common approach in modeling them, based on a clear separation of concerns between, on one hand, the models of the application logic and of the platform where the application will be eventually deployed and, on the other hand, the models of the logical and physical mobility. The underlying motivation has been to look at mobility (both physical and logical) as a feature that can be "plugged" into the system model, to support, for example, "what if" experiments concerning a mobile computing environment: for a given application logic and deployment environment (with possible physical mobility), what happens if different mobile code based adaptation strategies are plugged into the application? what if the physical mobility does change?

Note that, of course, "what happens" should be defined in terms of some observable application property (e.g. some performance measure). In this respect, we would like to remark that we have adopted a minimal approach in our modeling framework, including in it only aspects strictly related to mobility. We do not have included in it the modeling of other aspects that could be relevant in a given analysis domain (for example, resource features and utilization to be used for performance analysis). Depending on the type of analysis one is interested in, our modeling framework should be integrated with other modeling frameworks (e.g. the UML "Profile for Schedulability, Performance and Time Specification" in the case of performance analysis [2]).

The representation of mobility in computer systems has been treated in a number of work in the past. Some of them tackled this issue using UML based approaches [9, 4], while others have adopted more formal and rigorously defined frameworks [10, 11, 6, 5].

For what concerns the former approaches, the proposal in [9] requires a non-standard extension of UML sequence diagrams; on the other hand the proposal in [4] extends the UML class and activity diagrams allowing the representation of mobile objects and locations as well as basic primitives such as moving or cloning.

In this work both the mobility model (how objects move) and the computational model (which kind of computation they perform) are represented within the same activity diagram.

For what concerns the latter approaches, they in general provide useful insights for mobility related modeling problems, but the non widespread diffusion of the formal notations they are based on limits their direct use in real modeling problems.

The paper is organized as follows: in the next section we start identifying the key aspects that deserve to be modeled in mobile systems, introducing some conceptual schemata and a reference framework. In section 3 we define the profile modeling elements while in section 4 we give some examples to show how the profile and the conceptual guidelines sketched in section 2 can be used. Moreover in section 5 we use the profile to model some basic mobile code paradigms. Finally, in section 6 we draw some conclusions and outline a few interesting issues that could be the subject for further investigation and future works.

2 Modeling Mobile Systems

We are interested in devising a framework that gives the application designer the possibility of extending a basic model of a computer (software) system by adding or removing mobility at will, in order to experiment with different environment characteristics and design solutions since the earliest phases of the design process. In order to do so, we have to clearly define the following issues:

- how to model the movement of an entity;
- which entities move;
- what causes the movement of an entity.

Note that the above issues apply to both physical and logical mobility; hence, as far as possible, we will adopt a common approach to model them.

For what concerns the first issue, we believe that any attempt to represent movements requires that an underlying concept of location be defined. In our framework we model this concept as a relationship that binds two entities so that one acts as a container for the other, thus we will say that the latter is located in the former. We have derived from [5] the basic idea of modeling locations as nesting relationships among entities. However, with respect to the simple (and elegant) unifying model of [5], we have implemented in two different ways this idea for physical and logical mobility as shown in section 3, to remain compliant with the UML metamodel, trading off simplicity and elegance with usability. Given this basic model of location, a movement is modeled as a change in the relationship between a mobile entity and its container.

With regard to the second issue, both logical and physical mobile entities must be considered. A logical mobile entity can be, in principle, any kind of software artifact (run time entity), intended as the manifestation of a software component (design time entity) whose location can be an execution environment or a computing node.

On the other hand, the physical mobile entities can be computing nodes (and the execution environments inside them) whose location is a *place* (such as a building, a room or a vehicle). Places themselves can be mobile and can be located in other places (e.g. a car, which can be considered as a place on its own right, can be located inside a building) so that possibly complex hierarchical topologies can be conceived.

Any movement, either of a physical or a logical entity, should be constrained by a simple principle: it can happen only if the location where the moving entity currently is and the destination location are connected by a channel. Since this concept is so generic and abstract, the idea of a channel can be easily mapped, in a very intuitive way, onto different types of mobility. For instance a network link between two workstations can be described as a channel interconnecting two execution environments so that, under certain conditions, the software components located in one of the two workstations can flow across the channel and migrate towards the other workstation thus realizing software mobility. Similarly a corridor between two rooms can be thought of as a channel that allows a mobile device, such as a PDA (i.e. an execution environment) to move from one room to the other. It is important to observe that in this latter example the mobility of an execution environment, which is rendered explicitly, implies that all the software elements contained by the migrating entity move together with it.

Up to now, we have discussed issues concerning the phenomenology of mobility (how we can model the manifestation of a mobile behavior), but we have not tackled the description of what causes and triggers mobility. Our idea is to model this latter issue by means of the *mobility manager* concept whose main purpose is to encapsulate all the logic of mobility, separating it from the application logic. A mobility manager is characterized by the ability to perceive changes in its "environment" (which can be composed of both physical and software elements) and reacts to them by firing mobility activities, whose effect is to cause a movement (location change) of some mobile entity. We adopt this same concept for both physical and logical mobility. Note that, in principle, a mobility manager should be mainly intended as a modeling facility, that could not directly correspond to some specific entity in a real implementation of the system we are modeling, or whose responsibilities may be shared by several different entities; its modeling utility actually consists in providing an easily identifiable entity where we encapsulate the logic that drives mobility. This separation of concerns implies that different mobility managers, each modeling a different mobility policy, can be modularly plugged into some physical environment or software application model so that different environment dynamics and/or adaptation policies can be experimented.

The fundamental difference between mobility managers modeling physical and logical mobility is that the former are models of some existing physically observable behavior which is not modifiable by the software designer, whereas the latter are meant to model behaviors which are completely under the control of the designer, and that can be devised to realize some mobility based adaptation strategy.

3 The Profile

After the domain oriented survey of architectural and mobile code concepts provided in the previous section, we turn now to the very UML viewpoint focusing on the mapping of those concepts onto the UML metamodel. Here we define the semantics of the proposed extensions that build up the profile.

3.1 Place

Semantics and Rationale. The *Place* stereotype extends the metaclass *Node* and represents both the concept of location as delimited by concrete or administrative boundaries and the physical entities located in it (see figure 1). Examples of places are computing nodes, buildings, vehicles, rooms, persons and so on. Places can be nested (e.g. a building can contain rooms, which in turn can contain PCs).

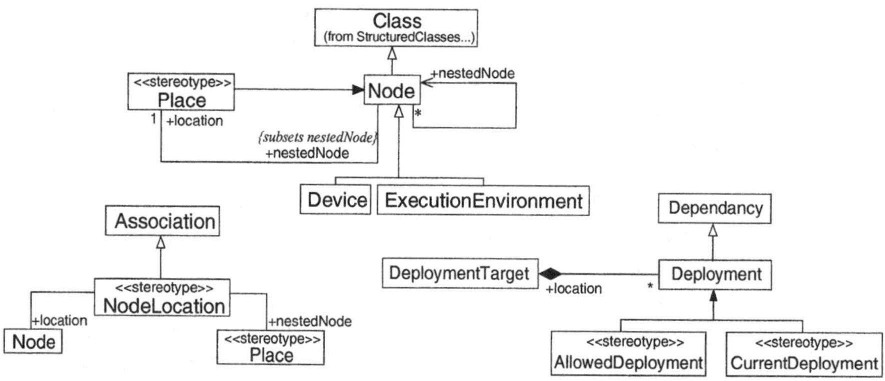

Fig. 1. UML metamodel fragment and some of the stereotypes introduced with the profile

3.2 NodeLocation

Semantics and Rationale. This stereotype is applied to associations that are defined between Nodes and Places, and it is used to express the location of Nodes (see figure 1). The Place that is attached to the *location* end of a *NodeLocation* association represents the location of the Node at the opposite end (nestedNode).

The profile supports the specification of activities that modify the value of the location of a given Node (see *MoveActivity* below).

3.3 MobileElement

Semantics and Rationale. This stereotype is used to mark an element as mobile. In particular a Place can be a MobileElement. The location of *MobileElements* can be changed by means of *MoveActivities*.

3.4 MobileCode

Semantics and Rationale. This stereotype is a specialization of *MobileElement.* It can be applied to components, classifiers, artifacts or other software level elements to specify that they can be treated as a piece of mobile code and as such can be copied and/or moved and possibly executed in different execution environments.

3.5 CurrentDeployment

Semantics and Rationale. This stereotype extends the semantics of the Deployment metaclass and specifies the deployment target where an artifact is currently deployed to.

The profile supports the specification of activities that modify the value of the *CurrentDeployment* of a given entity (see *MoveActivity* below).

3.6 AllowedDeployment

Semantics and Rationale. This stereotype extends the semantics of the Deployment metaclass and specifies which deployment targets are allowed for a MobileCode element. Such multiple specification is used to declare which locations a mobile component can be deployed to.

This stereotype can be used to introduce additional constraints on the mobility of a mobile software artifact, to reflect, for example, administrative or security related policies, besides those defined by the physical existence of channels between the execution environments that are the origin and the destination of a movement.

3.7 MobilityManager

Semantics and Rationale. The stereotype *MobilityManager* can be applied to state machines which are meant to control physical or logical mobility. The initial state of the state machine is entered as soon as the system is started.

Transitions are labeled with a guard condition (in square brackets) and with the name of an event (e.g. the execution of an activity). A transition is fired when the event specified by the label occurs, provided that the guard condition is satisfied. An activity that operates on one or more *MobileElements* can be associated to each state or transition of a mobility manager. Such an activity can be defined, in general, as a suitable composition of the activities listed below (3.8 - 3.13).

3.8 MoveActivity

Semantics and Rationale. The MoveActivity stereotype can be applied to activities whose execution results in a migration (i.e. change of location) of a MobileElement. Typically a MoveActivity receives in input the MobileElement and its destination location; when the activity is performed, the MobileElement is located in the specified location.

The concept of "being located" is represented differently for logical entities (i.e. Artifacts that manifest a software component or a class) and physical entities (i.e. hardware nodes or physical ambients), so the low level effect of the application of a MoveActivity is different according to the type of MobileElement it is invoked for (we call such element the *subject* of the migration). For physical mobile elements (i.e. Nodes) this is done by changing the association (stereotyped as *NodeLocation*) with their container Place, whereas for logical elements it is realized updating the *CurrentDeployment* dependency.

Constraints

1. Only MobileElements can be the subject of a MoveActivity
2. If the subject is a *MobileCode* element, the destination must be an allowed ExecutionEnvironment for it, i.e. an AllowedDeployment dependency must exist between the logical (mobile) element and the destination location.
3. A MoveActivity cannot act on MobileElements if a proper CommunicationPath (what is called a "channel" in section 2) does not connect the starting and the destination locations.

3.9 BeforeMoveActivity

Semantics and Rationale. The stereotype *BeforeMoveActivity* is used to define activities that are performed in order to prepare a *MobileCode* element to be copied or moved.

Examples of *BeforeMoveActivites* are the serialization of a component in a form that is suitable for transfer, the handling of bindings to resources or local data, encryption of confidential data that must cross untrusted channels and other preliminary tasks.

3.10 AfterMoveActivity

Semantics and Rationale. This stereotype is used for activities that operate on a *MobileCode* element right after its migration to a new execution environment. An *AfterMoveActivity* must follow a *MoveActivity*. Examples of operations that are good candidates to be stereotyped as *AfterMoveActivities* are those related to regenerate out of a serialized transferrable form a component that is capable to be run again. Other tasks that can be classified as *AfterMoveActivities* encompass handling of bindings to resources needed for proper operation of the migrated component in its new execution environment, recreating data structures and execution context that the component expects to find upon resuming, and so on.

3.11 AbortMoveActivity

Semantics and Rationale. The stereotype AbortMoveActivity is used to specify an activity whose execution aborts a migration that was formerly prepared by the invocation of a *BeforeMoveActivity.*

3.12 AllowDeploymentActivity

Semantics and Rationale. An *AllowDeploymentActivity* is a *CreateLinkActivity* that adds a deployment to the set of allowed deployments for a given *DeployedArtifact.*

3.13 DenyDeploymentActivity

Semantics and Rationale. This stereotype is complementary to *AllowDeploymentActivity* and can be used to mark activities that remove a deployment from the set of allowed deployments for a given *DeployedArtifact* (which means that any former AllowedDeployment of the same Artifact to the specified target is removed).

4 The Profile in Practice: Some Examples

In the following we give some simple examples to clarify the practical aspects of using the proposed profile, showing how to realize models of both structural and behavioral aspects of systems characterized by different forms of mobility. Anyway we remark that, since the profile is not supposed to force practitioners to follow a particular modeling methodology, these examples are only meant to give a few hints, not normative prescriptions.

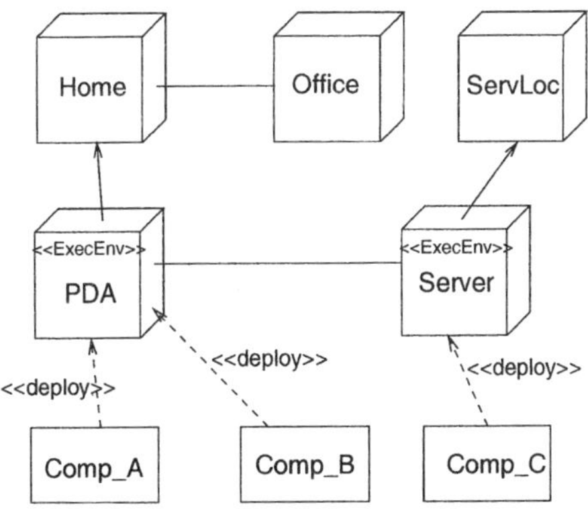

Fig. 2. Static system model

In the provided examples we refer to a basic system model depicted in figure 2; this model represents a "static" system where components deployment and nodes location are fixed. Then, we separately show how to use the profile to plug physical and logical mobility into this static model.

4.1 Modeling Physical Mobility

First of all we introduce in the basic example the provision for physical mobility. Dynamic topological models can be valuable in studying the software application behavior when the physical environment, e.g. the placement of locations and consequently the connectivity conditions, are subject to change.

If we want to allow the representation of physical mobility we need to enable hosts themselves and places to be contained in other places in a dynamically changing hierarchical structure composed of elements that are possibly nested and where the hosts are considered as *contained* entities themselves and not only as containers for software entities.

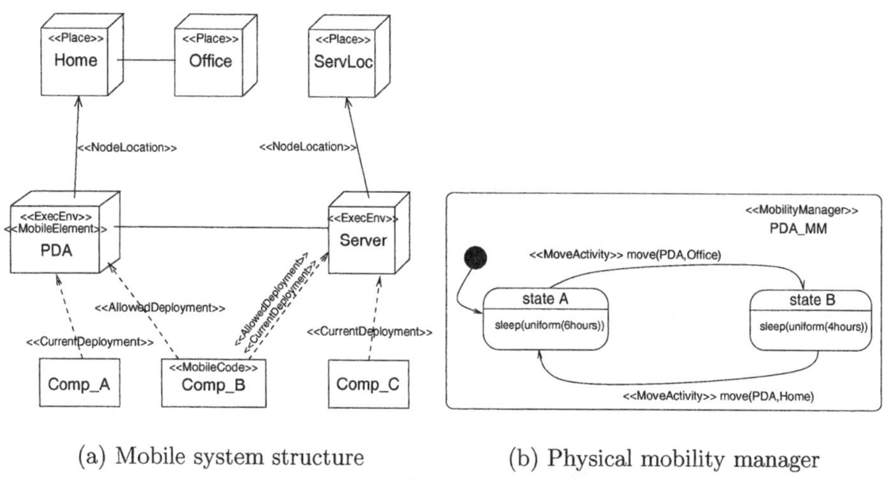

(a) Mobile system structure (b) Physical mobility manager

Fig. 3. Mobile system model

For the example of figure 2, figure 3 shows how we can plug into it physical mobility. Note that figure 3 also shows profile elements related to logical mobility, but we ignore them in this section.

As we can see, the PDA execution environment has been stereotyped as a *MobileElement*; since a link (modeling the channel concept of section 2) connects the Home and Office places, the PDA is enabled to move between them. Its actual mobility pattern is modeled by the mobility manager *PDA_MM* depicted in figure 3-b.

Note that, with respect to figure 2, figure 3 actually depicts a snapshot of one of the numerous allowed configurations. In the case of physical entities the only constraints to such configurations are enforced by the links that connect the nodes.

4.2 Modeling Code Mobility

As defined in the profile, the formal specification of a mobility manager modeling logical mobility does not basically differ from the definition of a mobility manager modeling physical mobility: also in this case, it consists of a state machine, whose state transitions are triggered by the occurrence of events, possibly conditioned by some guard condition. In the case of logical mobility, typical events triggering a transition are "internal" events of the software application (e.g. sending a message, completing an activity) or "external" events such as a modification of the application execution environment (e.g. a physical movement of a mobile host that causes a change in the available communication bandwidth).

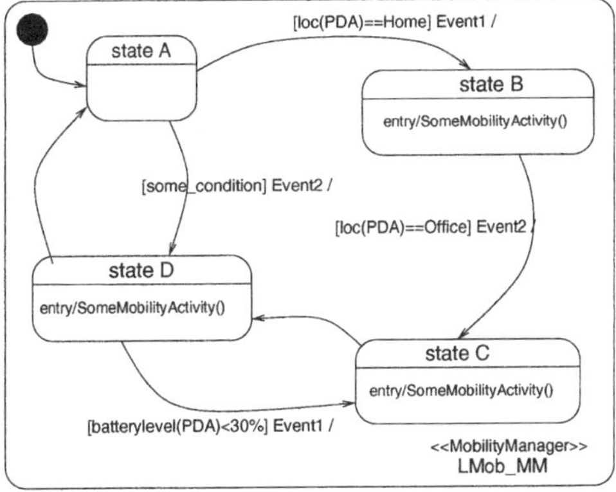

Fig. 4. Example of a logical mobility manager

As already remarked in section 2, the fundamental difference of logical mobility modeling with respect to physical mobility is that in the latter case the designer is forced to define a state machine modeling some given physical behavior (as the example in figure 3-b), while in the former he can freely select the states, the triggering events and the guard conditions to define some suitable code mobility based adaptation policy. This policy will be "implemented" by the code mobility activities dispatched by the state machine as a consequence of a state transition. In figure 3-a the Comp_B component has been labeled as *MobileCode* and two *AllowedDeployments* have been associated with it, so that any code mobility policy can move Comp_B between these two locations. In more complex settings, specifying within the same diagram the current location as well as the potential deployments for every mobile element could clutter the model. If this is the case, it might be more effective to use different diagrams to provide separate views for the possible and current deployments. Figure 4 shows an example of mobility manager that applies to the Comp_B mobile component implementing a given logical mobility policy. This mobility manager causes the migration of Comp_B when some (non specified here) events (Event1 and Event2) occur. The state transitions (and hence the Comp_B migration) also depend on some environmental conditions (in this example, battery level and PDA location). The migration of Comp_B is realized by a code mobility activity associated, in figure 4, to the states of the mobility manager.

As explained in section 3 the mobility activities dispatched by the mobility manager can be specified as a suitable composition of the basic activities defined in the profile (3.8-3.13). In this perspective some basic mobile code paradigms that can be used to implement a code mobility based adaptation policy have been identified in the literature, namely the Code on Demand (COD), Remote Evaluation (REV) and Mobile Agent (MA) paradigms [7]. In the next section we show how these paradigms and their introduction into an otherwise static application can be modeled, using our profile, by:

- a suitable definition of the event that triggers a state transition of some mobility manager;
- the code mobility activity dispatched by this state transition.

Before describing these paradigms and their models according to our profile, we would like to remark that modelers can refine in different ways a code mobility activity, by defining customized variants of the basic mobile code paradigms, for example adding special application-specific activities to the pre/post phases of code migrations.

5 Models of Basic Mobile Code Paradigms

The COD and REV paradigms can be defined as "location-aware" extensions of the basic "location-unaware" client-server (CS) interaction paradigm. Indeed, in the CS case, we have some software component that invokes an operation implemented by some other software entity; the operation result is then sent back to the caller. This interaction pattern is depicted by the activity diagram fragment of figure 5, and is realized independently of the location of the two partners, that does not change during the interaction.[1]

In the COD case, upon invocation of the operation, if the artifact that implements the operation is remotely located, a copy of it is first moved to the caller location and then executed. This interaction pattern can be modeled by

[1] Note that in this and in the following figures we give a different meaning to the activity diagram swimlanes, grouping in each swimlane activities performed within the same location, rather than by the same component (something similar is also used in [4]).

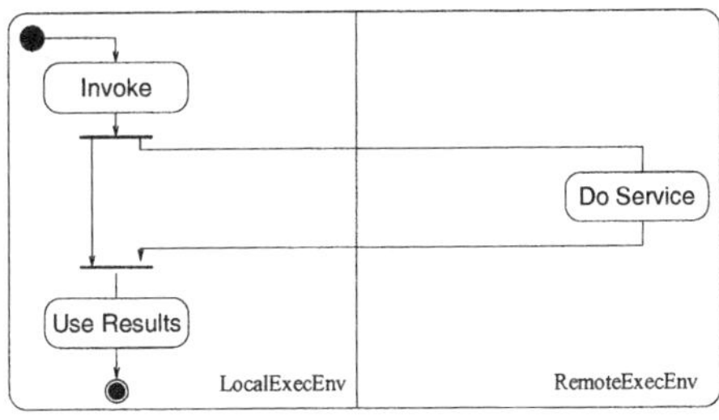

Fig. 5. Model of the Client/Server paradigm

defining the triggering event of the mobility manager as the operation invocation, possibly conditioned by some other guard condition (see figure 6-b), while the dispatched mobility action is the sequence of activities shown in figure 6-a surrounded by a dashed line. Figure 6-a also shows the whole activity diagram fragment obtained by plugging the COD paradigm into the basic CS interaction pattern of figure 5.

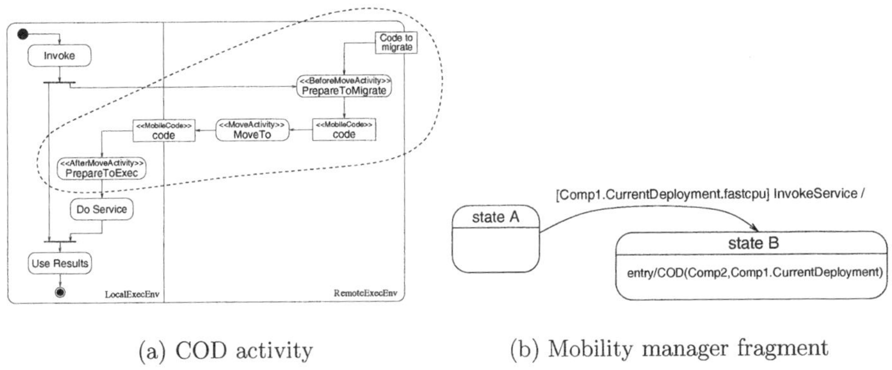

(a) COD activity

(b) Mobility manager fragment

Fig. 6. Model of the Code On Demand paradigm

Conversely, in the REV case, upon invocation of a locally available software artifact, a copy of it is first sent to a specified remote location, where it is executed. In this case the triggering event is again the operation invocation (see figure 7-b), while, analogously to figure 6-a, the corresponding sequence of activities and the result of plugging them into the basic CS pattern are shown in figure 7-a.

Finally, in the MA paradigm an active software component moves with its state, at some point of its execution, to a different location where it will resume its execution. In this case the triggering event in the mobility manager can be

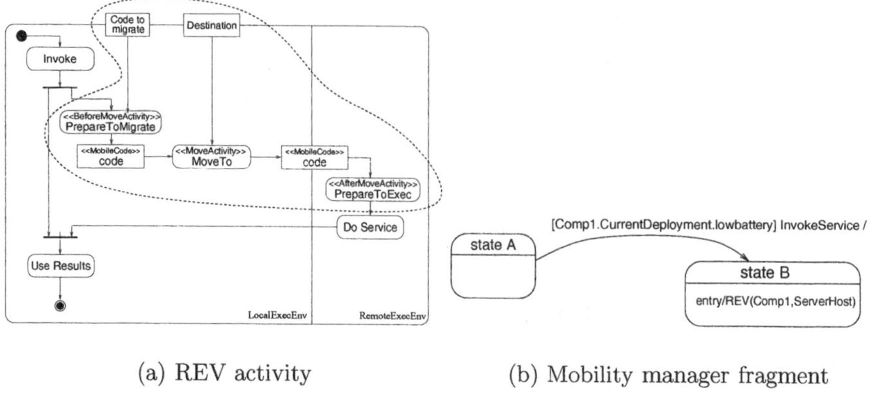

(a) REV activity

(b) Mobility manager fragment

Fig. 7. Model of the Remote Evaluation paradigm

any suitable event occurring in the application or its environment (according to some mobility policy the designer wants to model).

Figure 8-a shows an activity diagram modeling the behavior of some component, while figure 8-b shows the result of plugging into it the MA paradigm triggered by the mobility manager fragment depicted in figure 8-c.

6 Conclusion

We have defined a UML profile to deal with the fundamental aspects of mobile systems. One of the main goals that have driven the definition of this profile has been to look at mobility as a feature that can be easily added to a pre-existing model, to get (in the case of physical mobility) a more realistic and complete representation of the physical system that is modeled, and to allow (in the case of logical mobility) the easy experimentation of different code mobility based adaptation policies. An additional goal has been to remain fully compliant with the UML 2.0 metamodel. To meet these goals, we have modeled the location of physical and logical entities as suitable extensions of the *NodeNesting* and *Deployment* relationships defined in the UML 2.0 metamodel; moreover, we have introduced the concept of *Mobility Manager* to encapsulate the "logic" that drives the modifications of such relationships, thus modeling entities movement, keeping it separate from the model of the application logic.

Even though the profile proved to be good enough to express simple mobility scenarios and to model well established mobile code paradigms, nonetheless it requires further effort to validate its soundness and scalability with respect to real-life modeling needs. A preliminary test-bench for such an evaluation can be found in [8] where we elaborate on the proposed framework to make performance predictions in the context of a more complex case study.

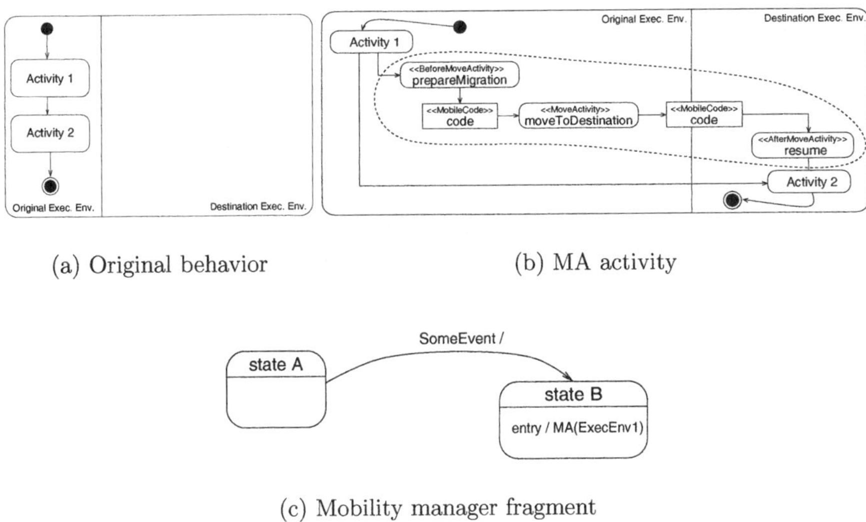

(a) Original behavior (b) MA activity

(c) Mobility manager fragment

Fig. 8. Model of the Mobile Agent paradigm

We would like to point out that this vision of mobility as a feature to be added to a pre-existing model can also be seen in a MDA perspective [1], where a basic (location and movement unaware) PIM is transformed into a "high level" (location and movement aware) PSM, where some assumptions are made about the platform where the software application will be deployed (the software components location), and about some software infrastructure enabling code mobility. This high level PSM can then be further refined to get a more detailed PSM corresponding to some specific platform and mobile code technology (e.g. Java based).

As a future work we plan to consider the full integration into a MDA framework of our modeling approach, and its extension to other kinds of adaptation, with the similar goal of supporting the experimentation with different adaptation policies.

References

[1] Model driven architecture. *OMG Technical report, http://cgi.omg.org/docs/ormsc/01-07-01.pdf*, July 2001.

[2] Uml profile for schedulability, performance, and time specification. *http://cgi.omg.org/docs/ptc/02-03-02.pdf*, 2002.

[3] *UML Superstructure 2.0 - Draft Adopted Specification (ptc/03-08-02).* OMG, 2003.

[4] H. Baumeister, N. Koch, P. Kosiuczenko, and M. Wirsing. Extending activity diagrams to model mobile systems. In *NetObject-Days 2002 (M. Aksit, M. Mezini, R. Unland Eds.), LNCS 2591*, pages 278–293, 2003.

[5] L. Cardelli and A. D. Gordon. Mobile ambients. In *Foundations of Software Science and Computational Structures (M. Nivat ed.), LNCS 1378*, pages 140–155. Springer-Verlag, 1998.

[6] R. De Nicola, G. Ferrari, R. Pugliese, and B. Venneri. Klaim: a kernel language for agents interaction and mobility. *IEEE Trans. on Software Engineering*, 24(5):315–333, May 1998.

[7] A. Fuggetta, G. P. Picco, and G. Vigna. Understanding code mobility. *IEEE Trans. on Software Eng.*, 24(5):342–361, May 1998.

[8] V. Grassi, R. Mirandola, and A. Sabetta. UML based modeling and performance analisys of mobile systems. *Technical Report, Universit di Roma "Tor Vergata" (submitted)*, July 2004.

[9] P. Kosiuczenko. Sequence diagrams for mobility. In *Proc. of MobIMod Workshop (J. Krogstie editor), Tampere, Finland*, October 2003.

[10] R. Milner. *Communicating and Mobile Systems: the π-calculus.* Cambridge University Press, 1999.

[11] G. P. Picco, G.-C. Roman, and P. McCann. Reasoning about code mobility in mobile unity. *ACM Trans. on Software Engineering and Methodology*, 10(3):338–395, July 2001.

[12] U. Varshney and R. Vetter. Emerging mobile and wireless networks. *Communications of ACM*, 43(6):73–81, June 2000.

Experimental Evaluation of the UML Profile for Schedulability, Performance, and Time

Andrew J. Bennett[1], A.J. Field[1], and C. Murray Woodside[2]

[1] Department of Computing,
Imperial College London,
London SW7 2AZ, United Kingdom
[2] Department of Systems and Computer Engineering,
Carleton University,
Ottawa K1S 5BG, Canada

Abstract. We present a performance engineering methodology based upon the construction and solution of performance models generated mechanically from UML sequence diagrams, annotated using the UML Profile for Schedulability, Performance and Time (SPT). The target platform for the performance analysis is the Labelled Transition System Analyser (LTSA) tool which supports model solution via discrete-event simulation. Simultaneously, LTSA allows functional properties of a system to be explored formally, and we show how this can be used to detect functional anomalies, such as unnecessary sequentialisation and deadlock, prior to analysing the performance aspects of a system. The approach is evaluated with reference to a case study – a simple robot-based manufacturing system. The main objective is to explore the ways in which UML, the SPT profile and the LTSA tool can be used to design systems that satisfy specified behavioural and performance properties, through successive refinement.

1 Introduction

Many modern software systems have performance requirements that must be met in order for them to be commercially viable. Due to the difficulty of building such systems, performance issues such as response times, scalability and resource usage are often largely ignored until a prototype has been built that can be tested under controlled loads. It may be possible to resolve any performance problems found at this stage by making small, targeted code changes. However, some performance characteristics are determined much earlier in the development cycle, and therefore the resolution of performance problems may require major changes to the architecture and design of the system, resulting in project delays and cost overruns. This has been documented by Smith [1].

In this paper we explore a design methodology that involves mechanically building performance models, in the form of stochastic process algebra programs, from UML sequence diagrams annotated using the UML Profile for Schedulability, Performance and Time (the SPT profile). These models can be analysed

T. Baar et al. (Eds.): UML 2004, LNCS 3273, pp. 143–157, 2004.

using conventional tools in order to establish functional correctness of the design and to verify that the design satisfies stated performance requirements. The process algebra itself does not need to be understood by the user, however; it merely provides the link between the UML and the underlying analysis tool.

The analysis tool we use in this paper is the Labelled Transition System Analyser (LTSA) tool [2], which is widely used to support the teaching of concurrency. The underlying process algebra supported by LTSA is FSP (Finite-State Processes) which is described in detail in [2]. This has recently been extended to support probabilistic choice and time delays and the LTSA has been extended to analyse stochastic FSP programs via discrete-event simulation [3].

The main objective of this paper is to explore the methodology and the application of the associated tools in the context of a worked example. We are not so much concerned with the detailed workings of the application, but rather the mechanics of how UML models can be constructed and later refined in the light of functional- and performance-related insights gained from the analysis of behaviour/performance models derived mechanically from the UML with SPT annotations. We found that the analysis is both straightforward and helpful in understanding the design.

The idea of building performance models from UML is by no means new. Several approaches have been explored in the literature using customised performance annotations and/or extensions to UML itself. In [4], UML statecharts and collaboration diagrams are used to derive performance models in the language PEPA – a stochastic process algebra. In [5] statecharts are again used, but these are extended with additional nodes representing probabilistic choice and events (actions) are additionally decorated with time delays. The modified statecharts that result essentially define a form of stochastic automaton that can be analysed by discrete-event simulation, or by a Markov analyser in specific cases. Various combinations of UML statecharts, activity diagrams and sequence diagrams have also been extensively studied as the basis of a performance modelling strategy based on stochastic Petri nets, as detailed in [6, 7, 8], for example.

Statecharts provide a fairly direct route to a performance model by virtue of their close correspondence with labelled transition systems, but they are not typically the formalism of choice for modellers. A more intuitive description of behaviour comes from sequence diagrams which define specific scenarios. Importantly, we are interested in studying systems very early in the development process, where the system is most easily expressed using only scenarios.

Sequence diagrams have been explored extensively for describing functional properties of a system, for example [9], and more recently for the extraction of performance models [10] in the form of layered queueing models. The more general issue of how to use the approach to optimise the design of real systems was explored separately in [11]. This represents the first study of a performance engineering methodology based on UML, the SPT profile and an underlying performance model generator and solver.

Like [11] we explore the role of sequence diagrams and the SPT profile, but the focus is on the added value of the underlying process algebra formalism and, specifically, the role of tools such as the LTSA to effect the combined behavioural and performance analyses. We are particularly interested in the mechanics of how a user moves from a UML/SPT specification to a fully working FSP model, how the LTSA tool can be used to do the analysis and how the user can employ feedback from the analysis tools to successively refine the design towards an acceptable solution. Specifically, the contributions of this paper are as follows:

- We describe a performance engineering methodology based on the analysis of stochastic process algebra models generated from UML sequence diagrams with standard SPT annotations (Sect. 2).
- We show how functional analysis of process algebra models by the LTSA tool can expose erroneous behaviour (e.g. deadlock) and also behavioural features which, although correct, can significantly affect performance (Sect. 3).
- We evaluate the approach with respect to a case study – an automated factory with real-time constraints – and show how results from the performance model can be used to successively improve the design (Sect. 3).
- We reflect on the use of sequence diagrams for this purpose and identify points in the translation to FSP that require intervention from the user. We also discuss the role of additional UML features that might be beneficial to enhance the methodology (Sect. 4).

2 Performance Modelling with UML and the SPT Profile

The UML diagrams that provide the key information required for performance analysis are those that describe behaviour and resources:

- Sequence or activity diagrams can be used to express those scenarios that have performance requirements.
- Statechart diagrams describe the behaviour of active objects, and the time required to respond to stimuli.
- Deployment diagrams define how active objects are mapped onto processing resources.

This work has concentrated on sequence diagrams because we are particularly interested in studying the performance of systems very early in the development process when they are best described by means of scenarios. However, we believe the approach can be applied to any behavioural specification in UML. For simplicity, it has been assumed that each active object (i.e. process or thread) has been assigned to its own processing resource (i.e. processor), obviating the need for deployment diagrams. Statechart diagrams have also not been used – instead we have taken the approach that the system is defined solely by sequence diagrams, and we mechanically generate state machines for each object, expressing them in FSP. Our work could, however, be extended to include statecharts when they become available later in the development process.

The decision to use only sequence diagrams has important implications for the designer – specifically they must be acutely aware of the way in which the processes corresponding to the various UML objects are composed. In the example covered here, the issue is side-stepped to some extent by defining the entire system in each case in a single UML diagram. This enables us to focus on the main issues at hand, but we come back to the general issue of composition in more detail in the discussion in Sect. 4.

2.1 The SPT Profile

The SPT Profile has recently been standardised [12]. It defines annotations that can be added to UML diagrams to show performance-related information such as the demand that an operation places on a processing resource, the load placed on the system by its users, and response time requirements.

A simple example is given in Fig. 1; this serves as an illustration of the use of the SPT profile and will be used to explain the principles of the translation to FSP. The <<PAcontext>> stereotype indicates that this diagram is a scenario involving some resources (software objects in this case) driven by a workload. The objects are a server (an active object, indicated by the heavy box), and a lock. The annotation on the lifeline of the user object has a <<PAopenLoad>> stereotype indicating that it is a workload, i.e. it defines the intensity of the demand made on the system by the users of this scenario; in this case there is an unbounded number of requests, with the interval between requests being exponentially distributed with a mean of 20 ms. A requirement that the mean response time is 70 ms is given, along with a placeholder variable (`$Resp`) for the predicted value that will be determined by simulation. The server offers a single operation, which requires the lock to be acquired and released – each of these operations takes 10 ms on average.

2.2 Performance Modelling with FSP

Our approach is to translate the set of sequence diagrams representing scenarios into an FSP program, with time delays to reflect the SPT delay annotations and performance measures to compute values (estimates) of the SPT placeholder variables.

The translation scheme generates an FSP process for each object specified in the UML diagram. This process is essentially a textual representation of the statechart for that object. We use the order of operations shown on the timeline of each object to determine the events available in each state. For example, the state machine corresponding to the lock shown in Fig. 1 will limit events to the order `lock -> unlock -> lock -> unlock`, etc.

The complete FSP script generated by translation of Fig. 1 is as follows:

```
RequestWorkload = ( enqueue -> <?exp(1.0/20)?> next
                         -> RequestWorkload ).
Server = ( request -> lock -> lock.response
                   -> unlock -> unlock.response
                   -> response -> Server).
```

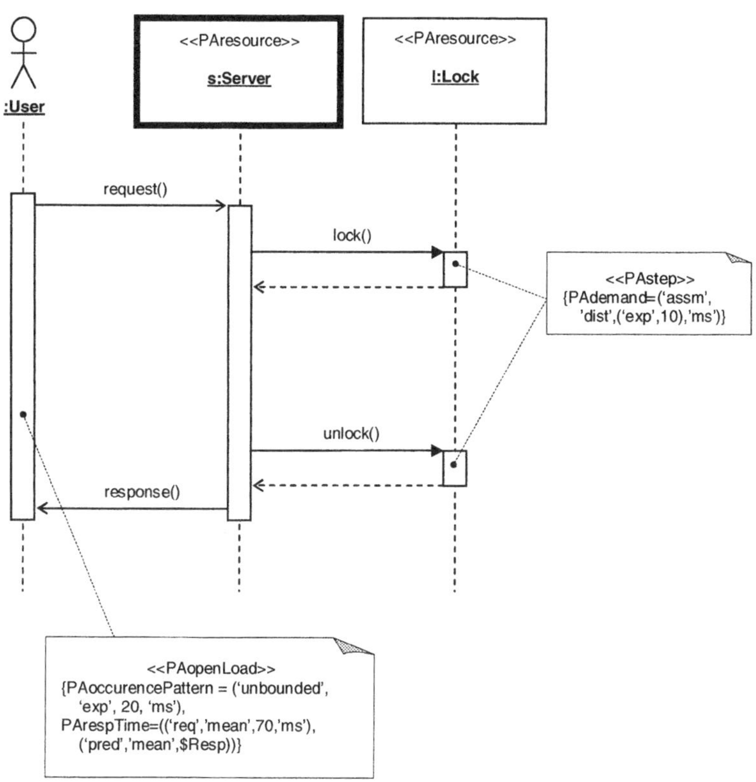

Fig. 1. A simple sequence diagram

```
Queue = Queue[0],
Queue[i:0..QMax] = ( when i < QMax enqueue -> Queue[i + 1]
                   | when i > 0    request -> Queue[i - 1]).
Lock = ( lock   -> <?c:exp(1.0/10)?> lock.response ->
         unlock -> <?c:exp(1.0/10)?> unlock.response -> Lock ).
timer RequestWorkloadResponseTime <enqueue, response>

||SYSTEM = ( RequestWorkload || Server || Queue || Lock ||
             RequestWorkloadResponseTime ).
```

The sequence of messages specified in the UML for each object are encoded as *actions* in the FSP, e.g. `enqueue`, `lock` and `unlock.response`. The open arrowhead on the `request` message in Fig. 1 implies that several users may be requesting the server at the same time and hence that there is an implicit queue (of undefined capacity) at the server. This is made explicit in the FSP via the auxiliary `Queue` process.

SPT Annotations. The various time delays are specified in the UML diagram using SPT annotations and these are straightforwardly translated into time delays in the corresponding FSP processes. For example, in the FSP shorthand: `<?exp(1.0/20)?> next`, an anonymous clock is set to run down for an exponentially-distributed time delay with mean 20 ms, after which time the action `next` is offered.

FSP supports `timers` and `measures`, which are *probes* that synchronise passively with specified actions in a program and change the internal state of the timer or measure. Timers record the distribution of the time between action occurrences in a given start and stop set. Measures record the distribution of the state of a system measure (queue length, server status, etc.). The `PArespTime` annotation specifies a performance measure that must be extracted from the FSP model – this generates automatically the timer process shown in the example.

Note that the example shown is a complete and fully "executable" FSP script once the queue capacity (`QMax` – a model parameter) has been specified.

Global Behaviour. The sequential constraints implied by the sequence diagram are understood in this work as follows: the diagram describes all global orderings or interleavings of messages and actions that preserve the specified sequential ordering of send and receive events in each individual object. That is, the diagrams specify the only valid behaviours. This is the widest interpretation that is consistent with sequential execution of the processes. If some of these global orderings are to be excluded, this can be specified by additional behaviour diagrams. This interpretation is required in order to model the behaviour by composing FSP processes, as in the example above.

3 Case Study: The Widget Factory

In this section, FSP programs generated from sequence diagrams are used with LTSA to analyse the performance of an example system. The first sequence diagram is created by studying a free-text description of the system – an automated factory with three machines that process components, and a robot that moves components between the machines on demand:[3]

> In an automated widget factory, widgets are assembled from two parts, an A part and a B part. A parts are processed by machine 1 while B parts are processed by machine 2; machine 3 then assembles one A part and one B part to make one widget. A single robot transports parts from a conveyor belt to the appropriate machine; it is also responsible for

[3] We use a description provided by Jane Hillston – the original source is unknown.

> moving completed A parts from machine 1 to machine 3, and completed B parts from machine 2 to machine 3.
>
> There are always A and B parts available from the conveyor belt. If both machine 1 and machine 2 need to use the robot at the same time they are equally likely to acquire it. Loading parts from the conveyor belt, or transferring them to machine 3 takes 10 seconds on average.
>
> The mean duration of processing A parts at machine 1 is 125 seconds, while the mean duration of processing B parts at machine 2 is 200 seconds. Assembling a widget from A and B parts takes 100 seconds on average. Unfortunately machine 1 is rather old and temperamental: for approximately 1 part in 20 it jams during processing and needs to be repaired. On average, the repair time is 500 seconds. The processing of that part then continues.

The task is to design a system that produces widgets at the fastest rate, i.e. with the smallest mean time between the completion of consecutive widgets.

3.1 Design 1: The Base Design

The sequence diagram that represents the production of one widget is shown in Fig. 2. This was produced by studying the interactions between objects in the system description. There are four active objects: three machines and the robot. There is a closed workload with a zero external delay – this effectively keeps machines 1 and 2 in busy loops, so that after processing a part, each machine takes another raw part from the conveyor.

The sequence diagram is mostly self-explanatory. Machine 1 instructs the robot to give it a part from the conveyor belt using the load operation. The machine has a delay with a probability attached to represent the time to fix the machine if it fails, and it has another delay to represent the time to process the part.[4] It then requests the robot to transport the part to machine 3. Machine 2 only has a delay to represent processing a B part. The robot offers three different operations: load, moveA, and moveB.

It is clear from this diagram that machines 1 and 2 can fetch and process new parts when each has handed a processed part to machine 3, i.e. the system consists of three pipelined processes.

It is a relatively straightforward task to translate the UML specification into an FSP program using the scheme outlined in [13]. An FSP process is generated for each class of object found in the sequence diagram and each process has a utilisation measure defined for it.

The first task is to ensure that no functional problems exist in the FSP program. The LTSA tool can be used to search for any possible deadlock and progress problems by examining explicitly the state space of the system. In this rendition of the system no such problems exist. Initial simulation experiments indicate that the system nears equilibrium after simulating approximately 200,000

[4] We omit details of how probabilities are specified in FSP, suffice it to say that the translation is straightforward.

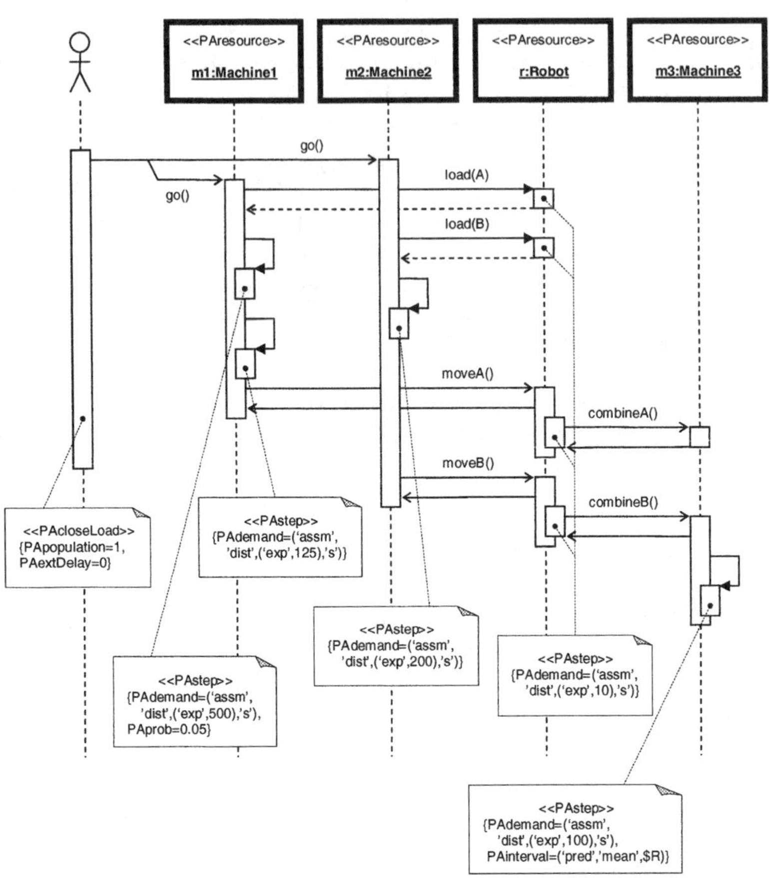

Fig. 2. Sequence diagram of widget factory design 1

seconds of execution time. Simulation runs of 30 million seconds were made, with performance measures being reset after 200,000 seconds to diminish the effects of the start-up transients. Twenty simulation runs were made, and the average of the results are shown in Table 1. The mean "interval" is the mean time between production of widgets. In all results presented in this paper, the maximum half-width of the 95% confidence interval was 4.3% of the mean.

A striking aspect of the performance results is the low utilisation of machine 2 – it is natural to expect its utilisation to approach 100% because its service time is the largest of all of the machines. This suggests a performance "bug" that needs to be fixed.

Table 1. Simulated performance of widget factory design 1

Mean interval (seconds)	Utilisations			
	Machine 1	Machine 2	Machine 3	Robot
316	0.48	0.63	0.32	0.13

3.2 Design 2: Reduced Robot Sequentialisation

How can the user exploit the LTSA tool to analyse problems such as the cause of the under-utilisation of machine 2? The proposed answer is to use the LTSA tool to explore the underlying labelled transition system, which is very much like a UML statechart for the composed system. Although the user is not required to specify a state chart at any point, the assumption is that they can interpret the transition system generated automatically from their UML design.

By using the animator functionality of the LTSA tool it becomes clear that the system is unnecessarily sequentialised, in particular part A is always moved to machine 3 before part B, regardless of whether an A part is available before B or vice versa. Figure 3 shows the state machine of the robot in the form of an FSP transition system, taken from a screenshot of the LTSA tool. The problem is now clear: the robot has been defined to move part A before part B. The timeline of the robot in Fig. 2 indicates that part A is moved before part B, but presumably the system designer would want the robot operations to take place in any order. We have borrowed the coregion concept from message sequence charts [14] to indicate that the actions can occur in any order in the sequence diagram. The translation scheme for coregions uses FSP's choice operator (`P | Q | ... | R`) to ensure that the load activities are offered simultaneously when the robot is not in use. Corresponding changes are required to machine 3. An alternative approach would be to define a separate sequence diagram for each possible ordering – the generated FSP would allow any order, but clearly this approach would be cumbersome when many possible orders need to be specified.

The translation scheme can be used to generate new versions of the FSP processes that represent the robot and machine 3. The system is now tested for functional errors, revealing a potential deadlock. After producing a B part, machine 2 gives it to the robot to move to machine 3, allowing machine 2 to process another part from the conveyor, which it gives to the robot. Machine 3 is unable to accept the second B part until it has received an A part from machine 1. However, machine 1 is now unable to send an A part to machine 3 because it cannot acquire the robot, i.e. the single shared robot is held by a blocking operation. This is a classic deadlock scenario, but it might easily be missed when making incremental changes to a UML specification. Figure 4 shows a screenshot of the LTSA tool displaying the offending sequence of actions.

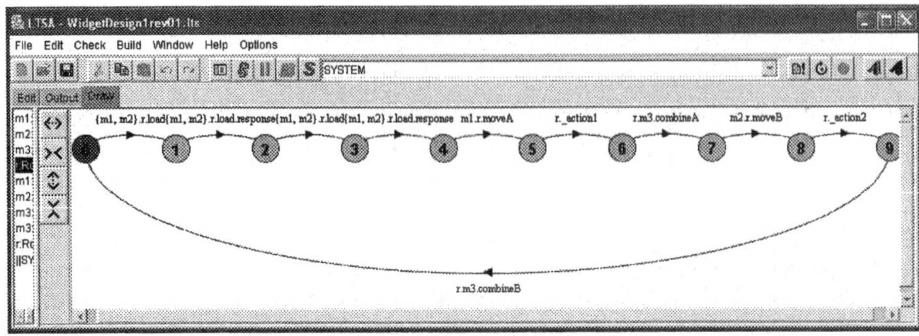

Fig. 3. Screenshot of LTSA showing the state machine of the robot

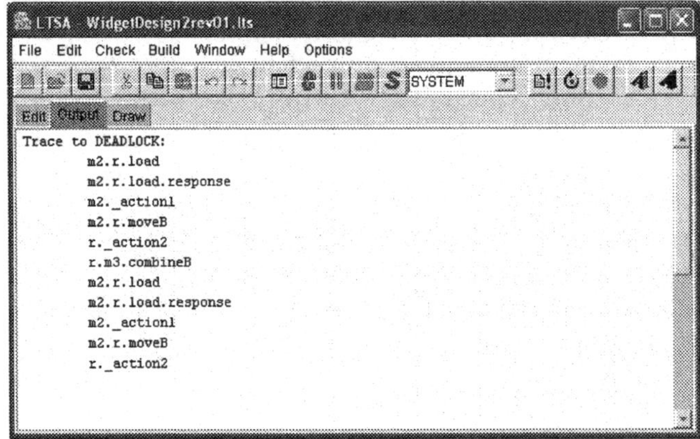

Fig. 4. Screenshot of LTSA diagnosing deadlock

3.3 Design 3: Deadlock Elimination

There are several possible solutions to the deadlock problem – one approach is to arrange for machines 1 and 2 to send messages to machine 3 when they have parts ready to move, leaving machine 3 to issue the move requests to the robot. In this way, move requests will only be made when both the generating and receiving machines are ready, and it is no longer possible for the robot to be held in a blocking operation. The revised sequence diagram is shown in Fig. 5. For clarity, we identify the sets of activations that can execute in any order by enclosing them in boxes.

No functional problems are found with this design. Simulations conducted using the same parameters as for design 1 yield the results shown in Table 2. These results show around a 10% improvement in the time between the production of consecutive widgets; the utilisations of all objects is also seen to be higher.

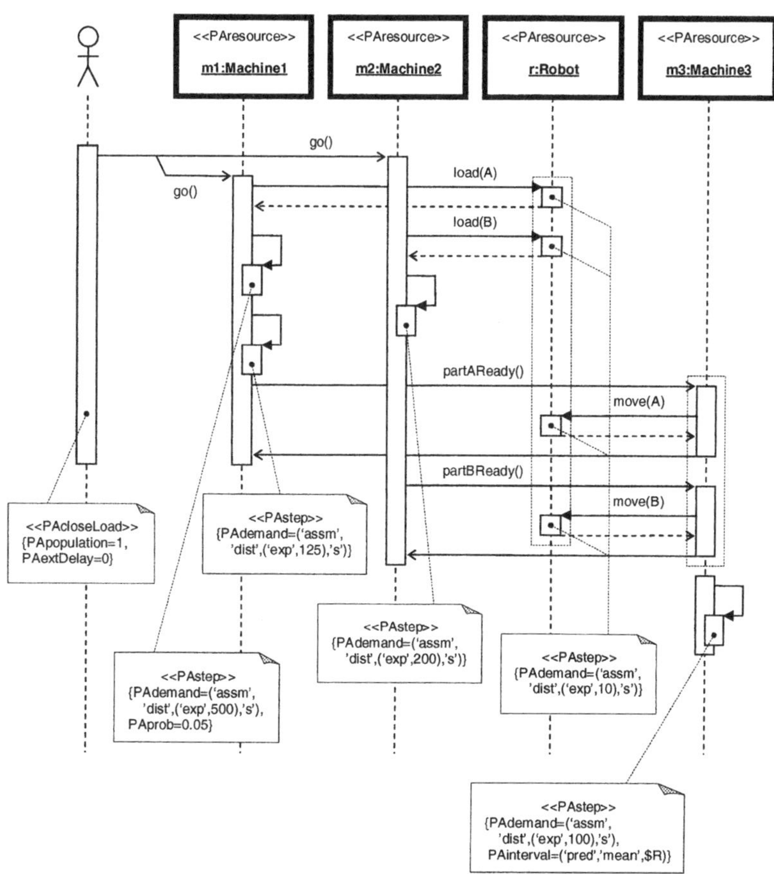

Fig. 5. Sequence diagram of widget factory design 3

3.4 Design 4: Buffering at Machine 3

A natural way to improve performance of the system is to add a buffer between machine 1 and machine 3. This would allow variations in the time to process an A part to be smoothed. The sequence diagram is shown in Fig. 6. Note that the buffer is represented explicitly by a passive object, and its capacity (denoted by the `PAcapacity` annotation) is a variable – this will be a simulation parameter.

Again no functional problems are found in this design and the simulation results are shown in Table 3. These show an improvement over design 3, even with a buffer capacity of 1. The performance also improves as the capacity of the buffer is increased but with diminishing returns. Clearly the utilisation of machine 2 is constrained by the processing rate of machine 3 – if it has assembled

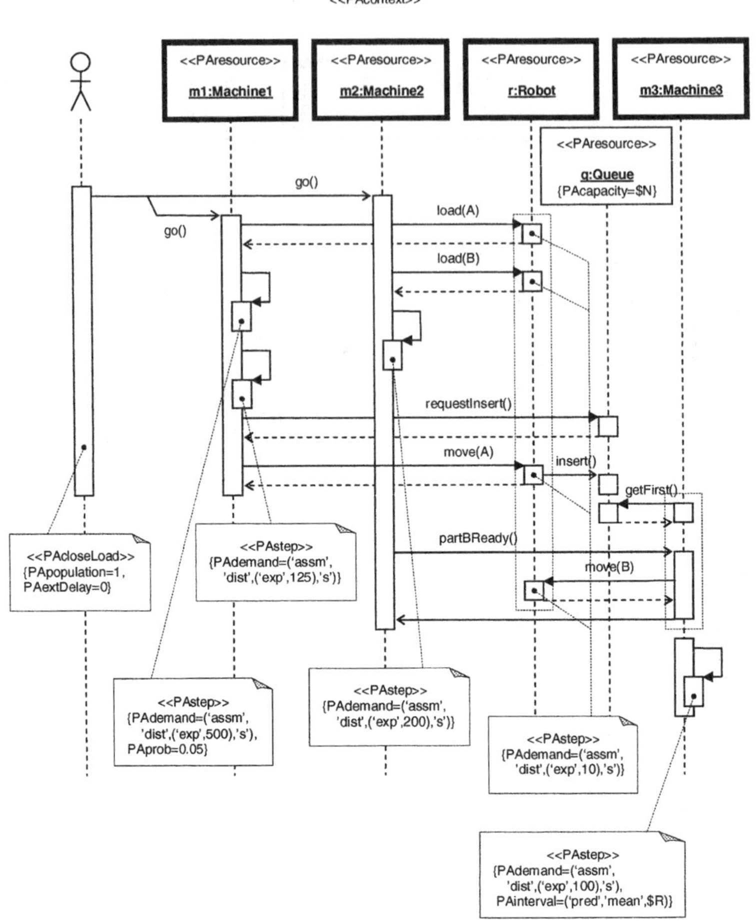

Fig. 6. Sequence diagram of widget factory design 4

a B part it must wait for machine 3 to complete its next widget. By the reverse argument machine 3's utilisation is similarly constrained by machine 2. Machine 1's utilisation improves slightly as the buffer capacity increases, but the buffer utilisations found suggest that it frequently blocks awaiting spare buffer capacity. One can imagine many ways of modifying the system to improve throughput and/or assembly times, but for the purposes of this paper, we terminate the exercise at this point.

4 Discussion

We have deliberately simplified things to explore how far we can get with sequence diagrams alone. For this case study, where the UML is confined to a

Table 2. Simulated performance of widget factory design 3

Mean interval	Utilisations			
(seconds)	Machine 1	Machine 2	Machine 3	Robot
285	0.53	0.70	0.36	0.14

Table 3. Simulated performance of widget factory design 4

Buffer	Mean interval	Utilisations				
capacity	(seconds)	Machine 1	Machine 2	Machine 3	Robot	Buffer
1	270	0.56	0.74	0.37	0.15	0.62
2	263	0.57	0.76	0.38	0.15	1.38
3	259	0.58	0.77	0.39	0.15	2.20
4	256	0.59	0.78	0.39	0.16	3.06
5	255	0.59	0.78	0.39	0.16	3.95
6	254	0.59	0.79	0.39	0.16	4.87
7	253	0.59	0.79	0.40	0.16	5.80
8	252	0.60	0.79	0.40	0.16	6.73
9	252	0.60	0.80	0.40	0.16	7.71
10	251	0.60	0.80	0.40	0.16	8.68

single sequence diagram, we have essentially avoided the issue of composition. How much did we have to "tweak" the FSP code generated for each design to build a usable model? The answer is none at all. In this example we are able to capture fully the required behaviour in a single UML diagram; applying the translation mechanically generated completely functioning (and correct) FSP code. All we had to do was specify the model parameters, which in this case comprised just the capacity of the buffer.

Compiling and executing the resulting FSP code is straightforward. The LTSA functional analyser is very intuitive, although, as we have already highlighted, the user needs to be able to relate the states and transitions in the underlying transition system to the objects and messages in the UML. The naming convention we used to translate UML messages to FSP actions helped enormously in this respect (some action names can be seen in Fig. 4). Executing the code, i.e. invoking the simulation, had to be done explicitly within the LTSA tool as there are currently no tools to link the UML and the simulation directly. In a production environment we would not expect the user to see the FSP code, and we would expect everything to be controlled via the UML interface, including UML/SPT input and the monitoring and analysis of the simulation output. The development of tools to support the methodology is the subject of ongoing work.

As a passing remark, we were surprised by how easy it can be to introduce deadlocks by making changes to the UML. As an example, in moving from design

1 to design 2 we allowed the robot to move A and B parts to machine 3 in either order. Simultaneously, we had to allow machine 3 to receive A and B parts in either order. The system will now deadlock if the robot moves two B parts in succession because machine 3 is still expecting an A part, and the robot is held by machine 2. Undoubtedly, in larger systems such "bugs" may be harder to spot by hand. Automation of the process via the LTSA proved extremely useful and reassuring in this case study and is likely to be more so for larger systems.

The process applied above also applies for more than one sequence diagram. Each will translate into its own FSP processes, which will be created with distinct names even when they represent the same process. All these processes will synchronise on messages by name (names must be consistent, if a message in one diagram triggers an action in another diagram). Mutual exclusion must be added for FSP processes that represent the same active object, and this can be imposed by the queue process which activates the active object. The details of this extension are postponed to later work.

5 Summary, Conclusions, and Future Work

In this paper we have demonstrated that UML sequence diagrams with annotations taken from the SPT profile can be represented in the stochastic process algebra FSP, and that the performance of the design can be systematically improved using a combination of functional and performance analyses. We have illustrated the ideas with reference to a case study and have shown how the LTSA tool can be used as a unifying framework to support the general methodology. Although the case study system presented here was composed of physical machines, our approach is equally applicable to software systems – we adopted the case study for simplicity of presentation. The case study is actually an example of a network of servers and queues – a common architectural feature of many modern software systems.

We have deliberately focused on sequence diagrams because they are widely understood. They are also used early in the development cycle to express requirements, whereas statecharts are used later during design. It would be useful to extend this method to include statecharts in order to have the analysis track the design as it develops.

Analysis of systems described by multiple behaviour diagrams of multiple types seems to be practical, and is the subject of our current research.

Acknowledgements

We wish to thank Prof. Alan Smith of the Centre for Systems Engineering at University College London for his insightful comments throughout this work. This work was partially funded by the U.K. Engineering and Physical Sciences Research Council through grant GR/R02238/01.

References

[1] Smith, C.U.: Performance Engineering of Software Systems. Addison-Wesley, Reading MA (1990)

[2] Magee, J., Kramer, J.: Concurrency: State Models and Java Programs. John Wiley and Sons, Chichester, England (1999)

[3] Ayles, T., Field, T., Magee, J., Bennett, A.J.: Adding performance evaluation to the LTSA tool. Technical report, Department of Computing, Imperial College London (2003)

[4] Canevet, C., Gilmore, S., Hillston, J., Prowse, M., Stevens, P.: Performance modelling with UML and stochastic process algebras. In: 18th UK Performance Engineering Workshop, Glasgow, Scotland. (2002)

[5] Jansen, D.N., Hermanns, H., Katoen, J.P.: A QoS-oriented extension of UML statecharts. In: UML 2003: The Unified Modeling Language, Modeling Languages and Applications, Lecture Notes in Computer Science, volume 2863, Springer-Verlag, Berlin (2003) 76–91

[6] Merseguer, J., Campos, J., Bernardi, S., Donatelli, S.: A compositional semantics for UML state machines aimed at performance evaluation. In: 6th International Workshop on Discrete Event Systems. (2002) 295–302

[7] Bernardi, S., Donatelli, S., Merseguer, J.: From UML sequence diagrams and statecharts to analysable Petri net models. In: WOSP 2002: Third International Workshop on Software and Performance, Rome, Italy. (2002)

[8] Tsiolakis, A.: Intergating model information in UML sequence diagrams. Electronic Notes in Theoretical Computer Science **50** (2001)

[9] Uchitel, S., Kramer, J., Magee, J.: Detecting implied scenarios in message sequence chart specifications. In: 8th European Software Engineering Conference, Vienna, Austria. (2001) 74–82

[10] Petriu, D., Woodside, M.: Software performance models from system scenarios in use case maps. In: Computer Performance Evaluation, Modelling Techniques and Tools: Twelfth International Conference (TOOLS 2002), Lecture Notes in Computer Science, volume 2324, Springer-Verlag, Berlin (2002) 141–158

[11] Xu, J., Woodside, M., Petriu, D.: Performance analysis of a software design using the UML profile for schedulability, performance and time. In: Conference on Computer Performance Evaluation, Modelling Techniques and Tools (TOOLS 2003), Lecture Notes in Computer Science, volume 2794, Springer-Verlag, Berlin (2003) 291–310

[12] Object Management Group: UML profile for schedulability, performance and time specification (2002)

[13] Bennett, A.J.: Software performance engineering with the UML profile for schedulability, performance and time. MSc dissertation, Centre for Systems Engineering, University College London (2004)

[14] ITU Telecommunication Standardisation Sector: ITU-T Recommendation Z.120 Message Sequence Charts (1996)

A UML Profile for Executable and Incremental Specification-Level Modeling

Risto Pitkänen and Petri Selonen

Tampere University of Technology
Institute of Software Systems
PO Box 553, FIN-33101 Tampere, FINLAND
{risto.pitkanen, petri.selonen}@tut.fi

Abstract. Model executability is widely considered an important enabling factor for model driven development. However, executability of Unified Modeling Language (UML) models tends to imply quite a low level of abstraction, which causes executable models to resemble diagrammatically structured program code. In this article, a UML profile that enables executable specification-level modeling using an incremental approach is proposed. The profile employs the Object Constraint Language (OCL) with multi-object joint actions to declaratively specify behavior on a higher level of abstraction than sequences of messages between objects. A nondeterministic mode of execution removes the need for explicit control flow, greatly simplifying the models. A variant of superposition is used to construct specification models incrementally, utilizing aspect-oriented layers, and preserving safety properties. The proposed mechanism also aims at bridging the gap between use cases and design level specifications. As the profile is based on ideas taken from the DisCo modeling language, originally designed for formal specification of reactive systems, there is a straightforward mapping that enables use of existing DisCo tools for animation, verification and synthesis. A running example is presented to illustrate the use of the proposed approach.

1 Introduction

Model executability has lately received much attention from the research community, partly due to the popularity of OMG's Model Driven Architecture [17], for which it is an important enabling factor. Mellor and Balcer [15] motivate executable modeling by stating that agile processes require the capability of immediate validation of constructed models. Executability also enables rapid model prototyping and test case generation, and facilitates communication between different stakeholders.

Work has been done in the field of UML model executability (e.g. [15, 12, 23]) at a level of abstraction we consider to be the *design level*. Design is more abstract than implementation; it does not necessarily address issues such as exact technology platforms, distribution, concurrency, etc. Still, it already includes a number of design choices regarding the architecture of the system, patterns, and communication models. In contrast, *specification level* executability of UML still largely remains unad-

T. Baar et al. (Eds.): UML 2004, LNCS 3273, pp. 158-172, 2004.

dressed. Specification level utilizes domain concepts, and addresses structure and behavior to the bare minimum extent, while still being able to describe the system unambiguously enough to capture a clear idea of what is being built.

Besides executability, another goal of our work is to facilitate incremental specification-level modeling. By definition, no clear idea of the system as a whole yet exists in the specification phase, and therefore it is essential to be able to work incrementally to develop such an understanding. Our approach enables utilization of aspect-oriented increments that may be superposed on each other.

Use case driven processes are widely utilized by the UML-based software engineering community, although UML has very limited facilities for expressing use cases. One contribution of the presented work is to give a concrete proposal on formalizing executable use cases, accompanied by a feasible diagram-based visualization scheme.

Technically, we define a UML profile for executable and incremental specification-level modeling. It is based on ordinary UML class diagrams, the main differences being that classes do not have operations, and that stereotyped packages called *layers* may be superposed on each other. Instead of operations, multi-object *joint actions* are used to specify behavior.

2 Related Work

2.1 Use Cases and Use Case Driven Development

In the mainstream of software engineering research, use cases are often seen as the main tool for capturing requirements and driving the whole development process. Among others, the Unified Process (Jacobson *et al.*, [8]) emphasizes use cases and employs them in a very informal fashion, mainly resorting to UML use case diagrams and textual descriptions.

Use cases have been criticized for not being object oriented, and for easily leading to a functional decomposition of a system. A further problem with use cases is their lack of precise semantics, or them hardly having semantics at all. Users of use cases often employ notions such as pre- and postconditions (e.g. [15], pp. 55), but these kinds of semi-formalizations do not really mean much in a formal sense as the objects and attributes referred to have not been defined anywhere.

The Catalysis approach (D'Souza and Wills, [6]) formalizes use cases as *joint actions* that in fact originate from the DisCo language [5], which is also the inspiration for our approach. Catalysis joint actions are interactions between multiple objects, specified by a list of participants and parameters, along with a postcondition given either using natural language or OCL. Consider an example of a joint action in Catalysis ([6], pp. 89) defining an abstraction of interaction between two instances of class Instructor, one of which as a result becomes the mentor of the other:

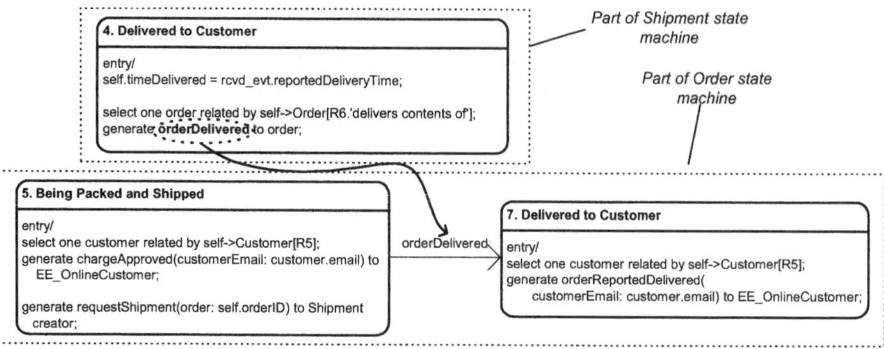

Fig. 1. Communicating state machines (adopted from [15], pp. 171)

```
action assign_mentor(subject: Instructor, watchdog: Instructor)
post   subject.mentor = watchdog and
       let ex_mentee = watchdog.mentee@pre in
          ex_mentee <> null ==> ex_mentee.mentor = null
```

Catalysis joint actions have a close resemblance to ours, but there are two significant differences: first, our joint actions have preconditions in addition to postconditions, and second, a certain restriction is placed on the form of postconditions. The latter property permits execution of use cases in most real-life cases. In addition, our approach addresses incremental modeling and aspect-orientation in a way that differs from Catalysis.

Li *et al.* [14] give use case formalizations as joint actions using a generic mathematical notation. Joint actions are used in conjunction with a structural domain model given in the form of a restricted class diagram.

2.2 Executable UML

Executable modeling in UML has been discussed by many authors, e.g. Mellor and Balcer [15], Kennedy Carter [12], and Sunyé *et al.* [23], all of which use slightly different approaches. However, a common denominator is the use of Action Semantics for specifying behavior.

In [15], behavior is specified using communicating state machines with operations. Fragments of two state machines are shown in Fig 1. They reside inside classes Shipment and Order, which are specified in a separate class diagram. States contain actions that are executed upon entry. In state 4 of the Shipment state machine, the order associated with this Shipment is looked up, and a signal is sent to its state machine, causing a transition from state 5 to state 7. While this sort of executable behavioral modeling might in some sense be more abstract than program code, it is quite low-level compared to use cases. Responsibilities have already been divided between classes, and the behavior of the system as a whole is obtained by composing the behaviors of the individual state machines.

A different approach to using actions to make models executable is described in [23], where actions are used inside ordinary operations of classes, much like method implementations in object-oriented programming:

```
Package::removeClass(class: Class)
  -- precondition and postcondition are specified using OCL in [23], but are not shown here
actions:
  let aCollection := class .allSuperTypes
  class .allSubTypes!forAll(sub : Class j
        aCollection!forAll(sup : Class j sub.addSuperClass(sup)))
  class . delete
```

The above is a definition for an operation removeClass of the UML Package metaclass. Again, the level of abstraction corresponds to design, and a model is not that far from diagrammatically structured program code.

Executable specification-level modeling has been studied extensively in the context of the DisCo method (e.g. Järvinen and Kurki-Suonio, [9]). A recent survey article about many of the ideas behind DisCo is presented by Kurki-Suonio [13]. Several executable formal specification languages exist in addition to DisCo. For example, Grieskamp and Lepper [7] describe how use cases can be formalized in executable Z. There are some similarities with our work, especially with the underlying DisCo model.

Oliver and Kent [19] describe a method for executing operations specified using OCL pre- and postconditions. Execution semantics are defined using a series of transformations that apply to UML object diagrams. The approach is able to handle a certain degree of nondeterminism in specifications. The main difference in our approach is that while Oliver and Kent animate ordinary methods of classes, we lift the specification of functionality outside classes, focusing on high-level collective behavior.

2.3 Incremental and Aspect-Oriented Modeling

Aspect-oriented modeling in UML, using an approach that has some resemblance with ours, has been discussed by Katara and Katz [10]. The main difference is that the authors stick to conventional classes and operations, their focus being on the design level. From the viewpoint of Subject-Oriented Design (Clarke *et al.*, [4]), our incremental approach can be seen as a technique for composing a system from UML model fragments, each describing a single aspect or a concern. The research done with Theme/UML by Clarke [3] addresses this problem with composition semantics that provides the merging of the individual UML model fragments.

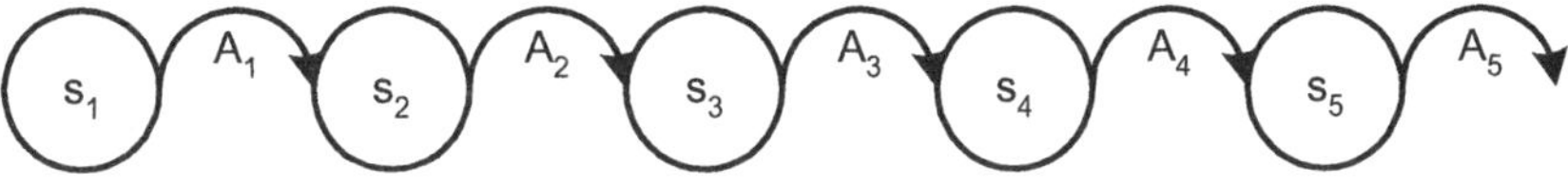

Fig. 2. A behavior of a model

3 Executable Specifications and Layered Action Diagrams

3.1 Abstract Execution Model

Our abstract execution model for specifications is based on using joint actions as formalizations of use cases. A behavior of a model is depicted in Fig. 2. Each s_i corresponds to a global state of the system, while each A_j denotes a joint action, which is a relation between two global states.

As an example, consider a use case, informally expressed as *"transfer xxx dollars from x to y ensuring that x stays zero or positive"*, specified by the joint action:

transfer: x – xxx >= 0 → x' = x – xxx and y' = y + xxx

The part before "→" is the *guard* or the *precondition,* i.e. a condition restricting the start state for this joint action, the rest being the *body* or the *postcondition.* Unprimed variables are used to denote variable values before, and primed variables after, the joint action. Note that although we do not indicate the difference explicitly in this example, *x* and *y* are variables that contribute to the system state, while *xxx* is just a transient value.

Assuming that there are joint actions *deposit* and *withdraw* in addition to transfer, each step in the execution of such a model now corresponds to the disjunction *transfer or deposit or withdraw.* To obtain a complete, declaratively specified executable model, also an initial state needs to be specified. An operational interpretation for such a declarative behavioral specification is that in each state, all actions whose preconditions hold true are candidates for execution. One of them is nondeterministically selected, and the next state will be such that it satisfies the postcondition.

3.2 Layered Action Diagrams

To facilitate executable and incremental specification-level modeling, we introduce *Layered Action Diagrams (LADs)* using a UML profile based on class diagrams. The key difference is that classes do not have operations. Instead, behavioral aspects are modeled using joint actions, which are nondeterministically scheduled, atomic units of execution in which one or more objects participate (Fig. 3). The joint actions used in LADs are parameterized versions of those of the abstract execution model described in the previous subsection: a LAD joint action is a class for a potentially infinite number of joint action instances.

An example of a joint action is depicted in Fig. 3, consisting of three parts: *signature, precondition* and *postcondition.* Signature comprises a name and a list of formal parameters. The precondition and postcondition are OCL expressions. In addition, joint actions can have *participant associations* with classes. Classes that a joint action has participant associations with are called *participant classes.* A joint action is said to be *enabled* if there exists a combination of participant class instances (*participants*) and parameter values such that the precondition evaluates to true, i.e. there is an enabled *joint action instance.* As the multiplicity of a participant association is always "*" on the joint action side, we use the drawing convention of not marking it explicitly. Furthermore, on the participant class side, multiplicity defaults to "1", which does not have to be explicitly marked. Optionally, it may be specified as "0..1". No other alternatives are allowed.

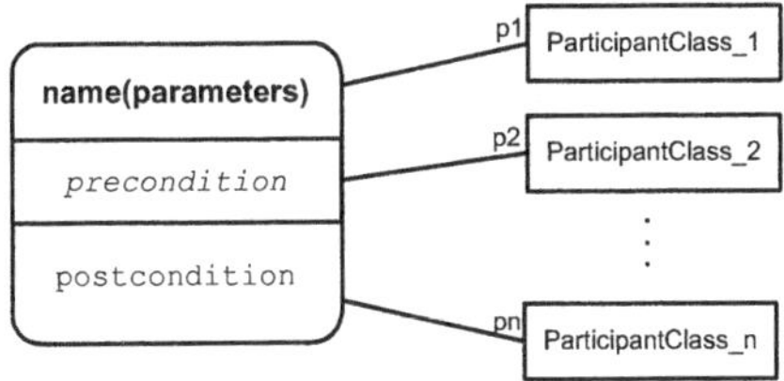

Fig. 3. Action and its participant associations and participant classes

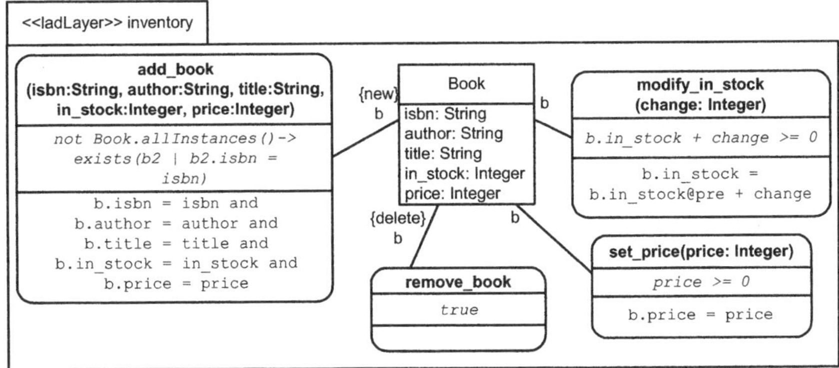

Fig. 4. Layer *inventory*

For a model to be *canonical,* each postcondition must be of the form

participant_object_attribute_or_association$_1$ = expression$_1$ and
...
participant_object_attribute_or_association$_n$ = expression$_n$

where all variable references in the right-hand-side expressions refer to precondition-time values of participant class attributes or associations. In other words, postconditions of canonical models may be operationally interpreted as parallel multiple assignments that may only alter participant object states. In addition, implications could be allowed as well to facilitate specifying conditional effects.

3.3 Example: A Web Bookstore

As an example, we develop a specification model of a web bookstore. LADs are used to specify aspect-oriented views to the system. The first aspect, represented by a package with stereotype «ladLayer», is about managing the inventory (Fig. 4). Class Book represents an item in the inventory. Its attributes are isbn, author, title, in_stock (the number of copies of the book currently in stock) and price.

Joint action add_book in Fig. 4 has a participant association with Book. As the association is marked with {new}, the joint action has implicit conditions that the participating Book instance does not exist at precondition time, but does exist at postcondition time.

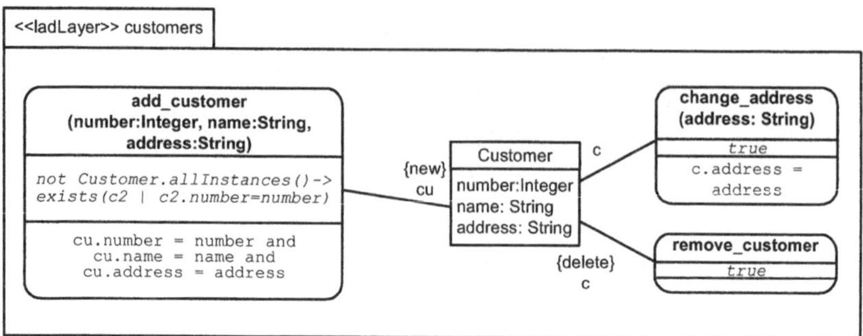

Fig. 5. Layer *customers*

Layer inventory states that books may be added to the store inventory as long as there exists no other book with the same ISBN. Books in the inventory may be removed at any time: {delete} in a participant association is syntactic sugar for the postcondition requiring that the other end of the participant association is undefined. In addition, in_stock and price of existing books may be altered as long as both will remain zero or positive.

A layer such as the one in Fig. 4 may be used somewhat similarly to a UML use case diagram together with use case descriptions. To gain the advantages of precise behavioral semantics, and to achieve executability, we specify classes explicitly together with those attributes that joint actions – or use cases – refer to. Classes belong to the problem domain and thus do not necessarily directly correspond to implementation classes: they may be mapped to implementation in various ways. LADs can also be used for quick sketching by leaving out the details about classes and joint actions; typically, one would just give the names of both, together with participant associations and perhaps some of the most important associations between classes.

An orthogonal aspect of the web bookstore, specifying how the customer database is managed, is modeled by layer customers in Fig. 5. There are no new modeling constructs here, and thus no further explanations are required.

A more interesting aspect of the model is depicted in Fig. 6. Layer shopping is a refinement of both of the previous layers, superimposing new constructs onto the old ones. Imported, old model elements are drawn with dashed lines with their details suppressed. The layer introduces a new class, ShoppingCart, together with joint actions to create carts and modify their contents. When wanted, a shopping cart may be asso ciated with a certain customer. A customer may have at most one shopping cart. Each shopping cart may contain any number of books.

The behavioral parts are modeled by three new joint actions. Create_cart instantiates a new shopping cart. Its precondition states that a Customer instance participating as cu cannot have a previously assigned shopping cart. The postcondition requires the cart items are initialized to an empty set, and that the cart is associated with the participating Customer, if there is one. Create_cart can also be executed without a Customer instance.

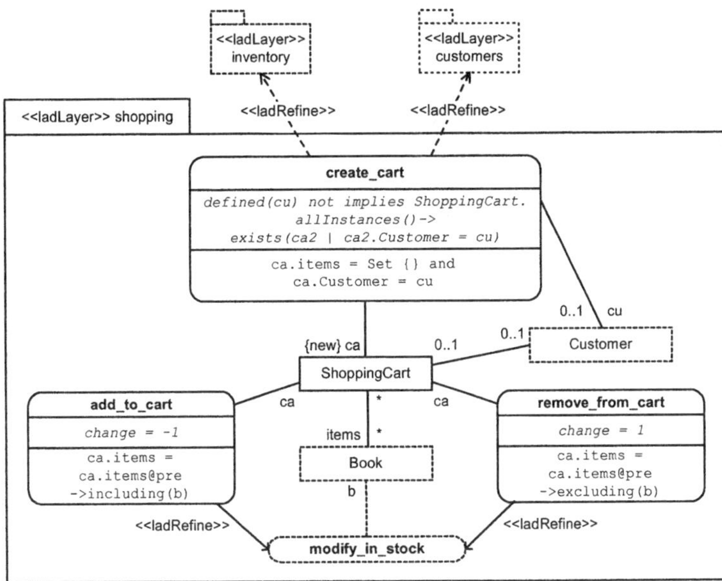

Fig. 6. Layer *shopping*

Joint actions add_to_cart and remove_from_cart both refine modify_in_stock introduced in layer inventory. This means that they implicitly have the participant associations, parameters, precondition and postcondition of the base action. In addition, they may have new participants and parameters, and they may strengthen the pre- and postconditions. Both joint actions have an additional participant association with ShoppingCart, they strengthen the precondition by requiring that in_stock is modified by –1 or 1, and their postconditions require that the ShoppingCart contents have been modified appropriately. Note that we do not have to check in add_to_cart whether there is an available copy of the book in stock, as the guard of the original modify_in_stock already does that.

A nice property of this kind of refinement by superposition is that safety properties (of the form "something bad never happens") are preserved by construction. This holds true as long as we refrain ourselves from "assigning" new values to variables already introduced in previous layers in new (parts of) joint actions. With refinement, we might for example be able to prove that, at any given point in time, no two books with the same ISBN already exist in layer inventory. Obeying the rules of superposition will guarantee that no later refinement would violate this property.

3.4 Executing Layered Action Diagrams

Any of the above layers may be executed. As layers that refine earlier layers also contain all the old parts, executing layer *shopping* would mean executing the whole model so far. For execution, LADs are mapped into the DisCo modeling language. This translation is quite straightforward, as DisCo has been used as the basis for designing LADs.

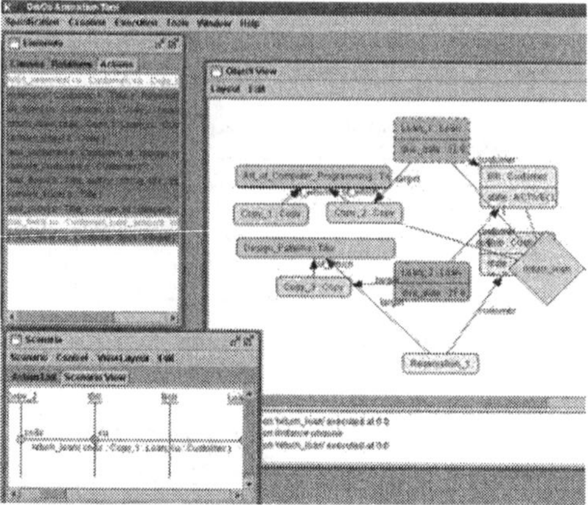

Fig. 7. DisCo Animator

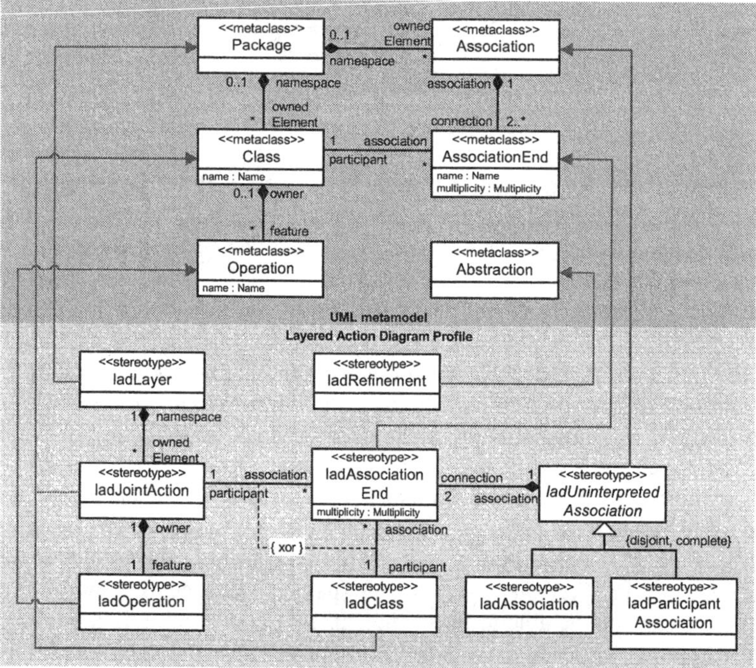

Fig. 8. Profile for Layered Action Diagrams

The compiler embedded in the execution tool, DisCo Animator, translates DisCo models to executable Java code, and the execution of a model may be graphically controlled and observed. Fig. 7 shows a snapshot of execution of a model. Animation of a model can proceed in various ways: the user may manually select enabled actions for execution, he can let the animator execute enabled actions randomly, or he can load and execute pre-created scenarios. A scenario view resembling generalized sequence diagram can be used for inspection of execution history, while the Object View window depicts the current dynamic state of the model. The screen has been grabbed in the middle of executing an action.

4 Profile for Layered Action Diagrams

4.1 Profile Definition

To establish a UML compliant presentation for LADs, a UML profile is defined. The applied *reference metamodel*[1] is UML 1.4 with Action Semantics [16]. A non-normative view of the LAD profile is shown in Fig. 8. The figure outlines the new user-defined stereotypes together with their base classes, and also explicitly shows the further restrictions on the inherited meta-associations[2].

There are in total nine new stereotypes, summarized in Table 1, each representing a particular concept described in Section 3.2. LAD layers (ladLayer) can contain a set of classes (ladClass), joint actions (ladJointAction with a ladOperation), and associations (ladAssociation or ladParticipantAssociation with two ladAssociationEnds) connecting them. The classes can have attributes with primitive data types but no operations. The associations are always binary and connect either a class and a joint action, or two classes. To ensure support by existing UML CASE tools, ladJointAction is derived from UML Class. Each joint action always has exactly one operation with parameters, a precondition, and a postcondition.

Well-formedness rules for the stereotypes are shown informally in Table 2. Some of the rules are already present in Fig. 8 (e.g. LAD associations being binary) while others are complementary to the profile. The general approach taken in the LAD profile is to restrict the usage of the elements preferably as little as possible. Since DisCo animator tools are being used for instance-level visualization, UML-level instantiation has been left outside the scope of this paper.

OCL is not always explicitly used with joint actions: drawing conventions and notations are utilized as shorthands when convenient (e.g. for new and delete). For example, when the designer wants to visually emphasize that a given LAD Joint Action results in the creation of a new instance of a LAD Class it is associated with, this can be done by marking the association end at the LAD Class side with constraint "{new}". This implies that the postcondition of the LAD Joint Action declares the creation of the corresponding instance using "oclIsNew()". Similarly, the deletion of an LAD Class instance is marked with constraint "{delete}".

[1] While UML 2.0 [18] indeed imposes major improvements to the metamodel, their effects to the selected extended metamodel subset remain mostly syntactic in nature.

[2] Here, the profile mechanism itself is adopted from UML 2.0. When necessary, the restricted meta-associations can be transformed into OCL constraints and removed from the profile, making the profile compliant with UML 1.4.

Table 1. Summary of Layered Action Diagram stereotypes

Stereotype	Description
«ladLayer»	A LAD Layer is a grouping mechanism for encapsulating certain behavioral viewpoints or aspects. It can refine other LAD Layers.
«ladJointAction»	A LAD Joint Action is a class of execution unit. LAD Joint Action instances are actual units of execution.
«ladOperation»	A LAD Operation is an operation placeholder for a LAD Joint Action. The pre- and postcondition, and signature of the LAD Operation define the pre- and postconditions and the signature of the corresponding LAD Joint Action, respectively.
«ladClass»	A LAD Class represents a classifier taking part in actions.
«ladUninterpreted Association»	A LAD Uninterpreted Association is an abstract stereotype representing a generic association between LAD Joint Actions and LAD Classes.
«ladParticipant Association»	A LAD Participant Association connects a LAD Joint Action and a LAD Class.
«ladAssociation»	A LAD Association connects two LAD Classes.
«ladAssociationEnd»	A LAD Association End represents an association end, connected to a LAD Uninterpreted Association, pointing to a LAD Joint Action or LAD Class.
«ladRefine»	A LAD Refinement represents a refinement relationship between two LAD Layers, LAD Joint Actions or LAD Classes, indicating a superposition relationship.

The execution model for joint actions is as follows:

1. Generate all possible joint action instances, connected to all possible combinations of class instances,
2. find all enabled joint action instances whose guard conditions hold true, and
3. nondeterministically select one enabled joint action instance and execute it.

To be precise, LADs are only semi-executable in the sense that it is not always possible to find all enabled actions mechanically. The enabledness of a joint action is an intractable problem in the general case. However, most practical models can be mechanically executed, and for the rest, the user can usually supply the extra information required for simulation to proceed in all situations.

4.2 LAD Diagrams as UML Metamodel Instances

The left-hand side of Fig. 9 shows a subset of the LAD diagram taken from Fig. 5. The right-hand side of the figure shows the diagram as a UML metamodel instance, extended with the LAD profile.

To use the LAD notation in practice, the UML CASE tool in question should provide support for introducing custom stereotype-related adornments. However, most CASE tools only allow the user to provide a new bitmap for existing UML metaclasses (e.g. Rational Rose). In such a case, the visualization of the properties specific to a given stereotype can be done as suggested in UML 2.0: for extended element, a UML note is attached to the stereotyped element, together with the property name and accompanied value ([18], pp. 582). While certainly clumsy, this mechanism provides modest means for introducing LAD diagrams into virtually any UML CASE tool supporting class diagrams.

Table 2. Well-Formedness rules for Layered Action Diagram stereotypes

Stereotype	Well-formedness rules
«ladLayer»	LAD Layer can contain LAD Joint Actions, LAD Classes, LAD Associations, LAD Participant Associations, LAD Refinements, and standard UML Constraints and Tagged Values.
«ladJointAction»	LAD Joint Action takes part in associations via LAD Association Ends. LAD Joint Action always owns exactly one LAD Operation.
«ladOperation»	LAD Operation always belongs to exactly one LAD Joint Action. LAD Operation has only parameters with primitive types.
«ladClass»	LAD Class connects to associations only via LAD Association Ends. LAD Class can only contain Attributes with primitive data types.
«ladUninterpreted Association»	LAD Uninterpreted Association is binary. LAD Uninterpreted Association connects only via a LAD Association End.
«ladParticipant Association»	LAD Participant Association only connects a LAD Joint Action to a LAD Class.
«ladAssociation»	LAD Association can only connect two LAD Classes.
«ladAssociation End»	LAD Association End can only belong to a LAD Uninterpreted Association. LAD Association End can only connect to a LAD Joint Action or LAD Class. LAD Association End connected to a LAD Joint Action has always multiplicity of 1 or 0..1
«ladRefine»	LAD Refinement is binary LAD Refinement has element of the same type as its client and supplier LAD Refinement connects LAD Layers, LAD Joint Actions or LAD Classes.

4.3 Refinement of LAD Layers

Each LAD layer can refine of one or more existing LAD layers through a *LAD Refinement* relationship. For example, LAD classes can be refined by adding new attributes, and LAD joint actions can be refined by adding new parameters, new preconditions and new postconditions.

However, the relationship between models and respective views is not well-defined in UML, leaving the interpretation, on purpose, up to the individual CASE tool manufacturers. Instead of supporting the construction of larger models from smaller model fragments, the UML specification implicitly assumes a single, complete UML model at all times.

Each LAD diagram is seen as a visualization of a stand-alone model fragment, formed by the transitive closure of the LAD Layer namespace. For refining the LAD layers as individual model fragments, a mechanism for merging of model fragments must be provided. It is assumed that a *correspondence* relationship between the model elements in different LAD diagrams representing the same semantic concept can be derived. Taken the name uniqueness requirement inherited by the LAD Layer from the UML Package into account, this is quite straightforward. Refinement can then be implemented with a mechanism for merging models by assimilating corresponding elements. In addition to refining layers, the user can explicitly state when a model element (i.e., LAD Joint Action or LAD Class*)* is refined into another model element (as seen in e.g. Fig. 6). The composition is performed at a given point in time, after which the resulting LAD layer and elements have been merged with all refined layers. The operation is recursively performed as follows:

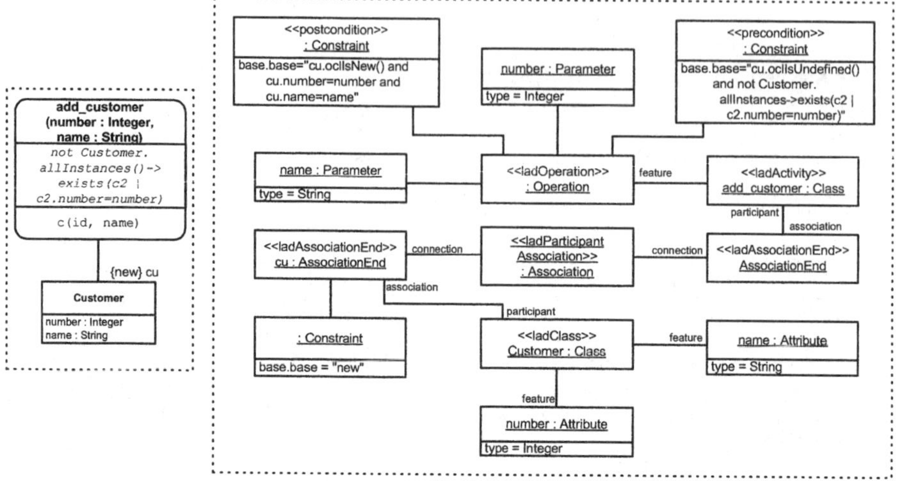

Fig. 9. An example Layered Action Diagram and its metamodel instance

```
Refine( L : layer )
   for all layers M refined by L:
      Refine( M )
      L = Merge( L, M )
   for all elements e1 refining e2 contained by L:
      L = Merge( L, Merge( e1, e2 ) )
      Remove the refinement relationship
```

In UML terms, the assumed merging capabilities resemble the PackageMerge ([18], Section 7.13.2) mechanism introduced in UML 2.0, which is "a relationship between two packages, where the contents of the target package is merged with the contents of the source package through specialization and redefinition". PackageMerge is intended to be used in situations where "elements of the same name are intended to represent the same concept, regardless of the package in which they are defined". However, the semantics of PackageMerge are, up to date, ambiguously defined. In practice, the assumed mechanism closely resembles a UML-based composition of design models, addressed, for example, by Clarke (e.g. [3]) with *composition relationships*, and by Selonen [22] with UML *union set operation*. Repository based merging of UML models has also been addressed by e.g. Alanen and Porres [2].

5 Discussion

We have described an approach to executable and incremental specification-level modeling using the UML profile mechanism. The Layered Action Diagrams (LADs) can be used as more precise, aspect-oriented replacements for use cases. Our work complements existing research on executable UML by extending executability to early stages of the development cycle, and addressing issues on incremental specification and aspect-oriented structuring of high-level models.

LADs bring all tool support available for the DisCo method within close reach of UML users. In addition to the already introduced Animator [1], there is experimental tool support for verification [11] and code generation [21]. DisCo has traditionally been applied as the sole language for both specification and design. This has hindered its adoption in industrial settings where UML and its predecessors, together with processes that utilize them, have dominated the field. With LADs, the specification power of DisCo can be taken advantage of without letting go of otherwise tried and proven tools.

Tool support for our approach needs to be further investigated, both from the point of view of integration with UML CASE tools, and developing tool support on top of an existing UML model processing platform [20] to assist in implementing the required model operations, i.e. interpreting refinement of layers and transforming LADs into DisCo specifications for execution and verification.

In the future, we also plan to address the issue of moving from a specification model expressed using LADs to a design model using more conventional form of executable UML. From the point of view of Model Driven Architecture, LADs are used to construct Computation Independent Models (CIM). Research on MDA model transformations has focused primarily on the Platform Independent Model (PIM) to Platform Specific Model (PSM) transformations, which would make it all the more interesting to try and give a CIM-to-PIM mapping whose domain is LADs. Experiences of a similar mapping [21] in the context of DisCo is expected to be utilized in this work.

Acknowledgements

The authors wish to thank Kai Koskimies, Tommi Mikkonen, Jari Peltonen, and Tarja Systä at Tampere University of Technology for their valuable comments on this paper.

References

1. Aaltonen, T., Katara, M., Pitkänen, R.: DisCo toolset – the new generation. Journal of Computer Science, 7(1) (2001) 33–18
2. Alanen, M., Porres, I.: Difference and Union of Models. In Proc. of UML 2003, October, 2003, San Francisco, CA, USA (2003) 3–17
3. Clarke, S.: Composing Design Models: An Extension to UML. In Proc. of UML 2000, York, UK (2000) 338–352
4. Clarke, S., Harrison, W., Ossher, H., Tarr, P.: Subject-Oriented Design: Towards Improved Alignment of Requirements, Design and Code. In Proc. of OOPSLA'99, Denver, Colorado, USA (1999) 325–339
5. The DisCo Home Page (2004). On-line at http://disco.cs.tut.fi
6. D'Souza, D.F., Wills, A.C.: Objects, Components, and Frameworks with UML: the Catalysis Approach. Addison-Wesley (1999)
7. Grieskamp, W., Lepper, M.: Using Use Cases in Executable Z. In Proc. of ICFEM'00 (2000) 111–120

8. Jacobson, I., Booch, G., Rumbaugh, J.: The Unified Software Development Process. Addison-Wesley (1999)
9. Järvinen, H.-M., Kurki-Suonio, R.: DisCo specification language: marriage of actions and objects. In Proc. of ICDCS'91 (1991) 142–151.
10. Katara, M., Katz, S.: Architectural Views of Aspects. In Proc. of the 2nd AOSD, Boston, MA, USA (2003) 1–10
11. Kellomäki, P.: Verification of Reactive Systems Using DisCo and PVS. In Proc. of FME'97 (1997) 589–604.
12. Kennedy Carter Ltd: Supporting Model Driven Architecture with Executable UML. Technical note (2002). On-line at http://www.kc.com
13. Kurki-Suonio, R.: Action systems in incremental and aspect oriented modeling. Distributed Computing, 16 (2003) 201–217
14. Li, X., Liu, Z., He, J.: Formal and Use-Case Driven Requirement Analysis in UML. In Proc. of COMPSAC2001, Chicago, USA, October (2001) 215–224
15. Mellor, S.J. and Balcer, M.J.: Executable UML: A Foundation for Model-Driven Architecture. Addison-Wesley (2002)
16. The Object Management Group: UML 1.4 with Action Semantics, Final Adopted Specification, January (2002). On-line at http://www.omg.org/uml/
17. The Object Management Group: MDA Guide, version 1.0.1. OMG (2003). On-line at http://www.omg.org/mda/
18. The Object Management Group: UML 2.0 Superstructure Specification, OMG Adopted Specification ptc/03-08-02, August (2003). On-line at http://www.omg.org/uml/
19. Oliver, I., Kent, S.: Validation of Object Oriented Models using Animation. In Proc. of EUROMICRO (1999). On-line at http://www.cs.kent.ac.uk/pubs/1999/755/
20. Peltonen, J., Selonen, P.: An Approach and a Platform for Building UML Model Processing Tools. In Proc. of WoDiSEE'04, Edinburgh, UK (2004) 51–57
21. Pitkänen, R.: A Specification-Driven Approach to Development of Enterprise Systems. In Proc. of NWPER'04, Turku, Finland, August (2004). To appear.
22. Selonen, P.: Set Operations for the Unified Modeling Language. In Proc. of SPLST'03, Kuopio, Finland (2003) 70–81
23. Sunyé, G., Pennaneac'h, F., Ho, W.-M., Le Guennec, A., Jézéquel, J.-M.: Using UML Action Semantics for executable modeling and beyond. In Proc. of CAiSE 2001, Interlaken, Switzerland, June (2001) 433–447

Applying Refactoring Techniques to UML/OCL Models

Alexandre Correa, Cláudia Werner

COPPE/UFRJ – Computer Science Department
Federal University of Rio de Janeiro
C.P. 68511, Rio de Janeiro, RJ, Brazil – 21945-970
{alexcorr, werner}@cos.ufrj.br

Abstract. The Object Constraint Language (OCL) plays an important role in the elaboration of precise UML models. Although OCL was designed to be both formal and simple, UML/OCL models may be difficult to understand and evolve, particularly when constraints containing complex or duplicate expressions are present. Moreover, the evaluation of how changes in the definition of the underlying classes impact the OCL part of a model may be a difficult and time-consuming task. In this paper, we discuss how refactoring techniques can be applied in order to improve the understandability of a UML/OCL model and how to support its evolution. In particular, we present a collection of refactorings and discuss how they can be specified and automated. We also show how the model animation features can be used to increase our confidence that the semantics of a model is preserved when a refactoring is manually performed.

1 Introduction

The Model Driven Architecture (MDA) is gradually becoming an important aspect of software development. MDA is a framework for model-based software development that is currently under development by the Object Management Group (OMG) [1]. In MDA, platform independent models, platform dependent models and automatic model transformations have a key importance in the software development process. In order to apply the MDA approach, we must produce models that can be understood by computers. In this context, the Object Constraint Language (OCL) plays an important role because it allows the elaboration of precise, consistent and computer-processable models. Besides, OCL can also be used in the context of a model transformation language, as demonstrated by some recent responses for the OMG QVT (Query, Views and Transformations) standard RFP [2].

Although OCL was designed to be both formal and simple when compared to formal specification languages such as Z and VDM-SL, UML/OCL models may be difficult to understand and evolve, particularly when they contain several complex or duplicate OCL expressions. Moreover, the evaluation of how changes in the underlying classes impact the OCL part of a model may be a difficult and time-consuming task when done by hand.

Changes in a software model or implementation can be divided in two main categories: semantics-preserving changes, usually aiming at improving quality factors

T. Baar et al. (Eds.): UML 2004, LNCS 3273, pp. 173-187, 2004.

such as understandability, modularity, efficiency, etc; and non-semantics-preserving changes. This paper focuses on semantics-preserving changes, also known as restructuring [3] or refactoring [4]. Refactoring is considered an essential technique for handling software evolution [5]. This importance has been acknowledged by recent software development methods such as Extreme Programming [6], for example, in which refactoring is a key practice. The automated support for this practice has increased in the last few years, mainly at the code level, and most programming environments currently implement some set of code refactorings.

Since models are the central point of software development in the MDA approach and, in the best scenario, code is automatically generated by formally defined model transformations, we argue that refactoring techniques and tools should also be developed at the model level. Since UML has several different views and diagrams, this paper discusses how refactoring techniques can be applied to a particular subset of UML elements that, to our knowledge, have not been explored so far in this context: UML class diagrams and OCL expressions.

The rest of this paper is structured as follows: section 2 presents common constructions in UML/OCL models that are amenable to refactorings. A collection of refactorings that can be applied to UML/OCL models is presented in section 3. Section 4 shows how these refactorings can be defined and automated. Some related works are discussed in section 5, and concluding remarks are drawn in section 6.

2 Common Problems in UML/OCL Models

In order to better motivate our work, this section shows an example of a UML/OCL model that presents several opportunities for the application of refactoring techniques.

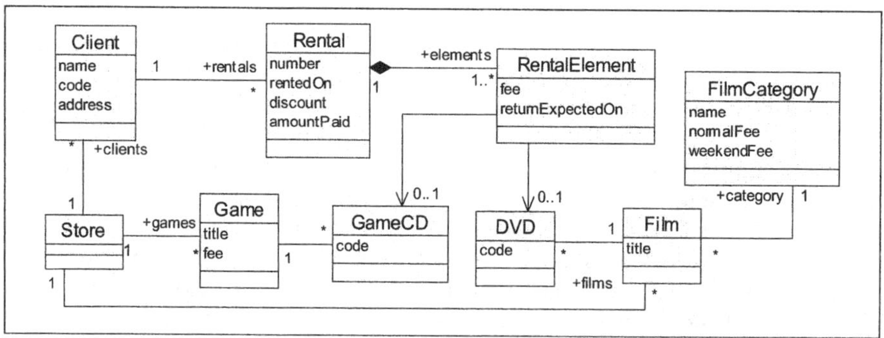

Fig. 1. Class diagram of a video rental software

2.1 UML Class Diagram Example

Figure 1 shows an excerpt of a class diagram corresponding to some business classes of a video rental software. The video store rents game cd-roms and dvd films to registered clients. Some improvements could be applied to this diagram. One example would be the introduction of a generic class *Item* associated to the *RentalElement* class in place of the specific associations to *GameCD* and *DVD* classes. However, such changes could affect OCL expressions that complement this diagram, as will be shown afterwards.

2.2 OCL Example

Figure 2 shows an invariant associated to the class diagram of the video rental model. It states that a *RentalElement* must be associated to only one element, a *GameCD* or a *DVD* film, and that the expected date of return for a rented element must be at least one day after the rental pickup date. This invariant and all examples discussed in this paper follow the OCL 2.0 specification [7].

```
context RentalElement
inv: (self.GameCD->notEmpty() xor self.DVD->notEmpty()) and
       self.returnExpectedOn.isAfter(self.Rental.rentedOn)
```

Fig. 2. Constraints associated to the video store example

Figure 3 shows an example of a system-level operation specification (*rent*) that states the preconditions and the effects expected on the system state after its execution. A system-level operation is very similar to the *operation schema* concept defined in the Fondue method [8] or to Catalysis's *joint action* [9]. It only states the expected results, abstracting away from all the internal collaborations that may occur in order to generate these results. In this example, the preconditions are stated in lines 4-18: the client's registration must not be in the cancelled state (line 5); the balance of the client's account (total due – total paid) must be less than 50 (lines 6-8); the limit of rented items is 5 for normal clients (lines 9-12) and 10 for premium clients (lines 13-16); all requested *DVD* and *GameCD* must be available for rental (lines 17-18). The post conditions are stated in lines 20-38: a new *Rental* should be created and associated to the client (line 21); the expected values for the attributes of the new *Rental* are defined in lines 22-25; a new *RentalElement* should be created for each requested *DVD* (lines 26-33) and *GameCD* (lines 34-38).

Although the refactorings described in this paper can be applied to UML models at any level of abstraction, we have noticed that they can be particularly helpful when applied at early modeling stages. The examples shown in Figures 2 and 3 reveal that understanding and changing specifications of relatively simple operations can become a difficult task depending on how they are written. Since system-level operation specifications have a wide scope, special care must be taken in order to produce an understandable and maintainable model.

2.3 OCL Smells

Code smell is a popular expression among Extreme Programming practitioners corresponding to signs that suggest that some parts of the code are problematic or violate programming guidelines. These problematic parts can be restructured by applying refactorings. Analogously, we define the term *OCL smell* as a hint that some

```
 1 context VideoRentalSystem::rent (theClient : Client,
 2    dvds : Set(DVD), gameCds : Set(GameCD), amountPaid : Money)
 3
 4 pre:
 5 not theClient.oclInState(Cancelled)and
 6 (theClient.rentals.elements.fee->sum()-
 7       theClient.rentals.discount->sum()) -
 8       theClient.rentals.amountPaid->sum() < 50.0 and
 9 theClient.oclInState(Normal) implies
10    theClient.rentals.elements->select(element|
11    element.oclInState(Pending))->size() +
12    dvds->size() + gameCds->size() <= 5  and
13 theClient.oclInState(Premium) implies
14    theClient.rentals.elements->select(element |
15    element.oclInState(Pending))->size() +
16    dvds->size() + gameCds->size() <= 10 and
17 dvds->forAll(dvd | dvd.oclInState(Available)) and
18 gameCds->forAll(cd | cd.oclInState(Available))
19
20 post:
21 theClient.rentals->one(newRental | newRental.oclIsNew() and
22   newRental.amountPaid = amountPaid and
23   newRental.discount = if theClient.oclInState(Premium)
24     then newRental.elements.fee->sum() * 0.1 else 0 endif   and
25   newRental.rentedOn = Date::now and
26   dvds->forAll(dvd | newRental->one(elem | elem.oclIsNew() and
27       elem.DVD = dvd and   elem.fee
28       = if newRental.rentedOn.dowIsBetween(DayOfWeek::Monday,
29                                DayOfWeek::Thursday)
30         then dvd.Film.category.normalFee
31         else dvd.Film.category.weekendFee endif and
32      elem.oclInState(Pending)) and
33      dvd.oclInState(Rented)) and
34   gameCds->forAll(cd | newRental->one(elem | elem.oclIsNew() and
35      elem.GameCd = cd and
36      elem.fee = cd.Game.fee and
37      elem.oclInState(Pending)) and
38      cd.oclInState(Rented)) )
```

Fig. 3. Example of a system-level operation specification

part of an OCL specification or even of the underlying class model should be refactored. Due to space constraints, this section only describes some examples of OCL smells that are often found in UML/OCL models, especially in those produced by OCL novices.

a) Magic Literal

Magic literal corresponds to a numeric or string literal that appears in the middle of an expression without explanation. In the example shown in Figure 3, 50.0 (line 8), 5 (line 12) and 0.1 (line 24) are examples of *magic literal* OCL smells. *Magic literals* make the specification less readable and less maintainable, especially if they are spread among different parts of the model.

b) And Chain

And chain corresponds to a single constraint (invariant, precondition or postcondition) composed of two or more expressions connected by *and* operators.

In general, it is much better to split an *and chain* into several separate constraints. This separation improves the readability and maintainability of the model and makes the identification of broken constraints much easier during program execution or model animation. The invariant shown in Figure 2, and the preconditions of the *rent* operation illustrated in Figure 3 are examples of *and chains*.

c) **Long Journey**
Long Journey is an OCL expression that traverses many associations between different classes of the model. A long navigation makes the expression more sensitive to changes in the underlying associations. *Long Journey* is similar to a violation of the Law of Demeter heuristic [10]. The expression `dvd.Film.category.weekendFee` (line 31) is an example of a *Long Journey* OCL smell.

d) **Rules Exposure**
Rules Exposure occurs when business rules details are specified in the preconditions or postconditions of system-level operations. The specification of a system-level operation can be greatly simplified if these details are encapsulated in other model elements. This is especially true for inferred knowledge and computation rules as shown in the example in Figure 3, where the details of how the system infers if a set of items can be rented to a client (lines 5-16) and how the rental fee is calculated (lines 27-31) make the specification lengthy and less readable.

e) **Duplicated Code**
Duplicated Code corresponds to the presence of duplicate OCL expressions. It is well known that duplication can lead to serious problems in software evolution. As illustrated in Figure 3, the expressions `theClient.rentals.elements->select(element | element.oclInState(Pending))` `(lines 10-11 and 14-15)` and `elements.fee->sum()` `(lines 6 and 24)` are examples of this OCL smell. *Duplicated Code* can also occur when two expressions have several equal sub-expressions and one or more slightly different sub-expressions. It is usually the result of a copy-paste-modify process, indicating a possible lack of generalization in the model. The final part of the *rent* operation postconditions shown in Figure 3 (lines 26-33 and 34-38) is an example of this situation.

3 Refactoring UML/OCL Models

This section presents a number of refactorings that can be applied to UML/OCL models in order to remove OCL smells such as the ones presented in the previous section. The proposed refactorings are classified into three categories:

- *OCL-exclusive* refactorings: those that result in changes that affect only OCL expressions;
- *UML diagram* refactorings: changes in the underlying class definitions that may have an impact in OCL expressions. Addition, removal or renaming of

classes, attributes, associations and operations are examples of such refactorings;

- *OCL definition constraint* refactorings: changes made to OCL expressions that introduce new elements in the underlying class definitions or that are related to OCL definition constraints.

The rest of this section informally presents some refactorings of each category. In section 4, we show how they can be formally specified and automated.

3.1 OCL-exclusive Refactorings

OCL-exclusive refactorings are changes that only affect OCL expressions, i.e., the underlying class model remains the same. Most of them are related to OCL *let* expressions, resulting in the definition, renaming or deletion of OCL variables. This section briefly discusses some examples of this type of refactoring.

a) Add Variable From Expression (source expression, variableName)
This refactoring inserts a variable declaration into an OCL expression. The inserted variable has the same type as the source expression and its value is linked to a copy of the source expression. The exact place where this new variable declaration is inserted depends on the existence of other variable definitions in the scope of the source expression. No variable named *variableName* can exist in the target scope and the source expression must not contain sub-expressions beginning with inner scope variables for this to be a legal refactoring.

b) Replace Expression By Variable (source expression, variableDeclaration)
This is one of the simplest refactorings that can be applied in order to simplify OCL expressions or to eliminate expression cloning, and it is usually applied after the *Add Variable From Expression* refactoring. It replaces the *source expression* with a variable expression (OCL VariableExp metaclass) which references the *variableDeclaration* defined in a previous let expression. The *source expression* must be equal to the initialization expression associated to *variableDeclaration*. Figure 4 shows, schematically, a refactored version of the preconditions for the *rent* operation obtained after applying this refactoring, combined with the previous one, twice.

```
pre:
 let clientIsAllowedToRent : Boolean = not theClient … <=
       gameCds->size() <= 10
     allItemsAvailable : Boolean = dvds->forAll(…) … and
       gamesCds->forAll(…) in
 clientIsAllowedToRent and allItemsAvailable
```

Fig. 4. *Add Variable From Expression* and *Replace Expression By Variable* refactorings

c) Split AND Expression (selected expression, name)
This refactoring is applied to invariants, preconditions and postconditions that are composed of two or more expressions connected by *ands*. A new constraint is

created from the selected expression with the same context and stereotype as the original constraint. A name can optionally be assigned to the created constraint. All let expressions corresponding to variables used in the selected expression must be introduced into the new constraint. Figure 5 shows an example of this refactoring.

original constraint:
```
context RentalElement
inv: (self.GameCD->notEmpty() xor self.DVD->notEmpty()) and
       self.returnExpectedOn.isAfter(self.rental.rentedOn)
```
---
selected expression:
```
self.returnExpectedOn.isAfter(self.rental.rentedOn)
```
name: `legalDate`

---
refactored constraint:
```
context RentalElement
inv: (self.GameCD->notEmpty() xor self.DVD->notEmpty())
inv legalDate:
       self.returnExpectedOn.isAfter(self.rental.rentedOn)
```

Fig. 5. Example of a ***Split AND Expression*** refactoring

3.2 UML Diagram Refactorings

In [11], Sunyé et al. discussed a set of refactorings that could be applied to class diagrams. These refactorings can be summarized in five basic operations: addition, removal, move, generalization and specialization of model elements (class, attributes, association ends and operations). To this set, we have added renaming refactorings because we consider them to be particularly relevant in situations where the OCL constraints are specified in separate files, since all significant name changes must be reflected in the concrete syntax used in the OCL part of the model.

Removal of UML model elements can be performed only when these elements are not referenced in the whole model. This implies that no OCL element must be associated to the UML element to be removed. Adding and removing classes can also be applied in an inheritance hierarchy. The *Insert Generalizable Element* refactoring replaces a generalization between two elements with two other generalizations, having a new element between them. The *Remove Generalizable Element* refactoring does the inverse, i.e., it removes an element without defined behavior and links its subclasses directly to its superclasses. As in any removal operation, the target element must not be referenced directly or indirectly by any UML or OCL model element.

Addition of attributes, operations, methods and associations to a class can be done when the added element does not have the same signature as any other elements owned by the target class and its parents. In his PhD thesis [5], Roberts states that a method with the same signature can be added to a subclass as long as it is semantically equivalent to the method defined in the superclass. In UML diagrams, the same rule can be applied to the addition of operations. However, whilst the structural equivalence of attributes, association ends and operation signatures can be verified by a straightforward comparison, the semantic equivalence between methods or operations can be a rather complex task.

Sunyé et al [11] also define Generalization and Specialization refactorings. Generalization is the integration of two or more elements into a single one, which is transferred to a common superclass. Specialization is the opposite of Generalization, since it pushes an element down to all direct subclasses of its owner. The Generalization refactoring can be easily applied in cases where the target elements are not involved in OCL constraints. However, complex constraints, especially those involving type casting and polymorphic operations, can lead to the same equivalence complexity problem previously described.

Therefore, as an initial step towards a fully automated support for refactoring UML models in a scenario where OCL is heavily used, we have adopted a more pragmatic approach by just supporting class diagrams refactorings based on rules that can be verified through structural relationships between model elements. Refactorings that demand more complex semantic equivalence analyses have been deferred to a future work.

3.3 OCL Definition Constraint Refactorings

In OCL 2.0 [7], reuse of variables/operations over multiple OCL expressions can be achieved through the use of *definition constraints*. Definition constraint is a constraint with the stereotype «definition» in which helper attribute/operation definitions, stereotyped as <<OclHelper>>, are attached to a classifier. Figure 6 shows some examples of definition constraints. In lines 1-2, a new attribute (*totalFee*) has been added to the *Rental* type, and in lines 4-7, a new operation (*areDebitsAboveLimit*) has been added to the *Client* type.

```
1 context Rental
2 def: totalFee : Money = self.elements.fee->sum()
3
4 context Client
5 def: areDebitsAboveLimit (limit : Money) : Boolean =
6   (self.rentals.totalFee->sum() - self.rentals.discount->sum()) -
7   self.rentals.amountPaid->sum() < limit
```

Fig. 6. Examples of definition constraints

Several OCL smells, especially those related to duplicate or complex expressions, can be removed by applying OCL refactorings based on definition constraints. This section briefly describes some refactorings of this type.

a) Add Operation Definition From Expression (source expression, targetClassifier, operationName, parameters)

This refactoring consists of adding an operation, stereotyped as <<OclHelper>>, and its respective definition constraint to the *targetClassifier*. The return type of the operation will be equal to the type of the *source expression*. Each *parameter* has a name and corresponds to a sub-expression selected from the *source expression*. Each parameter type matches the type of its corresponding sub-expression. The same preconditions for a conventional *Add Operation* refactoring apply here. Moreover, *source expression* must have an abstract syntax tree such that all expressions located at the leaves correspond to either literal expressions, references to *let* variables defined inside the *source expression,* or variable expressions linked to the same variable declaration. The type of that variable declaration must conform to the type of the *targetClassifier*. The references to the variable associated to all these variable expressions at the leaves are replaced by a reference to a "*self*" variable. Figure 7 shows an example of this refactoring.

source expression:
```
  if  newRental.rentedOn.dowIsBetween
          (DayOfWeek::Monday, DayOfWeek::Thursday)
  then        dvd.Film.category.normalFee
  else        dvd.Film.category.weekendFee
  endif
```
---

targetClassifier: `DVD`
operationName: `fee`
parameters:
parameter name: *day*   sub-expression: *newRental.rentedOn*
parameter.type: *Date*

---

added operation definition:
```
  context DVD
  def: fee(day : Date) : Money     =
        if day.dowIsBetween (DayOfWeek::Monday, DayOfWeek::Thursday)
        then  self.Film.category.normalFee
        else  self.Film.category.weekendFee
        endif
```

Fig. 7. Example of an *Add Operation Definition From Expression* refactoring

b) Replace Expression By Operation Call Expression (source expression, targetObject, targetOperation, arguments)

This refactoring is usually applied after the *Add Operation Definition From Expression* refactoring. It replaces the desired expression with an operation call expression linked to the *target operation.* The *source expression* must be equal to the expression associated to the *target operation* definition, except for references to the "*self*" variable that are part of the operation definition. The *source expression* must be either a property call expression or the body of a loop expression. Moreover, the type of the *source expression* or the associated iterator must conform to the return type of the *target operation. Arguments* are sub-expressions selected from the *source expression* that correspond to argument OCL expressions associated to the operation call expression that will be created. Figure 8 shows an example of this refactoring.

Due to space constraints, other refactorings such as *Add Attribute Definition From Expression*, *Replace Expression by Attribute Call Expression (*which are analogous to the refactorings based on operation definitions described previously), *Remove Attribute Definition* and *Remove Operation Definition* (which replace all uses of an attribute or operation by its corresponding expression) will not be detailed. The Rename Attribute/Operation refactorings mentioned in section 3.2 can also be applied to the attribute/operation definition constraints discussed in this section.

source expression:
```
    if newRental.rentedOn.dowIsBetween
          (DayOfWeek::Monday, DayOfWeek::Thursday)
    then  dvd.Film.category.normalFee
    else  dvd.Film.category.weekendFee
    endif
```
---

targetObject: dvd
targetOperation: *DVD::fee(day:Date) : Money*
arguments:
parameter: *day : Date* sub-expression: *newRental.rentedOn*

---

refactored expression: `dvd.fee(newRental.rentedOn)`

Fig. 8. Example of a *Replace expression by operation call expression* refactoring

It is important to notice that although the set of add and replace refactorings described in this section are distinct, they can be combined and automated in several different ways. For example, from an add refactoring, a refactoring tool can automatically apply the replace refactoring in the source expression, and it can also search for other possible targets for the application of the replace refactoring. This separation results in more compact and simple formal definitions of each refactoring and allows the definition of complex refactorings from more primitive ones in a way similar to the one described in [4].

4 Refactoring Automation

In this section we will show how OCL refactorings are defined and automated in Odyssey-PSW (Precise Specification Workbench), a prototype tool that is currently under development at our research lab. The main goal of our research is to develop tools and techniques that could make OCL more attractive to industrial settings. Odyssey-PSW is designed as an add-in to existent OO CASE tools and is able to access a UML model through a XMI interface.

4.1 Refactoring Definition

According to the UML standard [12], a UML model is organized as an instance of a MOF compliant metamodel. Therefore, any UML model can be represented by a graph of instances of the UML metamodel. Version 2.0 of the OCL standard also defines a MOF compliant metamodel for OCL expressions, and there are associations between OCL and UML metaclasses. A UML/OCL model can be viewed as a graph of instances of both UML and OCL metamodels. Figure 9 illustrates, schematically, an OCL expression and part of its corresponding graph.

A refactoring is defined as an update operation on the graph of instances representing a UML/OCL model. This operation has a name, a textual documentation, a sequence of parameters, preconditions that describe the model restrictions that must be satisfied before applying the refactoring, postconditions that state what properties are guaranteed by the refactoring, and a body that actually implements the refactoring.

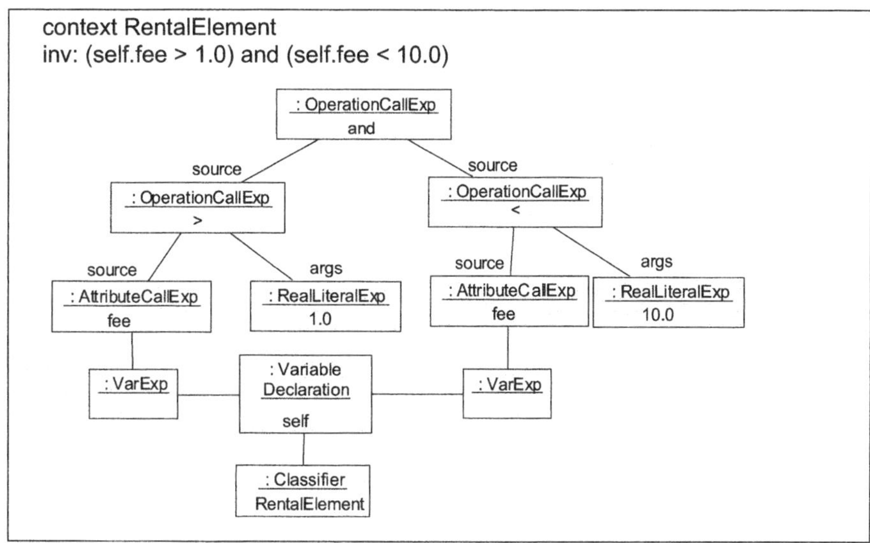

Fig. 9. Part of the abstract syntax tree of an OCL 2.0 expression

Pre and postconditions are defined in OCL. Since OCL is a side-effect free language, it cannot be used to update the graph of instances. Because of that, OCL-Script, our own scripting language, is used to define the body of a refactoring. OCL-Script is an imperative language, largely based on OCL, that allows actions such as creation and deletion of instances of a MOF compliant metamodel, assignment to attributes and association ends, operation calls, and operations that modify the contents of a collection, among others. All queries and link traversals are done using conventional OCL syntax.

Figure 10 shows how the *Replace expression by variable* refactoring can be defined using this structure. The first version of this refactoring was produced using the OCL metamodel as defined in the official standard and resulted in a very complex implementation. The reason for this complexity resides in the lack of support for generic traversals in an OCL abstract syntax tree. Since refactoring operations can be viewed as graph transformations, generic graph traversals and manipulation (creation and deletion of links, for example) are very important in this context. As it can be observed from the example shown in Figure 9, an OCL abstract tree is mostly composed of several linked expressions that must be traversed and modified by refactoring operations. However, since in the OCL 2.0 metamodel all associations between instances of the OclExpression metaclass are defined as specific composition associations, a simple traversal over an abstract syntax tree may result in lots of conditional code such as "*if appliedProperty->notEmpty() ... else if parentOperation ->notEmpty() ...*". An additional reason for this lack of generality is the fact that the VariableDeclaration metaclass has no superclass in the OCL metamodel.

The refactoring implementation shown in Figure 10 is based on a slightly modified version of the OCL 2.0 metamodel that greatly simplifies traversals over OCL abstract syntax trees. The proposed modifications to the OCL metamodel are shown in Figure 11. It contains a new metaclass named OCLModelElement that is the ancestor of all OCL metaclasses, except for the OCL types. The proposed metamodel also defines a composition association between instances of the OCLModelElement metaclass that can be used for generic abstract syntax tree traversals. Each association end of this added association is defined as a derived union of its subsets. To each composition association defined in the original OCL metamodel, a pair of *subsets* constraints was added (see the association between PropertyCallExp and OclExpression for an example). As an alternative, we could have used the self-association of the Element metaclass defined in the UML 2 Infrastructure Specification. In this case, we would have had to modify the OCL metamodel by defining the *subsets* constraints as explained before, and by defining the VariableDeclaration metaclass as a subclass of the UML 2 Element metaclass. Instead, we have chosen to add the OCLModelElement metaclass in order to make the solution more independent of the UML metamodel version. This independency is achieved in Odyssey-PSW by a bridge that is responsible to isolate the OCL metamodel elements from changes that may occur in the UML metamodel. Currently, Odyssey-PSW has bridges to the UML 1.3 and 1.4 metamodels.

```
context RefactoringComponent::ReplaceExpressionByVariable
 (sourceExpression : OclExpression, variable : VariableDeclaration)
-- sourceExpression is the root of a sub-graph that will be replaced by a variable expression
-- variable is a node corresponding to the Variable Declaration that will be linked to a new
-- variable expression

-- sourceExpression must have a sub-graph equivalent to the one referred by the target
-- variable declaration. areOclSubGraphsEquivalent is a query operation that evaluates
-- equivalence between OCL expressions
pre:sourceExpression.areOclSubGraphsEquivalent
(variable.initExpression)
-- variable must be visible in the source expression. variablesInScope is a query operation
-- that returns all variables visible to an OCL expression.
pre: sourceExpression.variablesInScope()->includes(variable)
post:
 let ownedElements : Set(OclModelElement) =
       sourceExpression.owner@pre.ownedElements,
     newVarExp : VariableExp = ownedElements->any(element |
       element.oclIsTypeOf(VariableExp) and
       element.oclIsNew()).oclAsType(VariableExp) in
 newVarExp.referredVariable = variable and
 ownedElements->excludes(sourceExpression)

actions:
  varExp : VariableExp;          -- variable definition

-- creates an instance of VariableExp, a link between this instance and the variable
-- parameter, and assigns to varExp variable a reference to the created instance
  varExp := new VariableExp(referredVariable => variable);
-- connects the variable expression to the owner node and disconnects sourceExpression
-- from it. ReplaceLink is a polimorphic operation since each expression type has specific
-- associations.
  sourceExpression.owner.replaceLink(sourceExpression, varExp);
-- deletes the source expression from the graph
  sourceExpression.deleteOclSubGraph();
```

Fig. 10. Formal definition of *Replace Expression by Variable* refactoring

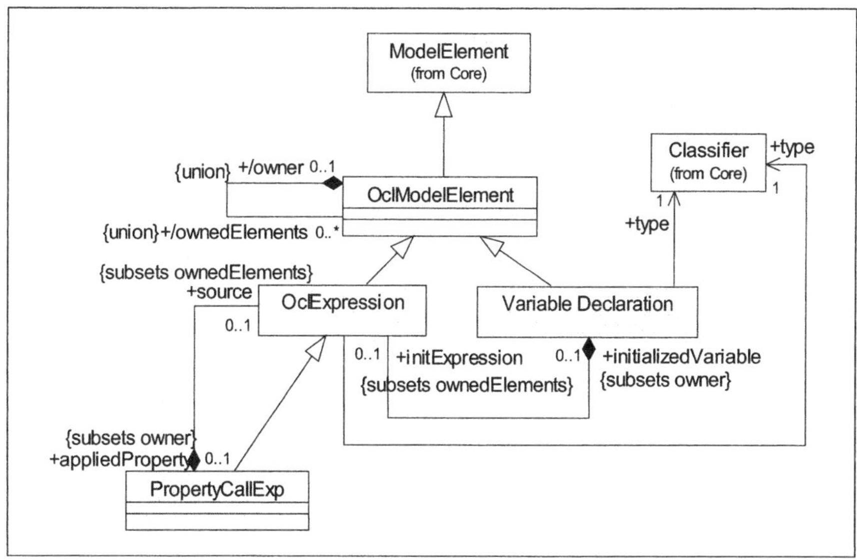

Fig. 11. The modified OCL 2.0 metamodel

4.2 Manual Refactorings and Animation

Although several useful model changes can be safely performed by applying automated refactorings, what if the modeler needs to do a modification to the UML/OCL model that is either not yet supported by the implemented refactorings or too complex to be implemented, such as the ones involving complex semantic analyses? In these situations, the modeler should manually modify the model, and in order to get more confidence that the model semantics were preserved, he can use the model animation features of Odyssey-PSW, applying the regression animation technique. This technique is inspired on the automated regression tests that support refactoring activities in the Extreme Programming method.

To be animated by Odyssey-PSW, the UML/OCL model must be compliant with the following requirements: query operations must have its body expression defined in OCL and non-query operations must have its body defined in OCL-Script. The Odyssey-PSW animation module checks if any invariant, precondition or postcondition is violated during an animation scenario. To perform a regression animation on a UML/OCL model, the modeler must specify test cases that define model snapshots corresponding to the instant right before and after the execution of some operation defined in the model. All test cases in which the actual results are different from the expected ones are shown to the user.

5 Related Work

The basic ideas of UML model refactoring were presented in [11], where the authors explored how the integrity of class diagrams and statecharts could be maintained after refactorings. Moreover, some statecharts refactorings were formally defined using OCL pre and postconditions.

Porres [13] proposed model refactorings as rule-based update transformations. In that proposal, refactorings are implemented through rules that have a guard (preconditions) and a body implemented in SMW, a script language based on Python. However, post conditions are not specified in these rules. While SMW is an extension for the Python language that implements many but not all OCL constructions using the Python syntax, our scripting language (OCL-Script) is an extension for the OCL itself, i.e., it supports all OCL features using the standard OCL syntax and provides additional constructions for producing side-effects.

Van Gorp et al [14] proposed an extension to the UML metamodel in order to support refactorings consistent with the source code through refactoring contracts. The proposed refactoring contract defines the pre and postconditions for a refactoring but leaves its implementation to CASE tool vendors.

The strategy for refactoring formalization presented in section 4 has been mainly inspired by these three papers. In our approach, refactoring preconditions and postconditions are written in OCL, as described in [11] and [14], but each refactoring is implemented using the proposed OCL extension, named OCL-script, in a way similar to the one described in [13].

Some OCL smells and refactorings described in this paper are closely related to the ones described in [15]. Although the smells described in that work are related to the implementation of methods, many of them can be adapted to UML/OCL specifications. The *Duplicated Code* OCL smell described in section 2.3 is an example of such adaptation. Some of the refactorings described in section 3.1 (*Add Variable From Expression, Replace Expression By Variable*) can also be viewed as adaptations of the *Introduce Explaning Variable* refactoring described in [15].

6 Conclusions

In this paper, we have discussed how refactoring techniques can be applied to a UML/OCL model. The main contributions of this work are: some OCL smells that can often be found in OCL specifications were presented and some refactorings that can be applied in order to remove these problematic constructions were proposed. We have also discussed how a refactoring can be formally defined and automated. A change in the OCL metamodel was proposed in order to ease the traversal and modification of an OCL abstract syntax tree. Finally, we briefly discussed the usefulness of the animation regression technique in the context of manually performed refactorings.

As future work, we plan to incorporate refactorings involving complex semantic analyses, as discussed in section 3, and develop an refactoring agent that will be able to analyze a specification searching for OCL smells and to automatically suggest better alternatives to the modeler.

References

[1] OMG. Model Driven Architecture (MDA), document number ormsc/2001-07-01 - July 2001.
[2] OMG. MOF 2.0 query/views/transformations RFP. OMG Document ad/02/04/10.
[3] William G. Griwswold. *Program Restructuring as an Aid to Software Maintenance.* PhD thesis, University of Washington, August 1991.
[4] William F. Opdyke. *Refactoring: A Program Restructuring Aid in Designing Object-Oriented Application Frameworks.* PhD thesis, University of Illinois at Urbana-Champaign, 1992.
[5] Don Bradley Roberts. *Practical Analysis for Refactoring.* PhD thesis, University of Illnois at Urbana-Champaign, 1999.
[6] Kent Beck. *Extreme Programming explained.* Addison-Wesley, 2000.
[7] OMG. UML 2.0 OCL Specification. October 2003.
[8] Shane Sendall. *Specifying Reactive System Behavior.* PhD thesis, Swiss Federal Institute of Technology in Lausanne, School of Computer and Communication Sciences, 2002.
[9] Desmond D'Souza and Alan Wills. *Objects, Components and Frameworks with UML: The Catalysis Approach.* Addison-Wesley, 1998.
[10] Karl Lieberherr and Ian Holland, Formulations and Benefits of the Law of Demeter. SIGPLAN Notices 24(3), pages 67-78, March 1989.
[11] Gerson Sunyé, Damien Pollet, Yves Le Traon and Jean-Marc Jézéquel. *Refactoring UML models.* In UML 2001, Lecture Notes of Computer Science vol. 2185, pages 134-148, Springer Verlag, 2001.
[12] OMG. Unified Modeling Language (UML), version 1.5, March 2003.
[13] Ivan Porres. *Model Refactorings as Rule-Based Update Transformations.* In UML 2003, Lecture Notes of Computer Science vol. 2863, pages 159-174, Springer Verlag, 2003.
[14] Pieter Van Gorp, Hans Stenten, Tom Mens and Serge Demeyer. *Towards Automating Source-Consistent UML Refactorings.* In UML 2003, Lecture Notes of Computer Science vol. 2863, pages 144-158, Springer Verlag, 2003.
[15] Martin Fowler. *Refactoring – Improving the Design of Existing Code.* Addison-Wesley, 1999.

Detecting OCL Traps in the UML 2.0 Superstructure: An Experience Report

Hanna Bauerdick, Martin Gogolla, and Fabian Gutsche

University of Bremen, Computer Science Department
Database Systems Group, D-28334 Bremen, Germany
[hanna|gogolla|gutsche]@informatik.uni-bremen.de
http://www.db.informatik.uni-bremen.de

Abstract. Currently, the OMG is developing a new version of the Unified Modeling Language (UML), UML 2.0, which involves major innovations in its metamodel. As for previous versions of the UML, the Object Constraint Language (OCL) is employed to give restrictions on the use of UML and for the formulation of additional operations. It seems that the OCL expressions in the current version of the UML 2.0 Superstructure have not been checked with a tool. In this paper we report on an experiment in checking and validating the well-formedness rules and operation definitions of the UML 2.0 Superstructure w.r.t. syntax and type checking by using our tool USE (UML-based Specification Environment). For this purpose we classify the errors detected by USE in appropriate error categories. We develop statistical information on error frequencies w.r.t. package location and error category. All errors detected by USE and their detailed description are made available in a separate EXCEL file.

1 Introduction

Today, the Unified Modeling Language (UML) [5,4] is commonly used as a description language within object oriented software development. For UML models, the Object Constraint Language (OCL) [5,7] is often applied to describe details of a model more precisely.
In the near future, a new version of UML will be released, UML 2.0 [6]. Apart from two parts dealing with OCL and diagram interchange, this UML version consists of two complementary documents: The UML Infrastructure defines the elementary language constructs and therefore provides the basic architecture for the UML Superstructure, which allocates the user constructs. Both parts, the Infrastructure and the Superstructure, are described with UML class diagrams and OCL expressions. In order to get more insight into the use of OCL within the UML metamodel, we have analyzed and categorized the OCL expressions of UML 2.0 by using our OCL tool USE [3]. The result of this validation process is collected in a comprehensive EXCEL file [1] and shows that many OCL errors arise due to errors in the underlying class diagrams.

T. Baar et al. (Eds.): UML 2004, LNCS 3273, pp. 188–196, 2004.

The aim of this study is first to give concrete hints to improve technical details of the UML 2.0, second to provide a larger case study showing the applicability of our tool USE, and third to make first steps for a test methodology for UML models with significant OCL parts and in particular to explore possibilities to document OCL errors appropriately.
The rest of the paper is structured as follows. Section 2 discusses extracts of the comprehensive validation, such as error categories which we found out to be adequate and expressive examples demonstrating typical problems which frequently occurred. In Sect. 3, statistical information about error frequencies will be presented. The paper closes with a short conclusion in Sect. 4.

2 OCL Traps in the UML 2.0 Superstructure

USE offers the possibility to check UML models on inconsistencies w.r.t. the class structure and OCL constraints. To validate the UML 2.0 Superstructure we have utilized this feature of USE. We have converted the superstructure MDL [2] file of the OMG into a USE compliant format to accomplish the validation process. We identified the following five main error categories: Category E1 is for plain syntax errors; category E2 describes minor inconsistencies; category E3 classifies type checking errors; category E4 stands for general problems; category E5 registers inconsistencies with USE. Errors which occurred more often were parameterized and consequently they have their own sub-category. In the following we will explain the different categories and give typical examples.

2.1 Category E1: Syntax Error

The first category E1 describes syntactical errors. The additional operation `inherit` of `Kernel::Class` (page 87 in [6]) is a typical example for this category.

```
inherit(inhs:Set(Kernel_NamedElement)):Set(Kernel_NamedElement)=
  inhs->excluding( inh | ownedMember
    ->select( oclIsKindOf(Kernel_RedefinableElement) )
      ->select( redefinedElement->includes(inh) ) )
```

The defining expression of the operation `excluding` is syntactically incorrect, because the bar | is not allowed in this place, as the original OCL syntax shows [7]:

```
set->excluding(object:T):Set(T)
```

As an example for a parameterized error sub-category for syntax errors we mention 'E1.1(boolValue)' which describes all errors, where a boolean value was used like an enumeration value. An example occurs in the following invariant of `IntermediateActions::AddStructuralFeatureValueAction` (page 219 of [6]):

```
inv: let insertAtPins=self.insertAt in
     if self.structuralFeature.isOrdered=#false
       then insertAtPins.isUndefined()
       else ... endif                          -- details left out
```

The literals `true` and `false` are predefined values in OCL, which means that the sharp `#` has to be omitted. The following further sub-categories of syntax errors E1 were identified as well:

- E1.2(X): 'X' is missing in the expression. With 'X' element of {(,),[,],...}.
- E1.3: Parentheses '[' ']' are not allowed here.
- E1.4: Too many right parentheses.
- E1.5: 'endif' is missing in the expression.
- E1.6: 'if' expression must have an 'else' expression.

2.2 Category E2: Minor Inconsistency

Errors which result from minor inconsistencies are described in the second category E2. One representative example for this category provides the following operation `is` of `Kernel::MultiplicityElement` (page 240 of [6]):

```
is(lowerbound:Integer, upperbound:UnlimitedNatural):Boolean=
  (lowerbound=self.lowerbound and upperbound=self.upperbound);
```

The identifiers (probably intended attributes or rolenames) `self.lowerbound` and `self.upperbound` are not defined in the context class or one of its superclasses. However there are derived attributes `lower` and `upper` and additional operations `lowerbound()` and `upperbound()` declared in this context. Probably one of these both possibilities is meant.
The single error sub-category identified within category E2 represents errors resulting from an erroneous multiplicity check:

- E2.1(X): Use OCL construct 'X.isDefined()' instead of 'X.multiplicity.is(1,1)' which is not defined as an operation (X being a rolename).

The navigation 'multiplicity' is not allowed in connection with 'X'.

2.3 Category E3: Type Checking Error

Very common OCL traps are type checking errors which are denoted here by E3. Type checking errors are easy to make and difficult to recognize. The operation `visibleMembers` is defined within the class `Kernel::Package` (page 100 of [6]) and shows the difficulty of this error category:

```
visibleMembers():Set(Kernel_PackageableElement)=
  member->select( m | self.makesVisible(m))
```

As Fig. 1 shows, the identifier `member` refers to a rolename of an association between the superclasses `Kernel::Namespace` and `Kernel::NamedElement`. Thus the above operation body returns a set of `Kernel::NamedElement`. This type is not compatible with the return type `Set(Kernel::PackageableElement)`.
One more example of this error category can be found in Appendix A.

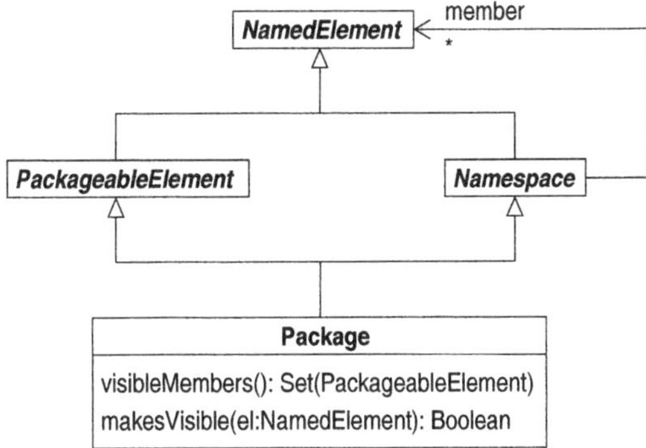

Fig. 1. Context Class Diagram for Operation `visibleMembers()`

2.4 Category E4: General Problems

Category E4 characterizes rather general problems. One typical example deals with the following additional operation of `BehaviorStateMachines::StateMachine` (page 491 of [6]):

```
LCA(s1:BehaviorStateMachines_State,s2:BehaviorStateMachines_State)
  :BehaviorStateMachines_State=
if ancestor(s1,s2) then s1 else
  if ancestor(s2,s1) then s2 else
    LCA(s1.container,s2.container) endif endif
```

The operation `LCA` possesses two parameters of type `BehaviorStateMachines::State`. However the recursive call of `LCA` assigns objects of type `BehaviorStateMachines::Region` to these parameters. This assignment leads to a type mismatch.
In Appendix B one further example of this category can be found.
'E4.1(member)' is a sub-category within E4 and describes errors where an attribute or rolename that is identified by the parameter 'member' is not defined. As an example consider the first invariant of `Kernel::Association` (page 81 of [6]) which uses the identifier `memberEnd`.

```
inv: self.parents()->forAll( p |
  p.memberEnd.size()=self.memberEnd.size() )
```

An attribute or rolename `memberEnd` is not defined in the UML 2.0 superstructure specification in this context. We also mention the last sub-category of the general problems which will not be described in detail:

- E4.2(X): Class 'X' is not defined (X being a class).

For us it was interesting that the OCL syntax check revealed places where the UML 2.0 class diagrams were inconsistent, i.e., places where names of attributes, rolenames, or classes are used but these names are not properly declared. Therefore, the OCL check offers much more than the analysis of the pure OCL expressions: The OCL check also makes statements about the correctness of the UML 2.0 class diagrams.

2.5 Category E5: Inconsistency with USE

Errors that utilize unsupported features of USE are described in the final category E5. One representative example for this category can be found in the following invariant of the class `Templates:: RedefinableTemplate-Signature` (page 557 of [6]):

```
inv: inheritedParameter = if extendedSignature->isEmpty()
        then Set{}
        else extendedSignature.parameter
     endif
```

The construct `Set{}` is not supported by USE. Instead USE offers the syntax `oclEmpty(Set(X))` where the specific type `X` must be substituted. The type of these expressions, e.g., `oclEmpty(Set(State))` or `oclEmpty(Set(String))`, is then uniquely defined in contrast to `Set{}` which has many types. In this case `Set{}` must be replaced by `oclEmpty(Set(Templates::TemplateParameter))`.

2.6 Changes Made Before Validating

Before we were able to employ USE, we had to make the following small modifications to the original description:

- We appended an underscore to identifiers which are keywords in USE, e.g., instead of the rolename `class` we use `_class`.
- The respective package names were added to the class names, e.g., instead of `Kernel::Namespace` we employ `Kernel_Namespace`, because USE is unaware of packages.
- The new primitive data type `UnlimitedNatural` was realized as a class, because it is not supported by USE.

All other necessary changes were explicitly identified in the validation process as error category E5 'Inconsistency with USE' and can be viewed in detail in the provided EXCEL file [1].

3 Results of the Validation

This section deals with the achievements of the validation. In the following, the structure of the EXCEL file and statistical issues will be discussed.

3.1 Error Documentation Structure in the EXCEL File

Every recognized error is documented in the mentioned EXCEL file [1]. The errors can be identified by their page location in the UML 2.0 Superstructure Specification [6]. The columns of the EXCEL file can be classified as follows:

- Page number of the offending entity (if applicable),
- page number of the corresponding diagram (if applicable),
- package name of the enclosing package,
- nature of the offending entity (e.g., class or invariant),
- context classifier of the offending entity,
- name of the participating classes (for associations, if applicable),
- type of the offending member (e.g., operation or rolename),
- name of the offending member,
- our error category,
- our error description, and
- location in our related USE file [1].

Column	Column description
Page	page 491 (Acrobat Reader page 507)
Figure	Figure 354, page 457 (Acrobat Reader page 473)
PackageName	BehaviorStateMachines
Classifier	Class
ClassEnumName	StateMachine
ParticipatingClassNamesForAssocs	((not applicable in this example))
MemberKind	operation
MemberRoleInvName	LCA(s1:BehaviorStateMachines::State, s2:BehaviorStateMachines::State)
ErrorCategory	E4
ErrorDescription	Operation call of LCA has 's1.container' as parameter. 's1.container' is of type 'Region' but a 'State' is expected.
USELine	1443

Fig. 2. Example Line of the EXCEL File

Figure 2 shows an example line from the EXCEL file (rotated by 90 degrees) which corresponds to the above example of the E4 category. This format is also the format in which a directly readable version of the EXCEL file is provided, namely the PDF file in [1].

3.2 Error Statistics

The UML 2.0 Superstructure contains 36 packages with 294 classes and 14 enumerations. 246 invariants and additional operations were defined with OCL and were taken into account during the validation process. We discovered 361 errors

Packages	#OCL exprs	#E	ERatio	#E1	#E2	#E3	#E4	#E5
AssociationClasses	2	7	3.5	2			5	
BasicActivities	1	2	2.0	1			1	
BasicInteractions	2	3	1.5				3	
BehaviorStateMachines	38	46	1.2	18		6	22	
Communications	1	1	1.0				1	
CompleteActions	26	27	1.0	6	9		12	
Fragments	1	2	2.0				2	
Interfaces	1	0	0.0					
IntermediateActions	51	105	2.0	28	15	5	51	6
Kernel	98	104	1.0	24	1	24	31	24
ProtocolStateMachines	2	0	0.0					
StructuredActivities	2	8	4.0	5			3	
Templates	17	20	1.1	3		4	8	5
UseCases	4	4	1.0	1				3
Associations		32					13	19
Sums	246	361		88	25	39	152	57
Percentages		100%		24%	7%	11%	42%	16%

Fig. 3. Numbers for the Validation

within these 246 OCL expressions. But also inconveniences and incompatabilites of our tool USE are included within this number.
The table in Fig. 3 lists all packages of UML 2.0 that use OCL. There are also 22 packages which do not use OCL at all. The line 'Associations' does not refer to a package, but to the errors which occurred during association handling, e.g., due to wrong rolenames. The table gives the number of OCL expressions (invariant or operation definition) in that package and shows the number of errors encountered. The five columns #E1, #E2, #E3, #E4, and #E5 in the right of the table refine the total number of errors #E according to our error categories. The fourth column entitled ERatio gives the number of errors per OCL expression. Accordingly, if one regards only our numbers, there are good and bad packages, e.g., the package StructuredActivities has the highest ERatio (4.0), the packages Interfaces and ProtocolStateMachines have the lowest ERatio (0.0). But both packages use only few OCL expressions. We found it also interesting that even packages with intensive use of OCL, namely the packages having more than ten OCL expressions, have a relatively high ERatio, i.e., an ERatio between 1.0 and 2.0.

4 Conclusion

In this paper, we have analyzed the OCL expressions in the UML 2.0 superstructure. Within the 246 OCL expressions we have found 361 places where our OCL tool USE had complaints. Many errors had its origin not in bad use of OCL, but in deficiencies of the underlying class diagrams. We think that all parts of an important standard like UML should be error-free and have provided detailed

information about the errors and possible corrections in the accompanying EXCEL file.
However, in our validation we have not exhausted the power of our validation tool USE. USE allows for example to instantiate the class diagrams by snapshots. With such an instantiation one could show the consistency of the invariants (Are there contradictory invariants?). Furthermore, in principle USE also allows to check whether one invariant is a consequence of a given set of invariants. Thus a redundancy check is imaginable as well (Are all invariants independent from each other?). Nevertheless, in addition to checks performed by machines one will still need developers enhancing the design quality through model inspection and discussions made with other modeling experts.

Acknowledgements

We would like to thank Bran Selic for pointing to the importance of the OCL part within UML 2.0.

References

1. Hanna Bauerdick, Martin Gogolla and Fabian Gutsche. UML 2.0 Validation Results in Form of an EXCEL, PDF, AND USE File. University of Bremen. 2004. `ftp://ftp.informatik.uni-bremen.de/local/db/papers/uml2004/ocl_uml2.[xls|pdf|use]`.
2. IBM Corporation, Rational Software: Rational Rose. http://www.rational.com.
3. Mark Richters and Martin Gogolla. Validating UML Models and OCL Constraints. In Andy Evans, Stuart Kent and Bran Selic, editors, UML 2000 - The Unified Modeling Language. Advancing the Standard. Proc. 3rd International Conference, LNCS 1939, pages 265-277. Springer, 2000.
4. Jim Rumbaugh, Ivar Jacobson and Grady Booch. The Unified Modeling Language Reference Manual. Addison-Wesley, 2nd Edition, 2004.
5. OMG. Unified Modeling Language Specification, Version 1.5, March 2003. Object Management Group, Inc., Needham, MA, http://www.omg.org, 2003.
6. OMG. UML 2.0 Superstructure Specification. Version ptc/03-08-02. Object Management Group, Inc., Needham, MA, http://www.omg.org, 2003.
7. Jos Warmer and Anneke Kleppe. The Object Constraint Language: Precise Modeling with UML. Addison-Wesley, 2nd Edition, 2003.

A Further Example for Error Category E3

One further interesting error example can be found in the second invariant of class `Templates::NamedElement` (page 560 of [6]).

```
inv: nameExpression.oclIsKindOf(Kernel_LiteralString)
       implies name = nameExpression.value
```

First of all there exists an inconsistency between the superstructure pdf document from the OMG and the superstructure MDL file. The rolename `nameExpression` references in the OMG document an association between `Templates::NamedElement` and `Templates::Expression`. However, in MDL file this rolename leads us to the class `Templates::StringExpression`.
Independent from the above inconsistency, this invariant will always be evaluated to true since the expression `nameExpression` can never be of type `Kernel::LiteralString` as you can conclude from the class diagram in Fig. 4.

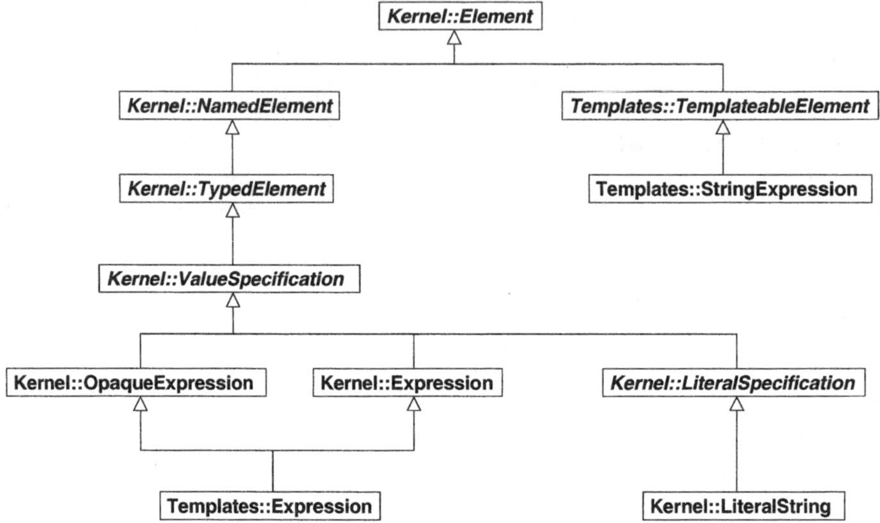

Fig. 4. Context Class Diagram for second invariant of class `Templates::NamedElement`

B Further Example for Error Category E4

The following excerpt from an invariant of class `IntermediateActions::-LinkEndCreationData` (page 238 of [6]) reveals another interesting error which ocurrs quite often within the superstructure document.

```
... insertAtPin.type = UnlimitedNatural ...
```

The rolename `type` returns an instance of `Kernel::Type`. With the use of the equality = operator the types of `insertAtPin.type` and `UnlimitedNatural` are tried to be compared. However in OCL the type comparison must be realized with the operation `oclIsTypeOf`.

From Informal to Formal Specifications in UML

Martin Giese and Rogardt Heldal

Chalmers University of Technology
Gothenburg, Sweden
{giese|helda}@cs.chalmers.se

Abstract. In this paper, we consider a way of bridging informal and formal specification. Most projects have a need for an informal description of the requirements of the system which all people involved can understand. At the same time, there is a need to make some of the requirements more formal. We present a way to relate informal requirements, in form of use cases, to more formal specifications, written in the Object Constraint Language (OCL). Our approach gives the customers of software systems a way of guiding the development of formal specifications. Conversely, the formal specification can improve the informal understanding of the system by exposing gaps and ambiguities in the informal specification.

1 Introduction

The development of software systems using the Unified Modeling Language (UML) [14, 13] has become the *de facto* standard for modeling object-oriented software systems. There are several reasons for this: it is relatively easy to understand and learn, it permits several views of software systems, and it gives a good overview of the software's architecture.

The simplicity of UML has its cost: it is less precise than many other specification languages, for example that of the B-method [1]. Some of the strength of these other specification languages can be obtained by adding Object Constraint Language (OCL) [13, 17] constraints to UML models. The added precision of a formal specification can greatly enhance the quality of the produced software. Tools like the KeY system [2] can be used to assist the authoring of OCL constraints, to check their consistency, and even to verify that an implementation adheres to the constraints.

On the other hand, it is not at all clear at which point in the development process OCL constraints should be written. Who is going to add them to the UML diagrams: customers, analysts, or designers? Who should understand OCL? This missing integration into the development process might be a reason why OCL is hardly used in industry.

We believe that the customers of the software system to be built need to be one of the driving forces behind producing OCL constraints. After all, only the customers can know what behavior they want from the system. However to expect the customer or even all of the developers to know OCL is unrealistic.

T. Baar et al. (Eds.): UML 2004, LNCS 3273, pp. 197–211, 2004.

Thus, there is a need for an informal description that everybody involved in the project can understand.

This is indeed the purpose of use cases. Use cases describe the system behavior in an informal way, usually using only text. In contrast to some research [7] which tries to add formal specifications directly to use cases, we will stick to text, because we believe that there needs to be an informal description of the system *somewhere*. Even for informal, textual use cases however, templates are used to structure the descriptions, e.g. the base use case description template in the Rational Unified Process (RUP), and these templates normally include pre- and post-conditions. In contrast to the OCL constraints usually attached to operations in a class diagram, these textual constraints can be understood by and negotiated with the customer.

In this paper, we investigate the *relationship* between the informal, textual pre- and post-conditions of use cases and the formal OCL pre- and post-conditions of operations in the class diagram. Apart from being a step from informal to formal specification, this is also a step from the analysis phase (use cases) to the design phase (sequence and class diagrams). The primary goal will be to make sure that all the behavior specified together with the customer in the use cases is also captured by the formal OCL specification attached to operations in the class diagrams.

Another important aspect when going from informal to formal description is the need to become more precise. It is often necessary to add contextual information in a formalization that was implicitly assumed, or simply forgotten in the textual use case description. We will consider ways to cope with such additional information, either by enhancing the use case text or at by acknowledging contextual information as such, thus making the formalization process more transparent. In other words, not only does the informal specification help in writing the formal one, but the formalization can also help in improving the informal one. Including customers in the development of the formal specification in this way gives them more power, but also more responsibility. We believe that it can add significantly to the value of a formal specification.

We should note that our method does not, in general, give OCL specifications for all operations in the model. In fact, there will usually be two categories of constraints: The first kind directly reflects the customer's requirements, and it is only this kind we consider in this paper. The other kind relates to the internal structure of the system, and is dependent on the design. Conditions on the type and range of method arguments belong to this category, as well as specifications of auxiliary methods used to implement the required functionality. Although this second kind of constraints is also important, they cannot easily be linked to the information in use cases.

This work is concerned with three types of UML diagrams: use case diagrams, state chart diagrams and class diagrams. Before we explain the approach itself, we briefly discuss use cases and state chart diagrams. In Sect. 2, we present the theoretical basis of our approach, which we then use in a case study in Sect. 3. The case study suggests a refinement of the theory which is presented in Sect. 4.

1.1 Use Case Diagrams

Use cases were invented by Jacobson [10]. They are part of the UML [13] and supported by UML tools, and widely used in the industry. There are a number of books dedicated only to use cases and countless papers discussing possible interpretations of use cases. Some of the more recent papers which have influenced our understanding of use cases are [5, 6, 9] and the book [3].

The informal nature of use cases allows more or less any textual description of a system to be categorized as a use case. This is both a strength and a weakness: on one side they can be used in many contexts, but on the other side their informal nature creates problems like choosing the right level of abstraction and ensuring inconsistency both inside and between use cases. Writing good use cases is a far from trivial task, but they can make a valuable contribution to the understanding of a project.

In our work, the style of writing use case descriptions is less important, as long as they create a common understanding between customers and developers, in such a way that sensible pre- and post-conditions can be obtained. In our case study, we describe the flows of the use cases in an abstract way, keeping out details like the user interface, in a style often referred to as essential use cases [5, 4]. This style of use cases was enough to obtain the required pre- and post-conditions. The text of pre- and post-conditions should be precise, but there is no need for formal or mathematical notation at this level.

Alternative flows [3] are crucial for our usage of use cases. There is nearly always more than one path through a use case, and the user should specify what happens in these alternative scenarios. Technically, alternative flows may be split into separate use cases, but we think having a use case for what is actually an error condition goes against the intention of use cases as satisfying a goal.

On the other hand, we do not explicitly consider 'include' and 'extends' [3] relationships for the time being. They may be treated by a transformation to 'flat' use cases that moves the extensions, resp. inclusions into the extended, resp. including use case.

1.2 State Chart Diagrams

We want to consider all scenarios, i.e. all possible paths through a use case. To describe all paths, we use a state chart diagram [13]. We are only interested in a limited part of the state chart: the final call event for each path, together with all the branching conditions for that path. In Sect. 2, we will show that this information suffices to capture the properties we want to hold.

Sequence or collaboration diagrams are commonly used to illustrate a scenario of a use case. The problem with these diagrams for our purpose is that they generally show only one path through a use case.[1]

Even though we use state chart diagrams to model all possible paths through a use case, it is useful to start with a sequence diagram for some of the important

[1] It might be possible to use generic interaction diagrams[16] instead, including conditional behavior and iteration.

scenarios. This simplifies the process of creating the state chart diagram, since it helps to identify the important calls.

2 From Use Cases to Operation Post-conditions

We start from a use case *UC* equipped with a post-condition $Post_{UC}$ formulated in natural language. We will not consider pre-conditions of use cases in this work, because the usual understanding of a pre-condition is that the post-condition need only be guaranteed if the pre-condition is met before the use case. In other words, having "the customer entered the correct PIN" as a pre-condition means that we will not specify what happens if the customer enters a wrong PIN. This is a much weaker statement than saying that the use case cannot be executed if the pre-condition is not met. It is easy to get confused by these two readings. To avoid this trap, we leave use case pre-conditions completely empty.

In the implementation, we expect the use case *UC* to correspond to a sequence of calls into the system, which we model as a single system object s. This is the only object we will talk about, and all OCL constraints are to be understood in the context of s, i.e. `self` $= s$. Depending on what exactly the user does, the sequence of operations might be different. Whatever the sequence is however, $Post_{UC}$ should finally hold, so ultimately it needs to be guaranteed by the post-condition of the last operation.

A post-condition $Post_{UC}$, given in natural language by the customer, will probably refer not only to the final state. It is natural to refer to the *sequence* of events, like in "when the customer entered the wrong PIN three times, ...". We will capture the possible sequences of events in a state chart which we attach to the system object s. Paths through the state chart correspond to possible sequences of events. The important aspects of this state chart are the events that correspond to operation calls from the outside, i.e. from the agent. The state chart can also contain conditions which refer to the arguments of these events.

The goal of this section is to match the post-conditions of the operations and conditions from the state chart to the use case post-condition. While the use case post-condition $Post_{UC}$ is an informal artifact of the analysis phase, and thus necessarily informal, the conditions in the state chart and the post conditions of the operations are written in OCL as part of the design.

Given a state chart, we can collect the set Σ of all paths π from the initial state to some final state. Depending on the state chart, there may be infinitely many of these. For every path π with events $op_1(args_1), \ldots, op_k(args_k)$ let

$$final(\pi) := op_k$$

be the last operation called. For correctness, we want every final state that the post condition of this method allows to also be permitted by the post condition of the use case. As a first approximation, we want the post-condition of the last operation to *imply* the post condition of the use case:

$$Post_{final(\pi)} \rightarrow Post_{UC}$$

Now, as $Post_{UC}$ includes requirements for all possible different paths, this implication will usually hold only if we add information about the path taken. As OCL does not allow to refer to the values of attributes in different states, we have to impose the restriction that the conditions (guards) in the state chart do not refer to attributes, and that the names for event arguments are all distinct. Let $Cond(\pi)$ be the conjunction of the conditions encountered on the path π, together with an expression of the form `oclInState@pre(x)` which expresses the state before the call of the last operation. What we want is then the weaker statement

$$Cond(\pi) \rightarrow (Post_{final(\pi)} \rightarrow Post_{UC})$$

or equivalently $(Cond(\pi) \wedge Post_{final(\pi)}) \rightarrow Post_{UC}$. Finally, this should be the case for all paths $\pi \in \Sigma$:

$$\bigwedge_{\pi \in \Sigma} \big((Cond(\pi) \wedge Post_{final(\pi)}) \rightarrow Post_{UC}\big) \qquad (I)$$

Note that we do not require $Post_{UC}$ to be given in formal syntax. Instead, we will consider all paths π, *formally* calculate the conjunction $Cond(\pi) \wedge Post_{final(\pi)}$ and then *informally* ask ourselves whether the formal post-condition does enough and whether all it does is intended. We shall see in the case study that it is valuable to ask this question, even without fully formal reasoning.

So far, we have considered only correctness, in the sense that every behavior allowed by the formal specification is also allowed according to the informal one. We shall see that it is also interesting to investigate the opposite direction, namely whether every behavior the informal specification allows is still allowed by the formal one. This would be the case if

$$Post_{UC} \rightarrow Post_{final(\pi)}$$

holds on every path, so

$$\bigwedge_{\pi \in \Sigma} \big((Cond(\pi) \wedge Post_{UC}) \rightarrow Post_{final(\pi)}\big) \qquad (II)$$

Typically, as we will see in the case study, information is added when an informal specification is formalized. This might be domain knowledge that is taken for granted by the authors of the informal specification, or even simple everyday knowledge (*red* $\neq$ *green*). In such cases, requiring (*II*) to hold would make the informal post specification $Post_{UC}$ unnecessarily verbose. After all, $Post_{UC}$ should be something that can be negotiated with a customer. We could however keep track of the added information $Extra(\pi)$ (which might be formal or informal) for every path and require

$$\bigwedge_{\pi \in \Sigma} \big((Cond(\pi) \wedge Post_{UC} \wedge Extra(\pi)) \rightarrow Post_{final(\pi)}\big) \qquad (III)$$

This would ensure that every requirement expressed in the formal post condition could be traced either to $Post_{UC}$ or to $Extra(\pi)$.

3 Case Study

We take a simple automated teller machine (ATM) scenario as a case study. We will look at only one use case, named "withdraw", in which the customer attempts to withdraw money from a bank account, see Fig. 1. For this, a PIN has to be entered and the requested amount must not exceed the balance on the customer's bank account. If the wrong PIN is entered three times, the card should be retained.

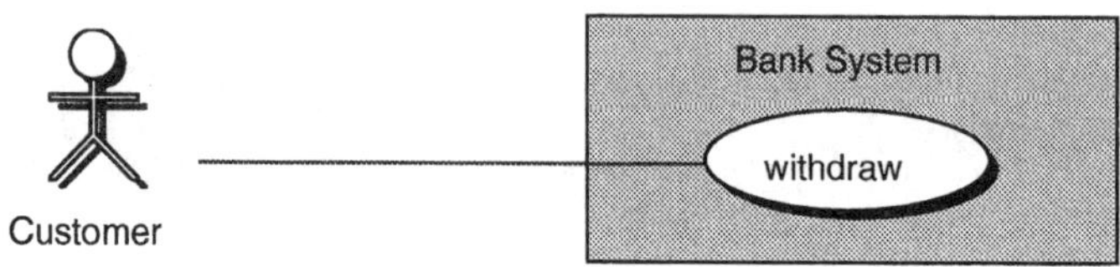

- If the customer entered the PIN stored on the Card, and the customer's balance was greater or equal to the requested amount, then the customer got the requested amount and the amount was deducted from the balance.
- If the customer entered the wrong PIN three times, the card was retained.
- If the customer requested too much money, the card was returned to the customer.

Fig. 1. The 'withdraw' use case for the ATM example, with its textual post condition

We can phrase these requirements as a *post-condition* for the withdraw use case, as shown in Fig. 1. Note that this postcondition is stated in natural language, in accordance with the informal nature of Use Cases. Also, it refers to the course of events in the past tense, that is from the perspective of having gone through the use case.

The normal flow of control is illustrated in Fig. 2. The whole sequence of events is initiated by the user presenting the card to the ATM, which is modeled by the call `insertCard(card)` to the system object `atm`. To be able to check the PIN entered by the user, the card is queried for the correct PIN, `cardPin`.

We neglect the modeling of other ATM operations, for example balance inquiry. As is customary, we do not model the control of the user interface, which would of course request the user to enter the PIN number at this point. We just assume that the completed PIN is given to the ATM controller with the call `givePin(userPin)`. For the normal flow of control, the subsequent call of `checkPinsEqual()` would return `true`.

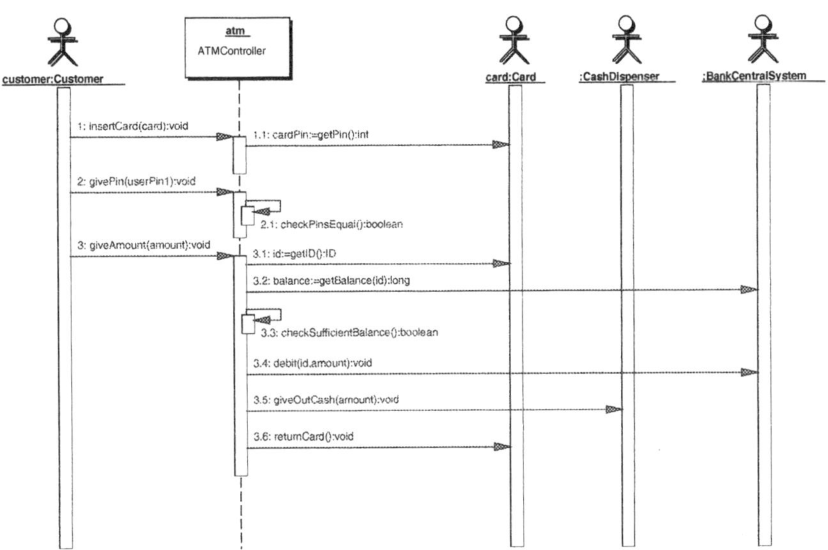

Fig. 2. Sequence diagram for the normal flow of the "withdraw" use case

Now, the user interface would be updated to ask the customer for the desired amount, which is passed to the controller in the call `giveAmount(amount)`. This amount needs to be compared to the customer's bank account balance. For this purpose, an identification `id` of the bank account is fetched from the card, and used to query `balance` from the bank's central system. After checking that the balance is sufficient, the `CashDispenser` unit is instructed to deliver the required amount to the user. Finally, the card is returned to the user.[2]

Comparing the post condition in Fig. 1 with this sequence diagram, one immediately notices the shortcoming of the latter: it does not say anything about the alternative flows of control. What happens if the call to `checkPinsEqual` or `checkSufficientBalance` returns `false`? For the normal flow of control, it is obviously the operation `giveAmount` which is responsible for ensuring the post-condition of the use case, simply because it is the last operation called. But what if the user enters the wrong PIN three times? Then the customer will never be asked to enter an amount. In that flow of control, the `giveAmount` operation will never be called, so it can no longer be responsible for ensuring the post-condition.

[2] It can be questioned where the call of `returnCard()` should be directed. We chose `card`, because the controller obviously communicates directly only with the card reading device and not with the card itself. If `card` stands for the card reader, than it is the right goal for the `returnCard()` call. One might also argue that the initial `insertCard()` call should then come from the card reader and not from the `customer` actor. However, this confuses more than it helps, and it is not really essential to our investigation.

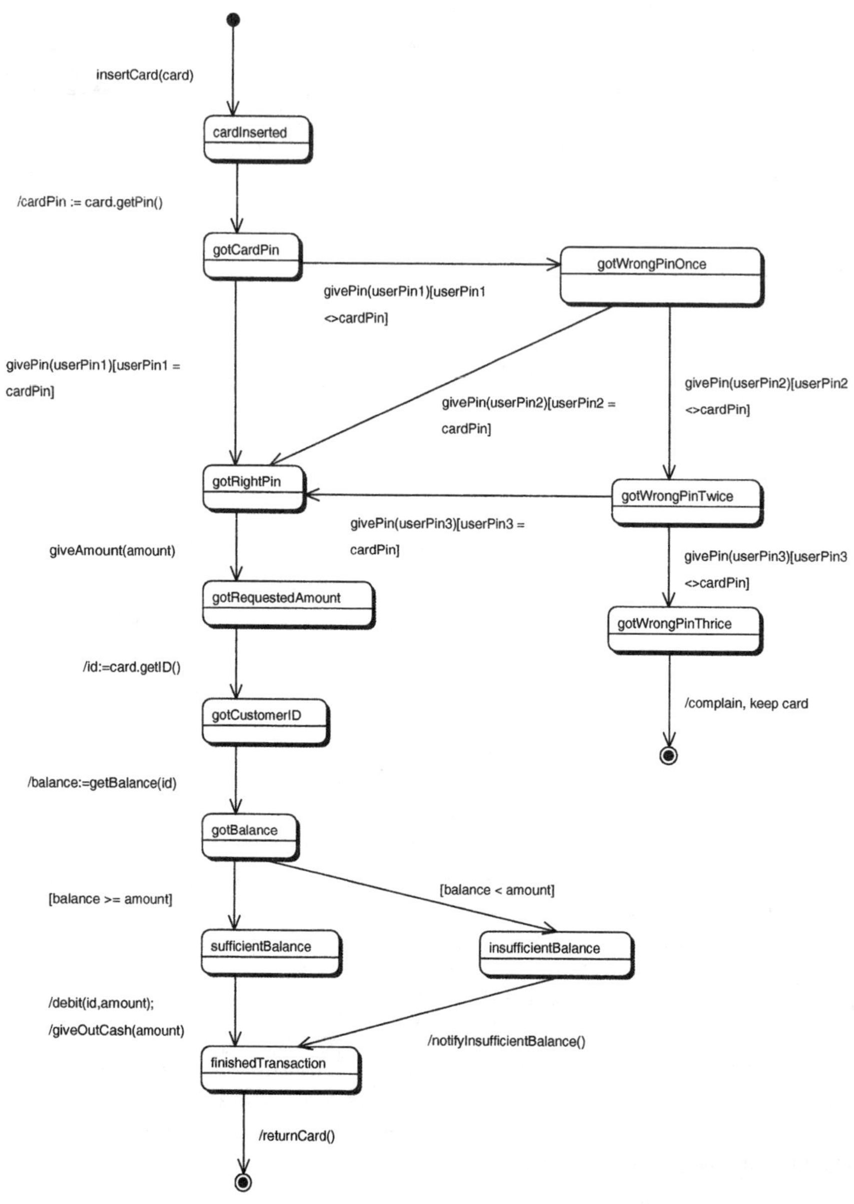

Fig. 3. State Chart for the "withdraw" use case of the ATM example

In order to cope with all the different possible flows of control, we attach a state chart to the system object `atm`, which we use essentially as a condensation of all sequence diagrams for all the flows of control of this use case. The following parts are captured here:

1. The *events* which correspond to the calls into the system in the sequence diagram. These are the calls `insertCard(card)`, `givePin(userPin)` and `giveAmount(amount)`. Some transitions have no event associated to them. This is convenient to capture a sequence of actions (e.g. get the `id`, get the balance, check the balance) triggered by a single event. In some paths, the `givePin` method gets called several times, so we call the argument `userPin1`, `userPin2`, etc. to ease later reference.
2. The *conditions* which determine which transitions will be chosen, depending on the data coming with the events. These are the items in square brackets, like `[userPin=cardPin]` or `[balance<amount]`.[3]

Due to the structure of the state chart, we can now see at a glance that there are at most 7 possible flows of control, one for each path from the initial state to some final state. In fact, one can check that the conditions on each of these paths are non-contradictory, so there are actually exactly 7 flows of control. One also sees immediately that the last event, and thus the last operation called for 6 of these is `giveAmount` and for one flow it is `givePin`.

According to the plan outlined in Sect. 2, we want the post condition of the last operation on every path, together with the accumulated conditions, to imply the post condition of the use case. So the post condition of `givePin` will have to take care of the situation that the wrong PIN was entered three times, while the post condition of `giveAmount` will cover all other cases.

To start with the simpler case, here is a possible OCL formulation of a post condition for `givePin`:

```
Context ATMController::givePin(userPin:int):void post:
  if (userPin = card.getPin()) then
    oclInState(gotRightPin)
  else if (oclInState@pre(gotCardPin)) then
    oclInState(gotWrongPinOnce)
  else if (oclInState@pre(gotWrongPinOnce)) then
    oclInState(gotWrongPinTwice)
  else
    not card^returnCard()
```

Note that we use the expression `card.getPin()` for the PIN stored on the card. Using an operation in an OCL constraint requires it to be free from side effects, i.e. a *query*. We assume that this is no problem for `getPin()` of `Card`. Finally, we use the 'has Sent' operator `^` of OCL 2.0 to express that the `returnCard()` method of `card` has not been called.

The post condition of `giveAmount(amount:long)` has to take care of all paths through the state chart where the correct PIN was eventually entered. Here is a possibility:

[3] In this diagram, the conditions unambiguously determine which transitions will be taken. This need not be the case in every diagram. Our method applies without changes even for indeterministic state charts.

```
Context ATMController::giveAmount(amount:long) post:
  if ( amount <= bank.getBalance(card.getID()) ) then
        cashDispenser^giveOutCash(amount)
    and   bank.getBalance(card.getID())
        = bank.getBalance@pre(card.getID()) - amount
    and card^returnCard()
  else
        not cashDispenser^giveOutCash(?)
    and   bank.getBalance(card.getID())
        = bank.getBalance@pre(card.getID())
    and card^returnCard()
```

We see that there are two cases, according to whether the required amount is below the bank account balance or not. The methods `getID()` of `Card` and `getBalance(id:ID)` of `BankCentralSystem` are both queries.

Now we can investigate the relationship of these post conditions to that of the use case, given in Fig. 1. We will only do this for four of the paths:

1. The "normal flow" with no wrong PIN entered and a sufficient balance.
2. First PIN entered is correct, but insufficient balance.
3. First PIN entered is incorrect, then like in normal flow
4. Three wrong PINs entered.

The three remaining flows are very similar to these four.

Normal flow of control. Let π_1 be the normal flow of control. The last operation $\mathit{final}(\pi_1)$ is `giveAmount()`. The conditions gathered on the normal path are

$$\mathit{Cond}(\pi_1) \quad = \quad (\texttt{userPin1 = cardPin} \land \texttt{balance >= amount})$$

Using the logical tautology $A \land (\texttt{if } A \texttt{ then } B \texttt{ else } C) \leftrightarrow A \land B$, we can simplify the conjunction

$$\mathit{Cond}(\pi_1) \land \mathit{Post}_{\mathit{final}(\pi_1)}$$

to

```
    userPin1 = cardPin
and balance >= amount
and cashDispenser^giveOutCash(amount)
and   bank.getBalance(card.getID())
    = bank.getBalance@pre(card.getID()) - amount
and card^returnCard()
```

One can now easily check that this implies *all three* of the points expressed informally in Fig. 1: the first point because the actions prescribed (give out cash, deduce amount from balance) have taken place. The other two, because the conditions ("If the customer...") of $Post_{UC}$ are contradicted by the gathered conditions $Cond(\pi_1)$. Of course, they will receive proper treatment when we look at the other flows of control. One difficulty here is that expressions using `@pre` refer to the state before the execution of `giveAmount`, instead of that before the use case. We have to convince ourselves that the balance has not been changed by the previous operations. Alternatively, one might introduce a means of referring to the state before the use case in the post condition. How to avoid this problem is a topic for future research.

So, for the normal flow of control, the post condition of `giveAmount` is powerful enough: if the implementation of that operation fulfills the post condition, then it will also correctly fulfill the post condition of the use case. But there is another aspect: in the informal post condition $Post_{UC}$, there was no mention of the card being returned. The clause `card^returnCard()` is something we added when we formulated the OCL constraints. Maybe the author of the informal specification forgot about this information, in which case it should probably by added to $Post_{UC}$. But it might also be information that may be taken for granted, and would only encumber the informal specification. It is hard to decide in general what to do with such added information, but our methodology does not depend on the choice taken. If the instruction to return the card is not added to $Post_{UC}$, it might still be added to $Extra(\pi_1)$, and then (*III*) holds, as one easily sees. The main point here is that a careful comparison of $Cond(\pi_1) \wedge Post_{final(\pi_1)}$ and $Post_{UC}$ can reveal such extra information added during the formalization, and that tool support could help to keep track of it.

Correct PIN but insufficient balance. Let π_2 be the flow of control where the correct PIN is entered at the first attempt but the amount requested is too high. The final operation is still `giveAmount`, but the gathered conditions are now:

$$Cond(\pi_2) \quad = \quad (\texttt{userPin1 = cardPin} \wedge \texttt{balance < amount})$$

For $Cond(\pi_2) \wedge Post_{final(\pi_2)}$, we get

```
    userPin1 = cardPin
and balance < amount
and not cashDispenser^giveOutCash(?)
and   bank.getBalance(card.getID())
    = bank.getBalance@pre(card.getID())
and card^returnCard()
```

Now the condition of the first two items in $Post_{UC}$ are not fulfilled, but that of the third ("If the customer requested too much money") is. And indeed, the conjunction of conditions and post condition states that the card was returned. Again, there is additional information that was missing in $Post_{UC}$, namely that no cash was delivered to the customer, and that the balance on the bank account did not change.

Correct PIN at second attempt. Let π_3 be the flow of control where the correct PIN is entered at the first attempt but the amount requested is too high. The final operation is `giveAmount` again, the conditions are

$$Cond(\pi_3) \quad = \quad \begin{pmatrix} \quad \texttt{userPin1 != cardPin} \\ \wedge \ \texttt{userPin2 = cardPin} \\ \wedge \ \texttt{balance >= amount} \end{pmatrix}$$

$Cond(\pi_3) \wedge Post_{final(\pi_3)}$ is

```
    userPin1 != cardPin
and userPin2 = cardPin
and balance >= amount
and cashDispenser^giveOutCash(amount)
and   bank.getBalance(card.getID())
    = bank.getBalance@pre(card.getID()) - amount
and card^returnCard()
```

Except for the slightly changed conditions, this is the same as for the normal flow π_1. Indeed, $Post_{UC}$ is implied for the same reason as in π_1, as it says "If the user entered the PIN on the card..." and does not specify in which attempt the correct PIN was entered. We will come back to this observation in Sect. 4.

Wrong PIN three times. We call π_4 the flow of control where the customer enters the wrong PIN three times in a row. The final operation $final(\pi_4)$ is the fatal third `givePin`. The gathered conditions are

$$Cond(\pi_4) \quad = \quad \begin{pmatrix} \quad \texttt{userPin1 != cardPin} \\ \wedge \ \texttt{userPin2 != cardPin} \\ \wedge \ \texttt{userPin3 != cardPin} \end{pmatrix}$$

$Cond(\pi_4)$ includes the information that `oclInState@pre(gotWrongPinTwice)` is true, so $Cond(\pi_4) \wedge Post_{final(\pi_4)}$ reduces to

```
not card^returnCard()
```

This obviously implies $Post_{UC}$, the second point being the relevant one in this case. Note that we have to assume that the condition "If the customer requested too much money" is not met. In fact, the customer did not get a chance to request any amount of money at all. That there is a problem here can be seen by considering the condition "If the requested amount lies below the customer's balance", which on one hand looks like the negation of the one above, but on the other hand might *also* be considered false in the present case where no amount was requested. One sees that the handling of undefined values is by no means trivial.

There are three more paths in the state chart, but they are very similar to the ones discussed. We think that this case study shows the validity and relevance of the theoretical concepts developed in Sect. 2. There is however a question of practicality remaining, which we will discuss in the following section.

4 Grouping Similar Paths

In our case study, there were only seven possible paths through the state chart. But in general, there might be very many, even infinitely many paths. In that case, it becomes impractical to consider each path separately. On the other hand, we already noticed in the previous section, that similar paths can require similar reasoning. It is therefore worthwhile to divide the set of possible paths into partitions which require similar reasoning. How this is best done is research in progress, but we want to give some ideas in this section.

We first remark that the post condition $Post_{UC}$ is actually composed of a number of clauses, each of which contains some condition on the path taken. The structure in the case study is

$$Post_{UC} = (C_1 \rightarrow P_1) \wedge (C_2 \rightarrow P_2) \wedge (C_3 \rightarrow P_3)$$

To show condition (I) of Sect. 2, it is sufficient to show

$$\bigwedge_{\pi \in \Sigma} \left((Cond(\pi) \wedge Post_{final(\pi)} \wedge C_i) \rightarrow P_i\right)$$

for $i = 1, 2, 3$. We now have three conditions to show, but for each of them, many paths are immediately excluded by C_i. For instance

$$C_3 = \text{“If the customer requested too much money”}$$

is only fulfilled on the three paths that go through the state ‘insufficientBalance’ in the state chart. Further, note that the last operation $final(\pi)$ is `giveAmount` on all these paths and that the condition `balance < amount` is on all three paths. It is thus sufficient to show

$$(\texttt{balance < amount} \wedge Post_{\texttt{giveAmount}} \wedge C_3) \rightarrow P_3$$

which can easily been seen to hold, because neither $Post_{\texttt{giveAmount}}$ nor P_3 require the information about the PIN verification process that was lost in taking only the conditions that were present on all three paths.

We believe that this approach can be generalized to reduce the number of paths that need to be considered in many practical cases.

5 Related Work

Grieskamp and Lepper [7] used executable Z to describe use cases. The benefit is that this gives a complete formal specification which can even be run. This is good for testing use cases. The drawback is the lack of informal description of the system to be made. It is hard for people without formal specification skills to understand the use cases. This makes use cases difficult to use as communication between customers and developers.

There have been a number of papers about relating the formal specification language B to UML [11, 12, 15]. In the papers [11, 15] the focus is on deriving a B model from a UML class description. Neither of these papers has a customer focus. The work of Levy, Marcano and Souquières [12] considers the mapping from informal to formal specification in a way similar to ours, using the B specification language instead of OCL. It is a short paper which gives a very brief overview of their process. They have not made clear the relationship between informal and formal specification, and no theory is stated in the paper.

6 Conclusion

Both informal and formal specification has its merits. A formal specification is more precise and therefore better suited for supporting the production of code, testing and proving. On the other hand, formal specifications are harder to read, and therefore informal specifications are needed. But for both the informal and formal specification to make sense, there has to be consistency between them – at least in those places where the system is described in both ways. In this paper, we have shown a process of relating informal specifications on use cases to formal OCL specifications on operations. Without a process like the one presented in this paper it is hard to justify the forces behind the writing of OCL constraints related to the customer's requirements. We have shown how to obtain formal specifications from informal ones, but also how the formal specification can improve the informal one.

One important field for further research is to find ways to handle state charts with infinitely many paths, extending the ideas from Sect. 4. Also, ways to handle `@pre` in post conditions correctly need to be investigated.

We also plan to provide a certain extent of tool support within the KeY system [2], to help developers in documenting and tracing the process of formalizing the customers requirements.

Finally, we want to try to automatically translate OCL constraints back to natural language: To automatically go from informal descriptions to formal descriptions is very hard. The other way around is more feasible, since a formal description is unambiguous. There is work by Hähnle, Johannisson, and Ranta [8] in going from OCL constraints to text descriptions. Having OCL pre and post conditions make it possible to obtain better textual description for use cases. The text produced might be used to validate the original description – even the customer can take part in this process since no OCL constraints are involved. Furthermore, the original text might be strengthened or replaced by the new text. This kind of round-trip engineering, involving a formally untrained customer on one side and a precise, formal specification on the other, would add tremendously to the value of formal specifications.

Acknowledgments

We would like to thank Wolfgang Ahrendt, Peter Gammie, and the anonymous referees for their helpful comments on drafts of this paper.

References

[1] J. R. Abrial. *B-Book*. Cambridge Univ. Press, 1996.

[2] W. Ahrendt, T. Baar, B. Beckert, R. Bubel, M. Giese, R. Hähnle, W. Menzel, W. Mostowski, A. Roth, S. Schlager, and P. H. Schmitt. The KeY tool. *Software and System Modeling*, 3, 2004. To appear.

[3] F. Armour and G. Miller. *Advanced Use Case Modeling*. Addison-Wesley, 2001.

[4] A. Cockburn. *Writing Effective Use Cases*. Addison-Wesley, 2001.

[5] L. L. Constantine and L. A. D. Lockwood. *Structure and Style in Use Cases for User Interface Design*, chapter 7, pages 245–279. Object Technology. Addison-Wesley, 2001.

[6] G. Génova, J. Llorens, and V. Quintana. Digging into use case relationships. In J.-M. Jézéquel, H. Hussmann, and S. Cook, editors, *UML 2002*, volume 2460 of *LNCS*, pages 115–127. Springer Verlag, 2002.

[7] W. Grieskamp and M. Lepper. Using use cases in executable Z. In *ICFEM*, pages 111–120, 2000.

[8] R. Hähnle, K. Johannisson, and A. Ranta. An authoring tool for informal and formal requirements specifications. In R.-D. Kutsche and H. Weber, editors, *Fundamental Approaches to Software Engineering*, volume 2306 of *LNCS*, pages 233–248. Springer Verlag, 2002.

[9] S. Isoda. A critique of UML's definition of the use-case class. In P. Stevens, J. Whittle, and G. Booch, editors, *UML 2003*, volume 2863 of *LNCS*, pages 280–294. Springer Verlag, 2003.

[10] I. Jacobson, M., Christerson, P. Johnsson, and G. Övergaard. *Object-Oriented Software Engineering: A Use Case Driven Approach*. Addison-Wesley, 1992.

[11] R. Laleau and F. Polack. Coming and going from UML to B : A proposal to support traceability in rigorous IS development. In *ZB'2002 – Formal Specification and Development in Z and B*, pages 517–534. Springer Verlag, 2002.

[12] B. N. Levy, R. Marcano, and J. Souquières. From requirements to formal specification using UML and B. In *International Conference in Computer Systems and Technologies, CompSysTech'2002*, Sofia, Bulgaria, 2002.

[13] OMG. *Unified Modeling Language Specification*.

[14] J. Rumbaugh, I. Jacobson, and G. Booch. *The Unified Modeling Language Reference Manual*. Object Technology. Addison-Wesley, 1999.

[15] C. Snook and M. Butler. Verifying dynamic properties of UML models by translation to the B language. In *Proceedings UML 2000 WORKSHOP Dynamic Behaviour in UML Models: Semantic Questions*, York, October 2000.

[16] P. Stevens and R. Pooley. *Using UML: software engineering with objects and components*. Object Technology Series. Addison-Wesley, 2000. Updated edition for UML1.3: first published 1998.

[17] J. Warmer and A. Kleppe. *The Object Constraint Language*. Object Technology. Addison-Wesley, 2003.

Building Precise UML Constructs to Model Concurrency Using OCL

Agustín Goñi and Yadran Eterovic

Pontificia Universidad Católica de Chile
Department of Computer Science
Vicuña Mackenna 4860, Santiago, Chile
agoni@puc.cl, yadran@ing.puc.cl

Abstract. The UML has established itself as the main tool for building software designs. However, one area that hasn't been completely explored is the semantically precise specification of behavior for concurrent programs. We have studied the feasibility of creating precise, unambiguous UML concurrency specifications using the Object Constraint Language (OCL) as a cornerstone, particularly focusing on constructs for concurrent access to shared variables. In this paper, we show that such specifications are possible, and that we can create basic concurrency abstractions that are precise, specifically semaphores and monitors. These constructs can be successfully applied to model solutions to classic concurrent problems, as we show in a monitor-based solution to the Sleeping Barber problem.

1 Introduction

The advent of the UML and its standarization by the OMG in 1997 has had a profound impact in the software community, both at an academic and industry level. The UML is used to specify and design all sorts of software systems, of varying degrees of complexity.

However, one area that hasn't been properly explored is the semantically precise specification of concurrent behavior in UML. Since UML was conceived as a semi-formal language, and since its greatest strength lies in its easy to grasp graphical notation (which often makes it preferable to a formal and complete design mechanism), the development of fine-grained, unambiguous specifications in UML is not a common practice.

There have been suggestions that, for a variety of reasons, UML is a less than adequate tool for modeling concurrency([2], [6]). On the other hand, some efforts have been made to create methods that allow developers to apply several concepts of the UML to concurrent problems correctly([4], [5], and [3]), but these works have not focused on providing precisely defined, semantically clear constructs to aid modeling. We have explored the possibility of combining UML [8] and OCL ([8], [9]) to generate concurrent models that are semantically precise, and that can be used as building blocks to specify these types of systems without having to deal with all the complex details involved. In this work in particular,

T. Baar et al. (Eds.): UML 2004, LNCS 3273, pp. 212–225, 2004.

we analyze concurrent systems in which several processes share memory blocks, and have to synchronize access to common variables.

Our objective is to be able to use a (mainly) graphical notation, supported by a well defined set of OCL specifications, and extensible by the developer through constraints of his or her own, to be able to model concurrent problems with a greater degree of precision than what standard UML offers today. To take full advantage of the notation, we use OCL version 2.0.

The rest of this paper is organized as follows. Section 2 introduces a model for a basic construct widely used to solve concurrent programming problems: the semaphore. Section 3 shows the other common abstraction, the monitor. Section 4 shows how these constructs can be used to model a solution to a well-known problem. Finally, section 5 presents the results and conclusions obtained in this work, as well as future areas of research.

2 Basic Constructs for Concurrency I: Semaphores

We start by analyzing how to model a semaphore. We base our discussion on the semaphore concept as presented in [1].

All we need to model and specify a semaphore is a class with one attribute, a non-negative integer **s**, and two methods, **P**() and **V**(), used to modify the value of **s**. Additionally, we provide a creation method to initialize the semaphore. All implementation considerations, such as handling explicit process scheduling or time slicing, are omitted here, as we focus exclusively on the semaphore's *behavior*. A basic **Semaphore** class is shown in figure 1.

Our goal is to specify the correct semantics for **P(s)** and **V(s)** and for that we use OCL. We must first find a way to link a process with the **Semaphore** class in a way that provides information we can manipulate in the semaphore specification: we need an association class to model this relationship.

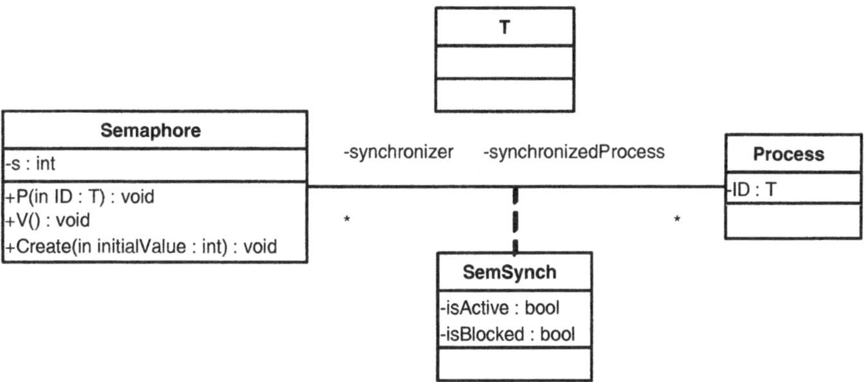

Fig. 1. Association class for semaphores and processes

The association class **SemSynch** shown in figure 1 captures the information of an interaction between a semaphore and a process. This class has only two Boolean attributes and no methods. Each attribute represents a state.

- If *isActive* is true, the process is executing.
- If *isBlocked* is true, the process has been blocked by the semaphore.

We also introduce a **Process** class that represents an abstract process. The only necessary attribute for such a class is an identifier of an arbitrary type **T**. This process represents an active object that uses the services provided by the semaphore.

For any given semaphore there will be any number of processes requesting synchronization, and any process, in turn, can be attached to an arbitrary number of sempahores. This means the semaphore needs a mechanism to discern which of the processes it is handling is the source of a particular call, and the state of that process. The association objects contain the necessary information for this.

The OCL specification for the **Semaphore** class is as follows:

```
context Semaphore inv:
    self.s >= 0

context Semaphore
    def:     waiting : Sequence{}

context Semaphore::P(ID : T) : void
    body:    if self.s@pre > 0 then
                 self.s = self.s@pre - 1
             else
                 self.synchronizedProcess->select( p : Process |
                     p.ID = ID ).semSynch.isActive = false
                 self.synchronizedProcess->select( p : Process |
                     p.ID = ID ).semSynch.isBlocked = true
                 self.waiting = self.waiting@pre->append(ID)
             endif

context Semaphore::V() : void
    body:    if self.s@pre = 0 then
                 if self.waiting@pre->isEmpty() = false then
                     self.synchronizedProcess->select(
                         p : Process | p.ID = self.waiting@pre->first()
                             ).semSynch.isBlocked = false
                     self.synchronizedProcess->select(
                         p : Process | p.ID = self.waiting@pre->first()
                             ).semSynch.isActive = true
                     self.waiting = self.waiting@pre->Subsequence(
                         2, self.waiting@pre->size() )
                 endif
             endif
             else
                 self.s = self.s@pre + 1
```

A detailed explanation of the way we approached these specifications can be found in the next section.

Both semaphore operations must be atomic. To accomplish this, we use the *concurrency* attribute, which UML defines for operations to control the concurrent behavior of calls. In this case, semaphores must execute with their *concur-*

rency attributes set to *guarded.* By definition, this means that multiple concurrent threads can invoke a method from the same instance of the class, but only one is allowed to commence, and all the others must block and wait for it to finish. Thus, atomicity is guaranteed.

We also provide a specification for the association class.

```
context SemSynch inv:
    ( isActive xor isBlocked ) = true

context SemSynch::isActive
    init: true

context SemSynch::isBlocked
    init: false
```

The **SemSynch** class has only two attributes, both of them of type Boolean, and the only constraint imposed is that only one of them can be **true** at any given time. This characteristic effectively provides the notion of state to the relationship between the **Semaphore** class and the calling process.

3 Basic Constructs for Concurrency II: Monitor

The other widely used construct created to synchronize concurrent access to shared variables is the monitor. In this section, we analyze a model for a monitor as presented in [1].

The basic behavior of a general purpose monitor can be encapsulated in a simple class in an object-oriented system. This class is depicted in figure 2. Once again, we need to model the interaction between the monitor and the processes that use its services. To do this we introduce an association class, called MonSynch, akin to the one used for the **Semaphore** class. This can also be seen in figure 2.

We have a **Process** class that represents an active object with a certain identifier of an arbitrary type **T**. This process will access some shared resource through the monitor.

We introduce the **MonSynch** class, which has only Boolean attributes, each of them representing a particular state of the monitor-process interaction. The possibilities are:

- If *isTryingEntry* is true, the process tried to enter the monitor and found it busy, so it is waiting.
- If *isInMonitor* is true, the process is executing within the monitor.
- If *isWaiting* is true, then the process has executed within the monitor and has called a **Wait** operation on a condition variable, and is therefore waiting for another process to signal that condition.
- If *isOutOfMonitor* is true, the process has either exited the monitor or hasn't yet commenced its interaction with it. This is always the initial state.

For the purposes of our model, each one of these synchronization objects will link one monitor to an arbitrary number of processes. To make sure that

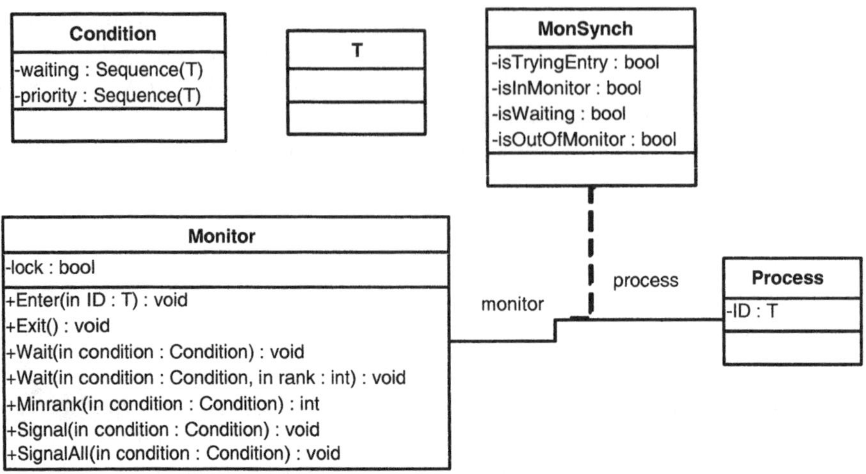

Fig. 2. Association class for monitors and processes

operations are atomic, all methods in the monitor must have their *concurrency* attributes set to *guarded.*

We now proceed to present a detailed specification of the **Monitor** class.

First of all, the monitor invariant establishes that there can be at most one process executing in the monitor at any given time, i.e., no more than one **MonSynch** object can have its *isInMonitor* attribute set to true. We can obtain this information by navigating the association and finding the set of processes that meet this requirement, which must have a size of 1 or less.

We also define a sequence, called *waiting*, to store the IDs of the processes that are interacting with the monitor.

```
context Monitor inv:
    --No more than one process executing in the monitor
    self.process->select( p : Process |
        p.monSynch.isInMonitor )->size() <= 1

context Monitor
    def:  waiting : Sequence{}
```

All of the specifications for the operations on this monitor rely on navigating the associations of the model, and on the use of a Boolean variable *lock.*

The first method to specify is **Enter**. In this case, if *lock* is false, we set it to true and navigate towards the process objects that are attached to the monitor, to find the one whose ID is the same as the parameter received in the call. This process's state has to be changed to *isInMonitor.* In case the lock was already true, we have to queue the process in the waiting sequence and set the state of the association to *isTryingEntry.* Again, we use Boolean conditions to navigate the association and identify the process whose state will be changed.

```
context Monitor::Enter( ID: T ) : void
    body:     if self.lock@pre = false then
                   self.lock = true
                   --Enter monitor
                   self.process->select( p : Process |
                       p.ID = ID ).monSynch.isOutOfMonitor = false
                   self.process->select( p : Process |
                       p.ID = ID ).monSynch.isInMonitor = true
              else
                   --Queue the process
                   self.waiting = self.waiting@pre->append(ID)
                   --Change process state
                   self.process->select( p : Process |
                       p.ID = ID ).monSynch.isOutOfMonitor = false
                   self.process->select( p : Process |
                       p.ID = ID ).monSynch.isTryingEntry = true
              endif
```

The next basic operation is **Exit**. In this case, there is a precondition: there must be a process executing in the monitor. To ensure this, we check if there exists a process whose association object has its *isInMonitor* attribute set to true.

We change the state of the process that leaves the monitor and find out if there are any processes waiting to enter. If there are, we find the one that occupies the first spot in the waiting sequence and change its association state from *isTryingEntry* to *isInMonitor*. After that, we have to eliminate that reference from the sequence, so we extract a subsequence that omits the first element. In case there aren't any processes waiting to execute in the monitor, all we have to do is set the lock to false.

```
context Monitor::Exit() : void
    pre:     --There must be a process executing in the monitor
             self.process->exists( p : Process |
                 p.monSynch.isInMonitor = true )
    body:    --Process leaves monitor; changes states
             self.process->select( p : Process |
                 p.monSynch.isInMonitor@pre = true
                     ).monSynch.isInMonitor = false
             self.process->select( p : Process |
                 p.monSynch.isInMonitor@pre = true
                     ).monSynch.isOutOfMonitor = true
             --Find out if there is another process waiting to enter
             if  self.waiting@pre->isEmpty() = false then
                 --Extract process; put it in monitor
                 self.process->select( p : Process |
                     p.ID = self.waiting@pre->first()
                         ).monSynch.isInMonitor = true
                 self.process->select( p : Process |
                     p.ID = self.waiting@pre->first()
                         ).monSynch.isTryingEntry = false
                 --Eliminate from waiting sequence
                 self.waiting = self.waiting@pre->subSequence( 2,
                         self.waiting@pre->size() )
             else
                 --If no process was waiting, the lock is now open
                 self.lock = false;
             endif
```

A process executing in the monitor can call a **Wait** method. When this happens, we change the state of the association object for that process from *isInMonitor* to *isWaiting*. Then we add it to the waiting sequence of the condition, and give it a priority of 0 (a "don't care" value). As before, if there is a process waiting to execute, it will enter the monitor.

```
context Monitor::Wait(condition : Condition) : void
    pre:     self.process->exists( p : Process |
                 p.monSynch.isInMonitor = true )
    body:    --The current process stops executing in monitor.
             self.process->select( p : Process |
                 p.monSynch.isInMonitor@pre = true
                     ).monSynch.isWaiting = true
             self.process->select( p : Process |
                 p.monSynch.isInMonitor@pre = true
                     ).monSynch.isInMonitor = false
             --Queue the process
             condition.waiting = condition.waiting@pre->append(
                 self.process->select( p : Process |
                 p.monSynch.isInMonitor@pre = true ).ID )
             condition.priority = condition.priority@pre->append(0)
             --If a process is waiting it will go in.
             if  self.waiting@pre->isEmpty() = false then
                 --Extract process; put it in monitor.
                 self.process->select( p : Process |
                     p.ID = self.waiting@pre->first()
                         ).monSynch.isInMonitor = true
                 self.process->select( p : Process |
                     p.ID = self.waiting@pre->first()
                         ).monSynch.isTryingEntry = false
                 --Eliminate from waiting sequence.
                 self.waiting = self.waiting@pre->subSequence( 2,
                     self.waiting@pre->size() )
             else
                 self.lock = false
             endif
```

Another option is the priority **Wait** operation. This is the same as the regular **Wait** method, except this time we append a meaningful number to the condition's priority sequence. This number allows us to discern which process in the sequence is to be awaken next. Echoing the recommendation in [1], our advice is to use only one type of **Wait** operation in the same system to avoid confusion.

```
context Monitor::Wait(condition : Condition, rank : Integer)
    pre:     self.process->exists( p : Process |
                 p.monSynch.isInMonitor = true )
    post:    --The current process stops executing in monitor.
             self.process->select( p : Process |
                 p.monSynch.isInMonitor@pre = true
                     ).monSynch.isWaiting = true
             self.process->select( p : Process |
                 p.monSynch.isInMonitor@pre = true
                     ).monSynch.isInMonitor = false
             --Queue the process with its priority
             condition.waiting = condition.waiting@pre->append(
                 self.process->select( p : Process |
                 p.monSynch.isInMonitor@pre = true).ID )
             condition.priority =
                 condition.priority@pre->append(rank)
             -- If there are processes waiting one will go in
             if  self.waiting@pre->isEmpty() = false then
                 --Extract process; put it in monitor
                 self.process->select( p : Process |
                     p.ID = self.waiting@pre->first()
```

```
                ).monSynch.isInMonitor = true
          self.process->select( p : Process |
              p.ID = self.waiting@pre->first()
                ).monSynch.isTryingEntry = false
          --Eliminate from waiting sequence.
          self.waiting = self.waiting@pre->subSequence( 2,
              self.waiting@pre->size() )
      else
          self.lock = false
      endif
```

Closely related to the priority **Wait** operation is **Minrank**. This method return the lowest rank value of all the processes delayed on a certain condition variable.

```
context Monitor::Minrank(condition : Condition) : Integer
    post:   result = condition.priority->iterate( i : Integer;
                value : Integer = condition->at(0) |
                    value = value.min( condition.priority->at(i) ) )
```

When a **Signal** call occurs, we have to check if the condition's waiting sequence is empty. If it isn't, one process has to be awaken. We must find the process that has the lowest rank (highest priority). We first find the element with the lowest rank in the priority sequence and then find that element's index. After that, we switch that process's state from *isTryingEntry* to *isInMonitor*, and then eliminate the respective elements from the monitor's waiting sequence and the condition's waiting and priority sequences.

```
context Monitor::Signal(condition : Condition) : void
    pre:    self.process->exists( p : Process |
                p.monSynch.isInMonitor = true )
    post:   if condition.waiting@pre->isEmpty() = false then
                --Awake one process waiting on condition
                let maxPriority = condition.priority@pre->iterate(
                    i : Integer;
                    value : Integer = condition.priority@pre->at(0) |
                    value = value.min( condition.priority@pre->at(i) ) )
                let nextIndex =
                    condition.priority@pre->indexOf( maxPriority )
                --Awake the process
                self.process->select( p : Process |
                    p.ID = condition.waiting@pre->at( nextIndex )
                        ).monSynch.IsInMonitor = true
                self.process->select( p : Process |
                    p.ID = condition.waiting@pre->at( nextIndex )
                        ).monSynch.IsTryingEntry = false
                --Eliminate process from the sequences.
                self.waiting = self.waiting@pre->iterate(
                    i : Integer; New : Sequence = Sequence{} |
                    if self.waiting@pre->at(i) <>
                        condition.waiting@pre->at(nextIndex)
                            New->append( self.waiting@pre->at(i) ) )
                condition.waiting = condition.waiting@pre->exclude(
                    condition.waiting@pre->at(nextIndex) )
                condition.priority = condition.priority@pre->exclude(
                    condition.priority@pre->at(nextIndex) )
            endif
```

The *SignalAll* method is the same as before, except we awake all processes waiting on the sequence, irrespective of priorities.

```
context Monitor::SignalAll(condition : Condition) : void
    pre:     self.process->exists( p : Process |
                 p.monSynch.isInMonitor = true )
    post:    if condition.waiting->isEmpty() = false then
                 --Awake all processes waiting on condition
                 self.process->select( p : Process |
                     condition.waiting@pre->includes( p.ID )
                         ).monSynch.isTryingEntry = true
                 self.process->select( p : Process |
                     condition.waiting@pre->includes( p.ID )
                         ).monSynch.isWaiting = false
                 --Eliminate all pertinent processes from sequence.
                 self.waiting = self.waiting@pre->reject( p:Process |
                     condition.waiting@pre->includes( p.ID ) )
                 --Flush the condition sequence.
                 condition.waiting =
                         condition.waiting@pre->select(false)
             endif
```

4 Modeling Solutions to Concurrency Problems

In this section we show how to use the specifications we obtained to model the solutions to well-known synchronization problems. Due to space constraints we will only analyze the use of monitors.

There are many problems that can be modeled using the **Monitor** class, such as the Readers and Writers problem, the Producers and Consumers problem, and the Sleeping Barber problem (all described in [1]). For our analysis, we focus on the latter.

Sleeping Barber There is a barbershop with two doors and some chairs. Customers enter through one door and exit through the other. As long as there are no customers requesting a haircut, the barber sleeps in his chair. When a customer arrives he awakes the barber, sits on the chair, and goes to sleep while the barber cuts his hair. If a customer arrives while the barber is busy he goes to sleep in one of the other chairs. After the barber has finished the haircut, he opens the door for the customer to exit and closes it once the customer has left. If there are any more customers waiting, the barber awakens one of them and waits until the customer sits in the chair before cutting his hair. Otherwise he goes to sleep again.

To model this problem we need three procedures: a customer must be able to request a haircut using the **GetHaircut()** method, and the barber must call **GetNextCustomer()** and **FinishedCut()** to bring in the next customer, and to indicate he has finished cutting the current customer's hair, respectively.

In order to specify synchronization we can use incrementing counters. In particular, we consider two important states for customers: sitting in the barber's chair and leaving the barber shop. We use counters to specify how many customers have been in each state, *customerInChair* and *customerLeave*. Similarly, the barber goes repeatedly through three states: available, busy, and done. We use counters *barberAvailable*, *barberBusy*, and *barberDone* to represent them.

The first thing we want to do is define an invariant for the barber shop. It has three parts:

- The states for both the customers and the barber obey the aforementioned sequences, so the counters have to follow this order. The number of customers that have left the barber shop after getting their haircut cannot be greater than the number of customers that have sat on the barber chair. Likewise, the number of times the barber has finished a haircut cannot be greater than the number of times he has become busy, which in turn cannot be greater than the number of times he has been available.

```
I1: customerInChair >= customerLeave
      ^ barberAvailable >= barberBusy >= barberDone
```

- The number of customers that have sat on the chair cannot be greater than the number of times the barber has been available, and the barber cannot have been busy more times than the number of customers that have sat on the chair.

```
I2: customerInChair <= barberAvailable
      ^ barberBusy <= customerInChair
```

- The number of customers that have left the barbershop cannot be greater than the number of times the barber has finished cutting someone's hair.

```
I3: customerLeave <= barberDone
```

Considering the above, the invariant for the barbershop is given by:

```
BARBER: I1 ^ I2 ^ I3
```

A model for this solution is shown in figure 3. Class BarberShop encapsulates all the logic above and is the one that is affected by this invariant, as can be seen in the OCL specification. As a matter of convenience, and since we are not interested in the counters themselves but rather in their differences, we define variables *barber*, *chair*, and *open* of type Integer to maintain them.

```
context Barbershop
  def:  barber : Integer = barberAvailable - customerInChair

  def:  chair : Integer = customerInChair - barberBusy

  def:  open : Integer = barberDone - customerLeave

context BarberShop
  inv:  ( customerInChair >= customerLeave )
        and ( barberAvailable >= barberBusy >= barberDone )

  inv:  ( customerInChair <= barberAvailable )
        and ( barberBusy >= barberDone )

  inv:  customerLeave <= barberDone

  inv:  barber >= 0 and barber <= 1

  inv:  chair >= 0 and chair <= 1
```

```
  inv:   open >= 0 and open <= 1

context BarberShop::GetBarberValue() : int
  post:  result = barber

context BarberShop::GetChairValue() : int
  post:  result = chair

context BarberShop::GetOpenValue() : int
  post:  result = open

context BarberShop::IncrementBarberValue() : void
  post:  barber = barber@pre + 1

context BarberShop::IncrementChairValue() : void
  post:  chair = chair@pre + 1

context BarberShop::IncrementOpenValue() : void
  post:  open = open@pre + 1

context BarberShop::DecrementBarberValue() : void
  post:  barber = barber@pre - 1

context BarberShop::DecrementChairValue() : void
  post:  chair = chair@pre - 1

context BarberShop::DecrementOpenValue() : void
  post:  open = open@pre - 1
```

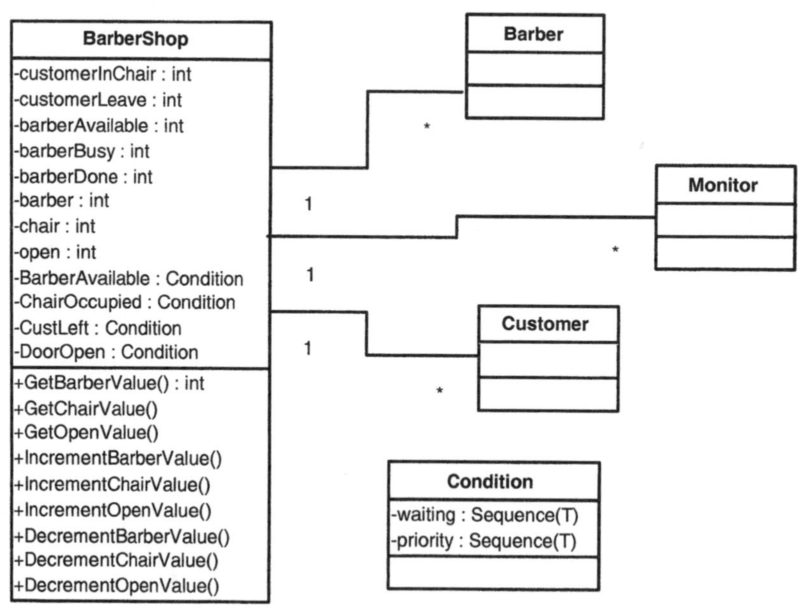

Fig. 3. Class diagram for the Sleeping Barber problem

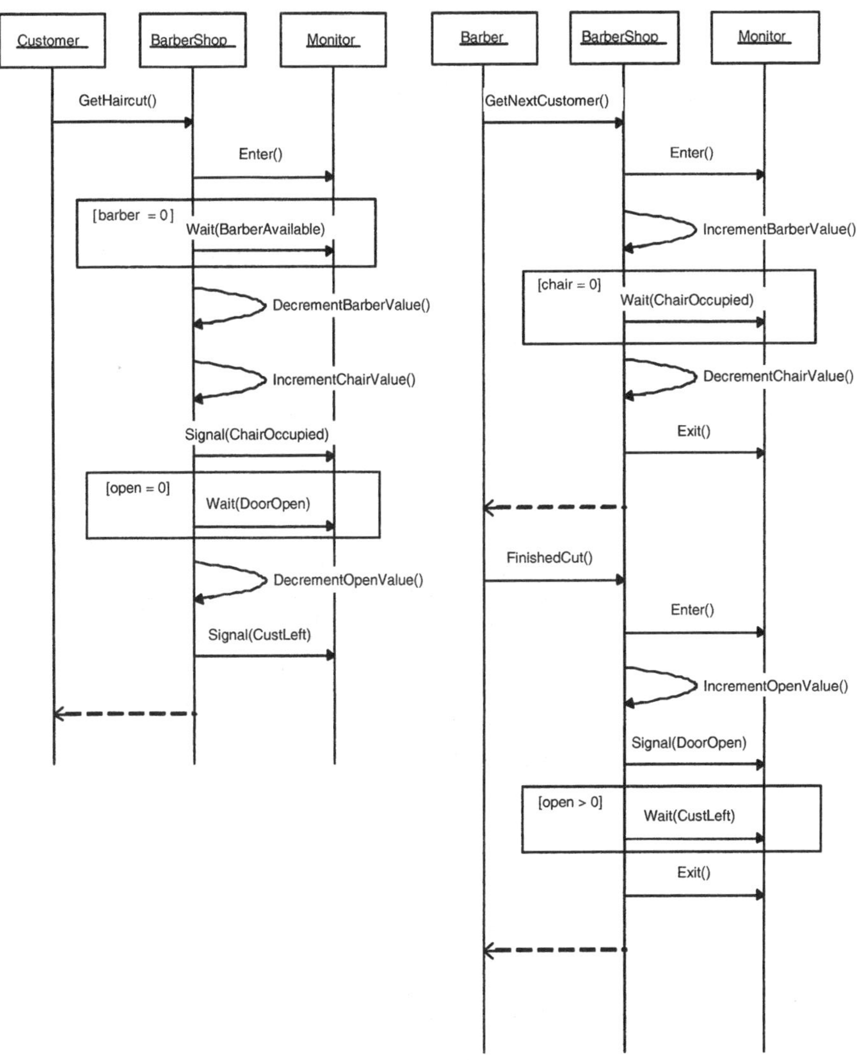

Fig. 4. Class diagram for the Sleeping Barber problem

The dynamic behavior of the proposed system is shown in figure 4. Notice how the problem can be modeled using a fairly simple diagram that encapsulates all the synchronization logic in the **BarberShop** class, which in turn communicates with the monitor. The **Barber** and **Customer** classes don't need to have any information about the rest of the system. Also notice that, even though the diagrams show the calls to the different operation in order, they could in fact interleave in any combination without affecting the correctness of the solution.

5 Conclusions

In this work we showed that it is possible to obtain precise UML specifications of commonly used concurrency constructs. To do this, we created new UML classes and made extensive use of OCL to write constraints on these classes. These constraints refer to the value of internal attributes of the classes, and the behavior of the operations defined in them. This method allowed us to come up with two basic data types, **Semaphore** and **Monitor**, with well-defined semantics.

One of the biggest challenges of this work was to create a specification that is oblivious to implementation issues, but that remains realistically implementable at the same time. This property can be noticed in various aspects of the specification, e.g., the use of OCL sequences to represent an abstract queue, or the use of association objects to represent the behavior an operating system scheduler process would have. These are abstract concepts, but there are well known mechanisms to implement them. By doing this we have ensured that our constructs can be implemented in any platform of choice, and they are not dependent on coding details.

Since we are examining the use of UML, we made sure our specifications are firmly rooted in the object-oriented programming paradigm. In that sense , both the **Semaphore** and **Monitor** class represent an encapsulation of a data type, and they have well-defined interfaces, and expose services that are accessible only through these interfaces. Additionally, our Sleeping Barber example shows that peripheral classes (in this case, **Customer** and **Barber**) don't need any information about the synchronization mechanism used, and they simply request the desired services.

These results allowed us to model a solution to well-known concurrent problems in a simple way. For instance, in the example shown in the previous section, the resulting sequence diagram is as simple as the problem allows, without any unnecessary complexities added. The implication of this finding is that by using OCL as a mechanism to extend and complete diagrams, we can make a UML model as precise as we want it to be, without making it visually complex. In particular, we have provided typical concurrency constructs (**Semaphore** and **Monitor**) that hide the complexity of concurrent interaction and possess unambiguous behavior.

Future work in this avenue includes finding a convenient and easy way to use these constructs as part of the toolbox for modeling concurrency, and incorporating them seamlessly into the standard UML resources. This could lead to the generation of a profile for the specification of concurrent access to shared variables.

References

[1] Andrews, Gregory R.: Foundations of Multithreaded, Parallel, and Distributed Programming, Addison-Wesley Longman, Inc., 2000

[2] Börger, E., Cavarra, A., Riccobene, E.: Solving Conflicts in UML State Machines Concurrent States, Workshop on Concurrency Issues in UML, October 2001

[3] Chrichton, C., Cavarra, A., Davies, J.: A Pattern for Concurrency in UML, Workshop on Concurrency Issues in UML, October 2001

[4] Gomaa, Hassan.: Designing Concurrent, Distributed and Real-Time Applications with UML, Addison-Wesley, 2000

[5] Gomaa, Hasan.: Concurrent Software Design with UML, Revised Version, August 2001

[6] Ober, I., Stan, I.: On the Concurrent Object Model of UML, Workshop on Concurrency Issues in UML, October 2001

[7] Sendall, S., Strohmeier, A.: Merging Fine-Grained and Coarse-Grained Concurrent Behavior Specifications in UML, Position Statement for the "Workshop on Concurrency Issues in UML", Workshop on Concurrency Issues in UML, October 2001

[8] Unified Modeling Language (UML), Version 1.5, 2003 http://www.omg.org/technology/documents/formal/uml.htm

[9] Warmer, J., Kleppe, A.: The Object Constraint Language, Second Edition. Addison-Wesley, Object Technology Edition, 2003

An ASM Definition of the Dynamic OCL 2.0 Semantics

Stephan Flake[1] and Wolfgang Mueller[2]

[1] ORGA Systems GmbH
Am Hoppenhof 33, 33104 Paderborn, Germany
[2] Paderborn University / C-LAB
Fürstenallee 11, 33102 Paderborn, Germany

Abstract. The recently adopted OCL 2.0 specification comes with a formal semantics that is based on set theory with a notion of an object model and system states. System states keep the runtime information relevant for the evaluation of OCL expressions. However, not all new language concepts of OCL 2.0 are already addressed in that formal semantics. We show how to overcome this by introducing new components to the object model and system states defining a dynamic semantics of OCL. In order to give precise rules that determine when the current system state has to be updated according to a change in the referred UML model, we make use of adequate mathematical means, namely Abstract State Machines (ASMs). Though our ASM specification also gives a clear definition for the evaluation of OCL constraints, it leaves sufficient flexibility for application specific implementations that have to determine when constraints are to be checked.

1 Introduction

The recently adopted OCL 2.0 specification provides both a metamodel-based as well as a formal semantics definition [11]. The formal semantics is based on set theory with the notion of an object model, which is basically a formalization of UML Class Diagrams. An instantiation of an object model is called a *system*. A system changes over time, i.e., the (number of) objects, their attribute values, and other characteristics change during system execution. The information that is needed to evaluate OCL expressions is stored in *system states*, which represent snapshots of the running system. For the evaluation of OCL expressions, the adopted OCL 2.0 specification provides a denotational semantics by interpretation functions over *environments*, i.e., tuples of system states and OCL-specific variable assignments.

Several new language concepts have been introduced to OCL 2.0, like tuples, messages sent, and ordered sets. However, not all of the new concepts are already addressed in the formal semantics. In particular, the formal OCL 2.0 semantics currently lacks a formalization of

- operations on predefined collection type `OrderedSet`,
- global variable definitions, called *def-clauses*[3],

[3] Leaving out this language concept leads to a significant loss in the expressiveness of OCL. See [4] for more details.

T. Baar et al. (Eds.): UML 2004, LNCS 3273, pp. 226–240, 2004.

- operations on State Diagram states, and
- operators to access OCL messages and operations to reason about them.

Note that operations defined for ordered sets are basically the same as for sequences and that def-clauses are mapped to so-called `OclHelper` variables and operations [11, Section 7.4.4]. `OclHelper` variables and operations, in turn, are stereotyped attributes and operations of classifiers. Such variables and operations can be used in OCL expressions just like common attributes and operations. Thus, it only has to be ensured that no naming conflicts occur.

We already integrated UML State Diagrams to OCL and defined a formal semantics for the predefined operation `oclInState()` [6] and also formally defined operators and operations for OCL messages [5]. These definitions are based on extensions of the work by Richters which heavily influenced the formal semantics of OCL 2.0 [13]. We introduced additional components to the object model and system states and could then give a denotational semantics by interpretation functions for the predefined OCL operations that are still missing in the formal semantics of OCL 2.0, e.g., the message-related operations `hasReturned()` and `result()`.

This extension is also the foundation for defining a *dynamic semantics* of OCL, which is in the focus of this article. Note that the (extended) denotational semantics allow to evaluate OCL 2.0 expressions over given system states, but there are no precise rules that determine *how* system states have to be updated in relation to the execution of the referred UML model. To overcome this, we make use of adequate mathematical means for state-oriented operational definitions, namely Abstract State Machines (ASMs).

ASMs were introduced by Gurevich [7]. Based on the notion of a virtual machine execution in combination with a mathematically precise notion of states and state transitions known as *algebras*, they provide a concise and rigorous but yet intuitive way to define system semantics. ASMs are well-established in the domain of formal specification and have already been successfully applied to define the semantics of, e.g., UML Activity Diagrams [1] and the run-to-completion step of UML State Diagrams [2].

The remainder of this article is structured as follows. The next section briefly outlines the basics of ASMs. In Section 3, we present the extensions to the object model and system states that are necessary to be able to evaluate OCL expressions that also make use of state- and message-related operations. Section 4 then presents the dynamic semantics of OCL with ASMs. In Section 5, we briefly discuss related work. Section 6 closes with a conclusion.

2 Abstract State Machines

Abstract State Machine (ASM) specifications can be understood as *pseudocode over abstract data* without any particular theoretical prerequisites. We here only list the basic definitions and refer to [7, 3] for a formal introduction and more details. An ASM specification comes in form of guarded function updates, called *rules*, of the form

$$\textbf{if}\ Condition\ \textbf{then}\ <Updates>\ \textbf{else}\ <Updates>\ \textbf{endif}$$

Rules are presented as nested if-then-else clauses with a set of function updates in their body. When executing the rules, the underlying ASM abstract machine executes state transitions with *algebras* as states. An algebra can be seen as a *database of functions* [3]. Basically, an algebra is a mathematical structure over abstract objects that are elements of a domain (or: universe). A particular function or relation for an object obj is described by a parameterized function f, which assigns to each x the value $f(obj, x)$. Partial functions are turned into total functions by setting $f(obj, x) = undef$, where $undef$ is a special predefined value denoting that $f(obj, x)$ is undefined. Note that 0-ary functions play the role of variables known from imperative programming languages.

Functions have a well-defined signature and mapping. ASMs distinguish static and dynamic functions. Static functions do not change during executions of the ASM, i.e., the function values do not depend on the states of the ASM. In contrast, the values of dynamic functions might change, either because of an update in the ASM itself or by the environment. ASMs distinguish between four kinds of dynamic functions, i.e., *controlled*, *monitored*, *interaction*, and *out* functions. Controlled functions can only be read and changed by the ASM itself, while monitored functions can only be read by the ASM and are changed by the environment. Interaction (or shared) functions can be changed by both the ASM and the environment, but then some mechanism is necessary to guarantee consistency. Finally, out functions are changed but cannot be read by the ASM.

Firing a set of rules in one step performs a *state transition*. Only those rules are fired whose guards (i.e., *Condition*) evaluate to true. At each step, the guards evaluate to a set of *function updates*, each of the form $f(t_1, ..., t_r) := t_0$, where t_i are terms (including functions). A *block* is a set of function updates which we separate by commas. The individual function updates of each block are collected in a so-called *update set* and are simultaneously executed in the same step. Each function update changes a value at a specific *location* that is given by the left hand side of the update. Functions are considered to be global, such that two or more simultaneous updates of the same location in one update set define inconsistency.

In the case of inconsistency no state transition is performed and no update is being executed.

We demonstrate a simple guarded update by the following example:

$$\textbf{if } true \textbf{ then } A := B, B := A \textbf{ endif}$$

That definition gives an simultaneous update of the 0-ary functions A and B. Since both updates are simultaneously executed, the values are swapped (A becomes the value of B and vice versa). Due to its true condition, the rule fires at each step.

ASMs are multi-sorted based on the notion of universes. We presume the standard mathematic universes of booleans, integers, lists, etc. as well as the standard operations on them without further mention.

The **choose** constructor defines an arbitrary selection of one element in a universe

$$\textbf{choose } v \textbf{ in } Universe \; <\!Rule\!> \; \textbf{endchoose}$$

where v is (non-deterministically) selected from the given universe. The **choose** constructor can be qualified by an additional condition indicated by the keyword **satisfying**.

The **var** rule constructor defines the simultaneous instantiation of a rule:

$$\textbf{var } v \textbf{ ranges over } Universe \ <Rule> \textbf{ endvar}$$

Executing the constructor means to execute the rule for each element in $Universe$ simultaneously, i.e., the constructor basically spawns n rules where n is the number of elements in $Universe$.

3 Extended Object Model and System States

The formal definition of the object model in OCL 2.0 is based on the object model of Richters [13]. However, this formalization lacks some of the new OCL 2.0 language concepts. We therefore define an extension of the object model called *extended object model*, in which a number of concepts are newly introduced (cf. Section 3.1). Correspondingly, additional information has to be stored in system states to be able to evaluate OCL 2.0 expressions (cf. Section 3.2). The completed system state description then allows to define a high-level dynamic semantics for OCL by means of *traces* (cf. Section 4).

3.1 Syntax

In the remainder of this article, let $\mathcal{A}$ be an alphabet, $\mathcal{N}$ be a set of names over $\mathcal{A}^+$, and T a set of types. In particular, $T = T_B \cup T_E \cup T_C \cup T_S$ comprises a set of basic standard library types T_B, i.e., $Integer$, $Real$, $Boolean$, and $String$, a set T_E of user-defined enumeration types, a set T_C of user-defined classes, $c \in CLASS$, and a set of special types $T_S = \{OclVoid, OclState, OclAny\}$.

We call the value set $I(t)$ represented by a type t the *type domain*. For convenience, we presume that `OclUndefined` (in the following denoted by symbol $\perp$) is included in each type domain, such that we have, e.g., $I(OclVoid) = \{\perp\}$ and $I(OclAny) = \bigcup_{t \in T_B \cup T_E \cup T_C \cup \{OclState\}} I(t)$.

Furthermore, let $c \in CLASS$ be a class and $t_c \in T_C$ be the type of class c.[4] Each class c has a set ATT_c of attributes that describe characteristics of their objects. An attribute has a name $a \in \mathcal{N}$ and a type $t \in T$ that specifies the domain of attribute values. A class c is also associated with a set OP_c of operations and a set SIG_c of signals.

We define the *Extended Object Model* $\mathcal{M}$ by the tuple

$$\begin{aligned}\mathcal{M} = \langle\ & CLASS, ATT, OP, paramKind, isQuery, SIG, SC, \\ & ASSOC, \prec, \prec_{sig}, associates, roles, multiplicities\ \rangle\end{aligned}$$

with

- a set $CLASS = ACTIVE \cup PASSIVE$ of active and passive classes,
- a set of attributes, $ATT = \bigcup_{c \in CLASS} ATT_c$,

[4] Each class $c \in CLASS$ induces an object type $t_c \in T$ that has the same name as the class. The difference between c and t_c is that we have the special value $\perp \in I(t_c)$ for all $c \in CLASS$.

- a set OP of operations, $OP = \bigcup_{c \in CLASS} OP_c$,
- a function $paramKind : CLASS \times OP \times \mathbb{N} \to \{in, inout, out\}$ that gives for each operation parameter its parameter kind,
- a function $isQuery : CLASS \times OP \to Boolean$ that determines whether an operation is a query operation or not,
- a set SIG of signals, $SIG \supseteq \bigcup_{c \in CLASS} SIG_c$,
- a set SC of State Diagrams (or: StateCharts), $SC = \bigcup_{c \in ACTIVE} SC_c$,
- a set $ASSOC$ of associations between classes,
- generalization hierarchies $\prec$ for classes and $\prec_{sig}$ for signals, and
- functions $associates$, $roles$, and $multiplicities$ that define a mapping for each element in $ASSOC$ to the participating classes, their corresponding role names, and multiplicities, respectively.

That definition should be sufficient for the remainder of this article. For more details about sets $CLASS$, ATT, OP, and $ASSOC$, readers are referred to the corresponding sources [13, 11]. We also omit the formal syntax definitions for signals and State Diagrams and refer to [6] for further details. Concerning State Diagrams and their inheritance among classes, we assume that they comply to some *inheritance policy*. Though the UML standard suggests some informal policies [12, Section 2.12.5], different other formal notions for behavioral consistency have been identified in the literature, e.g., [14].

The set of characteristics defined in a class together with the inherited characteristics is called the *full descriptor of a class*. Formally, this is a tuple

$$FD_c = \langle \; ATT_c^*, OP_c^*, paramKind_c^*, isQuery_c^*, SIG_c^*, SC_c, navEnds^*(c) \; \rangle$$

with the complete sets of attributes, operations, signals, navigable role names, and – in the case of an active class – the associated State Diagram. For example, the complete set of attributes of a class c is defined by

$$ATT_c^* = ATT_c \cup \bigcup_{c' \in parents(c)} ATT_{c'},$$

where $parents(c)$ denotes the set of (transitive) superclasses of c. The complete sets OP_c^*, SIG_c^*, and $navEnds^*(c)$ of operations, signals, and navigable role names are defined correspondingly. Functions $isQuery_c^* : OP_c^* \to Boolean$ and $paramKind_c^* : OP_c^* \times \mathbb{N} \to \{in, inout, out\}$ are derived from functions $isQuery$ and $paramKind$, respectively.

3.2 System State

The domain $I_{CLASS}(c)$ of a class $c \in CLASS$ is the set of objects of class c and all of its child classes. For technical purposes, we define $I_{CLASS} = \bigcup_{c' \in CLASS} I_{CLASS}(c')$. Objects are referred to by object identifiers that are unique in the context of the whole system. The set of object identifiers of a class $c \in CLASS$ is defined by an infinite set $oid(c) = \{oid_1, oid_2, \ldots\}$.

Note that – in contrast to the current OCL semantics – we distinguish between 'real' objects $\underline{oid}$ and their identifiers oid in the remainder of this article, simply by using underlines.

The current notion of a system state with only three components (i.e., current objects, their attribute values, and the established links) is not sufficient to be able to evaluate OCL 2.0 expressions. Additionally, we need information about currently activated states, operations called, signals sent, currently executed operations, etc. In this context, we adopt ideas of Ziemann and Gogolla [16] to formalize currently executed operations and define further functions to capture the required additional information. Formally, a *system state* over the extended object model $\mathcal{M}$ is a tuple

$$\sigma(\mathcal{M}) = \langle\ \Sigma_{CLASS}, \Sigma_{ATT}, \Sigma_{ASSOC}, \Sigma_{CONF}, \Sigma_{currentOp}, \Sigma_{currentOpParam}, \Sigma_{sentMsg}, \Sigma_{sentMsgParam}, \Sigma_{inputQueue}, \Sigma_{inputQueueParam}\ \rangle\ .$$

We explain the components of system states in more detail, but note that Σ_{CLASS}, Σ_{ATT}, and Σ_{ASSOC} are already defined in [13, 11].

(1) $\Sigma_{CLASS} = \bigcup_{c \in CLASS} \sigma_{CLASS}(c)$. The finite sets $\sigma_{CLASS}(c)$ comprise all currently existing objects of class c, i.e., $\sigma_{CLASS}(c) \subseteq oid(c) \subseteq I_{CLASS}(c)$. For further application, we define $\sigma_{ACTIVE}(c)$ for active classes correspondingly.

(2) The current attribute values are kept in set Σ_{ATT}. It is the union of functions $\sigma_{ATT}(a) : \sigma_{CLASS}(c) \to I(t)$, where $a \in ATT_c$ and t is the type specified for a. Each function $\sigma_{ATT}(a)$ assigns a value to attribute a for each currently existing object of class c.

(3) $\Sigma_{ASSOC} = \bigcup_{as \in ASSOC} \sigma_{ASSOC}(as)$ comprises the finite sets $\sigma_{ASSOC}(as)$ that contain links that connect objects. We refer to the sources mentioned above for detailed information about links.

(4) The current State Diagram configurations are kept in set

$$\Sigma_{CONF} = \bigcup_{c \in ACTIVE} \{\ \sigma_{CONF}(c) : \sigma_{ACTIVE}(c) \to I_{SC}(c)\ \}\ .$$

Each function $\sigma_{CONF}(c)$ assigns an active state configuration to each object of a given class $c \in ACTIVE$. Set $I_{SC}(c)$ denotes the set of valid state configurations of the State Diagram SC_c. For a formal definition of state configurations, see [6].

The following subsections describe the new system state components that relate to the *local snapshots* of the metamodel-based semantics of OCL 2.0 [11, Section 10.2.1].

Currently Executed Operations. Let $\mathcal{ID}$ be an infinite enumerable set, e.g., $\mathcal{ID} = \mathbb{N}$, and let $Status = \{executing, returning\}$. At the starting point of an operation execution, a unique identifier $opId \in \mathcal{ID}$ is associated with the current operation execution. Thus, an operation execution can uniquely be identified by a given object identifier, an operation signature $op \in OP$, and an operation identifier $opId \in \mathcal{ID}$. The set of currently executed operations is defined by

$$\Sigma_{currentOp} = \bigcup_{c \in CLASS} \{\ \sigma_{currentOp,c} : \sigma_{CLASS}(c) \times OP_c^* \to \mathcal{P}(I_{CLASS} \times OP \times \mathcal{ID} \times \mathcal{ID} \times Status)\ \}\ .$$

Each function $\sigma_{currentOp,c}$ gives a set of tuples of the form $\langle srcId, srcOp, srcOpId, opId, status\rangle$ that uniquely identify all currently executed operations for a given object and operation name. Elements $srcId$, $srcOp$, and $srcOpId$ refer to the operation execution that originally invoked the considered operation op with identifier $opId$. These elements are necessary to have a reference for returning a result value after operation termination.

A flag $\in Status$ indicates the current status of operation execution. Compared to the messaging actions specified in UML 1.5, we here omit statuses $ready$ and $complete$ [12, Section 2.19.2.3], as they are not necessary in the context of OCL.

Actual parameter values of executed operations are kept in $\Sigma_{currentOpParam} =$

$$\bigcup_{c \in CLASS} \{ \sigma_{currentOpParam,c} : \sigma_{CLASS}(c) \times OP_c^* \times \mathcal{ID} \rightarrow I^?(t_1) \times ... \times I^?(t_n) \times I^?(t) \} .$$

Each function $\sigma_{currentOpParam,c}$ gives the actual parameter values of the currently executed operations. In the definition above, we applied sets $I^?(t) = I(t) \cup \{?\}$ for any $t \in T$. Symbol ? denotes the *unspecified status* of a value. This symbol must not be mixed up with the *undefined value* denoted by $\perp$ (or `OclUndefined` in the concrete OCL syntax) and is also different from the String literal `'?'`. Only operation parameters i with $paramKind(c, op, i) = out$ and the return value carry the unspecified value during operation execution.

Messages Sent. To be able to evaluate OCL expressions that reason about messages, we have to store the *history of messages sent* for each executed operation. For each object $\underline{oid} \in \sigma_{CLASS}(c)$ and each of its currently executed operations op with identifier $opId$, we define a function $\sigma_{sentMsg,c}(\underline{oid}, op, opId)$ that gives the set of messages sent with their corresponding destination objects. We then define $\Sigma_{sentMsg} =$

$$\bigcup_{c \in CLASS} \{ \sigma_{sentMsg,c} : \sigma_{CLASS}(c) \times OP_c^* \times \mathcal{ID} \rightarrow \mathcal{P}(I_{CLASS} \times (SIG \cup OP) \times \mathcal{ID}) \} .$$

Set $\mathcal{ID}$ in $\mathcal{P}(I_{CLASS} \times (SIG \cup OP) \times \mathcal{ID})$ is used to refer to the correct message identifier when returning a value for synchronous operation calls. We here require a total order for $\mathcal{ID}$, such that it is possible to uniquely build sequences of messages sent.

An element $\langle destId, msg, callId\rangle \in \sigma_{sentMsg,c}(\underline{oid}, op, opId)$ denotes that a message with signature msg and call identifier $callId$ has been sent from object $\underline{oid}$ to the (not necessarily still existing) object with identifier $destId$ as part of operation execution op with identifier $opId$.

Additionally, we have to store the actual parameter values of each message sent. The formal definition of functions $\sigma_{sentMsgParam,c}$ is very similar to the definition of the functions for parameters of currently executed operations presented before. We therefore omit further descriptions here and refer to [5] for more details.

Input Queues. Set $\Sigma_{inputQueue}$ is used to store events, i.e., operation calls and signals that are sent to objects and still waiting to be dispatched. While other events like *change events*, *time events*, and implicit *completion events* invoked by (an implementation of) a State Diagram have to be considered in a general notion of an input queue, it is sufficient for us to consider only those events that are relevant for the evaluation of OCL expressions. We later refer to input queues to update the system state when a signal or operation is dispatched. This enables us to change the set of currently executed operations accordingly, which is essential for a well-defined semantics of OCL message operations. Formally, we have $\Sigma_{inputQueue} =$

$$\bigcup_{c \in CLASS} \{ \ \sigma_{inputQueue,c} : \sigma_{CLASS}(c) \rightarrow \mathcal{P}(I_{CLASS} \times OP \times \mathcal{ID} \times \ (SIG_c^* \cup OP_c^*) \times \mathcal{ID}) \ \},$$

where each function $\sigma_{inputQueue,c}$ maps to a set of sent signals and operations. The actual parameter values of waiting messages are kept in set $\Sigma_{inputQueueParam}$, and again we omit a formalization here for the sake of conciseness.

We now have all necessary components defined to evaluate general OCL 2.0 expressions and we refer to [6, 5] for the formal semantics of the predefined state- and message-related operations. In the remainder of this article, we make use of the presented extended object model and system states for an ASM definition of the dynamic semantics of OCL.

4 ASM Definition of the Dynamic OCL Semantics

In the simplest case, i.e., when (the implementation of) the system is executed on a single CPU, there is a clear temporal order on the system execution. But when the system is distributed, there is a partial order among the system execution. This problem can be treated in an ideal case by introducing a *global clock* that allows for a global view on the system. For the evaluation of OCL constraints, we assume that we have this global view on the system.

The basic idea of our approach is that the system states are stored such that it is possible to access them at a later point of time. There are two reasons for this approach, both in the context of postcondition evaluation. Firstly, it is possible in postconditions to refer to values at the precondition time of the corresponding operation execution. Secondly, the sequence of messages sent during an operation execution has to be stored to be able to evaluate message-related operations in postconditions.

To record the system changes we are interested in w.r.t. OCL constraints, we first identify the set of *noteworthy changes* which may affect the evaluation of OCL expressions. Each time such a noteworthy change occurs, a new system state is built and appended to the current sequence of system states. This sequence is also called a *trace* in the remainder. A *trace* for an instantiation of an extended object model $\mathcal{M}$ is an (infinite) sequence of system states, i.e.,

$$trace(\mathcal{M}) = \langle\langle \ \sigma(\mathcal{M})_{[0]}, \sigma(\mathcal{M})_{[1]}, \ldots, \sigma(\mathcal{M})_{[i]}, \ldots \rangle\rangle.$$

The first trace element $\sigma(\mathcal{M})_{[0]}$ denotes the initial system state in which all components are empty. Given a system state $\sigma(\mathcal{M})_{[i]}$, $i \in \mathbb{N}_0$, the next system state $\sigma(\mathcal{M})_{[i+1]}$ is added to the trace when at least one *noteworthy change* occurs. The particular noteworthy changes are further explained in the rule *updateSystemState* of the ASM definition in Subsection 4.2.

4.1 When to Check Constraints

We take a general approach and abstract from the fact *when* OCL constraints are to be evaluated and *what* to do in the case of a constraint failure. This is completely in sense of the OCL developers [15], as they state at the beginning of the corresponding Section 4.6 (page 90):

> *When implementing constraints, you must decide when to check them and what to do when a constraint fails.*

We make use of the monitored ASM function *evaluateConstraints* of type Boolean to trigger the evaluation of OCL constraints. As explained before, it is out of the scope of this definition when this function actually becomes true.

We define $INV = \bigcup_{c \in CLASS} inv(c)$ as the set of all invariants, where $inv(c)$ denotes the set of invariants over class c of the referred UML model. Let $inv^*(c)$ be the full set of invariants for a given class c, i.e., $inv^*(c) = inv(c) \cup \bigcup_{c' \in parents(c)} inv(c')$. Similarly, let PRE and $POST$ represent the sets of all pre- and postconditions, respectively.

The three monitored functions $checkInv : \Sigma_{CLASS} \rightarrow \mathcal{P}(INV)$, $checkPre : \Sigma_{currentOp} \rightarrow \mathcal{P}(PRE)$, and $checkPost : \Sigma_{currentOp} \rightarrow \mathcal{P}(POST)$ provide the invariants, pre-, and postconditions that have to be checked over particular objects and operations when *evaluateConstraints* becomes true. In the remainder, we may also write $\langle obj, inv \rangle \in checkInv$ to refer to an invariant $inv \in checkInv(obj)$. The same holds for pre- and postconditions $\langle opExec, pre \rangle \in checkPre$ and $\langle opExec, post \rangle \in checkPost$. Of course, we require that the constraints are well-defined for the objects and operations, e.g., for all $\langle obj, inv \rangle \in checkInv$ holds that $obj \in \Sigma_{CLASS}(c)$ implies $inv \in inv^*(c)$. Similar restrictions apply for pre- and postconditions.

4.2 ASM Rules

The left hand side of Figure 1 illustrates the general approach of the ASM definition for the dynamic OCL semantics. On the right hand side, the figure gives the corresponding sequential ASM steps until the system execution is stopped. The individual steps are given as ASM *macro* definitions. Macros are placeholders for ASM rules in order to achieve a better readability of the ASM specification.

In state *updateSystemState*, the OCL evaluation continuously updates the system state until *evaluateConstraints* becomes true. When *evaluateConstraints* is true, the evaluation of constraints is started with an initialization. In the next phase, the constraints under investigation, i.e., the elements of $checkInv$, $checkPre$, and $checkPost$, are checked. A Boolean function $violation$ is set to `true` if at least one of the considered constraints is violated. Note here that not only an evaluation to `false`, but also an evaluation to the undefined value $\perp$ is a violation.

In the remainder, we provide the ASM rules that reflect the OCL evaluation cycle of Figure 1. We follow a state-based definition of the individual steps. The individual states

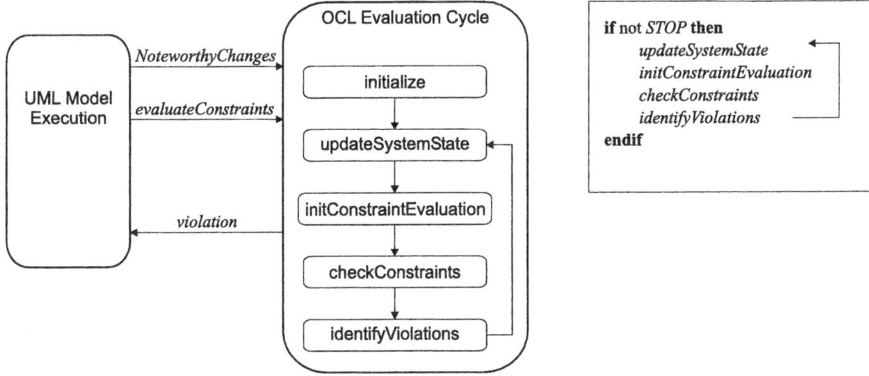

Fig. 1. Overview of the OCL Evaluation Cycle

are represented by the variable *phase* which is checked by each rule and is thereafter set to the corresponding next state.

Initialization. Initially, *phase* is set to *initialize* and *TRACE* is an empty sequence. In the following rule, setting $\sigma(\mathcal{M})_{[0]}$ to $\langle\emptyset,\ldots,\emptyset\rangle$ means that all tuple components are initially empty.

$$
\begin{array}{l}
\textbf{if } \mathit{phase} = \mathit{initialize} \textbf{ then} \\
\quad i := 0, \\
\quad \mathit{TRACE}.\mathit{append}(\sigma(\mathcal{M})_{[0]} := \langle\emptyset,\ldots,\emptyset\rangle), \\
\quad \mathit{phase} := \mathit{updateSystemState} \\
\textbf{endif}
\end{array}
$$

Update System State. Once entering phase *updateSystemState*, we continuously check for noteworthy changes in the running system. The kinds of noteworthy changes are listed in Table 1.

Note that different kinds of noteworthy changes might occur in parallel at the same instant of time, such that several of the macros have to be executed simultaneously and build a new system state $\sigma(\mathcal{M})_{[i+1]}$. For example, a number of objects can be created at the same time on different nodes in a distributed system, and in addition one or more new links can be established.

$$
\begin{array}{l}
\textbf{if } \mathit{noteworthyChange} = \mathit{true} \wedge \mathit{phase} = \mathit{updateSystemState} \textbf{ then} \\
\quad \mathit{UpdateClasses}, \mathit{UpdateAttributes}, \mathit{UpdateLinks}, \\
\quad \mathit{UpdateConfigurations}, \mathit{UpdateSignals}, \mathit{UpdateOperations}, \\
\quad \mathit{UpdateInputQueues}, \mathit{UpdateMessagesSent}, \\
\quad \mathit{TRACE}.\mathit{append}(\sigma(\mathcal{M})_{[i+1]}), \\
\quad i := i + 1, \\
\quad \textbf{if } \mathit{evaluateConstraints} = \mathit{true} \textbf{ then} \\
\quad\quad \mathit{phase} := \mathit{initConstraintEvaluation} \\
\quad \textbf{endif} \\
\textbf{endif}
\end{array}
$$

Table 1. Noteworthy Changes for OCL Evaluation

$NewObjects := \{\underline{oid}_1, \ldots, \underline{oid}_n\}$, where $\underline{oid}_1, \ldots, \underline{oid}_n$ are the **objects** of classes $c_j \in CLASS, 1 \leq j \leq n$, that are newly **created**.
$DestroyedObjects := \{\underline{oid}_1, \ldots, \underline{oid}_m\}$, where $\underline{oid}_1, \ldots, \underline{oid}_m$ are the **objects** of classes $c_j \in CLASS, 1 \leq j \leq m$, that are **destroyed**.
$NewAttributeValues := \{a_1, \ldots, a_l\}$, where $a_1, \ldots, a_l$ are the **attributes** of objects $\underline{oid}_j, 1 \leq j \leq l$, whose values are **changed**.
$NewLinks := \{l_{as_1}, \ldots, l_{as_k}\}$, where $l_{as_1}, \ldots, l_{as_k}$ are the **links** of associations $as_j \in ASSOC, 1 \leq j \leq k$, that are newly **established**.
$DestroyedLinks := \{l_{as_1}, \ldots, l_{as_p}\}$, where $l_{as_1}, \ldots, l_{as_p}$ are the **links** of associations $as_j \in ASSOC, 1 \leq j \leq p$, that are **removed**.
$NewConfigurations := \{cfg1, \ldots, cfg_q\}$, where $cfg1, \ldots, cfg_q$ are the **new state configurations** that are **reached** for objects $\underline{oid}_j$ of active classes $c_j, 1 \leq j \leq q$.
$MessagesSent := \{opExec_1, \ldots, opExec_r\}$, where $opExec_j$ denotes an operation execution with name op_j and identifier $opId_j, 1 \leq j \leq r$, of objects $\underline{oid}_j$ from classes $c_j \in CLASS$ that **sent a message** named msg_j with identifier $msgId_j$ and actual parameter values $v_{j,1}, ..., v_{j,n_j}$ to object $destId_j$ with identifier $callId_j$.
$MessagesReceived := \{\underline{oid}_1, \ldots, \underline{oid}_v\}$, where $\underline{oid}_j$ denotes an object of class $c_j \in CLASS, 1 \leq j \leq v$, that **receives a message** named msg_j with call identifier $callId_j$ invoked by an operation execution of object $srcId_j$ of a class c'_j (where c'_j is identified by $srcOp_j$ and $srcOpId_j$).
$ConsumedSignals := \{sigSent_1, \ldots, sigSent_w\}$, where $sigSent_j = \langle srcId_j, srcOp_j, srcOpId_j, sig_j, callId_j \rangle, 1 \leq j \leq w$, is a **signal** that is **consumed** by objects $\underline{oid}_j$ of classes $c_j \in CLASS$.
$DispatchedOperations := \{opCalled_1, \ldots, opCalled_x\}$, where $opCalled_j = \langle srcId_j, srcOp_j, srcOpId_j, op_j, callId_j \rangle, 1 \leq j \leq x$, is a **waiting operation call** that is **dispatched** by objects $\underline{oid}_j$ of classes $c_j \in CLASS$.
$TerminatedOperations := \{opExec_1, \ldots, opExec_y\}$, where $opExec_j, 1 \leq j \leq y$, denotes an **operation execution** with name op_j and identifier $opId_j$ of an object $\underline{oid}_j$ that **terminated**.
$ReturnedOperations := \{opExec_1, \ldots, opExec_z\}$, where $opExec_j, 1 \leq j \leq z$, denotes a **terminated operation** with name op_j and identifier $opId_j$ of an object $\underline{oid}_j$ that **returns** with its result value $result$.

In the preceding rule, condition $noteworthyChange$ is defined by

$$noteworthyChange \equiv \bigvee_{X \in Changes} X \neq \emptyset,$$

where the elements of $Changes$ are the sets of Table 1, i.e., $NewObjects$, $Destroyed$-$Objects$, ..., $ReturnedOperations$.

The macros with the prefix *Update* in the preceding rule are for building the new system state $\sigma(\mathcal{M})_{[i+1]}$ w.r.t. the sets of current objects, attribute values, links, configurations, received signals, currently executed operations, and sent messages. All of these update rules are very similar and explained in more detail in [5], but it is sufficient to give just an example rule here to understand the general idea, i.e., the functions of the previous system state are copied and updated corresponding to the given changes in terms of Table 1.

$$
\begin{aligned}
& UpdateMessagesSent \equiv \\
& \quad \forall j \in \{1, \ldots, r\} : \\
& \quad\quad \sigma_{sentMsg,c_j}(\underline{oid}_j, msg_j, msgId_j)_{[i+1]} := \\
& \quad\quad\quad \sigma_{sentMsg,c_j}(\underline{oid}_j, msg_j, msgId_j)_{[i]} \cup \{\langle destId_j, op_j, callId_j \rangle\}, \\
& \quad\quad \sigma_{sentMsgParam,c_j}(\underline{oid}_j, op_j, opId_j, destId_j, msg_j, callId_j)_{[i+1]} := \\
& \quad\quad\quad \langle v_{j,1}, \ldots, v_{j,n_j}, ? \rangle,
\end{aligned}
$$

Constraint Evaluation. In the phase *initConstraintEvaluation*, we initialize some help variables that are for documenting potential constraint violations and set *phase* to the next step.

$$
\begin{aligned}
& \textbf{if } phase = initConstraintEvaluation \textbf{ then} \\
& \quad violation := false, \\
& \quad violatedConstraints := \emptyset, \\
& \quad undefinedConstraints := \emptyset, \\
& \quad UpdateOclVariableAssignments, \\
& \quad phase := checkConstraints \\
& \textbf{endif}
\end{aligned}
$$

Phase *checkConstraints* then comprises the evaluation of the considered constraints of $checkInv$, $checkPre$, and $checkPost$. We partition this phase as follows.

$$
\begin{aligned}
& \textbf{if } phase = checkConstraints \textbf{ then} \\
& \quad CheckInvariants, \\
& \quad CheckPreconditions, \\
& \quad CheckPostconditions, \\
& \quad phase := identifyViolations \\
& \textbf{endif}
\end{aligned}
$$

The validity of OCL expressions is determined by an interpretation function $I[[\ ]]$ over so-called *environments* τ [11, Section A.3.1.2]. An environment $\tau = \langle \sigma(\mathcal{M}), \beta \rangle$ comprises the system state $\sigma(\mathcal{M})$ and an OCL-specific variable assignment β that maps variable names to values. Function β determines values for those variables that appear in OCL let expressions and as iterator variables of predefined collection operations. Note that we specified a macro *UpdateOclVariableAssignments* in the rule for *phase* = *initConstraintEvaluation* to indicate the update of β at trace position i. But as β is precisely defined in the formal OCL 2.0 semantics [11, Section A.3.1.1], we omit further details of the variable update here.

Generally, the semantics of an OCL expression $expr \in Expr_t$ of type t is a function $I[[expr]] : Env \to I(t)$ from the set Env of all environments to the semantic domain of t, i.e., $I(t)$. However, for postconditions *two* environments have to be considered, i.e., the current environment τ and the past environment τ_{pre} that represents the system state at the time of the start of the investigated operation execution.

As invariants, pre-, and postconditions are OCL expressions with Boolean result type, we here simply apply the expression interpretation function $I[[\ ]]$ as defined in the OCL 2.0 semantics [11, Section A.3.1]. However, note that we annotate function $I[[expr]]$ by obj to denote that $expr$ is evaluated w.r.t. that object.[5] The resulting rule for checking invariants is then defined by

$$
\begin{array}{l}
CheckInvariants \equiv \\
\quad \forall \langle obj, inv \rangle \in checkInv : \\
\quad\quad \textbf{if } I[[inv]]_{obj}(\tau) = false \textbf{ then} \\
\quad\quad\quad violatedConstraints = violatedConstraints \cup \{ \langle obj, inv \rangle \} \\
\quad\quad \textbf{endif} \\
\quad\quad \textbf{if } I[[inv]]_{obj}(\tau) = \bot \textbf{ then} \\
\quad\quad\quad undefinedConstraints = undefinedConstraints \cup \{ \langle obj, inv \rangle \} \\
\quad\quad \textbf{endif}
\end{array}
$$

As the rule for checking preconditions is defined in a very similar way, we here just present the more interesting rule for postconditions, as two system states have to be considered in this case:

$$
\begin{array}{l}
CheckPostconditions \equiv \\
\quad \forall \langle opExec, post \rangle \in checkPost : \\
\quad\quad \textbf{choose } \tau_{pre} = \langle \sigma(\mathcal{M})_{[j]}, \beta_{[j]} \rangle \textbf{ in } TRACE \\
\quad\quad\quad\quad \textbf{satisfying } \sigma(\mathcal{M})_{[j]} \text{ is the system state in which } opExec \text{ has started} \\
\quad\quad\quad \textbf{if } I[[post]]_{opExec}(\tau_{pre}, \tau) = false \textbf{ then} \\
\quad\quad\quad\quad violatedConstraints = violatedConstraints \cup \{ \langle obj, inv \rangle \} \\
\quad\quad\quad \textbf{endif} \\
\quad\quad\quad \textbf{if } I[[post]]_{opExec}(\tau_{pre}, \tau) = \bot \textbf{ then} \\
\quad\quad\quad\quad undefinedConstraints = undefinedConstraints \cup \{ \langle obj, inv \rangle \} \\
\quad\quad\quad \textbf{endif} \\
\quad\quad \textbf{endchoose}
\end{array}
$$

Constraint Violations. Finally, we set the function *violation* to true if there is a violated constraint. We keep the violations in dedicated sets for further usage by the system, e.g., for a *violation report*. However, we do not define *what* has to be done if a constraint fails. This is left to a user-defined mechanism in the system (e.g., exception handling, transaction rollback). That mechanism might benefit from our approach and check for a violation report at completion of the current evaluation cycle, i.e., when state *identifyViolations* is reached.

[5] This is in contrast to the OCL semantics in which an invariant is always evaluated for *all objects* of the invariant's context class [11, Section A.3.1.5]. Our model of course also allows for this. However, we find it more flexible to also allow that only particular invariants are evaluated for particular objects.

if $phase = identifyViolations$ **then**
  if $violatedConstraints \neq \emptyset \vee undefinedConstraints \neq \emptyset$ **then**
    $violation := true$
  endif,
  $phase := updateSystemState$
endif

5 Related Work

Various works on the semantics of OCL have been published, ranging from early definitions for OCL version 1.1 back in 1998 to the most recent version OCL 2.0 in March 2004. A good overview of the work is given in [4]. However, none of the existing formal OCL semantics covers all language features. This is due to the fact that the standard leaves several issues open since they are still under investigation, e.g., non-determinism, empty collections, and recursive specifications.

Especially language features for checking activated states and sent messages have not received much attention. Although it is possible to refer to State Diagram states and check for activated states with operation `oclInState()` since OCL version 1.3, only the authors of this article have presented a formal integration of State Diagram states with OCL yet [6]. Concerning OCL messages, which was originally proposed in [8, 9], we only know of one other approach that deals with the corresponding formal semantics [10]. However, we are not aware of any other OCL semantics that supports the OCL message concept and precisely defines when OCL constraints have to be checked.

6 Conclusion

Our ASM definition of the semantics of OCL makes use of a flexible, generic approach that allows the executed model (or: the system) to trigger the evaluation of OCL constraints at arbitrary times. This is in accordance with the OCL language definition that deliberately leaves it open when to check OCL constraints, which is mainly due to performance aspects of the individual application. Our approach allows to rigorously check constraints at all relevant times, namely by synchronization of noteworthy changes with the evaluation trigger *evaluateConstraints*. For constraint evaluation in sequential implementations, the system has to be interrupted until the evaluation is completed in order to extract the evaluation result. This, however, is not very efficient for general application. Therefore, we see our approach as a prerequisite framework for modellers that want to precisely define *when* to check OCL constraints. Generally, there are a number of aspects that have an impact on this issue, e.g., the different phases of the development process or the specific application domain.

As a next step, we want to use our ASM definition as a basis to precisely identify and check which constraints have to be evaluated in what states. Our application domain is the modelling of time-critical manufacturing systems. For this, we also plan to combine the presented ASM definition with related definitions for State and Activity Diagrams.

Acknowledgements

This work receives funding through the DFG project GRASP within the DFG priority programme 1064 'Integration von Techniken der Softwarespezifikation für ingenieurwissenschaftliche Anwendungen' and partial funding through the DFG Research Centre 614 'Selbstoptimierende Systeme des Maschinenbaus'.

References

[1] E. Börger, A. Cavarra, and E. Riccobene. An ASM Semantics for UML Activity Diagrams. In *AMAST 2000, Iowa City, USA*, volume 1816 of *LNCS*, pages 293–308. Springer, 2000.

[2] E. Börger, A. Cavarra, and E. Riccobene. Modeling the Dynamics of UML State Machines. In *Abstract State Machines, Theory and Applications (ASM 2000), Monte Verità, Switzerland*, volume 1912 of *LNCS*, pages 223–241. Springer, 2000.

[3] E. Börger and R. Stärk. *Abstract State Machines – A Method for High-Level System Design and Analysis*. Springer, 2003.

[4] M. V. Cengarle and A. Knapp. OCL 1.4/1.5 vs. OCL 2.0 Expressions: Formal Semantics and Expressiveness. *Software and Systems Modeling (SoSyM)*, 3(1):9–30, March 2004.

[5] S. Flake. Towards the Completion of the Formal Semantics of OCL 2.0. In *27th Australasian Computer Science Conference (ACSC 2004), Dunedin, New Zealand*, pages 73–82, 2004.

[6] S. Flake and W. Müller. Formal Semantics of Static and Temporal State-Oriented OCL Constraints. *Software and System Modeling (SoSyM)*, 2(3), October 2003.

[7] Y. Gurevich. Evolving Algebra 1993: Lipari Guide. In E. Börger, editor, *Specification and Validation Methods*. Oxford University Press, Oxford, UK, 1994.

[8] A. Kleppe and J. Warmer. Extending OCL to Include Actions. In *UML 2000 – Advancing the Standard. York, UK*, volume 1939 of *LNCS*, pages 440–450. Springer, 2000.

[9] A. Kleppe and J. Warmer. The Semantics of the OCL Action Clause. In T. Clark and J. Warmer, editors, *Object Modeling with the OCL*, pages 213–227. Springer, 2002.

[10] M. Kyas and F. de Boer. On Message Specifications in OCL. In *UML 2003 Workshop on Compositional Verification of UML Models*, San Francisco, CA, USA, October 2003.

[11] OMG, Object Management Group. UML 2.0 OCL Specification. OMG Adopted Specification ptc/03-10-14, October 2003.

[12] OMG, Object Management Group. Unified Modeling Language 1.5 Specification. OMG Document formal/03-03-01, March 2003.

[13] M. Richters. *A Precise Approach to Validating UML Models and OCL Constraints*. PhD thesis, Universität Bremen, Bremen, Germany, 2001.

[14] M. Stumptner and M. Schrefl. Behavior Consistent Inheritance in UML. In *19th Int. Conf. on Conceptual Modeling (ER 2000), Salt Lake City, UT, USA*, volume 1920 of *LNCS*, pages 527–542. Springer, 2000.

[15] J. Warmer and A. Kleppe. *The Object Constraint Language – Getting your Models Ready for MDA*. Addison-Wesley Object Technology Series. Pearson Education, Inc., 2003.

[16] P. Ziemann and M. Gogolla. An Extension of OCL with Temporal Logic. In J. Jürjens et al., editors, *Critical Systems Development with UML*, pages 53–62. Technische Universität München, Institut für Informatik, 2002.

Towards a Framework for Mapping Between UML/OCL and XML/XQuery

Ahmed Gaafar[1] and Sherif Sakr[2]

[1] Faculty of Computers and Information, Cairo University
agaafar@cu.edu.eg
[2] Department of computers and information science, University of Konstanz
sakr@inf.uni-konstanz.de

Abstract. The Unified Modeling Language is the standard language for modeling systems. UML has been extended to model web applications. At the same time, Web technology has become largely relying on XML documents. The structure of XML documents, namely the XML schema or DTD for these documents can be modeled using UML data structures. UML tools are usually concerned with the generation of the structure and behavior of the system that is captured by models in their equivalents in the selected platform. In this paper we introduce a novel approach for the integration between UML and XML families of technologies. We model the structure of XML using UML class diagrams and based on this, we study how queries on XML documents, namely XQuery expressions can be described using UML techniques. Here we show that modeling of XML documents and its queries represented by XQuery expressions is possible using the querying capabilities of UML Class diagram and the Object Constraint Language (OCL). As a result, we see how these two technologies compare, what the advantages of both technologies are and how they can be combined.

1 Introduction

The eXtensible Markup Language XML [6] has become the defacto standard to exchange structured data over the web. The Document Type Definition (DTD) language, was initiated as the most common method for describing the structure of XML instance documents. But DTD lacks enough expressive power to properly describe highly structured data. The World Wide Web Consortium (W3C) realized the limitations of DTDs and proposed other alternatives. Nowadays, XML Schema has become the most common method for defining and validating structured XML documents. It solves the limitations of DTD by providing a much richer set of structures, types and constraints for describing data. Since XML documents are viewed as a source of storing and exchanging information in XML format, it is logical to pose queries against those XML documents [1]. XQuery is the current W3C standard language for querying XML documents.

At the same time the Unified Modeling Language UML [20] is the OMG's standard language for object oriented analysis and design. UML defines modelling languages that span a range from functional requirements and activity workflow models to class

T. Baar et al. (Eds.): UML 2004, LNCS 3273, pp. 241-259, 2004.

structure design and component diagrams. These models, and a development process that uses them, improve and simplify communication among the application's many diverse stakeholders. Class diagram is a UML diagram that shows the static structure of the domain abstraction (classes) of the described model. It describes the types of objects in the system and various kinds of static relationships that exist among them. It shows the attributes, operations and the constraints of each class in the model. XML Schemas are static by nature so the most appropriate UML diagram to express them is the class diagram. A UML class diagram is very suitable as a tool for visual representation of the elements, relationships, and constraints of an XML vocabulary. Class diagrams allow complex XML vocabularies to be understood by non-technical business stakeholders.

There was much work done in this area to introduce different approaches for graphically and visually representing XML document structure in the form of DTD or XML Schema using UML Class diagram and other different models [13][14]. Although UML sustain many aspects of software engineering, it does not provide explicit facility for writing queries. UML provides a textual Object Constraint Language OCL which can be used to express detailed aspects of the modelled system. OCL [16] was originally designed for expressing constraints on a UML Model. However its ability to navigate through the model types has lead to attempts for using it as a query language [15]. We suggest that OCL can play for UML the same role XQuery plays for XML. There are many similarities between OCL and XQuery. Detailed explanation of these similarities will be represented in section 3.

In this paper we show the possibility of establishing mapping scheme between XQuery and OCL as query languages. Figure 1 shows our proposed framework for the mapping between UML/OCL and XML/XQuery. In the right side of the framework we can see how UML family of technologies are used in the different steps of software design phase (dark blocks). In the left side of the framework we can see how XML family of technologies are used in the different steps of the software implementation phase. There are two bridges connect and integrate both phases and both families of technologies. The first bridge is to map between UML class diagram and XML Schema. As we previously mentioned there was a lot of work already done in establishing this bridge. Discussion of this bridge is beyond the scope of this paper, nevertheless we will employ it. In this paper we focus on the second bridge. We show the possibility to close the framework cycle by establishing mapping scheme between OCL and XQuery as query languages.

The rest of the paper is organized as follows. In section 2 we briefly give an overview of XML, XML schema, XQuery and OCL. In section 3 we show the similarities between XQuery and OCL which motivate us for such mapping framework. In section 4 we represent our case study then we show our idea for the possibility of representing XQuery expressions using OCL. Finally, section 5 concludes the paper and outlines issues for further research.

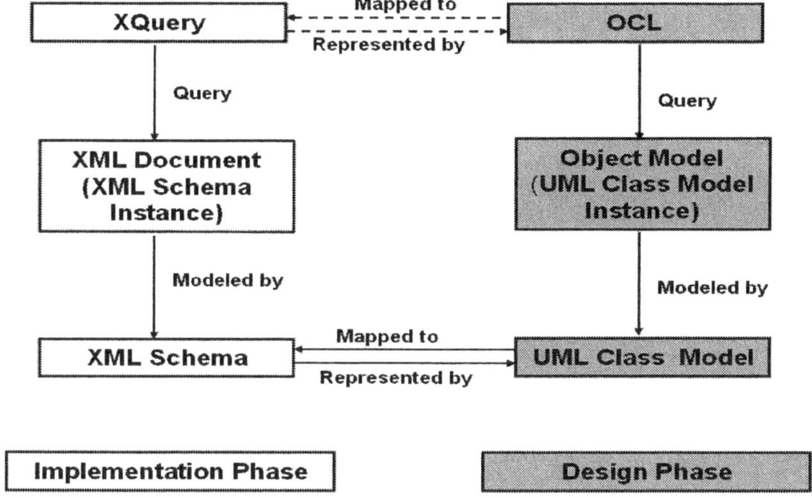

Fig1: Proposed UML/OCL and XML/XQuery integration framework

2 Background: XML, XML Schema, XQuery, and OCL

In this section we give a brief overview over the technologies and standards used in this paper. We give an overview on XML as a standard format for exchanging structured data, XML Schema, the current W3C standard for modeling the structure of XML document, and XQuery as the most expressive language for querying XML documents and at last about OCL.

2.1 XML

XML has become the most popular format for marking up all kinds of data, from web content to data used by applications. XML is a mark-up language for structured documentation. XML provided a simple and general facility, which is useful for data interchange. It is intended to make it easy and straightforward to use SGML on the web and to make it easy to define document types and easy to transmit and share them across the web. XML enables independent computer systems to exchange, interpret, and act on data, even if those systems run on different hardware and are programmed in different languages [6].

It is also a Meta mark-up language, which can be used to describe the logical structure of a wide variety of documents and data in different ways according to the application. It does not truly understand the content of document. What the tags actual conceal is entirely up to the user and application. XML specifies neither semantics nor a tag set. It only provides a facility to define tags and the structural relationship between them. All of the semantics will be defined either by the application that process the documents or by style sheets.

The basic construct of an XML document is the element. Elements can be nested at any depth and can contain other elements (sub-elements). An element contains a portion of the document delimited by two tags: the start tag, at the beginning of the element, of the form <tag-name>, and the end tag, at the end of the element, of the form </tag-name>. Empty elements of the form <tag-name/> are also possible.
A list of attributes can also be specified for an element. Attributes are of the form name = value, where name is a label and value is a quoted string, and are listed within the start tag of the element. Attributes can have different types allowing one to specify an element identifier (attributes of type ID often called id), links to other elements of the document (attributes of type IDREF, referring to a single target, or IDREFS, referring to multiple targets), or additional information about the element. Figure 2 shows an XML document example for representing book store items.

```
<bookstore>
	<topic>
		<name>Database Systems</name>
		<book>
			<title>... </title>
			<title>... </title>
			<title>... </title>
		</book>
	</topic>
</ bookstore >
```

Fig 2: XML Document example

2.2 XML Schema

An XML document is essentially a structured medium for storing and exchanging information. In order to assess the validity of an XML document, we need to establish exactly to which structure the information within the document must adhere. This is accomplished with a schema, which is a model used to describe the structure of information within an XML document. Schemas are used to model a class of data. Once a data model is in place for a particular class of data, we can create structured XML documents that adhere to that model [7] [18].
A schema describes the arrangement of markup and character data within a valid XML document. In other words, an XML document must adhere to a schema in order to be valid. We can think of a schema as an agreement between an XML application and the XML document on which it is based on.
There exits two approaches for modeling XML documents: Modeling XML documents with DTD (Document Type Definition) and Modeling XML documents with XML Schema language. We choose XML schema to be our alternative for modeling XML document structure for the following reasons: XML Schema is the current standard of W3C to model the XML document structure, XML Schema has more expressive power and modeling capabilities than DTD, And the most important reason to our work is mapping XML schema to the UML class diagram is more

preserving for the XML document semantics rather than mapping DTD to the class diagram.

XML Schema is a new approach defining the schema for XML documents that uses an XML vocabulary (XML-Data). XML Schema is used to establish the schema of a class of documents [7] [8]. XML Schemas describe the elements and their content model so that documents can be validated. However, XML schemas go several steps further than DTDs by allowing associating data types with elements. This allows XML processor to perform data validation, which is an extremely significant benefit of using XML Schema instead of traditional DTD. One of the most interesting aspects of XML schemas is that they are expressed in XML syntax. This means that we create an XML schema as an XML document. So, the familiar tag approach to encoding XML documents is all we need to code an XML schema. XML Schema also provides the facility to make description of the content models and to reuse the elements via inheritance. Also XML Schema supports namespace integration and attributes groups which allow to logically combining attributes. Figure 3 shows an XML Schema example describes the structure of book store item.

2.3 XML Query Language: XQuery

Since XML documents are viewed as a source of storing and exchanging information in XML format, so it is logical to pose queries against that XML documents. This is the basic reason why a query language for XML data is extremely important. The W3C provides two textual languages to formulate XML queries and express document transformations, XQuery and XSLT. XQuery is designed to be a language in which queries are concise and easily understood, and to be flexible enough to query a broad spectrum of information sources, including both databases and documents[1] [3]. XQuery is defined in terms of XQuery1.0 and XPath 2.0 data model. The Query data model [9] represents XML data in the form of nodes and values, which serve as the operands and results of the XQuery operators.

XQuery is closed under the Query data model, which means that the result of any valid XQuery expression can be represented in this model. In the Query data model, every value is an ordered sequence of zero or more items. An item can be either an atomic value or a node. An atomic value has a type, which is one of the atomic types defined by XML Schema or is derived from one of these types by restriction. A node is one of the seven kinds of node defined by XPath, called document, element, attribute, text, comment, processing instruction, and namespace nodes. Nodes have identity, and an ordering called document order is defined among all the nodes that are in scope.

XQuery is a functional language and instead of executing commands as procedural languages do, every query is an expression to be evaluated, and expressions can be combined quite flexibly with other expressions to create new expressions so the basic building block of XQuery is the expressions [1]. In XQuery, Several types of expressions are possible: *Primary expressions, Path expressions, Sequence expressions, Arithmetic expressions, logical expressions, Comparison expressions, Conditional expressions, Quantified expressions, FLOWR expressions, Element*

Construction expressions, Validate expressions and Unordered expressions. We will present all these types of expressions with more details in section 4.

```
<schema>
        <element name="bookstore" type="bookstoreType"/>
        <complexType name="bookstoreType" >
                <sequence>
                        <element name="name" type="xsd:string"/>
                        <element name="topic" type="topicType" minoccurs="1"/>
                </sequence>
        </complexType>
        <complexType name="topicType">
                <element name="name" type="xsd:string"/>
                <element name="book" type="bookType" minoccurs="0"/>
        </complexType>
        <complexType name="bookType">
                <element name="title" type="xsd:string"/>
                <element name="author" type="xsd:string"/>
                <element name="isbn" type="isbnType" />
        </complexType>
        <simpleType name=" isbnType">
                <restriction base="xsd:string"/>
                <pattern value="[0-9]{3}[-][0-9] {3}[-][0-9] {3}">
        </simpleType>
</schema>
```

Fig 3: XML Schema example

2.4 OCL

The Object Constraint Language [16] is a textual specification language, designed especially for the use in the context of diagrammatic specification languages such as UML .OCL was always used to add well-formedness rules on both the model and metamodel levels within UML. OCL is tightly connected to UML diagrams, as it is used as textual addendum within the diagrams, e.g. to define pre- and post-conditions, invariants, transition guards. OCL also uses the elements defined in the UML diagrams, such as classes, methods (side effect free) and attributes. The language is based on types. Each OCL expression evaluates to a type either predefined by the language or defined by the model on which the expression is built. Composing an expression comes out through the concept of navigation. Navigation in OO modeling means to follow links from one object to locate other object(s). Navigation in OCL is one of the following [16] [19]:

- *Navigating from an object to a property:* an example of this is accessing the value of an object's attribute or method like
  ```
  context Person inv:
  self.age > 25.
  ```
  The size of the result in this type of navigation is always of maximum 1.

- *Navigating from type to type:* this happens when the expression moves from one object type to another through associations. For example
```
context NaturalPersoninv:
self.address->size() > 0.
```
In this expression we started at the type represented by the variable "`self`" which is an instance of "`NaturalPerson`", through the "." a navigation through the association took place and the result of the expression at this moment is a set containing all address object that matches the self object. In this case also the type of result is compound on the following form Collection (destination object type). In our case it will be the following Collection (Address). Since Collection is an abstract type in the OCL metamodel, we have to refine the type by selecting from one of three types Set, Sequence, or Bag. The selection of the correct type depends mainly on the semantics of the association between the source and destination types. By default the type is Set. If the association is labeled with {ordered} then the collection is of type Sequence. If it is possible that navigation will generate duplicate elements then the collection type is Bag.
- *Operations over collections:* this is a special type of navigation in which a Boolean predicate is examined against collection elements, either for testing that all, some, none of the elements match this predicate. An example on this navigation:
```
context NaturalPerson inv:
self.address->select(attrStateOfapartment = #main)->
size() =1.
```

In this constraint an operation is made on the set of addresses a person might have to select only those addresses that are the main residence for the person. The purpose of this constraint is to state that a person must have only one main address. It is clear that within one expression the three different types of navigation can occur (which is very common with complex expressions). Almost all uses of OCL before were as a constraint language. Constraints expression are subset sub set if the OCL expressions that evaluate to the type Boolean. In this paper we are about to use the querying features of OCL and see the possibility to map them to XQuery expressions as an implementation for these queries.

3 Motivations for the Mapping Between OCL and XQuery

The purpose of OCL is to specify constraints on UML Model Elements and to limit the possible system states. OCL can be used also to query the models [17] [15]. In [15] OCL was not considered as a complete query language because of lacking expressions that evaluate to tuple types. But with the emergence of OCL 2.0, tuples are now possible to be expressed using OCL. On the other hand the purpose of XQuery is to provide flexible and powerful query facilities to extract data from a collection of real and virtual XML documents. In XQuery everything is an expression that evaluates to a value. An XQuery program or script is a just an expression. XQuery Core supports the equivalent of selection, projection, and set operators, and thus is arguably relationally complete. We believe that OCL can play for UML models the same role XQuery plays for XML documents. We justify our belief by showing the following similarities between OCL and XQuery.

- *Path Expressions vs. Navigation*
  Both languages support the notion of moving between types (in OCL) and nodes (in XQuery) [10]. The three different types of OCL navigation expressions we showed in section 2.4 with the set of its predefined operations over collections can cover the different XQuery expressions that we cover in detail in section 4.
- *Type based Expressions*
  XQuery is strongly typed language, meaning that the types of values and expressions must be compatible with the context in which the value or expression is used. Types can be imported from one or more XML Schemas that describe the input documents and the output document. XQuery language can then perform operations based on these types [5]. For example, this expression raises a type error because when "`isbn`" attribute is defined as string and then compared with an integer value.

  /book[isbn] = 1234

  In the same way OCL expression must evaluate to a type that is either predefined in the language or defined in the model to which the expression is attached.
- *Declarative nature of queries*
  Queries of both languages are declarative in nature where we specify *what* we need rather than specifying *how* to reach it.
- *Common constructs*
  Both of the languages are able to represent different control, and logic constructs like if statements, looping, arithmetic operations, and logical comparison, etc.

4 Mapping Between XQuery and OCL

We are looking for complete mapping scheme between XQuery and OCL. In section 4.1 we represent a case study that describes our suggested scenario of integration between UML, OCL, XML and XQuery. In section 4.2 we give an overview over the different types of expressions supported by XQuery, We represent our idea of the direct mappings and matches exist between some XQuery expressions and OCL. For the expressions which are not possible to be mapped directly, that will be future work to make it possible.

4.1 Case Study

Our proposal of integration between UML, OCL, XML and XQuery is based on the idea that Each XML document is an instance of XML schema. Each XML schema can be graphically modelled using UML class diagram notations. So we believe that we can find mapping schema that enables us to represent each query expressed by XQuery language as an OCL expression over the UML class diagram.

```
<Schema name="OrderSchema">
 <ElementType name="firstName" content="textOnly" dt:type="string"/>
 <ElementType name="lastName" content="textOnly" dt:type="string"/>
 <ElementType name="customerID" content="textOnly" dt:type="string"/>
 <ElementType name="addressID" content="textOnly" dt:type="string"/>
 <ElementType name="city" content="textOnly" dt:type="string"/>
 <ElementType name="state" content="textOnly" dt:type="string"/>
 <ElementType name="orderID" content="textOnly" dt:type="string"/>
 <ElementType name="quantity" content="textOnly" dt:type="float"/>
 <ElementType name="shipDate" content="textOnly" dt:type="date"/>
 <ElementType name="productName" content="textOnly" dt:type="string"/>
 <AttributeType name="price" dt:type="float"/>
 <ElementType name="product" content="mixed">
  <element type="productName" minOccurs="1" maxOccurs="*"/>
  <attribute type="price"/>
 </ElementType>
 <ElementType name="Customer" content="eltOnly">
  <description>
   This element type represents the customer information
  </description>
  <element type="firstName" minOccurs="1" maxOccurs="1"/>
  <element type="lastName" minOccurs="1" maxOccurs="1"/>
  <element type="custID" minOccurs="1" maxOccurs="1"/>
 </ElementType>
 <ElementType name="Address" content="eltOnly">
  <description>
   This element type represents the address information of an order invoice
  </description>
  <element type="addressID" minOccurs="1" maxOccurs="1"/>
  <element type="street" minOccurs="1" maxOccurs="1"/>
  <element type="city" minOccurs="1" maxOccurs="1"/>
  <element type="state" minOccurs="1" maxOccurs="1"/>
 </ElementType>
 <ElementType name="Shipto" content="eltOnly">
  <element type="Customer" minOccurs="1" maxOccurs="1"/>
  <element type="Address" minOccurs="1" maxOccurs="1"/>
 </ElementType>
 <ElementType name="order" content="eltOnly">
  <description>
   This element type represents the order information
  </description>
  <element type="orderID" minOccurs="1" maxOccurs="1"/>
  <element type="quantity" minOccurs="1" maxOccurs="1"/>
  <element type="product" minOccurs="1" maxOccurs="1"/>
  <element type="shipDate" minOccurs="1" maxOccurs="1"/>
 </ElementType>
 <ElementType name="orderInvoice" content="eltOnly">
  <element type="Shipto" minOccurs="1" maxOccurs="1"/>
  <element type="order" minOccurs="1" maxOccurs="1"/>
 </ElementType>
</Schema>
```

Fig 4: Case study XML Schema example

```
<orderInvoice>
    <shipTo>
        <customer>
            <firstName>Folkert</ firstName >
            < lastName >Wilken</ lastName >
            <custID>123C</ custID >
        </customer >
        <Address>
            <addressID>212</addressID>
            <street>206 Soflinger Street</street>
            <city>ULM</city>
            <state>Baden-Wuerttemberg<state>
        </Address>
    </ shipTo>
    <order>
        <orderID>ord123</orderID>
        <quantity>3</quantity>
        <product price="40"> PC Monitor</product>
        <shipDate>12.12.2004</ shipDate >
    </order>
</ orderInvoice >
```

Fig 5: Instantiated XML document

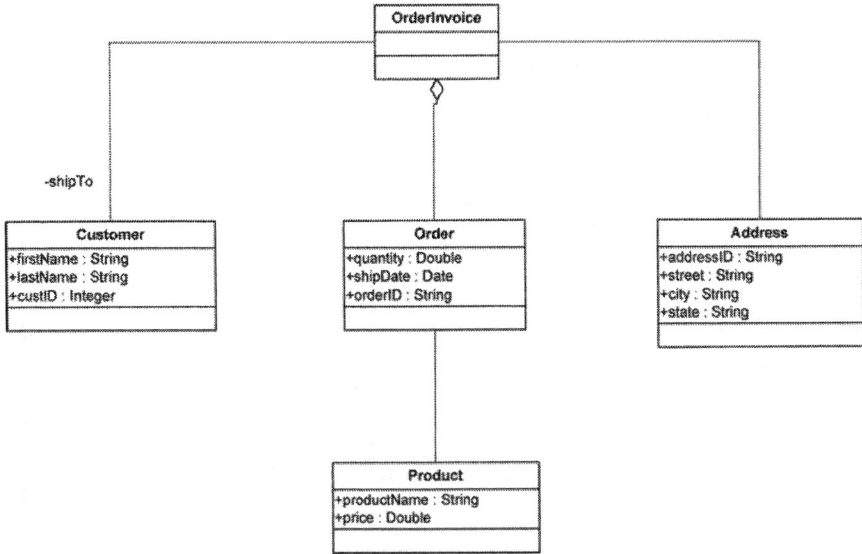

Fig 6: Class model representing our sample XML Schema

In this section we represent our case study according to the suggested integration scenario represented in figure 1 and in section 4.2 we will represent the possibility of mapping between XQuery and OCL. Figure 4 shows the XML schema example.

Figure 5 shows an example of XML document instantiated according to that XML schema. Figure 6 shows the representation of the XML Schema using UML class diagram notations. There are many advantages for using UML class diagram to model the XML document structure. UML syntax is generally more widely understood than XML Schema syntax. This is due to the graphical representation of UML models. It is much easier to grasp a general picture from UML diagrams. UML is independent of the XML schema, which will be used on the implementation level [22]. There are different approaches for representing XML document structure using UML class diagrams [21] [22] [23]. In our case study we have chosen simple one that represent each simple element type contains only text as an attribute for the class and each complex element type contain elements as separate class. We choose the class diagram association relationship to represent the relationship between the elements of our classes. Our idea of representing XQuery using OCL is independent from this step of representing XML Schema using UML class diagram so any other approach can be used without affecting the idea or results.

4.2 Mapped Expressions

- **Path expression**

Path expressions are used to locate nodes in XML data. Consist of a series of one or more steps separated by "/" or "//". Every step is evaluated to a sequence of nodes. Each operation E1/E2 is evaluated as follows: E1 is evaluated and its node sequence result serves in turn to provide an inner focus for an evaluation for E2.

```
Ex1: List the first names of all customers.
("Sample.xml")/orderinvoice/shipto/customer/firstName.
```

This expression can be represented in OCL using the navigation between object types. If we refer to figure 6 and we try to query the names of customers for whom invoices have been issued; then the start of the navigation will be the "OrderInvoice" class. Navigation flows through the association link "Shipto" now the expression "OrderInvoice.Shipto" will evaluate to a *collection of objects* (*sequence of nodes in XML document*) of type "Customer". To reach the information we need (list of first names) we need to make an extra navigation from the type "Customer" to the attribute "FirstName". At the end of this navigation we have reached the information we need from this query. The equivalent OCL expression is

```
OrderInvoice.shipTo.firstName
```

- **Positional Predicates**

Predicates are Boolean conditions that select a subset of the nodes computed by a step expression.

```
Ex2: Return the first Customer in the document
("Sample.XML")/OrderInvoice/ShitpTo/Customer[1].
```

To return a certain element at certain position in a collection of objects we need to use the subsequence operation defined in OCL document [12]. The equivalent OCL expression is

```
OrderInvoice.shipTo-> asSequence->subSequence(1,1)
```

- **FLOWR expression**

XQuery provides a feature called a FLOWR expression that supports iteration and binding of variables to intermediate results. It is similar to the SELECT-FROM-WHERE statements in SQL. The name FLOWR is an acronym, standing for the first letter of the clauses that may occur in FLOWR expression. *For and let clauses,* generate a sequence of bound variables called the tuple stream. *Where clause* serves to filter the tuple stream retaining some tuples and discarding the others. *Order by clause* improves an ordering on the tuple stream. *Return clause* evaluated once for every tuple in the tuple stream.

```
Ex3: Return the ID of all orders which have quantity
greater than 10
For $X in ("Sample.xml")/orderInvoice/order
  Where $X/quantity > 10
Return  $X/orderID
```

To represent a query where some objects are filtered according to a given selection criteria we can use the Select operation from OCL to make this filtration. The navigation starts from "OrderInvoice" using the association to the class "Order OrderInvoice.Order" the expression now evaluates to a set of objects of type "Order" on this set we need to select only orders which have quantity greater than 10. The expression now becomes `OrderInvoice.Order-> select(quantity > 10)`. This expression also evaluates to set of orders but for which the expression `quantity > 10` holds. To reach the information we need to make one more navigation to the attribute "orderID". The complete expression will be.

```
OrderInvoice.Order-> select(quantity >10).orderID
```

- **Conditional expression**

XQuery conditional expressions are used in the same way as conditional expressions in other languages. It is a Very well known and common type of expressions. *IF* test expression *Then* then-expression *Else* else-expression.

```
Ex4: Return the ID of all orders which have quantity
greater than 10 (rewriting of Ex3 using of conditional
expression format instead of where clause format)
For $X in ("Sample.xml")/orderInvoice/order
   If $X/quantity > 10 then
      Return  $X/orderID
   Else
      ()
```

OCL has a direct representation for the conditional expressions like all other language, the equivalent OCL expression is:

```
If OrderInvoice.Order.quantity > 10 then
    OrderInvoice.Order.orderID
Else
    NULL
End if
```

- **Arithmetic expression**

XQuery support the arithmetic operators +,-,*, /, div, mod. Each operand of the arithmetic expression should be represented by sequence with length exactly equal to one and then normally apply the expression operators over the sequence values. The result of arithmetic expression is a sequence with exactly one element.

```
Ex5: let X = 3 + 4
```

The equivalent OCL expression is:

```
let X = 3 + 4
```

- **Quantified expression**

Quantified expressions support existential and universal quantification. The value of a quantified expression is always true or false. If the quantifier is *some* then the quantified expression is true if at least one evaluation of the expression is true. If the quantifier is *every* then the quantified expression is true if every evaluation of the expression is true.

```
Ex6: this expression returns true if there exist any
instance of order that have quantity greater than 10
Some $X in ("Sample.xml")/orderInvoice/order Satisfy
$X/quantity > 10.
```

This expression can be represented in OCL using "Exists" operation defined for collection types. This expression evaluates to the Boolean type

The OCL expression will be

```
OrderInvoice.Order-> exists (quantity > 10)
```

- **Logical expression**

A logical expression is either "and-expression" or an "or-expression". Its value is always one of the Boolean values true or false.

```
Ex7: return all products which have prices in the range
between 10 and 20
("Sample.xml")/orderInvoice/order/product[@price > 10 and
@price < 20].
```

The equivalent OCL expression will be

```
OrderInvoice.Order.Product-> select( price > 10 and price
< 20)
```

- **Sequence expression**

XQuery supports operators to construct and combine sequence of items. Sequences are never nested. Also XQuery provides the *union, intersect* and *except* operators for combining sequences of nodes

```
Ex8: let s1=(1,2,3)
        let s2= (4,5,6)
        let s3 = (s1,s2)
       for $X in s2
       return $X
```

The equivalent OCL expression is:

```
let  s1 : Sequence(Integer)  = (1,2,3)
let s2: Sequence(Integer) = (4,5,6)
let s3: Sequence(Integer) = s1->union (s2)
```

```
for I = 1 to s3->size()
{
       s3->subSequence(I,I)
}
```

- **Value comparison expression**

Value comparison expressions are intended for comparing single values. Each operand must contain exactly one atomic value. The result of the expression is true if the value of the first operand satisfy the comparison operation (eq – ne – lt – le – gt - ge)to the value of the second operand otherwise the result of the comparison is false.

```
Ex9:
("Sample.xml")/orderInvoice/Shipto/customer/firstName eq
"Ahmad"
```

Representation of value comparison expressions can be represented using OCL with a navigation path that ends at an attribute and then the value of this attribute is compared to the value. The OCL expression for this is `OrderInvoice.shipTo.firstName = "Ahmad"`. The XQuery value comparison necessitate that the expression evaluates to a single node and its value is compared. The previous OCL expression lacks this restriction as it will evaluate to true only if all the "FirstName" value for all objects are equivalent to the value "Ahmad". In the following we add the condition that the navigation results in only a single object which "FirstName" value is equivalent to "Ahmad".

```
OrderInvoice.shipTo.firstName-> size() = 1 and
OrderInvoice.shipTo.firstName = "Ahmad"
```

- **General comparison expression**

General comparison expressions are existentially quantified comparisons that may be applied to operand sequences of any length. The result of the expression is true if there is a pair of atomic values, one belonging to the first operand and the other belongs to the second operand which are satisfying the comparison operation (= , !=, < , <=, >, >=) otherwise it is false

```
Ex10:
("Sample.xml")/orderInvoice/Shipto/customer/firstName =
"Ahmad".
```

The equivalent OCL expression is

```
OrderInvoice.shipTo-> exists(firstName = "Ahmad")
```

- **Unordered function**

XQuery expressions return sequences that have well-defined order. The *unordered* function takes any sequence of its argument and returns the same sequence of items in a nondeterministic order. A call to the *unordered* function is permission for the argument expression to be materialized in whatever order the system finds most efficient.

```
Ex11:
unordered(("Sample.xml")/orderInvoice/Shipto/customer/
firstName)
```

The equivalent OCL expression is

```
OrderInvoice.shipTo.firstName -> asSet ()
```

- **Built-in functions**

XQuery has a set of built-in functions and operators including many that are familiar from the other languages and some that are used in customized XML processors. These built-in functions include (min() – max () – count() - … etc)

```
Ex12: return the number of orders in this document
Count(("Sample.xml")/orderInvoice/order).
```

The count function in XQuery has a direct equivalent in OCL which is the operation **size** defined for collection types. The equivalent OCL expression is

```
OrderInvoice.Order-> size()
```

- **Element construction expression**

XQuery provides constructors that can create XML structures with in a query. Constructors are provided for every kind of node in XQuery data model.

```
Ex13:
For $X in ("Sample.xml")/orderInvoice/order
          Where $X/quantity > 10
      Return  <bigQuantity> <OrderID>$X/orderID</OrderID>
         <quantitv>$X/quantity<quantity></bigQuantity>
```

Such expression was not possible in OCL versions prior to Version 2.0. with the addition of tuple types to OCL it is capable of modeling the previous query where the expression evaluates to a tuple or a collection of tuples that have elements each of which belongs to possibly different type. In the equivalent OCL expression we first need to define the tuple type for this query, and then we define the expression which evaluates to this type.

```
Def:
bigQuantity: Set (Tupletype(orderID: String, quantity:
Integer))= OrderInvoice.Order->select(quantity > 10) ->
Tuple [orderID = orderID, quantity = quantity
```

- **Node Comparison (is and isnot operators)**

Each operand must be either single node or an empty sequence. A comparison with the *"is"* operand is true if the two operands have the same identity otherwise it is false. A comparison with the *isn't* operand is true if the two operands have different identities otherwise it is false.

```
Ex14:("Sample.xml")/orderInvoice/Shipto/customer[CustID =
1000] isnot
("Sample.xml")/orderInvoice/Shipto/customer[CustID =
1000]/firstName
```

Comparison between nodes is no longer made according to the content of the node. Figure 7 shows the generalization of different node types of an XML document. In order to find an equivalent representation for this type of queries in OCL all objects being compared must be instantiated from the same class. Figure 8 is a capture from the OCL metamodel, type hierarchy which shows that the class *oclAny* can play the role (in OCL expressions) *node* plays (in XQuery expressions) in figure 7

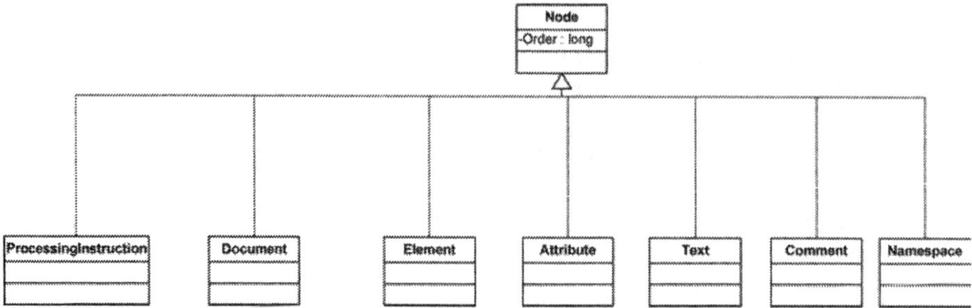

Fig 7: XML document node types

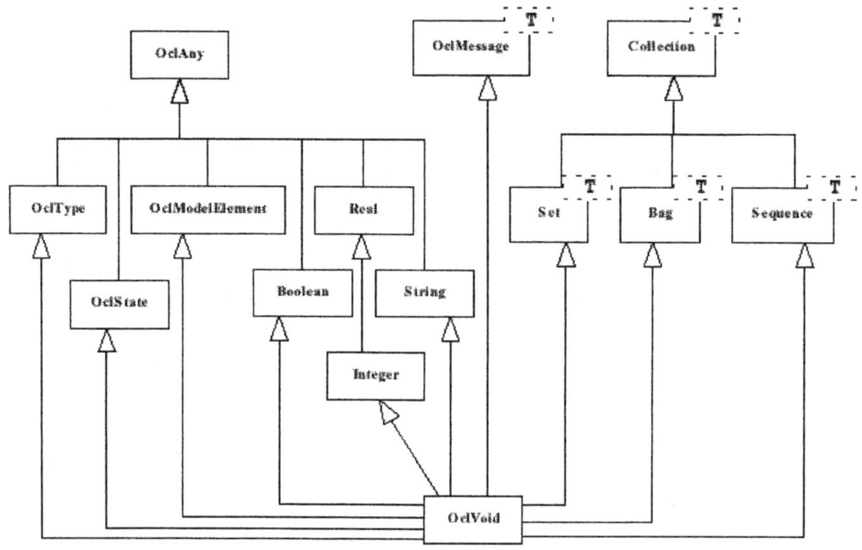

Fig 8: OCL data types

One possible way to simulate the XQuery is/isnot operator is to use the oclAny.=. That means all objects are represented as instance of the *oclAny* class. An equivalent OCL expression to the XQuery in Ex14 would be:

```
OrderInvoice.shipTo->select(custID = 1000)->
oclAsType(OclAny) <> OrderInvoice.shipTo->select(custID =
1000).firstName->oclAsType(OclAny).
```

To be compatible with the definition of the operation is/isnot the navigation in each operand must evaluate to a single object or empty collection. In the previous example selecting customer objects based on CustID attribute guarantees that selection returns with single or empty collection. If selection could be based on other attributes we can add an extra condition to check that at most one object is found at the end of the navigation expression.

```
(OrderInvoice.shipTo->select(firstName = "Ahmad")->
oclAsType(OclAny) <> OrderInvoice.shipTo->
select(firstName = "Ahmad").firstName->oclAsType(OclAny))
and OrderInvoice.shipTo->select(firstName = "Ahmad")->
size() = 1.
```

4.3 Unmapped Expressions

- **Order comparison (<< and >> operators)**

Each operand must be either single node or an empty sequence. A comparison with the << operand is true if the first operand node is earlier than the second operand node in document tree otherwise it returns false. A comparison with the >> operand is true if the first operand node is later than the second operand node in document tree otherwise it returns false.

```
Ex15:
("Sample.xml")/orderInvoice/Shipto/customer/firstName <<
("Sample.xml")/orderInvoice/Shipto/customer/firstName
```

Such operation can be partially simulated with slight modification to associations between classes with adding the {ordered}, and the two compared operands must lye on the same navigation path so that the {ordered} stereotype has meaning. XML documents define a total ordered between all nodes in them; such order is not possible between objects of different classes in UML. Defining a total order between objects of different classes needs extensions that are considered as future work.

5 Conclusion and Future Work

In this paper we have shown the possibility of representing most of XQuery expressions using OCL. In the usual software life cycle, the modelling and design activities normally precede the implementation activities. So we believe that the common way of using this approach will be to map OCL expressions describing queries over UML class diagrams into XQuery expressions on XML documents. Therefore, our plan in the future work is to design a complete framework for mapping between UML/OCL on one hand and XML/XQuery on the other.

In this work UML and OCL will play the role of modelling the data structure and the queries in the design. The modelled data structure and queries will be mapped to an XML schema and XQuery expressions in the XML implementation layer.

To reach this goal we will introduce our own mapping rules between UML class models into XML schema, then the mapping of different OCL expressions into XQuery equivalents. As we have seen in section 4.3 due to the technology differences between UML and XML, some XQuery expressions cannot be directly modelled unless UML metaclass *Classifier* is extended to act as a node in an XML tree.

We believe that as a side effect of this work the XML layer can be replaced with any other implementation layer (Relational Database and SQL – Object Oriented Database and OQL -…). In our work we choose to use the XML as an implementation target layer because the current widespread of usage of XML and to introduce new line for using UML in the web environment. We expect our work to continue and evolve in the future. The authors are currently planning to build a prototype tool that represents their proposed framework of integration and can implement their future complete mapping scheme. Also another point for future work will be to build extra metamodels for the XQuery and the XML documents to let UML and OCL understand the tree structure which makes mapping of the currently unmapped expressions possible.

References

1. Denise Draper, Peter Fankhauser, Mary F. Fernandez, Ashok Malhotra, Kristoffer Rose, Michael Rys and Philip Wadler. :XQuery 1.0 and XPath 2.0 Formal Semantics. Technical Report W3C Working Draft, World Wide Web Consortium, May 2003.
2. S.Alagic. : Type-Checking OQL Queries In the ODMG Type Systems. Transactions on Database Systems, 24(3), 1999.
3. J.Robie.: An Introduction to XQuery. in XQuery from the Experts. A Guide to the W3C XML Query Language edited by Howard Katz, Addison-Wesley, 2003.
4. D.Chamberlin. : Influences on the Design of XQuery. In XQuery from the Experts: A Guide to the W3C XML Query Language, edited by H. Katz, Addison-Wesley, 2003.
5. M.Fernandez, J.Simon, P.Wadler. : Static Typing in XQuery. In XQuery from the Experts: A Guide to the W3C XML Query Language, edited by H.Katz, Addison- Wesley, 2003.
6. Tim Bray, Jean Paoli, C.M.Sperbrag, Ere Maler. : eXtensible Markup Language (XML) 1.0 specification. W3C Recommendation. October 2000.
7. Henry S.Thompson, David Beech, Murray Maloney, Noah Mendelsohn. : XML Schema Part 1: Structures. W3C Recommendation. May 2001.
8. Paul V.Biron, Ashok Malhotra. : XML Schema Part 2: Datatypes. W3C Recommendation, May 2001.
9. XQuery 1.0 W3C Working Draft, May 2003.
10. XPath 2.0 data model, W3C Working Draft, May 2003.
11. OMG, editor. The Common Warehouse Metamodel Specification. OMG, 2000.
12. Rational Software Corporation: The Object Constraint Language specification,Version 1.4. 1999.
13. S.Ceri, S.Comai, E.Damiani, P.Fraternali, S.Paraboschi, L.Tanca. : XML-GL: a Graphical language for Querying and Restructuring XML Documents. Computer networks 31, 1999.
14. Enrico Augurusa, Daniele Braga, Messandro Campi, Stephano Ceri. : Design and implementation of a graphical interface to XQuery. SAC2003.
15. D.H.Akehurst, B.Bordbar. : On Querying UML Data Models with OCL. UML 2001 - The Unified Modeling Language. Modeling Languages, Concepts, and Tools: 4th International Conference, Toronto, Canada, October 1-5, 2001, Proceedings, 2001
16. J.Warmer, A.Kleppe, T.Clark, A.Ivner, J.Hogstrom, M.Gogolla, M.Richters, H.Hussmann, S.Zschaler, S.Johnston, D.S.Frankel, and C.Bock.: Object Constraint Language 2.0. Technical report, Submission to the OMG, 2001
17. Martin Gogolla and Mark Richters. : On constraints and queries in UML. In Martin Schader and Axel Korthaus, editors, The Unified Modeling Language - Technical Aspects and Applications, pages 109-121. PhysicaVerlag, Heidelberg, 1998.

18. Sherif Sakr, Mokhtar Boshra. : Using relational metadata to generate enhanced XML document structure. In proceedings of INFOS, Cairo University, November 2001.
19. Ali Hamie, John Howse, Stuart Kent. : Navigation Expressions in Object-Oriented Modeling Proceedings Fundamental Approaches to Software Engineering, 1st International Conference, 1998.
20. OMG, Unified Modeling Language Specification, version 1.4, 2001.
21. John Heintz, W. Eliot Kimber. : Using UML to define XML document types. isogen international, 2000.
22. Juho Tikkala.:Modeling W3C XML Schemas using UML. 2003
23. Rainer Conrad, Dieter Scheffner, J.Christof. :XML Conceptual Modeling using UML. 2003

Model-Driven Architecture for Automatic-Control: An Experience Report

Pierre-Alain Muller, Didier Bresch, Philippe Studer

ESSAIM
Université de Haute-Alsace
12 rue des Frères Lumière
68093 Mulhouse Cedex, France
pa.muller@uha.fr, d.bresch@uha.fr, ph.studer@uha.fr

Abstract. In the context of teaching distributed and embedded process-control it is difficult to bring students to perform efficient practical work, because the low-level underlying software technologies require too much time investment. Object-oriented modeling together with model-driven architecture provides a good solution to simplify such practical work, by automating the generation of the low-level code directly from the specifications of the process-control application. To support this approach, we have developed a model-driven application framework of about 130 distributed and embedded real-time components for RISC microcontrollers. This way, students can focus on the process-control side of their work, without having to dive (and often get lost) in the platform complexity.

1 Introduction

This work takes place in the context of practical work at ESSAIM, a school of engineering, where we teach process-control to students (in the second semester of a six semester engineer curriculum) who do not yet master the complete production line of low-cost distributed and embedded real-time applications.

We have been facing the problem of students who get lost in the complexity of the hardware and software platforms for distributed and embedded real-time systems. The problem is that the students get overwhelmed by the platform details, to the point that they are not able anymore to focus their effort on the process-control applications that they are supposed to develop during their practical work.

As a first attempt to simplify their work, we have been developing components, following an object-oriented style of writing assembly language, mainly based on the use of macro-instructions. However, this was still too much of an effort for the students, because there was no real enforcement of the object-orientation (and also because they were only starting to study object-oriented concepts).

Consequently, we have been looking for a more abstract way to deploy these components. Our goal has been to provide the students with tools that they could use to build process-control applications, without entering the details of programming, exactly as they would do when building electronic equipments from hardware components.

T. Baar et al. (Eds.): UML 2004, LNCS 3273, pp. 260-274, 2004.

We have followed an MDA approach, defined a meta-model for the components and a textual object-based language for the specification of the components, as well as transformation rules to target the commercial development tools for the various RISC microcontrollers that we use.
This specification language can in turn be generated from platform independent UML models. This way, students can focus on their domain, process-control, and forget about the details of the platform. The result is better understanding of the real issues, higher productivity and less frustration.
In this paper we give first an overview of model-driven engineering, as promoted by the OMG. Then, we describe the constraints of the distributed embedded applications that we want our students to deploy in their practical work, and we explain why the students face serious difficulties with these developments. Next we explain and motivate our model-driven framework for process-control, and give an example of application. Finally we report some lessons learned, and we draw final conclusions.

2 Model-Driven Architecture

Model-Driven Architecture (MDA) [1], as promoted by the OMG (Object Management Group), is an alternative to the traditional development of software by programming, moving from object composition to model transformation [2]. MDA is based on the well-known idea of separation between specification and implementation.
To achieve its three main goals, portability, interoperability and reusability, MDA promotes architectural separation of concerns, and provides ways to model systems, platforms, as well as transformations of platform independent models (PIMs) into platform specific models (PSMs).
The OMG has defined a four level meta-modeling architecture, and UML is playing a key role in this architecture, being both a general purpose software modeling language, and also a language to define meta-models (actually a subset of UML, known as the MOF [10] for Meta-Object Facility, used for meta-modeling). The following diagram shows the conventional representation of the OMG meta-modeling stack, with MOF being used for the meta-meta-model.

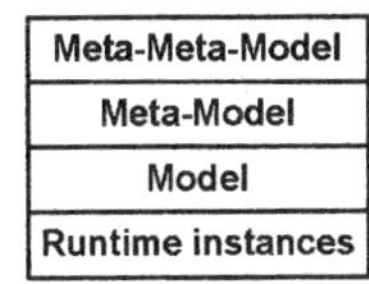

Fig. 1. Meta-modeling architecture for MDA

Beyond models, transformations seem to be at the heart of MDA [3]. As shown in the diagram below, transformations may themselves be considered as models; they explain how a model (instance of a given meta-model) may be mapped to another model (instance of another meta-model). In the ideal world, transformations are readily accessible to and modifiable by users (as models are), in the real world, transformations are still often hard-wired.

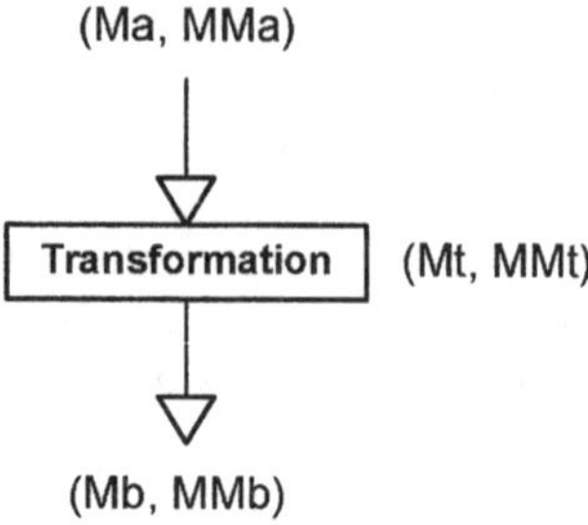

Fig. 2. Transformation of a model Ma (based on a meta-model MMa) into a model Mb (based on a meta-model MMb)

A meta-model is a model of models. In the MDA architecture, meta-models conform to the MOF and provide support for domain-specific languages and models. In our case, we have defined a meta-model for distributed and embedded components for low-cost microcontrollers.

It is likely that in the near future, the MDA approach will be applied to a wide range of domains and applications. Process-control engineering and embedded software will offer a good field of applicability for model-based software techniques [7], especially as modeling is already genuine to automatic-control engineering.

3 Constraints of Low-Cost Distributed and Embedded Applications for Process-Control

Among all the different kinds of embedded systems, we are most interested in distributed and embedded process-control applications, deployed and running on low-cost RISC microcontrollers (like PIC16F874, PIC18F458, or SAB-167C). These targets are very small standalone computer systems; they embed CPU, memory resources, digital and analog inputs/outputs, and a CAN controller for field-network access. They are typically designed to be tightly integrated into the systems that they contribute to control.

As an example, we summarize below the main technical characteristics of the SAB-167C chip:

- 16 bits CPU with 4 levels of pipeline, cycle of 100 ns at 20 MHz frequency clock
- 16 Mb address space (256 Kb external RAM available)
- 2 x 2 Kb RAM and 128 Kb ROM on chip
- 8 interrupt channels, 16 analog/digital converter channels (10 bits, 9.7μs)
- 4 PWM units, 10 timers, 2 serial ports, CAN interface (15 object messages)

It is important to note that such a chip is already a powerful one in its category; others do usually have more scarce resources, and writing software applications requires a good sense of optimization to fit into the capabilities and constraints of these chips.

Traditional developments for this kind of targets are based on low level primitive functions, and a software application is merely seen as a collection of tasks, whose synchronization is quite difficult to achieve. The situation is even worse in case of networks of heterogeneous low cost targets, as found in distributed process-control applications [4, 5].

Communication between microcontrollers is achieved via a field-network. We use the FullCAN protocol (a type of CAN), which provides message storage and enhanced filtering capabilities. CAN is dedicated to embedded process-control (mostly in the automotive industry), and provides reliable support for the exchange of small messages under real-time constraints, typically to retrieve the states of sensors, or to send commands to actuators.

The main characteristics of CAN field-networks are summarized below:

- hierarchical messages
- deterministic latency times
- error detection
- automatic retransmission of altered messages
- multi-master
- automatic defect nodes canceling

The typical topology for a distributed application built with these microcontrollers is given in the figure below. Microcontrollers execute in parallel, and communicate over the field-network. Tasks may exchange signals and synchronize, either inside a microcontroller, or over the network.

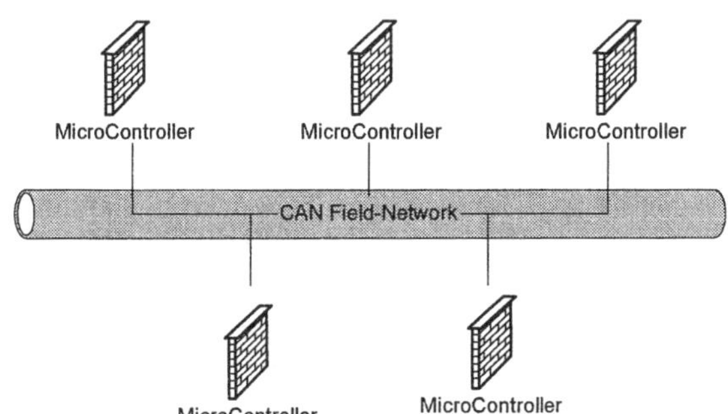

Fig. 3. Application topology, the microcontrollers are connected via the CAN field-network

Obviously, one way to simplify the developments would be to use the development tools and runtime executives for these kinds of processors. Unfortunately, earlier experience conducted targeting the SAB-166C chip, with the preemptive real-time kernel RTX166, showed us that the runtime introduced significant time overhead, and moreover that it was not possible to certify that a task would be allocated sufficient CPU resources to activate all its components within a cycle of 10 ms. As a consequence, we could not achieve the level of performances required to build the kind of process-control applications that we wanted to develop.

We then decided to bypass real-time kernels, and to write directly assembly code, using a reactive model of components, based on a perception-decision-action cycle as found in multi-agents approaches [8]. Components were no more scheduled by a preemptive monitor; instead they were using collaborative scheduling, within an activation main loop, leading to the expected maximal performance of giving CPU resource to all components within each 100 µs iteration.

This time, we were able to cope with our performance requirements, but introduced a lot more low-level details in the programs, which made them quite obscure to understand for beginners.

As one might expect, the students faced a lot of difficulties during their practical work with this kind of platforms and their software development constraints. The point was that the students almost got lost in the platform complexity, as they had to understand a lot of technical details related both to hardware and software, and this before they could even write a single line of code.

It became obvious that we had to raise the level of abstraction again.

As we could not do it in the assembly code, we decided to develop an intermediate pseudo-code (which could be considered as a PIM) and started to experiment with transformations between this pseudo-code and the macro-assembly language described earlier (a PSM in MDA jargon).

At this point in time we had the roots of a model-driven architecture. The next paragraph will describe how we have proceeded to build a model-driven production line for low-cost microcontrollers.

4 Model-Driven Framework

To promote high level reusability and help the students to master the complexity of distributed and embedded applications, we have developed a model-driven architecture platform for distributed process-control applications.

As shown is the picture below, this architecture is made of the following layers:

- The process-control application layer to be written by the students.
- The automatic control component framework, which contains about 130 highly reusable classes dedicated to process-control, available both as a PIM and as PSMs for the various microcontrollers that we target.
- The component execution subsystem, which contains the base classes required to implement collaborative scheduling.

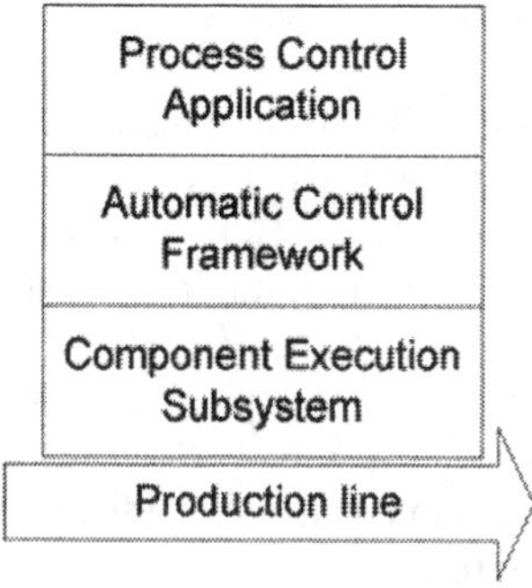

Fig. 4. Architecture for MDA distributed and embedded process-control

This approach, which is mixing object-technology with components, is particularly well adapted for distributed and embedded applications which do not necessarily follow a simple master-slave schema. A process-control application is represented as a set of distributed components, interconnected and communicating by broadcast of events. Basic components include real-time clocks, inputs and outputs, interfaces, behaviors, commands, but also messages, signals and network access. Higher level components include state-machines, multi-meters, frequency-meter, wave-front generators, modulators, coders-decoders, regulators…

The component framework, the component execution subsystem and the production line, are presented more in depth in the following sub-paragraphs.

4.1 Automatic-Control Component Framework

Almost all automatic-control applications can be built from a well defined set of basic components, supplemented by about 10 % application specific components. The goal of the component framework is to provide this set of highly reusable components, both under the form of a platform independent description (a PIM) and as specific implementations (PSM) for the various microcontrollers that we use. These PSM, depending on the kind of chip, will either be expressed in assembly or in C language.

From a PIM point of view, the components are organized into the following nine families drawn from the domain of automatic-control engineering [6].

Controllers	Programmable logic controllers, state machines, PID controllers, speed controllers, parallel communication controllers…
Actuators	On/Off switches, periodic switches, proportional control laws, DC motors, step-by-step motors, switched current sources…
Measurement	Analog probes, automatic multimeters, frequency-meters, pulse-meters…
Interface	Keyboard interfaces, code-bar readers, multiplexed displays, LCD displays, digital and analog trimmers, filtered push-buttons, latches…
Network	Field-networks, CAN controllers, event publishers and subscribers…
Synthesizer	Wave-front generators, pulse width modulators, real-time clocks, timers…
Operator	Transfer functions, Schmitt-triggers, edge detectors, filters, coder-decoders, multiplexer-demultiplexers, periodic and programmable counters, frequency dividers, discriminators, differentiators-integrators, adders, amplifiers…
Communication	Asynchronous serial controllers, RM611 and RC5 infrared controllers, V23 modems…
System	Development utilities, debuggers, PIC programmers and various sharewares…

4.2 Component Execution Meta-model

Our components are reactive entities, able to answer to external requests in real time, by producing states and data.

A component is designed to have the largest autonomy as possible; it self manages its execution and idle time, controls its synchronization with other components (via external signals, either synchronous our asynchronous) and masters its termination.
There is neither real-time operating system nor external task scheduler taking care of the components. Fair allocation of the CPU is based on the components good-will. A single activation loop invokes the `run` methods of all the components in a sequence. Each component is a generic template and can be instantiated as many times as needed, potentially having up to the complete CPU resources of a microcontroller. Of course, this scheme works only if all the components follow the same design style, and effectively do their best to minimize their activation time.
The following class diagram shows the mainloop constituents. The stereotypes `<<singleton>>` are used to show that there is only one instance of the mainloop running on a single microcontroller. The pseudo-code describes the content of the mainloop.

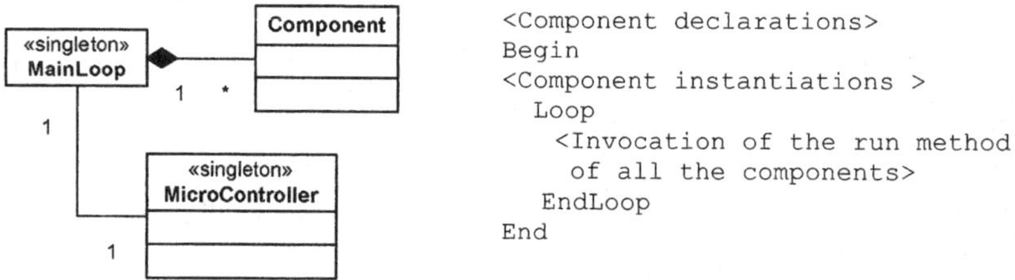

Fig. 5. The activation mainloop controls the CPU allocation to the various components

Bypassing a real-time kernel maximizes the CPU time available for the components and opens the way to a very vide range of control applications which can be developed on low-cost microcontrollers. Considering that typical component activation requires between 1 and 5 μs, our current technology is able to handle about up to 30 components by slice of 100 μs, and this for each station connected to the network. Each single component is therefore given a chance to execute and handle events at least every 100 μs.
The goal of the metamodel is to capture the few rules which have to be followed for this real-time execution model to be usable. These rules are summarized below, either in pseudo-code or as UML classes.
The meta-model of our components is made of the following modeling elements:

- Input and output ports, either for variables (whose values are maintained) or events (available during one activation cycle).
- A constructor used for initial setup of the component.
- Accessors for the output ports of the components.
- One `run` method, to define the behavior of the components and the input ports whose connections have to be setup in the main loop.

The following class diagram shows these modeling elements and their relations. The `source` class is abstract and can sub-classed by any of `variable`, `message` or `signal`. The pseudo-code describes the template for the `run` method of the components.

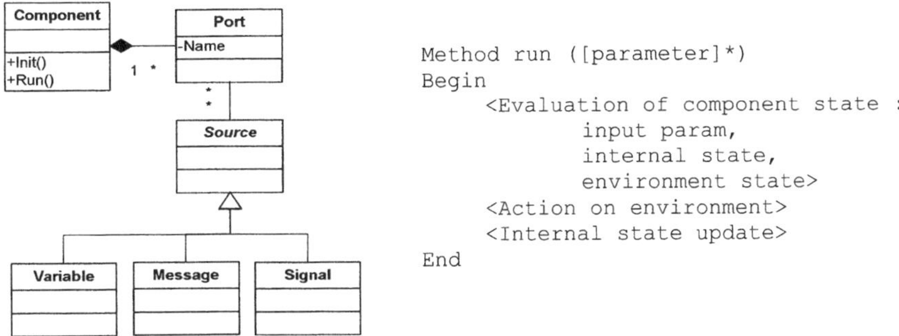

Fig. 6. Excerpt of the meta-model for components

4.3 Transformation-Based Production Line

We have implemented a production line which relies on model transformations, going from high-level UML diagrams down to assembly code. The line is organized as follows:

- A subset of UML is used to model the application independently of the final target (but using the component framework). We consider these models as PIMs, although we understand that some readers may believe that they are already PSMs. However, it must be stated that PIM and PSM are always defined relatively to a given platform [14]. There is no absolute PIM, or PSM.
- A first transformation takes the PIM and generates an intermediate textual specification language, under the shape of a PIM pseudo-code, that we use as isolation layer. This pseudo-code may be enriched manually, for instance to specify the code of the methods, in which case it acts as action language [12] as well (a language to express the behavior of the methods, independently of the final target-language). At this time we have no plan to implement backward engineering, to rebuilt UML models from modified pseudo-code.
- A second transformation merges the user models with the component models and generates PSM (under the form of either assembly or C language, depending on the final target). The reader may note that we consider here that programming languages are a kind of PSM.
- The PSM is fed into commercial compilers or assemblers and the final application is generated.

As said earlier, microcontrollers have limited resources, and therefore we have profiled UML to restrict the modeling elements which can be used.
Class diagrams can contain classes (with attributes and operations), binary associations and aggregations. They specify the components to be deployed on a given microcontroller.
Interaction diagrams describe the sequence of messages exchanged between the objects, only in the context of the mainloop.
The production line is showed in the following diagram.

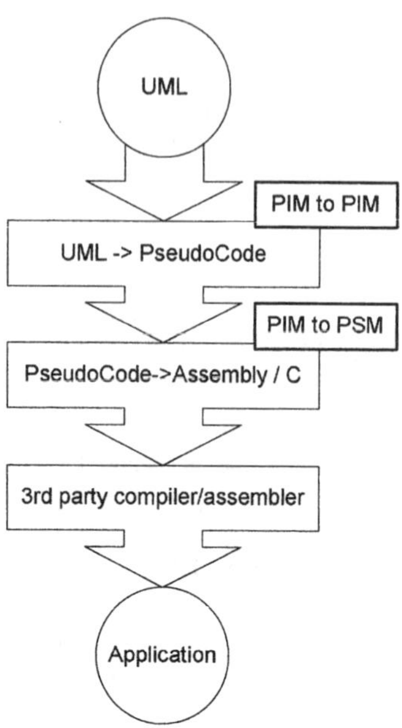

Fig. 7. Transformation-based production line

Our current implementation of these transformations is hard-wired in Java. While it is possible to customize the PSM generation, by changing the PSM of the component framework, it is not possible to change the transformation process itself. This is an area that we would like to explore in future work, as soon as QVT [13] compliant transformation engines will be available.

5 Example – A Lamp Controller

In this example, we are going to switch on/off a lamp. Obviously there is no need to use a microcontroller to commute a lamp, but we wanted to find a simple example.

The hardware is composed of one microcontroller board, one push-button and one lamp.

As shown below, the overall class diagram contains one domain class (the lamp) and two framework classes (a flip-flop latch and a push-button). A lamp is made of a flip-flop and has a connection to a push-button. Depending on the view-point, such representation could be considered either as a PIM or a PSM. In our prospective, this is a PIM as it involves abstractions from the automatic-control domain (FlipFlop and PushButton) but does not go into the details of the platform (target language, run-time environment) where these components will be deployed.

The push-button component provides a jitter-free image of the state of a physical push-button. The `is_on` method returns the state of the button. A state change is triggered as soon as the components detects that the button has been pressed during at least 10 ms.

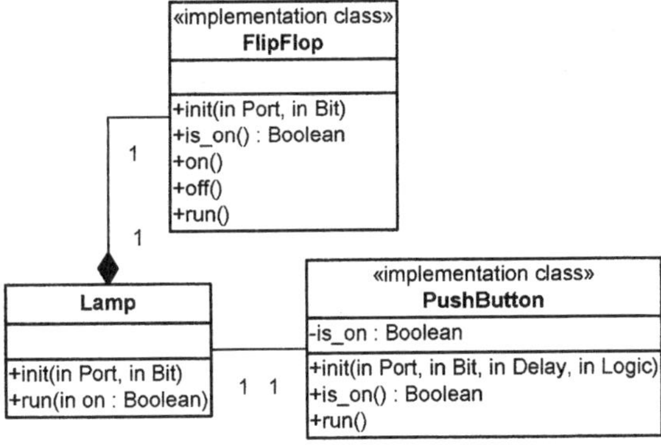

Fig. 8. Class diagram of the lamp controller

The behavior of the flip-flop latch can be described by the following state diagram.

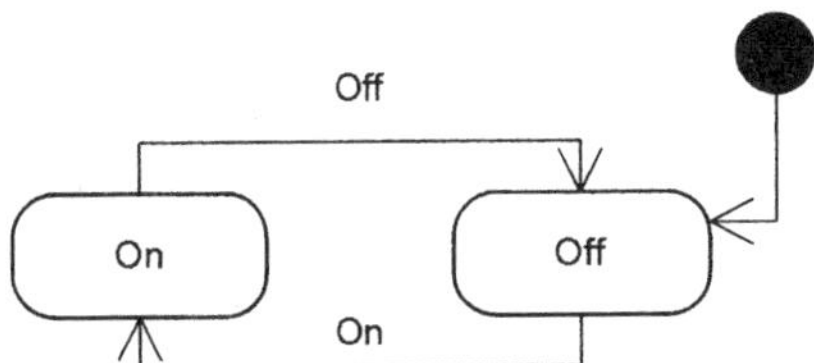

Fig. 9. Behavior of a flip-flop component

The flip-flop controls a digital output accordingly to its internal state, which is controlled by two different input signals: on and off. Having two separate input signals ensures that the flip-flop is latching the latest desired state.
The output of the flip-flop can then be used to switch on or off an electrical device such as a lamp, via a relay.
The stereotype `<<implementation class>>` instructs the production line that a PSM representation is available for merging during the PSM generation.
At transformation time, the PSM of the flip-flop is macro-expanded in the overall PSM which is generated for the activation mainloop.
As for all the framework components, the flip-flop PSM is available either in C language for the SAB-167C target, or in assembly language for the PIC16 family.
As an example, we give below the assembly source code for the flip-flop component.

```
c_flipflop.dcl  macro name
                var name.ev,1
name.var        equ name.ev
name.Q          equ 0
                endm

c_flipflop.init macro name
                bcf name.ev,name.Q
                // initial state Q = 0
                endm
```

```
c_flipflop.run  macro name, objSet,, evSet,
                     objReset,
                     evReset
                btfsc bjSet.ev,objSet.evSet
                bsf name.ev,name.Q //set Q
                btfsc objReset.ev,
                      objReset.evReset
                bcf name.ev,name.Q //resetQ
                endm
```

Obviously, it is much easier to work at the model level than to try to understand such kind of low-level rcpresentation.

5.1 Object Collaboration

An object-oriented application is made of collaborating objects [9]. The behavior of the lamp controller is achieved by a collaboration of objects, instances of the classes shown earlier.

We use a sequence diagram to specify the objects that participate to a given collaboration. From this diagram, we can derive the overall shape of the activation mainloop, which may then later be complemented by hand-written pseudo-code. This pseudo-code step is often required, because describing parameter passing in the UML diagrams is not always very convenient.

The following sequence diagram shows the objects involved in the lamp controller.

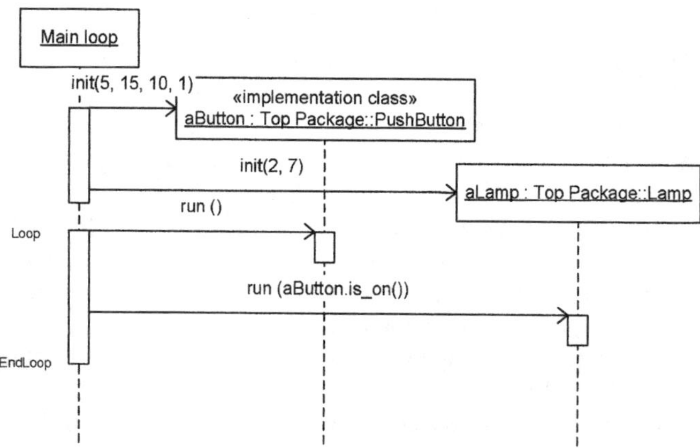

Fig. 10. Overall sequence diagram

The first activation contains the various object creations and initialization, the second activation corresponds to the mainloop.

From this diagram, an intermediate PIM representation is generated in pseudo-code, which can be enhanced manually. In the example given below, the pseudo-code can be considered as a textual representation of the previous interaction diagram.

```
aButton : PushButton
aLamp : Lamp
Begin
  aButton<=init (5,15,10,1)
  aLamp<=init (2,7)
  Loop
    aButton<=run
    aLamp<=run(aButton<=is_on)
  EndLoop
End
```

This pseudo code is then transformed into a platform dependent representation, either in C or in assembly language, depending on the kind of development environment available for the chosen target.
In this example, let's say that we target a SAB-167C and that we have a C compiler available. The transformation process would then lead to the PSM given below (remind that we consider the programming languages as some kind of executable PSM).
The transformation process adds the required headers, creates variables for the objects which belong to the interaction, then initializes the components, including default components for CPU initialization and for the real-time clock.
In the end, the activation mainloop contains the calls to the `run` methods of all the components, therefore giving a chance to every component to execute at least every 100 μs, which is the upper limit that we allow for a cycle (as we know exactly the processor instructions that get generated, we can easily compute the total cycle time).

```
#include "cpu.h"
#include "clock.h"
#include "lamp.h"
#include "button.h"

void main (void){
  struct c_button aButton;
  struct c_lamp aLamp;

  cpu_init();
  clock_init();
  c_button_init(&aButton,5,15,10,1);
  c_lamp_init(&aLamp,2,7);
  while (1) {
    cpu_run();
    clock_run();
    c_button_run(&aButton);
    c_lamp_run(&aLamp,
    c_button_is_on(&aButton));
  }
}
```

As can be seen from this example, building such a lamp controller at the model level, simplifies dramatically the development process. The software complexity of the platform is almost hidden to the users, who can focus on the application level, reusing the components from the automatic-control framework, while being assured to satisfy the real-time constraints.

At this time, we have had students' projects which implemented more than 30 different controllers, for various devices, including camera, webcam, HAM-radio, telescope, giant display, wash-machine, elevator, meteorological station, laser, traffic-light, mobile robot, heat regulator…

6 Lessons Learned

The lessons learned from our experience are manifold, and can be applied well beyond the context of teaching. We detail below one point related to teaching, and two more general points about the integration of model-driven development into an existing software development line.

Raising the Attractivity of Practical Work

Nowadays, it is difficult to find topics for practical work, because the level of achievement that students can reach in a 4 hour slot is low. This is especially true when programming is involved, as there is a tremendous gap between the kind of software that the students are used to (games, communication, internet…) and the kind of software they are able to write by themselves. This gap generates a lot of frustration, and tends to turn students away from programming.

Now, with our model-driven production line, they are able to tackle much more complex problems, and they can build significant process-control applications, within a few hours.

This is a major advantage, because it makes these practical work sessions attractive again for the students. We see that the students have more fun at learning, and that they get a much better feeling about developing software, because they can think in terms of *what they want to do*, instead of *how they have to do it.*

The software and hardware underlying complexity is hidden to the students. They are not required to master the details of microcontrollers, assembly or high-order languages, real time kernels and communication layers, and can focus on their main goal: process-control.

Faking Abstraction to Boost Performance

The model-driven approach is an interesting way of having both abstraction and performance at the same time. Contrary to runtime executives, which provide abstraction but at the cost of an expensive resource footprint at execution time, a model-driven approach associated to a set of transformations, makes it possible to fake abstraction. PIMs can be abstract (or provide the illusion of being so), while the generated PSMs can be made of calls to efficient low-level primitives. Layers of abstraction are for humans, but they can be bypassed for machines. The generated code may not be very readable, but the goal is not to read it anymore. The point here is really to achieve the same effect (abstraction) without paying the overhead at runtime. With our approach, the generated code is truly equivalent in terms of

performance to hand-written low-level code, and this is really important to convince practitioners of the viability of a model-driven approach.
An example of application of such an approach in another field would be the mapping of an object model onto a relational database, as was done in the Netsilon [15] project, where a multi-tier model is transformed into a flat implementation model.

Libraries Versus Metamodeling

In a broader perspective, we also found very interesting the ability to synchronize two different ways of handling extensibility. In our case, in the programming technological space [11], extensibility is achieved by incorporating libraries into generated code, whereas in the modeling technological space, extensibility is carried on via extension of the meta-model. In our experience, these two approaches complement themselves very well, and provide a nice support for the transition from PIMs to PSMs.
We see here an efficient way to incorporate existing libraries, or legacy code, in a model-driven approach, by combining the best of both world. This approach is purely pragmatic, because existing modeling tools support extensibility via stereotypes, and because existing reusable code is structured into libraries.

7 Conclusion

In this paper we have described a model-driven architecture framework for process-control, which is being used by students during their practical work.
The framework has proven to be especially suitable for the development of distributed process-control applications, such as quick data acquisition process, laboratory measurement, house automation, regulation and monitoring, and in any case where the number of sensor/actuators is large and/or when the resources are geographically distributed.
The major strength of this approach lies in the high ratio between level of achievement and required technical knowledge, ensured by the automatic transformation of platform independent models into realistic and efficient solutions, as soon as the platform independent specification activity is completed.
In the near future, we will investigate how to integrate our model-driven approach for micro-controllers, with the ACCORD UML [5] methodology.

References

[1] Object Management Group: MDA Guide (Draft Version 0.2). OMG document ab/03-01-03 (January 2003)
[2] J. Bézivin: From Object Composition to Model Transformation with the MDA. TOOLS'USA, Volume IEEE TOOLS-39, Santa Barbara (August 2001)
[3] J. Bézivin, N. Farcet, J.-M. Jézéquel, B. Langlois, and D. Pollet: Reflective Model Driven Engineering. Accepted for <<UML>>'03, SanFrancisco (October 2003)

[4] J.-M. Jézéquel, A. Le Guennec and F. Pennaneac'h: Validating Distributed Software Modeled with the Unified Modeling Language. <<UML>>'98, Mulhouse (June 1998)
[5] S. Gérard, N. S. Voros, C. Koulamas, and F. Terrier: Efficient System Modeling of Complex Real-Time Industrial Networks Using the ACCORD UML Methodology. DIPES'2000,Paderborn, Germany (2000)
[6] R. Dorf: Modern Control Systems. 6th edition, Series in Electrical and Computer Engineering, Addison Wesley (1992)
[7] G. Karsai, J. Sztipanovits, A. Ledeczi, and T. Bapty: Model-Integrated Development of Embedded Software. Proceedings of the IEEE, Vol. 91, Number 1 (January 2003) 145-164
[8] J. Ferber: Multi-Agent Systems. Addison-Wesley, Harlow, England (1999)
[9] G. Booch: Object-Oriented Analysis and Design. 2nd edition, Benjamin/Cummings, Redwood City, California (1994) 165
[10] OMG/MOF: Meta Object Facility (MOF). v1.4. OMG Document formal/02-04-03 (April 2002). Available from www.omg.org
[11] Y. Kurtev, J. Bézivin and M. Aksit : Technological Spaces: An Initial Appraisal. CoopIS, DOA'2002 Federated Conferences, Industrial track, Irvine (2002)
[12] S. Mellor, S. Tockey, R. Arthaud, P. Leblanc: An Action Language for UML: Proposal for a Precise Execution Semantics. UML 98, LNCS1618 (1998) 307-318
[13] OMG/RFP/QVT: Query/Views/Transformations RFP. OMG document ad/2002-04-10. Available from www.omg.org
[14] OMG/MDA Guide: MDA Guide. OMG Document omg/03-05-01 (May 2003). Available from www.omg.org
[15] P.-A. Muller, P. Studer, and J. Bezivin: Platform Independent Web Application Modeling. In P. Stevens et al. (Eds): UML 2003, LNCS 2863 (2003) 220-233

Model-Driven Development for Non-functional Properties: Refinement Through Model Transformation

Simone Röttger and Steffen Zschaler

Dresden University of Technology
Dresden, Germany
{Simone.Roettger, Steffen.Zschaler}@inf.tu-dresden.de

Abstract. Model driven architecture (MDA) views application development as a continuous transformation of models of the target system. We propose a methodology which extends this view to non-functional properties. Our basic idea is the separation of two different roles in the development process: the role of the measurement designer and the role of the application designer. The former provides a library of measurement definitions which is later used by the latter to annotate functional application models with non-functional property specifications. In this paper we define the notion of context models to allow the measurement designer to provide measurement definitions at different levels of abstraction independently of concrete applications.
Requiring the measurement designer to define transformations between context models and applying them to measurement definitions, enables us to provide tool support for refinement of non-functional constraints to the application designer. The concepts presented in this paper form the basis of a tool which we are currently developing.

1 Introduction

Non-functional properties of a system—for example, Quality of Service (QoS) or security aspects—need to be considered as early as possible in the development cycle to analyse the non-functional behaviour of the system. This is especially true for component-based systems because all context dependencies need to be made explicit. In the context of the COMQUAD project[1] we develop a methodology supporting the modelling of component-based systems with particular emphasis on non-functional aspects. In this paper we present the models required by the methodology. Although they are directly applicable to Quality of Service properties only (such as response time, delay, memory usage), we believe that they can be extended to cover other non-functional properties—such as security—as well. For the purpose of this paper we will consider the terms non-functional and QoS to be synonyms.

The core concept of QoS specifications is the measurement—or characteristic [8]. A measurement is a mapping from states, objects, or events of a physical system (e.g., an

[1] COMponents with QUantitative properties and ADaptivity at Dresden University of Technology and Friedrich-Alexander-University Erlangen-Nuremberg, Germany; supported by German Research Council; see www.comquad.org

T. Baar et al. (Eds.): UML 2004, LNCS 3273, pp. 275–289, 2004.

implemented and running application) to a formal system (e.g., the set of real numbers). Examples for measurements are: response time (a mapping from an operation call in a running system to a real number representing the time taken from invocation to return), or confidentiality (a mapping from a channel used to transfer information to a value indicating the level of confidentiality achieved by this channel). By using models of the relevant aspects of target applications—we call these *context models*—in the definition of measurements, these definitions can be made independent of specific applications. They will then be applicable to any system model that can be viewed as an instance of the context model used in the definition of the measurement. Non-functional specifications essentially constrain measurements applied to a functional model of a system. They are therefore application specific. From this duality it follows naturally to define two roles in the development process: The *measurement designer* and the *application designer*. The former creates a library of measurements, which are later used by the latter to annotate application models with non-functional specifications. This allows reuse of measurement specifications defined once.

The basic idea of existing development processes—especially MDA-based [12] approaches—is the refinement of system models from an abstract view of the system to a model close to the real implementation. The application designer creates, and thinks about, functional models at different levels of abstraction. He should be able to do so for non-functional models, too. We propose to use different context models to represent different *levels of abstraction* for a measurement. Requiring the measurement designer to define transformations between the different context models and applying them to measurement definitions forms the conceptual basis for providing tool support for the application designer's refinement of non-functional specifications. The application designer can then perform these refinements as prompted by refinements in the functional model of the system. We distinguish two kinds of non-functional refinement: *structural refinement* and *measurement refinement*, which will be explained later in Sect. 3.

This paper is an extended and refined version of [18]. It focuses on modelling issues related to measurement refinement. In Sect. 2 we give a short introduction to our overall development process, which forms the context of this work. The following sections describe measurement refinement and the related models in more detail: from the application designer's view (Sect. 3), from the measurement designer's view (Sect. 4), and from a more technical, tool-oriented perspective (Sect. 5). We use a simple example application with response time constraints throughout the paper to illustrate our approach. Finally, the conclusion points out the most important arguments of our work as well as issues for further research.

2 A Process for Component-Based Systems with Non-functional Properties

Fig. 1 gives an overview of our overall software development process for non-functional properties. After the requirements analysis the application designer begins to model the system. This includes modelling of non-functional properties by specifying non-functional constraints and attaching them to components and connectors. The application designer switches between modelling—and refining—non-functional properties

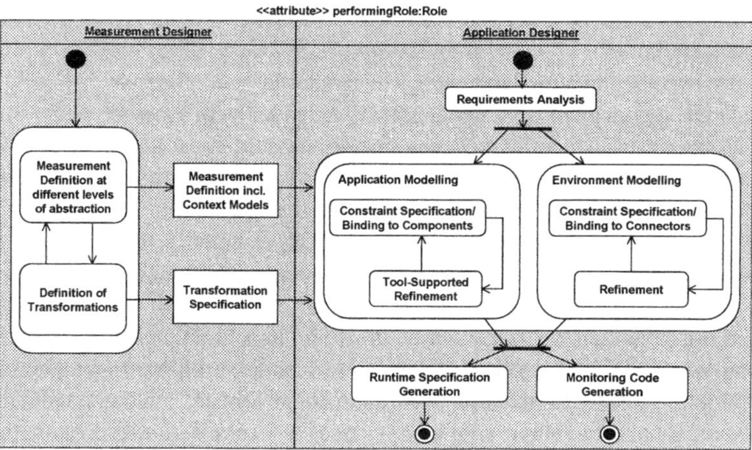

Fig. 1. Development process for non-functional properties overview

of the components (called "Application Modelling" in the figure) and of the components' environment (called "Environment Modelling" in the figure), using the concept of connectors for the latter part.

Our approach separates measurement definition from measurement usage; that is, specification of non-functional properties of applications using these measurements. Measurement definitions can be very complex, but on the other hand will be developed only once. Therefore, we separate the roles of measurement designer and application designer in our process. Their combined efforts lead to a specification of the system including its non-functional properties.

Our process comprises the following steps:

1. Definition of measurements at different levels of abstraction and provision of transformation rules for context models by the measurement designer (see Sect. 4). The measurement designer can do so independently of application development and even at a far earlier time.
2. Use of measurements during the specification process by the application designer. The application designer constrains measurements and binds these constraints to elements of the functional model.
3. Tool-supported refinement of measurements. The application designer chooses one out of different kinds of provided refined measurements. These have been previously provided by the measurement designer together with an informal description of each measurement.
4. Modelling and refinement of connectors between components during the assembly process. The application designer uses connectors to model the influence of the container on non-functional properties of the application.

The resulting non-functional specification is used for a variety of purposes. Besides generating code for runtime monitoring of QoS parameters, its main use is in providing a base for QoS contract negotiation and resource reservation in the running system—the component container.

We use two specification languages: For functional modelling we primarily use the component model element from UML 2.0 [16] extended with a stereotype for interfaces which allows us to distinguish between operational and streaming interfaces. For the non-functional specification we use CQML$^+$ [17] an extension to CQML [1]. Finally, we use a more compact XML-based representation in the runtime environment.

CQML$^+$ builds on quality characteristics, which essentially are definitions of measurements. Quality statements are used to specify constraints on characteristics. Both quality characteristics and quality statements are parametrised and can therefore be reused in different contexts. To actually attach the non-functional specification to the functional one, CQML$^+$ provides the construct of quality profiles. In such a profile current parameter values—for example, operations or streams of the component to which the non-functional constraint is applied—replace the formal parameters of quality statements. Quality statements can be associated to a component as offers (`provides`), requirements (`uses`), or resource demands (`resources`).

CQML$^+$ is a textual language comprising both measurement definition and measurement usage. For graphical modelling of measurement definitions we plan to use ideas proposed in [7]. For measurement usage we have defined a graphical notation allowing to attach constraints to parts of the functional model. The internal tool representation uses CQML$^+$, merging measurement definition and constraints into one specification.

For a more in-depth explanation, we describe the individual models as seen from the application designer's view as well as from the measurement designer's view in the following sections.

3 The Application Designer's View

The application designer obtains a target specification from the requirements analysis. Using this artefact, he starts to model an adequate system which fulfils the customer's requirements. He creates a functional model of the system, tagging non-functional aspects to it using a system modelling tool supporting graphical modelling. As he progresses in the development, the functional model gets more and more detailed. Correspondingly, the non-functional specification needs to be refined, too. We distinguish two kinds of non-functional refinement:

1. *Structural Refinement*: The application designer adds new model elements, as the functional model gets more refined. In this process, he may have to reassign non-functional property specifications that had been tagged to some model element to some newly added model element—or he may even have to distribute them to several new elements. For example, at a very early stage the application designer of a video server application may have modelled the complete application as one monolithic component, also tagging any non-functional specifications—for example, response time constraints—to this component. Later, he refines the component by decomposing its functionality into several subcomponents. In this step, he will also

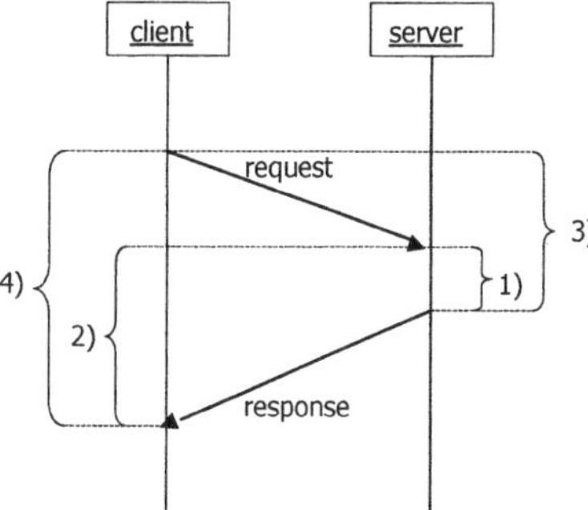

Fig. 2. A sequence diagram excerpt showing different kinds of response time specification

need to refine the non-functional properties tagged to the monolithic component by determining which of the subcomponents have to provide each non-functional property.

2. *Measurement Refinement*: With this type of refinement the application designer uses a more precise interpretation of the meaning of a certain characteristic. For example, he may wish to start out thinking about response time simply as the time between start and end of an operation call. Later he may wish to make more precise statements about response time. Fig. 2 shows his options: the time between 1) the reception of a request and the sending of the corresponding response, or 2) the reception of a request and the reception of the corresponding response, or 3) the sending of a request and the sending of the corresponding response, or 4) the sending of a request and the reception of the corresponding response.

This paper focuses on measurement refinement. Structural refinement remains an open issue. As a simple example imagine a login mechanism of a `VideoServer` component using another component `UserManager` that manages user data. At an early stage of development the application designer decides that the video server component provides an interface `ILogin` and uses an interface `IUserMgt`. The `UserManager` provides this interface `IUserMgt`. For operations of these interfaces he can specify different response times depending on the internal execution times of the components. This corresponds to Step 2 in Sect. 2. We are working to extend an existing CASE tool to provide support for our graphical notation for non-functional properties.

However, so far he has not thought about response time in detail, but only as the time between start and end of an operation call. Here, our mapping support is applied. If he wants to refine the response time of the operation `IUserMgt::checkPassWd` used by the `VideoServer`, the application designer asks the CASE tool to refine this non-functional aspect. The tool provides four different kinds of refined response times using a library where the information about the mapping is stored. Depending on what the application designer wants to model, he will choose one of the refined response times and the tool will update the internal model representation and tag the treated

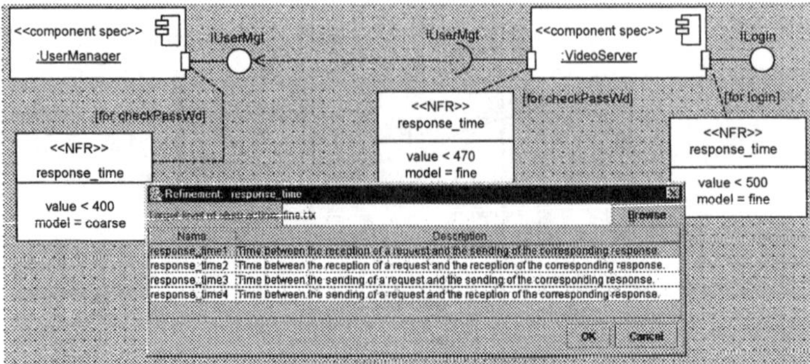

Fig. 3. Sample screen shot

characteristic as refined. This is Step 3 from Sect. 2. Figure 3 shows what the screen could look like after these two steps. It shows the two components `VideoServer` and `UserManager`, their used and provided interfaces, and the attached non-functional constraints. Some of these have already been refined—this can be seen from the line '`model = fine`'. The application designer has just opened the refinement dialogue for the last non-functional constraint to be refined and selected one of the possible refinements. Note that the application designer is completely shielded from the formal intricacies underlying the different response time definitions.

Once non-functional specifications have been created and connected with a functional specification, it becomes important to have analysis tools allowing for determination of various properties of the system. One property for which analysis is very important and helpful is to determine whether a component satisfies the non-functional demands of another component. For this it is necessary to compare the `used` properties of the "client" component with the `provided` properties of the "server" component.

In the example such an analysis becomes necessary between the `VideoServer` and the `UserManager`. The `VideoServer` requires the response time for `checkPassWd` to be less than 470ms, while the `UserManager` provides a response time for `checkPassWd` of less than 400ms. Analysis can conclude that the offered response time constraint is stronger than the required constraint. Thus, the two components can safely be plugged together.

After a refinement of the response time, the situation may well be different. For example, the application designer may have chosen variation 4 (cf. Fig. 2) for refining response time in `VideoServer` and variation 1 for `UserManager`. This corresponds to the principle of locality in component-based software engineering: no component specification makes constraining statements about anything beyond its own boundaries.

Trying to analyse whether or not these two components can work together yields no result as the two variations cannot directly be compared. This is not a shortcoming of the analysis, however, but a lack of the model. The application designer needs to add information about the delay of the communication channel between the two components. In other words, the refinement of the non-functional constraint prompts a refinement in the functional model: the designer needs to consider aspects of the communication between the components.

Communication between components is modelled using connectors in Architecture Description Languages (ADLs) [14]. This concept can be extended to provide non-functional properties of communication (cf., e.g., [5, 9, 20]). In our example, we might model the container-induced delay for communication to be 50ms. Given this additional information, the analysis tool should then be able to conclude, that the two components can safely be used together. This concludes Step 4 as described in Sect. 2.

In order to allow the application developer to concentrate on the business logic of his application, it seems reasonable to provide him with a library of connectors for different aspects of the container and of distribution. He would simply select an appropriate connector—or build a chain of connectors to combine non-functional effects of different connectors like distribution and encryption—from this library and plug it into his model.

4 The Measurement Designer's View

In the previous section we have had a look at the application designer's view. Now, let's have a look behind the scenes. This is where the measurement designer has done his work to make handling of non-functional properties easy for the application designer. He has specified individual measurements using CQML$^+$, defined context models for each measurement specification and level of abstraction, and performed transformations to provide measurement specifications at different levels of abstraction. This corresponds to Step 1 in Sect. 2.

Each CQML$^+$ specification—and in particular each definition of a quality characteristic—is written relative to what in [1] is called a computational model. We prefer the term *context model*, as it is really a model of the context of the characteristic definition—that is, it comprises the elements necessary for specifying the semantics of the characteristic. For each context model and each component model to be used, there needs to exist a mapping relating the concepts of the component model to concepts in the context model. For each concept of the component model (e.g., the concept of component itself) we need to identify the concept in the context model which represents it.

As we have shown in Sect. 3, at different stages in the development cycle it is helpful to use characteristics defined at different levels of abstraction. In order for this to be possible, we need to define context models at all these levels of abstraction. In effect, each context model represents the specification of a specific level of abstraction. This is different from what was proposed in [1], where one computational model was used for every CQML specification, independent of level of abstraction. Instead, we use multiple context models to represent different levels of abstraction.

Figures 4 and 5 show two examples of context models. Figure 4 shows a rather coarse—or more abstract—context model. All that one can talk about are components, interfaces, and operations on the static side and component instances and operation calls

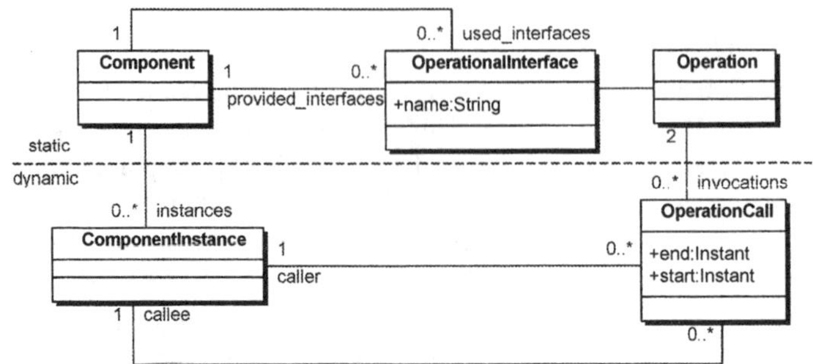

Fig. 4. Abstract context model

```
quality_characteristic response_time (op: Operation) {
  domain: numeric real [0..) milliseconds;

  values: op.invocations->last().end - op.invocations->last().start;
}
```

Listing 1.1. Abstract response time definition

between instances on the dynamic side.[2] For each operation it is possible to access the history of invocations of this operation. Each operation call connects two operations, one in the used interface of the calling component instance (`caller`) and one in the provided interface of the called component instance (`callee`).

Simple as it is, this context model already allows us to define the response time of an operation. Listing 1.1 shows the corresponding CQML$^+$ definition. The `domain` clause defines response times to be real values given in milliseconds. The `values` clause defines how response time values can be measured. It relates to the context model, using the start and end time of an operation call, which are stored in the attributes `start` and `end`, respectively.

The context model in Fig. 5 is much more detailed. It represents a much lower level of abstraction. In particular, it contains event sequences `SE` and `SR` for each operation. For each operation in a used interface, `SE` (short for "service emission") contains events fired whenever a request for an operation call was issued by the calling component; `SR` (short for "service reception") contains one event per result that was received by the calling component. On the other hand, for each operation in a provided interface, `SR` contains one event per request received, and `SE` one event per result sent out from the

[2] Although only structure is shown in the figure, each context model also has a behavioural aspect captured in a transition system. These specifications have been left out for lack of space. The term 'dynamic' in the diagrams refers to classes instances of which are created in the course of executing the transition system, while 'static' refers to those classes whose instances remain fixed over a complete run.

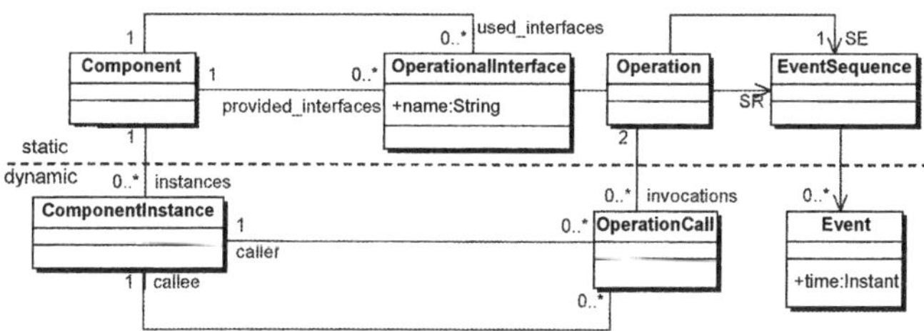

Fig. 5. More specialized context model

called component. This context model is already very close to Aagedal's [1] computational model.

To perform the interactive refinement described in Sect. 3, we have to specify the transformation between these two models. We need to say for each model element in the coarser model which model element(s) it should be mapped to in the finer model. This can be specified using a transformation language (as defined for MDA, e.g., in [12]) based on XML [3]. The transformation language and algorithm will be explained in more detail in Sect. 5.

After designing the finer context model and the transformations, the measurement designer who specified the response time characteristic in Listing 1.1 uses a transformation tool to apply the transformations to his specification of response time, and to generate refined versions of response time for the more detailed context model. Currently we are working on the implementation of such a tool using the concepts presented in this paper.

Listing 1.2 shows two of the four resulting versions of response time[3]. Note that the numbers appended to the characteristics' names correspond to the numbers from Fig. 2. The relationship between the more abstract response time definition and the newly created refined versions is stored as another transformation in the transformation specification. It remains the task of the measurement designer to give a clear textual explanation of the differences between the various types of response time, so that they can be used easily by an application designer. Of course, the measurement designer can also define additional measurements which could not be defined at the higher level of abstraction. Furthermore, application designers may require additional refinement patterns which they could communicate back to the measurement designer who would then provide the appropriate context models and transformation specifications.

5 The Transformation Language

In the previous section we explained that the measurement designer specifies context models and transformations between them, and uses these transformations to generate

[3] The remaining two versions have been left out for lack of space.

```
— Time between receipt of request and sending of response
quality_characteristic response_time1 (op: Operation) {
  domain: numeric real [0..) milliseconds;

  values: — The following has been substituted for
          — op.invocations->last().end
          (let op1 : Operation
                  = op.invocations->last()
                        .operation
                        ->select (operationalInterface
                                    .component
                                    .provided_interfaces
                                    ->contains (operationalInterface)
                        )
           in
             op1.SE->last().time()) -
          — The following has been substituted for
          — op.invocations->last().start
          (let op1 : Operation
                  = op.invocations->last()
                        .operation
                        ->select (operationalInterface
                                   .component
                                   .provided_interfaces
                                   ->contains (operationalInterface)
                        )
           in
             op1.SR->last().time());
}

...

— Time between sending of request and receipt of response
quality_characteristic response_time4 (op: Operation) {
  domain: numeric real [0..) milliseconds;

  values: — The following has been substituted for
          — op.invocations->last().end
          (let op1 : Operation
                  = op.invocations->last()
                        .operation
                        ->select (operationalInterface
                                   .component
                                   .used_interfaces
                                   ->contains (operationalInterface)
                        )
           in
             op1.SR->last().time()) -
          — The following has been substituted for
          — op.invocations->last().start
          (let op1 : Operation
                  = op.invocations->last()
                        .operation
                        ->select (operationalInterface
                                    .component
                                    .used_interfaces
                                    ->contains (operationalInterface)
                        )
           in
             op1.SE->last().time());
}
```

Listing 1.2. Refined versions of response time definition characteristic specifications at lower levels of abstraction from specifications at higher levels of abstraction. In this section we will look at the language used to describe the transformations as well as at the actual algorithm used by the transformation tool.

We have defined an XML-based language for the specification of transformations between context models. It expresses mappings between elements of a more abstract and a more detailed context model. An excerpt from the transformation descriptor for our two sample context models can be seen in Listing 1.3. Note that some of the text in the transformation specification is CQML$^+$ code. These pieces are code templates which are to be substituted for pieces of expressions in the more abstract model. We have omitted most of the trivial mappings, giving only the mapping for `Component` as an example. It can be seen that we distinguish two kinds of transformations:

1. *Classifier transformations* (cf. Line 2 in Listing 1.3) which are essentially type replacements.
2. *Feature transformations* which replace features from the coarse model with expressions in the finer model. The measurement designer specifies expressions giving the value of features from the coarser context model in terms of the elements of the finer context model. This is used for features which are no longer present in the finer model. For example the transformation definition on Line 8 defines expressions that can be used to determine the value denoted by the `start` attribute of the `OperationCall` classifier in the coarse model. The fact that there are two target expressions indicates that this aspect of the model has been enriched with information in the refinement.

We are aware that there may be other transformation types, but so far all examples we have looked up could be successfully handled with these two types. When transforming the specification of a characteristic, the transformation tool applies the transformations described by each `transform`-tag to each usage of the element/feature specified by the `element` attribute in the specification of the characteristic. Because there is some indeterminism in the mappings, the transformation will result in more than one version of response time. In one generated version the choice of target expression must be consistent for every `transform`-tag. Multiple occurrences of a feature in the original expression must be replaced by the same expression in the refined version.

There is some difference in the way classifier and feature transformations are handled. While classifier transformations are simple replacements of types by another type, feature transformations require some more work: Here the transformation rule defines a template expression that is to be substituted for the expression referencing the feature. Each expression referencing some feature has the general form `owner.feature`, where `owner` can be any expression and `feature` is the name of a feature. During the transformation, the owner part of this expression is inserted into the target expression at the places indicated by the identifier declared to be the `ownerRef` (see Line 8 of Listing 1.3) before the whole expression is substituted. Another issue to be taken into consideration is uniqueness of names. Names defined in the target expression template may clash with names defined or visible in the expression that is being transformed. To avoid such clashes, all names defined in `let`-statements in the target expression template are appended the smallest positive number that makes them unique.

```
<refinement_xform from="coarse.xmi" to="fine.xmi">
  <transform classifier="Component">
    <target classifier="Component"/>
  </transform>

  ...

  <transform feature="OperationCall::start" ownerRef="owner">
    <target_expression>
      let op : Operation
             = owner.operation->select (operationalInterface
                   .component
                   .provided_interfaces
                   ->contains (operationalInterface)
               )
      in
        op.SR->last().time()
    </target_expression>
    <target_expression>
      let op : Operation
             = owner.operation->select (operationalInterface
                   .component
                   .used_interfaces
                   ->contains (operationalInterface)
               )
      in
        op.SE->last().time()
    </target_expression>
  </transform>

  <transform feature="OperationCall::end" ownerRef="owner">
    <target_expression>
      let op : Operation
             = owner.operation->select (operationalInterface
                   .component
                   .provided_interfaces
                   ->contains (operationalInterface)
               )
      in
        op.SE->last().time()
    </target_expression>
    <target_expression>
      let op : Operation
             = owner.operation->select (operationalInterface
                   .component
                   .used_interfaces
                   ->contains (operationalInterface)
               )
      in
        op.SR->last().time()
    </target_expression>
  </transform>
</refinement_xform>
```

Listing 1.3. Sample transformation descriptor. The XML code has been slightly simplified to enhance readability

The response time specifications in Listing 1.2 have been generated from the definition in Listing 1.1 using the algorithm and the sample transformation descriptor above. The numbers correspond to Fig. 2. Note how the `start` and `end` expressions have been replaced by the corresponding target expressions. All combinations of target expressions have been used in generation. However, to save space, only the two most important versions have been included in this paper.

6 Related Work

VEST [22] is a design toolkit for component-based systems which focuses on non-functional properties. It uses an extended notion of aspects [11] to allow *en-bloc* modifications to the non-functional specifications of individual components, thus effecting changes to the global non-functional specification of a system. Our work does not use aspects, although they could probably be combined with our approach. The major difference between our approach and the VEST approach is that we use context models at different levels of abstraction, while all work in VEST is tied directly to the component model provided by the target environment (Boeing's Bold Stroke in this case).

Model-Driven-Architecture (MDA) [12] is an important current development. Transformation between models is at the heart of this technology. Our work fits well into this larger view, although to the best of our knowledge we are the first to apply model transformations to measurement refinement. The new Query/Views/Transformations specification for which the Object Management Group (OMG) has issued a request for proposals [15] will be of great importance for our work. We can use the concept of views to relate context models and application models, and we can use the transformation technologies defined to implement our transformation tool. [21] describes an MDA technology for the creation of QoS-aware applications. The main focus is on the transformation of application models and weaving in of non-functional aspects. Refinement of non-functional specifications is not considered. CoSMIC [6] is an MDA tool suite for supporting model driven middleware. The tool supports only application development, deployment and configuration, but no refinement of non-functional models.

QCCS [19] describes a methodology for the development of contract-aware components. This methodology covers only the application design. Our refinement step can be used both in requirements analysis and application design. It is embedded in a process which reckons with non-functional properties from requirements to code [2]. QCCS also provides UML model transformation based on aspect-oriented design [10]. The authors of [19] propose to weave non-functional constraints and functional aspects at application modelling time. In contrast, our methodology keeps non-functional and functional aspects separate until implementation time.

7 Conclusions and Open Questions

Non-functional properties must be considered throughout the development cycle of an application system. The application designer creates, and thinks about, functional models at different levels of abstraction. He should be able to do so with non-functional models, too. We have introduced the concept of explicitly defined context models of measurements which explicitly capture the level of abstraction of a measurement. Additionally, we enable tool support for refinement of non-functional specifications by requiring transformations between context models to be defined and applying them to measurement definitions.

Furthermore, we have outlined a software development process which separates the roles of measurement designer and application designer. It is the measurement designer's responsibility to specify measurements, context models and transformations between context models, all of which can then be used by the application designer when developing an application. Thus, the application designer is free to focus on the business logic.

The refinement process prompts for decisions when they are needed. We have indicated two points where this happens: a) in the actual refinement step, where the application designer needs to choose between different refinements of a measurement, and b) after a refinement has taken place, when the analysis tool cannot compare constraints on different refinements. In the latter case, the application designer will also need to refine the functional model by making explicit the effect caused by communication between components. We have shown how connectors can be used to model this. Defining these connectors, building libraries, and integrating the connectors into application models is still a research issue, although some approaches can be found in the literature. One important question, among others, is whether the usage of connectors we have sketched for response time also works for characteristics which are not time-related. On a more general note, we would like to propose the interaction of refinements to the functional and the non-functional model as an interesting research area.

It is important to point out, that, although we have explained our approach with two context models only, it is intended to be generic. For any one measurement there could be any number of context models and, correspondingly, any number of different levels of abstraction. How this large number of models can be managed in a way that further reduces the complexity for the application designer and makes choosing the next model for refinement easy, is an area for further research.

This paper has focused on measurement refinement. Structural refinement is also an important research topic. We plan to investigate this in our future work.

We are currently working on a tool set prototype to support our development process. This prototype implements the concepts presented in this paper. Context models are stored in a meta data repository [13], and we use model transformation techniques to describe the mapping between context model and application model.

Acknowledgements

We want to thank everybody in the COMQUAD project, Dr. Thomas Santen and the anonymous reviewers for their helpful comments on different versions of this paper.

References

[1] J. Ø. Aagedal. *Quality of Service Support in Development of Distributed Systems.* PhD thesis, University of Oslo, 2001.

[2] R. Aigner, M. Pohlack, S. Röttger, and S. Zschaler. Towards pervasive treatment of non-functional properties at design and run-time. In *16th Int'l Conf. on Software and Systems Engineering and their Applications (ICSSEA'03)*, Paris, France, 2–4 December 2003. CNAM-CMSL.

[3] T. Bray, J. Paoli, C. M. Sperberg-McQueen, and E. Maler. Extensible markup language (XML) 1.0 (second edition), October 2000. W3C Recommendation.

[4] J.-M. Bruel, editor. *Proc. 1st Int'l Workshop on Quality of Service in Component-Based Software Engineering, Toulouse, France.* Cépaduès-Éditions, June 2003.

[5] E. Demairy, E. Anceaume, and V. Issarny. On the correctness of multimedia applications. In *11th EuroMicro Conf. on Real Time Systems*. IEEE, June 1999.

[6] A. Gokhale, B. Natarajan, D. C. Schmidt, A. Nechypurenko, J. Gray, N. Wang, S. Neema, T. Bapty, and J. Parsons. Cosmic: An MDA generative tool for distributed real-time and embedded component middleware and applications. In *Proc. ACM OOPSLA 2002 Workshop on Generative Techniques in the Context of MDA*, Seattle, WA, November 2002.

[7] I-Logix Inc., Open-IT, and THALES. UML profile for modeling quality of service and fault tolerance characteristics and mechanisms: Revised submission. OMG Document, May 2003. URL http://www.omg.org/docs/realtime/03-05-02.pdf.

[8] Information technology – Quality of Service: Framework. ISO/IEC 13236:1998, ITU-T X.641, 1998.

[9] V. Issarny and C. Bidan. Aster: A framework for sound customization of distributed runtime systems. In *Int'l Conf. on Distributed Computing Systems*, pages 586–593. IEEE Computer Society, 1996.

[10] J.-M. Jézéquel, N. Plouzeau, T. Weis, and K. Geihs. From contracts to aspects in UML designs. In *AOSD Workshop on Aspect-Oriented Modeling with UML*, Enschede, The Netherlands, April 2002.

[11] G. Kiczales, J. Lamping, A. Mendhekar, C. Maeda, C. V. Lopes, J.-M. Loingtier, and J. Irwin. Aspect-oriented programming. In M. Akşit and S. Matsuoka, editors, *11th European Conf. on Object-Oriented Programming*, volume 1241 of *LNCS*, pages 220–242. Springer, 1997.

[12] A. Kleppe, J. Warmer, and W. Bast. *MDA Explained: The Model Driven Architecture: Practice and Promise*. Addison Wesley Professional, April 2003.

[13] M. Matula. Netbeans metadata repository, March 2003. http://mdr.netbeans.org/MDR-whitepaper.pdf.

[14] N. Medvidovic and R. N. Taylor. A framework for classifying and comparing architecture description languages. In *Proc. 6th European Software Engineering Conf. together with 5th ACM SIGSOFT Symposium on the Foundations of Software Engineering (ESEC-FSE97)*, pages 60–76, Zurich, Switzerland, September 1997.

[15] Object Management Group. MOF 2.0 query, views, transformations request for proposals. OMG Document, April 2002. URL http://www.omg.org/docs/ad/02-04-10.pdf.

[16] Object Management Group. Unified modeling language: Superstructure version 2.0. OMG Document, July 2003. URL http://www.omg.org/cgi-bin/doc?ptc/03-07-06.pdf.

[17] S. Röttger and S. Zschaler. CQML$^+$: Enhancements to CQML. In Bruel [4], pages 43–56.

[18] S. Röttger and S. Zschaler. A software development process supporting non-functional properties. In *Proc. IASTED Int'l Conf. on Software Engineering (IASTED SE 2004)*. ACTA Press, 2004.

[19] A.-M. Sassen, G. Amorós, P. Donth, K. Geihs, J.-M. Jézéquel, K. Odent, N. Plouzeau, and T. Weis. QCCS: A methodology for the development of contract-aware components based on aspect oriented design. In *AOSD Early Aspects Workshop*, Enschede, The Netherlands, 2002.

[20] M. Shaw, R. DeLine, and G. Zelesnik. Abstractions and implementations for architectural connections. In *3rd Int'l Conf. on Configurable Distributed Systems*. IEEE Press, May 1996.

[21] D. M. Simmonds, S. Ghosh, and R. France. An MDA framework for middleware transparent software development & quality of service. In Bruel [4], pages 1–7.

[22] J. A. Stankovic, R. Zhu, R. Poornalingam, C. Lu, Z. Yu, M. Humphrey, and B. Ellis. VEST: An aspect-based composition tool for real-time systems. In *Proc. 9th Real-Time and Embedded Technology and Applications Symposium (RTAS'03), Toronto, Canada*, pages 58–69. IEEE Press, May 2003.

Generic and Meta-transformations for Model Transformation Engineering*

Dániel Varró and András Pataricza

Budapest University of Technology and Economics
Department of Measurement and Information Systems
H-1117 Budapest, Magyar tudósok körútja 2.
{varro,pataric}@mit.bme.hu

Abstract. The Model Driven Architecture necessitates not only the application of software engineering disciplines to the specification of modeling languages (*language-ware*) but also to design inter and intra-language model transformations (*transformation-ware*). Although many model transformation approaches exist, their focus is almost exclusively put on functional correctness and intuitive description language while the importance of engineering issues such as reusability, maintainability, performance or compactness are neglected. To tackle these problems following the MDA philosophy, we argue in the paper that model transformations should also be regarded as models (i.e., as data). More specifically, we demonstrate (i) how *generic transformations* can provide a very compact description of certain transformation problems and (ii) how *meta-transformations* can be designed that yield efficient transformations as their output model.
Keywords: model transformation, metamodeling, meta-transformation, generic transformation.

1 Towards Model Transformation Engineering in MDA

MDA and language engineering. Recently, the Model Driven Architecture (MDA) of the Object Management Group (OMG) has become a dominant trend in software engineering. The main idea of the MDA framework is the use of models during the entire system design cycle. At first, the central business logic functionality on the target system is captured by the so-called platform-independent model (PIM). Information on the target software platform is added in a later phase when mapping PIMs into platform-specific models (PSMs). Finally, the entire source code of the target application can be generated automatically.

A key factor in the success of the MDA is thus the development of industrial-strength models in various modeling languages. Several metamodeling approaches [3, 6, 10, 24] have been flourishing to provide solid foundations for language engineering (or languagc-ware) to allow systems engineers to design a language for their own domain. As being the standard and visual object-oriented modeling language, UML obviously plays a key role also in language design.

* This work was partially supported by the Hungarian National Scientific Foundation Grant (OTKA 038027).

T. Baar et al. (Eds.): UML 2004, LNCS 3273, pp. 290–304, 2004.

Transformation engineering in MDA. Many methodologists and computer scientists have recently pointed out that the role of model transformations between modeling languages within MDA is as critical as the role of modeling languages themselves [4]. MDA requires various kinds of transformations including inter-model (for instance, from PIMs to PSMs) and intra-model transformations (such as transformations within PIMs), or model to code mappings. As these transformations will be mainly developed by software engineers, precise yet intuitive notations are required for model transformation languages. QVT [17], a recent initiative of the OMG, aims exactly at developing a standard for capturing Queries, Views and Transformations in MDA.

Many model transformation approaches exist (including the official proposals submitted to the QVT RFP and overviewed in [12]). An "ultimate debate" that separates these approaches is about the way of specifying transformations: declarative approaches (like [2, 13, 16]) define a relation between elements of the source and target modeling language while operational approaches (such as [20, 26, 14, 25, 23]) define rules to describe what steps are required to derive the target model from a given source model. Mixed approaches (see [21]) typically use declarative relations first which are manually refined into operational rules later on. In general, declarative approaches tend to be more intuitive for software engineers (i.e., it is easier to write and understand declarative transformations) while it is easier to automate operational approaches (i.e., it is easier to develop tools that execute operational transformations).

Problem statement. Due to the central role of model transformations in the MDA framework, transformations should be developed within MDA (thus, for instance, by distinguishing between platform-independent and platform-specific transformations as proposed in [4]). This also necessitates adapting the well-known principles of software engineering for transformation engineering (or *transformation-ware*, shortly, *transware*) to support the entire design cycle of model transformations. Despite the wide range of existing model transformation approaches, their focus is almost exclusively put on developing functionally correct model transformations using an intuitive notation while neglecting the importance of traditional software engineering issues such as reusability, maintainability, performance or compactness.

Objectives. To tackle (many of) these problems in a convenient way complying with the MDA philosophy, we argue in the paper that model transformations should also be regarded as models (or in other terms, as data). More specifically, we demonstrate (i) how *generic* (or higher-order) *transformations* can provide a very compact description of certain transformation problems in MDA (Sec. 3) and (ii) how *meta-transformations* (Sec. 4) can be designed that yield efficient transformations as their output model using VPM (Visual Precise Metamodeling), a multilevel and dynamic (rule-based) metamodeling framework. The concepts are demonstrated on a well-known (meta-)transformation problem of the MDA framework. Finally, we also discuss some tooling aspects for supporting our concepts (Sec. 5).

2 Motivating Example: Generating XMI Models

In order to motivate the need for generic and meta-transformations in MDA, we selected a well-known transformation problem, namely, generating standard XMI documents from MOF-based models. The relevance of this problem is also demonstrated by the fact that an official QVT submission [21] discusses this transformation for handling one specific modeling language, namely, UML.

However, it is worth pointing out that the XMI standard [18] is not related only to UML. In fact, it is a meta-standard in the sense that it specifies a corresponding XML format for an arbitrary modeling language defined by its MOF metamodel [19]. Although XMI is intended to serve as a common interchange format for the MOF-based models of UML tools, the XMI formats of these tools are essentially different from each other (despite the unique and standard UML metamodel). The lack of proper tool support for XMI export and import in off-the-shelf UML tools is a main motivation for discussing this transformation in the current paper. More specifically, we argue that capturing the XMI transformation in its generality is much easier than specifying it just for a single modeling language such as UML.

For an overview, a simplified variant of the MOF metamodel (i.e., the meta-metamodel in the MOF framework), and an XML metamodel are depicted in Fig. 1. Furthermore, an extract of a metamodel for the language of graphs (which is an instance of the MOF metamodel) and a sample XMI document are depicted in Fig. 2.

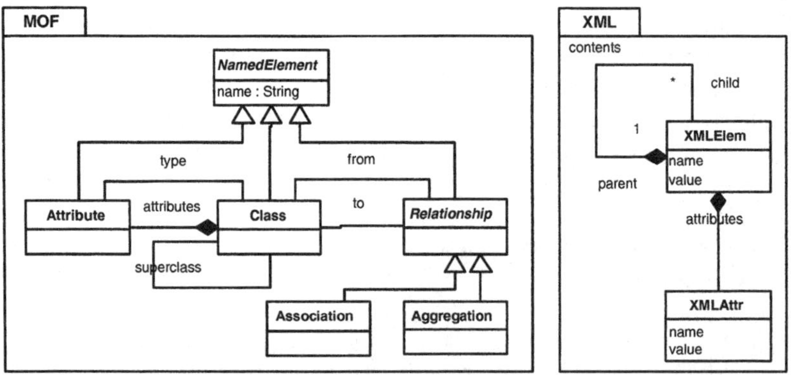

Fig. 1. The metamodels of MOF and XML

The main concepts of the MOF-model-to-XMI transformation are described informally below. For space limitations, we disregard the handling of inheritance, the navigability of association ends, and the sequencing of XML elements.

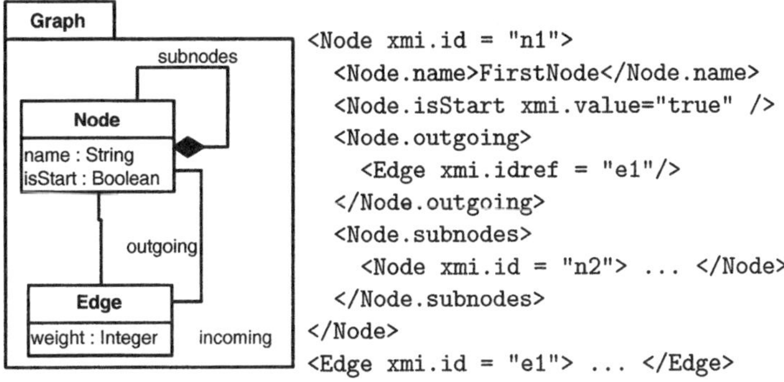

Fig. 2. A sample modeling language and XMI document

- The MOF metamodel of a language (e.g., the language of graphs in Fig. 2) defines the names and the structure of XML elements and attributes for the corresponding XMI format of the modeling language.
- Each instance of a MOF class *cls* (i.e., each object in traditional UML terminology) is transformed into a separate XML element (i) with a name corresponding to the name of the class (*cls*) and (ii) with a special attribute called *xmi.id* for storing the identifier of the instance. See the encoding of node *n1* in Fig. 2 for demonstration.
- Each instance of a MOF attribute *att* in a MOF class *cls* is mapped into an XML element with a name *cls.att* and placed inside the start and end tags of its owner element. If the type of an attribute is an enumeration type, then we use the special XML attribute *xmi.value* to store the value of the attribute instance (see attribute *isStart*). Otherwise, the value is stored within the start and end tags of the corresponding XML element as a string (as done in the case of attribute *name*).
- Each instance of a MOF aggregation is transformed into an XML element that encapsulates all the objects inside the container object (we assume that each object can be contained by exactly one other object to satisfy the tree criteria for XML models). XML elements of contained objects are placed inside this intermediate XML element representing the aggregation itself (see the aggregation *subnodes* in the example).
- Each instance of a MOF association is mapped into (i) an XML element corresponding to the association itself (such as *outgoing*) and (ii) an XML element corresponding to the target object at the other end of the association instance which contains a reference to the main XML element of the object appearing elsewhere in the XML document (see edge *e1*). This way, the complex graph structure of a MOF-based model can be encoded into the strict tree structure of an XML document.

3 Generic Transformations

Generic (or higher-order) transformations contain transformation rules where the types of certain objects are variables. An analogy can be made between general transformations and generic (or template) classes used in various object-oriented languages. However, while the parameters of generic classes are bound at design time, type variables in generic transformation rules are only substituted at transformation-time (run-time).

The advantages and drawbacks of higher-order transformations also show certain similarities with traditional logic frameworks. Higher-order logic is a very powerful description mechanism but it raises decidability (and performance) problems concerning automated reasoning when compared with traditional first-order logic. Still, several powerful (higher-order) theorem provers have been applied for a large scale of practical verification problems.

Analogously, generic transformation rules offer a very high level of generality and compactness when compared to other (first-order) model transformation frameworks (especially, for higher-level transformations). A single generic rule can handle several situations where essentially the same rule pattern should be applied on objects of different types. On the other hand, the foundations of their type system (metamodeling framework) require some precautions to avoid certain well-known problems (see [3]). Furthermore, degradation in performance has been experienced in rewriting logic systems like Maude [7] when working with the meta-representations of large models.

To overcome these problems, we will build on VPM [24], which is a dynamic metamodeling framework with fluid meta-levels. Moreover, generic transformation rules will be turned into traditional first-order ones by meta-transformations later on in Sec. 4 to tackle performance problems.

3.1 The Metamodeling and Transformation Framework

In the paper, we use the VPM metamodeling framework [24] to provide the theoretical foundations for our concepts. VPM is a multilevel framework in the sense that it introduces an explicit representation of both instance-of and inheritance relations, which is extended to handle associations, models and metamodels (in addition to classes) but the notions of metalevels are fluid. Furthermore, VPM is a dynamic framework, where inter and intra model transformations can be described by a visual, rule and pattern-based formalism provided by the paradigm of graph transformation [9].

VPM provides the following important features for supporting generic and meta-transformations.

- The instance-of relations between model elements are stored and manipulated as any other model elements (provided that the axioms of [24] are fulfilled). As a result, classes and objects can be represented uniformly as entities (nodes) with an explicit instance-of relation between them in order to avoid the "redefinition of concepts" problem [3].

– Transformation rules are also stored as ordinary models (or, in other terms, as data), therefore, we can easily develop transformation rules that process or generate transformation rules.

A transformation rule (see, e.g., *Obj2ElemR* in Fig. 3) is represented as a package having a source and a target pattern inside. Each entity in the pattern is either a constant or a variable (constants start with upper case initials or printed within in quotation marks). Correspondence between source and target elements are denoted by pentagons such as *Obj2Elem(o,e)* which is only syntactic sugar for correspondence objects of a specific class defined by the metamodel of the mapping (see [13] for the metamodeling of mappings).

A transformation rule can be applied on a given model by a transformation engine which first tries to match all the elements in the rule (patterns) that are not marked by {*new*} labels to model elements. A constant entity in the rule should be matched to the entity with the same identifier in the model while a variable entity can be matched to any type and edge-conforming entity of the model. Then, the images of all elements marked by {*delete*} labels in the rule are removed from the model (potentially including the removal of certain dangling edges). Finally, new nodes and edges are created that correspond to elements marked by {*new*} labels in the rule.

Instance-of relations are depicted either *explicitly* by dashed edges between two entities (an object and its class) and/or *implicitly* by using entity names of type *obj:class* to denote the fact that entity *obj* is an instance of entity *class*. However, it is crucial to point out that in generic transformation rules, both entities *obj* and *class* can be either constants (i.e., concrete objects or classes) or variables independently. For instance, a pattern where both *obj* and *class* are variables can be matched to all instances of all classes. If only *class* is a variable then pattern matching finds the type (or all types) of an object. Finally, if *class* is constant and *obj* is variable, then we have traditional first-class patterns. Note, however, that the type hierarchy of each rule should be upper closed, i.e., each entity should have (directly or indirectly) a constant entity as a type.

3.2 Details of the MOF-XMI Transformation

The rules of (a fragment of) the MOF-model-to-XMI transformation are now presented in Fig. 3 and 4 and explained below. The entire case study (that handles inheritance, the sequencing of XML elements, etc.) consists of less than 20 rules.

– *Obj2ElemR* (in Fig. 3). First each object *o* in our MOF-based model that is an instance of a MOF Class *x* in the metamodel is transformed into a corresponding XML element *e* with an XML attribute *a* (called *xmi.id*). In fact, *x* is, in turn, an instance of *Class* in the MOF metamodel as denoted by *x:Class*. The name of *e* equals to the name of class *x* while the identifier of *o* is mapped into the value of attribute (instance) *a*. The XML constructs *e* and *o* and the *Obj2Elem(o,e)* correspondence is generated as a result of the rule application.

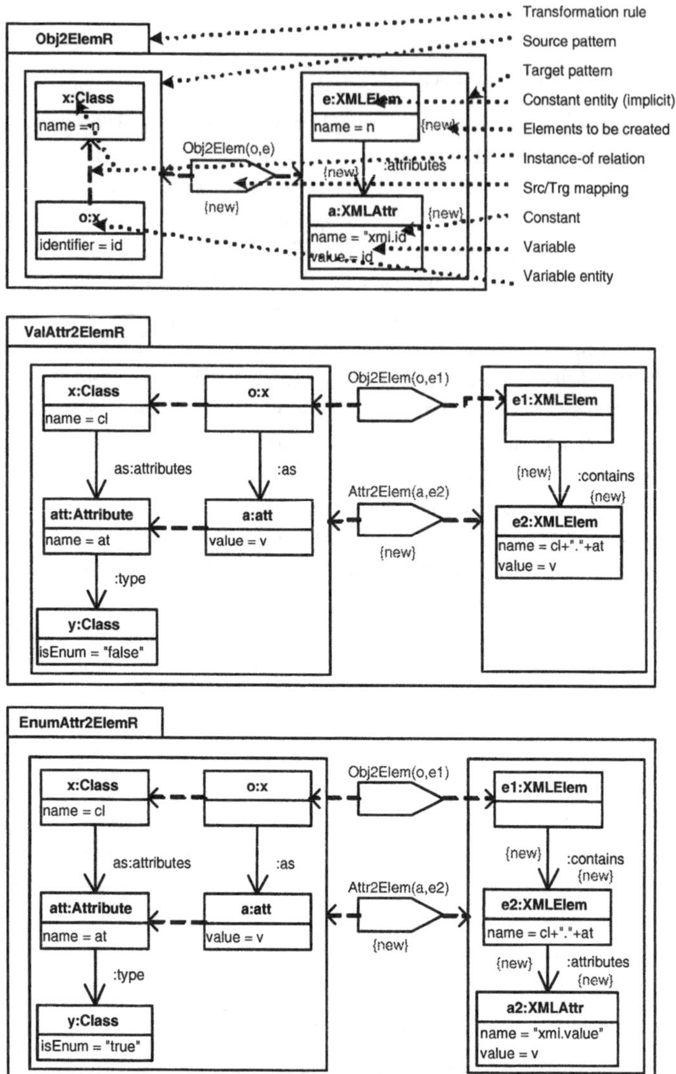

Fig. 3. Transforming objects and attributes

– *ValAttr2ElemR* (in Fig. 3). The handling of MOF attribute instances are dependent on the metamodel. If the type of an attribute *att* (in a class *x*) is not an enumeration type (i.e., *isEnum* = *false*) then the value of an attribute instance *a* is stored as a string between the start and end tag of an XML element *e2* and it is related to attribute instance *a* (by the *Attr2Elem(a,e2)* relation). Furthermore, we add *e2* to the content of the XML element *e1*

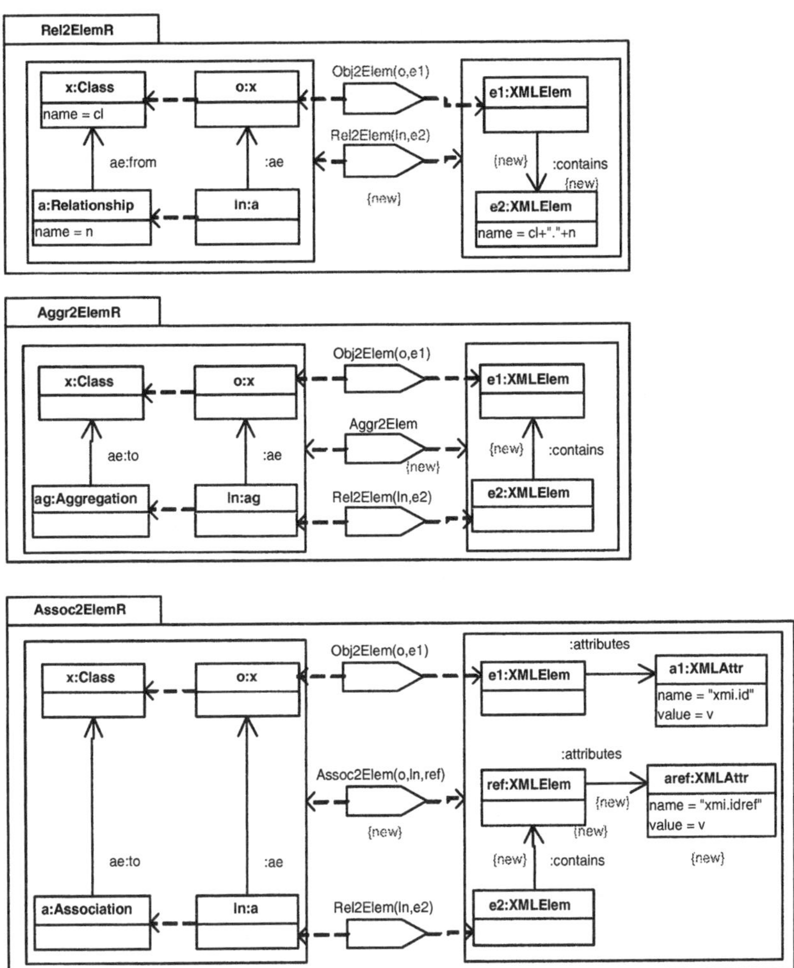

Fig. 4. Transforming associations and aggregations

which corresponds to the container object *o* of the attribute instance *a* (as denoted by checking the existence of an *Obj2ElemR(o,e1)* relation).

- *EnumAttr2ElemR* (in Fig. 3). If the type of an attribute *att* (in a class *x*) is an enumeration type (i.e., *isEnum = true*) then the value of an attribute instance *a* is stored in an XML attribute (*a2*) called *xmi.value* that belongs to XML element *e2*. Note that in both cases, the names of the new XML elements are created by concatenating the name of the class and the attribute (see *Node.isStart* and *Node.name* in Fig. 2).
- *Rel2ElemR* (in Fig. 4). For the sake of simplicity, both associations and aggregations are handled as directed relationships (with a source/from and a target/to class; see the MOF metamodel in Fig. 1). Rule *Rel2ElemR* handles

the source part of relationships. For a relationship instance *ln* it creates a new XML element *e2* and links it to an XML element *e1* that corresponds to the source object *o* of the relationship instance *ln*. The names of new XML elements are derived again as the concatenation of the names of the source class and the relationship.
- *Aggr2ElemR* (in Fig. 4). This rule simply places XML elements *e2* corresponding to the target object *o* of an aggregation instance *ln* into the (contents of) XML element *e1* which is related to the aggregation instance *ln* itself.
- *Assoc2ElemR* (in Fig. 4). Finally, in case of associations (references), we look up the corresponding XML element *e1* of the target end object *o*, and generate a new XML element *ref* referring to *e1* by the value of its *xmi.idref* attribute (see the main and the reference Edge element in Fig. 2).

As a conclusion, generic (graph) transformation rules provide an extremely compact and powerful platform-independent specification mechanism for model transformation problems in the MDA framework, especially, when more than two metalevels are involved in the transformation itself (as in case of the MOF-to-XMI transformation).

However, an increase in generality (naturally) causes a decrease in performance as experienced also in other meta-theoretical frameworks such as in [7]. Even if a clever pattern matching strategy is implemented (e.g., matching type variable nodes before instance variable nodes), higher-order transformations are necessarily slower than traditional first-order ones. To tackle performance (and maintainability) problems, we now introduce meta-transformations that will derive efficient, first-order from generic (higher-order) transformations.

4 Meta-transformations

Meta-transformations are transformations that operate on other transformations as their input or output. A prerequisite for meta-transformations is thus to store transformation rules also as ordinary models within the MDA framework. This idea is in direct analogy with the Neumann architecture of computers where programs are stored as data and only interpreted differently by the target machine.

Increasing performance of generic rules. A main goal of using meta-transformations is to increase the performance of generic transformations. Essentially, the pattern matching of a generic rule is split into two separate phases by creating rule-writing rules. Type variables are substituted in all possible ways, and each substitution yields a first-order transformation rule (which now only contains instance variables). Rule-writing rules are again higher-level, but (i) they are executed at design time, and (ii) they operate on the metamodels, which are several orders of magnitude smaller than the (system) models themselves, thus performance is not critical. Then, the main (model-level) transformation itself is carried out at transformation-time by efficient first-order rules.

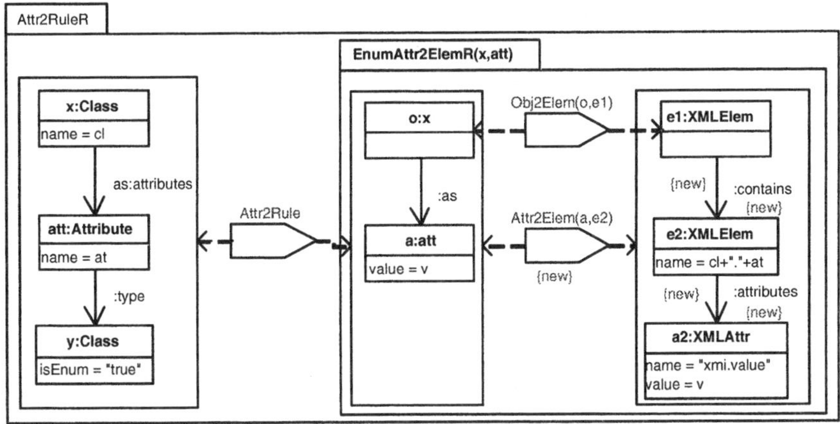

Fig. 5. A meta transformation rule for generating rules

A sample meta transformation rule that tailors the generic rule *EnumAttr2ElemR* to first-order rules is depicted in Fig. 5. When applied to the metamodel of graphs in Fig. 2, variables *x*, and *att* are substituted, therefore, the type variables in the target rule model *EnumAttr2ElemR(x,att)* are bound, for instance, to class *Edge* and attribute *weight*. In this respect, the generated rule (i.e., the target model of the meta-transformation) is now a traditional first-order rule (see Fig. 6) that can be used in any graph transformation engine. However, this rule was generated automatically which is much less error-prone than a copy-paste method with manual substitution of type variables.

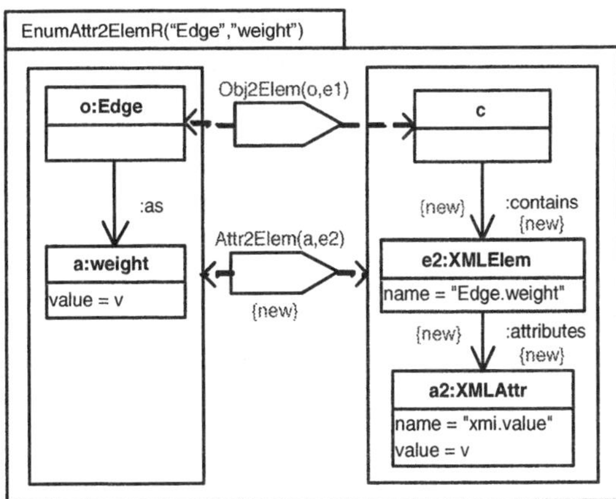

Fig. 6. A rule generated by applying the meta rule of Fig. 5 for the language of graphs

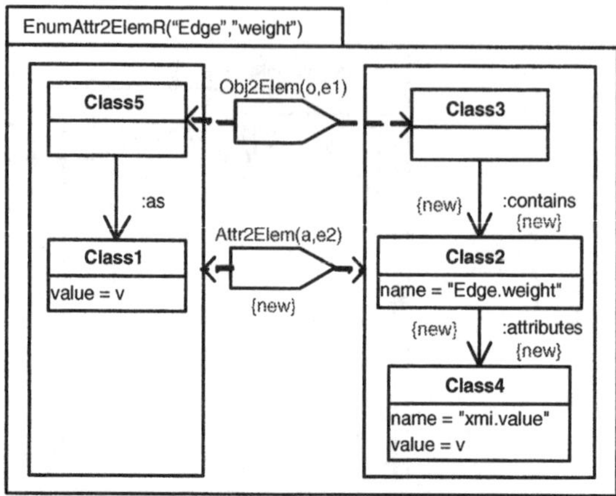

Fig. 7. Maintaining XMI models and rules

Increasing maintainability of transformations. An alternate main goal for the use of meta-transformations is concerned with the maintainability of transformation rules. As a motivation, it is not hard to imagine that we need to adapt our MOF-to-XMI transformation in practice to the XMI dialects of various tools (especially, as XMI versions 1.0 and 1.1 are very different).

For instance, a new XMI dialect no longer represents instances of MOF attributes as XML elements but as XML attributes (as done in XMI 1.1 to reduce the number of elements in the XML tree). Therefore, we created the rule of Fig. 7 to migrate the attribute changes of XMI 1.0 models into XMI 1.1 models. This rule also prescribes the deletion of certain model elements (such as the superfluous XML element *e2* for representing an attribute instance or its corresponding *xmi.value* attribute *a1*) in addition to creating a new XML attribute *a2* for storing the value of the attribute.

Now the rule of Fig. 7 can be applied directly on XMI 1.0 models to convert them into their XMI 1.1 equivalent. However, what is more interesting, we can use transformation rules (of Fig. 5-6) as source models of this maintenance rule so that the rules generating the XMI output are updated themselves. As a result, the same rule can be used for the maintenance of both transformation models and rules.

As a conclusion, meta-transformations are extremely powerful means (i) to increase the performance of generic rules by tailoring them into first-order rules of a specific domain, and (ii) to maintain or upgrade model transformations. These are achieved by treating transformation rules as ordinary models.

5 Tool Support

We have recently made major upgrades and re-engineering of VIATRA [25], our general model transformation framework, in order to support the dynamic,

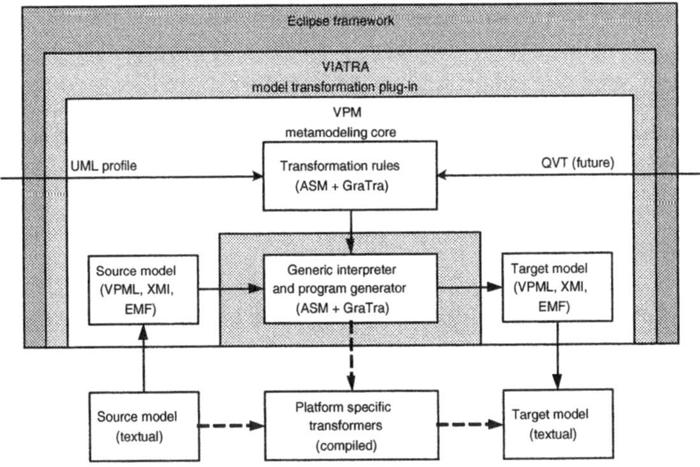

Fig. 8. The VIATRA model transformation architecture

multilevel metamodeling features of VPM [24], and the generic/meta transformational foundations presented in the current paper. The main intended usage of our framework is dependability evaluation and optimization of business workflow models and UML models.

The VIATRA 2.0 framework (see Fig. 8) is intended to be used in two alternate ways: platform-independent and platform-specific way.

- *Platform-Independent Transformations.* A source user model (which is a structured textual representation such as an XMI description of a UML model exported from a CASE tools) is imported into the VPM model space. Then, platform-independent transformation specifications can be constructed by combining graph transformation [9] and abstract state machine [5] rules. These rules can be created within the framework or in a UML tool using a special profile (and, in the future, using the QVT standard). The rules are then executed on the source VPM model by the generic (higher-order) VIATRA rule interpreter in order to yield the target (VPM) model. Finally, the target model can be serialized into an appropriate textual representation specific to back-end tools. This way, the transformation is kept within a single transformation framework (i.e., VIATRA) in order to ease the testing, debugging and validation of model transformations without relying on the highly optimized target transformation technology.
- *Platform-Specific Transformations.* The VIATRA engine also enables the design of meta-transformations that take an already validated transformation specification as the input and yield a platform-specific transformer (e.g., a Java program, or XSLT script) as the output. In other terms, the functionality of a transformation program is *compiled* into a more efficient (but less general) target transformation technology. In this respect, the transformation from a specific source model to its target equivalent can be performed

outside the VIATRA framework. This is especially important for integrating complex transformations into off-the-shelf CASE tools which, normally, have their own, tool-dependent way for writing transformation add-ons.

A main technological change is that VIATRA 2.0 is now implemented as a plug-in for the Eclipse framework [1] (in contrast to the previous Prolog version).

6 Related Work

The main point of the current paper is to draw attention to the fact that important MDA transformations can only be properly captured as a generic and/or meta-transformations. However, these issues are not addressed in the QVT RFP (thus not in any of the submissions), we can only find some weaker constructs. For instance, the use of multi-objects in patterns (e.g., in the QVT partners proposal [21]) still can only handle transformations on the same metalevel (while variables may appear on any metalevels in our approach). Using both classes and objects in transformation rules in a UML style is rather higher-level, but our approach can also handle an arbitrary number of metalevels, thus models can be taken from various technological spaces (with different meta-metamodels).

Existing graph transformation approaches and tools (e.g. AGG [11] or ATOM3 [8]) work with a fixed metamodel (type graph) for a given transformation disallowing higher-order variables. Only Progres [22] allows the use of type parameters in rules to support higher-order transformations, but meta-transformations are still not supported.

Probably, the closest theoretical correspondence is provided by (i) two-level graph grammars [15] introduced for the definition of context-sensitive language grammars, (ii) the meta-theoretical foundations in rewriting logic implemented in Maude [7] where arbitrary models can be transformed into their meta-representation; and (iii) object-based reflective programming languages such as Smalltalk. However, we believe that our proposal fits much better to the MDA framework for generic and meta-transformations due to its intuitive visual representation and relatedness to existing MDA standards.

The distinction between platform-independent and platform-specific transformation (see Sec. 5) was also facilitated in [4]. Here the authors propose the use of UML as the platform-independent language for designing transformations. In our approach, the PIT language is a combination of two formal notations (abstract state machines and graph transformation) but naturally, the mathematical background is hidden by using a UML-like visual syntax for transformation rules.

7 Conclusions

In the current paper, we proposed the use of *generic* and *meta-transformations* for solving transformation engineering problems within the MDA. Generic transformations (that allow the use of type (higher-order) variables in transformation rules) may capture transformation problems involving several metalevels in a very general, *compact* and platform-independent way. Meta-transformations (that are transformations operating on transformations) offer support for increasing the *performance* of generic transformations by tailoring them into different platforms (modeling languages). Furthermore, the *maintenence* of models and transformation can also be carried out in a uniform way by meta-transformations.

The two main prerequisites for such a high-level transformation framework are (i) the explicit representation of instance-of relations in the modeling space, and (ii) the handling of transformation rules as models (as data). In the paper, we used the dynamic and multilevel VPM metamodeling framework [24], which provides support for both of these features. In fact, VPM also supports the *reusability* of transformation rules by introducing rule inheritance. However, we disregarded this very important software engineering aspect in the current paper to clearly distinguish our new results from any previous work.

Acknowledgments. This paper was influenced by several fruitful discussions at the Dagstuhl Seminar on Language Engineering in the Model Driven Architecture (March 2004). We are grateful to many of the participants and organizers.

References

[1] The Eclipse project. www.eclipse.org.

[2] D. Akehurst and S. Kent. A relational approach to defining transformations in a metamodel. In J.-M. Jézéquel, H. Hussmann, and S. Cook (eds.), *Proc. Fifth Intern. Conference on the Unified Modeling Language – The Language and its Applications*, vol. 2460 of *LNCS*, pp. 243–258. Springer, Dresden, Germany, 2002.

[3] C. Atkinson and T. Kühne. The essence of multilevel metamodelling. In M. Gogolla and C. Kobryn (eds.), *Proc. UML 2001 – The Unified Modeling Language. Modeling Languages, Concepts and Tools*, vol. 2185 of *LNCS*, pp. 19–33. Springer, 2001.

[4] J. Bézivin, N. Farcet, J.-M. Jézéquel, B. Langlois, and D. Pollet. Reflective model driven engineering. In P. Stevens, J. Whittle, and G. Booch (eds.), *Proc. UML 2003: 6th Intern. Conference on the Unified Modeling Language*, vol. 2863 of *LNCS*, pp. 175–189. Springer, San Francisco, CA, USA, 2003.

[5] E. Börger and R. Stärk. *Abstract State Machines. A method for High-Level System Design and Analysis.* Springer, 2003.

[6] T. Clark, A. Evans, and S. Kent. The Metamodelling Language Calculus: Foundation semantics for UML. In H. Hussmann (ed.), *Proc. Fundamental Approaches to Software Engineering, FASE 2001 Genova, Italy*, vol. 2029 of *LNCS*, pp. 17–31. Springer, 2001.

[7] M. Clavel. *Reflection in Rewriting Logic: Metalogical Foundations and Metaprogramming.* CSLI Publications, Stanford University, 2000.

[8] J. de Lara and H. Vangheluwe. AToM3: A tool for multi-formalism and meta-modelling. In R.-D. Kutsche and H. Weber (eds.), *5th Intern. Conference, FASE 2002: Fundamental Approaches to Software Engineering, Grenoble, France, April 8-12, 2002, Proceedings*, vol. 2306 of *LNCS*, pp. 174–188. Springer, 2002.

[9] H. Ehrig, G. Engels, H.-J. Kreowski, and G. Rozenberg (eds.). *Handbook on Graph Grammars and Computing by Graph Transformation*, vol. 2: Applications, Languages and Tools. World Scientific, 1999.

[10] G. Engels, J. H. Hausmann, R. Heckel, and S. Sauer. Dynamic meta modeling: A graphical approach to the operational semantics of behavioral diagrams in UML. In A. Evans, S. Kent, and B. Selic (eds.), *UML 2000 - The Unified Modeling Language. Advancing the Standard*, vol. 1939 of *LNCS*, pp. 323–337. Springer, 2000.
[11] C. Ermel, M. Rudolf, and G. Taentzer. *In [9]*, chap. The AGG-Approach: Language and Tool Environment, pp. 551–603. World Scientific, 1999.
[12] T. Gardner, C. Griffin, J. Koehler, and R. Hauser. A review of OMG MOF 2.0 Query / Views / Transformations submissions and recommendations towards the final standard. In *Workshop on Metamodeling for MDA*, pp. 179–197. 2003.
[13] J. H. Hausmann and S. Kent. Visualizing model mappings in UML. In *SoftVis 03: ACM Symp. on Software Visualization*, pp. 169–178. San Diego, CA, USA, 2003.
[14] R. Heckel, J. Küster, and G. Taentzer. Towards automatic translation of UML models into semantic domains. In *Proc. AGT 2002: Workshop on Applied Graph Transformation*, pp. 11–21. Grenoble, France, 2002.
[15] W. Hesse. Two-level graph grammars. In V. Claus, H. Ehrig, and G. Rozenberg (eds.), *Intern. Workshop on Graph-Grammars and Their Application to Computer Science and Biology, October 30 - November 3, 1978*, vol. 73 of *Lecture Notes in Computer Science*, pp. 255–269. Springer, Bad Honnef, 1979.
[16] D. Milicev. Automatic model transformations using extended UML object diagrams in modeling environments. *IEEE Transactions on Software Engineering*, vol. 28(4):pp. 413–431, 2002.
[17] Object Management Group. *QVT: Request for Proposal for Queries, Views and Transformations.* http://www.omg.org.
[18] Object Management Group. *XML Metadata Interchange.* http://www.omg.org/technology/documents/formal/xmi.htm.
[19] Object Management Group. *Meta Object Facility Version 2.0*, 2003. http://www.omg.org.
[20] I. Porres. Model refactorings as rule-based update transformations. In P. Stevens, J. Whittle, and G. Booch (eds.), *Proc. UML 2003: 6th Intern. Conference on the Unified Modeling Language*, vol. 2863 of *LNCS*, pp. 159–174. Springer, San Francisco, CA, USA, 2003.
[21] QVT-Partners. Revised submission for MOF 2.0 Query / Views / Transformations RFP, 2003. http://qvtp.org.
[22] A. Schürr, A. J. Winter, and A. Zündorf. *In [9]*, chap. The PROGRES Approach: Language and Environment, pp. 487–550. World Scientific, 1999.
[23] J. Sprinkle, A. Agrawal, T. Levendovszky, F. Shi, and G. Karsai. Domain translation using graph transformations. In *Proc. Tenth IEEE Intern. Conference and Workshop on the Engineering of Computer-Based Systems*, pp. 159–168. Huntsville, AL, 2003.
[24] D. Varró and A. Pataricza. VPM: A visual, precise and multilevel metamodeling framework for describing mathematical domains and UML. *Journal of Software and Systems Modeling*, vol. 2(3):pp. 187–210, 2003.
[25] D. Varró, G. Varró, and A. Pataricza. Designing the automatic transformation of visual languages. *Science of Computer Programming*, vol. 44(2):pp. 205–227, 2002.
[26] J. Whittle. Transformations and software modeling languages: Automating transformations in UML. In J.-M. Jézéquel, H. Hussmann, and S. Cook (eds.), *Proc. Fifth Intern. Conf. on the Unified Modeling Language – The Language and its Applications*, vol. 2460 of *LNCS*, pp. 227–242. Springer, Dresden, Germany, 2002.

Supporting Model Refactorings Through Behaviour Inheritance Consistencies

Ragnhild Van Der Straeten[1], Viviane Jonckers[1], and Tom Mens[2]

[1] System and Software Engineering Lab
Vrije Universiteit Brussel
Pleinlaan 2, 1050 Brussel, Belgium
rvdstrae@vub.ac.be|viviane@info.vub.ac.be
[2] Service de Génie Logiciel
Université de Mons-Hainaut
Av. du Champs de Mars 6, 7000 Mons, Belgium
tom.mens@umh.ac.be

Abstract. This paper addresses the problem of consistency preservation in model-driven software development. Software models typically embody many different views that need to be kept consistent. In the context of *consistency within a model*, *behaviour inheritance consistencies* restrict the way the behaviour of a subclass can specialize the behaviour of a superclass. In the context of *model evolution*, *model refactorings* restructure a model while preserving its behavioural properties. It is still an open research question how to define behaviour preservation properties for model refactorings. We claim that behaviour inheritance consistencies correspond, in an evolution context, to the preservation of behavioural properties between model versions. To illustrate this claim, we implemented consistency rules and preservation behaviour rules in Racer, a reasoning engine for *description logics*. We show how the same logic rules can be used to detect behaviour inheritance inconsistencies in a model and to detect the preservation of call behaviour properties during model refactoring.

1 Introduction

During model-driven software development, models are built representing different views on a software system, or models can be evolved into a new version. Both situations may lead to inconsistencies. To address the first situation, so-called *behaviour inheritance consistencies* can be used to restrict the way the behaviour of a subclass should specialize the behaviour of a superclass in a class hierarchy (cf. Liskov's well-known substitutability principle). To address the second situation, so-called *model refactorings* can be used, because they have the important benefit that they restructure a model while preserving certain behavioural properties.

The aim of this paper is to explore the precise relation between behaviour inheritance consistencies and model refactorings. We claim that behaviour inheritance consistencies within a single model version correspond, in an evolution

T. Baar et al. (Eds.): UML 2004, LNCS 3273, pp. 305–319, 2004.

context, to the preservation of certain behavioural properties between model versions. In the remainder of the paper, we validate our claim in four successive steps.

First, we investigate and formalise behaviour as defined in UML 2.0 state machines and sequence diagrams (Section 3)[13]. Second, we express different kinds of behaviour inheritance consistencies in the context of UML 2.0 state machines and sequence diagrams, and found in literature [19] with our formalism (Section 4). Third, we investigate and formalise different kinds of behaviour preservation properties for model refactoring (Section 5). Finally, we show that these notions of consistency and preservation are closely related (Section 6). To this extent, we implement a set of logic rules in a reasoning engine based on the formalism of Description Logic (DL) [2], and show that the logic queries that are used to detect behavioural inconsistencies in a model, can also be applied to guarantee the preservation of behavioural properties between different model versions.

2 Motivating Example

The motivating example used throughout this paper, is based on the design of an automatic teller machine (ATM), originally developed by Russell Bjork for a computer science course at Gordon University. A possible usage scenario of an instance of *ATM* is shown in the sequence diagram in Figure 1. This sequence diagram shows part of an interaction between instances of the classes *ATM*, *Session*, *CardReader* and *CashDispenser*, when a user decides to make a withdrawal. The messages sent in the diagram verify if there is enough cash in the ATM. If so, the amount of cash is dispensed and the card is returned to the user.

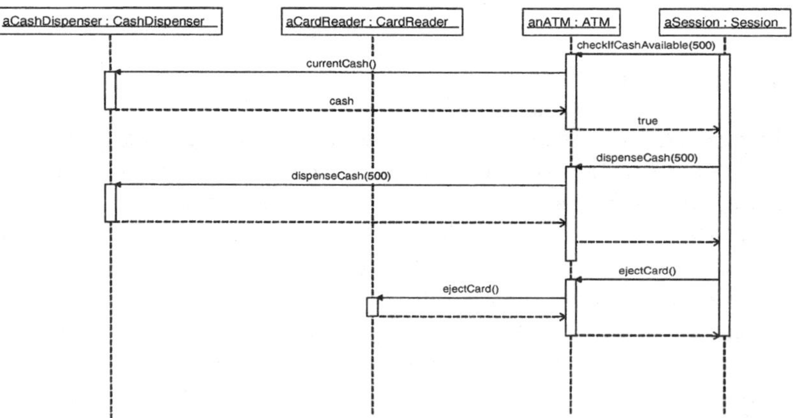

Fig. 1. Sequence diagram for withdrawal scenario on an *ATM*

The behaviour of the *PrintingATM* class, which is a subclass of *ATM* that has extra printing functionality, is represented by the state machine in Figure 2. When a customer wants to withdraw money from his account, he has to insert a bank card and enter the associated PIN number. If the PIN is not valid, the card is returned to the user. If a valid PIN has been entered, the *ATM* prompts the user to enter the amount to withdraw from his account. If the amount is less than *100*, the user is asked to re-enter an amount. In the other case, the *ATM* checks that the client's account has sufficient funds. If so, the *ATM* proceeds to check if it can dispense this amount. Once these checks have been passed, the *ATM* dispenses the money and at the same time, the *PrintingATM* class, unlike its parent, the *ATM* class, prints a receipt. Finally, the card is ejected.

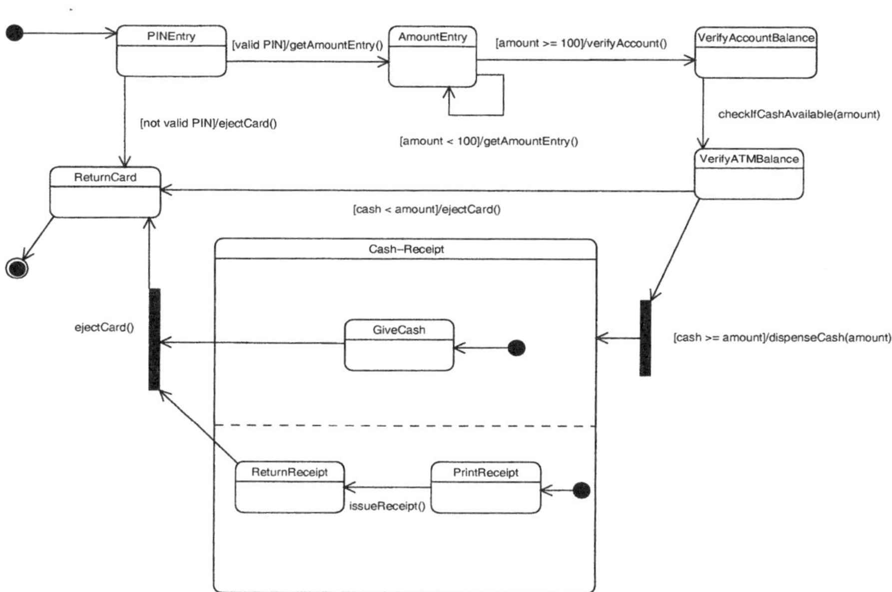

Fig. 2. UML protocol state machine for *PrintingATM* class

Consider the consistency relationship that an instance of *PrintingATM* must be usable in each situation where an instance of *ATM* is required (according to the substitutability principle). To guarantee this consistency relationship, *each sequence of the* ATM *sequence diagram of Figure 1 should be contained in the set of sequences of the* PrintingATM *state diagram of Figure 2*. In our case, *ATM* and *PrintingATM* do not obey this consistency rule, because an instance of *PrintingATM* will, after dispensing the cash, *always* print a receipt. It is not possible to skip this printing and immediately eject the card, which is the original behaviour of the *ATM* class.

Consider now an evolution of the *ATM* class obtained by extracting functionality contained in the *checkIfCashAvailable* method into a separate method. This *model refactoring* is comparable to the source code *Extract Method* refactoring [8], but at the design level we do not have source code at our disposal.

In our example, a new method *validate* is created, which takes two arguments, *amount* indicating the amount to withdraw and *cash*, the amount of money available in the *ATM*. This method checks if there is sufficient cash available. The sequence diagram in Figure 3 is the refactored version of the sequence diagram in Figure 1 where in the body of the method *checkIfCashAvailable*, the extracted method *validate* is called with arguments *500* and *cash*, which is the return value of the invoked *currentCash* method.

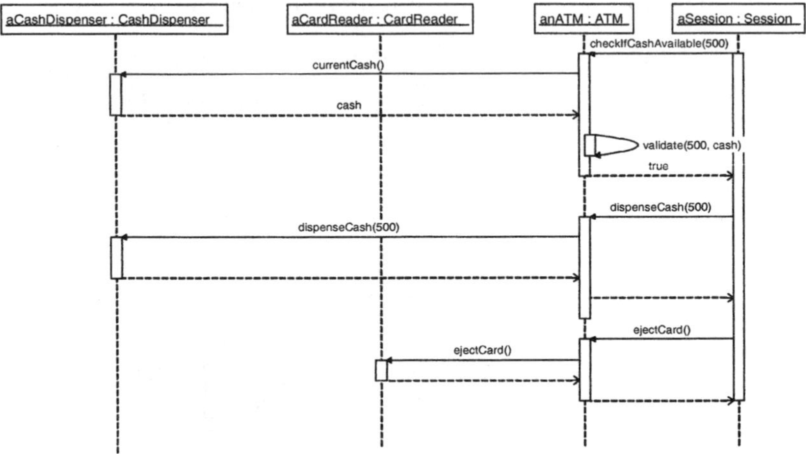

Fig. 3. Refactored sequence diagram for refactored *ATM* class

The behaviour specified in Figure 1 is not altered by this model refactoring. However, the call sequence in the method body of *checkIfCashAvailable* has been extended with a call to the new method *validate*.

3 Behaviour in UML 2.0

In this section, basic definitions of behaviour as defined in the UML 2.0 Superstructure and Infrastructure Specification [13] are given. These definitions enable a precise characterisation of behaviour inheritance consistencies and behaviour preservation in sections 4 and 5.

In UML 2.0, *Behaviour* is defined as a specification of how its context classifier changes state over time. *Behaviour* is an abstract metaclass and as such, the specification of a behaviour can take a number of forms, as described in its subclasses. A variety of specification mechanisms are provided by UML, such as *Statemachine*, *Activity*, *Usecase* and *Interaction*. To keep our experiments manageable, we deliberately confine ourselves to *Statemachine* and *Interaction* as specifications of behaviour.

3.1 Interaction

As described in chapter 14 of [13], " *Interactions are used in a number of different situations. They are used to get a better grip of an interaction situation for an individual designer or for a group that need to achieve a common understanding of the situation. Interactions are also used during the more detailed design phase where the precise inter-process communication must be set up according to formal protocols. When testing is performed, the traces of the system can be described as interactions and compared with those of the earlier phases.*"

The semantics of an *Interaction* is given by a pair of sets of traces [13] representing valid traces and invalid traces, respectively. Only the valid traces are described in [13].

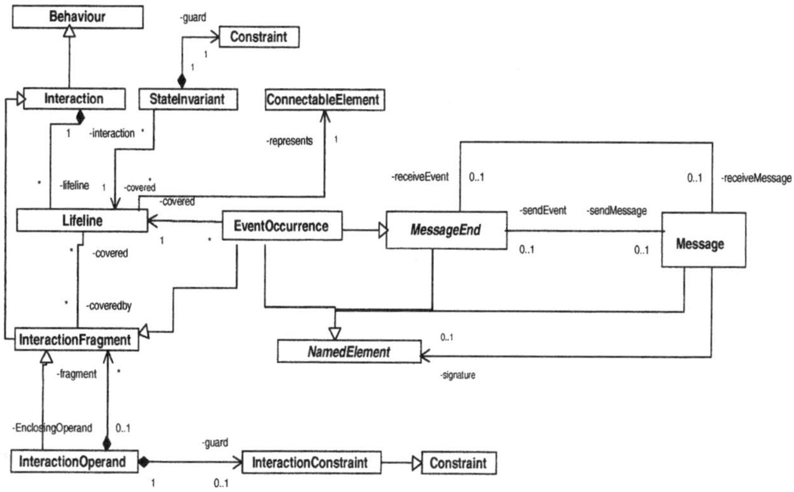

Fig. 4. UML meta model fragment for interactions

Figure 4 shows the relevant fragments of the UML meta model dealing with interactions. An *Interaction* consists of some *Lifelines* which are covered by *EventOccurrences*. *EventOccurrences* are *MessageEnds* representing either the receiving event of a *Message* or the sending event of a *Message*. A *Message* is a *NamedElement* that defines one specific kind of communication, represented by another *NamedElement*, e.g., an *Operation* in the case of an operation invocation. A *Lifeline* represents a *ConnectableElement*. A *ConnectableElement* represents a set of instances owned by a containing classifier instance. The UML meta class *InstanceSpecification* represents an instance in a modeled system. However, this meta class is not related to the *ConnectableElement* meta class in the UML 2.0 meta model. In this paper, a *Lifeline* is assumed to represent an *InstanceSpecification*. On a *Lifeline*, *StateInvariants* can be specified. An *InteractionFragment* is a piece of an interaction, which is an interaction in its own right. An *InteractionOperand* is an *InteractionFragment* with an optional guard expression. Only *InteractionOperands* with a guard that evaluates to true at this point in the interaction will be considered for the production of the traces of the enclosing *Interaction*.

The guards are *InteractionConstraints*, which are *Constraints*. In this paper, we typically consider constraints that represent pre- and postconditions.

Notation 1 *The* **set of all preconditions of an operation** *op* **of a class** *c, i.e., the set of conditions specifying the state of the system when the operation op is invoked, is denoted by* $Pre_{op,c}$. *The* **set of all preconditions** *of all operations of a class c is denoted by* Pre_c.
The **set of all postconditions of an operation** *op* **of a class** *c, i.e., the set of conditions specifying the state of the system when the operation op is completed, is denoted by* $Post_{op,c}$. *The* **set of all postconditions** *of all operations of a class c, is denoted by* $Post_c$.

Depending on its purpose, an *Interaction* can be displayed with different types of diagrams. For the sake of simplicity, we only consider sequence diagrams here. We formally define a *SD (sequence diagram) trace* as:

Definition 1. *A* ***SD trace*** ν_o *of an instance o of a class c is a sequence of event occurrences denoted* $< e_1, \ldots, e_n >$ *occurring on the lifeline of the instance o. An* ***event occurrence*** *e is defined as a couple* $(m, cons)$ *where m denotes the message that is associated to this event occurrence and cons represents the constraints valid on the lifeline of the instance o before the execution of the event occurrence e. The elements of cons are instances of the meta classes* StateInvariant *and* InteractionConstraint.

Note that this definition of SD trace indicates a subset of what is meant by the term "trace" in the UML 2.0 [13] chapter 14 on *Interactions*. A sequence diagram typically consists of several traces, as defined below:

Definition 2. *A* **sequence diagram** Δ *is a set of SD traces. This set typically contains SD traces for instances of different classes.*

For defining behaviour inheritance consistencies, we are only interested in the order of invocations of an object's operations. As such, the traces of event occurrences representing the receipt of a message are considered. Therefore, we define a *receiving SD trace* as follows:

Definition 3. *A* **receiving SD trace** $\nu_o/^{rec}$ *of an instance o of a class c is an SD trace* ν_o *for the instance o with only event occurrences representing the receipt of messages, which represents the invocation of an operation.*

Example 1. A receiving SD trace of the instance *anATM* of class *ATM* in the sequence diagram Δ of Figure 1 is $< e_1, e_2, e_3 >$, where e_1 represents the receipt (by *anATM*) of the message *checkIfCashAvailable*, e_2 represents the receipt of the message *dispenseCash* and e_3 represents the receipt of the message *ejectCard*.

Notation 2 *The* **set of all event occurrences denoting the receipt of a message** *for each instance o of a class c appearing in the sequence diagram Δ is denoted by* $\mathbf{E_{\Delta,c}}$.

Example 2. Let Δ and e_i be defined as in *Example 1.* Then $E_{\Delta,ATM} = \{e_1, e_2, e_3\}$

3.2 Statemachine

UML 2.0 differentiates between two kinds of state machines, *behavioural state machines* and *protocol state machines*. *Behavioural state machines* are used to specify the behaviour of various model elements. *Protocol state machines* are used to express usage protocols and are always defined in the context of a classifier, which can have several protocol state machines. These state machines express the legal transitions that a classifier can trigger. As such they are a convenient way to define a *lifecycle of an object* or an *order of the invocation of its operations.* Because in the context of behaviour inheritance consistencies, the order of invocation of operations is the most important, only protocol state machines are considered here.

A protocol transition specifies a legal transition for an operation. Transitions of protocol state machines have next to their trigger, which is an operation invocation, a pre- and a postcondition. We make some simplifying assumptions in this paper.[3]

A protocol state machine (PSM) can be defined as follows (based on the definition in [18] and in [19]) [4]:

Definition 4. *A* **protocol state machine** $\Pi_c = (S_c, T_c, L_c, \rho_c, \Lambda_c)$ *for a class c, consists of a set of states S_c and a labelled transition set $T_c \subseteq \mathcal{P}(S_c) \times L_c \times \mathcal{P}(S_c)$ containing labelled relations (S_1, l, S_2) such that l is a triple (op, g, h) where op is the operation, $g \subseteq Pre_{op,c}$ specifies the precondition of the transition (which is part of the precondition of the operation op), and $h \subseteq Post_{op,c}$ specifies the postcondition of the transition (which is part of the postcondition of the operation op). ρ_c denotes the initial state and Λ_c denotes the set of final states of the state machine.*

Example 3. The state machine specified in Figure 2 is a protocol state machine which has six states of which one is a concurrent state. This concurrent state is treated (as specified by the definition of a PSM) as a set of simple states. The concurrent state is entered in the set $\{GiveCash, PrintReceipt\}$, if *issueReceipt()* is called, the new state configuration is $\{GiveCash, ReturnReceipt\}$. This brings us to the next definition.

[3] UML provides special kinds of states and transitions, such as history states, stubbed transitions, junction and choice transitions. These concepts are not considered in this paper.

[4] Note that $\mathcal{P}(S)$ denotes the powerset of S.

The state of an object at a given point in time is defined by the set of states it occupies in the state machine. This set of states is referred to as the *life cycle state configuration* of the object.

Definition 5. *A* **life cycle state configuration** σ_o *of an instance o of a class c in a PSM* Π_c *is a subset of* S_c.

Definition 6. *A* **PSM trace** γ *of an instance o of a class c in a PSM* Π_c *is a sequence of life cycle state configurations* $< \sigma_1, \ldots, \sigma_n >$ *such that* $\sigma_1 = \{\rho_o\}$ *and, for* $i \in \{1 \ldots n-1\}$, $\sigma_{i+1} = \sigma_i$ *or* $\exists (\sigma_i, \tau_i, \sigma_{i+1}) \in T_c$.

Definition 7. *A* **call sequence** μ *of instance o of class c in a PSM* Π_c *is a sequence of labels* $< \tau_1, \ldots, \tau_n >$ $(n \geq 1)$, *where* $\tau_i \in L_c$.

Definition 8. *A* **call sequence** $\mu =< \tau_k, \ldots, \tau_n >$ **is valid** *on a state configuration* σ_k *of instance o, if there is a PSM trace* $\gamma =< \sigma_1 \ldots \sigma_k \ldots \sigma_{n+1} >$ *of o where for* $i \in \{k \ldots n\}$, $(\sigma_i, \tau_i, \sigma_{i+1}) \in T_c$.

Example 4. $< issueReceipt, ejectCard >$ is a valid call sequence on the state configuration $\{GiveCash, PrintReceipt\}$ of Figure 2.

4 Behaviour Inheritance Consistencies

The basic definitions given in the previous section enable the precise definition of behaviour inheritance consistencies in and between protocol state machines and sequence diagrams. It is expected that the behaviour specification of classes described by sequence diagrams and/or state machines is consistent with the behaviour specification of their superclasses. This kind of consistency is not defined in most object-oriented modeling languages and also not in UML 2.0.

In Ebert and Engels [5] two kinds of consistencies between state machines are defined, *observation* and *invocation* inheritance consistency.

Observation inheritance consistency means that *each sequence of calls which is observable with respect to a subclass must result (under projection of the methods known) in an observable sequence of its corresponding superclass. If a subclass reacts to the invocation of an operation op, where op is also known to the superclass, this reaction must also be reflected in the superclass behaviour specification.* Observation consistency can be defined between state machines, between sequence diagrams, and between a state machine and sequence diagrams.

In order to define this kind of consistency, we need some auxiliary definitions.

Definition 9. *The* **restriction** μ_L **of a sequence** $\mu =< \tau_1, ..., \tau_n >$ **to a set** *L is the sequence obtained from* μ *by removing all* $\tau_i \notin L$.

Definition 10. *Given a sequence diagram Δ and a PSM Π_c.*
The function **label$_c$** $: E_{\Delta,c} \rightarrow L_c : (m, cons) \rightarrow (op, g, h)$ *maps an event occurrence onto a label as follows:*

op is the operation corresponding to message m
g is a set of preconditions of op met by the set of constraints cons
h is a set of postconditions of op met by the set of constraints cons

Definition 11. Observation inheritance consistency. *Given a class c and a subclass c′ of c and instances o of c and o′ of c′.*

A PSM $\Pi_{c'} = (S', T', L', \rho', \Lambda')$ is observation consistent with a PSM $\Pi_c = (S, T, L, \rho, \Lambda)$ if, for every valid call sequence μ' of o', μ'_L is a valid call sequence of o.

A SD Δ' is observation consistent with a SD Δ with respect to c and c′ if, for every instance o′ of c′, if $\nu' = \nu_{o'}/^{rec}$ is an SD trace in Δ', then $\nu'_{E_{\Delta,c}}$ is an SD trace in Δ.

A SD Δ' is observation consistent with a PSM $\Pi_c = (S, T, L, \rho, \Lambda)$ with respect to c′ if, for every SD trace $\nu_{o'}/^{rec} = < e_1, \ldots, e_n >$ in Δ', there exists a valid call sequence $\mu_o =< \tau_1, \ldots, \tau_n >$, containing only labels τ_i for which $\tau_i = label_c(e_i)$

Remark that we do not define observation inheritance consistency between a PSM $\Pi_{c'}$ and an SD Δ with respect to the superclass c. Such a definition would imply that all possible scenarios are described by Δ, because every trace in the PSM $\Pi_{c'}$ must be observable in Δ under projection of the methods known. This demands completeness of the models which is not always the case, especially in early phases of the software development life cycle.

Example 5. Consider the protocol state machine $\Pi_{PrintingATM}$ of Figure 2, and the protocol state machine Π_{ATM} that is the same as $\Pi_{PrintingATM}$ except for the absence of substates *PrintReceipt* and *ReturnReceipt.* $\Pi_{PrintingATM}$ is observation consistent with Π_{ATM}. After hiding the message call {*issueReceipt*}, the behaviour of the subclass *PrintingATM* is identical to the behaviour of the superclass *ATM.*

Invocation inheritance consistency means that *any sequence of operations invocable on the superclass can also be invoked on the subclass.* This notion of behaviour inheritance consistency is based on the substitutability principle requiring that an object of subclass *B* of class *A* can be used where an object of class *A* is required.

Definition 12. Invocation inheritance consistency. *Given a class c and a subclass c′ of c and instances o of c and o′ of c′.*

A PSM $\Pi_{c'} = (S', T', L', \rho', \Lambda')$ is invocation consistent with a PSM $\Pi_c = (S, T, L, \rho, \Lambda)$ if every valid call sequence μ on $\{\rho\}$ in Π_c is also valid on $\{\rho'\}$ in $\Pi_{c'}$ and for their respective PSM traces γ and γ' it holds that $\gamma = \gamma'_S$.

A SD Δ' is invocation consistent with a SD Δ with respect to c and c′, if every SD trace $\nu_o/^{rec}$ in Δ is also a SD trace in Δ' for an instance o′ of class c′.

A PSM $\Pi_{c'} = (S', T', L', \rho', \Lambda')$ is invocation consistent with a SD Δ with respect to c if, for every SD trace $\nu_o/^{rec} =< e_1 \ \ldots \ e_n >$ in Δ, there exists a valid call sequence $\mu_{o'} =< \tau_1 \ldots \tau_n >$ such that, for each $i \in \{1 \ldots n\}$, $\tau_i = label_c(e_i)$.

Remark that, in this case, we do not define invocation consistency between a PSM Π_c and a sequence diagram Δ' with respect to a subclass c' of c. Such a definition implies completeness of the models involved.

Example 6. The behaviour of the sequence diagram Δ of Figure 1 is **not** invocation consistent with the PSM $\Pi_{PrintingATM}$ of Figure 2 with respect to class *ATM*. Indeed, the SD trace $< e_1, e_2, e_3 >$ of Example 1 does not correspond to a valid call sequence <*checkIfCashAvailable, dispenseCash, ejectCard*> in the PSM $\Pi_{PrintingATM}$, that always requires the message invocation *issueReceipt* between *dispenseCash* and *ejectCard*.

5 Behaviour Preservation

Model refactorings restructure a model while preserving its behavioural properties. On the source code level, refactorings of an object-oriented program are restructurings that preserve program behaviour. Despite the available tool support for source-code refactorings and also model refactorings, it is still an open research question how to define behaviour preserving properties for (model) refactorings. In [12], *call preservation* was defined for source code refactorings. This preservation property can be redefined for model refactorings as follows:

Definition 13. *A model refactoring is* **call preserving** *if each operation still invokes at least the same operations after the model refactoring as it did before the model refactoring.*

However, there are different variants of call preservation. Assume that we have a model M_1 and a refactored version M_2 of this model. The most restricted form of call preservation specifies that, if an operation m can invoke an operation n in M_1, the operation m can still invoke operation n in M_2, following exactly the same chain of messages as in M_1. A less restricted form of call preservation specifies that this message chain can be completely arbitrary in M_2, as long as n remains reachable from m. Another notion of call preservation we can define formally, is *observation call preservation.* In this case, every call sequence observable with respect to a class in M_2 must result in an observable call sequence of its corresponding class in M_1.

Definition 14. Observation call preservation. *Let c be a class, c' a refactored version of c and instances o of c and o' of c'.*

The behaviour specified by a PSM $\Pi_{c'} = (S', T', L', \rho', \Lambda')$ is observation call preserving with a PSM $\Pi_c = (S, T, L, \rho, \Lambda)$ if, for every valid call sequence μ' of o', μ'_L is a valid call sequence of o.

The behaviour specified by a SD Δ' is observation call preserving with a SD Δ with respect to c and c' if, for every instance o' of c', if $\nu' = \nu_{o'}/^{rec}$ is an SD trace in Δ', then $\nu'_{E_{\Delta,c}}$ is also an SD trace of Δ.

The behaviour specified by a SD Δ' is observation call preserving with a PSM $\Pi_c = (S, T, L, \rho, \Lambda)$ with respect to c' if, for every SD trace $\nu_{o'}/^{rec} = < e_1, \ldots, e_n >$ in Δ', there exists a valid call sequence $\mu_o =< \tau_1, \ldots, \tau_n >$, containing only labels τ_i for which $\tau_i = label_c(e_i)$.

Remark that Definition 14 is almost identical to Definition 11. The main difference is that the words *observation consistent* are replaced by *observation call preserving.* Also, c' does not represent a subclass of c anymore, but a new version of c in the refactored model.

Example 7. The behaviour specified by the refactored sequence diagram Δ' of Figure 3 is observation call preserving with the original sequence diagram Δ of Figure 1. The model refactoring presented here, abstracts existing behaviour into a new operation and as such, boils down to the addition of a message *validate* in Δ'. However, this does not affect the behaviour. All traces of the *ATM* class in Δ' are also traces in Δ if we exclude the message *validate.*

Another kind of call preservation, *invocation call preservation* guarantees that each call sequence invocable on the original version of a class, must also be invocable on the corresponding class in the refactored model. The definition of invocation call preserving is identical to Definition 12 by substituting *invocation call preserving* for *invocation consistency.*

Referring to Example 7 above, the behaviour specified by the refactored sequence diagram Δ' is *not* invocation call preserving with sequence diagram Δ. However, if we would ignore the message *validate* (because it can be considered as an auxiliary method that is of no interest to the user), the property would hold. This lead us to refine the two above notions of behaviour preservation into weaker, more specialised, variants, where the traces and call sequences can be restricted to a specific set of messages of interest to the user. As an example, we give the formal definition of *weak invocation call preservation* below:

Definition 15. Weak invocation call preservation. *Assume a class c, a refactored version c' of c and instances o of c and o' of c', and user-defined sets of labels $L_{user} \subseteq L'$ and $E_{user} \subseteq E_{\Delta',c'}$.*

A PSM $\Pi_{c'} = (S', T', L', \rho', \Lambda')$ is weak invocation call preserving with a PSM $\Pi_c = (S, T, L, \rho, \Lambda)$ if every valid call sequence μ on $\{\rho\}$ in Π_c is also valid on $\{\rho'\}$ in Π'' where $\Pi'' = (S', T'', L_{user}, \rho', \Lambda')$, where T'' is the restriction of transition relations of T' to the ones with only labels contained in L_{user}, and for their respective PSM traces γ and γ'' it holds that $\gamma = \gamma''_S$.

A SD Δ' is weak invocation call preserving with a SD Δ with respect to c and c', if every SD trace $\nu_o/^{rec}$ in Δ is also a SD trace in Δ' restrictred to E_{user} for an instance o' of class c'.

A PSM $\Pi_{c'} = (S', T', L', \rho', \Lambda')$ is weak invocation call preserving with a SD Δ with respect to c if, for every SD trace $\nu_o/^{rec} =< e_1, \ldots, e_n >$ in Δ, there exists a valid call sequence $\mu_{o'} =< \tau_1, \ldots, \tau_n >$ such that, for each $i \in \{1 \ldots n\}$, $\tau_i = label'_c(e_i)$, where $label'_c(e_i)$ is similar to $label_c(e_i)$, except that $label'_c(e_i)$ maps $E_{\Delta,c}$ on L_{user}.

Example 8. If the message *validate* is not considered in the sequence diagram Δ' in Figure 3, the sets $E_{\Delta,ATM}$, where Δ is the sequence diagram in Figure 1, and $E_{user} = \{< e_1, e_2, e_3 >\}$, where e_i is defined as in *Example 1*, are equal. This trivially implies invocation call preservation.

6 Tool Support

Consistency maintenance requires a decidable formalism to detect inconsistencies and also a generic framework to facilitate the addition, removal and modification of consistency specifications. In earlier work [22], we already proposed and used description logics (DL) [2] to detect and resolve inconsistencies; also the translation of the UML meta model and user defined models were described. A crucial property of DL is that it allows us to guarantee that the consistency rules that we can specify are *decidable.*

Given the similarity between the definitions for behaviour consistency and behaviour preservation, identified in the previous section, it is possible to use the same formalism in the context of checking the preservation of behavioural properties between a model and its refactored version.

To achieve this, we set up the following tool chain. UML design models are expressed in a UML CASE tool (Poseidon [9]) which exports UML models in XMI format. Using an XML parser (Saxon [17]), the models are translated into description logic statements. These are asserted into a knowledge base maintained by a description logic reasoning engine. We chose Racer [10] for this purpose as it is a state-of-the-art logic reasoning engine for DL.

To check behaviour inheritance consistency within a model and behaviour preservation between a model and its refactored version, rules are specified. These rules can be immediately translated into our logic framework using the query language of Racer (nRQL) [11]. For example, to check invocation consistency or preservation between the behaviour specified by a SD Δ with respect to a class c, and a PSM $\Pi_{c'} = (S', T', L', \rho', \Lambda')$ with c' subclass or refactored version of class c, the following rule (written in pseudo-code) needs to be checked:

consistent($\Pi_{c'}$, Δ, c) $\leftarrow$
  $query_1(events, c, \Delta)$,
  for each $e \in events$
    $query_2(e, op, startstate, target, \Pi_{c'})$
    if op = NIL then "consistency error at state" $startstate$

Consider, first of all, the $query_1$ that generates the SD traces for the sequence diagram Δ:

```
(retrieve (?events ?c ?seqinteraction)
 (and
  (?objectid ?c instance-of) ;retrieve the instances of class c
  (?objectid ?lifeline (inv represents));using the instance ?objectid the
                                         ;representing lifeline ?lifeline is retrieved
  (?seqinteraction ?lifeline ownedlifeline);only lifelines from the involved sequence diagram
  (?lifeline ?events eventoccurrences) ;the event occurrences ?events occurring on ?lifeline
  (?events (some receivemessage message)))) ;only receiving event occurrences
```

Using these events, the state machine $\Pi_{c'}$ is traversed. The next query $query_2$ checks if the operation belonging to the event $?e$ is also the operation referred to by the corresponding transition in the statemachine.

```
(retrieve (?e ?op ?startstate ?targetstate ?statemach)
  (and
   (?e ?msg receivemessage)    ;retrieve the ?msg related to event ?e
   (?msg ?op signature)        ;retrieve the invoked operation ?op
   (?transition ?op referred) ;?transition referring to ?op
   (?statemach ?transition owningtransitions) ;?transition owned by statemachine
   (?transition ?startstate source) ;?startstate must be the startstate of ?transition
   (?transition ?targetstate target))) ;the target state of the ?transitions
```

We applied the above mentioned rules to check the consistency of the sequence diagram in Figure 1 and the protocol state machine in Figure 2. Finally, we applied the rules to check observation and invocation consistencies and preservation, to the examples of Section 2. These experiments let us conclude that our framework for inconsistencies as presented in [22] is also suitable to check behaviour preservation for model refactorings.

7 Discussion and Related Work

Many notions of behaviour inheritance consistency can be found in literature. Compared to Schrefl *et al.* [19], our notions of behaviour inheritance consistency are more general, since they are defined independent of the kind of subtype relation between the superclasses and their subclasses. Engels *et al.* [5] define observable and invocation consistency using homomorphisms on state diagrams. Criteria for inheritance of object life cycles based on Petri nets are discussed in [19], [16] and [21]. Approaches based on CSP are discussed in [6] and [15]. CSP is used as a medium to check consistency, i.e., the UML model remains consistent if its CSP translation remains consistent. Moreover, CSP refinement relations are used to check and define several inheritance approaches and subtyping relations. In this approach, it is necessary to understand the effects that CSP refinement relations induce on UML models.

Research on model refactoring is less abundant. A set of basic UML refactorings is provided in [20] to improve the software design in a stepwise fashion. Boger *et al.* show how model refactorings can be integrated in the Poseidon UML refactoring browser [3]. Astels uses a UML tool to perform refactorings more easily, and also to aid in code smell detection [1]. Model refactorings are defined in [14] as a sequence of transformation rules. Surprisingly, none of the above approaches towards model refactoring takes behaviour preservation into account. One of the reasons is that there is no generally accepted behavioural interpretation of UML models. Therefore, we consider this as an important contribution of our paper.

The approach presented in our paper does not explicitly specify model refactorings as model transformations. In order to do this, the UML metamodel first needs to be extended with a model transformation language (e.g., based on the ideas of graph transformation [12]). We also need a formal means to prove that a transformation preserves precisely those behavioural properties that we want to reason about (e.g., observation and invocation call preservation). Using such a formalism, we can guarantee that the refactored model is still consistent, without needing to recheck all consistency rules. This is precisely the approach taken by [7] in the context of UML-RT. Transformation rules specify local modifications that preserve a local consistency property (e.g., absence of deadlocks) that can be checked locally. This enables an incremental approach to consistency checking.

The approach explained above also provides a promising alternative to traditional model checking approaches [4] that need to recheck the entire model whenever small and local changes have been made to a model.

8 Conclusion

In this paper, we have defined different kinds of behaviour inheritance consistencies between UML 2.0 state machines and sequence diagrams. We also have shown that those consistency specifications correspond to behaviour preservation properties between a UML model and its refactored version. Based on those consistency definitions, definitions of behaviour preservation are given. We also showed that our tool chain for detecting behavioural inconsistencies can be used to check the preservation of behaviour between different model versions.

We only carried out experiments on small examples, experiments on larger models must be done. As future work, we want to explore if other consistency specifications such as the ones defined in [22] correspond to the preservation of certain behavioural properties. We also need to extend our ideas to deal with consistency maintenance and behaviour preservation between different levels of abstraction. This will allow us to provide better formal support for the model-driven architecture process.

References

[1] D. Astels. Refactoring with UML. In *Proc. Int'l Conf. eXtreme Programming and Flexible Processes in Software Engineering*, pages 67–70, Alghero, Sardinia, Italy, 2002.

[2] F. Baader, D. McGuinness, D. Nardi, and P. Patel-Schneider. *The Description Logic Handbook: Theory, Implementation and Applications*. Cambridge University Press, 2003.

[3] M. Boger, T. Sturm, and P. Fragemann. Refactoring browser for UML. In *Proc. Int'l Conf. eXtreme Programming and Flexible Processes in Software Engineering*, pages 77–81, Alghero, Sardinia, Italy, 2002.

[4] E. M. Clarke, O. Grumberg, and D. A. Peled. *Model Checking*. MIT Press, 1999.

[5] J. Ebert and G. Engels. Specialization of object life cycle definitions. Fachbericht Informatik 19/95, Universität Koblenz-Landau, Fachbereich Informatik, Koblenz, 1995.

[6] G. Engels, J. Hausmann, R. Heckel, and S. Sauer. Testing the consistency of dynamic UML diagrams. In *Proc. Sixth Int'l Conf. Integrated Design and Process Technology (IDPT 2002)*, June 2002. Pasadena, CA, USA.

[7] G. Engels, R. Heckel, J. M. Küster, and L. Groenewegen. Consistency-preserving model evolution through transformations. In J.-M. Jézéquel, H. Hussmann, and S. Cook, editors, *UML 2002 - The Unified Modeling Language. Model Engineering, Languages, Concepts, and Tools. 5th International Conference, Dresden, Germany, September/October 2002, Proceedings*, volume 2460 of *LNCS*, pages 212–226. Springer, 2002.

[8] M. Fowler. *Refactoring: Improving the Design of Existing Programs.* Addison-Wesley, 1999.

[9] Gentleware. Poseidon, http://www.gentleware.com/products/poseidonpe.php3, March 18 2004.

[10] V. Haarslev and R. Möller. RACER system description. In *Int'l Joint Conf. Automated Reasoning (IJCAR 2001)*, 2001.

[11] V. Haarslev, R. Möller, R. Van Der Straeten, and M. Wessel. Extended query facilities for RACER and an application to software-engineering problems. In V. Haarslev and R. Möller, editors, *Proc. Int'l Workshop on Description Logic*, 2004.

[12] T. Mens, S. Demeyer, and D. Janssens. Formalising behaviour preserving program transformations. In *Proc. First Int'l Conf. Graph Transformation*, pages 286–301. Springer-Verlag, 2002.

[13] Object Management Group. Unified Modeling Language 2.0 Superstructure Draft Adopted Specification. ptc/03-08-02, February 2004.

[14] I. Porres. Model refactorings as rule-based update transformations. In P. Stevens, J. Whittle, and G. Booch, editors, *Proc. Int'l Conf. UML 2003*, volume 2863 of *LNCS*, pages 159–. Springer-Verlag, 2003.

[15] G. Rasch and H. Wehrheim. Checking consistency in UML diagrams: Classes and state machines. In *Formal Methods for Open Object-based Distributed Systems*, volume 2884 of *LNCS*, pages 229–243. Springer-Verlag, 2003.

[16] M. Schrefl and M. Stumptner. Behavior consistent specialization of object life cycles. *ACM Trans. Software Engineering and Methodology*, 11(1):92–148, January 2002.

[17] Sourceforge. Saxon, http://saxon.sourceforge.net/, March 18 2004.

[18] P. Stevens and J. Tenzer. Modelling recursive calls with UML state diagrams. In M. Pezzé, editor, *Proc. Fundamental Approaches to Software Engineering (FASE 2003)*, volume 2621 of *LNCS*, pages 135–149. Springer-Verlag, 2003.

[19] M. Stumptner and M. Schrefl. Behavior consistent inheritance in UML. In A. H. F. L. et al. editor, *Proc. 19th Int'l Conf. Conceptual Modeling (ER 2000)*, volume 1920 of *LNCS*, pages 527–542. Springer-Verlag, 2000.

[20] G. Sunyé, D. Pollet, Y. LeTraon, and J.-M. Jézéquel. Refactoring UML models. In *Proc. Int'l Conf. UML 2001*, volume 2185 of *LNCS*, pages 134–138. Springer-Verlag, 2001.

[21] W. van der Aalst. Inheritance of dynamic behaviour in UML. In D. Moldt, editor, *Proc. of the Second International Workshop on Modelling of Objects, Components and Agents (MOCA'02)*, pages 105–120, August 2002.

[22] R. Van Der Straeten, T. Mens, J. Simmonds, and V. Jonckers. Using description logic to maintain consistency between UML models. In P. Stevens, J. Whittle, and G. Booch, editors, *Proc. Int'l Conf. UML 2003*, volume 2863 of *LNCS*, pages 326–340. Springer-Verlag, 2003.

Determining the Structural Events That May Violate an Integrity Constraint

Jordi Cabot and Ernest Teniente

Universitat Politècnica de Catalunya
Dept. Llenguatges i Sistemes Informàtics
Jordi Girona 1-3, 08034 Barcelona (Catalonia)
[jcabot|teniente]@lsi.upc.es

Abstract. Any implementation of an information system must ensure that an operation is only applied if its execution does not lead to a violation of any of the integrity constraints defined in its conceptual schema. In this paper we propose a method to automatically determine the operations that may potentially violate an OCL integrity constraint in conceptual schemas defined in the UML. This is done by determining the structural events that may violate the constraint and checking whether those events appear in the operation specification. In this way, our method helps to improve efficiency of integrity checking since its results can be used to discard many irrelevant tests.

1. Introduction

A complete conceptual schema (CS) must include the definition of all relevant integrity constraints [6]. An integrity constraint states a condition that must be satisfied in each state of the information base (IB). Some constraints are inherent in the conceptual model in which the language is based but almost all constraints require an explicit definition [13, ch. 5]. Many constraints cannot be expressed using only the graphical constructs provided by the conceptual modeling language and require the use of a general-purpose (textual) sublanguage [4, ch.2]. In the UML this is usually done by means of invariants written in the OCL language [11].

The content of the IB changes due to the execution of the operations provided by the information system. Therefore, it must be guaranteed that the IB state resulting from these operations is consistent with regards to the set of integrity constraints specified over the CS. Moreover, if the application of an operation leads to an IB state where some integrity constraint is violated then the operation should be rejected and the contents of the IB should remain unchanged.

In general, the effect of an operation over the IB may be specified by means of a set of structural events (see for instance [8, 14]). A structural event is an elementary change in the population of an entity type (i.e. a class) or relationship type (i.e. an association) such as: create object, reclassify object, create link, etc. In particular, in the UML, structural events are a subset of the actions defined in the Actions Package [9, p.203+].

T. Baar et al. (Eds.): UML 2004, LNCS 3273, pp. 320-334, 2004.

We may assert that a given operation will not violate a certain integrity constraint if we know that none of its structural events may induce the violation of such constraint. In this context, our work is aimed at proposing a method that automatically determines the structural events that may violate a constraint.

Our approach allows detecting those constraints that are irrelevant to a given operation and thus must not be taken into account during the process of checking integrity constraints after the operation execution. Hence, we may substantially improve the efficiency of this process since only the constraints we know can actually be violated by the operation must be taken into account.

Roughly, the rationale of our method is to find out the set of potentially violating structural events (PSEs, from now on) for each constraint and then compare this set with the set of structural events included in the operation to see if the operation includes some of them, and thus, its execution can violate that constraint.

The knowledge provided by our method may also be useful in the area of schema validation. For instance, if after applying our method we realize that a particular constraint can never be violated (none of the operations affects it) we can think of removing the constraint.

To our knowledge, ours is the first proposal to address the problem of determining the exact set of PSEs for an integrity constraint in conceptual schemas defined in UML and OCL.

Previous work addressing similar problems can be found in the fields of deductive or relational databases. Therefore, an alternative approach to solve this problem could consist of translating the OCL constraints into logic or SQL (using [3], for instance) and then make use of the algorithms developed for those technologies to determine the set of PSEs of the constraint.

Unfortunately, algorithms for deductive databases are not powerful enough for dealing with the expressiveness of OCL since this language allows negation, recursion, bag semantics (also known as duplicate semantics) and aggregation operations (like *size* or *sum*) which are hardly handled by those algorithms (see [5] for a discussion of their limitations). On the other hand, algorithms for relational databases (like [2]) support the required OCL constructs but lack precision when determining the relevant PSEs that may violate a constraint. For this reason, we believe that using an ad-hoc method to reason directly about the OCL expression that defines the integrity constraint (like the one we propose in this paper) is the best solution to deal with this problem in conceptual models defined in UML.

Our work could be included in any architecture aimed at generating automatically the implementation of an information system from its specification like [7]. It is also helpful in the context of the MDA [10] when deriving platform specific models from a platform independent model.

The structure of the paper is as follows. The next section reviews structural events in the UML. Section 3 outlines how to obtain the simplified OCL expressions that our method will deal with. Section 4 presents our method to determine PSEs that may violate an integrity constraint. Finally, we present our conclusions and point out future work in Section 5.

2. Structural Events in the UML

The main goal of this paper is to determine the set of structural events that may (potentially) violate an integrity constraint defined over the conceptual schema by means of OCL. A structural event is an elementary change in the population of an entity type or a relationship type such as create object, reclassify object, create link, etc.

The precise number and meaning of structural events depends on the particular conceptual modeling language used. In UML, structural events are a subset of the actions defined in the Actions Package [9, p.203+]. Each action is a fundamental unit of behaviour specification. An action takes a set of inputs and converts them into a set of outputs. Structural events correspond to the actions that modify the contents of the IB. They are the only actions that, when applied, may cause the violation of a constraint.

In fact, we are only interested in base structural events. A structural event is base if its effect may not be specified by means of other (base) structural events. Intuitively, it is not difficult to see that determining whether a non-base structural event may violate an integrity constraint can be performed just by considering whether one of the events that define it may violate such constraint.

The base structural events that we find in the UML are the following (for more details about them see [9, p.203+]):

- *AddStructuralFeatureAction*: it adds values to a structural feature. It supports also the update of the current value of a structural feature by a new one. A structural feature may represent either an attribute or an association end.
- *CreateLinkAction*: it creates a new link of an association between a set of participants.
- *CreateLinkObjectAction*: it creates a new link when the association is an association class.
- *CreateObjectAction*: it creates a new object as an instance of a specified classifier.
- *DestroyLinkAction*: it destroys links and link objects
- *DestroyObjectAction*: it destroys an object.
- *ReclassifyObjectAction*: it replaces the current classifiers of an object by a new set of classifiers.
- *RemoveStructuralFeatureValueAction*: it removes a value from a structural feature.

We show in Figure 2.1 an example that will be used throughout the paper. It contains a conceptual schema that represents information about the departments of a company and their employees, which may be either freelance or not, and four integrity constraints specified in OCL. Those constraints ensure that each department has a worker older than 45 (constraint *OldEmployee*), that the department boss may not be a freelance (*NotBossFreelance)*, that two different employees may not have the same name (*UniqueName*), and that the assignment of each freelance must be between 5 and 30 hours (*ValidAssignment*).

We may be interested to specify also two different operations to update the contents of the previous conceptual schema. Since UML provides only a metamodel for structural events but no concrete syntax to define them, we have used in our examples the syntax proposed in [12]. Next to each concrete action we add the equivalent structural event of the UML.

ContractFreelance is aimed at contracting a new freelance for a given department. It creates a new instance for the classifier *Freelance*, initializes its values and relates it with the department passed as a parameter to the operation. On the other hand, *FireEmployee* fires an employee (either a normal employee or a freelance), deleting also its relationship with the department.

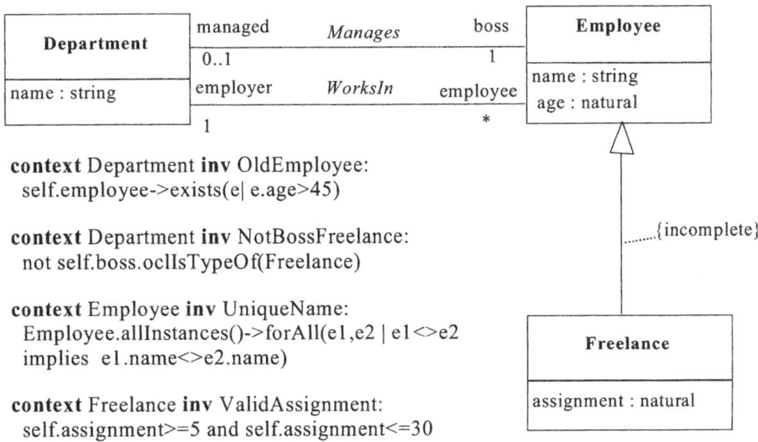


```
context System::ContractFreelance(name: string, age: natural, assig: natural, department: string)
  create object instance f of FREELANCE; -- CreateObjectAction
  f.name=name; --AddStructuralFeatureAction
  f.age=age; --AddStructuralFeatureAction
  f.assignment=assig; --AddStructuralFeatureAction
  select one d from instances of DEPARTMENT where selected.name=department;
  relate f with d across WORKSIN; -- CreateLinkAction

context System::FireEmployee(name:string)
  select one e from instances of EMPLOYEE where selected.name=name;
  select one d related by e->DEPARTMENT;
  unrelate e from d across WORKSIN; -- DestroyLinkAction
  delete object instance e; -- DestroyObjectAction
```

Figure 2.1 - Example of a conceptual schema

3. Simplifying OCL Expressions

Our method assumes a simplified representation of the OCL expression that defines an integrity constraint. Such a simplified representation may be automatically obtained from the original OCL expression and it does not entail a loss of expressive power on the constraints we may deal with.

First, we reduce the number of different operations that appear in an OCL expression by using some of the equivalences among operations already defined in the OCL Standard Libray [11, ch. 11]. Second, we simplify the structure of the OCL expressions by transforming them into conjunctive normal form. We provide in [1] the list of substitutions we perform to simplify the OCL expression and describe the rules to transform the expression into conjunctive normal form.

As a result of this transformation, each integrity constraint is a conjunction of disjunctions, where each OCL expression appearing in a disjunction is an expression that evaluates to a boolean type. Obviously, to satisfy the constraint the IB must satisfy each disjunction. A disjunction is satisfied if at least one of its literals is satisfied. The literal of a disjunction may be only a *forAll* iterator over an expression, an arithmetic comparison, an equality comparison between objects or sets, a boolean attribute, the not operator and the *oclIsTypeOf* and *oclIsKindOf* operators over an expression.

Applying the first step to our example, we get the following new expressions to define the constraints *OldEmployee* and *UniqueName* (the rest of constraints remain unchanged):

context *Department* ***inv*** *OldEmployee:*
self.employee->select(e| e.age>45)->size()>0

context *Employee* ***inv*** *UniqueName:*
Employee.allInstances()->forAll(e1,e2|not e1=e2 implies not e1.name=e2.name)

As a result of the second step, the expression defining *UniqueName* is converted to conjunctive normal form, resulting in:

context *Employee* ***inv*** *UniqueName:*
Employee.allInstances()->forAll(e1,e2 | e1=e2 or not e1.name=e2.name)

4. Our Method

A naïve approach to solve the problem of determining the structural events that may violate an OCL integrity constraint would conclude that any insertion, update or deletion over an entity or relationship type referenced within the OCL expression may violate the constraint since, obviously, any modification (insert/update/delete) of a model element not appearing in the expression may not cause its violation.

However, such naïve approach is not precise enough since it includes in the result events that will never violate the integrity constraint. In other words, the set of structural events provided by this naïve solution is a superset of the structural events that may actually violate the constraint. For instance, following this approach we would determine that nine base structural events may violate the constraint *OldEmployee*: insert / delete / update entity type Department, insert / delete / update relationship type WorksIn and insert / delete / update entity type Employee.

However, only four structural events may actually violate the constraint: insertion of Department, deletion and update of WorksIn and update of Employee. Intuitively, it is not difficult to see the other five events may never violate *OldEmployee*. So, the most precise solution contains just a 44% (4 of 9) of the events of the naïve one.

The goal of our method is to substantially improve the results obtained with the naïve solution by determining, at definition time, the exact set of base structural events that may actually violate an OCL integrity constraint. As we will see, our method will obtain in the previous example just the four structural events that may really violate the constraint.

We must note that the events we obtain may violate the constraint but this does not necessarily imply that the constraint is violated every time those events are executed (it depends on the exact parameters of the event at execution time). For this reason, we call the events obtained by our method *potentially violating structural events* (PSEs).

We consider that a state of the IB satisfies an integrity constraint *Ic* if *Ic* does not evaluate to false in that state. Then, we have that a base structural event is a PSE for a given constraint when such event can modify the state of the IB in a way that after the execution of the event the constraint evaluates to false. In a similar way, we assume that a *select* expression selects those elements that evaluate the select condition to true (but not when they evaluate to false nor undefined).

Our method assumes that the OCL expression that defines an integrity constraint is represented as an instance of the OCL metamodel [11, ch.8]. For this reason, we treat the OCL expression as a binary tree where each node represents an atomic subset of the OCL expression (an instance of any metaclass of the OCL metamodel: an operation, an access to an attribute or an association ...).

The left child of a node is the source of the node (the part of the OCL expression previous to the node). The right child of a node is the argument of the operation (i.e. the second argument, we can think of the left child, the source, as the first argument) if the node represents a binary operation (such as '>', *union*, '+',...) or the body [1] of the iterator if the node represents a loop expression (a forAll, select...).

We show in Figure 4.1 the constraint *OldEmployee* (*self.employee->select(e| e.age>45)->size()>0)* as an instance of the OCL metamodel.

The operator '>' (represented as an instance of the metaclass *OperationCallExp* having as a referred operation an operation called '>') is the root of the tree. The first child of the root is the source of the operator (*self.employee->select(e| e.age>45)->size()*) whereas the second child is the argument of the operation (the integer literal 0). The first child of the child node is an operation (*size*) with a single child (*select*). The *select* node has two children. The first one is its source, an access to an association end (*employee*) with a last child (the access to the variable *self*). The second one, its body, is the operation '>' between the attribute *age* (left child) and the integer *45* (right child).

Given the binary tree that represents the OCL constraint, our method performs two different steps to determine the base structural events that may violate it:

1. Marking the tree. It is needed to mark each node (i.e. each atomic subset of the OCL expression) with information about its context. This information allows us to discard the events that may not actually violate the constraint.

[1] The expression that is evaluated for each element in the collection.

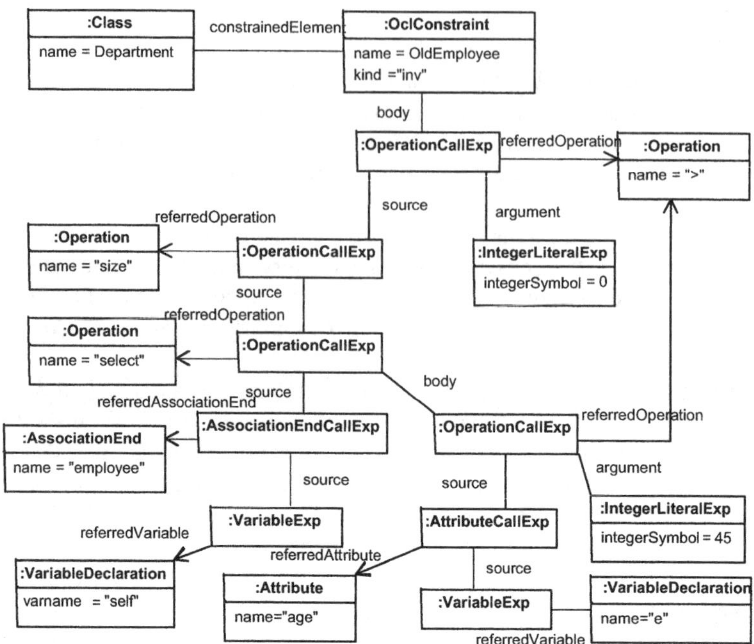

Figure 4.1 – Constraint *OldEmployee* as an instance of the OCL metamodel

2. Drawing base structural events. It determines the PSEs by taking the mark and the subexpression corresponding to each node into account.

This section is aimed at explaining these two steps in detail. We need first to introduce a set of internal events we use to determine the set of UML base structural events that may violate an integrity constraint.

We deal with a representative subset of possible OCL expressions. In particular, we cover the whole range of model element, boolean, collection and set operations and loop expressions. However, due to space limitations, we do not address expressions that contain operations over integers, reals or strings (except for the operation '+' chosen as a representant of this group of operations) nor specific operations for Bags, OrderedSets and Sequences.

We assume that taxonomies over relationship types are represented by converting both relationship types to a reified entity type (i.e. an association class) and then defining the taxonomies over them. We also assume that multivalued attributes are represented by means of a binary relationship between the entity type where the attribute is defined and the datatype of the attribute. In this way we do not need to provide a specific reasoning to deal with these two particular constructs since they are already dealt as taxonomies over entity types and as relationship types, respectively.

4.1 Internal Events

To determine the PSEs that may violate an OCL integrity constraint our method reasons about a set of internal events that do not correspond exactly to the base structural events of the UML. Nevertheless, the result of our method in terms of those internal events can be easily translated into the base structural events of the UML. The internal events we use are more basic and precise than those of UML. Besides this, their independence of a particular language allows us to incorporate our results to different sets of structural events providing that we define the correspondence between our internal events and those different sets.

The internal events we use are the following. We state in each case its correspondence with the base structural events of the UML.

- InsertET: insertion over an entity type *et*. It creates a new instance of *et*. The new object can have its attributes initialized but it does not participate in any relationship. It corresponds to a CreateObjectAction over the entity type, a CreateLinkObject (if *et* is an association class), any of them over a subtype of *et* (which induces an insertion over *et*) or by a reclassify action that adds the classifier *et* to an existing instance, plus several AddStructuralFeatureActions to initialize the attributes of the new object. An example is an insertion in the entity type *Employee*, which could be caused either by a CreationObjectAction over *Employee* or *Freelance*.
- UpdateAttribute: it updates the value of an attribute of an entity type *et*. It corresponds to an AddStrucuturalFeature for that attribute (possibly preceded by a RemovalStructuralFeatureAction) over an instance of *et* or any of its subtypes or supertypes. Example: a change in the salary of an employee.
- DeleteET: it deletes an instance of an entity type *et*. The corresponding actions are: a DestroyObjectAction over *et*, a DestroyLinkAction (if *et* is an association class), any of them over a supertype or subtype of *et* (both induce the deletion of the instance over *et*) or by a reclassify action that removes the classifier *et* from an existing instance. Example: the deletion of an employee.
- SpecializeET: it specializes an instance of a supertype of an entity type *et* to *et*. It is equivalent to a ReclassifyObjectAction with an empty set of old classifiers and only the entity type *et* in the set of new classifiers. Example: an employee becoming a freelance.
- GeneralizeET: it generalizes an instance of a subtype of an entity type *et* to *et*. It is equivalent to a ReclassifyObjectAction with an empty set of new classifiers and a direct subtype of *et* in the set of old classifiers. Example: an employee that finishes working as a freelance but remains as employee.
- InsertRT: creation of a new link in a relationship type *rt*. It can be produced by a CreateLinkAction or a CreateLinkObject (if *rt* is an association class) over *rt*. Example: the assignment of an employee to a department.
- UpdateParticipant: it updates one of the participants of a link of a relationshiptype *rt*. It corresponds to an AddStructuralFeature for the association end of that participant over a link of *rt*. Example: a change of the department boss.

- DeleteRT: it deletes a link of a relationship type *rt*. The equivalent action is a DestroyLinkAction over *rt*. Example: to remove an employee from a department.

4.2 Marking the Tree

To compute the set PSEs it is not enough to examine each part of the OCL expression separately. For instance, to determine whether constraint *OldEmployee* may be violated either by an employee assignment or by an employee dismission we may not take into account just the subexpression *self.employee->select(...)->size()*. In fact, both events may change the resulting value of evaluating this subexpression. However, since after the *size* operation we find the '>' operator, only firing an employee may induce the violation of this constraint. On the contrary, if we had used '<=' instead, the expression could be violated by employee assignments.

Each node of the binary tree that represents the OCL expression is marked to indicate which information of the node must be propagated to its children. There are four different symbols to propagate:

- '+': it indicates that the constraint can be violated by an increase in the value or in the number of items of the expression
- '-': it indicates that the constraint can be violated by a decrease in the value or in the number of items of the expression
- '**u**': it indicates that the constraint can be violated by a change in the value or in the items of the expression
- '**und**': it indicates the node does not propagate any kind of information

As an example of the first two symbols consider the operation '>'. A node representing a call to this operation propagates the symbol '-' to the left child (i.e. the first argument) and the symbol '+' to the right child (the second argument). The semantics of this operation justifies this propagation. To violate an expression like *'A > B'* there are two options: decrease the value of *A* (this is why we propagate the symbol '-' to the left) or increase the value of *B* (this explains the '+').

The symbol 'u' is used, for instance, when accessing an attribute. A reference to an attribute can be violated due to an update of the value of the attribute. The same happens with the *select* iterator. The result of a *select* can differ not only because an insertion or deletion on the collection where we apply the *select*. It can also change if we replace any of the objects of the collection (maybe the old object was not selected for the *select* expression but the new one is or vice versa). As an example, imagine that we replace the employee *e1* by the employee *e2* in the department *d1*. The number of employees of *d1* remains constant but if *e1* was the only employee older than 45 years old and *e2* is younger than that age, constraint *OldEmployee* will be violated since no employee will be returned by the select expression.

Finally, the symbol 'und' is used by operations like *'and'* or *'or'*. It denotes that the node does not influence its children expressions at all. The events that can violate *'A and B'* are the same that violate *A* plus those of *B* stand-alone.

To mark the nodes of the tree we traverse the tree in preorder. In a preorder traversal we process all nodes of the tree by first processing the root and then, recursively, processing in preorder the children subtrees. In each node, we take into account the kind of node and the information received from its parent node to decide which information propagates the node to its children.

Table 4.1 shows the symbol propagation for each kind of node and symbol. Sometimes we propagate more than one symbol. In such a case, the final value is obtained by applying the table information to each received symbol. When a cell contains *n/a* (not applicable) it means no constraint exists that includes such combination. When a node has two children the cell states the symbol (or symbols) for each child.

Table 4.1 - Marking the binary OCL tree

	1. and,or	2. >=,>	3. <,<=	4. =	5. not	6.oclIsType	7. attribute	8. forAll	9.assEnd, assClass[2]
1. und	und und	- +	+ -	+-u +-u	und	+u	+u	+u und	n/a
2. +	n/a	n/a	n/a	n/a	n/a	n/a	+u	n/a	+
3. -	n/a	n/a	n/a	n/a	n/a	n/a	+u	n/a	-
4. u	n/a	n/a	n/a	n/a	n/a	n/a	u	n/a	u

	10. select	11. size	12. sum	13. collect	14 U,∩ count	15. - (set)	16. allInstances	17.var or ct[3]	18. + (Integers)
1. und	n/a	n/a	n/a	n/a	n/a	n/a	n/a	n/a	n/a
2. +	+u und	+	+u	+ +	+ u +u	+u -u	und	und	+-[4] +-
3. -	-u und	-	-u	- -	-u -u	-u +u	und	und	+- +-
4. u	u und	n/a	n/a	u u	u u	u u	und	und	u u

We show in Figure 4.2 the result of marking the binary tree that represents the constraint *OldEmployee* (a simplified version of the tree of Figure 4.1). Next to each node we add information about the cell (or cells) used to process that node. *CX.Y* means that we access the cell at row *X* and column *Y*.

We start with the operation '>'. Since it is the root of the tree it does not receive any initial information. To mark its children we use the cell 1.2 (row 1, column 2) which states that the left child must be marked '-' while the right must be '+'. The *size* operation receives the symbol '-'. Thus, cell 3.11, we propagate the '-' to its child (the *select*). The *select* sends (cell 3.10) the symbols *–u* to its source (*employee*) and *und* to its body. *Employee*, in its turn, propagates *–u* (column 9 rows 3 and 4) to the variable self. The rest of the tree is marked in a similar way.

4.3 Drawing Base Structural Events

Once the tree is marked as explained in the previous section, we may determine the PSEs that may violate the integrity constraint. They are computed as the set of PSEs for the root of the constraint plus, recursively, the set of PSEs for each child node of

---

[2] A navigation through an association end or an association class.

[3] Node that represents any variable or constant (literal) appearing in the constraint.

[4] If we add natural values we only need to propagate the symbols '+' on row 2 and '–' on row 3. However, when adding integers, since they can be negative, we propagate both symbols.

the root. Hence, we need now to traverse the tree in postorder which implies to process all nodes of the tree by first recursively processing in postorder the children subtrees and then the root.

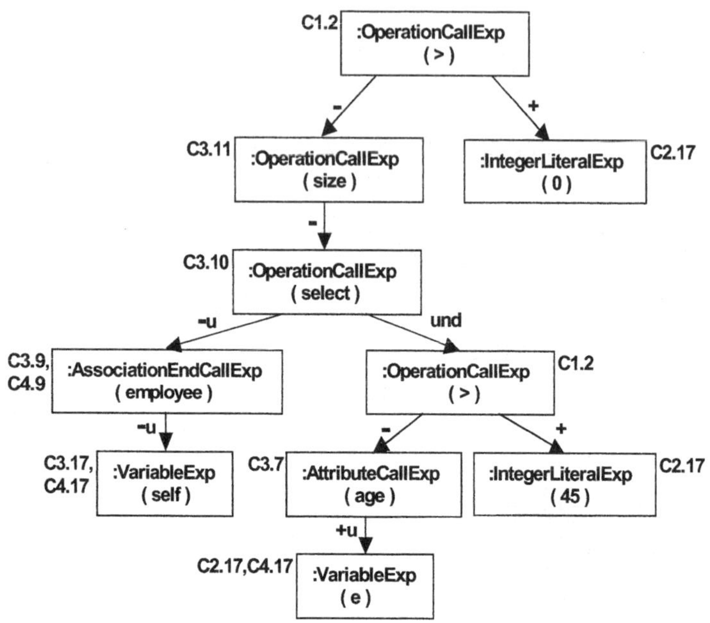

Figure 4.2 - Marking the constraint *OldEmployee*

Table 4.2 describes the set of PSEs we determine for each node in terms of the node type and its mark. Notation: *s(c1)* indicates that the set of PSEs for that node is the sum of the PSEs for its child, and so *s(c1,c2)* when the node has two children. *s(c1)* + *X* denotes that the node adds the event *X* to the set of PSEs of that node. Blank cells indicate the node does not affect the computation of the PSEs. In addition, to make the table clearer, we use shorthands to indicate the internal events: iET (insertET), uAt (updateAttribute), dET (deleteET), iRT (insertRT), uPa (updateParticipant), dRT (deleteRT), speET (specializeET), genET (generalizeET).

Of particular interest is the function *opp(X)*. This function is used to denote that the set of PSEs for a node is the opposite of the set of PSEs returned by its children. This is the case of nodes representing the *not* operator. The set of PSE for a *not* operator over an expression is defined as just the opposite of the set of PSEs for the expression stand-alone.

A similar thing happens with a *select* expression. An event that can violate the body of a *select* may decrease the number of elements returned by the *select* expression. Therefore, when we need to obtain the set of PSEs that increase the number of selected elements we apply the opposite function to the set of PSEs of the *select* body. The opposite of an insertion is a deletion and vice versa. The opposite of an update event is the event itself. Therefore, the opposites for each event are:

opp(iET)=dET, opp(uAt)=uAt, opp(dET)=iET, opp(iRT)=dRT, opp(dRT)=iRT, opp(uPa)=uPa.

Table 4.2 - Determining the set of PSEs

	1. and,or	2. >=,>	3. <,<=	4. =	5. not	6.oclIs Type	7. attribute[5]	8. forAll	9.assEnd , assClass
1.und	s(c1,c2)	s(c1,c2)	s(c1,c2)	s(c1,c2)	opp(c1)	s(c1)+ genET	s(c1)+ uAt	s(c1,c2)	n/a
2. +	n/a	n/a	n/a	n/a	n/a	n/a	s(c1)+ uAt	n/a	s(c1)+iRT[6]
3.-	n/a	n/a	n/a	n/a	n/a	n/a	s(c1)+ uAt	n/a	s(c1)+dRT[7]
4.u	n/a	n/a	n/a	n/a	n/a	n/a	s(c1)+ uAt	n/a	s(c1)+uPa

	10. select	11. size	12. sum	13. collect	14. U,∩ count	15. - (Set)	16. allIn stances	17.var or ct	18. +
1. und	n/a	n/a	n/a	n/a	n/a	n/a	n/a	n/a	n/a
2. +	s(c1, opp(c2))	s(c1)	s(c1)	s(c1,c2)	s(c1,a1)	s(c1,c2)	iET		s(c1,c2)
3.-	s(c1,c2)	s(c1)	s(c1)	s(c1,c2)	s(c2,a1)	s(c1,c2)	dET		s(c1,c2)
4. u		n/a	n/a						

As an example, we discuss the possible options when the node represents a reference to an association end involved in a navigation of the OCL expression (column 9 of Table 4.2). When the association end is labeled with a '+' the constraint may be violated by an insertion over the association (event insertRT) where the association end belongs. Remember that '+' pointed out that the constraint can be violated due to an increase of the number elements obtained through a navigation over the association using that association end, and thus, the events that can cause the violation are those events that increase such number. That is precisely what the event insertRT does.

In a similar way, if it is labeled with a '-', the critical event is the deletion of a link of the association (event deleteRT) since we are interested in reducing the number of links of the association. Finally, if it is labeled with the symbol 'u' the problematic event is the replacement of a participant in that association end (updateParticipant) even if the total number of elements does not vary.

Figure 4.3 applies table 4.2 to our example. Since the traversal is in postorder we start by processing the leaves of the tree. First, we process the access to the variable self, already marked with the symbols '-' and 'u'. We must then consider column 17 rows 3 and 4 of Table 4.2 which states that this subexpression does not produce any PSE. After this step, we consider the association end (*employee)* using row 3 and 4 of column 9 to initialize the set of PSE with the events insertET(*Department*, in this case), deleteRT(*WorksIn*) and updateParticipant (association end *WorksIn-Employee*). Next, we process the second child of the *select* expression (its body, e.*age>45*), which produces the event updateAttribute (attribute *age* of entity type *Employee*). After that, we analyse the *select* itself adding the events generated by its two children. The execution will continue with the process of the *size* operation (no additional

[5] When the attribute is preceded by *self* the event iET is added to the set of PSEs.

[6] If the association end is referenced inside the body of a select expression, the event dET is added to the set of PSEs.

[7] When *self* precedes the the association end the event iET is added to set of PSEs.

events) and the integer constant 0, to end up with the root of the tree, the operation '>' that returns the final set of PSEs for the whole expression.

At the end of this process, we have that the constraint *OldEmployee* may be violated by the internal events: updateAtribute(*age*), updateParticipant(*WorksIn-Employee*), deleteRT(*WorksIn*) or insertET(*Department*). Note that a deleteET over *Employee* does not violate the constraint. It is the deletion of the link between the employee and the department (deletion that can be a preliminary before deleting the employee itself), which may violate it.

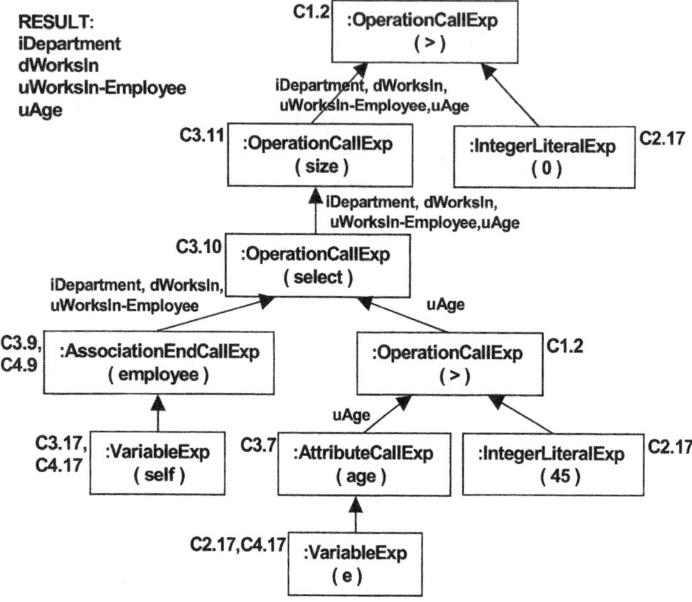

Figure 4.3 - Computing PSEs for *OldEmployee*

4.4 Applying the Method

After computing the set of PSEs for each constraint we compare its set of events with the events that appear in the operation specification to see which is the exact set of constraints each operation may violate.

There is only one step missing. The set of PSEs is described using our internal events while the system operation is specified using the set of external events provided by the specific conceptual modelling language used, UML in this case. Therefore, before doing the comparison, we transform the set of PSE into the set of corresponding external events using the rules described in section 4.1

As an example, we apply the method to the whole CS of figure 2.1, obtaining the following results:

1. Set of PSE for each constraint:
   a. *OldEmployee*: updateAtribute(*Age*), updateParticipant(*WorksIn-Employee*), deleteRT(*WorksIn*), insertET(*Department*)
   b. *NotBossFreelance*: specializeET(*Freelance*), insertRT(*Manages*), updateParticipant(*Manages-Boss*).
   c. *UniqueName*: insertET(*Employee*), updateAttribute(*Name-Employee*)
   d. *ValidAssignment*: insertET(*Freelance*), updateAttribute(*Assignment*).
2. Once transformed into the structural events of the UML, the set of events is:
   a. *OldEmployee*: AddStructuralFeature over the attribute *age*, and AddStructuralFeature over the association end *Employee*, a DestroyLinkAction over the association *WorksIn* and a CreateObjectAction over *Department*.
   b. *NotBossFreelance*: ReclassifyObjectAction adding the classifier *Freelance* to a non-freelance *Employee*, CreteLinkAction over *Manages* and an AddStructuralFeature over the associationEnd *boss*.
   c. *UniqueName*: CreateObjectAction over *Employee*, CreateObjectAction over *Freelance* and AddStructuralFeatureAction over the attribute *name*.
   d. *ValidAssignment*: CreateObjectAction over *Freelance* and AddStructuralFeatureAction over the attribute *assignment*.
3. Finally, with this information we can determine which constraints may be violated by each operation
   a. *ContractFreelance* may only violate *ValidAssignment* and *UniqueName* but not the other two constraints.
   b. *FireEmployee* may only violate *OldEmployee*

We would like to remark that with our method we provide an important efficiency improvement to integrity checking. As seen in the previous example, instead of checking all four constraints after the execution of each operation, we have that after *ContractFreelance* we only have to check two of them and just one after *FireEmployee*.

5. Conclusions and Further Work

We have proposed a new method to determine whether the execution of a given operation may potentially violate an integrity constraint. This is done by determining the structural events that may violate the constraint and comparing them with those events that appear in the operation specification.

The main contribution of our work is the use of this knowledge to check only those constraints that can actually be violated by the execution of an operation. We think this is an important contribution since all existing strategies that pursue an automatic code generation of the information systems from their specification can benefit from this knowledge (since they do not have to consider all constraints but just the relevant ones after each operation execution) to provide more efficient implementations.

Checking integrity constraints efficiently requires at least solving two different problems. The first one is the one we have addressed in this paper. The second one is to provide efficient (incremental) algorithms to check an integrity constraint when we know it can be violated by the execution of an operation. This is a direction in which we plan to continue our work.

Acknowledgements

We would like to thank people of the GMC group for their many useful comments to previous drafts of this paper. This work has been partially supported by the Ministerio de Ciencia y Tecnologia and FEDER under project TIC2002-00744.

References

[1] J. Cabot, E. Teniente, "Determining the structural events that may violate an integrity constraint", LSI Research Report, LSI-04-41-R, 2004

[2] S. Ceri, J. Widom, "Deriving Production Rules for Constraint Maintenance" , Proc. of the 16th VLDB Conference (VLDB'90), Morgan Kauffman, 1990, pp.566-577.

[3] B. Demuth, H. Hussmann, S. Loecher, "OCL as a Specification Language for Business Rules in Database Applications", Proc..of the 4th UML Conference (UML'01), LNCS 2185, Springer, pp. 104-117.

[4] D.W.Embley, B.D. Kurtz, S.N. Woodfield, "Object-Oriented Systems Analysis. A Model-Driven Approach", Yourdon Press, 302 p.

[5] A. Gupta, I.S. Mumick, "Maintenance of Materialized Views: Problems, Techniques and Applications", IEEE Data Engineering Bulletin, Volume 18, Number 2, June 1995, pp. 3-18

[6] ISO/TC97/SC5/WG3, "Concepts and Terminology for the Conceptual Schema and Information Base", J.J. van Griethuysen (ed.), March.

[7] S.J. Mellor, "Executable UML: A Foundation for Model Driven Architecture", Addison-Wesley, 2002

[8] A. Olivé. "Time and Change in Conceptual Modeling of Information Systems". In Brinkkemper, S.; Lindencrona, E.; Solvberg, A. "Information Systems Engineering. State of the Art and Research Themes", Springer, 2000, pp. 289-304.

[9] OMG, "UML 2.0 Superstructure Specification", OMG Adopted Specification.

[10] OMG."MDA Guide Versión 1.0.1", http://www.omg.org/docs/omg/03-06-01.pdf

[11] OMG, "UML 2.0 OCL", http://www.omg.org/docs/ptc/03-10-14.pdf, OMG Adopted Specification

[12] Project Technology, Object Action Language Manual, http://www.projtech.com/pdfs/bp/oal.pdf, visited March 2004.

[13] B. Thalheim, "Entity-Relationship Modeling", Foundations of Database Technology, Springer, 627 p.

[14] R. Wieringa, "A survey of structured and object-oriented software specification methods and techniques". ACM Computing Surveys, 30(4), 1998, pp. 459-527.

Deductive Verification of UML Models in TLPVS*

Tamarah Arons[1], Jozef Hooman[2,3], Hillel Kugler[1], Amir Pnueli[1], and Mark van der Zwaag[2]

[1] The John von Neumann Minerva Center for Verification of Reactive Systems, Weizmann Institute of Science, Rehovot, Israel
{tamarah.arons, hillel.kugler, amir.pnueli}@weizmann.ac.il
[2] Department of Computer Science, University of Nijmegen, The Netherlands
[3] Embedded Systems Institute, Eindhoven, The Netherlands
{hooman, mbz}@cs.kun.nl

Abstract. In recent years, UML has been applied to the development of reactive safety-critical systems, in which the quality of the developed software is a key factor. In this paper we present an approach for the deductive verification of such systems using the PVS interactive theorem prover. Using a PVS specification of a UML kernel language semantics, we generate a formal representation of the UML model. This representation is then verified using TLPVS, our PVS-based implementation of linear temporal logic and some of its proof rules. We apply our method by verifying two examples, demonstrating the feasibility of our approach on models with unbounded event queues, object creation, and variables of unbounded domain. We define a notion of fairness for UML systems, allowing us to verify both safety and liveness properties.

Keywords: Formal Verification, Deductive Verification, PVS, UML, State Machines, Semantics, Temporal Logic

1 Introduction

The Unified Modeling Language (UML) [26] is a flexible, general purpose modeling language that is widely used in a variety of domains. In recent years UML has been applied to the development of reactive safety-critical systems, in which the quality of the developed software is a key factor. In these domains, an executable model and the ability to generate production code from the model is an important advantage [21, 5]. This approach is supported by existing commercial case tools [8, 19, 23], which facilitate the generation of code from a subset of the UML diagrams (typically class diagrams and state machine diagrams) combined with a high level object oriented language or action language.

In this paper we present a methodology and tool-set that allow us to verify that various properties hold on a UML model. We take a formal verification

* This work has been supported by EU-project IST 33522 OMEGA [17], and by the John von Neumann Minerva Center for Verification of Reactive Systems.

T. Baar et al. (Eds.): UML 2004, LNCS 3273, pp. 335–349, 2004.

approach which enables us to derive a mathematical proof of correctness; in contrast, testing and other validation methods can raise the confidence in the developed system and help in finding bugs, but cannot guarantee correctness.

The two prevalent methods for formal verification are *model checking* and *deductive verification*. There are obvious advantages to the model-checking techniques, the most important being that it is fully automatic and requires no strong familiarity with the internal details of the design. A very serious limitation of model-checking techniques is the limited size of designs which can be fully automatically verified.

The alternative approach based on deductive verification does not suffer from such limitations and, in principle, can be used to verify very big designs provided their structure is based on regular patterns. The main drawback of the deductive approach to reactive system verification (as outlined, for example, in [12]) is that it is not fully automatic and requires much user ingenuity and supervision.

For this reason, we developed TLPVS [16], a system for the formal verification of linear temporal logic (LTL) properties built on the PVS [14] verification system. The system provides support for a number of proof rules. Special attention has been paid to the verification of systems with an unbounded number of processes, and our rules are robust for such systems. This means that TLPVS can be used in systems with dynamic object creation.

Like other formal verification systems, TLPVS depends on a notion of *fairness* for the verification of liveness properties. Intuitively, fairness is a means of restricting to the set of "reasonable" runs. To the best of our knowledge, no formulation of fairness requirements appears in the UML literature. In this paper we propose a definition, and illustrate its use.

The UML diagrams that we consider in this work are class diagrams and state machine diagrams. This choice is motivated by the fact that these are the diagrams that are considered to form the executable kernel in most approaches and advanced tools. At this stage of our work we avoided adding additional diagrams that may show a different behavioral view of the same aspects and may require us to address issues of consistency, even before addressing the challenges of formal verification which are complex enough in their own right.

The UML standard leaves certain semantic issues open and these are implemented differently in various tools and approaches. In order to perform formal verification a precise semantic definition must be taken, our semantic decisions follow [2, 7]. Our deductive verification methodology is, however, more general, and can also support semantic decisions other than the ones we took.

The executable kernel subset of the UML mentioned above supports complex features, and our approach treats some of the features that are most difficult for verification: dynamic object creation, active and passive objects, unbounded event queues, synchronous and asynchronous communication and unbounded domain variables. While working to develop a practical formal verification methodology we applied and tested this methodology on two examples, each of which illustrates different features. Eratosthenes' sieve (PRIME-SIEVE) provided an example of dynamic object creation, while a model based on a medium altitude reconnaissance system (MARS) included method calls, and allowed us to check how the methodology scales up in larger systems.

The structure of this paper is as follows. In Sect. 2 and 3 we outline the language and semantics we used, and detail the MARS example. Section 4 overviews TLPVS, and in Sect. 5 we demonstrate its application to the MARS example. Section 6 introduces the PRIME-SIEVE example. In Sect. 7 we give our fairness requirements, and show how they can be used to verify response properties in PRIME-SIEVE. In Sect. 8 we discuss related work and draw conclusions. The PVS files are available at [24].

2 Kernel Language

In this section we use a fragment of the so-called Medium Altitude Reconnaissance System (MARS) to introduce our kernel language. This example is part of a case study provided by the Dutch Aerospace Laboratory (NLR). The system controls the movement of a camera in an airplane; ground survey photographs are taken by the camera during the flight. The position and movement of the camera have to be adjusted to the altitude and speed of the plane.

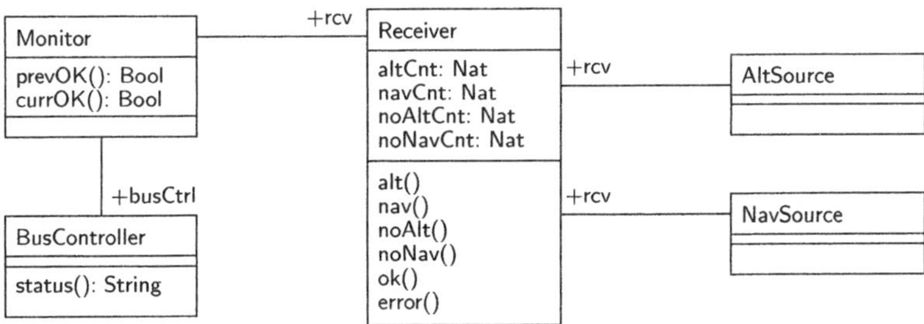

Fig. 1. Example class diagram

Here we present a part of the bus manager of the system; the class diagram is given in Fig. 1. For our purposes it suffices to know there is altitude data (*alt* messages), and there is navigation data (*nav* messages). In case a data source fails to send data, a time-out is issued. Since we did not model time explicitly for this example, we model these time-outs by failure signals (*noAlt*, *noNav*). The central object in the example is a receiver which processes the incoming data. The system further consists of a controller monitor and a bus controller which we do not present in detail here. The monitor can ask the bus controller for a status report by calling a method of the bus controller. In case of an error the monitor will send the *error* signal to the receiver in reaction to which the receiver enters the controller error location. The monitor sends the receiver the *ok* signal if the bus controller indicates that the error situation is resolved. The task that we concentrate on is the detecting of, and response to, failure of the data sources.

For each class the behavior of its objects is defined by means of a state machine and methods (program text) for its so-called *primitive operations*. Other operations are defined by means of the state machine. A state machine transition is labelled with a trigger event, a guard, and a list of actions (and each of these parts may be empty). A trigger event is either an operation call or a signal. The guard is a boolean expression which can be evaluated locally by the object without side-effects. The action part of a transition is a list of basic actions. We consider the following five basic actions: assign a value or reference to an attribute, create an object and assign a reference to it to an attribute, send a signal to a particular object, call an operation of a particular object and assign a result value to an attribute, return from a call.

Fig. 2. State machines for the altitude data source (left) and the navigation data source (right)

Both of the data sources (Fig. 2) have the repetitive nondeterministic choice between sending a data message or a failure message. For example, the action *rcv!alt* is the emission of an *alt* signal to the receiver.

The receiver (Fig. 3) can accept some failure from the data sources, but if either source fails to send data for three consecutive times, it enters an error state. The receiver recovers from the error state if it receives correct data for at least two consecutive times. Counters (with initial value 0) are used to count consecutively accepted signals of one kind. If the receiver is operational then it counts the number of consecutive failure messages it has accepted from each data source. If either of these failure counters has value 3, the receiver enters the bus error location (since it must *run to completion* before accepting a new signal, see Sect. 3). In the bus error location, positive acceptances of the data messages are counted.

3 Transition Systems

Intuitively, multiple objects each execute their own state machine concurrently. By interleaving and synchronizing the state machine transitions of the objects in the system we obtain a global transition system representing the system behavior on which we can express properties in temporal logic. Each step of this global transition system corresponds to either the execution of an action by one of the objects in the system, or to the triggering of a state machine transition for one of the objects. In the latter case we distinguish between transitions without

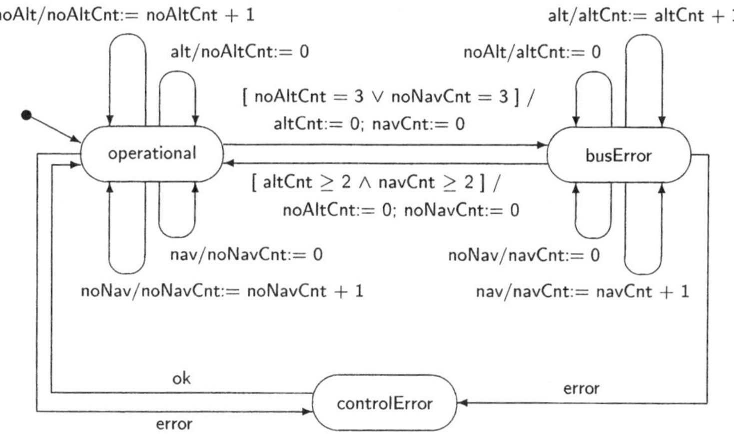

Fig. 3. Receiver state machine for the MARS example

a trigger (which are enabled if their guard is satisfied), and signal-triggered transitions. The triggering of a transition with an operation call as trigger is combined with the execution of the transition with the call action into one step of the system. (Note that if the action part of the callee also contains an operation call, this would lead to a cascading sequence of synchronizations. Since this greatly complicates the semantics, we currently do not support an operation call in the action part of a transition with a call trigger.)

The interleaving is restricted by the *run-to-completion* assumption (standard in UML 2.0 [26], see also [21]): when an object has been triggered by a call or a signal, it must become *stable* before it can accept a new event. An object is stable if, in its current location, it has no outgoing triggerless transitions for which the guard is satisfied; a stable object can only proceed by accepting an event. Thus transitions without a trigger have precedence over triggered transitions.

Concurrency can also be restricted by the sharing of control: only an object that has *control* is allowed to execute. To achieve this, the set of objects is partitioned into *activity groups* which are centered around active objects: a class can be active or passive, and this leads to active or passive objects. Control is shared within activity groups. During execution the control within a group may shift from one object to another. Control changes when performing a call inside the same group, otherwise an object may only lose control if it is stable. [4]

Operations are synchronous: a caller is suspended (blocked) until the callee executes the return. Signals are sent asynchronously: the sender may continue

[4] This notion of activity groups is comparable to that of *threads of control*; an active object corresponds to a thread of control and at most one thread is active in each object. To avoid confusion with, e.g., Java-like threads, we decided to avoid the term "thread" and use "activity group" instead.

immediately and the signal is put in a signal queue at the receiver side. Signals are selected from the queue in order of arrival.

The definition of the semantics in PVS is parametrized by the particular types that are to be instantiated by the model that we wish to verify: given that a model provides the names used for classes, attributes, locations, etc., and the set of state machine transitions, this theory defines a labelled transition system which is used as input to the verification in TLPVS as explained below in Sect. 4.

For more details of our semantics see [7], which also explains how we model features like inheritance, real-time, and primitive operations, that do not play a role in the examples presented in this paper.

4 A Brief Overview of TLPVS

To reduce the enormous manual effort required to complete deductive proofs, we developed TLPVS, a system which embeds temporal logic and its deductive framework within an existing powerful general-purpose high-order theorem prover, PVS [14]. This system includes a formal PVS specification of the LTL temporal logic based on [12] and a framework for defining systems.

A number of rules for proving safety and response properties are included in the system, each one accompanied by a strategy supporting its use. These rules and strategies greatly reduce the routine theorem proving interaction. All proof rules used are defined and proved correct within TLPVS. Using them we eliminate the pen-and-paper application of "known" rules typical in many proofs, and the validity of our final proof rests solely on the correctness of PVS.

4.1 Parameterized Fair Systems

The computational model of *parameterized fair systems* [16] is used for defining systems in TLPVS. This is a variation of the *fair discrete systems* of [9] which, in turn, are derived from the model of *fair transition systems* [12].

A *parameterized fair system* (PFS) is a tuple $S = \langle V, \Theta, \rho, \mathcal{F}, \mathcal{J}, \mathcal{C} \rangle$, where

- V is a finite set of typed *system variables.* We define a *state* to be a type-consistent interpretation of V. A *(state) predicate* is a function which maps states to truth values. A *bi-predicate* defines a binary relation over states.
- Θ is a predicate characterizing the initial states called the *initial condition.*
- $\rho(V, V')$ is a bi-predicate relating a state to its successors called the *transition relation.*
- $\mathcal{F}$ is a non-empty *fairness domain* which is used to parameterize the fairness requirements of justice and compassion.
- $\mathcal{J}$ is a *justice (weak fairness) requirement.* This is a mapping from $\mathcal{F}$ to predicates.
- $\mathcal{C}$ is a *compassion (strong fairness) requirement.*[5]

[5] We do not use compassion requirements in this paper, and omit them from the explanation. The interested reader is referred to [12, 16].

We define a *computation* of S to be an infinite sequence of states $\sigma : s_0, s_1, s_2, \ldots$ satisfying the following requirements:

- *Initiality*: s_0 is initial, i.e., $s_0 \models \Theta$.
- *Consecution*: For each j, the state s_{j+1} is a successor of the state s_j.
- *Justice*: For every $t \in \mathcal{F}$ there are infinitely many $\mathcal{J}[t]$-states in σ.

A typical justice requirement is that continuously enabled transitions are eventually taken. For example, in the MARS system we may require that the data sources of Fig. 2 send messages infinitely often.

The *henceforth* operator $\Box$ and the *eventually* operator $\Diamond$ are defined as:

$$(\sigma, j) \models \Box p \iff \text{for all } k \geq j,\ (\sigma, k) \models p,$$
$$(\sigma, j) \models \Diamond p \iff \text{exists } k \geq j,\ (\sigma, k) \models p,$$

where $(\sigma, j) \models p$ denotes that property p holds at position j in σ.

4.2 Parametrized Fair Systems for UML Models

A PFS is an unlabeled transition system. For this reason, our state data-structure includes, in addition to the state information defined in the kernel language, the label of the last transition that has been taken. We may also want to use auxiliary (history) variables in our proofs. The desired auxiliary information varies according to the system and properties to be verified.

The transition relation ρ is derived from the kernel semantics transition relation, and the transition relations for auxiliary variables. Similarly, the initial condition Θ requires that both the kernel semantics state and the auxiliary components satisfy their initial conditions.

4.3 Verifying Safety Properties

Intuitively, safety properties assert that "something bad does not happen." They are of the form $\Box a$, asserting that predicate a holds in every state that the system may reach.

The most frequently used rule for proving safety properties is the basic invariance rule, BINV [12]. This rule (Fig. 4) states that if a holds at the initial system state, and is preserved by all transitions, then a is a system invariant. It is the rule we use most often in verifying safety properties.

Rule BINV is implemented within TLPVS, and is applied using strategy *binv*. Strategy *binv* applies the rule, and typically manages to discharge premise B1 automatically. User interaction is then required to prove premise B2. However, the strategy does expand the kernel semantics definitions, labeling the different formulas, and distinguishes subsequent cases according to the kind of transition involved (discarding a signal, locally triggered transition, etc).

Rule BINV

For predicate a,

B1. $\Theta \longrightarrow a$

B2. $a(V) \wedge \rho(V, V') \longrightarrow a(V')$

$$\frac{}{\Box a}$$

Fig. 4. Rule BINV (basic invariance)

5 Verification of the MARS Example

In this section we describe how TLPVS was used to verify safety properties in the example of Sect. 2. We would like to verify the following property.

Property NoError: If the data sources never send *noAlt* and *noNav* messages, the receiver never reaches the bus-error location.

This property is not inductive (its holding in the current state does not ensure that it will hold in the next state). As is typically the case in theorem proving, to prove it, it is necessary to prove other, more basic, properties, and to strengthen the invariant. We derive a strengthened invariant:

Property NoError′: If the data sources never send *noAlt* and *noNav* messages, then:

- The receiver never has *noAlt* or *noNav* messages in its signal queue;
- The receiver's *noAltCnt* and *noNavCnt* counters remain at zero;
- The receiver does not reach the bus-error location.

This second property is inductive and can be proved using rule BINV. Thereafter it is easy to show that *NoError* is implied by the strengthened property.

Proving premise B1 was done by the *binv* strategy without user intervention. However, proving premise B2 (the property is invariant over the transition relation) did require user interaction. This invariance must be proved for each of the 26 state machine transitions, as well as for the auxiliary actions such as the discarding of signals.

The strategy breaks these transitions into groups according to type (e.g., triggered and untriggered transitions in different groups). Each such branch in the proof is dealt with uniformly, that is, we apply the same set of commands to prove the invariance over all triggered transitions (using the *then* sequencing strategy of PVS). Some transitions differ from others in their group, and must be dealt with separately. However, the majority are dealt with by a common procedure with no user interaction. The resulting proof was far less interactive than had been anticipated.

6 The Sieve of Eratosthenes

Eratosthenes' prime sieve algorithm is an ancient algorithm for identifying the prime numbers. The algorithm is inherently unbounded as it can be used to verify the primality of arbitrarily large numbers. We built a UML model of this algorithm, and then verified both the safety property that only primes are identified as prime, and the liveness property that every prime is eventually identified. Despite its simplicity, this example allows us to demonstrate our ability to model and verify object creation and unbounded systems.

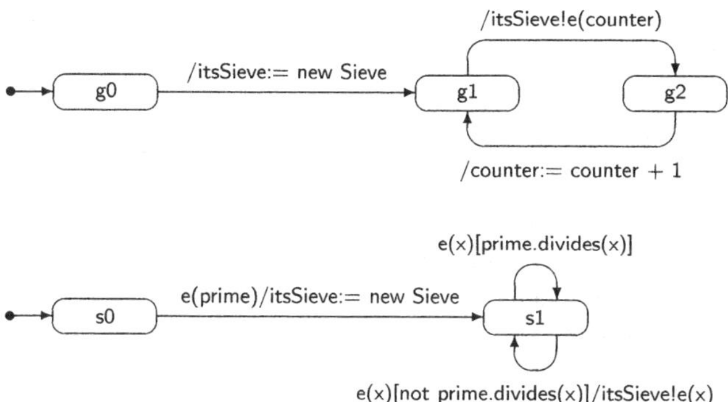

Fig. 5. State machines for the PRIME-SIEVE generator (above) and sieves (below)

The objects in the PRIME-SIEVE algorithm (Fig. 6) are a single generator and an unbounded number of sieves. Each object has a unique identifier: the generator has identifier 1, sieves are numbered from 2 upwards. The counter of the generator is initialized to two. After creating the first sieve, the sieve sends it all the natural numbers from two upwards (by repeatedly sending and then incrementing the value of its counter).

On receiving its first signal, a sieve stores this number as its prime, and creates the next sieve, while taking a transition from location `s0` to `s1`. A sieve which has received and stored a *prime* and is in location `s1` is called *looping*, while if it is at location `s0` it is called *non-looping*. Subsequent numbers received by a looping sieve are compared to its prime number, *prime*. Numbers which are not multiples of *prime* are passed on to the next sieve.

Intuitively, a number z which is not a prime will be eliminated when it reaches a looping sieve whose prime is a factor of z. If z is a prime, then no sieve will eliminate it and it will bubble through the system until it reaches a non-looping sieve, which will store z as its prime.

6.1 Primes Are Correctly Identified

In this section we outline the proof of the safety property that every number identified as prime by a sieve is truly prime:

Property SievesPrime: The number stored in the *prime* field of a sieve at location `s1` is prime.

This property is not inductive and can only be proved once we have proved some additional properties. We need to show that composite (non-prime) numbers are eliminated by the sieves before they reach a non-looping sieve. We note that a composite number n must have some prime factor $f < n$. This factor must precede n in the sequence of signal queues, until f is itself identified as prime by some sieve i. The number n should then be eliminated when it reaches sieve i (if it wasn't eliminated before). Our argument that n is removed from the system depends on f not being removed, a property which must also be proved.

So, to prove the invariance of *SievesPrime* we prove that every composite number is preceded by a prime factor (*FactorsPrecede*), a proof which itself depends on showing that primes are not eliminated (*PrimesRemain*). In addition, we found it useful to prove some technical system properties such as that all numbers in the queues and sieves are greater than one. These properties simplified our proofs, using BINV, of *FactorsPrecede* and *PrimesRemain*. Property *SievesPrime* follows quite simply from *FactorsPrecede* and is also proved using BINV. (The main idea is that when a number reaches a non-looping sieve there are no numbers preceding it in the system, and so it is prime.)

7 Fairness and Liveness

Intuitively, *liveness* properties assert that under certain conditions a given event will occur. They are generally more difficult to verify than safety properties, and entail the use of the system fairness requirements. They typically require that the user devise well-founded ranking functions, whose values decrease until the desired event occurs.

In this section we discuss first our proposed definition of fairness requirements for the UML diagrams under discussion (Sect. 7.1). We then discuss our response rule, DIST-RANK (Sect. 7.2), and finally demonstrate its use in PRIME-SIEVE (Sect. 7.3).

7.1 Fairness Requirements for UML Models

To the best of our knowledge, no formal definition of fairness requirements for UML models appears in the literature. We propose the following definition:

> For every activity group A, if there is always some transition of an object in A enabled, then A takes transitions infinitely often. More formally:
>
> $$\Box(\Box(\exists t : \mathit{enabled}(t, A)) \longrightarrow \Box\Diamond(\exists u : \mathit{taken}(u, A))),$$
>
> where t and u range over transitions.

Rule DIST-RANK
For PFS $S = \langle V, \Theta, \rho, \mathcal{F}, \mathcal{J}, \mathcal{C} \rangle$,
Given initial and goal predicates p, q, helpful predicates $\{h_t : t \in \mathcal{F}\}$,
ranking functions $\delta_t : \Sigma \mapsto \mathbb{N}$ with finite support

$$
\left.
\begin{array}{lll}
\text{D1. } p & \rightarrow & q \ \vee \ \bigvee_{t \in \mathcal{F}} h_t \\
\text{D2. } h_t \ \wedge \ \rho & \rightarrow & q' \ \vee \ h'_t \ \vee \ \left[\delta_t > \delta'_t \ \wedge \ \bigvee_{u \in \mathcal{F}} h'_u \right] \\
\text{D3. } h_t \ \wedge \ \rho & \rightarrow & q' \ \vee \ \bigvee_{d \in \mathcal{F}} \bigwedge_{u \in \mathcal{F}} (\delta_u \geq \delta'_u \ \vee \ \delta_d > \delta'_d \ \wedge \ \delta_d > \delta'_u) \\
\text{D4. } h_t & \rightarrow & \neg \mathcal{J}[t]
\end{array}
\right\} \text{For } t \in \mathcal{F}
$$

$$\square(p \longrightarrow \Diamond q)$$

Fig. 6. Rule DIST-RANK

Observe that fairness is not defined on the level of objects, but on activity groups (although this coincides if all objects are active). Moreover, it is not required that every transition that is continuously enabled be taken, or that the same transition remain continuously enabled – it is sufficient to take any transition currently enabled for the activity group. This is motivated by the observation that switching control between objects in an activity group may cause transitions to become disabled.

7.2 Verifying Response Properties in Unbounded Systems

Object creation complicates verification in that it is not known, a priori, how many objects will participate in a run. Devising appropriate ranking functions is complicated in such systems. We have developed a new rule, DIST-RANK, which is particularly suited to unbounded systems [16]. A derivation of the WELL rule [20], DIST-RANK allows us to distribute a ranking function over a potentially unbounded number of objects in the system.

Rule DIST-RANK (Fig. 6) traces the progress of a computation from an arbitrary p-state to an unavoidable q-state. Intuitively, a well-founded ranking function δ is distributed over the fairness domain. We show that until a q-state is found, δ decreases monotonically. The well-foundedness of δ then assures us that a q-state is eventually encountered.

With each *helpful* predicate h_t of the rule we associate the justice requirement $\mathcal{J}[t]$. Intuitively, the helpful predicate defines a set of states in which a just transition is enabled. When this just transition is taken, and ceases to be helpful, the rank decreases. Thus, the helpful set indicates a transition it would be “helpful” to take in order to decrease the rank.

Premise D2 ensures that the application of a transition to a state satisfying predicate h_t will cause the rank for fairness domain element t to decrease. When an element decreases, other elements are allowed to increase providing that their new values are strictly smaller than the old value of a decreasing element (D3). The net result is a reduction in the total system rank [16].

As long as the rank does not decrease h_t will continue to hold and $\mathcal{J}[t]$ will not (D4). Since the system is just $\mathcal{J}[t]$ must hold eventually (Sect. 4.1) and so the rank must eventually decrease. Due to the well-foundedness of the ranking functions, the rank cannot decrease infinitely often. Thus, we cannot have an infinite fair computation which avoids reaching a q-state.

The well-foundedness of the ranking function depends on it always having finite support. That is, it must be shown that only a finite number of fairness domain elements can have a positive rank at any point.

7.3 Verifying Response in the Sieve Example

In this section we demonstrate how the DIST-RANK rule can be used to verify that every prime number is eventually found (meaning, it is stored in the *prime* field of a looping sieve.)

Property PrimesFound: $\forall z : \Box(\texttt{prime}(z) \longrightarrow \Diamond(\texttt{found}(z)))$

We first define the system fairness requirements. In PRIME-SIEVE, every object is in its own activity group. The generator always has some transition enabled, and thus the requirement is that eventually it takes a step. A sieve has a transition enabled if its message queue is non-empty. In this case, the requirement is that a transition eventually be taken.

Whereas the generator changes location when it takes a step, a looping sieve remains at `s1`. A change in location can therefore not be used as an indication that a transition was taken. Instead we use an auxiliary boolean *flag* variable which changes value every time a sieve at location `s1` takes a transition.

We define the fairness domain as the tuple [`loc`, `pid`, `flag`], where `loc` is the object location, `pid` is the object identifier, and `flag` is an auxiliary variable. The justice conditions then state, intuitively, that the generator changes location infinitely often, and that a sieve with non-empty signal queue will either change location or change its flag variable.

We now define a ranking function. We first define a "rank" for objects, and then use this to define ranks for fairness domain elements.

We ensure that the rank of the generator decreases with time by making it inversely dependent on the value of the generator counter. It is defined as $2z - \mathit{counter} + 1$.

For sieve $i \leq z$ with a non-empty signal queue with value $h \leq z$ at its head, the rank is calculated as $2z - h - i + 1$. Since the numbers in the signal queues are monotonically increasing, the rank of the sieve decreases as it processes queue elements. A sieve with an empty signal queue is assigned rank 0. Therefore, when an element is pushed onto sieve i's empty signal queue, the rank of sieve i increases. The rank of sieve $i - 1$ will, however, decrease (its signal queue is either empty or has a larger value at its head). To ensure that the new rank of sieve i is smaller than the old rank of sieve $i-1$ (as required by premise D3 of DIST-RANK), we subtract the object (sieve) identifier from the rank.

We have now defined ranks for objects. The fairness domain element d is given the rank of object *d.pid*, provided the object *d.loc* is no larger than the current location of *d.pid* (where $\mathtt{g0} < \mathtt{g1} < \mathtt{g2}$, $\mathtt{s0} < \mathtt{s1}$). As the sieve progresses to location `s1` the rank of its various domain elements are set to zero. The *number* of domain elements with positive rank can thus be viewed as a counter of sorts, decreasing as the sieve approaches location `s1`. (On moving from location `s1` back to `s0`, a new, lower, rank is allocated to relevant fairness domain elements.)

Finite support is guaranteed by defining the rank of a sieve i to be zero if $h > z$ or $i > z$. It is easy to see that in both cases the activity of the sieve is no longer of interest for verifying the primality of z: if $h > z$ then z must already have passed through the sieve, or have been eliminated. The prime number of a looping sieve is never smaller than the sieve's identifier, and so for $i > z$, sieve i's prime cannot be a factor of z.

A transition of the generator is *helpful* if it is enabled, and the generator counter is less than z. Once z has been generated, the sieve transitions become helpful. A transition of sieve i is helpful if it is enabled and z is in queue i.

Having defined the necessary components, and some auxiliary properties (such as that the values in the signal queues are monotonically increasing) we are able to use TLPVS to verify *PrimesFound*. This property is non-trivial to prove, and its verification took over one person week. However, we regard the fact that it was tractable at all as an indicator of the appropriateness of TLPVS, and the DIST-RANK rule in particular, to the verification of UML models. The rule DIST-RANK is implemented in TLPVS together with a strategy for applying it. In addition, many generic theories and strategies of TLPVS proved very useful. For example, a theory of list properties was used when reasoning about messages in the signal queues, and much use was made of pre-existing simplification strategies.

8 Related Work and Conclusions

In this paper we have presented a methodology for the deductive verification of UML models, and demonstrated it on two examples. We present a new definition of fairness for such models. Future work includes the extension of the methodology to features not yet covered (such as orthogonal states) and timed systems.

Much work has been done on formal semantics of UML models (e.g., [18, 6]). A two-dimensional propositional linear temporal logic is used to define the semantics of real-time UML behavior [22]. A proof system using PVS is presented, but verification results were not reported. In contrast, we use transition systems to define the UML semantics, and standard LTL for verification. In [25] an axiom-based definition of UML semantics is given, along with a PVS-based verification environment (PrUDE). The authors demonstrate how simple safety properties can be specified and proved. However, it appears that the system does not include a formal specification of a verification logic (such as LTL) and its proof rules, which we believe are necessary for the specification and verification of more complex properties. For more details on various semantics efforts and a comparison to our work see [2, 7].

Model-checking has been applied to the verification of UML models in [15, 10, 4]. Apart from the state explosion problem which limits the size of the models that can be verified, these techniques can be applied directly only to finite models. Thus features like object creation, unbounded event queues and unbounded domain variables cannot be treated in a straightforward way. To overcome these limitations, [1] presents a symbolic analysis technique which can be tuned to give a finite, possibly inexact representation of the unbounded event queues. A natural class of protocols for which this representation is both finite and exact is studied. In [3] the symmetry-based technique of query reduction and the abstraction technique data-type reduction are applied in the verification of UML models. In [13] the IF tool-box is used for verifying UML models which have been mapped to communicating extended timed automata.

In contrast, our deductive approach allows us to verify models directly with unbounded queues and variables and object creation. There is a trade-off here between the added user-interaction in deductive proofs and the need to devise, and work with, specialized methods for model-checking unbounded systems.

Our work was done as part of the EU project Omega [17]. According to the Omega approach, users construct UML models using existing industrial case tools. An XMI representation of the model is then used as input to verification tools constructed by the academic partners of the consortium. Some automated preprocessing may be applied at this level, e.g., the flattening of state machines, and subsequently the representation of the model is translated to a representation of the model in PVS by the `uml2pvs` tool [11]. Future work in the Omega project considers the extension of the `uml2pvs` tool to translate OCL constraints to PVS.

References

[1] W. Damm and B. Jonsson. Eliminating queues from RT UML model representations. In *Proc. FTRTFT'02*, volume 2469 of *LNCS*, pages 375–393. Springer, 2002.

[2] W. Damm, B. Josko, A. Pnueli, and A. Votintseva. Understanding UML: A formal semantics of concurrency and communication in Real-Time UML. In *Proc. 1st Int. Conf. Formal Methods for Components and Objects (FMCO 2002)*, volume 2852 of *LNCS*, pages 71–98. Springer, 2003.

[3] W. Damm and B. Westphal. Live and let die: LSC-based verification of UML-models. In *Proc. 1st Int. Conf. Formal Methods for Components and Objects (FMCO 2002)*, volume 2852 of *LNCS*, pages 99–135. Springer, 2003.

[4] A. David, O. Moller, and W. Yi. Formal verification of UML statecharts with real-time extensions. In *Proc. 5th Int. Conf. Fundamental Approaches to Software Engineering (FASE 2002)*, volume 2306 of *LNCS*. Springer, 2002.

[5] D. Harel and E. Gery. Executable object modeling with statecharts. *Computer*, July 1997. Also in *Proc. 18th Int. Conf. Soft. Eng.*, Berlin, IEEE Press, 1996.

[6] D. Harel and O. Kupferman. On object systems and behavioral inheritance. *IEEE Trans. Software Engineering*, 28(9):889–903, 2002.

[7] J. Hooman and M. B. van der Zwaag. A semantics of communicating reactive objects with timing. Technical report, EU project IST 33522 OMEGA, 2004. Available at http://www-omega.imag.fr.

[8] Rhapsody. I-Logix, Inc., products web page. http://www.ilogix.com/products/.

[9] Y. Kesten and A. Pnueli. Verification by augmented finitary abstraction. *Inf. and Comp.*, 163:203–243, 2000.

[10] A. Knapp, S. Merz, and C. Rauh. Model checking – timed UML state machines and collaborations. In *Proc. FTRTFT'02*, volume 2469 of *LNCS*. Springer, 2002.

[11] M. Kyas, H. Fecher, F.S. de Boer, J. Jacob, M.B. van der Zwaag, J. Hooman, T. Arons, and H. Kugler. Formalizing UML models and OCL constraints in PVS. In *Semantic Foundations of Engineering Design Languages (SFEDL 2004)*, Electronic Notes in Theoretical Computer Science. Elsevier, 2004. To appear.

[12] Z. Manna and A. Pnueli. *Temporal Verification of Reactive Systems: Safety*. Springer, New York, 1995.

[13] I. Ober, S. Graf, and I. Ober. Validation of UML models via a mapping to communicating extended timed automata. In *Proc. 11th Int. SPIN Workshop on Model Checking of Software (SPIN'04)*, volume 2989 of *LNCS*. Springer, 2004.

[14] S. Owre, N. Shankar, J.M. Rushby, and D.W.J. Stringer-Calvert. *PVS System Guide*. Menlo Park, CA, November 2001.

[15] I. P. Paltor and J. Lilius. vUML: A tool for verifying UML models. In *Proc. of the 14th IEEE Int. Conf. on Automated Software Engineering (ASE'99)*. IEEE, 1999.

[16] A. Pnueli and T. Arons. TLPVS: A PVS-based LTL verification system. In *Verification: Theory and Practice*, pages 598–623. Springer, 2003.

[17] OMEGA. EU project IST 33522 (Correct Development of Real-Time Embedded systems). Homepage. http://www-omega.imag.fr/.

[18] G. Reggio, E. Astesiano, C. Choppy, and H. Hussmann. Analysing UML active classes and associated state machines – A lightweight formal approach. In T. Maibaum, editor, *Proc. Fundamental Approaches to Software Engineering (FASE 2000)*, volume 1783 of *LNCS*. Springer, 2000.

[19] Rational Rose Technical Developer. Rational, Inc., web page. http://www-306.ibm.com/software/awdtools/developer/technical/.

[20] E. Sedletsky, A. Pnueli, and M. Ben-Ari. Formal verification of the Ricart-Agrawala algorithm. In *FST TCS 2000: Foundations of Software Technology and Theoretical Computer Science*, volume 1974 of *LNCS*, pages 325–335. Springer, 2000.

[21] B. Selic, G. Gullekson, and P. Ward. *Real-Time Object-Oriented Modeling*. John Wiley & Sons, New York, 1994.

[22] S. Shankar and S. Asa. Formal semantics of UML with real-time constructs. In *Proc. 6th Inf. Conf. on the Unified Modeling Language (UML'03)*, volume 2863 of *LNCS*, pages 60–75. Springer, 2003.

[23] Telelogic TAU. Telelogic, Inc. http://www.telelogic.com/products/tau/.

[24] TLPVS. Homepage. http://www.wisdom.weizmann.ac.il/~verify/tlpvs.

[25] I. Traore, D. B. Aredo, and H. Ye. An integrated framework for formal development of open distributed systems. In *Proc. of ACM Symposium on Applied Computing, (ACM SAC2003)*, 2003.

[26] UML. Documentation of the Unified Modeling Language. Available from the Object Management Group (OMG), http://www.omg.org.

Integrating a Security Requirement Language with UML

H. Abie[1], D.B. Aredo[1], T. Kristoffersen[1], S. Mazaher[1], and T. Raguin[2]

[1] Norwegian Computing Center
P. O. Box 114 Blindern, N-0314 Oslo, Norway
[2] NetUnion sarl, Avenue de Villamont 19
CH-1005 Lausanne, Switzerland

Abstract. We present an approach that integrates a language for precise and high-level specification of application security requirements, the Security Requirement Language (SRL), with an existing modeling technique, namely, the Unified Modeling Language (UML). SRL is based on first-order logic extended with a small set of modal operators and a syntactic abstraction mechanism. It offers extensibility in that new application/domain-specific requirements can be defined and reused. The focus of SRL is the security of communication in distributed systems. The integrated framework enables developers to add to system models security requirements, such as confidentiality, non-repudiation, and authentication, at an early stage of development, making security an integral part of the system development process. We illustrate the practical usability of our approach by presenting an example, and discuss the experiences that the users of our approach, i.e., system developers, have reported.

1 Introduction

E-work systems, be it for commerce, government, learning, etc., have made their way into our everyday lives, and therefore, we are more vulnerable to the malfunctioning of these systems than ever before. One of the important aspects common to all these systems is that they are security-critical. Security attacks against, e.g., e-commerce systems, have already caused huge financial damage, and much confidential information has been compromised.

One of the major reasons behind the failure of many critical systems is that security mechanisms are added to them as afterthoughts and not integrated into them in the early phases of the development process. Moreover, it is seldom checked, if at all, whether the security mechanisms used indeed satisfy the security requirements of the systems. It is necessary to capture security requirements at an early stage and integrate the requirements into system specification and propagate them further to the design and implementation phases. Lastly, security analysis methodologies must be used to ensure that the provided security mechanisms satisfy the specified security requirements.

This paper presents the results of our work in the EU IST project CASENET [6], whose overall objective was to develop and implement a tool-supported integrated framework and methodology for the formal and systematic specification

T. Baar et al. (Eds.): UML 2004, LNCS 3273, pp. 350–364, 2004.

of security requirements, modeling and analysis of security protocols, and implementation of security-critical e-work systems. The focus of the work described is the *specification* of security requirements based on formal methods and its integration with the Unified Modeling Language (UML) [16]. UML is widely used by the software community for modeling software applications. UML is effective in modeling systems, and its graphical notation is intuitive to users. In contrast, formal methods are not so user-friendly but offer a well-defined semantics that enables them to precisely capture security requirements, thus paving the way for formal verification. Systematic integration of mathematically-based methodologies with semi-formal analysis and design techniques into a single development framework bridges the gap between the practical application of security requirements engineering and the formal methods used in design and analysis of security protocols. Such an integration is shown to be an efficient approach to formal development of critical systems as it pulls together the strengths of the mathematical foundation of formal methods and the user friendliness of UML and exploits their synergy effect [18].

To specify security requirements in a precise way, we have designed the Security Requirement Language (SRL) [2] based on first-order logic. There have been several goals guiding the design of SRL:

- When dealing with security requirements, our concern is to capture just the *what* - specification of the requirements - and not the *how* - mechanism for realization of the requirements.
- Security requirements specifications must be useful in the development of security critical systems, i.e., it must be possible to translate/refine the specified requirements automatically to input used in the formal design/analysis of security protocols. This makes it possible to show that the system indeed provides the specified requirements.
- Most users involved in specifying system requirements and functionalities are not familiar with mathematical notations and concepts underlying formal specification languages, and hence are reluctant to use them. A third goal is therefore to be able to specify security requirements in a way that is clear and easy to understand for end-users.

The first two goals have been addressed by the formal nature of SRL. First-order logic both allows the precise specification of the *what* and lends itself to an automated translation/refinement for use in the formal design/analysis of security protocols, i.e., the *how*. That is, requirements can be translated into goals/constraints to be satisfied in the formal design/analysis of security protocols. We have addressed the third goal by providing abstraction mechanisms that hide the mathematical complexity of the specification behind concepts familiar to the end-users, and by providing a methodology to integrate the language with UML.

The rest of the paper is organized as follows. In Sect. 2, we briefly introduce SRL. Section 3 discusses our methodology for integrating SRL with UML. In Sect. 4, we present an example from a real world problem - a *Document Approval*

Workflow for Public Administration, to illustrate the practical usability of our approach. In Sect. 5, other related approaches are discussed. Section 6 gives a summary of the work described and discusses future work.

2 The Security Requirement Language (SRL)

SRL is based on first-order logic extended with a small set of relations and modal operators. Its focus has so far been on security of communication in distributed systems. For a detailed description of the language the reader is referred to [2].

From the point of view of the specification, at any given time, the world consists of a set of *objects*, each object being an entity of a *type*, such as principal (people, computers, systems) or message. Some objects are *constant* and have a fixed value, while objects of type *variable* may change *value* over time.

SRL's primitives are comprised of:

- a set of **logical connectives**, such as the usual propositional connectives in first-order logic $\wedge$, $\vee$, $\neg$, and $\rightarrow$, logic quantifiers $\forall$ and $\exists$, and equality operators $=$ and $\neq$.
- the **relations** $\text{Writes}(P, m)$ and $\text{Reads}(P, m)$, to convey the sending and the receiving of messages m by principal P, respectively.
- the **functions** $Binding(P, X)$ that returns the value of X in the context of principal P (if P does not know the value of X it returns the null object, ϵ), and $Values(X)$ that returns the set of values that it is possible for an object X to be bound to.
- the **modal operators** believes and can_prove. Intuitively, P believes s means that P believes that s is true, and P can_prove s means that P believes that s is true and is able to prove s, i.e., it has a proof of the truth of s, denoted $proof(s)$, that it can present whenever necessary.
- a **macro facility** that allows for the definition of a shorthand for a formula, namely, a *macro*. A macro has a name and a body, and it may take typed parameters. In this way, mathematical formulae can be hidden behind concepts familiar to users.
- the **epoch** construct that allows for the definition of a period of time during which given security requirements apply to the interactions that take place during the defined period. The related **within** construct is used to specify the interactions that may occur during the epoch.
- the **sequence** construct that allows for the modeling of the application in terms of its interactions.
- a concept of **time** that allows to express a particular point in time in which a particular relation holds. For example, if P reads a message, m, at time t_1, we write $\text{Reads}_{t_1}(P, m)$. This makes it possible to place temporal constraints on relations.

The Macro Facility. The following example clarifies the concept of *macro*:
$\text{MessageAuthentication}(A : principal, B : principal, m : message) \equiv$

$$\text{Reads}_{t_2}(B, m) \rightarrow B \ \mathsf{believes}\ (\text{Writes}_{t_1}(A, m))) \wedge t_1 < t_2$$

introduces a macro by the name of MessageAuthentication, taking three parameters: the first two being principals and the last one a message. It expresses the requirement that m be authenticated for principal B. In other words, when receiving m, B knows it comes from A.

Macros are expanded by replacing their formal parameters with the given arguments. For example, the macro,

$$\text{MessageAuthentication}(Manager, Employee, CallForMeeting)$$

expands to

$$\text{Reads}_{t_2}(Employee, CallForMeeting) \rightarrow$$
$$Employee \textsf{ believes } (\text{Writes}_{t_1}(Manager, CallForMeeting))) \wedge t_1 < t_2$$

where $CallForMeeting$ is the message sent (an object in SRL).

A library of macros, called the *standard* library, is included in SRL. This library contains, among others, macros corresponding to common security requirements such as confidentiality, message authentication, non-repudiation, etc. Note that users can define their own macros, customized to their needs, and put them in a library, which can then be used in addition to or instead of the standard library. Libraries also facilitate reuse of requirements.

The Epoch Construct. An epoch is a period of time during which a given security requirement is in effect. It has associated with it an establishment phase and a termination phase that define the sequences of actions that establish and terminate the epoch, respectively. These phases delimit the duration of the epoch but are not part of the epoch themselves. The security requirement that is associated with an epoch applies to all interactions occurring during the corresponding period of time.

The interactions that may occur during a given epoch are specified using SRL's *within* construct which refers to the relevant epoch by its name.

The Sequence Construct. All the SRL primitives presented so far have to do with the specification of security requirements. The context of the security requirements is the application and especially the interactions to which they apply. To model the application, SRL provides the *sequence* construct that allows to group together related interactions of the application in a temporal order. A sequence can have a *name* and can be marked, using *within*, to take place within a given epoch.

3 The Integration Methodology

3.1 Design Decisions

To integrate SRL with UML, we identified constructs and concepts in the two worlds that best fit together and based the integration methodology on those.

Security requirements expressed in SRL are requirements on the interactions between the different entities in a system, and the *sequence* construct is used to model those interactions. Among the different types of UML diagrams, it is the sequence diagram that depicts these interactions and their temporal order explicitly; it is therefore the most appropriate type of diagram, with respect to SRL, for specifying security requirements.

On the SRL side, it is the macro facility that provides end-users with familiar terminology, which hides the mathematical formulae. To specify a requirement, the user only needs to know the name of the corresponding macro and its parameters; the body of the macro is of no concern to him. The arguments passed to the macro are taken from the context of the requirement, which is the application whose security requirements are being specified. The arguments will therefore be entities taken from the UML model of the application. Our integration methodology is therefore primarily based on combining SRL macros with UML sequence diagrams.

UML does not directly offer any constructs for the specification of security requirements, but it offers extension mechanisms that enable addition of new kinds of modeling elements. We wanted a flexible and uniform way to attach security-related properties, from requirements (by means of macros) to epoch definitions, to some of the elements of UML. The *Tagged-Value* extension mechanism was selected because of the flexibility it offers, especially for the values of the tags. In brief, SRL macros representing different security requirements, and other security-related information are attached to different elements of UML using the UML *Tagged-Value* mechanism.

Definition of epochs with their related *within* constructs, names for the sequence diagrams, definition of new macros, and security related assumptions, such as trust, comprise the other information that may be necessary when specifying the security requirements of a system. A special tag by the name CASENET is used for the purpose of supplying security information. Depending on their nature, the different types of information must be conveyed by tags on different elements of a UML model.

3.2 Applying the Methodology

Figure 1 illustrates the integration framework. In SRL security requirements apply to the interactions of a system. In UML, the corresponding parameterized

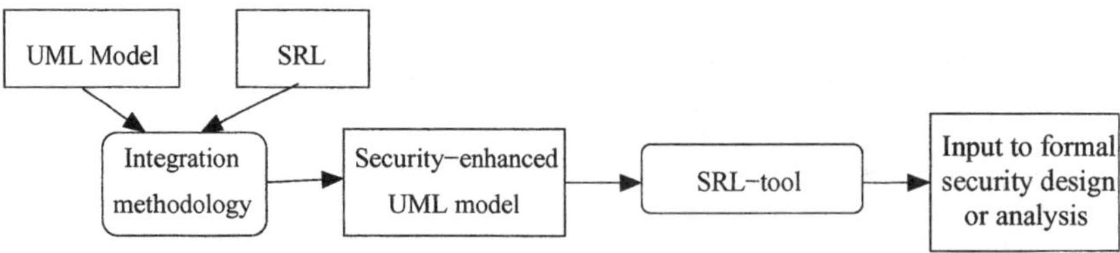

Fig. 1. The Integration Framework

macros are assigned to the CASENET tags of the appropriate interactions in sequence diagrams. That is, if an interaction in a sequence diagram has the requirement of *message authentication*, a CASENET tag whose value is the corresponding macro is used for that interaction. Note that the parameters of the SRL's `Message_Authentication` macro are replaced with values from the context of the macro, i.e., the corresponding interaction. Figure 2 illustrates the use of SRL macros in UML sequence diagrams where the comment box visualizes the value of the CASENET tag, and the dashed line indicates to which element it is attached (the tags themselves do not have a graphical notation). As for the

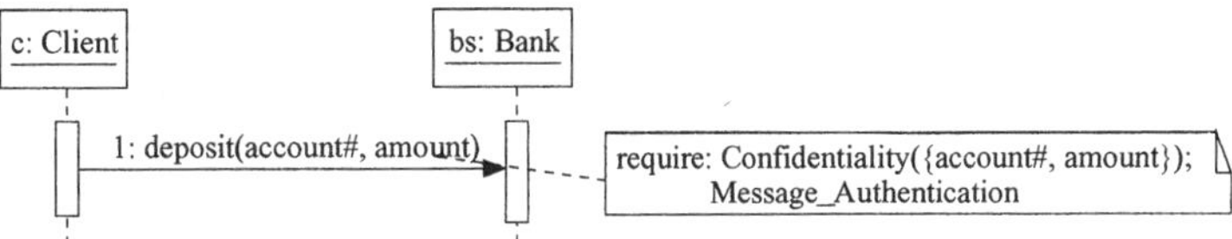

Fig. 2. Use of SRL Macros in UML

other types of information mentioned above, some apply to a sequence diagram as a whole, such as a name for a sequence diagram or the *within* construct, or to the system as a whole, such as the definition of an epoch or that of a new macro.

The natural place for the sequence diagram-related and the system-related information is the sequence diagram and the system model (within which all the diagrams are contained), respectively. But tagged-values are neither supported for UML sequence diagrams nor for the system model. We therefore had to make some compromises and these types of information were attached to other elements than where they belong.

For sequence diagram-related information, the use of the corresponding *collaboration* was considered; but, since the corresponding *collaboration* may contain several sequence diagrams, the information pertaining to a specific sequence diagram cannot therefore be used as the tag value for the *collaboration*. A completely different option was to use UML comment boxes instead of the *Tagged-Value* mechanism, but UML comments are not always carried through to the output generated by the UML tools, such as `.xmi` files. We therefore have opted for a less than elegant solution, i.e., to attach the information to one of the object elements of a sequence diagram.

Similarly, the system-related information is attached to one of the object elements of a sequence diagram. The rationale behind this choice was to make it easier for end-users by limiting the number of places for tags. Since that kind of information cannot be placed in its natural place, we chose to gather all types of security-related properties in one place such that the end-user can concentrate only on sequences diagrams. Figure 3 illustrates how a sequence diagram-related information is specified in UML. Some of these problems, namely, the naming of

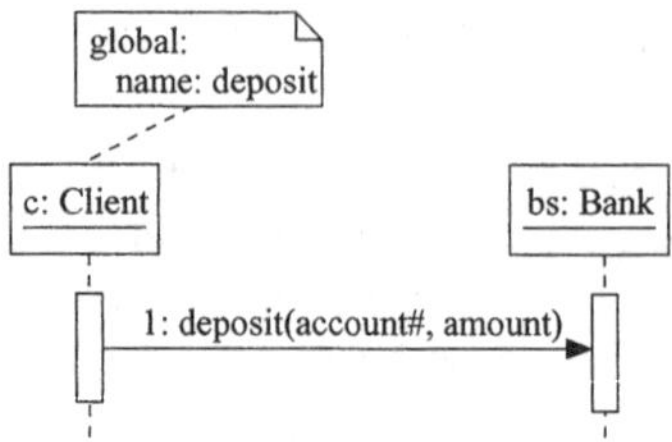

Fig. 3. An Example of Defining Sequence-related Information in UML

sequence diagrams, will be solved by the upcoming UML2.0 [17] specification, but this is only one of the types of information needed at the sequence diagram level. We believe that UML should support tags at the diagram and model levels, as illustrated by our work on SRL.

SRL is extensible in that, in addition to the predefined macros, new macros can always be defined for requirements specific to a system, as part of the specification of the system in SRL. To define new macros, a deeper knowledge of the language is required. But, once defined and tested, the macros can be reused thereafter. This extensibility is conveyed through the described integration methodology to the UML model. That is, new macro definitions can be tag-values and be used as requirements wherever needed.

Note that all requirements in comment boxes are valid SRL statements. A detailed syntax for the possible values of the CASENET tag is defined and can be found in [5].

3.3 Tool Support

The integration methodology described in the previous section, is supported by the SRL-tool. The input to the tool is the `.xmi` file generated by a UML tool from an application's model augmented with security requirements by means of tags. So far, our tool only supports the `.xmi` files generated by the PoseidonCE1.6.1 tool [3]. Figure 4 shows the SRL-tool, consisting of two components, and its input and output. Both components of the tool are implemented in Java. The front-end component uses an XML parser to extract the necessary information about both the sequence diagrams and the security requirements to generate a specification in SRL. The SRL file is input to the back-end of the tool, basically a compiler, to generate input for a given formal security design/analysis methodology. The code-generation part of the compiler must be rewritten for each new target formalism.

The SRL specification can set the constraints for the formal design or selection of appropriate security protocols for the application, or it can serve as the basis for specifying the goals of formal security protocol analysis methodologies.

[3] PoseidonCE1.6.1 is a product from Gentleware: http://www.gentleware.com

That is, SRL specifications can be translated to formal notations used in design or analysis processes of the security protocols. In the context of our work, the back-end of the SRL-tool translates SRL specifications to a notation used by the formal design methodology used in CASENET. Consequently, the process

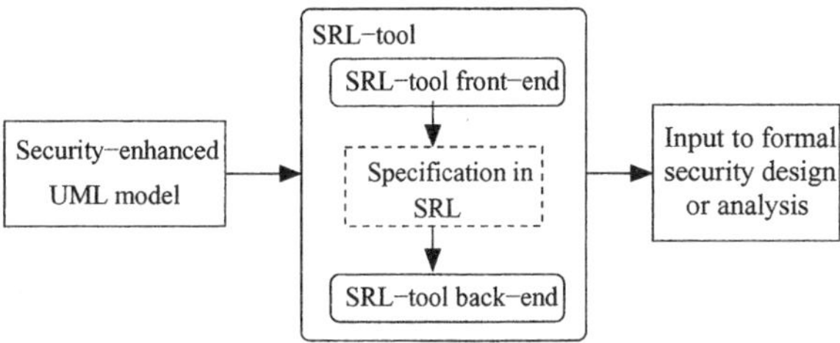

Fig. 4. The SRL-tool

from using SRL in connection with UML for the specification of the security requirements of an application, to generating input for a formal design/analysis process is supported by tools. This makes it possible to ensure that the security requirements are indeed satisfied by the implementation of the system.

4 Case Study: A Document Approval Workflow

4.1 Description of the System

As a proof of concept, our methodology has been applied to parts of the applications of the user-partners of the CASENET consortium. This section reports on one such trial where the example used is taken from a case study that NetUnion conducted for an online contracting application for public administration. The approach described in Sect. 3 is applied, by one of the members of NetUnion's design and development team, to the part of the process where an end-user digitally signs a previously submitted document.

4.2 Process Description

Once the to-be-signed document is stored on the server, the end-user can proceed with the *signDocument* process

The signing itself has always to take place on the end-user side where any appropriate security device for signing (SmartCard, software certificate, etc.) can be accessed. This implies the transmission of confidential data (the document to be signed and the created signature) over the Internet. The sequence diagrams shown in Fig. 5 illustrate the *signDocument* process. The user logs on to the server (5a), retrieves the document to be signed, does the signing, returns the signature to the server (5c), and logs off (5b).

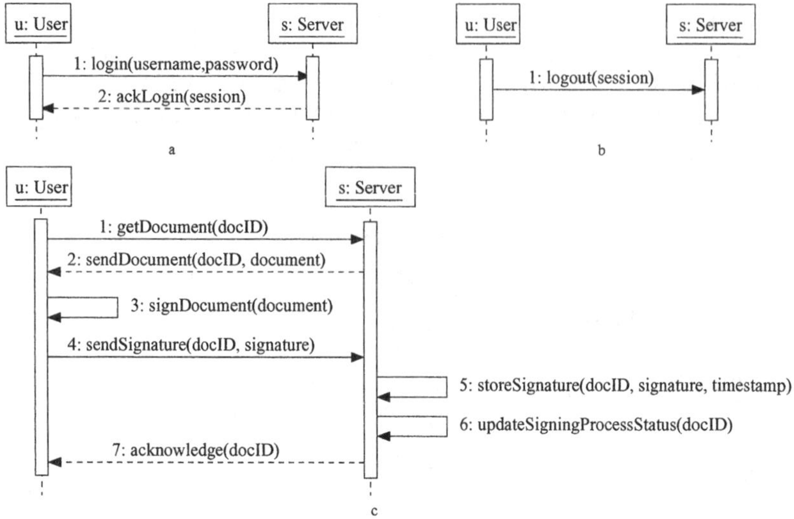

Fig. 5. Sequence Diagrams of the Signing Process

4.3 The Identified Security Requirements

NetUnion identified the following security requirements for the signing process:

1. authenticity of the user u to the server s;
2. authenticity of the server s to the user u;
3. authenticity of all messages sent by user u to the server s;
4. confidentiality of *password*;
5. confidentiality of *session*;
6. confidentiality of *document*;
7. confidentiality of *signature*;
8. non-repudiation of receipt for the *signature*.

4.4 Specification of the Security Requirements

The security requirements for the signing process being identified, the next step was to specify them on the sequence diagrams of Fig. 5. The appropriate macros were used as values of CASENET tags and attached to the relevant interactions by NetUnion.

The first two requirements on the list in the previous section imply that the messages exchanged in the login phase, depicted in Fig. 6, must be authenticated. This is specified by means of the *Message_Authentication* macro as the tag-value for both messages, namely, *login* and *ackLogin*, of *login_diag* as shown in Fig. 6. Furthermore, the confidentiality of *password* and *session* were required, the fourth and fifth requirements on the list above. This is achieved by using the *Confidentiality* macro as shown in Fig. 6.

The third requirement on the list above can be specified by means of SRL's epoch construct. We define an epoch, called the *secured_session*, which is established by the *login_diag* (Fig. 6) and terminated by the *logout_diag* sequence diagrams (Fig. 7), respectively. The predefined macro *Epoch_authentication*[4] expresses the desired requirement that all messages sent by u must be authenticated by s. This requirement applies to all interactions between u and s taking place in the period of time defined by the corresponding epoch, i.e., between login and logout. Note that the requirement does not apply to the interactions in the *login_diag* and *logout_diag* sequence diagrams.

Now that we have defined the epoch *secured_session*, we have to say what are the interactions that may occur within that epoch. This is done by means of SRL's *within* construct, which is used in the *signDocument* sequence diagram, as depicted in Fig. 8. The *within* construct expresses the fact that all of the interactions in the sequence diagram are permitted to occur within the epoch *secured-session*. Therefore, the epoch requirement, *Epoch_Authentication*, applies to all of those interactions. Fig. 8.

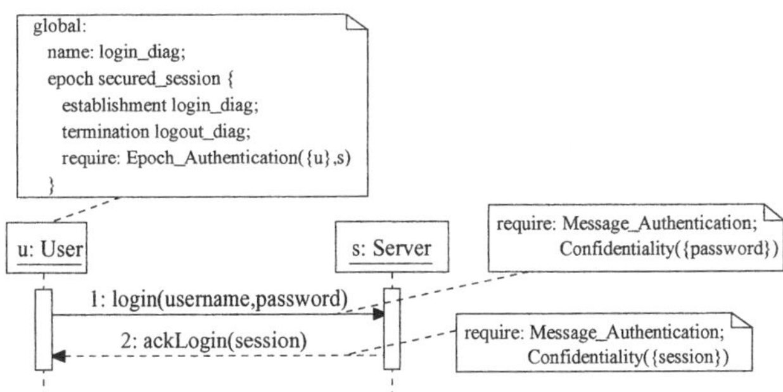

Fig. 6. Sequence Diagram of the Login Process with its Security Requirements

As mentioned earlier, the requirement of the epoch *secured_session* does not apply to the interactions of the *logout_diag* sequence diagram. Therefore, in order to completely specify the third requirement in the list, *Message_Authentication* is explicitly required for the *logout* message. Confidentiality of *session* being one of the identified requirements, the corresponding macro is also applied to that message.

In addition, the other identified requirements, namely,

- confidentiality of the *signature* and the *document*, and
- non-repudiation of receipt for the *signature*,

are explicitly specified by means of the corresponding predefined macros for the relevant interactions.

4 This macro is part of the standard macro library that is defined for SRL and can be used only within an epoch definition.

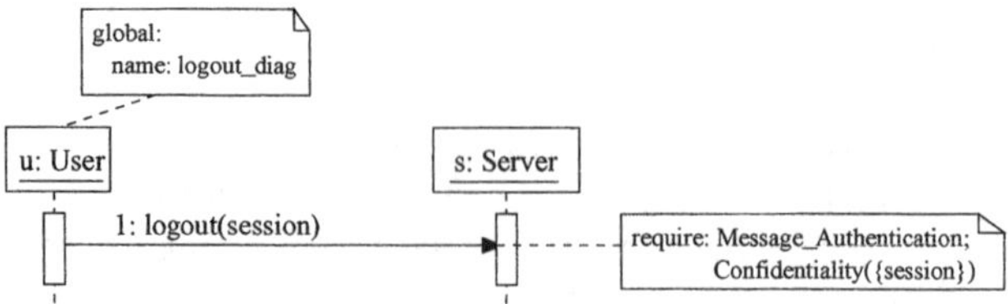

Fig. 7. Sequence Diagram of the Logout Process with its Security Requirements

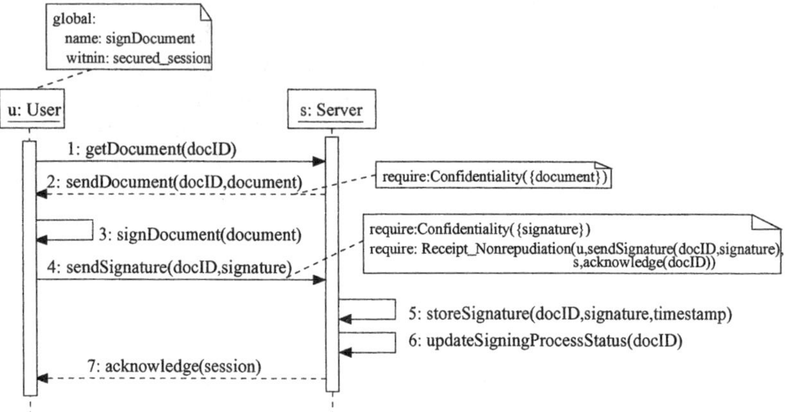

Fig. 8. Sequence Diagram of the Signing Process with its Security Requirements

An excerpt of the `.xmi` file generated by the Poseidon tool for these sequence diagrams and the corresponding class diagram is shown in Fig. 9. The different CASENET tags appear as instances of the `UML:TaggedValue` element. One such instance is shown in Fig. 9, and has the requirements for the *logout* message as its *dataValue*. The SRL specification generated by the SRL-tool for the example is presented in Fig. 10. This specification is further transformed by the back-end of the SRL-tool to the design formalism used in the CASENET project.

4.5 Experience with the Integration Methodology

The system designers at NetUnion reported that SRL is easy to use. Since SRL is combined with a software engineering standard, specifying security requirements for a complete application can be done quickly. SRL macros are easy to understand and to use; the syntax is clear and simple, and they cover a wide range of security requirements. In addition, it is possible to extend the language by creating new macros. When using the predefined macros, SRL only requires a basic knowledge of security engineering and therefore the learning curve is extremely low. For defining new requirements however a thorough knowledge of the language is necessary and some security expertise is needed.

```
<?xml version = '1.0' encoding = 'UTF-8' ?>
<XMI xmi.version = '1.2' xmlns:UML = .... >
  <XMI.header> ... </XMI.header>
  <XMI.content>
    ...
    <UML:CallAction xmi.id = 'a21' name = 'logout(session)' ... >
      ...
    </UML:CallAction>
    <UML:Stimulus xmi.id = 'a23' name = 's1' isSpecification = 'false'>
      <UML:ModelElement.taggedValue>
        <UML:TaggedValue xmi.id = 'a25' ... dataValue =
         'require: Message_Authentication; Confidentiality({session})'>
          ...
        </UML:TaggedValue>
      </UML:ModelElement.taggedValue>
      ...
      <UML:Stimulus.dispatchAction>
        <UML:CallAction xmi.idref = 'a21'/>
      </UML:Stimulus.dispatchAction>
    </UML:Stimulus>
    ...
  </XMI.content>
</XMI>
```

Fig. 9. Excerpt of the xmi File.

5 Related Work

To put our work in context, we give some background information and a brief overview of related work.

Work done on formalization of security has been mainly concerned with the formal specification of security protocols for the purpose of analysis. A few examples are [3], [19], [14], [4], [1], [11] and [7]. Protocols are specified in some formal notation, which are then input either directly or after undergoing some transformation to a suitable analysis methodology. Their correctness is established with respect to some goals or invariants defined by the specification.

Several of these efforts are based on modal logic, of which [4], better known as BAN logic, is perhaps the most widely known. SRL has some operators, e.g., *believes*, that are close to the ones used in BAN logic. It therefore should be investigated whether BAN logic is a particularly suitable target formalism for SRL.

None of the work cited above deals directly with the specification of security requirements at a high, abstract level suited for application modeling. Integrating security engineering into the software development process is of paramount importance [8], [15]. Instead of an after-thought, security requirements must be an integral part of the requirements of the system to be built. Work has been done on capturing the security aspects of a system when modeling software by using graphical notations, such as the Unified Modeling Language (UML) [16]. Some of the major efforts in this direction are secureUML [10], AutoFocus [20], and UMLsec [9].

```
import(standard);
environment {
  u, s: principal;
}
epoch secured_session() {
  establishment (u,s) {
    u -> s: login(username,password);
      require: MessageAuthentication(u,s,login(username,password));
      require: Confidentiality(u,s,{password});
    s -> u: ackLogin(session);
      require: MessageAuthentication(s,u,ackLogin(session));
      require: Confidentiality({session});
  }
  termination (u,s) {
    u -> s: logout(session);
      require: MessageAuthentication(u,s,logout(session));
      require: Confidentiality(u,s,{session});
  }
  EpochAuthentication({u},s);
}
sequence signDocument(within secured_session) {
  u -> s: getDocument(docID);
  s -> u: sendDocument(docID,document);
    require: Confidentiality(s,u,{document});
  u -> s: sendSignature(docID,signature);
    require: Confidentiality({signature});
    require: ReceiptNonrepudiation(s,sendSignature(docID,signature),
                                   u,acknowledge(docID));
  s -> u: acknowledge(docID);
}
```

Fig. 10. The SRL Specification of the Example

These approaches are similar to ours in the sense that they all introduce security related elements (concepts) into existing graphical modeling notations. The major difference is that our security related elements are based on a formal language with a well-defined semantics. This enables the automated refinement of the requirements for use in formal security design/analysis methodologies. secureUML is concerned only with access control requirements. AutoFocus and UMLsec mainly deal with confidentiality and authentication requirements. AutoFocus uses its structure diagrams, the equivalent of UML collaboration diagrams, to introduce security requirements. In UMLsec, different UML diagrams are used to capture security relevant information using extension mechanisms such as *Tagged-Value* and *stereotype*. A major limitation of these two approaches is that each deals with a limited set of security requirements and that it is not possible for the user to introduce new requirements. In contrast, SRL covers a wide range of requirements, and allows new application-specific requirements to be defined and reused; this capability is extended to UML through the integration methodology.

6 Conclusion

We have designed a language based on first-order logic to express systems' security requirements. A methodology for its integration with UML is also defined.

We have shown the practical usability of our approach by presenting a real world example and discussing user experiences.

SRL and its integration with UML have a number of advantages:

- Security requirements can be specified precisely and at a high level of abstraction, independently of the implementation mechanisms.
- SRL is extensible in that it allows experts to define new, application/domain-specific security requirements, which can be reused by end-users.
- The library of predefined security macros makes it possible to easily reuse security requirements.
- The formal nature of the language with its well-defined semantics makes it possible to transform a high-level security requirement specification systematically and automatically into input for formal security design/analysis methodology. This permits to verify whether the security requirements are satisfied by the implementation of the system. It also paves the way for automatic generation of executable security-preserving code.
- The integration of SRL into UML exploits the complementary properties of these languages: formality and usability.
- The integration of SRL into UML encourages focusing on security requirements at an early stage, raising developer's awareness of security.
- The integration of SRL into UML makes possible the automated processing of security requirements from an early stage of system development.

In our future work, we plan to make SRL easier to use for end-users and apply SRL to other types of security requirements.

As an example, one way to improve the user-friendliness of SRL would be to make it possible to specify global requirements, such as to express that some data, e.g., *pinCode*, is always to be kept confidential. This would express that whenever *pinCode* is used in an communication, then there is a confidentiality requirement for *pinCode*. This is not possible in the current version of SRL. In an extended, future version of SRL, the obvious place for such a requirement in the UML model of a system would be the class diagram; the security requirement will be given as a tag-value for the attribute in question.

As mentioned earlier, the focus of SRL has been to specify security requirements related to communication. We will continue our work by using SRL to express security requirements for other contexts, such as access management, and by including the resulting new concepts into the integration methodology described in this paper.

Acknowledgments

This work has been partially funded by the European Commission through the CASENET project, IST-2001-32446, in the Fifth Program Framework.

References

1. Abadi, M., Gordon, A. D.: A Calculus for Cryptographic Protocols, The Spi Calculus. Research Report, digital Systems Research Center, January 1998.

2. Aredo, D. B., Kristoffersen, T., Mazaher, S.: Abstract Security Requirement Specification. Technical Report DART/03/04, Norsk Regnesentral, Oslo, Norway, March, 2004.
3. Bieber, P.: A Logic of Communication in a Hostile environment. *Proceedings of the Computer Security Foundations Workshop III.* IEEE Computer Society Press. June, 1990.
4. Burrows, M., Abadi, M., Needham, R.: A Logic of Authentication. *ACM Transactions on Computer Systems*, 8(1), February 1990.
5. CASENET, IST project 2001-32446: User Trial Progress Report. Deliverable CASENET/WP5/D5.2, June, 2003.
6. CASENET, IST project IST-2001-32446: *http://www.casenet-eu.org/*,
7. Denker, G., Millen, J., Rues, H.: The CAPSL Integrated Protocol Environment. Technical Report SRI-CSL-2000-02, SRI International, Computer Science Laboratory, October 2000.
8. Higginbotham, M. D., Maley, J. G., Milheizler, A. J., Suskie, B. j.: Integrating Information Security Engineering with System Engineering with System Engineering Tools. *Proceedings of WETICE '98*, July, 1998.
9. Jurjens, J.: UMLsec: Extending UML for Secure Systems Development. *Proceedings of the 5th International Conference on the United Modeling Language* (UML 2002). Lecture Notes in Computer Science, vol. 2460. Springer Verlag, 2002.
10. Lodderstedt, T., Basin, D., Doser, J.: SecureUML: A UML-based modeling language for model-driven security. *Proceedings of the 5th International Conference on the United Modeling Language* (UML 2002). Lecture Notes in Computer Science, vol. 2460. Springer Verlag, 2002.
11. Lowe, G.: Breaking and Fixing the Needham-Schroeder Public-Key Protocol Using FDR. *Proceedings of TACAS 95.* Lecture Notes in Computer Science, vol. 1055. Springer Verlag, 1996.
12. Meadows, C., Syverson, P.: A Formal Language for Cryptographic Protocol Requirements. *Designs, Codes and Cryptography*, 7(1-2), January 1996.
13. Meadows, C.: The NRL Protocol Analyzer: An Overview. *Journal of Logic Programming*, 26(2), 1996.
14. Moser, L.: A Logic of Knowledge and Belief for Reasoning about Computer Security. *Proceedings of the Computer Security Foundations Workshop II.* IEEE Computer Society Press, June, 1989.
15. Mouratidis, H., Giorgini, P., Manson, G.: Integrating Security and Systems Engineering: Towards the Modeling of Secure Information Systems. *Proceedings of the 15th Conference on Advanced Information System Engineering* (CAISE*03), 2003.
16. OMG: The Unified Modeling Language Specification V1.5., Object Management Group, Needham, MA, U.S.A.", March, 2003.
17. OMG: *http://www.omg.org/technology/documents/modeling_spec_catalog.htm*
18. Shroff, M., France, R.: Towards a Formalization of UML Class Structures in Z. *Proceedings of COMPSAC'97*, August, 1997.
19. Syverson, P.: Formal Semantics of Logics of Cryptographic Protocols, *Proceedings of the Computer Security Foundations Workshop III.* IEEE Computer Society Press, June, 1990.
20. Wimmel, G., Wißpeintner, A.: Extended Description Techniques for Security Engineering. In M. Dupuy and P. Paradinas, editors, *Trusted Information, The New Decade Challenge*, Proceedings of the IFIP 16th International Conference on Information Security (Sec'01). Kluwer Academic Publishers, 2001.

Automated Verification of UMLsec Models for Security Requirements

Jan Jürjens* and Pasha Shabalin

Software & Systems Engineering, TU Munich, Germany
http://www4.in.tum.de/~juerjens, http://www4.in.tum.de/~shabalin

Abstract. For model-based development to be a success in practice, it needs to have a convincing added-value associated with its use. Our goal is to provide such added-value by developing tool-support for the analysis of UML models against difficult system requirements. Towards this goal, we describe a UML verification framework supporting the construction of automated requirements analysis tools for UML diagrams. The framework is connected to industrial CASE tools using XMI and allows convenient access to this data and to the human user.
As a particular example for usage of this framework, we present verification routines for verifying models of the security extension UMLsec of UML. These plug-ins should not only contribute towards usage of UMLsec in practice by offering automated analysis routines connected to popular CASE tools. The verification framework should also allow advanced users of the UMLsec approach to themselves implement verification routines for the constraints of self-defined stereotypes, in a way that allows them to concentrate on the verification logic. In particular, we focus on an analysis plug-in that utilises the model-checker Spin to verify security properties of UMLsec models which make use of cryptography (such as cryptographic protocols).

1 Introduction

Still only about 4% of software systems in practice are built using modeling techniques of some sort (most of them using UML). There needs to be a convincing added-value to the usage of model-based development techniques before it will be widely adopted in industry. Our goal is to provide such added-value by developing tool-support for the analysis of UML models against system requirements which can be formulated at the level of the system model, and which cannot be manually checked in a reliable and efficient way (such as security requirements). Here, we describe a UML verification framework supporting the construction of automated requirements analysis tools for UML diagrams. Its design is influenced by experiences from long-standing efforts at our group regarding the development of the AutoFocus CASE-tool [HMR+98]. The framework is connected to industrial CASE tools using data integration with XMI [Obj02] and allows convenient access to this data and to the human user.

* Supported by the Verisoft Project of the German Ministry for Research (BMBF).

T. Baar et al. (Eds.): UML 2004, LNCS 3273, pp. 365–379, 2004.

To be of interest in practice, the requirements that can be treated, and the method we propose for handling them, should fulfill the following constraints.

- The properties that can be specified and analysed should be important and sophisticated enough so that it is necessary to consider them and that it would be difficult to do so manually.
- The analysis should be automatic to prevent additional running costs in using it.
- It should efficient enough to be effectively and conveniently usable and an ongoing basis.
- It should be possible to use the approach with just a modest training effort.

As an example for such requirements, we focus on security aspects. We demonstrate how to instantiate this framework with analysis plug-ins at the hand of examples for verification routines for constraints associated with the stereotypes of the UML security extension UMLsec [Jür02, Jür04]. In particular, we focus on a plug-in that utilises the model-checker Spin to verify security properties of UMLsec models which make use of cryptography (such as cryptographic protocols). To do so, the analysis routine extracts information from different diagram types (class, deployment, and statechart diagrams) that may contain additional specific cryptography-related information. With respect to UMLsec, the goal here is thus two-fold. On the one hand, we aim to support the usage of UMLsec in practice by offering analysis routines connected to popular CASE tools which allow the automated verification of the constraints associated with the UMLsec stereotypes. One the other hand, the verification framework should allow advanced users of the UMLsec approach to themselves implement verification routines for the constraints of self-defined stereotypes, in a way that allows them to concentrate on the verification logic (rather than on user interface issues). This verification framework should then be useful beyond UMLsec, as well. For these purposes, the framework is available as open-source.

Sect. 2 presents the verification framework supporting the construction of automated requirements analysis tools for UML diagrams. We give a short overview over analysis tool plugins for the framework supporting verification of UMLsec models for the contained security requirements. In Sect. 3, we present one of these plug-ins, a binding with the Spin modelchecker for checking data security requirements, for example of cryptographic protocols. At the hand of a running example, the translation from UMLsec models to Promela code and its execution in Spin is explained. We close with comparisons to related work, a discussion of our work and an outlook on further developments. For background on data security and UMLsec, we refer to [Jür02, Jür04].

2 The UML Verification Framework

We present a framework supporting the construction of automated requirements analysis tools for UML diagrams. The framework is connected to industrial CASE tools using data integration with XMI [Obj02] and allows convenient access to this data and to the human user. The framework provides three input and output interfaces for the analysis plug-ins: a textual command-line interface, a graphical user interface, and a web-interface. Inputs can be UML diagrams in the form of XMI files, as well as textual parameters. (Alternatively, the diagrams can be input in the .zuml format of the Poseidon tool [Gen03], which also includes graphical information.) As output one can again have UML diagrams as XMI (or .zuml) files and text messages. The tool can access the information in the UML models on the conceptual level of UML model elements through Java Metadata Interface (JMI) methods [Dir02]. The plug-ins can have an internal state which is preserved between different executions of its commands. Any analysis tool written in Java and complying with the input and output interface of the framework can be plugged into the framework. To avoid having to parse XMI files, we use XMI data-binding offered by the Meta Data Repository (MDR) [Mat03], a XMI-specific data-binding library in Java Netbeans. Since MDR allows one to make use of the DTDs for XMI that are officially released, compatibility with the standard is ensured (and MDR is also used in Poseidon). The architecture and basic functionality of the UML verification framework are illustrated in Fig. 1. The framework can be offered as a web application (where the UML models are uploaded to the framework over the web). Additionally, a locally installable version is available. Exemplarily, the figure includes two of the UMLsec analysis plug-ins (a checker for static security properties, and a checker for dynamic properties using a model checker).

The usage of the framework as illustrated in Fig. 1 proceeds as follows. The developer creates a model and stores it in the UML 1.4/XMI 1.2 file format.[1] The file is imported by the UML verification framework into the internal MDR repository. Each plug-in accesses the model through the JMI interfaces generated by the MDR library, they may receive additional textual input, and they may return both a UML model and textual output. The two exemplary analysis plug-ins proceed as follows: The static checker parses the model, verifies its static features, and delivers the results to the error analyzer. The dynamic checker translates the relevant fragments of the UML model into the model-checker input language. The model-checker is spawned by the UML framework as an external process; its results (a counter-example in case a problem was found) are delivered back to the error analyzer. The error analyzer uses the information received from the static checker and dynamic checker to produce a text report for the developer describing the problems found, and a modified UML model, where the errors found are visualized. On any Java-enabled platform, the framework can run in one of three modi:

- as a console application, either interactive or in batch mode
- as a Java Servlet, exposing its functionality over the Internet
- as a GUI application with higher interactivity and presentation capabilities

To achieve a media-independent operation of the tools, input and output are handled by the framework. Each tool command defines a set of required input parameters (currently supported parameter types are Integer, Double, String

[1] This will be updated to UML 2.0 once the corresponding DTD is released.

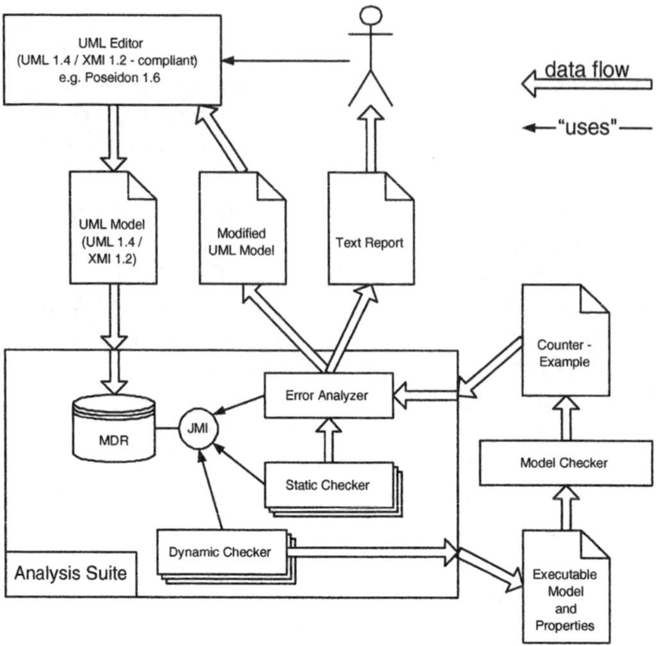

Fig. 1. UML verification framework: usage

and File; others can be easily added). On behalf of the tool, the framework collects the parameters from the user and returns the output to the user using the current input/output media (console, web, or GUI). To enable this, each tool that is integrated into the UML verification framework must implement a common interface (IToolBase), plus three media-dependent interfaces (IToolConsole, IToolWeb and IToolGui). For simplification, the framework provides default implementations for the IToolWeb and IToolGui interfaces. These default wrappers use the interface implemented by the tool IToolConsole and render the text output in HTML or in a text window format respectively. Each tool exposes a set of commands which can be executed through the functions of the corresponding interface (GetConsoleCommands, GetWebCommands and GetGuiCommands). Thus the tool can provide different functionality on different media, adopting to its specifics. The framework uses the IToolBase interface to retrieve general information about the tool, and one of the three media-specific tool interfaces to call a command provided by the tool and receive the output. This output is rendered by the framework on the current media. The tool can execute several commands subsequently; the internal state of the MDR repository and all tools is preserved between command calls. The set of available commands for each tool may vary depending on the execution history and current state. This allows to use the UML framework for complex and interactive operations on the UML model. The source code of the verification framework and the plug-ins is downloadable as part of the UMLsec tool from [UML], where they are also offered as a web-interface, including a small user tutorial.

We give a short overview over analysis tool plugins for the UML verification framework which support verification of UMLsec models for the security requirements contained as stereotypes and their constraints (see [Jür02]). One of them will be explained in more detail in the later sections (a binding with the Spin modelchecker for checking the constraints of the «data security» stereotype, for example to verify cryptographic protocols). When given a UMLsec model, the analysis tools automatically produce a semantic model and include a formalization of the security requirements or primitives contained as stereotypes and their constraints. These can be applied by a developer without specialized training in security or formal methods by simply including them in the UML model. The constraints associated with the stereotypes are translated to the formal model, protecting from errors that manual formalization is prone to (see [Jür02] for details about the formal semantics of a simplified fragment of UML we use). Since security requirements are usually defined relative to an adversary, to analyze whether the UML specification fulfills a security requirement, the tools automatically include the adversary model arising from the physical view contained in the UML specification as a deployment diagram. The UMLsec verification plug-ins fall into several different categories.

Static features: For each of the static security requirements in UMLsec (such as «secure links» and «secure dependency»), we have implemented an analysis plugin which directly checks the relevant conditions in a Java routine.

Simple dynamic features: For dynamic properties, we need a mapping from UMLsec models to a representation of their behavioral semantics as event histories. This is done for statecharts, activity diagrams, sequence diagrams, and for subsystems containing the above diagram types in four other plugins. The semantics is analyzed to verify basic security requirement, defined on the behavioral level (such as «fair exchange» and «guarded access»).

Complex dynamic features: For complex dynamic properties, the UMLsec model is translated into the input language of a suitable analysis tool. As an example, we describe a tool-binding to the model-checker Spin to verify the «data security» constraints in this paper.

External application binding There are also plug-ins analyzing security permissions from configurations for SAP R/3 business applications with respect to security rules and business processes formulated in UML [HJ03].

Note that the other stereotypes from [Jür02] not mentioned above do not entail any verification obligation, but just provide some security-relevant information which is used when defining constraints associated with other stereotypes: For example, «Internet» and other stereotypes include information about the physical security level used for example by the «secure links» constraint.

3 Model-Checking UMLsec Models

As an example for the verification routines implemented in the UMLsec tool, we present a tool-binding with the model-checker Spin [Hol03] for verifying cryptographic protocols following the «data security» requirement from [Jür02]. «data security» is a UMLsec stereotype for subsystems which one can use to specify that certain attributes in the subsystem that are marked using the «secrecy» stereotype are supposed to remain secret. These UML subsystems, such as cryptographic protocols, can be specified to make use of cryptographic algorithms. That the secrecy requirement is actually fulfilled (as far as one can determine from the model), is formalized using the constraint associated with «data security». This is done with respect to a formal semantics of (a restricted version of) the subsystem and its subdiagrams, and using an adversary model arising from the physical security specification given in the deployment diagram contained in the subsystem. This is shortly sketched at the end of this section; for details we refer to [Jür02]. In this section, we present work on how to provide tool-support for automatically verifying a UML specification for the «data security» constraint.

Spin supports automatic verification of finite-state reactive systems given in form of a state-transition system against properties expressed in Linear Time Logic (LTL). To check the constraint associated with «data security» attached to a subsystem, we collect information from the following diagrams contained in the subsystem:

Class diagrams In class diagrams, attributes and methods may be tagged for example with {secrecy} to specify that the relevant data should remain secret from an adversary.

Statecharts The behaviour of the instances of each class (for example, with a cryptographic protocol) is defined in a statechart diagram.

Deployment diagrams Deployment diagram are used to specify the physical security of communication links between objects within the system that are distributed, for example over the Internet.

Thus, from the information in the statecharts we construct a formal model of the system, which is augmented with an adversary model derived from the threat information in the deployment diagram. This formal model is then verified with respect to the security requirement contained in the class diagram.

Following [Jür02], we extend the UML notation with cryptography primitives, which can be used in *Guards* and *Effects* in UMLsec Statecharts and to define initial values for variables in the Class diagrams. The BNF representation of the cryptographic expressions is given in Fig. 2. Here, the object identifiers `identifier` are assumed to be given. The functions `SenderOf`, `PublicKeyOf`, `SecretKeyOf`, `SymmetricKeyOf`, and `NonceOf` return the corresponding attributes of the object. Note that the function `NonceOf` was introduced based on the assumptions that for protocols with symmetric session keys, at each iteration of the protocol a new object with a fresh session key is generated; it would alternatively be easily possible to modify the definition to allow

```
<expression>   ::=    <identifier> |
                      "SenderOf" "(" <identifier> ")" |
                      "PublicKeyOf" "(" <identifier> ")" |
                      "SecretKeyOf" "(" <identifier> ")" |
                      "SymmetricKeyOf" "(" <identifier> ")" |
                      "NonceOf" "(" <identifier> ")" |
                      "ApplyKey" "(" <expression> "," <expression> ")" |
                      "this" |
                      <expression> "::" <expression> |
                      <expression> "[" integer "]"
```

Fig. 2. UMLsec Cryptography Language

each object to have several symmetric keys. The function `ApplyKey` performs the cryptographic operations of encryption, decryption, signing, and extraction from signatures (as formalized below). Within a class, the keyword `this` references the class itself, and the other classes are referenced by the corresponding association end identifiers from the class diagram. Expressions can finally include the concatenation and indexing operators `::` and `[]` (where a concatenation of n expressions followed by `[`m`]` evaluates to the mth of these expressions if $m \leq n$. Furthermore, one can use the Boolean comparison operators `==` (equal) and `!=` (not equal) between expressions, the assignment `=` of expressions to attributes, as well as events (which specify incoming method calls at statechart transitions).

For any symmetric key k, any asymmetric key pair consisting of a secret key sk and a public key pk, and any message m, the following rules apply:

- $\texttt{ApplyKey}(\texttt{ApplyKey}(m, k), k) = m$ (symmetric encryption)
- $\texttt{ApplyKey}(\texttt{ApplyKey}(m, pk), sk) = m$ (asymmetric encryption)
- $\texttt{ApplyKey}(\texttt{ApplyKey}(m, sk), pk) = m$ (digital signature)

The first rule axiomatizes the functional properties of any symmetric encryption algorithm, the latter two rules the properties of the RSA asymmetric encryption algorithm [RSA78].

Example We introduce a UML specification of a simple cryptographic protocol, which we use in the remainder of this paper as a running example. In this simple (and obviously insecure) protocol, Alice (of class Initiator) wants to receive some

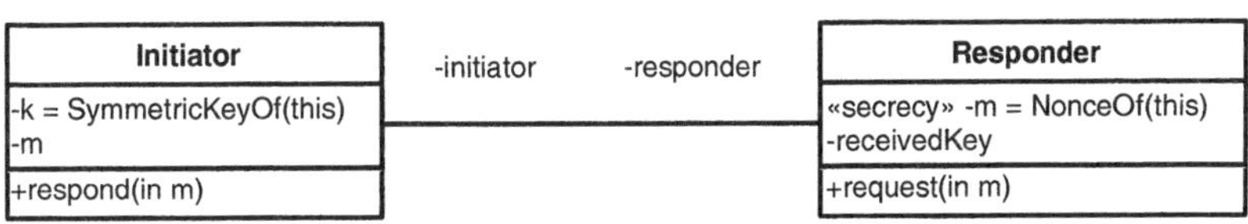

Fig. 3. Example Class diagram

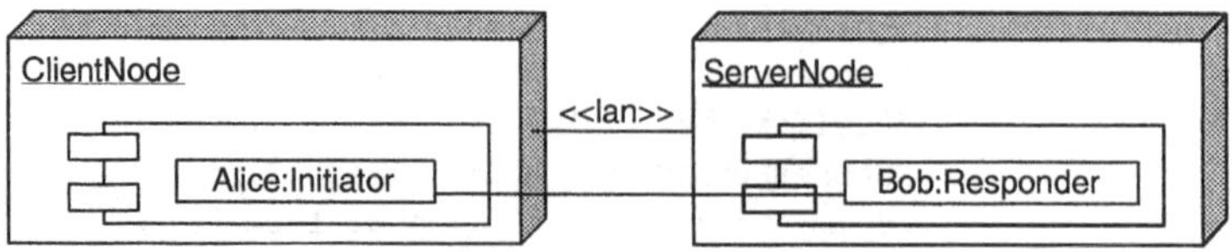

Fig. 4. Example Deployment diagram

secret information from Bob (of class Responder). Alice sends to Bob her key, and Bob returns the secret value encrypted under the key:

$$\begin{array}{llll} \text{Alice} & \rightarrow \text{Bob} & : & k \\ \text{Bob} & \rightarrow \text{Alice} & : & \{x\}_k \end{array}$$

The UML model of the example is presented in Figures 3 through 6. Fig. 3 contains a class diagram defining the data structure of the system consisting of the Initiator and the Responder. Note that the attribute m of the Responder class is marked with the «secrecy» stereotype, which expresses the requirement that the content of this attribute is never leaked to the adversary. Fig. 4 contains a deployment diagram describing the physical layer underlying the protocol. The communication link is marked with the «lan» stereotype, meaning that the communication link is supposed to be a connection in a local area network, which implies that the (internal) adversary we consider in this example is capable of reading and writing on the link. Fig. 5 contains a statechart specifying the behavior of the Initiator in the protocol sketched above, and Fig. 6 a statechart for the Responder.

Translation to Model-Checker We explain some key points in the automatic translation from UMLsec models to Promela code and its execution in Spin at the hand of our running example. We use the Spin model checker since we found it suitable for verification of distributed communicating systems. In particular, Spin's *on-the-fly* model checking allowing to partially verify a model without building the full state space seems suitable for verifying security requirements with their highly non-deterministic adversary models.

Parameters and Data Types In a UML model, developers can use a broad range of predefined data types, and can also define their own data types. In

Fig. 5. Example Initiator Statechart

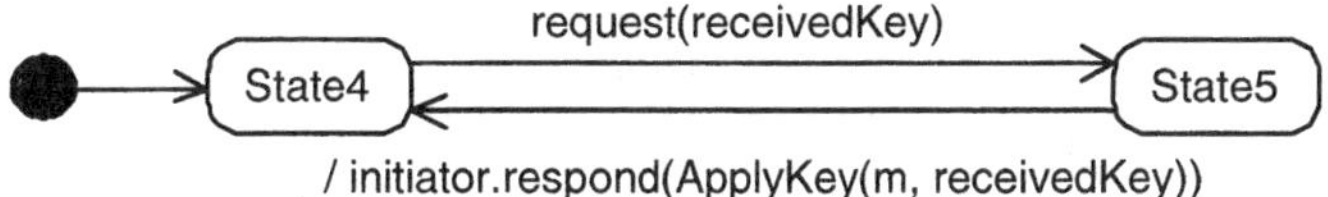

Fig. 6. Example Responder Statechart

contrast, model checker notations usually support only a very limited set of data types (in the case of Promela: Boolean, Integer and enumeration [Hol03]). For a given UML model, we thus need to define a mapping of complex UML data types onto the limited set of data types supported by the model checker. We discuss two obvious approaches for constructing such a mapping and explain why they are not sufficient for our needs, which motivates the solution we then propose. We use the term *atomic values* for values like an encryption key k, or a message v, which are considered to be unique and cannot be derived from other atomic values. We use the term *complex values* for data constructs received from applying operations (the *data transformation functions*) to atomic values, such as $\{v\}_k$ (x encrypted under the key k).

We consider a model with a base data type (say, Integer) supposed to include the atomic values to discuss three possibilities of representing and processing complex values:

Simple Enumeration We use the Integer data type to enumerate all possible data values. For the $\{v\}_k$ expression we assign a new integer value to every combination of atomic values v and k. The data transformation functions are represented by a simple mapping function. In this approach, it is difficult to decide which combinations of values are possible and need to be enumerated. The translation process and the resulting code are complex. The internal logic of different processes in the translated code becomes mutually dependent. Detecting and enumerating all possible combinations is in fact the task of the Model Checker. Implementing the same logic in the translator complicates the translation process and the resulting model. The HUGO UML to Promela translator [SKM01], for example, allows using native Model Checker data types in the function parameters in the UML Model. It does not explicitly implement enumerating of the all possible complex data values, but it may be possible to be extended in this way. However, taking the discussed drawbacks into account, we consider other possibilities.

Fixed Types The UML explicitly defines the data types of all variables, parameters and return values in the model. For every data type, it is then possible to enumerate all its values and define data transformation functions hardcoded in the translated Model Checker code according to the data type they process. We are not aware of any existing tools implementing this approach. Comparing to the first solution, it will result in a better structured code, and the translation logic will be cleaner and easier to understand. However, we then have to limit the developer to use only those data types known to our translator. Alternatively we can request the developer to provide mapping rules describing how the data types in the UML model relate to the translator data types. Both solutions mean significant additional effort which might prevent developers from using the technology. To handle these problems, we introduce dynamic handling of data types, where the message itself carries information about its type.

Dynamic Types The complex data type is defined during the translation process and holds any complex value which may appear in the system during its execution. For this, the tool builds a *Type Graph*. Starting from the root node of type *atomic*, and applying all expressions which are met in the model (namely, initial values, transition effects, and transition guards), the tool creates new vertexes in the graph as necessary. The data transformation functions are presented by edges, and the complex data types incarnations are presented by nodes.

The data graph for our example is presented in Fig. 7. It contains two vertices representing a simple variable (root) and an encrypted variable, and two edges representing encryption and decryption. Based on the data graph, the complex data type is encoded by a structure which holds as many atomic values as necessary to represent the most complex vertex plus a variable to encode the actual value type. Then the tool defines a set of data transformation functions which perform operations on the complex data type, for each edge in the graph. The translation result for our example in Promela language is presented in Fig. 8. The MSG structure is then used in the translated code to represent complex data type. The *messageType* field defines which vertex the structure represents. The *param*1 field stores the message v, and param2 stores the key k only when the structure represents vertex $\{v\}_k$. The *ApplyKey* function defines a transformation rule for the graph: encryption on a v-type vertex produces a $\{v\}_k$ vertex; decryption with a valid key on a $\{v\}_k$ vertex produces a v vertex.

UML Semantics We sketch how the analysis plug-in translates the UML model into the Promela notation, following the simplified UML semantics in [Jür02, Jür04]. The resulting model consists of a network of communicating objects, based on the deployment diagram. Each object has an input queue and an output queue for exchanging messages with other parts of the system. Each object has a separate thread of execution within the model. This is achieved by creating a Promela *proctype* definition for every UML class, and by instantiat-

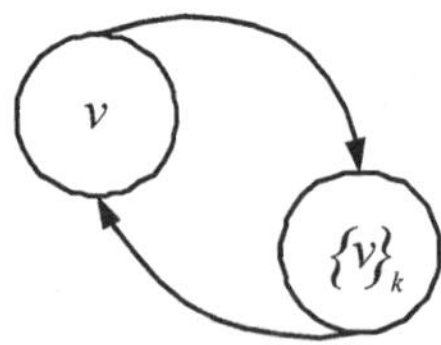

Fig. 7. Example Data Graph

```
typedef MSG {
TYPE_MSGTYPE messageType; TYPE_DATAVAL param1; TYPE_DATAVAL param2;}%
inline ApplyKey(message, key) {
if :: message.messageType == MT_GARBAGE -> ;
   :: message.messageType == MT_v -> message.messageType = MT_LvRk;
                                     message.param2 = key;
   :: message.messageType == MT_LvRk ->
      if :: message.param2 == InverseKey(key) ->
                                     message.messageType = MT_v;
         :: else -> message.messageType = MT_GARBAGE;
      fi;
fi;}
```

Fig. 8. Translated Example - fragment

ing it for every corresponding object in the deployment diagram. Each object in the resulted code receives a unique ID. From the class diagram, the tool collects information about the attributes and its associations with other classes; each association is resolved to an object ID based on the Deployment diagram. The behavior of each class is encoded in a loop following the UML *run-to-completion* semantics by repeatedly executing the following two steps:

- If not in the end state, all enabled actions are executed in a loop, without consuming external events. If more than one action is enabled, the selection of the executed action is non-deterministic.
- A single event is read from the input communication channel and the corresponding action is executed. The execution of the object is blocked if the channel is empty. The events which do not trigger any actions in the current object state are lost.

The tool uses a simplified UML semantics. Some of the other UML constructs can be reduced as usual to the subset the tool supports. In particular, composite and history states are not allowed, events cannot be deferred, and only asynchronous communication is supported at present.

Adversary To apply formal verification methods for verifying security properties of an open, distributed system, it is necessary to model all possible interactions between the system and the outside world. This includes behavior of an adversary trying to break or compromise the system. The adversary model is defined through certain basic capabilities, depending on the physical properties of the system, and on the strength of the adversary that is considered. This is specified in UMLsec using a function mapping an adversary type A and a stereotype s characterizing a physical property of the system in the deployment diagram (such as «Internet») to a set of threats $\mathsf{Threats}_A(s) \subseteq \{\mathsf{delete}, \mathsf{read}, \mathsf{insert}\}$ (see [Jür02]). Each of the threats is implemented by a possible adversary action in the system model. The behavior of the adversary is modeled by a separate Promela *proctype* process definition and instantiated with a separate execution thread.

```
never { T0_init: if  :: known_DV_Bob_nonce == true -> goto accept_all;
                     :: (1) -> goto T0_init;
                fi;
        accept_all:  skip}
```

Fig. 9. Never Claim in Promela

- **read** gives the adversary the capability to read the information from the communication link and store it in the internal variables.
- **insert** allows the adversary to insert his own messages into the communication link. The message is created from the information known to the adversary, constructed from the initial adversary knowledge and the information learned by the adversary from the previous communication.
- **delete** allows the adversary to remove a message from the communication link.

In our example, the adversary capabilities are limited to the subset {*read*, *insert*}, which results into the loop given in Fig. 10 in pseudocode. Note that in this case, the adversary cannot drop the message which is received, but always forwards it to the intended receiver, according to the missing *delete* capability.

Security requirement The security requirement from the UML model, expressed in our example by the stereotype «secrecy» on the variable m of the *Responder* class, is translated into the *never claim* construct in the Promela code, saying that the adversary should never get to know the secret values. It defines a process which runs in parallel with the rest of the system and monitors this property. The *never claim* for our example is presented in Fig. 9.

Verification results For space restrictions we cannot include the full Promela code for our example. It can however be downloaded from [UML]. Spin completes verification of this simple example within a minute after detecting a flaw in the protocol. Part of the Spin output is shown in Fig. 11, the complete verification result also can be found at [UML]. In the attack found in this simple example,

```
loop { do this { read message from Bob
                 send it to Alice
                 analyze and save the message }
       or this { generate a message from knowledge
                 send it to Bob }
       or this { read message from Alice
                 send it to Bob
                 analyze and save the message }
       or this { generate a message from knowledge
                 send it to Alice } }
```

Fig. 10. Example Adversary

```
Depth=      80  States= 122065 Transitions=   165114 Memory= 22.422
pan: claim violated! (at depth 82)
pan: wrote pan_in.trail (Spin Version 4.1.1 -- 2 January 2004)
```

Fig. 11. Fragment of the Spin output

the adversary sends his own key to Bob, pretending to be a legitime protocol participant, and receives back the secret value, encrypted under the key. The adversary can easily decrypt the message and obtain the plain text secret value. If we restrict the adversary from writing messages to the communication link, another attack is still found: the adversary records the key passed from Alice to Bob in the first protocol step, and uses it to decipher the message in the second.

As part of the verification process, Spin produces a trail file, which records the sequence of actions of the potential attack. This information can be used by the system developer to improve the protocol.

Related Work There are several tools for automated verification of UML models. The vUML Tool [LP99] analyzes the behavior of a set of interacting objects, defined in a similar way. The tool can verify various properties of the system, including deadlock freeness and liveliness, and find problems like entering a forbidden state or sending a message to a terminated object. The HUGO Project [SKM01] checks the behavior described by a UML Collaboration diagram against a transitional system comprising several communicating objects; the functionality of each object is specified by a UML Statechart diagram. Work on how to use XMI to provide tool support for UML includes [Ste03] (including an example using the Edinburgh Concurrency Workbench for analyzing UML models). [CBC+01] applies model checking to the formal verification of concurrent object-oriented systems, using the model checker SPIN. It uses an extension of the SPIN notation Promela with additional primitives needed to model concurrent object-oriented systems, such as class definition, object instantiation, message send, and synchronization. [EKHL03] presents automated verification of UML models using the model-checker FDR. [CRS04] presents a simulation framework for UML models based on a UML semantics using Abstract State Machines (ASMs).

To our knowledge, none of the existing bindings of UML to model checkers can be easily extended to analyze UMLsec models. The first reason is the support for security constructs. The second issue is the translation of complex data types, which is necessary for supporting the cryptography extension.

There is an increasing interest in using UML for the development of security-critical systems. For example, [KRFL04] describes an approach for specificating role-based access control policies in UML design models. It allows developers to specify patterns of violations against the policies. [BP04] presents an approach for the specification of user rights using UML. The approach is based on a first-order logic with a built-in notion of objects and classes with an algebraic semantics and can be realized in OCL. [HW04] defines a Security assessment Object Language to specify security requirements in UML.

4 Conclusion and Future Work

We presented work to support model-based development using UML by providing tool-support for the analysis of UML models against difficult system requirements. We described a UML verification framework supporting the construction of automated requirements analysis tools for UML diagrams which is connected to industrial CASE tools using XMI. As an example for its usage, we presented verification routines for verifying UMLsec models. Their aim was firstly to contribute towards usage of UMLsec in practice. Secondly, the verification framework should allow advanced users of the UMLsec approach to themselves implement verification routines for the constraints of self-defined stereotypes. We focussed on an analysis plug-in that utilises the model-checker Spin to verify systems which may use cryptographic algorithms.

The tools we presented are used in industrial projects involving a car manufacturer, a bank, and a telecommunications company. Several security design weaknesses could be demonstrated which have lead to changes in the designs of the systems that are being developed.

The verification framework has proven to be sufficiently flexible and expressive to support analysis plug-ins for a variety of checks. With respect to the tool-binding to the Spin model-checker presented here the Promela code that is generated consists to a large extent of general definitions and security analysis machinery which are always present. Thus the size and complexity of the code scale sufficiently well with increasing size of models. Although we focused on a core definition of the diagrams we used, the tools can be extended to support more complex features. The tools presented here can be downloaded from [UML] as open-source. A support mailinglist for users and developers is available.

In future work, our usage of model-checking can be further optimized in performance to deal with the state explosion problem inherent in model-checking; additionally, we work on the usage of automated theorem provers. We aim to to include feedback from the model checker back into the UML model. Also, we aim to further support extensibility of the approach by allowing advanced users to define stereotypes, tags, and first-order logic constraints which are then automatically translated for verification on a given UML model.

Acknowledgments Fruitful collaborations with about 25 students performing Masters and Bachelors theses and study projects on the construction and use of the UMLsec tools are very gratefully acknowledged; see [UML] for details. Special thanks go to Alexander Knapp for very helpful explanations on his work.

References

[BP04] R. Breu and G. Popp. Actor-centric modeling of user rights. In Wermelinger and Margaria [WM04], pages 165–179.

[CBC+01] Seung Mo Cho, Doo-Hwan Bae, Sung Deok Cha, Young Gon Kim, Byung Kyu Yoo, and Sang Taek Kim. Applying model checking to concurrent object-oriented software. In *ISADS 1999*, pages 380–383. IEEE Computer Society, 2001.

[CRS04] A. Cavarra, E. Riccobene, and P. Scandurra. A framework to simulate UML models: moving from a semi-formal to a formal environment. In *SAC*, pages 1519–1523. ACM, 2004.

[Dir02] R. Dirckze. Java Metadata Interface (JMI) API 1.0 Specification. Available at http://jcp.org/aboutJava/communityprocess/final/jsr040/index.html, June 2002.

[EKHL03] G. Engels, J. Küster, R. Heckel, and M. Lohmann. Model-based verification and validation of properties. *Electr. Notes Theor. Comput. Sci.*, 82(7), 2003.

[Gen03] Gentleware. http://www.gentleware.com (February 2004), 2003.

[HJ03] S. Höhn and J. Jürjens. Automated checking of SAP security permissions. In *6th Working Conference on Integrity and Internal Control in Information Systems (IICIS)*, Lausanne, Switzerland, November 13–14, 2003. IFIP, Kluwer.

[HMR+98] F. Huber, S. Molterer, A. Rausch, B. Schätz, M. Sihling, and O. Slotosch. Tool supported specification and simulation of distributed systems. In *International Symposium on Software Engineering for Parallel and Distributed Systems*, pages 155–164, 1998.

[Hol03] G. Holzmann. *The Spin Model Checker.* Addison-Wesley, 2003.

[HW04] S. Houmb and R. Winther. Security assessment object language (SOL). *Software and Systems Modeling*, 2004. Special issue on the CSDUML workshop, to be published.

[Jür02] J. Jürjens. UMLsec: Extending UML for secure systems development. In J.-M. Jézéquel, H. Hußmann, and S. Cook, editors, *UML 2002 – The Unified Modeling Language*, volume 2460 of *LNCS*, pages 412–425. Springer, 2002.

[Jür04] J. Jürjens. *Secure Systems Development with UML.* Springer, 2004.

[KRFL04] D. Kim, I. Ray, R. France, and Na Li. Modeling role-based access control using parameterized UML models. In Wermelinger and Margaria [WM04], pages 180 – 193.

[LP99] J. Lilius and I. Porres. Formalising UML state machines for model checking. In R. France and B. Rumpe, editors, *UML'99*, volume 1723 of *LNCS*, pages 430–445. Springer, 1999.

[Mat03] M. Matula. Netbeans Metadata Repository (MDR). Available from http://mdr.netbeans.org, 2003.

[Obj02] Object Management Group. OMG XML Metadata Interchange (XMI) Specification. Available at http://www.omg.org/cgi-bin/doc?formal/2002-01-01 (February 2004), January 2002.

[RSA78] R. Rivest, A. Shamir, and L. Adleman. A method for obtaining digital signatures and public-key cryptosystems. *Communications of the ACM*, 21:120–126, 1978.

[SKM01] T. Schäfer, A. Knapp, and S. Merz. Model checking UML state machines and collaborations. In S.D. Stoller and W. Visser, editors, *Workshop on Software Model Checking*, volume 55 of *ENTCS*. Elsevier, 2001.

[Ste03] P. Stevens. Small-scale XMI programming; a revolution in UML tool use? *Journal of Automated Software Engineering*, 10(1):7–21, 2003. Kluwer.

[UML] http://www4.in.tum.de/~umlsec.

[WM04] M. Wermelinger and T. Margaria, editors. *7th International Conference on Fundamental Approaches to Software Engineering (FASE)*, volume 2984 of *LNCS*. Springer, 2004.

Extending OCL for Secure Database Development

Eduardo Fernández-Medina and Mario Piattini

Escuela Superior de Informática. Universidad de Castilla-La Mancha
Paseo de la Universidad, 4. 13071, Ciudad Real (Spain)
{Eduardo.FdezMedina, Mario.Piattini}@uclm.es

Abstract. The Model Driven Architecture (MDA) is becoming an important aspect of software development, since it considers languages and models that can represent an information system at different abstraction levels, and makes it possible a coherent transformation of the system from the domain context into the machine context. In this paper, we present the Object Security Constraint Language V.2. (OSCL2), which is based on the well-known Object Constraint Language V.2. (OCL) of the Unified Modeling Language (UML), and which needs an extension of the UML[1] metamodel. This language is defined to be used in secure database development process, incorporating security information and constraints in a Platform Independent Model (UML class model). This security information and constraints are then translated into a Platform Specific Model (multilevel relational model). Finally, they are implemented in a particular Database Management System (DBMS), such as Oracle*9i* Label Security. These transformations can be done automatically or semi-automatically using OSCL2 compilers.

Keywords: OCL, security constraints, multilevel databases, UML, confidentiality.

1. Introduction

Organizations depend increasingly on IS, which rely upon large databases, and these databases need increasingly more quality and security. Indeed, the very survival of the organization depends on the correct management, security and confidentiality of this information [10].

As some authors remarked [9, 13], information security is a serious requirement which must be considered carefully, not as an isolated aspect, but as an element present in all stages of the development life cycle, from the requirement analysis to implementation and maintenance. For this purpose, different ideas for integrating security in the system development process have been proposed [16], but they only considered information security from a cryptographic point of view. Chung et al. also insist on integrating security requirements in the design, by providing designers with models specifying security aspects, but they do not deal with database specific issues [3]. There are a few proposals that try to integrate security into conceptual modeling such as the Semantic Data Model for Security [27] and the Multilevel Object Model-

[1] We based our extension on the UML 1.5 as this is the current accepted standard.

T. Baar et al. (Eds.): UML 2004, LNCS 3273, pp. 380-394, 2004.

ing Technique [23], but they have not been very spread. One more recent proposal is UMLSec [18] where UML is extended to develop secure systems. This approach is very interesting, but it -again- only deals with IS in general, whilst conceptual and logical databases design, and their implementation are not considered. All these proposals make important contributions that try to solve the problem of developing secure information (sometimes also database) systems, but they are not Model Driven Architecture (MDA) compliant [21]. In fact, they do not define neither development methodologies, nor several models at different conceptual levels. Nevertheless, a methodology and a set of models have been proposed [12] in order to design secure databases, and implement them with Oracle*9i* Label Security (OLS) [22]. This approach is important, because it considers security aspects in all stages of the development process, from requirement gathering to implementation, and it is also based on UML [1]. Together with the methodology mentioned above, a preliminary version of the Object Security Constraint Language (OSCL) has been proposed [25]. This language is based on the Object Constraint Language (OCL) [28, 29] of UML, and it allows us to specify security constraints in the conceptual and logical database design process, and to implement these constraints in a concrete database management system (DBMS), Oracle*9i* Label Security.

OCL is a precise textual language for describing constraints in object-oriented models. This language complements diagrammatic notations in modeling object-oriented systems, defining constraints which can not be described using the standard UML diagrammatic notation. The most important elements that are defined in OCL are invariants (constraints that establish a condition that must be always fulfilled by all the class instances, types and interfaces), preconditions (conditions related to class operations and which must be fulfilled when an operation is executed), and postconditions (conditions related to operations that generally specify the result of operations and which must be considered them true only at the moment the operation finishes).

In the past few years, some proposals to extend OCL to include new properties have been presented. In [14], an OCL extension in order to define real-time constraints is stated. Also, in [17], an approach for incorporating time-based constraints within OCL is described. Moreover, in [30], OCL is extended with temporal operators to formulate temporal constraints, and [5, 19, 20] present an extension of OCL in order to introduce dynamic semantics by adding an action clause to the language. OCL is being used and extended in order to model relational databases with UML [8], or even to model operation contracts to preserve low coupling [24]. Nevertheless, none of these proposals allows us to specify security constraints in conceptual database models. We have only found a work [2] that uses OCL to model software reliability constraints, but it does not match perfectly with the problem we are considering.

In this paper, we define some UML metamodel extensions to be used together with the second version of OSCL language, taking into account the new properties of OCL Version 2.0 [29]. OSCL allows us to define security information in the database conceptual model (through the UML class model) as well as security constraints that can be implemented in a concrete secure DBMS. Recently, several DBMS are including modules in order to manage and implement secure databases, such as OLS [22] and DB2 Universal Database (UDB) [6, 7]. In this work, according to MDA [21], we have considered the UML class model as Platform Independent Model (PIM), the multilevel relational model [12] as Platform Specific Model (PSM), and OLS as DBMS to implement the secure database. However, following the properties of MDA, it could be perfectly valid to consider another database logical paradigm and another secure DBMS.

The remainder of this paper is structured as follows: Section 2 briefly introduces the methodology we proposed for developing secure databases. Section 3 states OSCL2 language and necessary UML metamodel extensions. Section 4 shows an example where the new constraint language is used, and Section 5 presents our main conclusions and introduces our future work.

2. MDA-compliant Secure Database Development Methodology

The goal of the methodology presented in [12] is to be able to develop databases, but classifying the information in order to define what properties have to own the user to be entitled to access the information. In order to fulfill the previous goal, we need to carry out the following activities:

1. To precisely define the organization of the users that will have access to the database. We can define a precise level of granularity considering three ways of organizing the users: *Security hierarchical levels* (which indicate the level of accreditation the user owns), *Compartments* of users (which indicate a horizontal classification of users), and *user Roles* (which indicate a hierarchical organization of users according to the roles or responsibilities of users within the organization).
2. To classify the information within the conceptual database model. For each element of the model (classes, attributes and associations), we can define its security information, which is a tuple composed of a sequence of security levels, a set of user compartments, and a set of user roles. This information indicates the security properties that the users have to own to be able to access the information.
3. To enforce the mandatory access control [26]. The secure DBMS is in charge of ensuring the enforcement of the mandatory access control, and the security information that has been specified in the database conceptual model has to be kept.

These activities are embedded in a methodology for developing secure databases [12]. The general structure of this methodology can be observed in Fig. 1. The *requirements gathering*, *database analysis*, and *multilevel relational logical design* stages, allow us to build general (conceptual and logical) models of the secure database, and finally, the *specific logical design* stage adapts those general models to the particularities of Oracle9i Label Security.

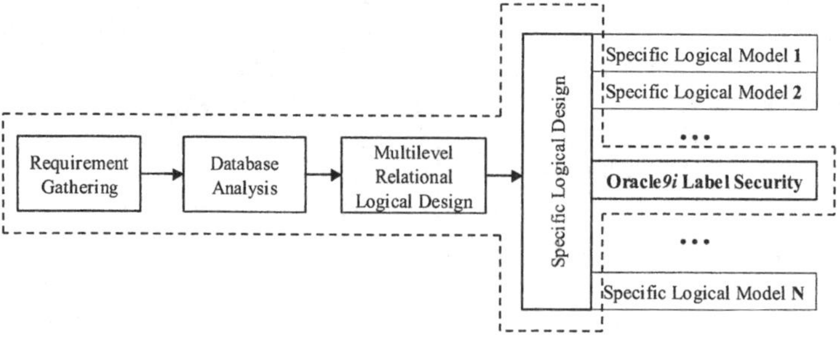

Fig. 1. Secure database development methodology stages

This methodology is MDA-compliant because it is open to integrate, after the database analysis stage (where the conceptual model is created), another logical design stage in order to create another secure logical model of the database (object-oriented, or object-relational). It is also open to integrate, after the multilevel relational logical design, other specific logical design in order to implement the secure database by other DBMS (See Fig. 2.).

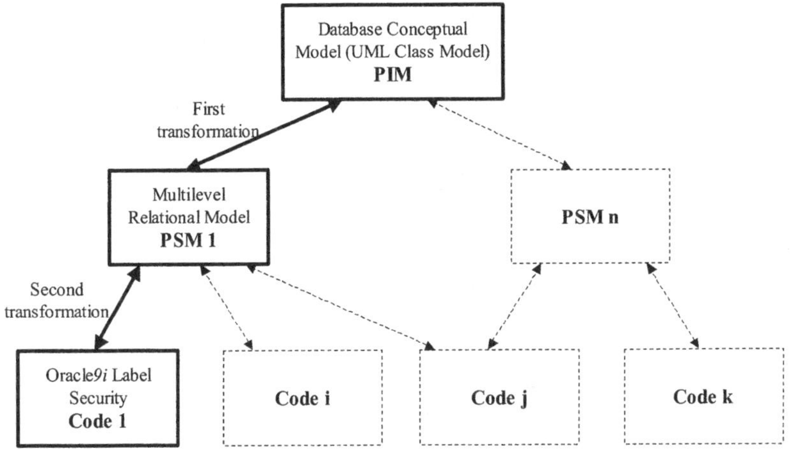

Fig. 2. MDA-compliant models

OSCL2 is integrated into the database analysis, where it helps in both the definition of security information of the conceptual database model elements and the definition of security constraints of the model. This security information and constraints are adapted to the logical model in the multilevel relational logical design, and finally, they are implemented in the specific logical design.

3. Object Security Constraint Language Version 2

According to [4], an extension to UML begins with a brief description and then it lists and describes all of the stereotypes, tagged values, and constraints of this extension. In addition to these elements, an extension contains a set of well-formedness rules. These rules are used to determine whether a model is semantically self-consistent. According to this quote, we define our OCL extension following the schema composed of these elements: Description (a little description of the extension in natural language), prerequisite extensions (they indicate whether the current extension needs the existence of previous extensions), stereotypes/tagged values (the definition of the stereotypes and/or tagged values), well-formedness rules (the static semantics of the metaclasses are defined as a set of invariants defined by means of OCL expressions), and comments (any additional comment, decision or example, usually written in natural language). For the definition of the stereotypes, we follow the structure suggested in [15], which is composed of a name, the base metaclass, the description, the tagged values and a list of constraints defined by means of OCL. For the definition of tagged values, the type of the tagged values, the multiplicity, the description, and the default value are defined.

3.1. Description

The extension we present in this section is not only an extension of the OCL, but also the definition of a new framework that needs the definition of some new data types, and that allows us to specify both security information of the different elements of the database conceptual model (through tagged values), and dynamic and static security constraints of these elements. These constraints, allow us to dynamically define the security information of instances of classes and its attributes, depending on the value of attributes of these instances. Moreover, in this framework, a set of inherent constraints are specified in order to define the well-formedness rules regarding the values of these tagged values.

This framework allows us to represent all the security information (both tagged values and constraints) in the same model and in the same diagrams that describe the rest of the system.

The security information that we will embed in the database conceptual model will be security levels, user compartments, and user roles. This information indicates the security properties that the users have to own to be able to access information. Fig. 3 shows an extension of the pattern that has been presented in [11], that explains the mandatory access control.

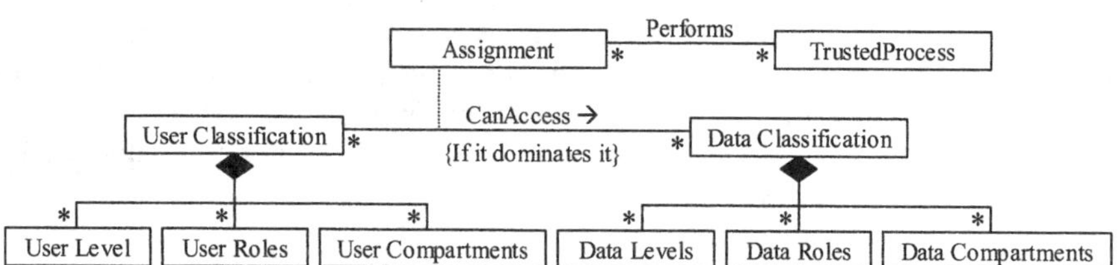

Fig. 3. Class model for the mandatory access control

3.2. Prerequisite Extensions

First of all, we need the definition of some new data types to be used in the tagged values definitions (see Fig. 4). The *Level* type will be the ordered enumeration composed by all security levels that have been considered (these values, are generally *unclassified*, *confidential*, *secret* and *top secret*, but they could be different). The *Levels* type will be an interval of levels composed by a lower level and an upper level. The *Role* type will represent the hierarchy of user roles that can be defined for the organization (in this case, we consider there is no multiple inheritance). The *Compartment* type is the enumeration composed by all user compartments that have been considered for the organization. All this information has to be defined for each database, depending on its confidentiality properties, and on the number of users and complexity of the organization which the database will be operative in.

Finally, we need some syntactic definitions that are not considered in the standard OCL. Particularly, in addition to *Set*, *OrderedSet*, *Bag* and *Sequence*, we need the following collection type:

- *Tree*: It is a collection that contains a root and a sequence of trees. A Tree can be empty.

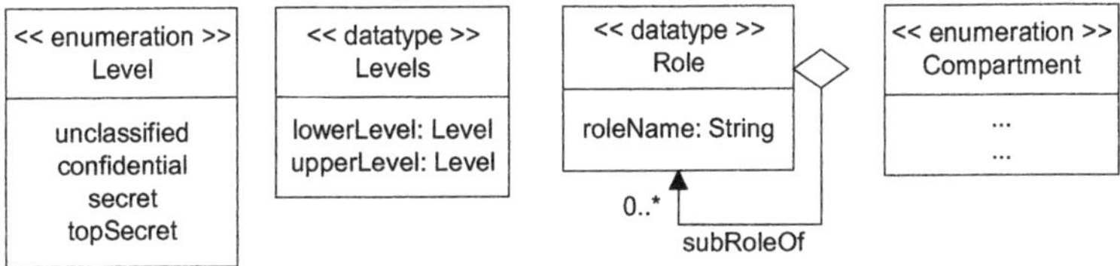

Fig. 4. New data types

Despite trees could be specified by complex OCL structures (see Fig. 5. (a) that shows the collections constant definition of the tree that is shown in Fig. 5. (b)), for the sake of simplicity, we prefer to use a new collection type.

```
Tree {
  'Employee',
  Sequence { Tree { 'System Administrator' , Sequence {} },
             Tree { 'Operator' , Sequence {} }
           }
    }
```

Employee

System Administrator

Operator

Fig. 5. (a) Example of Tree collection (b) Example of Tree

All the standard operations in this collection are applicable, but we need to define two new operations. Table 1 shows all these operations.

Table 1. Standard and new operations applicable to the *Tree* collection

Operation	Description
count (object)	The number of occurrences of the object in the tree
excludes(object)	True if the object is not an element of the collection
excludesAll(collection)	True if all elements of the parameter are not present in the current collection. This operation is applicable if the collection parameter type is Tree.
Includes(object)	True if the object is an element of the collection
includesAll(collection)	True if all elements of the parameter collection are present in the current collection. This operation is applicable if the collection parameter type is Tree.
IsEmpty()	True if the collection contains no elements
notEmpty()	True if the collection contains one or more elements
Size()	The number of elements in the collection
Sum()	The addition of all elements in the collection. The element must be of a type supporting addition
Root()	**The root of the tree**
Subtree(n)	**The subtree n of the sequence of subtrees of a tree**

3.3. Tagged Values

In this extension, the definition of several types of tagged values is necessary. We need to define tagged values for the conceptual database model, classes, attributes and associations.

Table 2. Tagged values of the model, classes and attributes

Tagged Values of the Model		
Name	Type	Description
Classes	Set(OclType)	It specifies all classes of the model. This new tagged value is useful in order to navigate over all classes of the model
securityLevels	Sequence (Levels)	It specifies all security levels (ordered from less to more restrictive) that can be used by the elements of the model
SecurityRoles	Role	It specifies the hierarchical role structure that has been defined for the organization. This type will be managed as a tree
security-Compartments	Set (Compartment)	It specifies the set of compartments that have been defined for the organization
Tagged Values of the Class		
Name	Type	Description
Attributes	Set(OclType)	It specifies all attributes of the model. This new tagged value is useful in order to navigate over all attributes of a class
associations-End	Set(OclType)	It specifies all associations in which a class is involved. This new tagged value is useful in order to navigate over all associations of a class
securityLevels	Levels	It specifies the interval of possible security level values, that an instance of this class can receive. If the upper and lower security levels are similar, all instances will have the same security level. Otherwise, the concrete instance security level will be defined according to a security constraint
SecurityRoles	Set(Role)	It specifies a set of user roles. Each role is the root of a subtree of the general user role hierarchy defined for the organization. All instances of this class can have the same user roles, or maybe subtrees of the roles that have been defined for the class. A security constraint can decide the user roles for each instance according to the value of some attribute of the instance
security-Compartments	Set (Compartment)	It specifies a set of compartments. All instances of this class can have the same user compartments, or a subset of them. A security constraint can decide the user compartments for each instance according to the value of some attribute of the instance
Tagged Values of the Attribute		
Name	Type	Description
securityLevels	Levels	It specifies the interval of possible security level values that an attribute of an instance can receive. If the upper and lower security levels are similar, all instances will have the same security level. Otherwise, the concrete instance security level will be defined according to a security constraint
SecurityRoles	Set(Role)	It specifies a set of user roles for this attribute. Each role is the root of a subtree of the general user role hierarchy defined for the organization. All instances for this attribute can have the same user roles, or maybe subtrees of the roles that have been defined for the attribute. A security constraint can decide the user roles for each instance according to the value of the attribute of the instance
security-Compartments	Set (Compartment)	It specifies the set compartments for an attribute. For this attribute, all instances can have the same user compartments, or a subset of them. A security constraint can decide the user compartments for each instance according to the value of this attribute

In Table 2 and 3 the tagged vaues of all elements of this extension are shown. The multiplicity of all tagged values is 1. All default values of security tagged values of the model are empty collections. On the other hand, the default value of security tagged values for each class is the less restrictive (the lower security level, the security role hierarchy that has been defined for the model, and the empty set of compartments). The default value of the security tagged values for attributes is inherited from the class they belong to. For associations, the security information is the most restrictive from all classes that are involved in this association (the security levels of the most restrictive class, the intersection of the security roles of the classes, and the intersection of the security compartments of the classes).

Table 3. Tagged values of associationEnd and instance

Tagged Values of the AssociationEnd		
Name	Type	Description
securityLevels	Levels	It specifies the interval of possible security level values that an association between two instances can receive. If the upper and lower security levels are similar, all links will have the same security level. Otherwise, the concrete link security level will be defined according to a security constraint
securityRoles	Set(Role)	It specifies a set of user roles for this association. Each role is the root of a subtree of the general user role hierarchy defined for the organization. All links of this association can have the same user roles, or maybe subtrees of the roles that have been defined for the association. A security constraint can decide the user roles for each link according to the value of the attribute of the instances
security-Compartments	Set (Compartment)	It specifies the set compartments for an association. For this association, all links can have the same user compartments, or a subset of them. A security constraint can decide the user compartments for each link according to the value of the attribute of the instances
Tagged Values of the Instance		
Name	Type	Description
securityLevel	Level	It specifies the security level of an instance
securityRoles	Set(Role)	It specifies a set of user roles for this instance. Each role is a subtree of the general user role hierarchy defined for the organization.
security-Compartments	Set (Compartment)	It specifies the set compartments for an instance

3.4. Stereotypes

Once we have all these tagged values available, we could specify security constraints in a class diagram, but all depending on the value of attributes and specified tagged values. In this extension, we need to define some stereotypes in order to specify other types of security constraints (see Table 4).

We define the *UserProfile* stereotype because it could be necessary to specify constraints depending on particular information of a user or a group of users, for instance, depending of the user citizenship, age, etc. We define the *Exception* stereotype because of the necessity of specifying different constraints which permit or deny access to information depending on information different from the security levels, roles or compartments. We also define the *Log* stereotype that can help us to identify and specify classes with special requirements of auditing.

For the sake of readability, the stereotypes *Exception* and *Log* can be graphically specified outside of the class.

Table 4. Extension stereotypes

Name	**UserProfile**
Base class	Class
Description	Classes of this stereotype contain all the properties that the systems manage from users

Constraints	- This class has no associations to other classes
	`Self.AssociationsEnd.size()=0`
	- There is no more than one class of this type
	`Context Model`
	`Inv self.classes->forAll(oclisTypeOf(UserProfile))->size()<=1`
	- The name of a class of this stereotype will be "UserProfile"
	`self.className="UserProfile"`

Tagged Values	None
Name	**Log**
Base class	Class
Description	Classes of this stereotype have special security constraints: the information of all accesses to this class has to be recorded in a log file for future audit
Constraints	None
Tagged Values	- Type - Type: {all, frustratedAttempt, successfullAccess} - Multiplicity: 1 - Description: It indicates whether the access has to be recorded: all accesses, only accesses that have been frustrated, or only successful accesses - Condition - Type: OCLExpression - Multiplicity: 0..* - Description: It indicates whether the access has to be recorded
Name	**Exception**
Base class	Class
Description	Classes of this stereotype will have a special security constraint. This constraint specifies an exception by which a user or a set of users (depending on a condition) can (or cannot) access to the corresponding class, independently of the its security information
Constraints	None
Tagged Values	- Sign - Type: {+,-} - Multiplicity: 1 - Description: It indicates if the exception permit (+) or deny (-) access to instances of this class to a user or a group of users - Privileges - Type: {read, insert, delete, update, all} - Multiplicity: 1..* - Description: It indicates the privileges the user specified in this constrain can receive or remove. - Condition - Type: OCLExpression - Multiplicity: 0..* - Description: It specifies the condition that users have to fulfill to be affected by this exception

3.5. Well-Formedness Rules

We can identify and specify with complex OSCL2 constraints many well-formedness rules. These rules are grouped as follows:

- Correct value of the tagged values:
  - The security levels defined for each class of the model, for each attribute, and for each association, have to belong to the sequence of security levels that has been defined for the model.

```
context Model
inv self.classes-> forAll(c | self.securityLevels -> includesAll
(subSequence2(c.securityLevels.lowerLevel, c.securityLevels.upperLevel))
inv self.classes-> forAll(c | c.attributes-> forAll(a |
self.securityLevels-> includesAll(subSequence(a.securityLevels.lowerLevel,
a.secrityLevels.upperLevel)))
inv self.classes-> forAll(c | c.associationsEnd-> forAll(a |
self.securityLevels-> includesAll(subSequence(a.securityLevels.lowerLevel,
a.secrityLevels.upperLevel)))
```

  - The set of user roles defined for each class, attribute, and association of the model has to be a subtree of the roles tree that has been defined for the model.

```
context Model
inv self.classes-> forAll(c | c.Roles-> forAll( r | self.Role-
>includesAll(r)))
inv self.classes-> forAll(c | c.attributes-> forAll(a | a.Roles-> forAll (r
| self.Role-> includesAll(r))))
inv self.classes-> forAll(c | c.associationsEnd-> forAll(a | a.Roles->
forAll (r | self.Role-> includesAll(r))))
```

  - The set of user compartments defined for each class, attribute and association of the model has to be a subset of the model compartments.

```
context Model
inv self.classes-> forAll(c | c.Compartments-> forAll( comp |
self.Compartments->includes(comp)))
inv self.classes-> forAll(c | c.attributes-> forAll(a | a.Compartments->
forAll (comp | self.Compartments-> includes(comp))))
inv self.classes-> forAll(c | c.associationsEnd-> forAll(a |
a.Compartments-> forAll (comp | self.Compartments-> includes(comp))))
```

- The security information of instances:
  - The security level of the instance of a class has to be included in the interval of security levels that has been defined for the class. The same rule is applicable to the instances of attributes and links.

```
context Model
inv self.classes-> forAll(c | c.allInstances -> forAll (i |
self.securityLevels-> subSequence(c.securityLevels.lowerLevel,
c.securityLevels.upperLevel)-> includes(i.securityLevel)))
```

  - The user roles of an instance of a class have to be subtress of the roles trees that have been defined for the class. The same rule is applicable to the instance of attributes and links.

```
context Model
inv self.classes-> forAll(c | c.allInstances -> forAll (i |
c.securityRoles-> includesAll(i.securityRoles)))
```

  - The user compartments of an instance of a class have to be a subset of the compartments that have been defined for the class. The same rule is applicable to the instance of attributes and links.

```
context Model
inv self.classes-> forAll(c | c.allInstances -> forAll (i |
i.securityCompartments-> includesAll(i.securityCompartments)))
```

- Relationship between the security information of classes, and its attributes:
  - The security levels defined for an attribute have to be equal or more restricted than the security levels defined for its class. The same rule is applicable to the role hierarchies and user compartments.

---

[2] The type of the arguments of *subSequence* collection is integer, but for the sake of readability, we consider that the arguments can be elements of the subSequence. The correct expression should be subSequence(self.securityLevels->indexOf(c.securityLevels.lowerLevel), self.securityLevels->indexOf(c.securityLevels.upperLevel). We consider this simplification in all uses of *subSequence* operation.

```
context Model
inv self.classes-> forAll(c | c.attributes-> forAll(a |
self.securityLevels-> subSequence(c.securityLevels.lowerLevel,
a.securityLevels.upperLevel)-> includesAll(self.securityLevels->
subSequence(a.securityLevels.lowerLevel,a.securityLevels.upperLevel)))
inv self.classes-> forAll(c | c.attributes-> forAll (a | c.securityRoles->
includesAll(a.securityRoles)))
inv self.classes-> forAll (c | c.attributes-> forAll (a |
c.securityCompartments-> includesAll(a.securityCompartments)))
```

- Relationship between the security information of classes, and its associations:
  - The security levels defined for an association between two classes have to be equal or more restricted than the security level of these classes. The same rule is applicable to the role hierarchies and user compartments

```
context Model
inv self.classes-> forAll(c | c.associationsEnd-> forAll(a | a.participant-
> forAll (ca | self.securityLevels->
subSequence(ca.securityLevels.lowerLevel, a.securityLevels.upperLevel)->
includesAll(self.securityLevels-> subSequence
(a.securityLevels.lowerLevel,a.securityLevels.upperLevel)))
inv self.classes-> forAll(c | c.associationsEnd-> forAll (a |
a.participant-> forAll (ca | ca.securityRoles->
includesAll(a.securityRoles)))
inv self.classes-> forAll (c | c.associationsEnd-> forAll (a |
a.participant-> forAll (ca | ca.securityCompartments->
includesAll(a.securityCompartments)))
```

- Generalization hierarchies:
  - The rule we consider for this type of relationships is as follows: The security level of the subclasses has to be equal or more restrictive than the security level of the superclass. This rule is applicable to user roles and compartments.

```
context Model
inv self.classes-> forAll(c | c.subClasses-> forAll(s |
self.securityLevels-> subSequence(c.securityLevels.lowerLevel,
s.securityLevels.upperLevel)-> includesAll(self.securityLevels->
subSequence (s.securityLevels.lowerLevel,s.securityLevels.upperLevel))
inv self.classes-> forAll(c | c.subClasses-> forAll (s | c.securityRoles->
includesAll(s.securityRoles))
inv self.classes-> forAll (c | c.subClasses-> forAll (s |
c.securityCompartments-> includesAll(s.securityCompartments)))
```

3.6. Comments

Many of the previous constraints are very intuitive, hence, we have to ensure their fulfillment since, in other case the system would be inconsistent. Additionally to these inherent constraints, the designer can specify security constraints with OSCL2. If the security information of a class or an attribute depends on the value of an attribute of an instance, it can be expressed as an OSCL2 expression (see Section 4).

4. Example Where OSCL2 Is Used

In this section, we apply the extension we are dealing with for the conceptual design of a secure database in the context of a typical health-care information system. We have only selected two classes in order to focus the example on the specification of security information and constraints. Fig. 6 (a) shows the simplified hierarchy of user roles of the system, and Fig. 6 (b) shows the security levels that have been defined. In this example, compartments have not been defined.

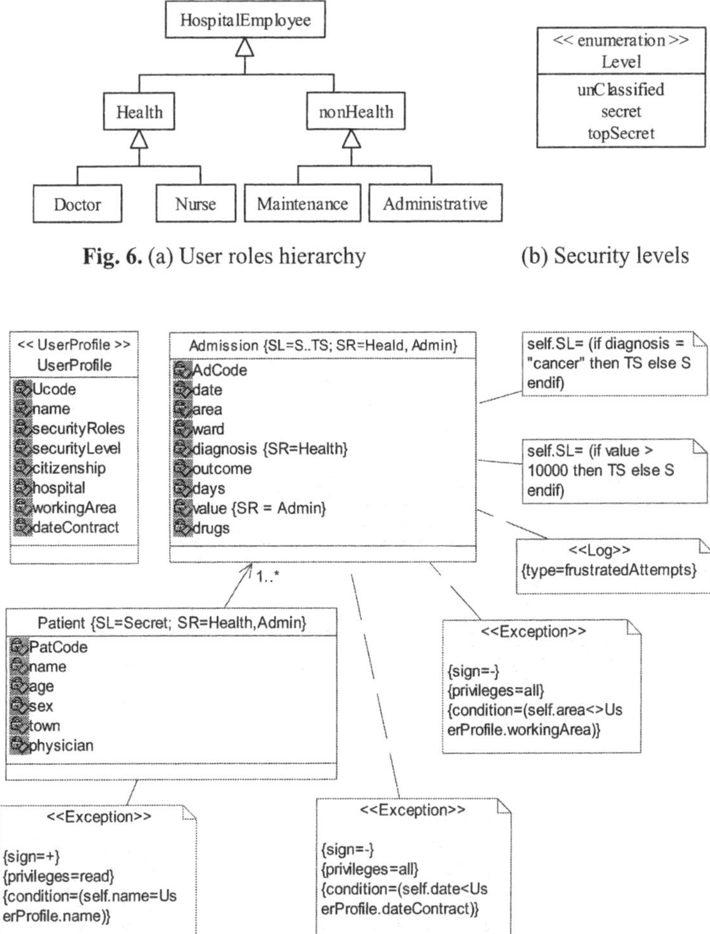

Fig. 6. (a) User roles hierarchy (b) Security levels

Fig. 7. Example of class diagram with security information and constraints[3]

Fig. 7 shows a class diagram that includes three classes: *UserProfile*, *Patient*, and *Admission*. *UserProfile* class contains the information of all users who will have access to this database. *Patient* class contains the information of hospital patients, and can be accessed by all users who have *secret* or *top secret* security levels, and play *health* or *administrative* roles. *Admission* class contains the information of all hospital admissions, and can be accessed by users who play *health* or *administrative* roles, and have *secret* or *top secret* security levels. We can analyze that *diagnosis* attribute can only be accessed by users who play *health* role, and *value* attribute can only be accessed by users who play *administrative* role. There is also an association between *Patient* and *Admission* classes. A patient can be related to one or more admissions,

---

[3] Version 2 of OCL considers a special syntax for enumerations (EnumTypeName::EnumLiteralValue), but in this example, for the sake of readability, we consider only EnumLiteralValue.

but an admission will always be related to a patient. Several security constraints have been specified by using the previously defined constraints and stereotypes:

- The security level of each instance of *Admission* is defined by a security constraint that is specified in the model. If the value of the attribute *diagnosis* is "cancer", the security level of this admission will be *top secret*, otherwise *secret*. The security level of each instance can also depend on the value of the *value* attribute, that indicates the price of the admission service.
- The stereotype *Log* has been defined for the *Admission* class, specifying the tagged value *type=frustratedAttempts*. This stereotype specifies that the system has to record, for future audit, the situation in which an user tries to access to information of this class, and the system denies it because of lack of permissions.
- Patients could be special users of the system. In this case, it could be possible that patients access to their own information as patients (for instance, for querying their personal data). This constraint is specified by using the *Exception* stereotype in the *patient* class.
- For confidentiality reasons, we could deny access to admission information to all doctors whose date of contract with the hospital is later than the date of admission of a patient. This is specified by an exception in the *Admission* class.
- Moreover, we could also deny access to admission information to users whose working area is different than the area of a particular admission instance. This is specified by another exception in *Admission* class.

We can notice that, using this extension, it is possible to specify a wide range of confidentiality constraints in the conceptual model of a database. All these security constraints are transformed along the stages of the methodology we have mentioned before, and finally they are implemented with OLS.

Additionally, an Add-in of Rational Rose has been developed to support most of the elements we have defined in this paper. This CASE tool can be used in the secure database conceptual modeling; with the advantage of the fact that Rational Rose is one of the most used CASE tools in the software development process with UML.

For space restrictions, we refer readers to [12], to analyze how these constraints are transformed in the methodology and implemented in OLS, and to see an overview of the CASE tool.

5. Conclusions and Future Work

In this paper, we have presented an extension of UML and OCL that allows us to represent sensitivity information and constraints in the database conceptual model. This extension contains the necessary stereotypes, tagged values and constraints for integrating security in the first stages of secure database development, and according to MDA ideas, it makes it easier the task of maintaining the security information and constraints along all the process, making it possible to compile constraints and, automatically or semi-automatically generating code that implements security control in a secure DBMS. One of the most important advantages of this approach is that it uses UML, a widely-accepted object-oriented modeling language, which saves developers from learning a new model and its corresponding notations for specific models.

We are currently working on extending the functionality of the Add-in of Rational Rose in order to automatically obtain the multilevel relational model, once the secure conceptual model has been developed, and automatically compile the security constraints and obtain code to OLS. Furthermore, in this extension, we are also considering new stereotypes and constraints regarding other security problems, such as integrity and availability.

Acknowledgements

This research is part of the CALIPO (TIC2003-07804-C05-03) and RETISTIC (TIC2002-12487-E) project, supported by the Dirección General de Investigación of the Ministerio de Ciencia y Tecnología. We would like to thank Luis Reynoso for his valuable comments in the paper review process.

References

1. Booch, G., Rumbaugh, J., and Jacobson, I., *The Unified Modeling Language, User Guide.* 1999, Redwood city, CA: Addison-Wesley.
2. Charpentier, R. and Salois, M. *Security Modelling for C2IS in UML/OCL.* in *8th ICCRTS.* 2003. Washington DC.
3. Chung, L., Nixon, B., Yu, E., and Mylopoulos, J., *Non-functional requirements in software engineering.* 2000, Boston/Dordrecht/London: Kluwer Academic Publishers.
4. Conallen, J., *Building Web Applications with UML.* Object Technology Series. 2000: Addison-Wesley.
5. Cook, S., Kleppe, A., Mitchell, R., Rumpe, B., Warmer, J., and Wills, A., *The Amsterdam Manifesto on OCL*, in *Object Modeling with the OCL*, Clark, T. and Warmer, J., Editors. 2002, Springer. p. 115-149.
6. Cota, S., *For Certain Eyes Only.* DB2 Magazine, 2004. **9**(1): p. 40-45.
7. Database, D.U., *DB2 UDB for Z/OS v.8.* 2004.
8. Demuth, B. and Hussmann, H. *Using UML/OCL Constraints for Relational Database Design.* in *The Unified Modeling Language.* 1999. Fort Collins, CO, USA: Springer, LNCS.
9. Devanbu, P. and Stubblebine, S., *Software engineering for security: a roadmap*, in *The Future of Software Engineering*, Finkelstein, A., Editor. 2000, ACM Press. p. 227-239.
10. Dhillon, G. and Backhouse, J., *Information system security management in the new millennium.* Communications of the ACM, 2000. **43**(7): p. 125-128.
11. Fernandez, E.B. and Pan, R.Y. *A pattern language for security models.* in *8th Conference on Patterns Languages of Programs (PLOP 2001).* 2001. Illinois, USA.
12. Fernández-Medina, E. and Piattini, M., *Designing Secure Database for OLS*, in *Database and Expert Systems Applications: 14th International Conference (DEXA 2003)*, Marik, V., Retschitzegger, W., and Stepankova, O., Editors. 2003, Springer. LNCS 2736: Prague, Czech Republic. p. 886-895.
13. Ferrari, E. and Thuraisingham, B., *Secure Database Systems*, in *Advanced Databases: Technology Design*, Piattini, M. and Díaz, O., Editors. 2000, Artech House: London.
14. Flake, S. and Mueller, W., *An OCL Extension for Real-Time Constraints*, in *Object Modeling with the OCL*, Clark, T. and Warmer, J., Editors. 2002, Springer. p. 150-171.
15. Gogolla, M. and Henderson-Sellers, B. *Analysis of UML Stereotypes within the UML Metamodel.* in *5th International Conference on the Unified Modeling Language - The Language and its Applications.* 2002. Dresden, Germany: Springer, LNCS 2460.

16. Hall, A. and Chapman, R., *Correctness by Construction: Developing a Commercial Secure System.* IEEE Software, 2002. **19**(1): p. 18-25.
17. Hamie, A., Mitchell, R., and Howse, J., *Time-Based Constraints in the Object Constraint Language.* 1999.
18. Jürjens, J., *UMLsec: Extending UML for secure systems development*, in *UML 2002 - The Unified Modeling Language, Model engineering, concepts and tools*, Jézéquel, J., Hussmann, H., and Cook, S., Eds. 2002, Springer. LNCS 2460.: Dresden, Germany. p. 412-425.
19. Kleppe, A. and Warmer, J., *Extending OCL to Include Actions*, in *UML 2002*, Evans, A., Kent, S., and Selic, B., Editors. 2000, Springer. LNCS 2460. p. 440-450.
20. Kleppe, A. and Warmer, J., *The Semantics of the OCL Action Clause*, in *Object Modeling with the OCL*, Clark, T. and Warmer, J., Editors. 2002, Springer. p. 213-227.
21. Kleppe, A., Warmer, J., and Bast, W., *MDA Explained; The Model Driven Architecture: Practice and Promise.* 2003: Addison-Wesley.
22. Levinger, J., *Oracle label security. Administrator's guide. Release 2 (9.2).* 2002: http://www.csis.gvsu.edu/GeneralInfo/Oracle/network.920/a96578.pdf.
23. Marks, D., Sell, P., and Thuraisingham, B., *MOMT: A multi-level object modeling technique for designing secure database applications.* Journal of Object-Oriented Programming, 1996. **9**(4): p. 22-29.
24. Nunes, I. *An OCL Extension for Low-coupling Preserving Contracts.* in *The Unified Modeling Language, Modeling Languages and Applications.* 2003. San Francisco, CA, USA: Springer, LNCS 2863.
25. Piattini, M. and Fernández-Medina, E. *Specification of Security Constraint in UML.* in *35th Annual 2001 IEEE International Carnahan Conference on Security Technology (ICCST 2001).* 2001. London (Great Britain).
26. Samarati, P. and De Capitani di Vimercati, S., *Access control: Policies, models, and mechanisms*, in *Foundations of Security Analysis and Design*, Focardi, R. and Gorrieri, R., Editors. 2000, Springer: Bertinoro, Italy. p. 137-196.
27. Smith, G.W., *Modeling security-relevant data semantics.* IEEE Transactions on Software Engineering, 1991. **17**(11): p. 1195-1203.
28. Warmer, J. and Kleppe, A., *The object constraint language.* 1998, Massachusetts: Addison-Wesley.
29. Warmer, J. and Kleppe, A., *The Object Constraint Language Second Edition. Getting Your Models Ready for MDA.* 2003: Addison Wesley.
30. Ziemann, P. and Gogolla, M. *OCL Extended with Temporal Logic.* in *Perspectives of Systems Informatics, 5th International Andrei Ershov Memorial Conference.* 2003. Akademgorodok, Novosibirsk, Russia: Springer LNCS.

Test Driven Development of UML Models with SMART Modeling System

Susumu Hayashi[1], Pan YiBing[1], Masami Sato[1], Kenji Mori[1], Sul Sejeon[1], and Shusuke Haruna[2]

[1] Kobe University, Nada, Kobe, Japan,
{shayashi,pybing,satoman,moriken,sejeon}@cs33.scitec.kobe-u.ac.jp
[2] Matsushita Electric Industrial Co., Ltd., Kadoma, Osaka, Japan,
haruna@isl.mei.co.jp

Abstract. We are developing a methodology for Test-Driven Development of Models (TDDM) based on an experimental UML 2.0 modeling tool SMART. Our experience shows that TDDM is quite useful for agile model developments. SMART provides guidance on how to build models based on compiler errors of testcases, something similar to what Quick Fix of Eclipse does. It also provides such guidance from failures of testcases, which seems difficult in the case of TDD of programs.

1 Introduction

The integration of Agile methods and Modeling is attracting considerable attention [1,2,5,6,11]. Test-Driven Development (TDD) is one of the central notions of Agile developments. In this paper, we present a method of TDD of Models with with an experimental UML 2.0 modeling tool called SMART.

The most important feature that distinguishes our method from other agile methods is the full scale realization of tool support of test-driven *guidance*. By "guidance", we mean "a suggestion of the next steps to be achieved and/or an aid to achieve them."

In the original TDD, compiler error messages were utilized as suggestions to inform us which classes and methods should be defined next [3]. Quick Fix of Eclipse [15,7] and certain other tools aid us in writing them by automatically generating stubs.

Thanks to UML architectures, we were able to take the idea of guidance forward even more than the original TDD for codes. Quick Fix guides which and how program elements such as classes and methods should be introduced. However, Quick Fix guidance is restricted to *syntactical* aspects, since it is made based on compiler errors (see [7,15]). Failures of testcases can provide us with behavioral information how to fix codes. SMART system supports even TDD of behavioral aspects based on failures of testcases and other execution information. Quick Fix generates stubs but our method can generate fakes as well. (A stub does nothing. It exists only for compilation. A fake returns a fixed correct value for a particular testcase. See p. 169 of [2].)

T. Baar et al. (Eds.): UML 2004, LNCS 3273, pp. 395–409, 2004.

Our technology is possible due to abstractness of UML modeling architecture. It might be difficult to realize similar tool supports for realistic programming languages. It is likely that TDD is more suitable for model-based development, such as AgileMDA, than for development of programs. This seemingly paradoxical fact was realized by a simple technique of logging, which we call *omnipresent log*, that is also possible by the abstractness of UML standard.

In section 2, we explain our method by examples. In section 3, we provide an overview of SMART system. In section 4, we describe the architecture of TDDM and discuss an advantage of modeling based developments over direct program developments for test-driven developments. In section 5, we compare our system with other systems.

2 TDD of Models by Example

In this section, we explain TDDM methodology using examples. The examples are on a room air conditioner with a remote controller.

2.1 TDD of State Machine

A development in our methodology starts with writing some requirements such as stories or usecases. As an illustration, we start with a very simple requirement, "the air conditioner may be turned on and off by pushing a power button."

The next step is to write a *testsuite table*, a table of testcases, that could be understood to be a formalized story or a scenario instances. The following is a testsuite table for the requirement.

Name	**Setup**	**Test Subject**	**Verification**
testcase1	`aircon^PowerOff`	`aircon.power`	`aircon^PowerOn`
testcase2	`aircon^PowerOn`	`aircon.power`	`aircon^PowerOff`

`aircon` signifies a room air conditioner. "air-con" is a common Japanese word for room air conditioners. `aircon^PowerOff` refers to a state of the state machine of `aircon`. `aircon.power` refers to an event in its state machine. The first row of the table reads "when `aircon` is in the `PowerOff` state, the triggering of a `power` event (a modelization of pushing the power button) changes the current state to `PowerOn`". The second line reads similarly.

SMART translates the testsuite table into a testsuite consisting of xUnit style testcases of an action language SAL (SMART Action Language) based on UML Action Semantics. SAL for SMART is used to program actions in models as OAL for Executable UML [10]. The version of SAL used to write testcases is enhanced for testing and is called Extended SAL. The following is the Extended SAL testcase translated from the first row of the testsuite table presented above:

```
begin
setCurrent(aircon^PowerOff); /* Setup part */
callEvent aircon.power;      /* Execution part */
```

```
isCurrent(aircon^PowerOn)     /* Verification part */
end
```

The setup part sets the current state of `aircon` to `PowerOff`. The execution part triggers the event `power`. The verification part is an assertion to check if the new current state of `aircon` is `PowerOn`. This kind of xUnit style testcases are automatically generated when the contents of testsuite tables are entered. To be more precise, all tests are written in and executed by Extended SAL. Testsuite tables serve as the user interface in order to enable an easier input of testcases. Although SAL programs must be directly written for complicated cases, testsuite tables are sufficient for most cases.

Next, we compile the testsuite. Then, some compilation errors are reported, since *no model* has been defined. Just as other xUnit-style test tools, SMART Test Tool has a bar that indicates if there is an error or not (see Figure 1 in 2.4 below). When we compile or run testcases, the bar turns green (no error) or red (some errors). We got a red bar this time. SMART tells us there are no objects called `aircon`, no state called `PowerOff` or `PowerOn`, and no event called `power`.

Besides the error reports, SMART also provides suggestions for possible fixes of the errors just as Quick Fix of Java development environment of Eclipse does [15]. For example, it asks if an object `aircon` shall be created. If we accept the suggestion, then SMART prompts us to choose one of the existing classes or enter a new class name. Since no class has been defined yet, we enter a new class name, e.g. `Air-Conditioner`. Then, SMART declares a new class with the name. Similarly, we are guided to declare other model elements. These kinds of suggestions by the tool are called *guidances.*

We will be guided and so declare a class, an object, an event and two states. When all the compilation errors are eliminated, we get a green bar. Subsequently, we run the testsuites created from the testsuite table. We get a red bar again, but this time the error is a failure. The assertion `isCurrent(aircon^PowerOn)` of **testcase1** failed. Failure is a behavioral error. Some conventional development tools fix structural errors such as lack of `aircon` object, but they do not fix behavioral errors. The guidance mechanism of SMART fixes even behavioral errors. SMART recognizes that the execution of the testcase requires three steps:

setup: set the current state to `PowerOff`,
execution: trigger the event `power`,
verification: verify if the current state is `PowerOn`.

Since all three steps take place within the state machine of `aircon`, SMART infers that we intend a transition from `PowerOff` to `PowerOn` triggered by `power`. Thus, it asks us if we would like to make such a transition. This is called *transition guidance.* Answering "yes" to this guidance creates a transition and the failure of the first testcase is eliminated. Similarly, we create the reverse transition driven by the failure of the second testcase. When it is done, the state machine **sm0** is obtained. What we

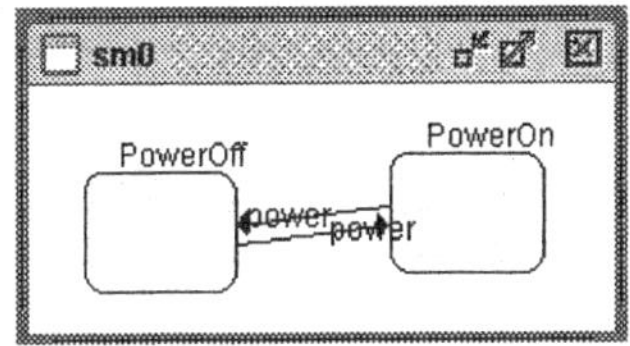

have input from the keyboard are only the name of the class `Air-Conditioner`, although we have accepted several guidances.

It must be noted that there are other possible solutions for the failure of **testcase1**. An air conditioner may enter into a warming up state, when the power button is pushed. On the event of "warming up finished" triggered by a sensor or something, it would make a transition to `PowerOn`. This kind of scenario is possible. Thus, guidance of SMART must be inspected and guaranteed by users to make models respect the intention of users.

2.2 Scenario Test and Testsuite

The testcases we have considered are all "unit tests". Let us now consider scenario tests. Scenario tests can be written as a sequence of unit tests. The following is a scenario test to change the status of the air-conditioner from Off to On and again to Off.

```
begin
setCurrent(aircon^PowerOff);  /* setup part */
callEvent aircon.power;       /* Execution part */
isCurrent(aircon^PowerOn);    /* Verification part */
callEvent aircon.power;       /* Execution part */
isCurrent(aircon^PowerOff)    /* Verification part */
end
```

This testcase can be represented by the following testsuite table:

Name	Setup	Test Subject	Verification
testcase3	`aircon^PowerOff`	`aircon.power`	`aircon^PowerOn`
		`aircon.power`	`aircon^PowerOff`

2.3 TDD of Collaboration

Let us consider an example of TDD of collaboration. We build `aircon` and then consider the following testsuite:

Name	Setup	Test Subject	Verification
tc1	`remocon^PowerOff`	`remocon.power`	`remocon^PowerOn`
tc2	`aircon^PowerOff;` `remocon^PowerOff`	`remocon.power`	`aircon^PowerOn`

The intention of the testsuite is "we can turn `aircon` on by `remocon`". `remocon` signifies a remote controller. "remo-con" is a Japanese word for remote controller. In the testcases of the previous subsection, only one object is concerned. Now two objects are involved. Compiling this, we create `aircon`, `remocon` and other elements. Then, we run the compiled testcase.

The assertion `isCurrent(aircon^PowerOn)` of **tc2** failed, since `aircon` is not turned on by the trigger `remocon.power`. The transition guidance is not provided this time. This is because `remocon.power` is targeted at another machine `aircon`. However, we are unaware of this. So we display a trace of the execution in a sequence diagram shown below to see what happened. This is called *sequence diagram guidance.*

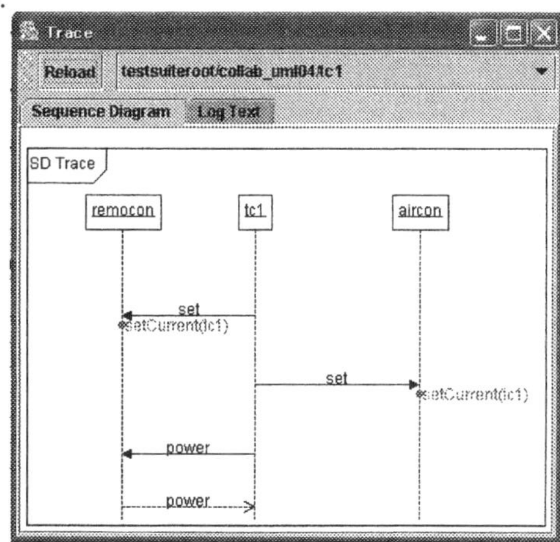

The sequence diagram clearly shows what happened. The testcase set the initial test states of the two models, but the models did not communicate at all during the send/return of `power` event. We have to make them collaborate.

We achive this by inserting `callEvent(aircon.power)` in the effect of the transition of `remocon` triggered by `remocon.power`. (Effect is the activity executed with the transition [12].)

Since the models `remocon` and `aircon` have started to collaborate, it would be a good idea to have a collaboration diagram. We declare a new model with a collaboration in its composite structure compartment. Then, we declare two parts of the collaboration `aircon` and `remocon`. Since the collaboration does not affect *behavior* of the model, the bar turns green when the testcase is run again. However, there might be some errors with the collaboration diagram. We have SMART check if the diagram is correctly drawn by pushing the button of "communication test". Then, it reports that although `remocon` communicated with `aircon`, a connector between them is not represented in the diagram. We drew the parts but did not draw any connectors. Since SMART has memorized communications between `remocon` and `aircon`, it guides us by asking if we would like to draw such a connector. We accept the guidance, execute the model, and check. The communication check passes this time. This kind of guidance is called *connector guidance.*

2.4 TDD of Actions: Change Summary Guidance

We present more elaborate developments in TDD of actions from [13]. Automatic inferences of actions are unrealistic. Thus, guidance is restricted to presentations of information collected from testcase executions. Although decisions are left entirely to the users, this kind of information is useful enough.

We enhance the aircon-remocon model with temperature controls. The controller has an up-button, a down-button and a liquid crystal display indicating the room temperature. Using up- and down-buttons, the temperature could be controlled by one degree. The highest and lowest limits of temperatures memorized by the controller are 26 and 16 degrees centigrade respectively. The memorized temperature does not change beyond the limits. When the up- or down-

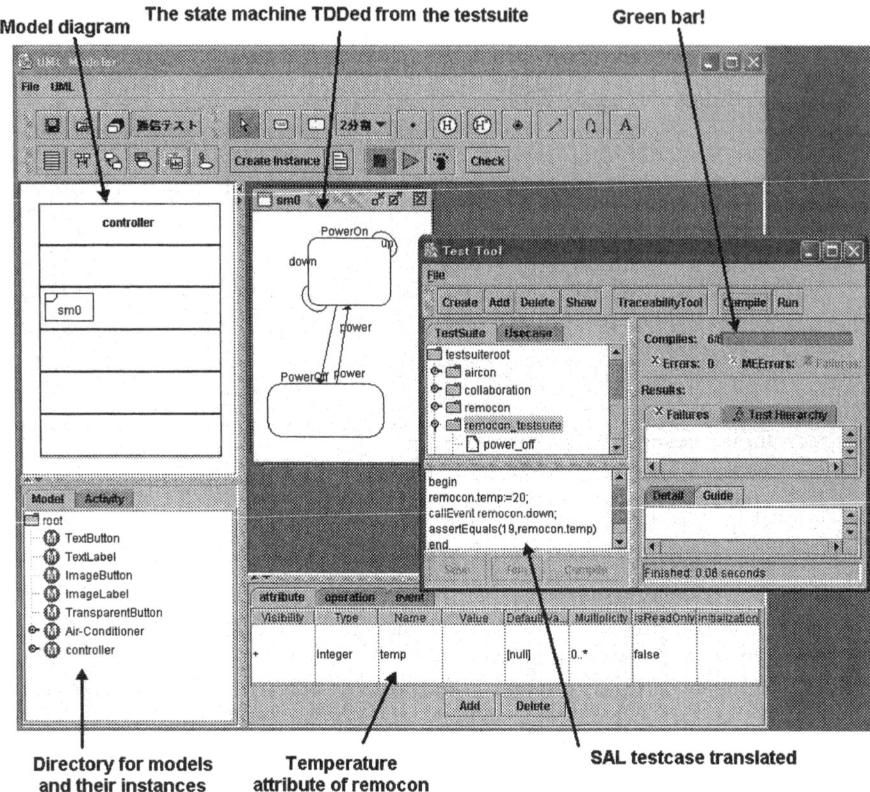

Fig. 1. A state machine made by TDD with SMART

button is pushed, the memorized temperature is transmitted to the air conditioner, and the temperature memorized by the air conditioner is set accordingly.

Firstly, we model `remocon`. The testsuite table is as follows:

Name	Setup	Test Subject	Verification
power_on	`remocon^PowerOff`	`remocon.power`	`remocon^PowerOn`
power_off	`remocon^PowerOn`	`remocon.power`	`remocon^PowerOff`
temp_up	`remocon.temp:=20`	`remocon.up`	`21=remocon.temp`
temp_up_max	`remocon.temp:=26`	`remocon.up`	`26=remocon.temp`
temp_down	`remocon.temp:=20`	`remocon.down`	`19=remocon.temp`
temp_down_min	`remocon.temp:=16`	`remocon.down`	`16=remocon.temp`

Figure 1 is a picture of the modeler, in which a state machine of `remocon` has been built by fixing all the structural errors of the testsuite mentioned above. Then, we run the testsuite. Some testcases fail. This is because the effects (actions) attached to the transitions have not been written yet. For example, **temp_up** testcase tells us that the temperature (20) does not rise. So we add the command `remocon.temp:=remocon.temp+1` in the effect of the transition triggered by `remocon.up`. The error is fixed and we do the same thing for **temp_down**. **temp_down** and **temp_up** run with the green bar. We run the entire testsuite. However, we have a red bar indicating failure again.

This is a good time to use *change summary guidance*. A sequence diagram guidance displays a particular execution of a testcase. On the other hand, change summary guidance displays change of attributes and state of models caused by an event or activity under test. In this case, change summary guidance for the testsuite looks as follows:

```
Created automatically when running TestCases:
From: testsuiteroot\remocon\temp_up
remocon.temp[0]: 20 ==> 21 true
remocon: PowerOn

From: testsuiteroot\remocon\temp_up_max
remocon.temp[0]: 26 ==> 27 false
remocon: PowerOn
```

The first unit for `testsuiteroot\remocon\temp_up` shows that **temp_up** is ok. The temperature `temp` changed from 26 to 27 as expected by the testcase. However, the second unit `testsuiteroot\remocon\temp_up_max` shows that **temp_up_max** for `remocon` failed. The temperature changes from 26 to 27, however, the expected value by the testcase is 26. Oops! We have forgotten to limit the temperature rise. We have to prevent the rise over 26 by putting a limit on the transition trigger. We have to do the same for "down". Now, we regain the green bar.

We do a similar thing for the `remocon` model. Subsequently, we make these two collaborate (communicate). A testsuite for the communication looks as follows:

Name	Setup	Test Subject	Verification
power_on	`remocon^PowerOff;` `aircon^PowerOff`	`remocon.power`	`remocon^PowerOn;` `aircon^PowerOn`
temp_up	`remocon.temp:=20;` `aircon.temp:=20`	`remocon.up`	`21=remocon.temp;` `21=aircon.temp`

The rest of the developments are essentially the same as the ones in 2.3.

3 SMART Modeling System

In this section, we will provide details of SMART modeling system. SMART modeling system is a UML 2.0 modeling tool used to realize our TDDM methodology. The main application targets of SMART are distributed embedded systems such as home electric appliances. The current version SMART 0.3 is based on UML 2.0 standard except its action language, which is still based on UML 1.5.

3.1 Model Concept of SMART

In the terminology of SMART system, a *system* is modeled as a behaviored and structured classifier with graphical user interfaces. A *SMART model* consists of its name, properties, operations, events, constructors, and the following five compartments: (i) Composite Structure, (ii) User Interface, (iii) State Machine, (iv) Interaction (as Sequence Diagram), and (v) Use Case. A SMART model is depicted by a table like diagram called a *model diagram* (see Figure 1 in 2.4). The concept of SMART model and model diagrams were introduced and discussed in [14].

SMART models can be nested. A distributed system, such as communicating electric appliances is modeled using the composite structure compartment. Formally, a distributed system is a SMART model whose composite structure compartment consists of a collaboration (of UML 2.0) and each part of the collaboration is again a SMART model. The aircon-remocon model mentioned in section 2 can be represented by a SMART model consisting of a collaboration of two SMART models of aircon and remocon. However, the collaborations need not be written explicitly.

SMART is intended to be a simulator for home network. Thus, it has a graphical tool to build GUIs for home appliances, such as a remote controller of an air conditioner or a TV. A GUI for the remote controller is easily made by placing some buttons and a text box on the picture of a controller body.

3.2 SAL: SMART Action Language

SAL (SMART Action Language) is our own action language based on UML Action Semantics. SAL compiles its programs into Actions and then Action Executions for execution. The current SMART 0.3 uses a sequential version of SAL based on UML 1.5 Action Semantics. A new version of SAL supporting concurrent data flow computations with multi-valued functions based on UML 2.0 Action semantics is nearing completion and is planned to replace the current SAL soon.

SAL is used to describe the effects of transitions of state machines and operations of classes. Conforming to UML 2.0 standard [12], actions are handled independently from these model elements. Namely, SAL programs are written and managed separately from these model elements and are then associated with them. SAL is also a language for testcases as explained in the next subsection.

3.3 STT: SMART Test Tool

STT (SMART Test Tool) is a test tool for TDDM introduced in [13]. It is implemented on the JUnit testing framework [4]. In a xUnit framework, test subjects and testcases are both written in the same language "x" for xUnit. The JUnit testcases are Java programs to test Java programs. In STT, test subjects are UML models and testcases are written in SAL programs enhanced with a test profile STP (SMART Test Profile). Since SAL is an action language for Action Semantics, this architecture conforms to UML except enhancements for STP.

Since testing is not considered in UML standard, we introduces a simple profile for testing called STP. To be precise, STP is a metamodel extension, although we call it a profile. Firstly, the concept of configurations of executing state machines is introduced so that state machines in execution can be dumped and restored. Metaclasses for state machines are hard-extended by them. Secondly, the Action metaclass is enhanced with actions for testing. New metaclasses for actions are:

1. *WriteStateMachineConfigurationAction* and *ReadStateMachineoConfigurationAction* for writing and reading configuration of state machines in order to set up and verify state machine configurations.
2. *DumpConfigurationAction* and *RestoreConfigurationAction* dump and restore executing models. At any stable moment, the entire models in execution can be dumped out and restored later. This makes setting up and tearing down for testing extremely easy. This is also quite useful for every day development of models. The implementation of these for SMART dumps/restores even the positions of model diagrams.
3. *AssertAction* extends Action Semantics with actions for xUnit-style assertions.

Extended SAL is an extension of SAL supporting STP. This is the language that was used for testcases shown in section 2. For example, `setCurrent` command sets up current state of state machines, and `isCurrent` checks if a state is the current state. `assertEquals` is a counterpart of `assertEquals`-assertion of JUnit.

Errors of testcases are classified into three categories: (i) Syntax error, (ii) ME error (Missing Element error), and (iii) Failure. A syntax error is an error of syntax on Extended SAL. This is not an error of a model, but an error of a testcase.

ME errors and failures are errors of models. ME errors are errors of missing model elements. If a token in a testcase refers to a model element but such an element does not exist, then an ME error is raised. As syntax errors, this type of errors are detected by the SAL compiler.

On the other hand, failures are behavioral errors. It is quite difficult to fix them automatically. It may even be dangerous to do so, since there are too many possible solutions and presenting a small number of them to users may guide them in the wrong direction which do not conform to their intentions. The behavioral guidance supported by the current version of SMART are *transition guidance*, *change summary guidance*, *connector guidance*, and *sequence diagram guidance* used in the examples of section 2.3. In section 4, we will discuss how these guidance are realized and how they can be extended.

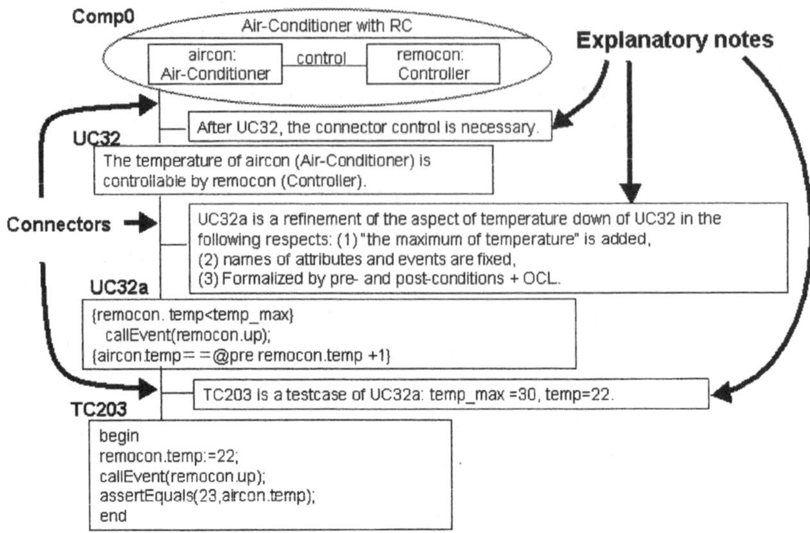

Fig. 2. The concept of STWT

3.4 STWT: SMART Traceability Web Tool

STWT (SMART Traceability Web Tool) is a tool that manages relationships between documents and elements in models developed with SMART. Figure 2 shows the concept of STWT. A SMART model consists of numerous documents such as testcases and model elements. All of them are related. For example, the testcase TC203 is an "instance" of the usecase UC32a, which is a refinement of the usecase UC32. The Comp0 presents the collaboration of `aircon` and `remocon` described in UC32.

When the designer of the system changes his mind, now deciding that the maximum of the temperature should be 28 degree, he changes the requirements. The testcases must then be changed accordingly. STWT is a web of STWT-documents that traces the dependence of these documents in such a case. Testcases, usecases, and model elements can be declared as STWT-documents. Change summary guidances, which are plain texts generated by STT, are declared as STWT-documents when they are generated. STWT-documents are related by connectors and connectors have meta-documents called *explanatory note* (see Figure 2), in which we can write how the parties at connector ends are related. In the current version of SMART, explanatory notes are plain texts.

To browse, the STWT web, SMART now has two "view" mechanisms. *Local view*, which is good for displaying each document, and *Global view* for displaying a birds-eye view of the web. STWT-documents may have "levels" and STWT-documents are deployed in positions specified by these levels.

4 Architecture of Guidance and Omnipresent Log

In this section, the architecture of guidance is explained and possible extensions of guidance are discussed. Guidance is a suggestion or aid made to help modeling. Guidance is classified into behavioral guidance and structural guidance. Guidance is behavioral when it is based on the results of executions of models and testcases. Guidance is structural when it is not behavioral. Since compilation takes place before executions, guidance based on compiler errors are structural. In fact, most structural guidances are driven by SAL compiler errors.

The realization of behavioral guidances is realized by recording all executions of testcases and actions (activities in UML 2.0 terminology). These records are called *omnipresent log*, since logging is present everywhere and anywhere. In reality, SMART does not maintain records of all the executions, but they are kept upto a certain limit.

The following shows parts of a real log:

```
begin-testcase:testsuiteroot\temp\testcase1,2004/1/22/13:28
write-attribute:controller.set\-temp,controller.set\-temp[0],24,24,24,...
setcurrent-state:aircon.poweron,testcase1
   :
transition-end:controller.transition1
message-send-return-event:push\-up,testsuiteroot\temp\testcase1,...
assert-equals:25,controller.set\-temp[0],25,24,false
```

The readers would see that it records call/return of messages, start/end of activities and testcases, call of each action, such as write-attribute action, errors, etc. Since practically all the executions of the models are recorded in this way, it is easy to create sequence diagram guidances and change summary guidances from the omnipresent log. By definition, *guidance is behavioral, when it is based on the omnipresent log.*

4.1 Transition Guidance and Some Related Guidance

Let us explain how the transition guidance is created from the omnipresent log. When a testcase is executed and a failure on current states occurs, the execution record of the failure is extracted from the omnipresent log and analyzed. If the test subject is an event for a model, the setup part sets a state to the current state of the model (a model has at most one state machine), the verification part checks if the state is the current state of the same model. Finally the check fails, and the transition guidance is then triggered. This triggering condition for the transition guidance is well represented by the following pre- and post-conditioned behavior by using a variable keeping the current state `current`:

{`current=PowerOff`} transition triggered by `power` {`current=PowerOn`}.

An obvious solution for "transition triggered by `power`" is `current:=PowerOn`, which means the transition to `PowerOn`. Note that this solution can be obtained by Dijkstra-Gries style top-down inference of programs from specifications by the axiom of assignment (e.g., [8]). The same consideration leads us to a guidance for the following behavior specification:

{`temp=22`} action triggered by `up` {`temp=23`}.

The solution following the Dijkstra-Gries style top-down inference is

{`temp=22`} `temp:=23` {`temp=23`}.

The inferred code `temp:=23` is not correct, but it is the standard fake used in TDD. Putting it in the effect of the transition triggered by `up`, a fake for the testcase is automatically generated. This will be called *assignment fake guidance*. Stub generation is currently supported by certain programming tools, such as Eclipse, IDEA, etc., but fake generation is not.

The same technique will produce fakes for communications. A fake for the testcase **tc2** in 2.3 could be generated by putting `setCurrent(aircon^PowerOn)` in the effect of the transition triggered by `remocon.power`. Fakes for change of values of properties caused by communications can also be generated.

There are no essential difficulties in the installation of these fake guidances and they are planned to be done very soon. However, they should not be used until an improvement of STWT is completed. Fake generation is useful but also dangerous. Such semi-automatically generated codes could be forgotten easily. When they are forgotten, they become *bugs* that which pass unit tests. Fakes must be marked and managed by STWT.

4.2 Modeling and Omnipresent Log

It must be noted that the technique of omnipresent log is the same as the one of record/reply debugger often used for debugging of nondeterministic systems such as multi-threaded Java programs. For such applications, the huge size of log causes difficulty.

In our case, the size of log is remarkably small. This fact seems to emerge from the abstractness of behavioral semantics of UML models. UML models are abstract even in their executions. We do not need to record accesses to registers, stack, changes of program counters, etc.

The current version of the omnipresent log records almost all actions performed by SAL activities and state machines but not all the executions. We expect that recording all the execution would not make the log much bigger but it would definitely increase the size. Thus, some techniques to reduce the size may be necessary. Techniques developed for record/reply debugger would be helpful. This would be an interesting research problem.

It must be noted that we may assume the *standard execution semantics* of UML for such research. Although the semantics is not completely defined, this would be a great advantage compared with record/replay debugger for programming languages and hardware.

Thus modeling has two significant advantages compared to programming languages, abstractness and standardization, for realization of the omnipresent log.

5 Comparison with the Other Test Tools

Several UML tools have facilities for testing. In this section, we compare them with our SMART system and its test tool. Testing tools for UML modelers are commonly used. Telelogic TAU Generation2 utilizes ITU TTCN-3 language for integration testing. IBM Rational Rose Technical Developer could be utilized with Test RealTime test tool. Most test tools for UML modelers, including these two, are used for test-after approach.

STT of SMART is a test tool used for test-first approach. TDD-style design is primarily a design strategy, and only secondarily a testing strategy. In the same vein, our STT test tool is primarily an aid for constructing models from *pointwise specifications* represented as pre- and post-conditioned behaviors represented as xUnit-style testcases as illustrated by an example in 4.1. This model design strategy and the semi-automated guidance mechanism is the main feature of our STT testing tool. STT is only secondarily a test tool. This is the discrepancy of SMART/STT from the other modeling and testing tools.

Although most testing and modeling tools differ from ours, there has been a notable pioneering study conducted in the test-first modeling approach prior to our work. Boger et al. have introduced a UML tool supporting TDD in [6].

In Boger's tool, users established testcases in Java codes and could conduct test-driven model construction. Note that we use an action language for Action Semantics instead of JAVA in Boger's system. Thus, our method is completely independent from any programming languages. Our exclusive concern is model construction. It seems that Boger's tool was aimed not only model consruction but also direct code developments, as they stressed interactions between testcases and codes written after the models in [6].

Contrary to Boger's approach, we prohibit programming languages at the model construction levels of developments. Due to this design decision, exceptions of errors and failures in testcases are all native and the omnipresent log was easily implemented. These made syntactical and semantical guidances easy. Adding features like semantical guidance to a modeling tool based on existing compiler languages would not be easy.

Note that we have not considered code developments in the present paper. In our approach, code developments should be done in the manner similar to MDA. Since our methodology is programming language independent, we are expecting that it will be particularly important for AgileMDA [11] as TDD is a very important factor in eXtreme Programming.

6 Conclusions

In this paper, a methodology of TDD of Models was introduced. The methodology is based on support with SMART UML modeling tool. The methodology was illustrated with examples and the architecture of the methodology and the system were explained. Possible extensions of TDDM were also discussed.

The novel feature of SMART system is test-driven behavioral guidance. This is possible by the abstract and standardized semantics of model executions. Thus this TDD methodology is more suitable for MDA than for code base developments.

Improvements of STWT is inevitable for further developments of TDDM technology. In the next version of SMART, STWT will be based on XML and Semantic Web like architecture.

Now we input testsuite tables from keyboards. However, contents of fields of testsuite tables are very simple and are easily specified graphically. Using the play-in technology in [9], such an interactive and graphical input tool for testsuite tables would be realized without great difficulty. Such a tool would make the entire development very graphical, interactive, and intuitive. An even more challenging research project is to use play-out technology in [9] to infer fake codes automatically and generically as we did in 4.1.

The concurrent version of SAL and SMART are planned to be launched very soon. This version of SMART is expected to be useful for simulation of home networks. However, if SMART supports asynchronous communications, there is a problem of timing the evaluation of testcases. An assertion verifying change of attribute set must be evaluated after the change of attribute. Such timing mechanism is not present in xUnit-style testcases and it is possible only when SMART/SAL supports concurrent realtime computing.

The guidance mechanisms are now coded in the system. By introducing a script language to describe actions of guidance, scripting of guidance for customization would be possible. The omnipresent log is an archive of complete execution traces. We may regard it as a huge archive and let scripted agents mine incidents from the archive. These agents are *investigators* of the archive and they could run even on other machines if the archive are shared through networks. The current version of SMART ignores invariants.

xUnit style testcases are not quite good for checking invariants. But we could ask investigators to check if the `temp` attribute is kept between 16 and 26 for *all* executions of the air conditioner model recorded in the log. Note that the check can be done even after the execution completed. In a sense, we can test the past.

We are planning to solve these problems soon to apply SMART to the problem of home network simulations. In the long term, we are also thinking of relating STWT to formal methods, including term rewriting systems and proof checkers, and Semantic Web.

Acknowledgments

We express our deepest appreciation to Tomoharu Yachikami, who designed and built the first version of SMART. He also directed our attention to TDD. Without his ideas and effort, our project would not have materialized. We thank Shingo Noguchi, Kazuto Aikou, and Hideyuki Kushida for their efforts in building a state machine tool from which SMART evolved.

References

1. Scott W. Ambler, http://www.agilemodeling.com, Agile Modeling site.
2. David Astels, *Test-Driven Development: A Practical Guide*, Printece Hall, 2003.
3. Kent Beck, *Test-Driven Development: By Example*, Addison-Wesley, 2002.
4. Kent Beck, Erich Gamma, http://www.junit.org, Junit site.
5. Barry Boehm, Richard Turner, *Balancing Agility and Discipline: A Guide for the Perplexed*, Addison-Wesley, 2004.
6. Marko Boger et al., Extreme Modeling, in Succi, G. and Marchesi, M. *Extreme Programming Examined*, 175–189, Addison-Wesley, 2000.
7. Erich Gamma and Kent Beck, *Contributing to eclipse*, Addison-Wesley, 2004.
8. David Gries, *The Science of Programming*, Springer Verlag, 1981.
9. David Harel and Rami Marelly, Specifying and Executing Behavioral Requirements: The Play-In/Play-Out Approach, *Software and System Modeling* **2**, 82–107, 2003.
10. Stephen J. Mellor, Marc J. Balcer, *Executable UML*, Addison-Wesley (2002)
11. Stephen J. Mellor, *Agile MDA*, www.projtech.com/pubs/current/agilemda.pdf.
12. OMG, *UML 2.0 Superstructure Specification*, http://www.omg.org (2003)
13. Yibing Pan, *Test Driven Development of UML Modeling* (in Japanese), master's thesis, Graduate school of Science and Technology, Kobe University, 2004.
14. Masami Sato, *Structural modeling based on UML2.0* (in Japanese), bachelor's thesis, Faculty of Engineering, Kobe University, 2004.
15. Sherry Shavor et al., *The Java Developer's Guide to Eclipse*, Addison-Wesley, 2003.

Behavioral Domain Analysis – The Application-Based Domain Modeling Approach

Iris Reinhartz-Berger[1] and Arnon Sturm[2]

[1]Department of Management Information Systems,
University of Haifa, Haifa 31905, Israel
iris@mis.hevra.haifa.ac.il
[2]Department of Information System Engineering,
Ben-Gurion University of the Negev, Beer Sheva 84105, Israel
sturm@bgumail.bgu.ac.il

Abstract. Being part of domain engineering, domain analysis enables identifying domains and capturing their ontologies in order to assist and guide system developers to design domain-specific applications. Domain analysis should consider commonalities and differences of systems in a domain, organize an understanding of the relationships between the various elements in that domain, and represent this understanding in a formal, yet easy to use, way. Several studies suggest using metamodeling techniques for modeling domains and their constraints. These metamodels are basically structural and present static constraints only. We propose an Application-based DOmain Modeling (ADOM) approach for domain analysis. This approach treats a domain as a regular application that needs to be modeled before systems of that domain are specified and designed. This way, the domain structure and behavior are modeled, enforcing static and dynamic constraints on the relevant application models. The ADOM approach consists of three-layers: the language layer handles modeling language ontologies and their constraints, the domain layer holds the building elements of domains and the relations among them, and the application layer consists of domain-specific systems. Furthermore, the ADOM approach defines dependency and enforcement relations between these layers. In this paper we focus on applying the ADOM approach to UML and especially to its class and sequence diagrams.

1 Introduction

Domain Engineering is a software engineering discipline concerned with building reusable assets and components in a specific domain [4, 5, 6]. We refer to a *domain* as a set of applications that use a common jargon for describing the concepts and problems in that domain. The purpose of domain engineering is to identify, model, construct, catalog, and disseminate the commonalities and differences of the domain applications [21]. As such, it is an important type of software reuse, verification, and validation [14, 15].

Similarly to software engineering, domain engineering includes three main activities: domain analysis, domain design, and domain implementation. *Domain*

T. Baar et al. (Eds.): UML 2004, LNCS 3273, pp. 410-424, 2004.

analysis identifies a domain and captures its ontology [24]. Hence, it should identify the basic elements of the domain, organize an understanding of the relationships among these elements, and represent this understanding in a useful way [4]. *Domain design* and *domain implementation* are concerned with mechanisms for translating requirements into systems that are made up of components with the intent of reusing them to the highest extent possible.

Domain analysis is especially crucial because of two main reasons. First, analysis is one of the initial steps of the system development lifecycle. Avoiding syntactic and semantic mistakes at this stage (using domain analysis principles) helps to reduce development time and to improve product quality and reusability. Secondly, the core elements of a domain and the relations among them usually remain unchanged, while the technologies and implementation environments are in continuous improvement. Hence, domain analysis models usually remain valid for long periods.

Several methods and architectures have been developed to support domain analysis. Most of them rely on Unified Modeling Language (UML) [3] and metamodeling techniques [25]. However, most of these works are concerned with domain structural elements and relations, neglecting domain behavioral constraints. Other techniques for domain analysis (e.g., [7, 23]) use UML extension mechanisms, or more accurately stereotypes. Yet, this mechanism provides no formal definition of domain models.

In this paper we present the Application-based DOmain Modeling (ADOM) approach which enables modeling domains as if they were regular applications. This approach enables the specification of both structural and behavioral aspects of any application within a domain. The ADOM approach consists of three layers: the application layer, the domain layer, and the (modeling) language layer. In the application layer, the required application is modeled as composed of classes, associations, collaborations, etc. In the domain layer, the domain elements and relations are modeled as if the domain itself is an application. Finally, the language layer includes metamodels of modeling languages (or methods). We also provide a set of verification and validation rules between the different layers: the domain layer enforces constraints on the application layer, while the language layer enforces constraints on both the application and domain layers. Thus, the contribution of this paper is twofold. First, we provide an approach for modeling the structure and behavior of domains and for validating application models against domain models. Secondly, basing the ADOM approach on UML, we provide a formal framework for defining and constraining stereotypes.

The structure of the rest of the paper is as follows. In Section 2 we review existing works in domain analysis, dividing them into single-level and two-level domain analysis approaches. Section 3 introduces our three-level ADOM approach, elaborating on its applicability to UML class and sequence diagrams. We exemplify the approach stages and validation constraints on a domain of sensor-based machines and an elevator system. Finally, Section 4 summarizes the strengths of this approach and refer to the future research plan.

2 Domain Analysis – Literature Review

Referring to domain analysis as an engineering approach, Argano [1] suggested that domain analysis should consist of conceptual analysis combined with infrastructure specification and implementation. Meekel et al. [15] suggested that in addition to its static definition, domain analysis may be conceived of as a development process, which identifies a domain scope, builds a domain repository (model), and validates that model. Since the domain keeps evolving as new requirements are introduced, domain analysis in not a one-shot affair [5, 6]. Gomaa and Kerschberg [12] agreed that the domain model lifecycle is constantly evolving via an iterative process. Supporting this domain evolution concept, Drake and Ett [9] claimed that domain analysis gives rise to two concurrent, mutually dependent lifecycles that should be correlated: the fundamental system lifecycle and the domain lifecycle. Becker and Diaz-Herrera [2] proposed that the two concurrent streams are the design for reuse (i.e., the domain model) and the design with reuse (i.e., the application model). Following this spirit, the Model-Driven Architecture (MDA) [19], which originally aimed to separate business or application logic from underlying platform technology, observes that system functionality will gradually become more knowledge-based and capable of automatically discovering common properties of dissimilar domains. In other words, the aim of MDA is to eventually build systems in which considerable amount of domain knowledge is pushed up into higher abstraction levels. However, this vision is supported in a conceptual level and not in a practical one.

Several methods and techniques have been developed to support domain analysis. We classify them into two categories: single-level and two-level domain analysis approaches.

2.1 Single-Level Domain Analysis Approaches

In the single level domain analysis approaches, the domain engineer defines domain components, libraries, or architectures. The application designer reuses these domain artifacts and can change them in the application model. Meekel et al. [15], for example, propose a domain analysis process that is based on multiple views. They used Object Modeling Technique (OMT) [22] notations to produce a domain-specific framework and components. Gomaa and Kerschberg [12] suggest that a system specification will be derived by tailoring the domain model according to the features desired in the specific system.

Feature-Oriented Domain Analysis (FODA) [13] defines several activities to support domain analysis, including context definition, domain characterization, data analysis and modeling, and reusable architecture definition. A specific system makes use of the reusable architecture but not of the domain model.

Clauss [7] suggests two stereotypes for maintaining variability within a domain model: <<variation point>>, which indicates the variability of an element, and <<variant>>, which indicates the extension part. These stereotypes seems to be weak when defining a domain model and validating a specific application model of that domain.

Catalysis [10] is an approach to systematic business-driven development of component-based systems. It defines a process to help business users and software developers share a clear and precise vocabulary, design and specify component interfaces so they plug together readily, and reuse domain models, architectures, interfaces, code, etc. Catalysis introduced two types of mechanisms for separating different subject areas: package extension and package template. Package extension allows definitions of language fragments to be developed separately and then merged to form complete languages. Package templates, on the other hand, allow patterns of language definition to be distilled and then applied consistently across the definition of languages and their components. Both package extension and package template mechanisms deal basically with classes and enable renaming of the structural elements when reusing them in particular systems.

2.2 Two-Level Domain Analysis Approaches

In the two-level domain analysis approaches, connection is made between the domain model and its use in the application model. Contrary to the single-level domain analysis approaches, the domain and application models in the two-level domain analysis approaches remain separate, while validation rules between them are defined. These validation rules enable avoiding syntactic and semantic mistakes during the initial stages of the application modeling, reducing development time and improving system quality. Petro et al. [20], for example, present a concept of building reusable repositories and architectures, which consist of correlated component classes, connections, constraints, and rationales. When modeling a specific system, the system model is validated with respect to the domain model in order to check that no constraint has been violated.

Schleicher and Westfechtel [23] discuss static metamodeling techniques in order to define domain specific extensions. They divide these extensions into descriptive stereotypes for expressing the elements of the underlying domain metamodel, restrictive stereotypes for attaching constraints to stereotyped model elements, regular metamodel extensions, and restrictive metamodel extensions. They mostly deal with packages and classes, but not with behavioral elements.

Gomma and Eonsuk-Shin [11] suggest a multiple view meta-modeling method for software product lines. They solve model commonalty and variability problems within a specific domain (the product line) by defining special stereotypes which are used in the use case, class, collaboration, statechart, and feature model views. These stereotypes are modeled in the metamodel level by class diagrams, while the relations among them are modeled in Object Constraint Language (OCL) [26]. The main shortcoming of this method is in changing the core UML notation (e.g., by adding alternating paths) and in using structural metamodels that capture only the static constraints of the extension.

Morisio et al. [16] propose an extension to UML that includes a special stereotype indicating that a class may be altered within a specific system. The extension is demonstrated by applying it to the UML class diagram. The validation of an application model with respect to its domain model entails checking whether a class appears in the application model along with its associate classes, but not if the class is correctly connected.

The Institute for Software Integrated Systems (ISIS) at Vanderbilt University suggested a metamodeling technique for building a domain-specific model [17] using UML and OCL. The application models are created from the domain metamodel, enabling validation of their consistency and integrity in terms of the domain analysis [8]. While the ISIS project provides an environment for performing the tasks of building domain metamodels and domain application models, it is not clear how the domain dynamics is specified and validated, as the metamodel technique is basically static.

3 The Application-Based Domain Modeling (ADOM) Approach

Application models and domain models are similar in many aspects. An application model consists of classes and associations among them and it specifies a set of possible behaviors. Similarly, a domain model consists of core elements, static constraints, and dynamic relations. The main difference between these models is in their abstraction levels: domain models are more abstract than application models. Furthermore, domain models should be flexible in order to handle commonalities and differences of the applications within the domain.

The classical framework for metamodeling is based on an architecture with four abstraction layers [18]. The first layer is the information layer, which is comprised of the desired data. The model layer, which is the second layer, is comprised of the metadata that describes data in the information layer. The third metamodel layer is comprised of the descriptions that define the structure and semantics of metadata. Finally, the meta-metamodel layer consists of the description of the structure and semantics of meta-metadata (for example, metaclasses, metaattributes, etc.). Following this general architecture, we divide our Application-based DOmain Modeling (ADOM) approach into three layers: the application layer, the domain layer, and the (modeling) language layer. The application layer, which is equivalent to the model layer (M1), consists of models of particular systems, including their structure and behavior. The domain layer, i.e., the metamodel layer (M2), consists of specifications of various domains. The language layer, which is equivalent to the meta-metamodel layer (M3), includes metamodels of modeling languages. The modeling languages may be graphical, textual, mathematical, etc. In addition, the ADOM approach explicitly enforces constraints among the different layers: the domain layer enforces constraints on the application layer, while the language layer enforces constraints on both the application and domain layers. Figure 1 depicts the architecture of the ADOM approach. The application layer in this figure includes three applications: *Amazon*, which is a Web-based book store, *eBay*, which is an auction site supported by agents, and *Kasbah*, which is a multi-agent electronic marketplace. Each one of these systems may have several models in different modeling languages. The domain layer in Figure 1 includes two domains: *Web applications* and *multi agent systems*, while the language layer in this example includes only one modeling language, *UML*. Since UML is the current standard (object-oriented) modeling language, we apply the ADOM approach to UML in this work.

Figure 1 also shows the relations between the layers. The black arrows indicate constraint enforcement of the domain models on the application models, while the grey arrows indicate constraint enforcement of the language metamodels on the application and domain models.

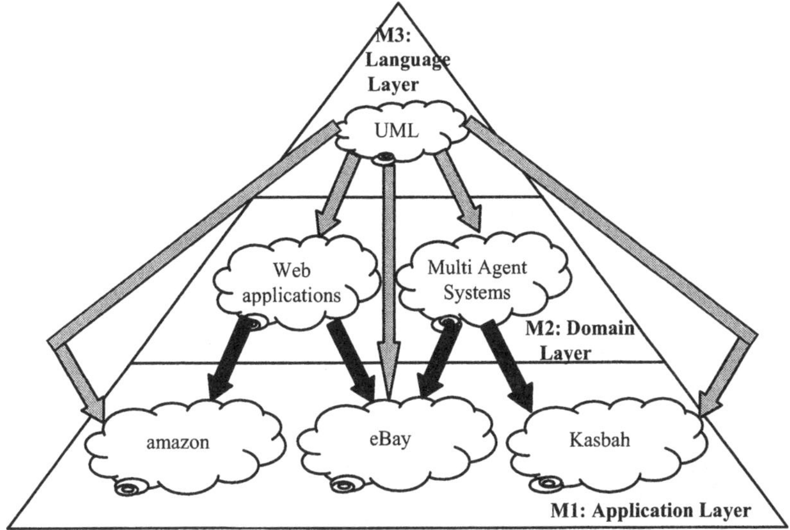

Figure 1. The Application-based DOmain Modeling (ADOM) architecture

The rest of this section elaborates on the domain and application layers, while the language layer is restricted to the UML metamodel except of two minor changes:

1. A model element (e.g., attribute, operation, message, etc.) has an additional feature, "multiplicity", which represents how many times the model element can appear in a particular context. This feature appears as <<min..max>> before a relevant domain element in a domain model, while <<1..1>> is the default (and, hence, does not appear).
2. A model element can have several stereotypes, which are separated by commas.

3.1 The Domain Layer of the ADOM Approach

In the domain layer, the domain engineer specifies the structural and behavioral elements of a specific domain. This is done using UML structural and behavioral views. Figures 2-4 are a (partial) UML model that describes a domain of sensor-based machines. Figure 2 is the class diagram of the domain, which includes the basic elements of the domain and the static relations among them. The top-level class is **machine** which may have any number (including 0) of attributes of any type, as the **"<<0..m>> anyAttribute: anyType"** declaration indicates. The scope of these attributes in the application models must be private. The order of scopes (from the least resticted to the most restricted) is public, package, protected, and private. A scope of a model element defined in a domain model is the least restricted scope that this element can get in any application model of that domain[1].

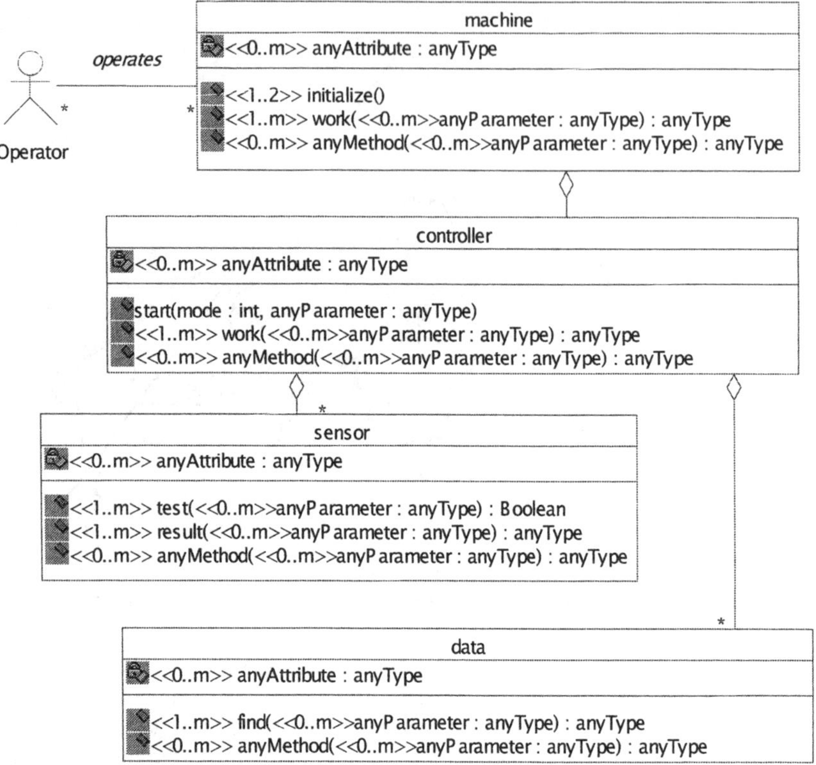

Figure 2. A UML class diagram describing a domain of sensor-based machines

Figure 2 also specifies that **machine** has one or two operations of type **initialize** and at least one operation of type **work**. The **initialize** operations get no parameters and their return type is void, while the **work** operations can get any number of parameters of any type and their return types are not specified in the domain layer, as indicated by the "**: anyType**" declaration at the end of the operation signature. In addition to these types of operations, **machine** may have any number (including 0) of operations (as the reserved word **anyMethod** indicates) with any type of signature. All the operations of a **machine** (as all the operations in this domain model) are defined as public in the domain model and, hence, their scopes are not restricted in the domain-specific application models, i.e., they can be public, package, protected, or private.

A **machine** consists of one **controller**, which is composed of any number of **sensors** and any number of **data** items. A **controller** may have any attributes of any type, exactly one **start** operation with one **mode** parameter of type integer and any

[1] Enforcing a specific scope on a model element (e.g., public) can be done by defining an OCL constraint.

number of additional parameters of any type, at least one **work** operation, and other possible operations. A **sensor** should have at least one **test** operation and at least one **result** operation, in addition to other attributes and operations. A **test** operation gets any number of parameters of any type and returns a Boolean value, while a **result** operation may have any signature. Finally, **data** should have at least one **find** operation with any signature. Figure 2 also shows that an **operator** (a system actor) has a relation with the class **machine**, labeled "**operates**".

Using UML sequence diagram notation, **Figure 3** describes a possible scenario of initialization in the domain of sensor-based machines. According to this scenario, the **operator** invokes an **initialize** operation of a **machine**. As a consequence, the **machine** invokes a **start** operation of its **controller**, which immediately invokes at least one **test** operation of the relevant **sensors**. All these messages are synchronous, enforcing that the corresponding messages in the application models will be synchronous too. Specifying a message to be asynchronous in a domain model enables defining this message as either synchronous or asynchronous in an application model of that domain[2].

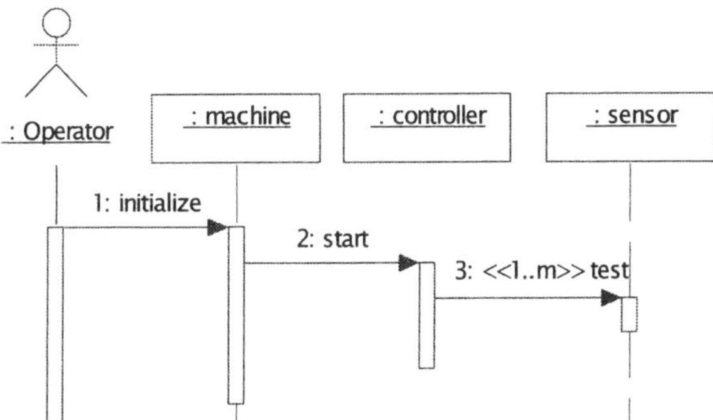

Figure 3. A UML sequence diagram describing an initialization operation in the domain of sensor-based machines

The ADOM approach also supports conditional messages and loops. Figure 4 describes a possible scenario of the machine work:

1. The operator invokes a work operation of a machine.
2. The machine invokes a work operation of its controller.
3. The controller invokes at least one result operation of its sensors. This invocation can be conditional and/or run in a loop, as indicated by [anyCondition] and [anyLoop], respectively.
4. The controller invokes zero or more find operations of its data items. This invocation can run in a loop, but it is not conditional.
5. Finally, the controller invokes at least one work operation of itself. This invocation can be conditional and/or run in a loop.
6. Steps 3-5 can run in a loop, as indicated by the <<1..m>> anyLoop note enclosing steps 3-5.

---

[2] Enforcing a message to be only asynchronous can be done by introducing a new type of an OCL constraint.

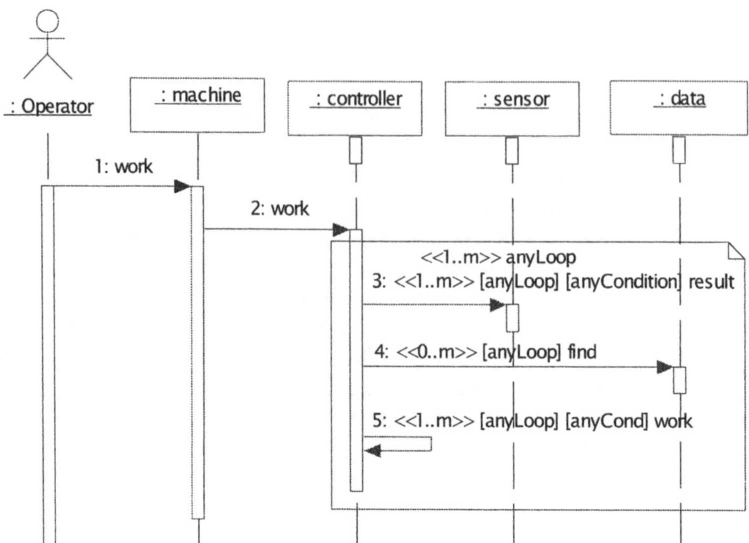

Figure 4. A UML sequence diagram describing a machine work operation in the domain of sensor-based machines

3.2 The Application Layer of the ADOM Approach

An application model uses a domain model as a validation template. All the static and dynamic constraints enforced by the domain model should be applied in any application model of that domain. In order to achieve this goal, any element in the application model is classified according to the elements declared in the domain model using UML built-in stereotype mechanism. As defined in the UML user guide [3], a *stereotype* is a kind of a model element whose information content and form are the same as a basic model element, but its meaning and usage are different. The ADOM approach requires that a model element in an application model will preserve the static and behavioral relations of its stereotypes in the relevant domain model(s).

Returning to our example of the sensor-based machine domain, we describe in this section a model of an elevator system in that domain. Figure 5 is the class diagram of the elevator system. Following the class hierarchy of the domain, shown in Figure 2, the **elevator** (classified as a machine) consists of an **elevator controller** (classified as a controller). The **elevator controller** consists of two types of sensors, a **door sensor** and a **button sensor**, and **music** items (classified as data items). Two types of operators are defined: **user** who **uses** the **elevator** and **technical person** who **fixes** the **elevator**.

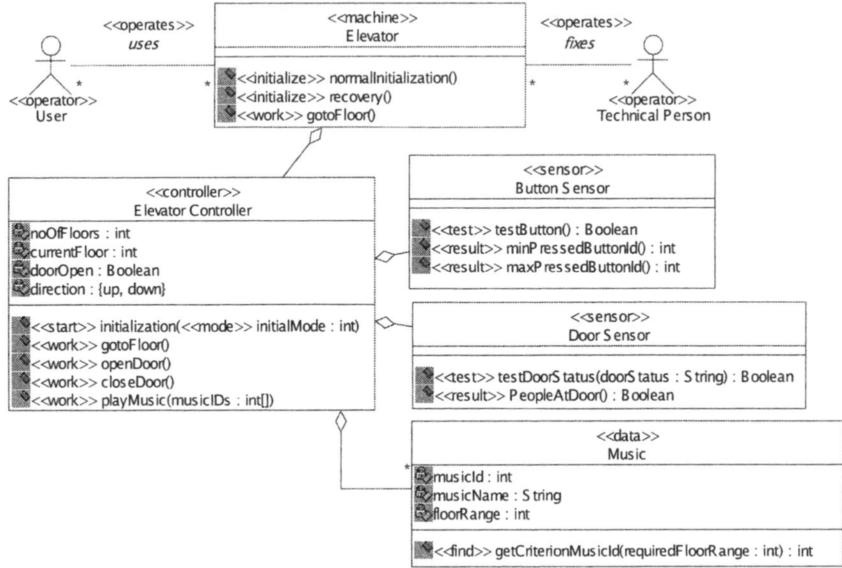

Figure 5. A UML class diagram describing an elevator system in the domain of sensor-based machines

Table 1. The domain constraints and their fulfillment in the elevator system model – comparing the class diagrams

Class	Feature	Feature Constraint	Allowed Feature Multiplicity	Actual Feature Multiplicity
Machine	General attribute	Private	0..∞	0
	Initialize operation	No parameters No return type	1..2	2
	Work operation	---	1..∞	1
	General operation	---	0..∞	0
Controller	General attribute	Private	0..∞	4
	Start operation	Mode:int parameter No return type	1..1	1
	Work operation	---	1..∞	4
	General operation	---	0..∞	0
Sensor	General attribute	Private	0..∞	0
	Test operation	Boolean return type	1.. ∞	1
	Result operation	---	1..∞	1* / 2**
	General operation	---	0..∞	0
Data	General attribute	Private	0..∞	3
	Find operation	---	1..∞	1
	General operation	---	0..∞	0

* for door sensor, ** for button sensor

Table 1 summarizes the domain constraints of the four basic domain elements, machine, controller, sensor, and data, and how they are correctly fulfilled in the class diagram of the elevator system. As can be seen, none of the constraints expressed in Figure 2 are violated by the application model shown in Figure 5.

Figure 6 includes two possible scenarios for initializing the elevator system: Figure 6(a) describes a normal initialization of the elevator, while Figure 6(b) describes an initialization operation that occurs after recovery (due to electrical power interruption, for example). These scenarios follow the guidelines of an initialization operation in the sensor-based machine domain as expressed in **Figure 3**. In these scenarios, no conditions and no loops are defined; hence, the ADOM approach validates only the order of the stereotyped operations and their multiplicities.

Table 2 summaries the constraints on an initialization operation in the domain of sensor-based machines and how the various constraints are fulfilled by the sequence diagrams of the elevator system specified in Figure 6. Note that the validation is done with respect to the stereotype of a model element in the application layer, which is itself an element in the domain layer.

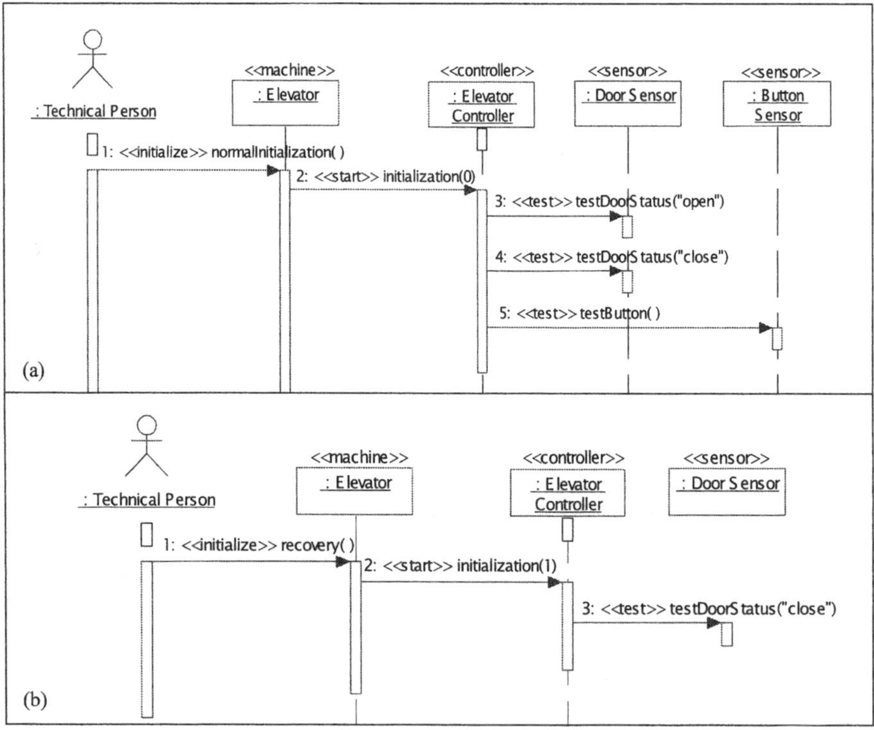

Figure 6. UML sequence diagrams describing initialization operations. (a) Normal initialization. (b) Initialization after recovery.

Table 2. The domain constraints and their fulfillment in the elevator system model – comparing the sequence diagrams of the initialization operations

Layer/ Sequence	Operation	Source	Destination	Mult.
Domain/ Initialization	initialize	operator	machine	1..1
Application/ normal init.	normalInitialization	technical person	elevator	1
Application/ recovery	recovery	technical person	elevator	1
Domain/ Initialization	Start	machine	controller	1..1
Application/ normal init.	initialization(0)	elevator	elevator controller	1
Application/ recovery	initialization(1)	elevator	elevator controller	1
Domain/ Initialization	test	controller	sensor	1..∞
Application/ normal init.	testDoorStatus("open")	elevator controller	door sensor	3
	testDoorStatus("close")	elevator controller	door sensor	
	testButton()	elevator controller	button sensor	
Application/ recovery	testDoorStatus("close")	elevator controller	door sensor	1

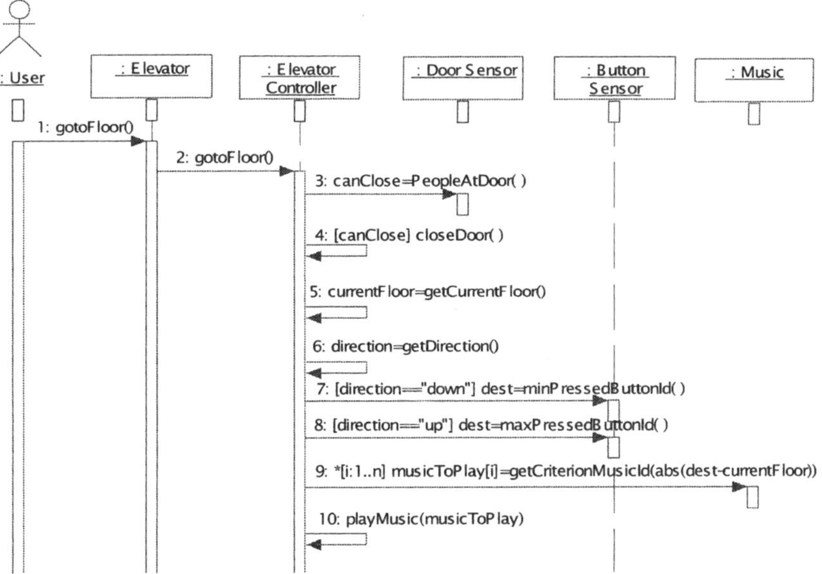

Figure 7. A UML sequence diagram describing an elevator work operation called gotoFloor

Figure 7 describes a possible work scenario of the elevator system. According to this scenario, called "go to floor", after the **user** pressed a button, the **elevator** (through its **controller** and **door sensor**) checks if the door can be closed, close it (if so), check the travel length, and choose **music** accordingly[3].

Table 3. The domain constraints and their fulfillment in the elevator system model – comparing the sequence diagrams of the work operation

Layer/ Sequence	Operation	Cond./ Loops	Source	Destination	Mult.
Domain/ work	work	None	operator	machine	1..1
Application/ go to floor	gotoFloor()	None	user	elevator	1
Domain/ work	work	None	machine	controller	1..1
Application/ go to floor	gotoFloor()	None	elevator	elevator controller	1
Domain/ work	result	Any	controller	sensor	1..∞
Application/ go to floor	peopleAtDoor()	None	elevator controller	door sensor	1
Domain/ work	find	AnyLoop	controller	data	0..∞
Application/ go to floor					0
Domain/ work	work	Any	controller	controller	1..∞
Application/ go to floor	closeDoor()	canClose	elevator controller	elevator controller	1
Domain/ work	result	Any	controller	sensor	1..∞
Application/ go to floor	minPressedButtonId()	direction= "down"	elevator controller	button sensor	2
	maxPressedButtonId()	direction= "up"	elevator controller	button sensor	
Domain/ work	find	AnyLoop	controller	data	0..∞
Application/ go to floor	getCriterionMusicId(abs(dest-currentFloor))	*[i:1..n]	elevator controller	music	1
Domain/ work	work	Any	controller	controller	1..∞
Application/ go to floor	playMusic(musicToPlay)	None	elevator controller	elevator controller	1

Table 3 summarizes the fulfillment of the constraints enforced by the domain sequence diagram expressed in Figure 4 on this particular scenario. Note that in Figure 7 there are several calls for operations that were not explicitly specified within

[3] For simplicity, the stereotypes of the messages and the objects in Figure 7 are suppressed.

the domain sequence diagram in Figure 4, for example, **getDirection()** and **getCurrentFloor()**. These operations are categorized as the additional methods allowed by the domain class diagram (Figure 2) for the **controller** class. They can be invoked in any stage in a sequence diagram, since they are basic operations (getter methods in this case).

4 Summary and Future Work

In this paper we introduced the Application-based DOmain Modeling (ADOM) approach which enables domain engineers to define structural and behavioral constraints that are applicable to all the systems within a specific domain. When developing a system, its domain (or domains) should be defined in order to enforce domain restrictions on the system. The advantages of this approach are twofold. First, it validates system models against their domain models in order to detect semantic errors in early development stages. These errors cannot be automatically found when using syntactic modeling languages alone. Secondly, the usage of the same modeling language for the application and domain layers reduces the ontological gap and the communication problems between the different stakeholders in the system development process. Applying ADOM specifically to UML, the standard object-oriented modeling language, also benefits from the maturity of the UML environment, including its CASE tools. Furthermore, this combination of ADOM and UML establishes a formal framework for defining and constraining stereotypes in UML. However, the separation of the ADOM architecture into three layers (application, domain, and language) makes it flexible enough to be applied to other languages as well.

Further work is planned to develop a domain verification tool that will check a system model against its domain model and will even guide system developers according to given domain models. An experiment is also planned to classify domain-specific modeling errors when using the ADOM approach and other domain analysis methods. This experiment will also check the adoption of several different domains to the same application following the ADOM approach.

References

1. Arango, G. "Domain analysis: from art form to engineering discipline", Proceedings of the Fifth International Workshop on Software Specification and Design, p.152-159, 1989.
2. Becker, M. and Diaz-Herrera, J. L. "Creating domain specific libraries: a methodology, design guidelines and an implementation", Proceedings of the Third International Conference on Software Reuse, pp. 158-168, 1994.
3. Booch, G., Rumbaugh, J., and Jacobson, I. The Unified Modeling Language User Guide, Addison-Wesley, 1998.
4. Carnegie, M. "Domain Engineering: A Model-Based Approach", Software Engineering Institute, http://www.sei.cmu.edu/domain-engineering/, 2002.
5. Champeaux, D. de, Lea, D., and Faure, P. Object-Oriented System Development, Addison Wesley, 1993.
6. Cleaveland, C. "Domain Engineering", http://craigc.com/cs/de.html, 2002.

7. Clauss, M. "Generic Modeling using UML extensions for variability", Workshop on Domain Specific Visual Languages, Object-Oriented Programming, Systems, Languages, and Applications (OOPSLA'01), 2001.
8. Davis, J. "Model Integrated Computing: A Framework for Creating Domain Specific Design Environments", The Sixth World Multiconference on Systems, Cybernetics, and Informatics (SCI), 2002.
9. Drake, R. and Ett, W. "Reuse: the two concurrent life cycles paradigm", Proceedings of the conference on TRI-ADA '90, p.208-221, 1990.
10. D'Souza, D. F., Wills, A.C. Objects, Components, and Frameworks with UML – The CatalysisSM Approach. Addison-Wesley, 1999.
11. Gomma, H. and Eonsuk-Shin, M. "Multiple-View Meta-Modeling of Software Product Lines", Proceedings of the Eighth IEEE International Confrerence on Engineering of Complex Computer Systems, 2002.
12. Gomaa, E. and Kerschberg, L. "Domain Modeling for Software Reuse and Evolution", Proceedings of Computer Assisted Software Engineering Workshop (CASE 95), 1995.
13. Kang, K., Cohen, S., Hess, J., Novak, W., and Peterson, A.,"Feature-Oriented Domain Analysis (FODA) Feasibility Study", CMU/SEI-90-TR-021 ADA235785, 1990.
14. Massonet, P., Deville, Y., and Neve, C. "From AOSE Methodology to Agent Implementation", Proceedings of the First Joint Conference on Autonomous Agents and Multi-Agents Systems, pp. 27-34, 2002.
15. Meekel, J., Horton, T. B., France, R. B., Mellone, C., and Dalvi, S. "From domain models to architecture frameworks", Proceedings of the 1997 symposium on Software reusability, pp. 75-80, 1997.
16. Morisio, M., Travassos, G. H., and Stark, M. "Extending UML to Support Domain Analysis", Proceedings of the Fifth IEEE International Conference on Automated Software Engineering, pp. 321-324, 2000.
17. Nordstrom, G., Sztipanovits, J., Karsai, G., and Ledeczi, A. "Metamodeling - Rapid Design and Evolution of Domain-Specific Modeling Environments", Proceedings of the IEEE Sixth Symposium on Engineering Computer-Based Systems (ECBS), pp. 68-74, 1999.
18. OMG, "Meta-Object Facility (MOF™)", version 1.4, 2003, http://www.omg.org/docs/formal/02-04-03.pdf
19. OMG, "Model Driven Architecture (MDA™)", version 1.0.1, 2003, http://www.omg.org/docs/omg/03-06-01.pdf
20. Petro, J. J., Peterson, A. S., and Ruby, W. F. "In-Transit Visibility Modernization Domain Modeling Report Comprehensive Approach to Reusable Defense Software" (STARS-VC-H002a/001/00).
21. Pressman, R.S. "Software Engineering: A Practitioner's Approach", 5th Edition, New York: McGraw-Hill, 2000.
22. Rumbaugh, J., Blaha, M., Premerlani, W., Eddy, F., and Lorensen, W. Object-Oriented Modeling and Design, Prentice-Hall International, Inc., Englewood Cliffs, New Jersey, 1991
23. Schleicher, A. and Westfechtel, B. "Beyond Stereotyping: Metamodeling Approaches for the UML", Proceedings of the Thirty Fourth Annual Hawaii International Conference on System Sciences, pp. 1243-1252, 2001.
24. Valerio, A., Succi, G., and Fenaroli M. "Domain analysis and framework-based software development", ACM SIGAPP Applied Computing Review, 5 (2), 1997.
25. Van Gigch, J. P. System Design Modeling and Metamodeling. Kluwer Academic Publishers, 1991.
26. Warmer, J. and Kleppe, A. The Object Constraint Language: Precise Modeling with UML. Addison-Wesley, 1998.

Using UML-based Feature Models and UML Collaboration Diagrams to Information Modelling for Web-Based Applications

Peter Dolog and Wolfgang Nejdl

L3S Research Center
University of Hannover
Expo Plaza 1, 30539 Hannover, Germany,
{dolog, nejdl}@l3s.de

Abstract. Web oriented software technology has provided access to information serving environments for a broad audience. This situation requires web-based software applications which satisfy increasing variety of requirements of the broad audience. Such variability can be found in requirements for information but also for environment which is serving the information. In this paper, we discuss a method which utilizes the UML-based feature modelling to support the need to model the variability. The information and environment configurations are modelled as common and variable features of application domain and environment concepts. Separation of feature models into application domain and environment allows us to select several configurations of environments to deliver particular information. The UML collaboration diagrams model collaborations between the application domain and environment concept and feature instances as an abstraction for presented information fragments in a web application.

Keywords: Feature modelling, information modelling, web-based application, UML collaboration diagrams

1 Introduction

Open environments such as Internet provide us with possibility to serve information to users with different goals, background, interests and so on. To build applications for such an environment requires to focus on diversity of features user of the applications can require in case of information provided and also in case of how the provided information is re-/presented.

Explicit information about a purpose of already authored content and the purpose of the information being described by the content can help requirements analyst, designer or author of the content to compare existing material with the diverse requirements of users and to say whether the content can be reused or new content should be provided. Current established modelling methods for web based applications do not provide sufficient mechanisms to express such information.

This paper explores an approach to information modelling which is based on the idea of information product line and is inspired by domain engineering approaches

T. Baar et al. (Eds.): UML 2004, LNCS 3273, pp. 425–439, 2004.

for building software systems like generative programming [6] or product line practices [23] where feature models play an important role. Our method is also based on the idea that an information is communicated usually using several concepts to a user. We use the UML collaboration diagrams to model such a design view where information features collaborate together to fulfill a main information goal. This extends our previous work on feature modelling for the domain engineering approach for hypermedia engineering (DEAHE) [7]. Our approach is based on:

- Two views on information: domain and environment;
- Feature models which model common and variable features of concepts and variation points in both views;
- Collaboration diagrams which refine and integrate feature models of both views.

Feature modelling allows us to capture common and variable features of concepts being covered by an application. Common and variable features reflect diverse requirements of different current and possibly future users of particular application for the information and also environment through which it is served. Collaborations between different features are determined by roles. The roles reflect the context in which information can be used and presented in an environment component.

The feature and collaboration models allow us to specify conditions in which features from two separate models can be used. The conditions determine which combinations of features provide us with meaningful information. Different configurations of features and roles represent possible web based applications which form an application family. Such an approach provides us with following advantages:

- The separation of the domain and information/environment models allows us to provide information about concepts in different environment and vice versa;
- Mandatory and optional features together with variation points in both models allow us to maintain information which reflect different successful implementations of web-based application;
- Instance roles and their collaborations allow us to maintain information how domain features collaborated in information serving environments installed at a customer site.

1.1 Motivating Scenario

To illustrate our approach, we refer to a scenario where a training company needs to be able to configure a training suite where, besides other courses, Java course is provided. The suite will be provided for a group of people with a background in electrical engineering — *tutorial*. They would like to gain an overview of the Java language and possibly ideas where they can use it.

On the other hand, the company needs to configure the training suite for a group of people from a software company which just acquired a project where Java language was chosen as a programming language — *detailed course*.

In addition, in both cases the training material has to be provided with different environments as it is needed to support mobile learners and also learners in offices.

The company's vision is that similar situation can happen in the future. Due to this they decide to document design models in a way which is suitable for the varying requirements.

As this situation shows, information about the same concepts has to be presented in a different way according to whether a detailed presentation is needed or just overview. In both cases the information is articulated by several concepts playing different roles. For example, to give an introduction to Java objects in a simple Java tutorial, object state and object behavior concepts are needed. This can be called the smallest meaningful set of concepts to present the Java object in any content configured for the Java lecture. Additional concepts might be suited to describe other aspects of the object state for example. Information modelling framework has to provide tools for modelling the concept configurations by means of mandatory and optional features of the concept and configuration dependencies between them.

As the information can be delivered by different environments, the domain concepts which are used to model information have to be separated form the environment concepts used to model the environment. On the other hand, interconnections between domain concepts and the environment concepts have to be modelled to document successful cases of training suite applications. The information modelling framework has to provide means for modelling such collaboration interconnections between several roles the concepts and features play in the environment.

1.2 Paper Structure

The rest of the paper is structured as follows. Section 2 provides a brief overview of an approach and its context in web-based application development. Section 3 describes UML-based feature modelling for information and environment. Section 4 discusses collaboration model and its refinements. A short summary of application and experiences with this approach is given in Sec. 5. Section 6 discusses our approach in the context of related work. The paper concludes with some remarks and proposals for further work (Sec. 7).

2 Overview of a Modelling Framework

Figure 1 depicts a framework for engineering web-based information intensive product lines [7]. This paper focuses mainly on the shaded areas in Fig. 1. In this paper we discuss a method where:

- *Domain and information conceptual models* are used to model concepts and their mutual relationships;
- *Domain and information/environment feature models* are used to maintain common and variable features of concepts and their dependencies as companies' experience in how different concepts can help in presenting another concept;
- *Collaboration models* refine the feature models and are used to express how features from domain and information/environment feature models collaborate together to achieve a main information goal.

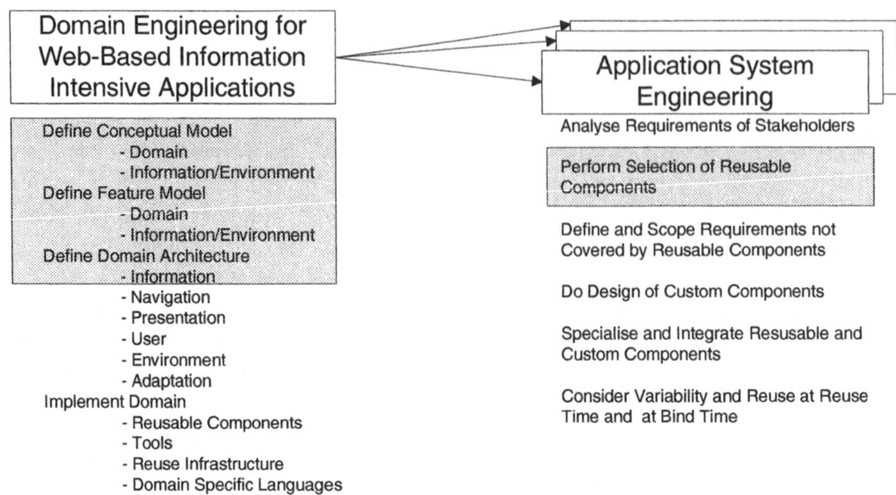

Fig. 1. Domain engineering based approach for engineering web-based information intensive product lines

The purpose of the conceptual models is to document domain and environment vocabulary used in all other models. As the domain/content presented in a training suite in case of Java lecture from our example scenario, the domain conceptual model will refer to concepts from Java programming language. As the environment mentioned in the scenario is a course, the course structure and some other concepts will depict in the environment conceptual model.

The purpose of the feature models is to document presentation relations of all concepts from the conceptual models to other concepts in that model; i.e. which other concepts are used to articulate particular concept, e.g. on Java objects.

The purpose of the collaboration models is to connect the instances from the two models according to a selection performed by a designer. In addition, the purpose of the collaboration models is to model messages needed to be sent between the roles of those instances depicted in the models when an interaction with particular role instance was requested by a user.

The process of such information modelling can be summarized in the following steps:

1. Define a conceptual model for a domain and environment (e.g. concepts used to teach Java programming language served in a course as an environment);
2. Define a feature model for all concepts from the domain and environment conceptual models being used in the application;
3. Refine domain feature models into the domain collaboration model based on features selected for final application;
4. Refine the domain collaboration models
   (a) Introduce collaborations with information/environment features in place of selected collaboration links from the domain collaboration models;

(b) Introduce messages being sent between the participants in the collaborations and constraints for determination which message applies in a specific situation;

5. Update conceptual and feature models of domain and environment if new concepts and/or features have been developed.

3 Commonalities and Variabilities in Domain and Environment

Conceptual Models. Let us recall our application scenario. The company has an experience with serving a Java tutorial. Information usually exposes one or more concepts from a domain where general conceptual models, taxonomies or ontologies can already exist. For example Java tutorial serves an information which belongs to computer science domain. There are several taxonomies which are used for example to classify computer science literature (ACM CCS[1]) or to describe a computing body of knowledge and curricula[2]. Companies use also their own conceptual models to communicate terminology used in their information systems.

Figure 2 depicts an excerpt of such a *domain conceptual model* modelled by the UML class diagram with basic object-oriented programming concepts (annotated by the `Concept` stereotype) and their mutual relationships. The figure expresses a company's general view on relationships between `Object`, `Class`, object's `State` and `Behaviour` using `Methods` and `Variables`.

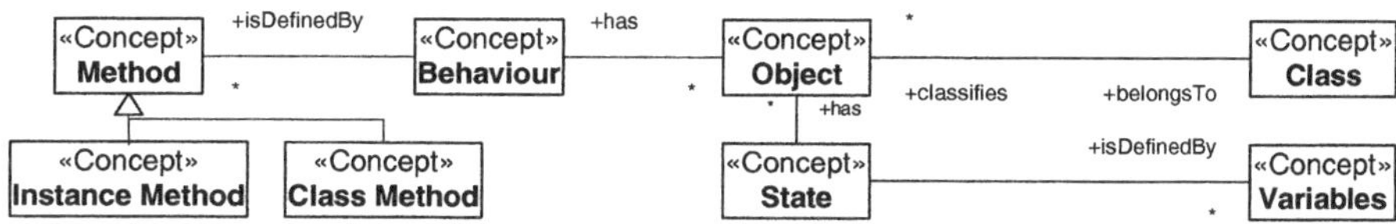

Fig. 2. An excerpt of conceptual application domain model

As the training suite is provided with several possible virtual environments, a company needs to communicate how the environments are structured. The example of such an environment suitable for the Java tutorial can be a virtual course. Concepts such as `Course`, `Lectures`, `Modules`, `Learning Object`, `Lecturer`, and `Provider` would then appear in a similar UML class diagram for *environment conceptual model* (Fig. 3).

Feature Models. According to our scenario, the company needs two different configurations of a content and several configurations of environment for two different audiences. Some features are common for both configurations and some vary.

As scenario pointed, the content is intended to be served through different environments which is selected according to requirements. Feature models have to be created

---

[1] http://www.acm.org/class/1998/

[2] http://www.computer.org/education/cc2001/

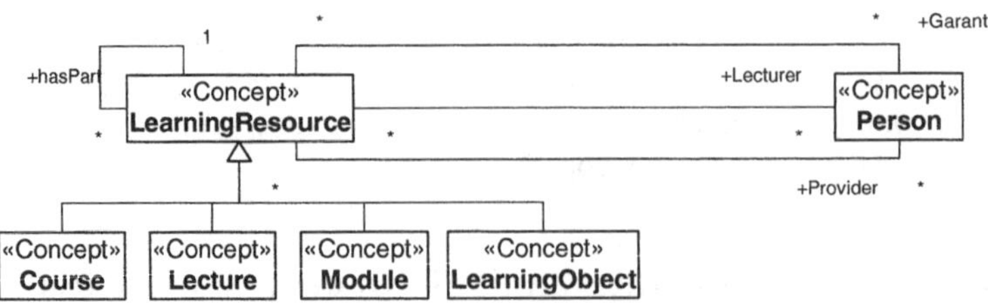

Fig. 3. An excerpt of conceptual environment/information model

for both views. The main elements in feature models are *concepts*, *features*, *variation points*, and *relationships* between them. A *concept* in feature models represents:

- *in a domain model* — an information, which is of the main purpose (main information goal) of the content which author had when authored the content,
- *in an environment/information model* — a main structural unit of a content in particular web-based application (different representations are modelled by different concepts).

A feature model has to be maintained for all concepts from conceptual model which are going to be depicted as main information entities in an environment. Figure 4 depicts an excerpt of such a feature model for the `Object` concept.

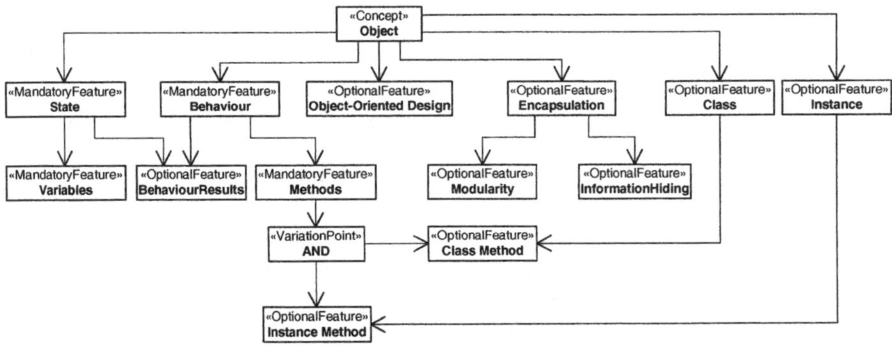

Fig. 4. An excerpt of *Object* feature model

Other concepts needed to communicate the main information goal represented by a concept in a feature model are selected and transformed to *features* of the concept. According to our scenario for example, the `Object` concept is usually described with the help of the concept of its `State` and `Behaviour`. Both appear as concepts in the conceptual model in Fig. 2. They appear as the `Object`-s features in Fig. 4.

All other concepts from the conceptual model (Fig. 2) have usually such feature models if they are communicated to learners as available in the application. For space limitation we do not show them here. Note also that the models depicted in our examples are not intended to provide a one and only solution, but just to exemplify how to create own feature models which report on best practices for information being served in web based applications.

The fact that there are some features which are common to all configurations and some vary has to be also reflected in the model. According to that we consider (in both, domain and information/environment models):

- *mandatory features* — form common or core features for all considered situations which will be covered in our applications (application family), and
- *optional features* — form variable features needed only in specific context.

In our example scenario from Fig. 4, the `State` and `Behaviour` are considered as mandatory features (annotated with `MandatoryFature` stereotype). The concepts annotated by `OptionalFeature` stereotype do not appear in all applications (e.g., `Object-Oriented Design`, `Encapsulation`, `Class`, and `Instance`).

Sometimes some features need to be presented together with other information features to provide sufficient explanations to understand presented information. Some other information features cannot be presented together because they could confuse a learner. In some cases the combination of features is not so relevant. For this purpose *variability relationships* have been introduced between features and they are usually denoted as *variation points* [22] or *variations* [9]. The variation point can define:

- *mutually exclusive variants,*
- *mutually required features, and*
- *mutually inclusive features.*

Figure 4 depicts a variation point shown for `Methods` mandatory feature. The model defines that the `Methods`have to be described also on `Instance Method` and `Class Method`.

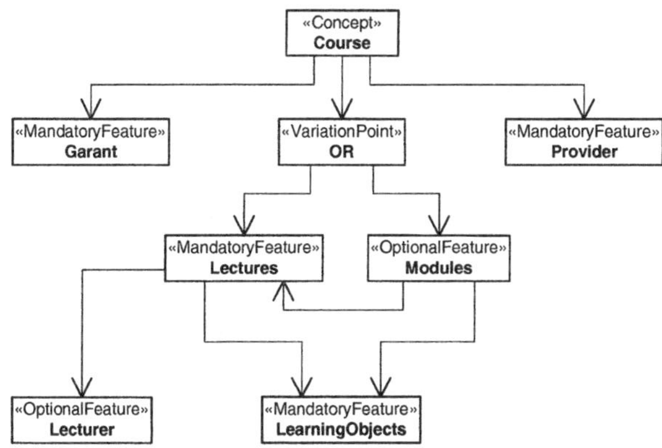

Fig. 5. An excerpt of *Course* feature model

Similarly, a feature model is needed for the information/environment concepts. Figure 5 depicts an excerpt of such a feature model of a virtual environment from our example scenario for the `Course` concept. Usually, information feature model for one virtual environment consists just of one feature model for the most general concept. The `Course` has to have a `Provider` and also a `Garant` (modelled by so called mandatory features). Then, according to requirements of a customer, the `Course` can consist of either `Lectures` where some of them can be encapsulated into thematic `Modules` or just from `Lectures` (this is reflected by the `OR` variation point of the `Course`). The `Lecture` can have a `Lecturer` provided who plays a role of a tutor when somebody needs to consult something related to the lecture. Both, `Lectures` and `Modules`, refer to learning objects.

4 Information Collaboration Modelling

In this section we will show just a collaboration model made according to a selection of features for the simple Java tutorial from our example scenario.

The Java tutorial provides a small lecture on introduction to the Java objects, which are introduced by it's state and behaviour. The features which are needed to communicate this introduction are depicted in Fig. 4. At runtime, the feature instances collaborate to create a content. The idea of collaboration is based on the notion of active learning objects which provide a defined interface to access their content and presentation. With this idea in mind, dependencies from the domain feature models can be transformed into collaboration links. The collaboration models are created as refinements of the feature models. The refinement consists of:

- Instantiating concepts and features from feature model;
- Identifying roles of the instances in collaborations;
- Transforming associations between features and concept in feature models into collaboration links.

Roles are used to model different purposes of a particular feature or concept in an environment/information component. We use the following notation:

$$O/R : P :: C$$

where O is a Classifier or Feature instance,
R is a Classifier or Feature role,
P (optional) is a Package name where Feature or Classifier belongs to, and
C is a Classifier or a Feature.

Roles terminology can form a complex structures. The UML class diagram can be employed to model such a structure [1]. This model can be used similarly to the domain and environment/information conceptual models; i.e. as a mean for communicating the roles terminology to be used in the web-based training suite.

Domain Features Collaborations. The first refinement of the feature models is refinement into domain features collaborations. The refinement is based on defining concept and feature *instances and roles* and *links* between them as instances of associations between the concept and features.

Instances and Roles. Figure 6 depicts an excerpt of a collaboration model of features from the `Object` feature model (the feature model depicted in Fig. 4). Roles of domain features used in the collaborations are *definition*, *example*, *exercise*, *description*, and so on. The `Definition` and `Example` roles played by the `Object` concept instances are used to model a situation where a term `JavaObject` is defined and then showed on the example. The term `JavaObject` is defined using the `JavaObjectState` and `JavaObjectBehaviour` definitions. The `Variable` definition is used define the state variables.

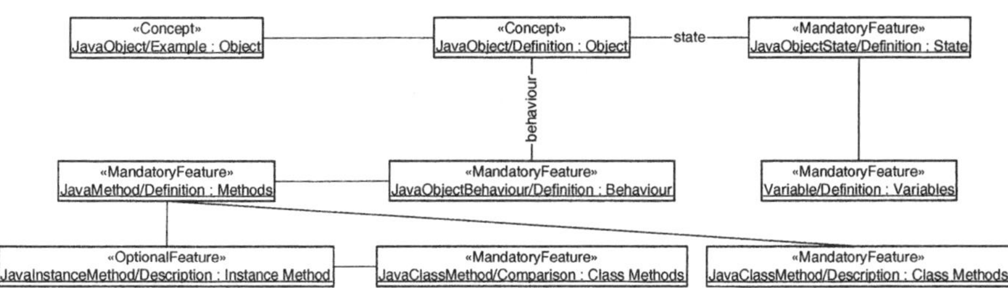

Fig. 6. An excerpt of a collaboration model showing features from *Object* feature model

The `JavaObjectBehaviour` collaborates with the `JavaMethod` definition, as the behavior of an object is exposed by its methods. The `JavaInstanceMethod` and `JavaClassMethod` descriptions are provided as two alternatives for the Java methods (they play a description role in collaboration with the `JavaMethod` definition). In addition, a comparison of the class method and instance method is provided to improve an understanding of the difference between these kinds of methods. This is reflected by additional comparison role of the `JavaClassMethod` in collaboration with the `JavaInstanceMethod`.

Links. The collaboration links are defined mostly as straitforward mappings from associations in the feature model. Special attention has to be paid in case of several instances and roles of the domain features in the model. A designer has to decide which roles and instances will be linked together. In our example, two instances of the `Object` concept appear in the collaboration model. We created a link just between the `Definition` roles of the `JavaObject` and the `JavaObjectBehaviour`. The `Example` role of the `JavaObject` contributes just to the collaboration with `Definition` role of the `JavaObject` role in our example application, so the link to the `JavaObjectBehaviour` is not created. Similarly, the AND variation point in the feature model from Fig. 4 was resolved as several links between the participating feature instance roles.

Names of the links are suppressed in the model except of the `state` link between `JavaObject` and `JavaObjectState` and the `behaviour` link between `JavaObject` and `JavaObjectBehaviour`, which we will use for the purpose of description later.

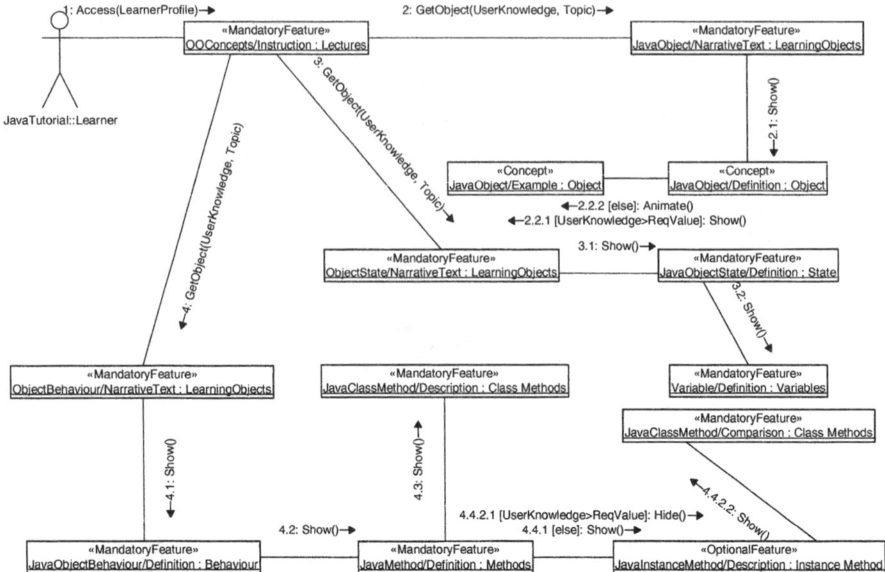

Fig. 7. An excerpt of a collaboration between feature from *Course* and *Object* feature model

Collaborations of Domain Features with Information/Environment Features. Second refinement of the abstract feature models which follows the domain feature collaborations described above is the refinement into so called *information components*. By information components we mean accessible environment components which are accessed through their interfaces and are able to deliver concrete information about particular domain concepts.

This is achieved by linking the instances of the domain features to the instances of the environment/information features. The refinement extends above described collaboration models with:

– *Instance roles of environment/information features* to model mainly pedagogical style and purpose of the information component;
– *Links* between instance roles of environment/information features and domain features instance roles which replaces some of the links between domain feature roles (collaboration is being delegated to the information components);
– *Messages* being sent between environment/information feature roles and domain feature roles when a user performs an act of interaction.

Instance Roles of Environment/Information Features. Roles of information features in collaborations with domain features are usually *container*, *provider*, or more domain specific like *narrative text*, *simulation*, *problem statement*, *instruction*, and so on. Some of the roles are suitable just for higher level information objects like lecture or module. This is, for example, the *instruction* role which refers to the learning theory used to construct an information component. Similar concepts are used in the learning object metadata standard [12].

Figure 7 depicts an excerpt of such a collaboration model which links environment features to domain features. NarativeText role is introduced for the JavaObject, the ObjectState, and the ObjectBehaviour instances of LearningObjects. The learning objects can be accessed through the OOConcepts instruction which is an instance role of the Lectures. In a final training suite this lecture of Java tutorial collaborates with other lectures.

Additional Links — Collaboration Delegation. The three learning objects introduced in the Fig. 7 are linked to the corresponding domain features and/or concepts. The JavaObject is linked to the Definition role of the JavaObject. The Object-State is linked to the Definition role of the JavaObjectState. The Definition role of the JavaObjectBehaviour is linked to the ObjectBehaviour. Note that these domain features are connected by the state and the behaviour links in the Fig. 6. These links are replaced by introduced environment feature instance roles and the collaborations are delegated to information feature roles accessible by a user (in this case the OOConcept/Instruction). Remaining links between domain features are derived from the Fig. 6. The collaboration links between environment/information features are created as instances of the associations in environment/information feature models. Similarly as in case of the domain features collaborations, collaboration links have to be resolved by a designer when several roles and instances of one feature or concept appear in the collaboration model and when variation point has to be transformed.

Messages. In addition, links are annotated by messages which are sent between the roles. User interaction generates the Access(...) message to the OOConcepts lecture. The OOConcepts lecture generates several GetObject(...) messages which are sent to the learning objects. Those learning objects request a content from the domain feature instance roles like JavaObject by sending for example the Show() messages. A content is propagated to the user as the result of interaction between the instance roles.

The LearnerProfile parameter of the Access(...) message is propagated by several GetObject(...) messages to domain features instance roles. Just fragments of the profile relevant to prerequisite competencies and/or topics of the learning objects are transferred by the GetObject(...) messages. These fragments are used to determine which presentation options are valid for a learner with particular level of knowledge, e.g. the two conditionally constrained messages at the link between the Definition and Example roles of the JavaObject. The UserKnowledge parameter is used to determine whether the example is just statically shown (Show() message) or animated (Animate() message). The ReqValue is a predefined constant which sets which level of knowledge is required to switch between the presentation options. The conditionally constrained messages at the link between JavaMethod and JavaInstanceMethod can be interpreted similarly.

5 Applications and Experiences

Figure 8 depicts an example of the lesson or lecture from Java tutorial with some concepts used in our modelling approach.

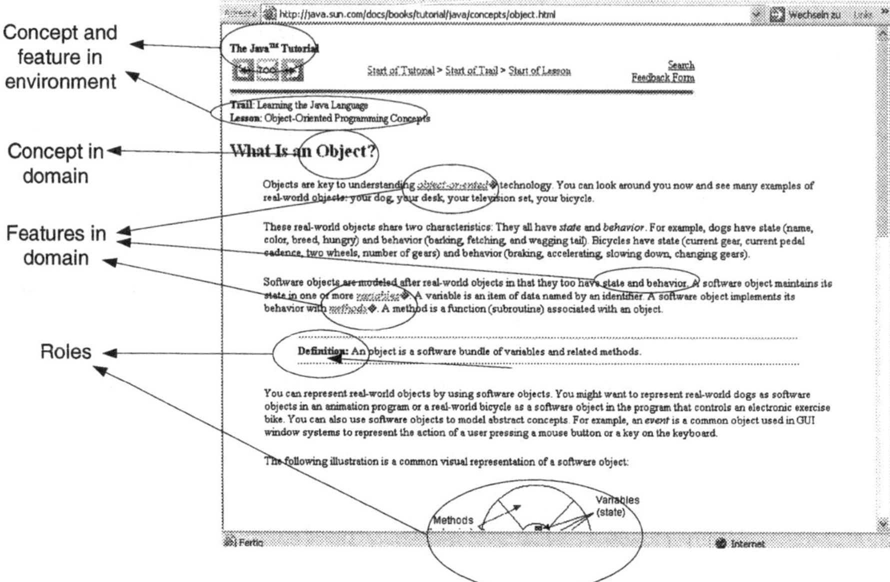

Fig. 8. Modelling concepts of our approach highligted at a web-based Sun Java tutorial

The collaborations are presented as a web page showing content about several features we modeled in our models. There are two roles highlighted: the definition and example modeled for the Object concept in our feature model. Object-oriented design, behavior, state, methods and variables are similarly highlighted as the features from the domain. The lesson and course are also highlighted as environment features.

This information modelling approach resulted from several experiences with modelling and developing learning oriented web-based systems. First of all, it served as an underlying information modelling for the applications generated by the UML-Guide [8] where a very basic environment considered was environment of web pages.

In another EU/IST project — Elena[3] — we gained experiences in information modelling for information sources connected to a network and accessed through applications making use of services such as recommendation, booking, and delivery. The information sources have been connected by Edutella [15], a p2p infrastructure for the semantic web. Resource Description Format (RDF) [13] was employed as the physical data model for metadata about information being served by the Edutella peers. The physical model for accessing the content varied. The metadata have been structured into two separated models, domain and information/environment. A subset of the ACM CCS system

[3] www.elena-project.org

was used as concept ontology. Applications developed on top of the information provision infrastructure used defined interfaces encapsulating queries to application services and to the information provision infrastructure to provide tutorials, course, or learning resources through environments defined in the network.

6 Related Work

Recently, role oriented modelling was applied as a promising modelling approach for design and development of software applications [21,20] or databases [10]. The notion of role is used to identify different purposes of classes and objects in collaborations with different classes and objects available in a design framework. The importance of roles in modelling is apparent from the work on topic maps standard [16]. The concept of role is used in the topic map similarly to our approach: a topic plays particular role in association to other topics. Knowledge modelling community also reflects on notion of roles for example in [19]. There, the structural types can be associated to each other through roles the types play in the associations.

Feature modelling is another modelling technique which has been successfully applied in reuse oriented community [22,6,23,9]. The main idea is to explicitly represent information about different possible combinations of features a concept can have in software system for different purposes.

Our approach extended and integrated the ideas from the role oriented and feature oriented approaches for purposes of information modelling of information intensive web-based applications.

Tropos approach [4] relates to our work by considering variation of goals as a main concept which drives its requirements engineering phase. The goal oriented early requirements analysis can be suitable as a pre-step to feature modelling in our approach, as it is intended to provide a broader view for all interacting actors. Our approach also emphasizes on a conceptual model which is used as a vocabulary for the feature models documenting suitable configurations of information being provided in different environments. Refining technique of goal models into sequence diagrams in Tropos relates to our refinements from feature models into collaboration diagrams.

The information models in web applications modelling approaches usually reflect either an application domain point of view or environment point of view. OOHDM [18], W2000 [3], UWE [11], WebML [5], and UML extension for web engineering [14] model information from application domain perspective. ADM [2] concentrates on logical model of a web site where E-R model is used to specify data to be used in sites and page schema is used to specify pages. The work [17] relates to our approach by employed application domain.

Our approach introduces several new models, separating domain from environment modelling. Feature and collaboration models which are not considered in the mentioned approaches are used to represent additional design views needed in cases similar to our example scenario. This of course brings additional overhead arisen from creation and maintenance of those additional models. Therefore, our approach is beneficial when there is a knowledge or assumption that the models will help in other projects to reuse content and implementation from previous projects.

The approach introduced in this paper is highly complemental to those approaches introduced in recent web application design methods and can be integrated with them. The integration as pointed above have to be justified by the need to ease the future development projects.

7 Conclusions and Further Work

We discussed the UML-based feature modelling with the UML collaboration diagrams for information modelling for web-based applications in this paper. The core features of the approach are:

- Separation of domain and information/environment models;
- Making use of feature models in both design views to communicate best practices in information product line;
- Making use of the UML collaboration diagrams to configure a web-based information provision application with a specific virtual environment.

The models provide a designer of a web-based application with necessary information about which feature configurations make sense, what are important features to be considered and how their roles determine their use in provided environments.

In our further work we would like to investigate possibilities to automate some of the steps which now have to be performed by a designer. We also would like to further investigate how to improve a tool support for such information modelling described here. This comprises especially domain specific query language for more effective selection of features when building the collaboration models.

Acknowledgement. We would like to thank anonymous reviewers whose comments helped to improve the work presented in this paper. This work is partially supported by EU/IST ELENA project IST-2001-37264.

References

1. Heidrun Allert, Peter Dolog, Wolfgang Nejdl, Wolf Siberski, and Friedrich Steimann. Role-oriented models for hypermedia construction — conceptual modeling for the semantic web. Technical Report. Learninglab Lower Saxony, University of Hannover, February 2003.
2. Paolo Atzeni and Alessio Parente. Specification of web applications with adm-2. In Patrick van Bommel, editor, *Information Modelling for Internet Applications*, pages 127–143. Idea Group Publishing, 2002.
3. Luciano Baresi, Franca Garzotto, and Paolo Paolini. Extending UML for modeling web applications. In *Proc. of 34th Anual Hawaii International Conference on System Sciences (HICSS'34)*, Maui, Hawai, January 2001. IEEE Press.
4. Jaelson Castro, Manuel Kolp, and John Mylopoulos. Towards requirements-driven information systems engineering: the Tropos project. *Information Systems*, 27(6):365–389, September 2002.
5. Stefano Ceri, Piero Fraternali, and Maristella Matera. Conceptual modeling of data-intensive web applications. *IEEE Internet Computing*, 6(4), August 2002.

6. Krysztof Czarnecki and Ulrich Eisenecker. *Generative Programing: Principles, Techniques, and Tools*. Addison Wesley, 2000.
7. Peter Dolog and Mária Bieliková. Towards variability modelling for reuse in hypermedia engineering. In Yannis Manolopoulos and Pavol Návrat, editors, *Proc. of Advances in Databases and Information Systems : 6th East European Conference, ADBIS 2002, Bratislava, Slovakia, September 8-11, 2002.*, vol. 2435 of *LNCS*, pages 388–400. Springer.
8. Peter Dolog and Wolfgang Nejdl. Using UML and XMI for generating adaptive navigation sequences in web-based systems. In Perdita Stevens, Jon Whittle, and Grady Booch, editors, *Proc. of UML 2003 - The Unified Modeling Language. Model Languages and Applications. 6th International Conference, San Francisco, CA, USA, October 2003,*, vol. 2863 of *LNCS*, pages 205–219. Springer.
9. Martin L. Griss, John Favaro, and Massimo d' Alessandro. Integrating feature modeling with the RSEB. In P. Devanbu and J. Poulin, editors, *Proc. of 5th International Conference on Software Reuse*, pages 76–85, Victoria, Canada, June 1998. IEEE Computer Society Press.
10. Terry Halpin. *Information Modeling and Relational Databases: From Conceptual Analysis to Logical Design*. Morgan Kaufmann, 2001.
11. Rolf Hennicker and Nora Koch. A UML-based methodology for hypermedia design. In S. Stuart A. Evans and B. Selic, editors, *Proc. of UML 2000 Conference*, York, England, October 2000, vol. 1939 of *LNCS*. Springer.
12. IEEE Learning Technology Standards Committee. IEEE standard for learning object metadata (IEEE 1484.12.1–2002). http://ltsc.ieee.org/, July 2002.
13. O. Lassila and R. Swick. W3C Resource Description framework (RDF) Model and Syntax Specification, 2001. http://www.w3.org/TR/REC-rdf-syntax/.
14. David Lowe, Brian Henderson-Sellers, and Alice Gu. Web extensions to UML: Using the MVC triad. In S. Spaccapietra, S.T. March, and Y. Kambayashi, editors, *Proceedings of 21nd International Conference on Conceptual Modeling*, pages 105–119, Tampere, Finland, October 2002, vol. 2503 of *LNCS*. Springer.
15. W. Nejdl, B. Wolf, C. Qu, S. Decker, M. Sintek, A. Naeve, M. Nilsson, M. Palmr, and T. Risch. EDUTELLA: a P2P Networking Infrastructure based on RDF. In *In Proc. of 11th World Wide Web Conference*, Hawaii, USA, May 2002.
16. Steven R. Newcomb, Sam Hunting, and Jan Algermissen. Reference model for ISO 13250 topic maps (RM4TM) v. 1.0, 2002. http://www.isotopicmaps.org/rm4tm/.
17. Joerg Pleumann and Stefan Haustein. A model-driven runtime environment for web applications. In Perdita Stevens, Jon Whittle, and Grady Booch, editors, *Proc. of UML 2003 - The Unified Modeling Language. Model Languages and Applications. 6th International Conference, San Francisco, CA, USA, October 2003,*, vol. 2863 of *LNCS*, pages 190–204. Springer.
18. Daniel Schwabe and Gustavo Rossi. An object-oriented approach to web-based application design. *Theory and Practise of Object Systems (TAPOS), Special Issue on the Internet*, 4(4):207–225, October 1998.
19. John F. Sowa. *Knowledge Representation: Logical, Philosophical and Computational Foundations*. Brooks/Cole, 2000.
20. Friedrich Steimann. On the representation of roles in object-oriented and conceptual modelling. *Data and Knowledge Engineering*, 35(1):83–106, 2000.
21. Trygve Reenskau with P. Wold and O.A. Lehne. *Working with objects The OOram Software Engineering Method*. Manning/Prentice Hall, 1996.
22. James V. Withey. Implementing model based software engineering in your organization: An approach to domain engineering, 1994. CMU/SEI-94-TR-01, see also http://www.sei.cmu.edu/mbse/index.html.
23. James V. Withey. Investment analysis of software assets for product lines, 1996. CMU/SEI-96-TR-010.

Workshops at the UML 2004 Conference

Ambrosio Toval (Ed.)

Departamento de Informática y Sistemas
Facultad de Informática
Universidad de Murcia
30100 Espinardo Murcia, ESPAÑA
atoval@um.es

Abstract. UML 2004 conference hosts twelve workshops. These selected events cover a wide range of hot topics related to the Unified Modeling Language. In the following, a brief summary of each workshop, along with the list of organizers and references for further information are given.

1 Introduction

Following the tradition of previous UML conferences, UML 2004 hosts a number of workshops, which this year reaches twelve. Workshops provide a collaborative forum for a group of (typically 15 to 30) participants to exchange recent or preliminary results, to conduct intensive discussions on a particular topic, or to coordinate efforts between representatives of a technical community. Each workshop lasts for a full day. The workshops take place during the first three days of the conference.

As mentioned, this year the conference includes 12 workshops. This figure confirms the increasing importance given to workshops in this conference, and the growing trend with respect to the latest editions. For instance, last year (2003), the conference held 9 workshops while in previous editions the number was 5 or 6. A novelty with respect to previous UML conferences is the inclusion of a Doctoral Symposium, which has had a wide acceptance, to provide an explicit space for young researchers developing their theses on some aspect related to UML. Another novelty of this year's edition is that the workshop selection process has benefited from the participation of a Selection Committee, formed by the following prestigious researchers :

> Eric Dubois (Public Research Centre), Henri Tudor (Luxembourg), Jean Michel Bruel (University of Pau, France), Juan Hernández (University of Extremadura, Spain), Ivan Porres (Turku Centre for Computer Science, Finland), Roel Wieringa (University of Twente, The Netherlands).

Special thanks are given to all of them for their valuable support.

Although at the time of writing this report, July 2004, it is not possible to know the success of each workshop, the interest of the themes selected and the quality of the proposals is highly promising.

T. Baar et al. (Eds.): UML 2004, LNCS 3273, pp. 440–448, 2004.

Workshops web pages (indicated below) provide access to the variety of position papers presented and/or the information needed to access them. We also include in the following a brief summary of each workshop, as provided by their organizers. Detailed technical reports describing the variety of issues discussed in each workshop are included in a separate LNCS volume [1].

2 Detailed List of Workshops

Workshop 1: Consistency Problems in UML-based Software Development III — Understanding and Usage of Dependency Relationships

Organizers: Zbigniew Huzar (Department of Computer Science, Wrocław University of Technology, Wrocław, Poland), Ludwik Kuzniarz, (School of Engineering, Blekinge Institute of Technology, Ronneby, Sweden) and Jean Louis Sourrouille (Department of Computer Science, INSA, Lyon, France)

URL: http://uml04.ci.pwr.wroc.pl/

Abstract: A UML-based software development can be considered as a modeling process. Software development process yields a partially ordered set of UML models the should be inter-consistent. The problem is how to define relationships between models reflecting the property. A similar problem relates to elements of individual model that should be intra-consistent. Different kinds of dependency relationships are used to describe relationships between models and their elements. However, the meaning of the UML dependency and their specializations are still not precisely defined. It raises the problem of how to understand and how to check consistency between modeling artifacts.

Workshop 2: Aspect Oriented Modeling

Organizers: Omar Aldawud (Lucent Technologies, USA), Mohamed Kandé (Condris Technologies, Switzerland), Grady Booch (Rational, USA), Bill Harrison (IBM Thomas J. Watson Research Center, USA), Jeff Gray (University of Alabama at Birmingham, USA), Siobhán Clarke (Trinity College, Dublin, Ireland), Jörg Kienzle (McGill University, Canada), Atef Bader (Lucent Technologies, USA), Dominik Stein (University of Duisburg-Essen, Germany) and Faisal Akkawi (North Western University, USA)

URL: http://www.cs.iit.edu/~oaldawud/AOM

Abstract: The Aspect-Oriented Modeling (AOM) Workshop brings together researchers and practitioners from two communities, aspect-oriented software development (AOSD) and software model engineering. This workshop provides a forum for presenting new ideas and discussing the state of research and practice in modeling various kinds of crosscutting concerns at different levels, software architecture, detailed design, and testing, and mapping the models onto aspect-oriented programs. Important goals are to identify and discuss the impacts of aspect-oriented technologies on model engineering, especially UML, and to set up a shared agenda for future research in aspect-oriented modeling of software systems.

Workshop 3: Software Architecture Description & UML

Organizers: Nenad Medvidović (University of Southern California, USA), Paris Avgeriou (University of Luxembourg, Luxembourg) and Nicolas Guelfi (University of Luxembourg, Luxembourg)

URL: http://uml2004.uni.lu

Abstract: The description of software architectures has always been concerned with the definition of the appropriate notations or languages for designing the various architectural artifacts. The past ten years, formal or less formal Architecture Description Languages (ADLs) and supporting methods and tools have been proposed by researchers. Recently UML is being widely accepted in both industry and academia as a language for architecture description, and there have been approaches of UML-based AD either by extending the language, or by mapping existing ADLs onto it. The upcoming UML 2.0 standard has also created great expectations about the potential of the language to capture software architectures and especially allow for early analysis of systems under development. The interest in this field is also raised by the IEEE 1471 standard for AD that can foster the use of UML through defined viewpoints. Furthermore, MDE and MDA are tightly connected with both UML and AD, thus promoting new approaches of combining these two. This workshop aims to bring together researchers and practitioners that work on all aspects of Architectural Description (AD) of software systems, relating to the Unified Modeling Language. It will foster a presentation of the latest approaches on the field from both industry and academia, as well as a creative discussion between the participants in specific themes.

Workshop 4: Specification and Validation of UML Models for Real Time and Embedded Systems, SVERTS

Organizers: Susanne Graf (Verimag, France), Øystein Haugen (Ericsson, Norway), Bran Selic (Rational, Canada) and Ileana Ober (Verimag, France)

URL: http://www-verimag.imag.fr/EVENTS/2004/SVERTS

Abstract: Today's applications often have strong constraints with respect to time related aspects. Moreover, overall systems may be huge, and even if the embedded hard real-time components are relatively small, there is some global interdependence, and the existence of a global model in a uniform framework is an important issue. The Unified Modeling Language UML can play this role, even if the real-time aspects are not really integrated today. The definition of UML has been motivated by the need for a standard notation for modelling system architectures and behaviours at functional and implementation level. UML aims at providing an integrated modelling framework encompassing architecture descriptions and behaviour descriptions. A first step to the integration of extra functional characteristics into the modelling framework has been achieved by the "UML profile for Schedulability, Time and Performance"; it provides the basic concepts and a first attempt for a common syntax. Nevertheless, in order to be able to exchange models and to build validation tools, it is important to have also a common understanding of the semantics of the given notations. Other important issues in the domain of real-time is methodology and modeling paradigms allowing break down of the complexity, and tools which are able to verify well designed systems. This workshop should bring together researchers to discuss different time related issues in the context of modeling, design and validation of real-time systems, such as notations for expressing time and related requirements, semantic issues and tools, and modeling paradigms for real-time systems. The workshop aims to gather people from academia and industry to discuss the needs and possible solutions for handling time and scheduling related issues which should help to define a work programme in this field.

Workshop 5: 3rd UML Workshop in Software Model Engineering (WiSME 2004)

Organizers: Martin Gogolla (University of Bremen, Germany), Paul Sammut (Xactium, Great Britain) and Jon Whittle (QSS/NASA Ames, USA)

URL: http://albini.xactium.com/wisme

Abstract: Model Driven Architecture (MDA) is an OMG initiative that attempts to separate business functionality specification from the implementation of that functionality on specific middleware technological platforms (e.g., CORBA, C#/DotNet, Java/EJB, XML/SOAP). This approach is intended to play a key role in the fields of information system and software engineering. MDA is supposed to provide a basic technical framework for information integration and tools interoperation based on the separation of platform specific models (PSMs) from platform independent models (PIMs). Models of low granularity and high abstraction will represent the various functional and non-functional aspects of computer systems. In the long term there will be well defined operations, implemented by commercial tools that will allow us to build, transform, merge or verify these different models. Key standards in the MDA will be based on OMG recommendations like UML, MOF, XMI, CWM, QVT. In fact, MDA can be considered an implementation of a more general trend that has been gathering momentum in recent years called Model Driven Development (MDD). This aims to make models the primary driving assets in all aspects of software development, including system design, platform and language definition and mappings as in MDA, but also to design data integration, design analysis, tool specification and product family development.

Workshop 6: Open Issues in Industrial Use Case Modeling

Organizers: Gonzalo Génova (Carlos III University of Madrid, Spain), Juan Lloréns (Carlos III University of Madrid, Spain), Pierre Metz (Cork Institute of Technology, Ireland), Rubén Prieto-Díaz (James Madison University, VA, USA) and Hernán Astudillo (Universidad Técnica Federico Santa María, Chile)

URL: http://www.ie.inf.uc3m.es/uml2004-ws6

Abstract: Use Cases have achieved wide use as specification tool for observable behavior of systems. However, there is still much controversy, inconsistent use, and free-flowing interpretations of use case models: in practice, they are dangerously ambiguous. The workshop purpose is to identify and characterize some ambiguity sources. It will gather specialists involved in modeling use cases to exchange ideas and proposals, with an eye to both clear definition and practical application. Some proposed topics are: Alignment of textual specification and graphical representation: use case relationships, use case standard templates, use case contracts, etc. Little semantic connection between use case specification items and UML use case diagrams. Collaboration vs. participation among actors of a use case. Functional vs. structural view of use cases. Use cases composition. Adding potentially missing relationships among use cases, and, finally, other topics including novel applications of use case models. The target audience is researchers, lecturers and practitioners interested in use case modeling. The workshop will produce identification and characterization of open issues and promising avenues of inquiry.

Workshop 7: Models for Non-functional Aspects of Component-Based Software

Organizers: Jean-Michel Bruel (University of Pau France), Geri Georg (Colorado State University, USA), Heinrich Hußmann (University of Munich, Germany), Ileana Ober (Verimag, France), Christoph Pohl (Technical University Dresden, Germany), Jon Whittle (NASA Ames Research Center, USA) and Steffen Zschaler (Technical University Dresden, Germany)

URL: http://www.comquad.org/nfc04

Abstract: Developing reliable software is a complex, daunting, and error-prone task. Therefore, many researchers are interested in improving the support for developers creating such software. Component-based software engineering has emerged as an important paradigm for handling complexity. The goal of this workshop is to look at issues related to the integration of non-functional property expression, evaluation, and prediction in the context of component-based software engineering. In this area it is our main focus to look at model-based approaches, preferably, but not limited to, UML-based approaches. This includes semantic issues, questions of modelling language definition, but also support for automation, such as analysis algorithms, MDA-based approaches, or tool-support for refinement steps. As models are only really meaningful if used in the context of a software development process, we also welcome work in this area. We expect the workshop to foster cooperation between the various research groups in the field. One important expected outcome is a joint workshop report as well as ongoing discussions, e.g., on a workshop mailing list.

Workshop 8: OCL and Model Driven Engineering

Organizers: Thomas Baar (EPFL Lausanne, Switzerland), Jean Bézivin (University of Nantes, France), Tracy Gardner (IBM in Hursley, United Kingdom), Martin Gogolla (University of Bremen, Germany), Reiner Hähnle (Chalmers University, Gothenburg, Sweden), Heinrich Hußmann (University of Munich, Germany), Octavian Patrascoiu (University of Kent, United Kingdom), Peter H. Schmitt (Universität Karlsruhe, Germany) and Jos Warmer (De Nederlandsche Bank, The Netherlands)

URL: http://www.cs.kent.ac.uk/projects/ocl/oclmdewsuml04

Abstract: Precise modeling is essential to the success of the OMG's Model Driven Architecture initiative. OCL can play a role at multiple levels. At the meta-level (M2), queries, views and transformations are subjects that will be vital to the success of the OMG's Model Driven Architecture Initiative. Will OCL 2.0 become an essential part of the Queries/Views/Transformations standard and what will its application areas in industry be? At the modeling level (M1) OCL allows for the precision needed to write executable models. Currently OCL is restricted to side-effect free queries. Can OCL be extended to become a full high-level executable language with side-effects? How will the powerful features of OCL 2.0 be used in the Model Driven Engineering approach? Is OCL 2.0 more powerful than needed, or is not powerful enough? This workshop aims at bringing together people from academia that are expected to report on inspiring ideas for innovative application scenarios and tools, and industrial practitioners, which are expected to provide statements on their view of the future of OCL in the context of Model Driven Engineering.

Workshop 9: Critical Systems Development with UML

Organizers: Eduardo B. Fernandez (Florida Atlantic University, USA), Robert France (Colorado State University, USA), Jan Jürjens (TU Munich, Germany) and Bernhard Rumpe (TU Braunschweig, Germany)

URL: http://www4.in.tum.de/~csduml04

Abstract: The high quality development of critical systems (be it real-time, security-critical, dependable/safety-critical, performance-critical, or hybrid systems) is difficult. Many critical systems are developed, deployed, and used that do not satisfy their criticality requirements, sometimes with spectacular failures. Part of the difficulty of critical systems development is that correctness is often in conflict with cost. Where thorough methods of system design pose high cost through personnel training and use, they are all too often avoided. UML offers an unprecedented opportunity for high-quality critical systems development that is feasible in an industrial context. As the de-facto standard in industrial modelling, a large number of developers is trained in UML. Compared to previous notations with a user community of comparable size, UML is relatively precisely defined. A number of tools have been developed to assist with the operational use of UML. To exploit this opportunity, some challenges remain which include the following: Adapting UML to critical system application domains. Encouraging the correct use of UML in the application domains. Avoiding conflict between flexibility and unambiguity in the meaning of a notation. Improving tool-support for critical systems development with UML. The workshop aims to gather practitioners and researchers to contribute to overcoming these challenges.

Workshop 10: QUEVER — UML Workshop on QUantitative-Based Evaluation, Visualization, and Refactoring

Organizers: Fernando Brito e Abreu (Universidade Nova de Lisboa, Portugal), Geert Poels (Ghent University & Katholieke Universiteit Leuven, Belgium), Houari A. Sahraoui (Université de Montréal, Canada) and Jan Hendrik Hausmann (Universität Paderborn, Germany)

URL: http://ctp.di.fct.unl.pt/UML2004/quever2004.htm

Abstract: The main objective of this workshop is to bridge the research being produced in the areas of Evaluation, Visualization and Refactoring (briefly EVR), within the wider community of UML users. Although these areas have obvious intersections, there is no known forum where the three are addressed in conjunction. QUEVER is intended to fulfill this gap.During the workshop there will be some sessions for presenting position papers, a hands-on session where a cooperative problem solving approach will be applied to a proposed problem and a closing session for summarizing, evaluating and assembling the research results and for identifying future research opportunities. Participation in the workshop is by invitation only, i.e. based on the submission of a position paper. All submitted position papers will be formally reviewed by the workshop organizers for originality, relevance, quality and clarity. We specially encourage the submission of new ideas, even if not fully validated yet. All invited participants will be asked to summarize the contributions and limitations of the work they will present. A paper-based proceedings of QUEVER'2004, including all accepted position papers, will be distributed to the participants. An electronic-based edition of the same proceedings will be made available in the workshop website.

Workshop 11: SIVOES 2004: Behavior in Model Driven Approaches

Organizers: Sébastien Gérard (Centre d'Etudes de Saclay / List, France), Pierre-Alain Muller (Université de Haute Alsace, ESSAIM, France), Colin Atkinson (University of Mannheim, Germany) and Bran Selic (IBM Rational Software Canada, Ontario, Canada)

URL: http://www.sivoes.org

Abstract: The latest OMG initiative (already three years old), called MDA – for "Model Driven Architecture" - puts forward the idea that future process development will be centred around the models, thus keeping independent development from underlying platform technology. Concretely, OMG initiated activities (e.g. MOF 2.0 Query/View/Transf. RFP) in order to promote all the technologies that should ensure that this principle becomes a reality in industry. The first significant result of the MDA paradigm for engineers is the possibility for them to build application models that can be conveniently ported to new, emerging technologies - implementation languages, middleware, etc.- with minimal effort and risk. In the DRES area, this model-oriented trend is also very active and promising. But DRES are different from general-purpose systems, at last because of their behavior aspects. Indeed, it is one of the main issue in their development. The purpose of this workshop is to serve as an opportunity to gather researchers and industrialists in order to survey some existing experiments related to behavioral issues related to DRES development in the context of the model-driven paradigm. This workshop aims to bring together members of the various communities concerned by the behaviour across a wide range of domains. The workshop will provide them with a central forum where to debate the place of behaviour in analysis, design, implementation and maintenance of software and systems in the context of the distributed, real-time and embedded areas. This workshop seek contributions from researchers and practitioners interested in all aspects of the representation and implementation of behaviour. We are especially interested in papers outlining how behaviour is addressed in the different communities and how these communities see the balance between structure and behaviour in software and systems. To achieve this purpose, SIVOES-Behavior solicits abstract papers (about 4 pages) related to, but not limited to, the following principal topics: Models and metamodels. Simulation. Verification and validation. Automation. Code generation. Real-time and reactive systems.

Workshop 12: Doctoral Symposium

Organizers: Marcus Alanen (Åbo Akademi University, Finland), Jordi Cabot (Universitat Oberta de Catalunya, Spain), Miguel Goulão (New University of Lisbon, Portugal), Na Li (Colorado State University, USA) and José Sáez (University of Murcia, Spain)

URL: http://ctp.di.fct.unl.pt/UML2004/phdSymp.htm

Abstract: The UML'04 Doctoral Symposium is the first Doctoral symposium in the UML Conference series. The Doctoral Symposium seeks to bring together PhD Students working in areas related to UML and modeling in general. Selected students will have the opportunity to present and to discuss their research goals, methods and results within a constructive and international atmosphere. The symposium is intended for students who have already settled on a specific research proposal and have some preliminary results, but still have enough time remaining before submitting their dissertation. Thus, they will benefit from the Symposium discussions.

References

[1] N. J. Nunes, B. Selic, A. Silva, and A. Toval, editors. *UML Modeling Languages and Applications. UML 2004 Satellite Activities. Revised Selected Papers. Lisbon, Portugal, October 11-15, 2004*, volume 3297 of *LNCS*. Springer Verlag, 2004.

Tutorials at the UML 2004 Conference

Ezra K. Mugisa (Ed.)

Department of Mathematics & Computer Science
The University of the West Indies (Mona)
Kingston 7, Jamaica
ezra.mugisa@uwimona.edu.jm

Abstract. The UML 2004 conference provides six half-day tutorials on advanced topics related to UML, presented by recognized worldwide experts. A short summary of each tutorial and a list of its respective presenters are given in section 2.

1 Introduction

Tutorials afford opportunities for conference attendees to get new knowledge, insights and abilities on key subjects and typically relate up to date techniques. The tutorial program of the UML 2004 conference seeks to continue this tested tradition. This program is intended for practitioners, researchers, educators and students looking for a better and deeper understanding of UML-related topics.

The quality of tutorial proposals this year was very high and it is a pity that we had space for only six. As a result, a number of good proposals were not accepted as we sought to maintain strong attendances at each tutorial. We hope the prospective presenters will be encouraged to submit again next year.

In the six that were selected we have a good mixture of tutorials covering areas that are topical and have great appeal and relevance to the modeling community. We summarise these tutorials in the following section. Further detailed information on these tutorials can be accessed at the UML 2004 conference website: http://www.umlconference.org

2 Detailed List of Tutorials

Tutorial T1: Constructing Tool-Support for Sophisticated Analysis of UML Models: A Hands-On Introduction

Presenter: Jan Jürjens (TU Munich, Germany)

Abstract: UML is now widely used as a notation to support informal discussions between customers and developers, and among developers, and for basic tasks such as generating class definitions. There is, however, a potential for a more far-reaching use of UML within model-based development that could increase efficiency and quality. This potential can be realized by making a tool-supported use of the UML models for

T. Baar et al. (Eds.): UML 2004, LNCS 3273, pp. 449–452, 2004.

- mechanical analysis of (potentially complicated) system requirements on the model level (for example by tool-bindings to model-checkers, constraint solvers, automated theorem provers), consistency checks etc.
- generation of behavioral code from the models
- generation of test-sequences for conformance testing
- mechanical analysis of system configurations against UML models

The tutorial aims to give a hands-on introduction to developing advanced tool-support for model-based development with UML.

Tutorial T2: MDA Standards for Ontology Development

Presenter: Dragan Gašević, Dragan Djurić and Vladan Devedžić (all from FON - School of Business Administration, Belgrade, Serbia and Montenegro)

Abstract: The Semantic Web is the main direction of the future Web development. Domain ontologies are the most important part of Semantic Web applications. Artificial intelligence techniques are used for ontology creation, but those techniques are more related to research laboratories. Recently, there are many proposals to use software engineering techniques, especially the UML since it is the most accepted software engineering standard, in order to bring ontology development process closer to wider practitioners' population. However, UML is based on object oriented paradigm, and has some limitation regarding ontology development. These limitations can be overcome using UML's extensions (i.e. UML profiles), as well as other OMG's standards (i.e. Model Driven Architecture - MDA). Currently, there is an initiative (i.e. RFP) within the OMG aiming to define a suitable language for modeling Semantic Web ontology languages in the context of the MDA.

The main goal of this tutorial is to present comprehensive introduction into MDA-based ontology development. It will provide an introduction to the field of the Semantic Web and ontology engineering, a description of several UML- and metamodeling- based solutions and tools for ontology development, an overview of the OMG's MDA effort and related standards (Meta-Object Facility - MOF, UML, XML Metadata Interchange - XMI), a detailed overview of the OMG's proposal for Ontology Definition Metamodel (http://ontology.omg.org). Finally, we will describe our experiences in developing and employing an MDA-based infrastructure for ontology engineering we defined using the OMG's recommendations.

Tutorial T3: An Overview of UML 2.0

Presenter: Bran Selic (IBM Software Group - Rational Software, Kanata, Ontario, Canada)

Abstract: The first major revision of the UML standard, UML 2.0, has recently been submitted for adoption to the Object Management Group. This revision was strongly influenced by the current heightened interest in model-driven development methods. This approach requires modeling languages that are precisely defined and which can cope with the complexities of large-scale software systems. We start the tutorial with an explanation of the essential characteristics of model-driven development and how those are reflected in modeling languages. This is followed by a brief objective critique of the pros and cons of the current version of UML. The formal requirements for UML 2.0 are reviewed next. Finally, we examine the proposed revision itself: its structure, its conceptual foundations, and its salient new features. Since the presenter was a direct participant in the definition of the submission, the design philosophy and rationale behind each aspect are clearly explained.

Tutorial T4: Guided Inspection of UML Models

Presenter: John D. McGregor (Clemson University, USA)

Abstract: There is widespread agreement that finding defects as early in the development life cycle as possible is cost-effective; however, there are few systematic techniques for accomplishing this goal. Guided inspection is an inspection technique that is"guided" by test cases. By constructing a "complete" set of test cases, the guided inspection technique identifies elements missing from the model as well as evaluating the quality of those that are present. This tutorial illustrates the technique using design models created using the Unified Modeling Language. Checklists designed for use at various points in a typical development process assist the inspector in selecting the most effective test cases.
Guided Inspection has several benefits:

Objectivity - systematically selects test cases to give all portions of the model equal coverage.
Traceability - links the faults detected back to specific requirements
Testability - identifies portions of the design that are complex and require much effort to test.

Tutorial T5: Model-Centric Enterprise Architecture

Presenter: Desmond D'Souza (Kinetium Inc., Austin, TX, USA)

Abstract: The architecture of an enterprise is described by a set of models of that enterprise, expressing key aspects of the business domains themselves, the goals and challenges of the enterprise, it's processes, people, and organizations, the software applications and components that support it, the software and hardware infrastructure they run on, and the interrelationships, commonalities, and standards across these. The main reason for investing in an enterprise architecture is to better understand the enterprise with its current and ideal operating characteristics, in order to best design, manage, and guide the evolution of its supporting systems.

Enterprise architecture involves multiple viewpoints, spanning business goals through technology platforms. It must handle heterogeneous and overlapping systems, short and long-term migration planning, medium to large-grained components and applications, and mixtures of logical and highly platform-oriented views.

UML 2.0 and MDA provide facilities that help with some aspects of enterprise architecture, but do not address several others. In this tutorial we will describe an approach to enterprise architecture, based on models and their interrelationships, and using UML 2.0 and ideas from MDA where appropriate.

Tutorial T6: How to Design and Use Domain Specific Modeling Languages

Presenter: Alan Cameron Wills and Stuart Kent (both from Microsoft Corporation, Cambridge, UK)

Abstract: Software development can be accelerated and made more agile, by designing a language that is specialised to model your domain of interest. A user interface, a database queries, or a page layout is rarely designed these days without using a language (and supporting tools) specific to that purpose - a language that may be textual or graphical or both. A domain-specific language captures an ontology of its domain; and each implementation (a generator, interpreting engine, or simulator that executes the language's statements) encapsulates a framework of components and design patterns. This tutorial will explain how to create and use domain specific languages, and how to make this pattern more applicable to narrower and more specialized domains. We will discuss some related patterns such as adaptive assembly, software product lines and model driven development, and how these form an integrated pattern language we call the "Software Factory". Finally, we will explore in some detail techniques for designing a domain specific language; and look at the tools and processes that go along with such a language.

Acknowledgments

I would like to thank Alessandra Cavarra, Robert France, Ivan Porres and Shane Sendall for their contributions during the selection process and João Araújo for passing on the experience from last year.

Author Index

Lecture Notes in Computer Science

For information about Vols. 1–3162

please contact your bookseller or Springer

Vol. 3274: R. Guerraoui (Ed.), Distributed Computing. XIII, 465 pages. 2004.

Vol. 3273: T. Baar, A. Strohmeier, A. Moreira, S.J. Mellor (Eds.), «UML» 2004 - The Unified Modeling Language. XIII, 454 pages. 2004.

Vol. 3271: J. Vicente, D. Hutchison (Eds.), Management of Multimedia Networks and Services. XIII, 335 pages. 2004.

Vol. 3270: M. Jeckle, R. Kowalczyk, P. Braun (Eds.), Grid Services Engineering and Management. X, 165 pages. 2004.

Vol. 3266: J. Solé-Pareta, M. Smirnov, P.V. Mieghem, J. Domingo-Pascual, E. Monteiro, P. Reichl, B. Stiller, R.J. Gibbens (Eds.), Quality of Service in the Emerging Networking Panorama. XVI, 390 pages. 2004.

Vol. 3263: M. Weske, P. Liggesmeyer (Eds.), Object-Oriented and Internet-Based Technologies. XII, 239 pages. 2004.

Vol. 3260: I. Niemegeers, S.H. de Groot (Eds.), Personal Wireless Communications. XIV, 478 pages. 2004.

Vol. 3258: M. Wallace (Ed.), Principles and Practice of Constraint Programming – CP 2004. XVII, 822 pages. 2004.

Vol. 3256: H. Ehrig, G. Engels, F. Parisi-Presicce, G. Rozenberg (Eds.), Graph Transformations. XII, 451 pages. 2004.

Vol. 3255: A. Benczúr, J. Demetrovics, G. Gottlob (Eds.), Advances in Databases and Information Systems. XI, 423 pages. 2004.

Vol. 3254: E. Macii, V. Paliouras, O. Koufopavlou (Eds.), Integrated Circuit and System Design. XVI, 910 pages. 2004.

Vol. 3253: Y. Lakhnech, S. Yovine (Eds.), Formal Techniques, Modelling and Analysis of Timed and Fault-Tolerant Systems. X, 397 pages. 2004.

Vol. 3250: L.-J. (LJ) Zhang, M. Jeckle (Eds.), Web Services. X, 300 pages. 2004.

Vol. 3249: B. Buchberger, J.A. Campbell (Eds.), Artificial Intelligence and Symbolic Computation. X, 285 pages. 2004. (Subseries LNAI).

Vol. 3246: A. Apostolico, M. Melucci (Eds.), String Processing and Information Retrieval. XIV, 332 pages. 2004.

Vol. 3245: E. Suzuki, S. Arikawa (Eds.), Discovery Science. XIV, 430 pages. 2004. (Subseries LNAI).

Vol. 3244: S. Ben-David, J. Case, A. Maruoka (Eds.), Algorithmic Learning Theory. XIV, 505 pages. 2004. (Subseries LNAI).

Vol. 3242: X. Yao, E. Burke, J.A. Lozano, J. Smith, J.J. Merelo-Guervós, J.A. Bullinaria, J. Rowe, P. Tiňo, A. Kabán, H.-P. Schwefel (Eds.), Parallel Problem Solving from Nature - PPSN VIII. XX, 1185 pages. 2004.

Vol. 3241: D. Kranzlmüller, P. Kacsuk, J.J. Dongarra (Eds.), Recent Advances in Parallel Virtual Machine and Message Passing Interface. XIII, 452 pages. 2004.

Vol. 3240: I. Jonassen, J. Kim (Eds.), Algorithms in Bioinformatics. IX, 476 pages. 2004. (Subseries LNBI).

Vol. 3239: G. Nicosia, V. Cutello, P.J. Bentley, J. Timmis (Eds.), Artificial Immune Systems. XII, 444 pages. 2004.

Vol. 3238: S. Biundo, T. Frühwirth, G. Palm (Eds.), KI 2004: Advances in Artificial Intelligence. XI, 467 pages. 2004. (Subseries LNAI).

Vol. 3236: M. Núñez, Z. Maamar, F.L. Pelayo, K. Pousttchi, F. Rubio (Eds.), Applying Formal Methods: Testing, Performance, and M/E-Commerce. XI, 381 pages. 2004.

Vol. 3235: D. de Frutos-Escrig, M. Nunez (Eds.), Formal Techniques for Networked and Distributed Systems – FORTE 2004. X, 377 pages. 2004.

Vol. 3232: R. Heery, L. Lyon (Eds.), Research and Advanced Technology for Digital Libraries. XV, 528 pages. 2004.

Vol. 3229: J.J. Alferes, J. Leite (Eds.), Logics in Artificial Intelligence. XIV, 744 pages. 2004. (Subseries LNAI).

Vol. 3225: K. Zhang, Y. Zheng (Eds.), Information Security. XII, 442 pages. 2004.

Vol. 3224: E. Jonsson, A. Valdes, M. Almgren (Eds.), Recent Advances in Intrusion Detection. XII, 315 pages. 2004.

Vol. 3223: K. Slind, A. Bunker, G. Gopalakrishnan (Eds.), Theorem Proving in Higher Order Logics. VIII, 337 pages. 2004.

Vol. 3222: H. Jin, G.R. Gao, Z. Xu, H. Chen (Eds.), Network and Parallel Computing. XX, 694 pages. 2004.

Vol. 3221: S. Albers, T. Radzik (Eds.), Algorithms – ESA 2004. XVIII, 836 pages. 2004.

Vol. 3220: J.C. Lester, R.M. Vicari, F. Paraguaçu (Eds.), Intelligent Tutoring Systems. XXI, 920 pages. 2004.

Vol. 3219: M. Heisel, P. Liggesmeyer, S. Wittmann (Eds.), Computer Safety, Reliability, and Security. XI, 339 pages. 2004.

Vol. 3217: C. Barillot, D.R. Haynor, P. Hellier (Eds.), Medical Image Computing and Computer-Assisted Intervention – MICCAI 2004. XXXVIII, 1114 pages. 2004.

Vol. 3216: C. Barillot, D.R. Haynor, P. Hellier (Eds.), Medical Image Computing and Computer-Assisted Intervention – MICCAI 2004. XXXVIII, 930 pages. 2004.

Vol. 3215: M.G.. Negoita, R.J. Howlett, L.C. Jain (Eds.), Knowledge-Based Intelligent Information and Engineering Systems. LVII, 906 pages. 2004. (Subseries LNAI).

Vol. 3214: M.G.. Negoita, R.J. Howlett, L.C. Jain (Eds.), Knowledge-Based Intelligent Information and Engineering Systems. LVIII, 1302 pages. 2004. (Subseries LNAI).

Vol. 3213: M.G.. Negoita, R.J. Howlett, L.C. Jain (Eds.), Knowledge-Based Intelligent Information and Engineering Systems. LVIII, 1280 pages. 2004. (Subseries LNAI).

Vol. 3212: A. Campilho, M. Kamel (Eds.), Image Analysis and Recognition. XXIX, 862 pages. 2004.

Vol. 3211: A. Campilho, M. Kamel (Eds.), Image Analysis and Recognition. XXIX, 880 pages. 2004.

Vol. 3210: J. Marcinkowski, A. Tarlecki (Eds.), Computer Science Logic. XI, 520 pages. 2004.

Vol. 3209: B. Berendt, A. Hotho, D. Mladenic, M. van Someren, M. Spiliopoulou, G. Stumme (Eds.), Web Mining: From Web to Semantic Web. IX, 201 pages. 2004. (Subseries LNAI).

Vol. 3208: H.J. Ohlbach, S. Schaffert (Eds.), Principles and Practice of Semantic Web Reasoning. VII, 165 pages. 2004.

Vol. 3207: L.T. Yang, M. Guo, G.R. Gao, N.K. Jha (Eds.), Embedded and Ubiquitous Computing. XX, 1116 pages. 2004.

Vol. 3206: P. Sojka, I. Kopecek, K. Pala (Eds.), Text, Speech and Dialogue. XIII, 667 pages. 2004. (Subseries LNAI).

Vol. 3205: N. Davies, E. Mynatt, I. Siio (Eds.), UbiComp 2004: Ubiquitous Computing. XVI, 452 pages. 2004.

Vol. 3203: J. Becker, M. Platzner, S. Vernalde (Eds.), Field Programmable Logic and Application. XXX, 1198 pages. 2004.

Vol. 3202: J.-F. Boulicaut, F. Esposito, F. Giannotti, D. Pedreschi (Eds.), Knowledge Discovery in Databases: PKDD 2004. XIX, 560 pages. 2004. (Subseries LNAI).

Vol. 3201: J.-F. Boulicaut, F. Esposito, F. Giannotti, D. Pedreschi (Eds.), Machine Learning: ECML 2004. XVIII, 580 pages. 2004. (Subseries LNAI).

Vol. 3199: H. Schepers (Ed.), Software and Compilers for Embedded Systems. X, 259 pages. 2004.

Vol. 3198: G.-J. de Vreede, L.A. Guerrero, G. Marín Raventós (Eds.), Groupware: Design, Implementation and Use. XI, 378 pages. 2004.

Vol. 3195: C.G. Puntonet, A. Prieto (Eds.), Independent Component Analysis and Blind Signal Separation. XXIII, 1266 pages. 2004.

Vol. 3194: R. Camacho, R. King, A. Srinivasan (Eds.), Inductive Logic Programming. XI, 361 pages. 2004. (Subseries LNAI).

Vol. 3193: P. Samarati, P. Ryan, D. Gollmann, R. Molva (Eds.), Computer Security – ESORICS 2004. X, 457 pages. 2004.

Vol. 3192: C. Bussler, D. Fensel (Eds.), Artificial Intelligence: Methodology, Systems, and Applications. XIII, 522 pages. 2004. (Subseries LNAI).

Vol. 3191: M. Klusch, S. Ossowski, V. Kashyap, R. Unland (Eds.), Cooperative Information Agents VIII. XI, 303 pages. 2004. (Subseries LNAI).

Vol. 3190: Y. Luo (Ed.), Cooperative Design, Visualization, and Engineering. IX, 248 pages. 2004.

Vol. 3189: P.-C. Yew, J. Xue (Eds.), Advances in Computer Systems Architecture. XVII, 598 pages. 2004.

Vol. 3188: F.S. de Boer, M.M. Bonsangue, S. Graf, W.-P. de Roever (Eds.), Formal Methods for Components and Objects. VIII, 373 pages. 2004.

Vol. 3187: G. Lindemann, J. Denzinger, I.J. Timm, R. Unland (Eds.), Multiagent System Technologies. XIII, 341 pages. 2004. (Subseries LNAI).

Vol. 3186: Z. Bellahsène, T. Milo, M. Rys, D. Suciu, R. Unland (Eds.), Database and XML Technologies. X, 235 pages. 2004.

Vol. 3185: M. Bernardo, F. Corradini (Eds.), Formal Methods for the Design of Real-Time Systems. VII, 295 pages. 2004.

Vol. 3184: S. Katsikas, J. Lopez, G. Pernul (Eds.), Trust and Privacy in Digital Business. XI, 299 pages. 2004.

Vol. 3183: R. Traunmüller (Ed.), Electronic Government. XIX, 583 pages. 2004.

Vol. 3182: K. Bauknecht, M. Bichler, B. Pröll (Eds.), E-Commerce and Web Technologies. XI, 370 pages. 2004.

Vol. 3181: Y. Kambayashi, M. Mohania, W. Wöß (Eds.), Data Warehousing and Knowledge Discovery. XIV, 412 pages. 2004.

Vol. 3180: F. Galindo, M. Takizawa, R. Traunmüller (Eds.), Database and Expert Systems Applications. XXI, 972 pages. 2004.

Vol. 3179: F.J. Perales, B.A. Draper (Eds.), Articulated Motion and Deformable Objects. XI, 270 pages. 2004.

Vol. 3178: W. Jonker, M. Petkovic (Eds.), Secure Data Management. VIII, 219 pages. 2004.

Vol. 3177: Z.R. Yang, H. Yin, R. Everson (Eds.), Intelligent Data Engineering and Automated Learning – IDEAL 2004. XVIII, 852 pages. 2004.

Vol. 3176: O. Bousquet, U. von Luxburg, G. Rätsch (Eds.), Advanced Lectures on Machine Learning. IX, 241 pages. 2004. (Subseries LNAI).

Vol. 3175: C.E. Rasmussen, H.H. Bülthoff, B. Schölkopf, M.A. Giese (Eds.), Pattern Recognition. XVIII, 581 pages. 2004.

Vol. 3174: F. Yin, J. Wang, C. Guo (Eds.), Advances in Neural Networks - ISNN 2004. XXXV, 1021 pages. 2004.

Vol. 3173: F. Yin, J. Wang, C. Guo (Eds.), Advances in Neural Networks – ISNN 2004. XXXV, 1041 pages. 2004.

Vol. 3172: M. Dorigo, M. Birattari, C. Blum, L. M. Gambardella, F. Mondada, T. Stützle (Eds.), Ant Colony, Optimization and Swarm Intelligence. XII, 434 pages. 2004.

Vol. 3171: A.L.C. Bazzan, S. Labidi (Eds.), Advances in Artificial Intelligence – SBIA 2004. XVII, 548 pages. 2004. (Subseries LNAI).

Vol. 3170: P. Gardner, N. Yoshida (Eds.), CONCUR 2004 - Concurrency Theory. XIII, 529 pages. 2004.

Vol. 3166: M. Rauterberg (Ed.), Entertainment Computing – ICEC 2004. XXIII, 617 pages. 2004.

Vol. 3163: S. Marinai, A. Dengel (Eds.), Document Analysis Systems VI. XI, 564 pages. 2004.